I am Here! 2

Volume 2

Ema Toyama

Translated and adapted by
Joshua Weeks

Lettered by
North Market Street Graphics

KC
KODANSHA
COMICS

A Kodansha Comics Trade Paperback Original

I Am Here! volume 3 copyright © 2008 Ema Toyama
I Am Here! volume 4 copyright © 2008 Ema Toyama
I Am Here! volume 5 copyright © 2009 Ema Toyama
English translation copyright © 2011 Ema Toyama

Published in the United States by Kodansha Comics, an imprint of Kodansha USA Publishing, LLC, New York.

Publication rights for this English edition arranged through Kodansha Ltd., Tokyo.

First published in Japan in 2008-2009 by Kodansha Ltd., Tokyo, as *Ko Ko Ni Iru Yo!* volumes 3, 4 and 5.

ISBN 978-1-935-42943-2

Printed in the United States of America.

www.kodanshacomics.com

9 8 7 6 5 4 3 2 1

Translator/Adapter: Joshua Weeks
Lettering: North Market Street Graphics

CONTENTS

Honorifics Explained

Throughout the Kodansha Comics books, you will find Japanese honorifics left intact in the translations. For those not familiar with how the Japanese use honorifics and, more important, how they differ from American honorifics, we present this brief overview.

Politeness has always been a critical facet of Japanese culture. Ever since the feudal era, when Japan was a highly stratified society, use of honorifics—which can be defined as polite speech that indicates relationship or status—has played an essential role in the Japanese language. When addressing someone in Japanese, an honorific usually takes the form of a suffix attached to one's name (example: "Asuna-san"), is used as a title at the end of one's name, or appears in place of the name itself (example: "Negi-sensei," or simply "Sensei!").

Honorifics can be expressions of respect or endearment. In the context of manga and anime, honorifics give insight into the nature of the relationship between characters. Many English translations leave out these important honorifics and therefore distort the feel of the original Japanese. Because Japanese honorifics contain nuances that English honorifics lack, it is our policy at Kodansha Comics not to translate them. Here, instead, is a guide to some of the honorifics you may encounter in Kodansha Comics books.

-san: This is the most common honorific and is equivalent to Mr., Miss, Ms., or Mrs. It is the all-purpose honorific and can be used in any situation where politeness is required

-sama: This is one level higher than "-san" and is used to confer great respect.

-dono: This comes from the word "tono," which means "lord." It is an even higher level than "-sama" and confers utmost respect.

-kun: This suffix is used at the end of boys' names to express familiarity or endearment. It is also sometimes used by men among friends, or when addressing someone younger or of a lower station.

-chan: This is used to express endearment, mostly toward girls. It is also used for little boys, pets, and even among lovers. It gives a sense of childish cuteness.

Bozu: This is an informal way to refer to a boy, similar to the English terms "kid" and "squirt."

Sempai/
Senpai: This title suggests that the addressee is one's senior in a group or organization. It is most often used in a school setting, where underclassmen refer to their upperclassmen as "sempai." It can also be used in the workplace, such as when a newer employee addresses an employee who has seniority in the company.

Kohai: This is the opposite of "sempai" and is used toward underclassmen in school or newcomers in the workplace. It connotes that the addressee is of a lower station.

Sensei: Literally meaning "one who has come before," this title is used for teachers, doctors, or masters of any profession or art.

-[blank]: This is usually forgotten in these lists, but it is perhaps the most significant difference between Japanese and English. The lack of honorific means that the speaker has permission to address the person in a very intimate way. Usually, only family, spouses, or very close friends have this kind of permission. Known as *yobisute*, it can be gratifying when someone who has earned the intimacy starts to call one by one's name without an honorific. But when that intimacy hasn't been earned, it can be very insulting.

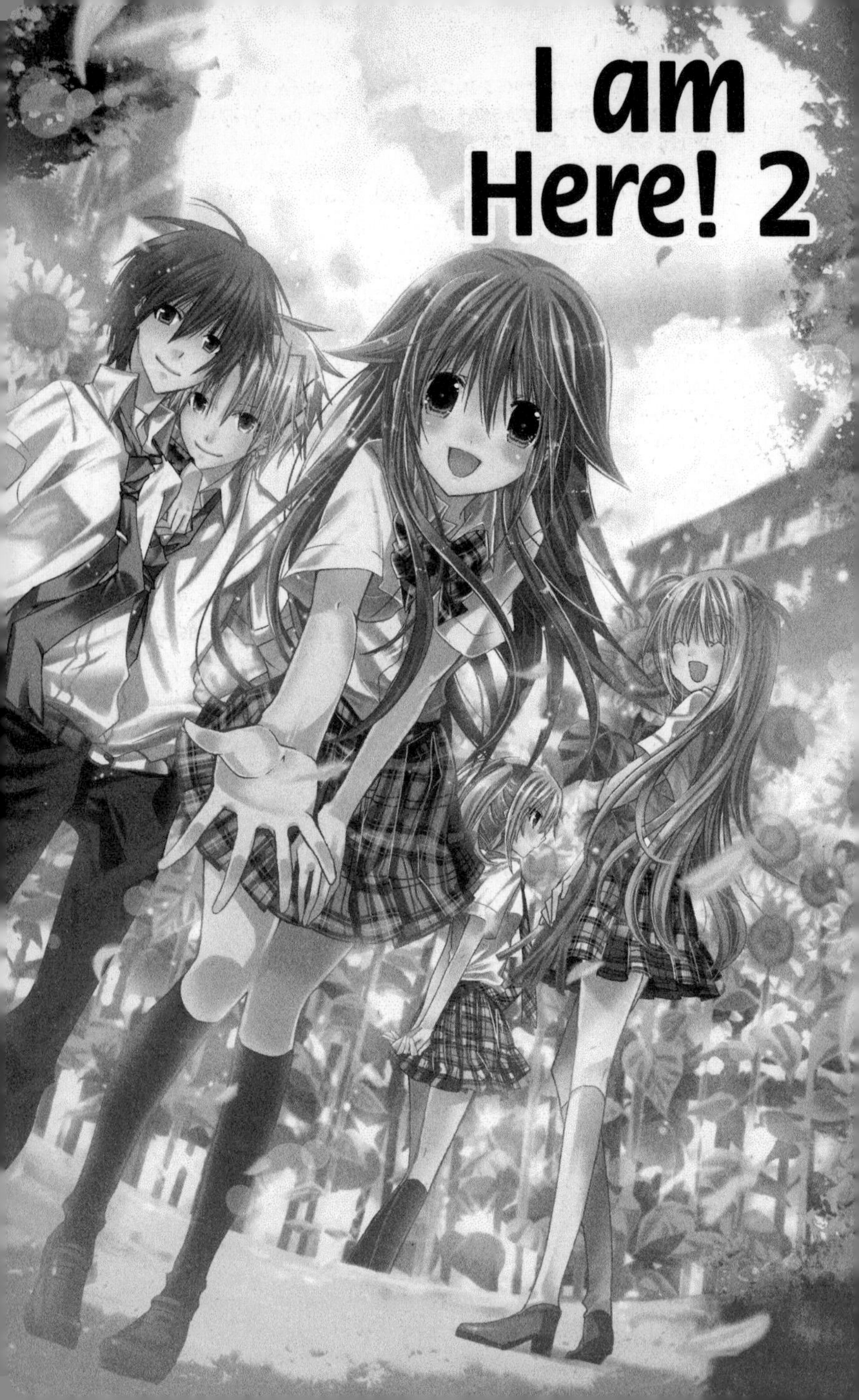
I am
Here! 2

I Am Here! Story

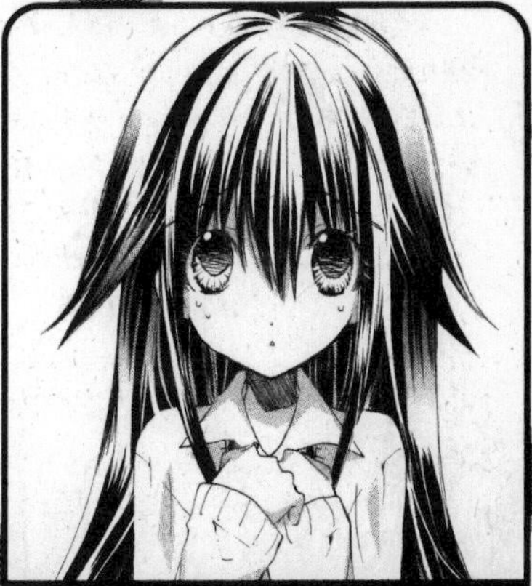

Hikage Sumino
Eighth grader. The main character, who nobody notices.

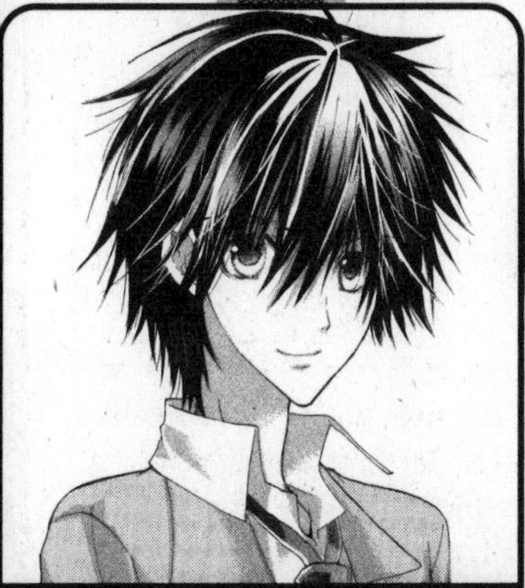

Hinata Mutō
Excels at school and at sports. He likes Hikage.

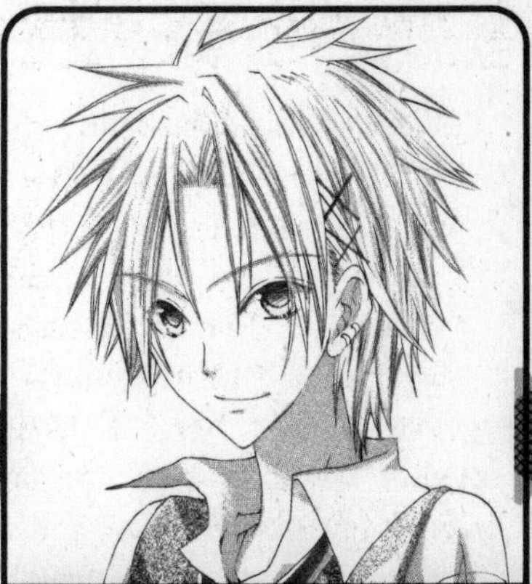

Teru Mikami
A rich kid with model looks. Hinata's best friend.

Regular Blog Visitors

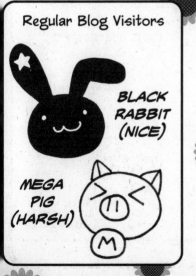

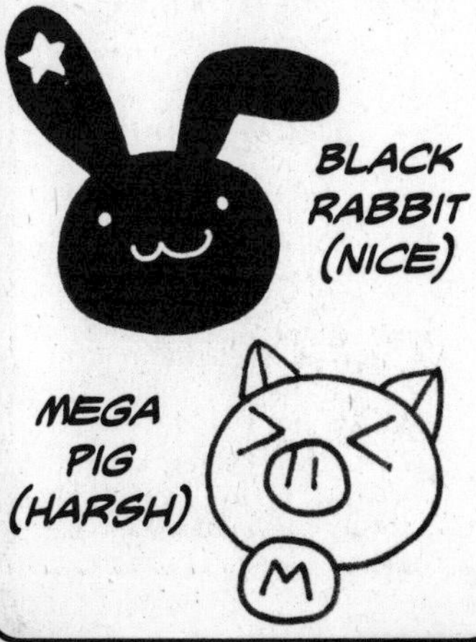
BLACK RABBIT (NICE)
MEGA PIG (HARSH)
M

Hikage Sumino was so invisible that even her classmates didn't remember her name. Her only friends were the regular visitors to a blog that she keeps as a hobby. But one day, Hinata confessed to her, "I've been watching you," and Hikage's world began to change, bit by bit.

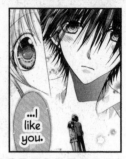

...I like you.

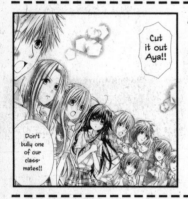

Cut it out Aya!!

Don't bully one of our classmates!!

After a brief moment of feeling accepted by her classmates, a group of girls who like Hinata start to bully Hikage, and she becomes so scared that she refuses to go to school. But her blog friends coach her through this, and she musters up the courage to tell the girls her mind, and is once again accepted by her classmates.

Black Rabbit has always had kind words for Hikage. But all of a sudden he disappears from her blog, with a good-bye message. She suspects that Hinata is Black Rabbit, which complicates their friendship... Then, Black Rabbit sends her a message, saying that he's ready to "tell her everything"...!!?

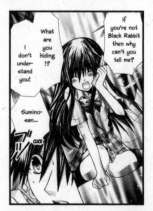

If you're not Black Rabbit then why can't you tell me?

What are you hiding !?

I don't understand you!

Sumino-san...

click

I am Here!
CONTENTS

Do you believe in destiny?

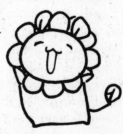

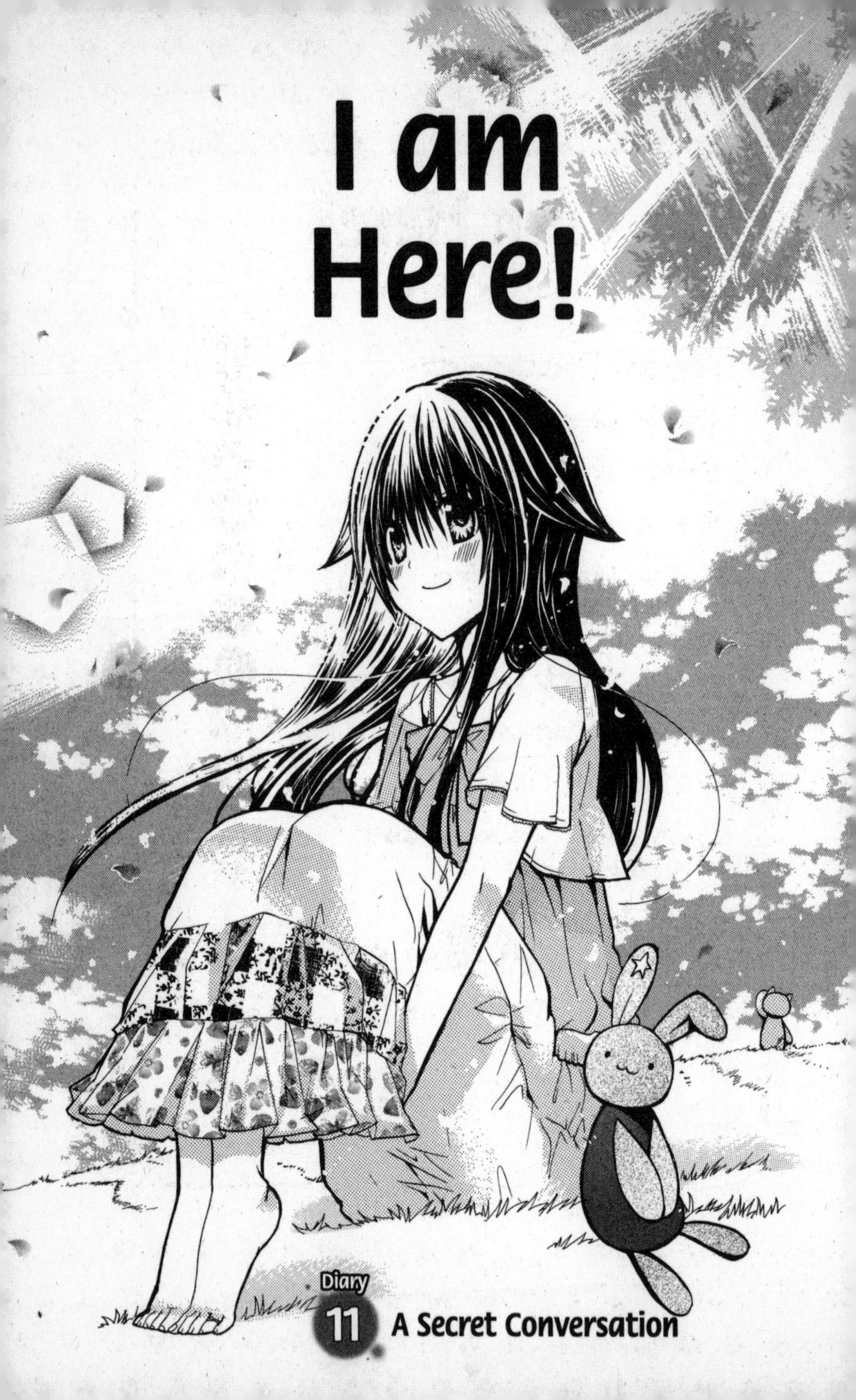
I am Here!
Diary 11 A Secret Conversation

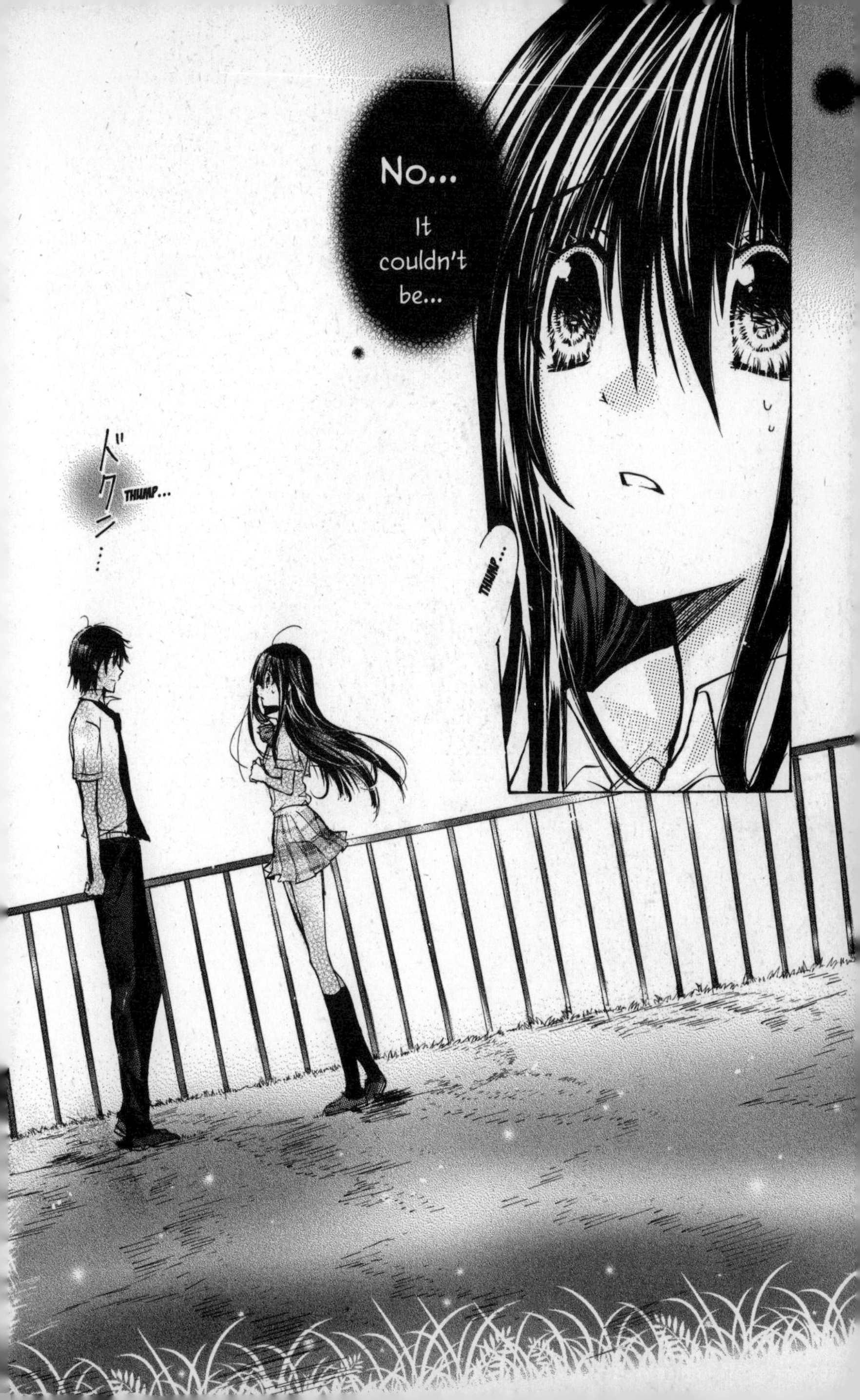
No...
It couldn't be...
THUMP...
ドクン…
THUMP...

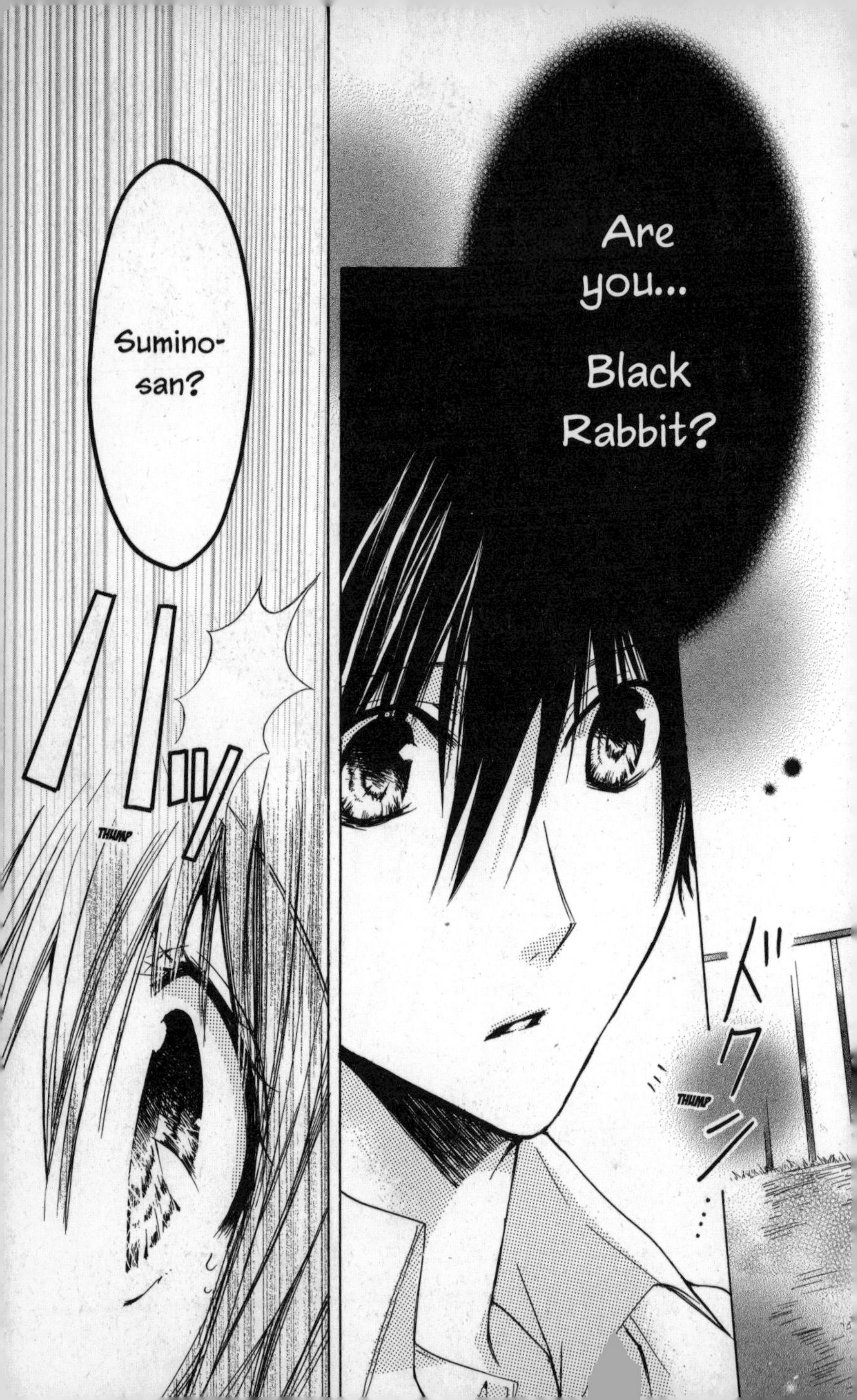
Are you...
Black Rabbit?
THUMP
Sumino-san?
THUMP

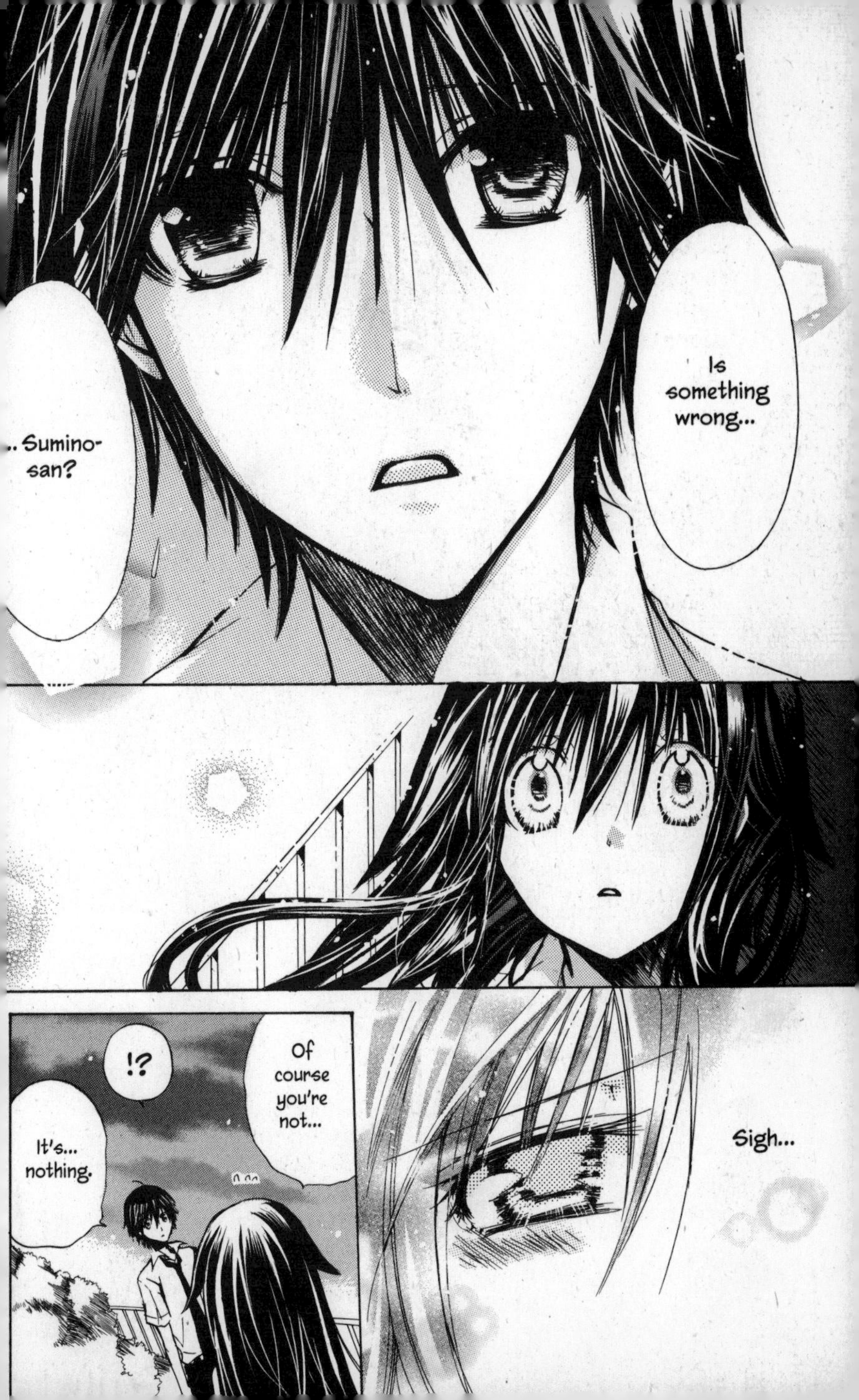

Is something wrong...
.. Sumino-san?
Sigh...
Of course you're not...
!?
It's... nothing.

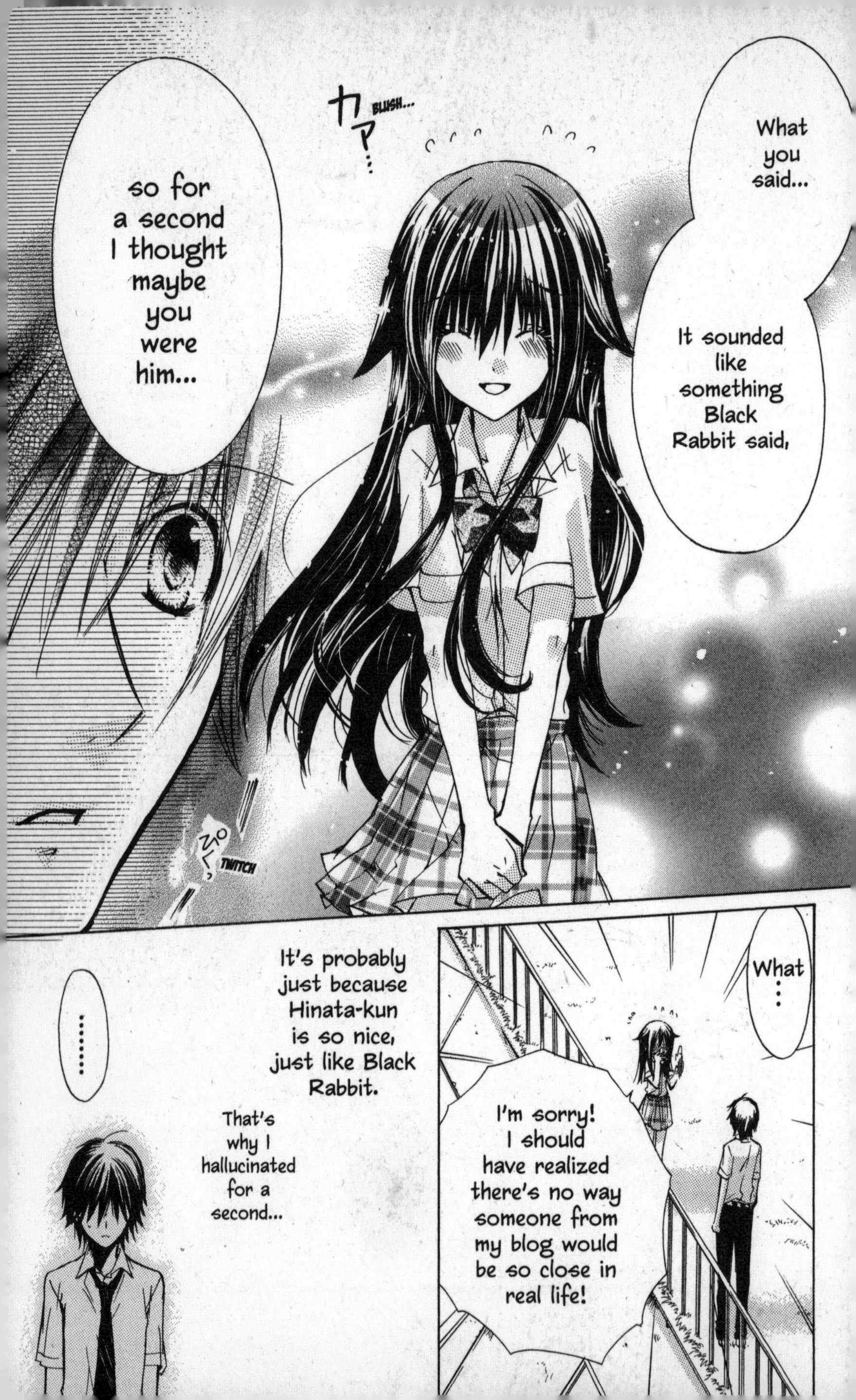
What you said...
It sounded like something Black Rabbit said,
BLUSH...
so for a second I thought maybe you were him...
TWITCH
What...
I'm sorry! I should have realized there's no way someone from my blog would be so close in real life!
It's probably just because Hinata-kun is so nice, just like Black Rabbit.
That's why I hallucinated for a second...
....

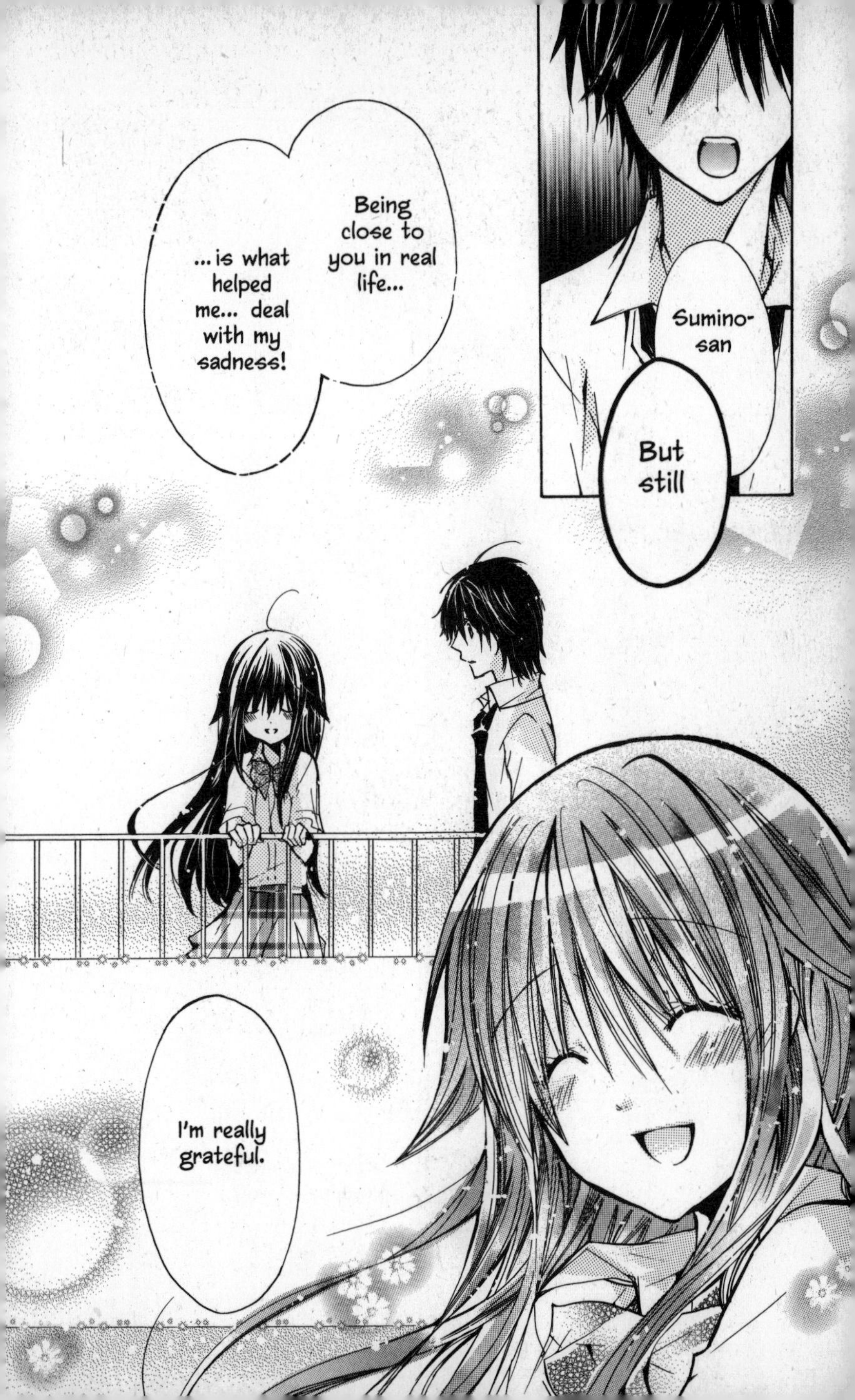
Sumino-san
But still
Being close to you in real life...
...is what helped me... deal with my sadness!
I'm really grateful.

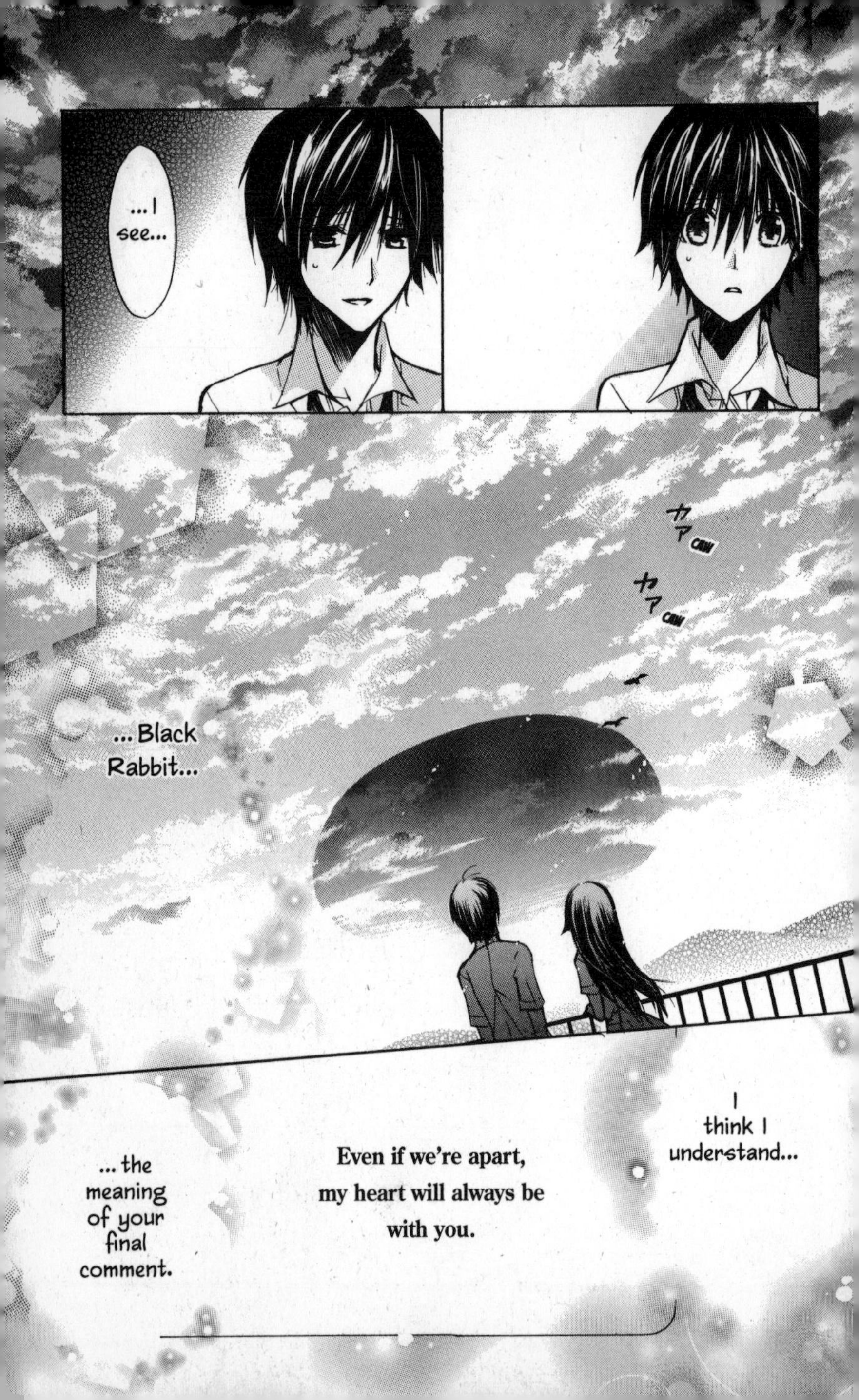
...I see...
カァ CAW
カァ CAW
...Black Rabbit...
I think I understand...
Even if we're apart, my heart will always be with you.
...the meaning of your final comment.

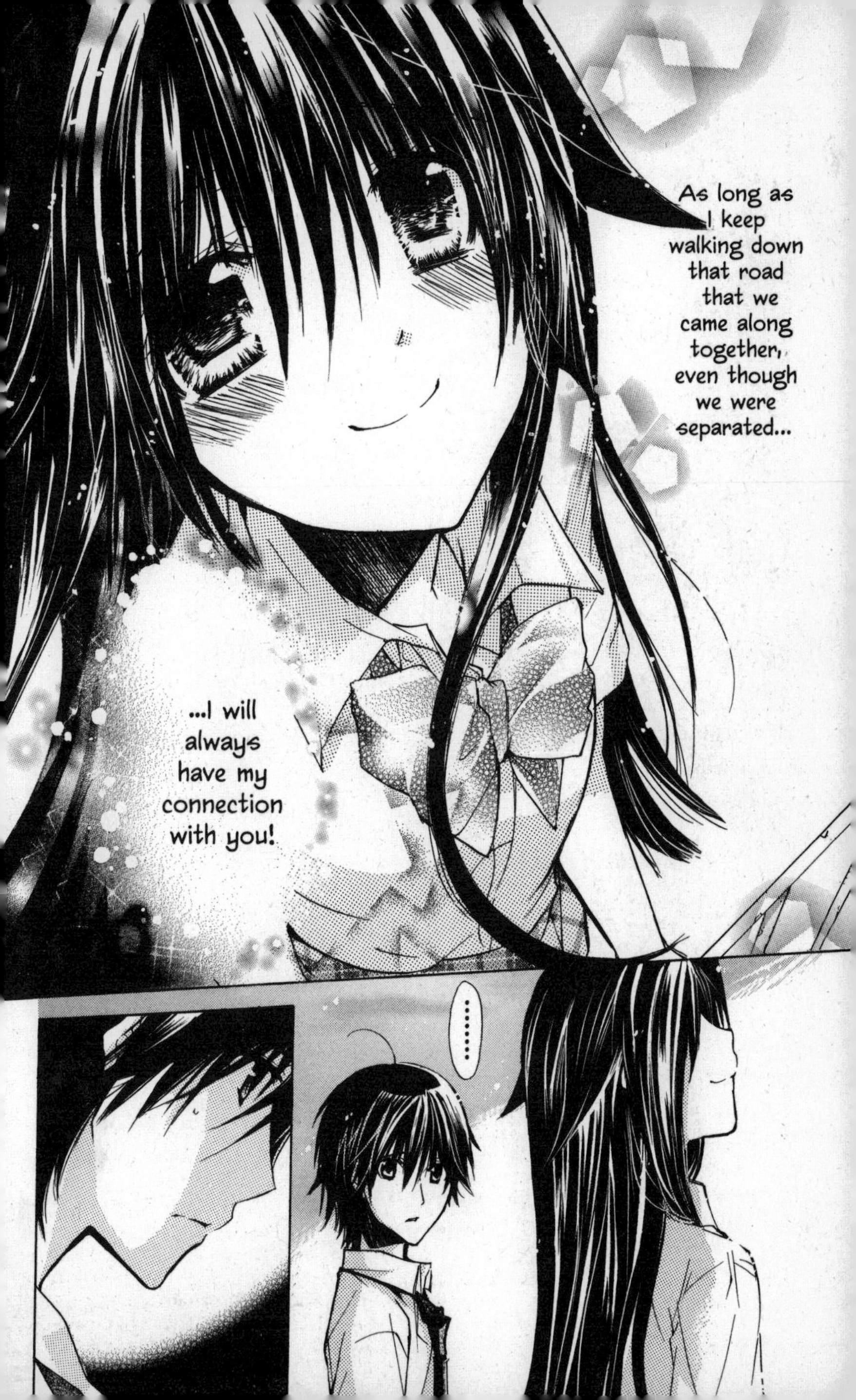
As long as I keep walking down that road that we came along together, even though we were separated...
...I will always have my connection with you!
....

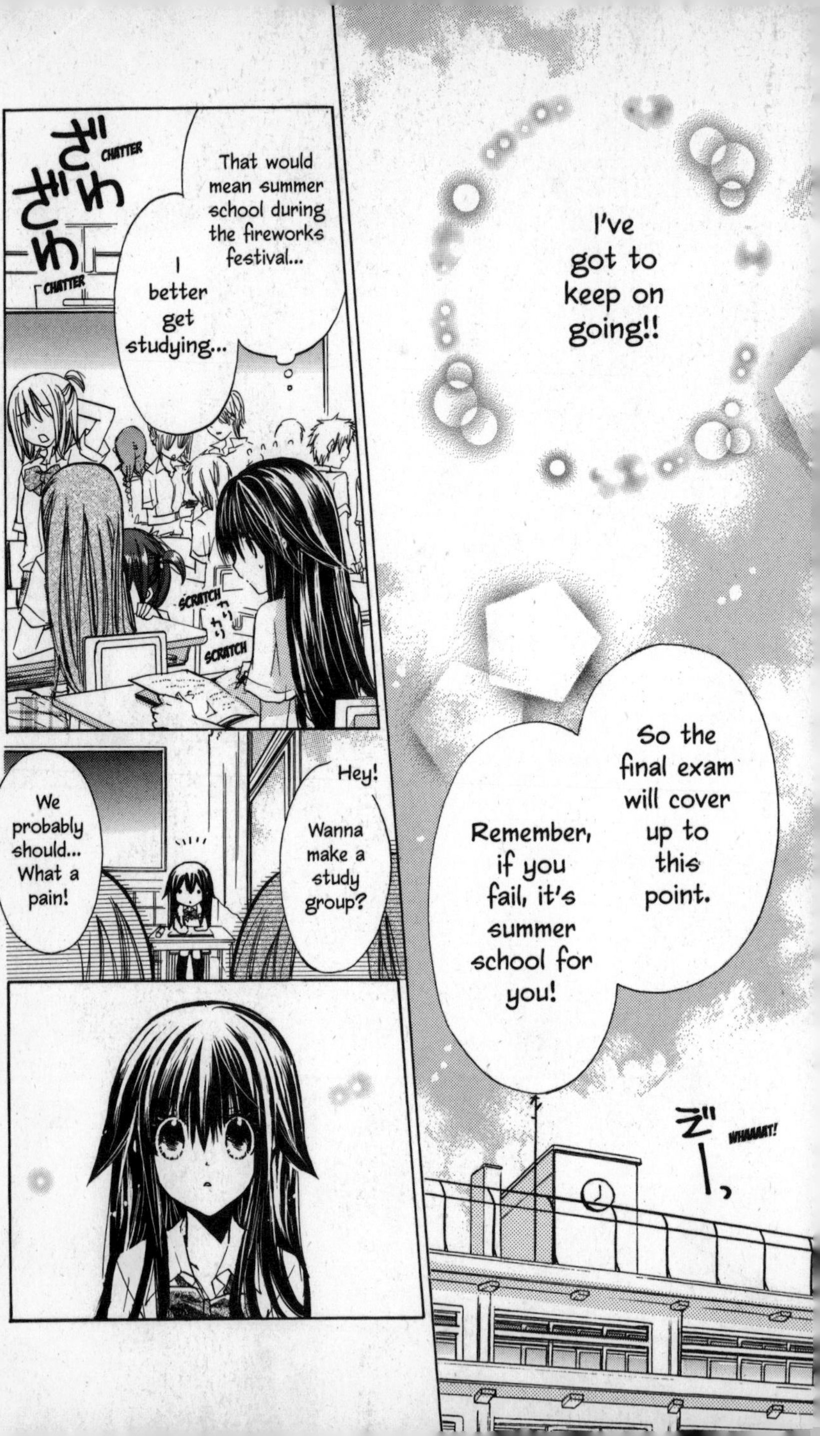
I've got to keep on going!!
So the final exam will cover up to this point.
Remember, if you fail, it's summer school for you!
WHAAAAT!
ざわ ざわ
CHATTER
CHATTER
That would mean summer school during the fireworks festival...
I better get studying...
SCRATCH
SCRATCH
Hey! Wanna make a study group?
We probably should... What a pain!

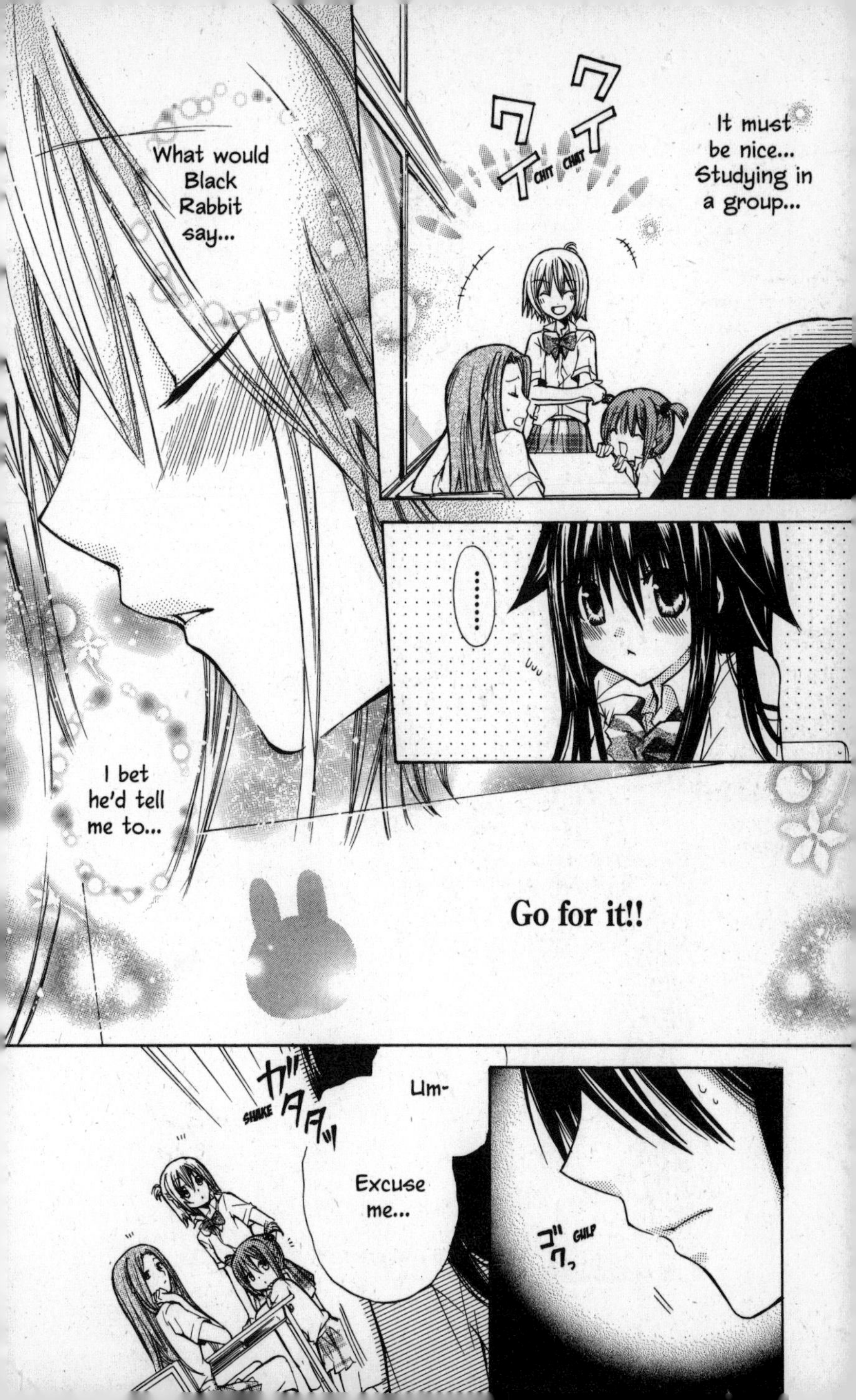

ワイワイ
CHIT CHAT
It must be nice... Studying in a group...
......
What would Black Rabbit say...
I bet he'd tell me to...
Go for it!!
ゴクッ
GULP
Um-
Excuse me...
ガタタッ
SHAKE

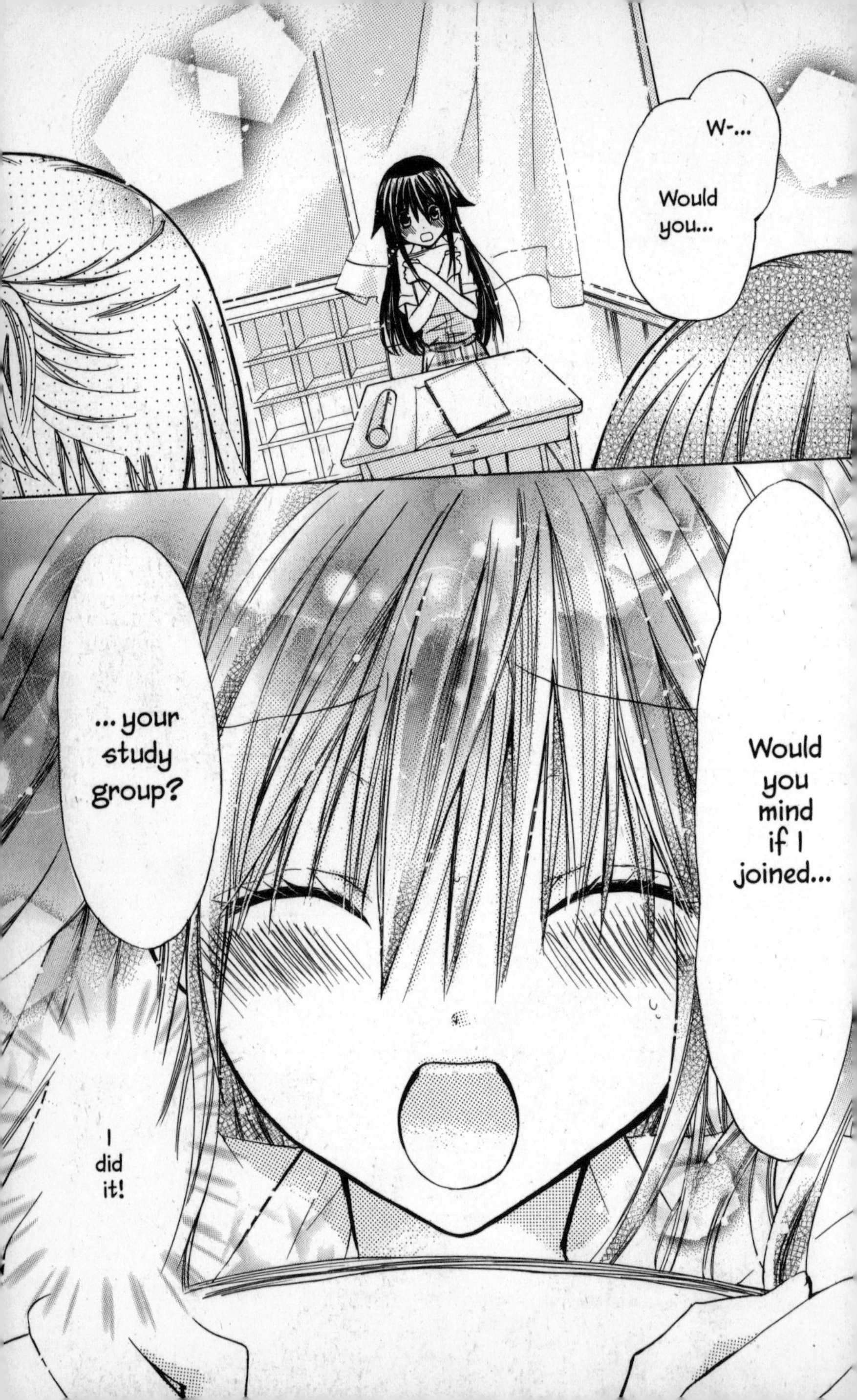
W-...
Would you...
Would you mind if I joined...
... your study group?
I did it!

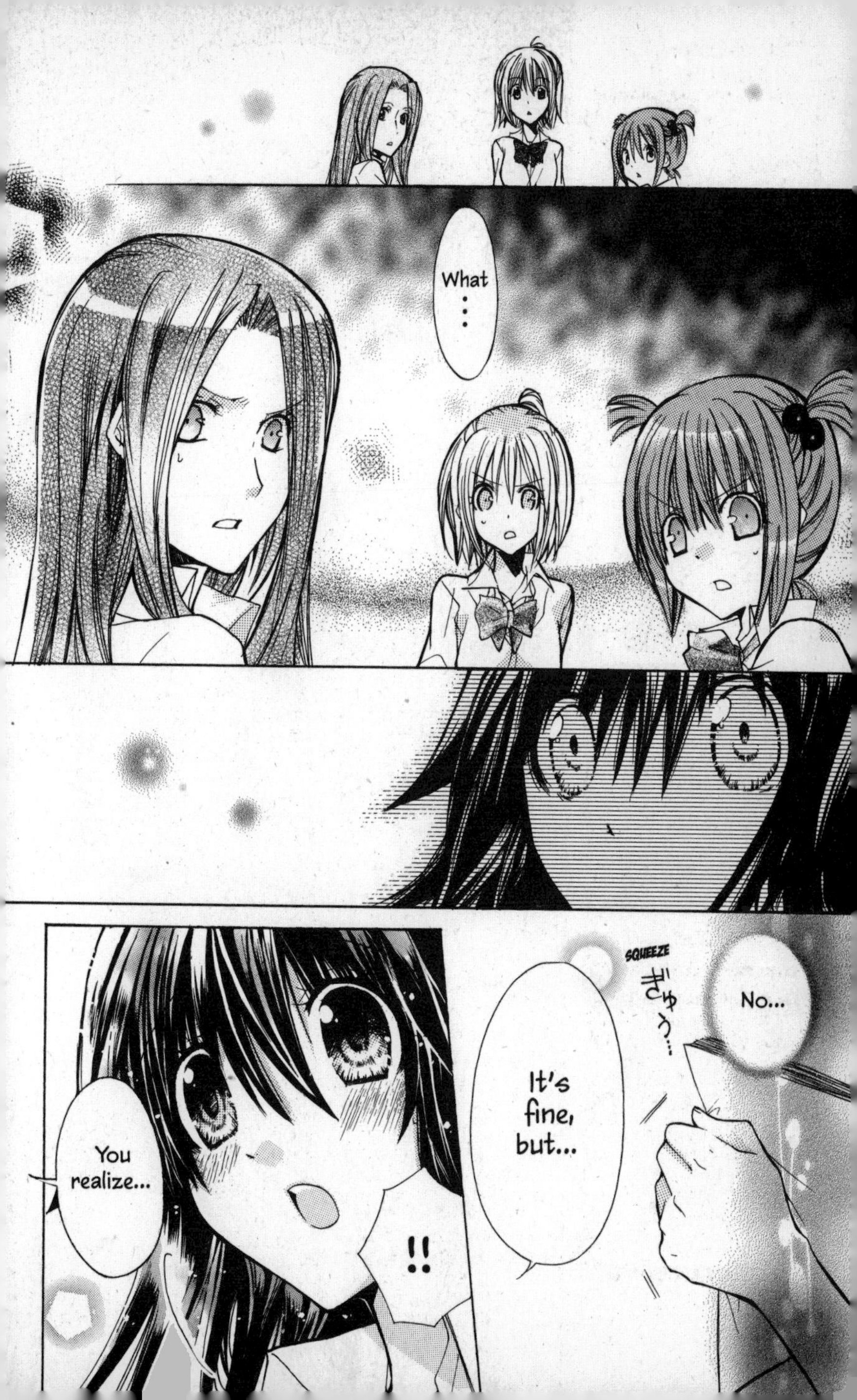
What...
No...
SQUEEZE
ぎゅう...
It's fine, but...
You realize...
!!

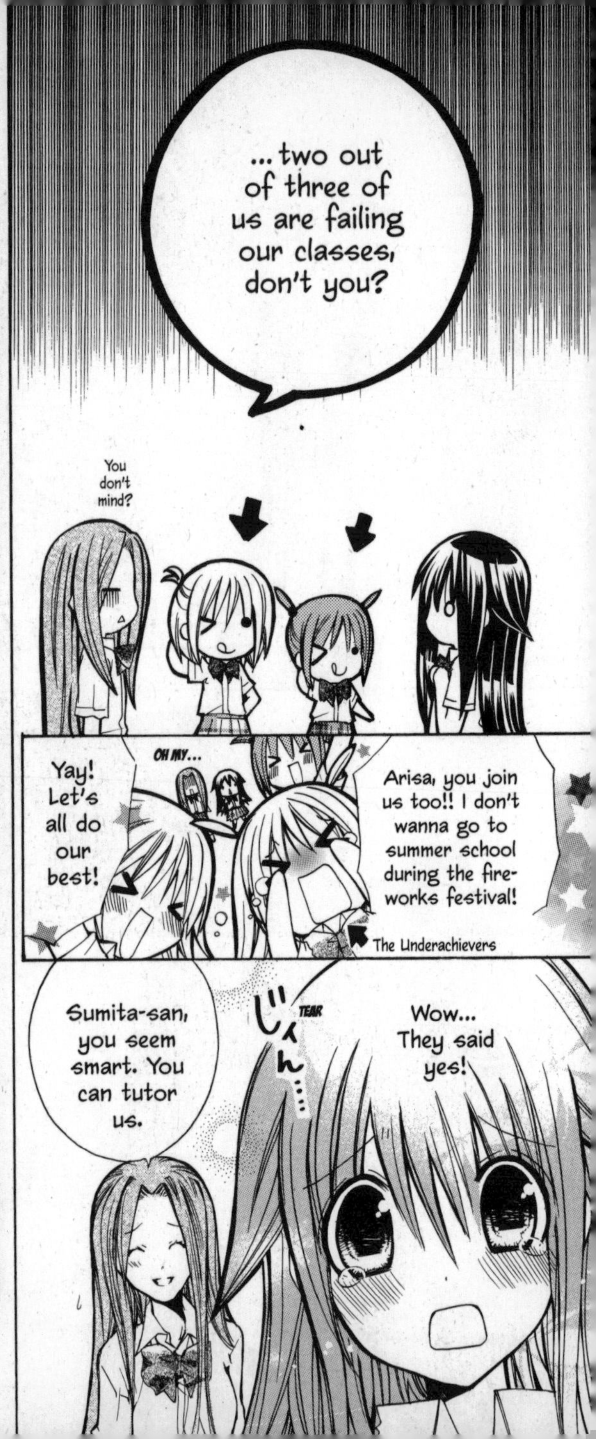
...two out of three of us are failing our classes, don't you?
You don't mind?
Arisa, you join us too!! I don't wanna go to summer school during the fire-works festival!
OH MY...
Yay! Let's all do our best!
The Underachievers
Wow... They said yes!
じ~ん...
TEAR
Sumita-san, you seem smart. You can tutor us.

The Adventures of Mahimahi 3

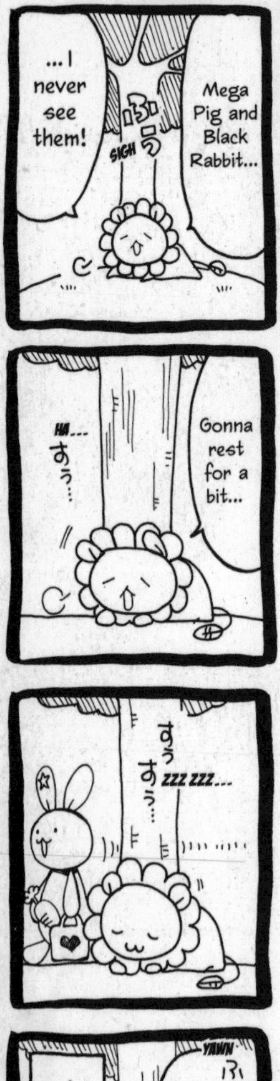
Mega Pig and Black Rabbit...
ふぅ
SIGH
...I never see them!
Gonna rest for a bit...
HA...
すぅ...
すぅ すぅ...
ZZZ ZZZ...
YAWN
ふわあ~
I slept well!
Life is full of missed chances.

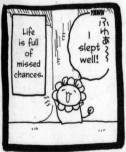

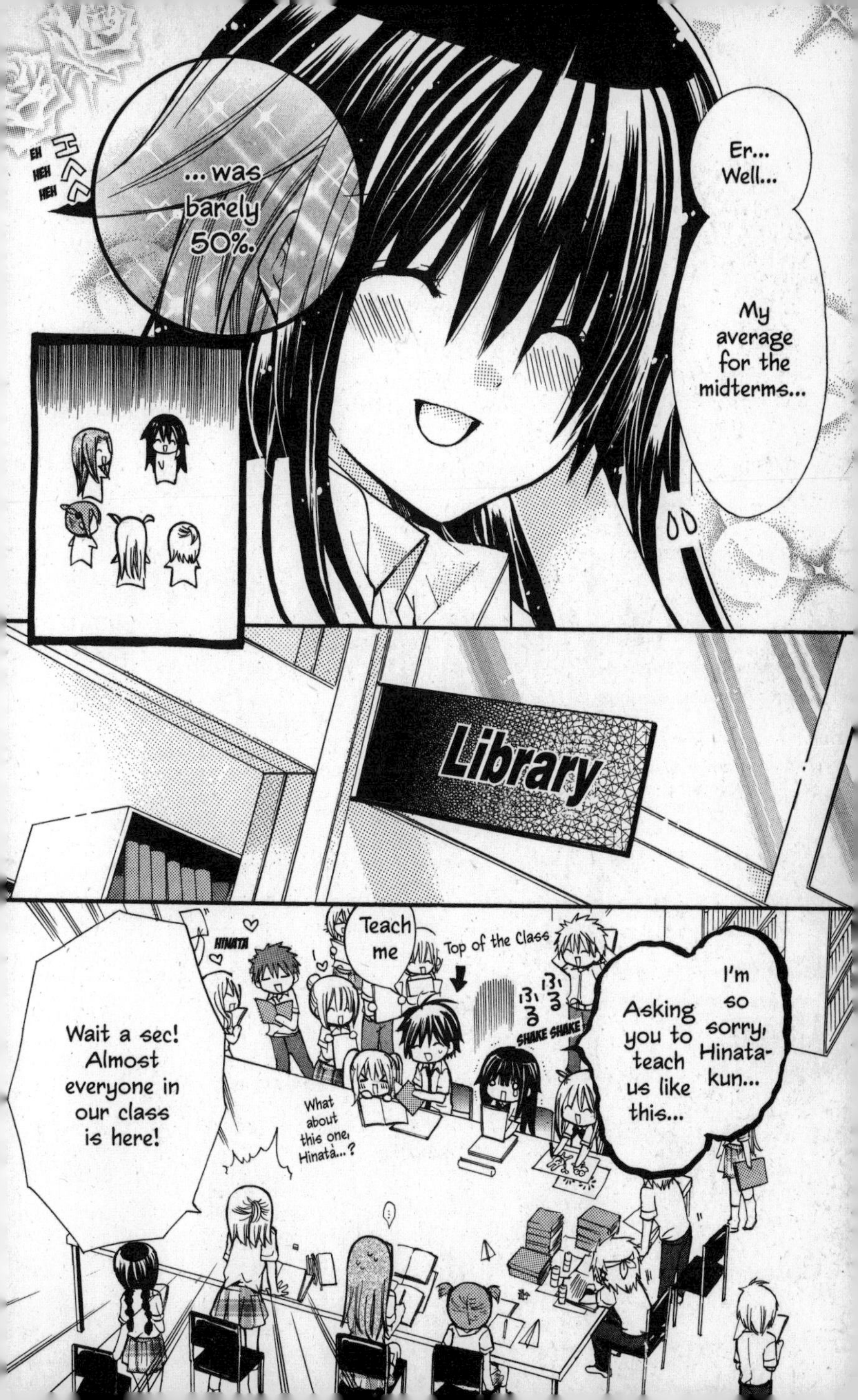
Er... Well...
My average for the midterms...
... was barely 50%.
EH HEH HEH
Library
I'm so sorry, Hinata-kun... Asking you to teach us like this...
ふるふる
SHAKE SHAKE
Top of the Class
Teach me
HINATA
What about this one, Hinata...?
Wait a sec! Almost everyone in our class is here!

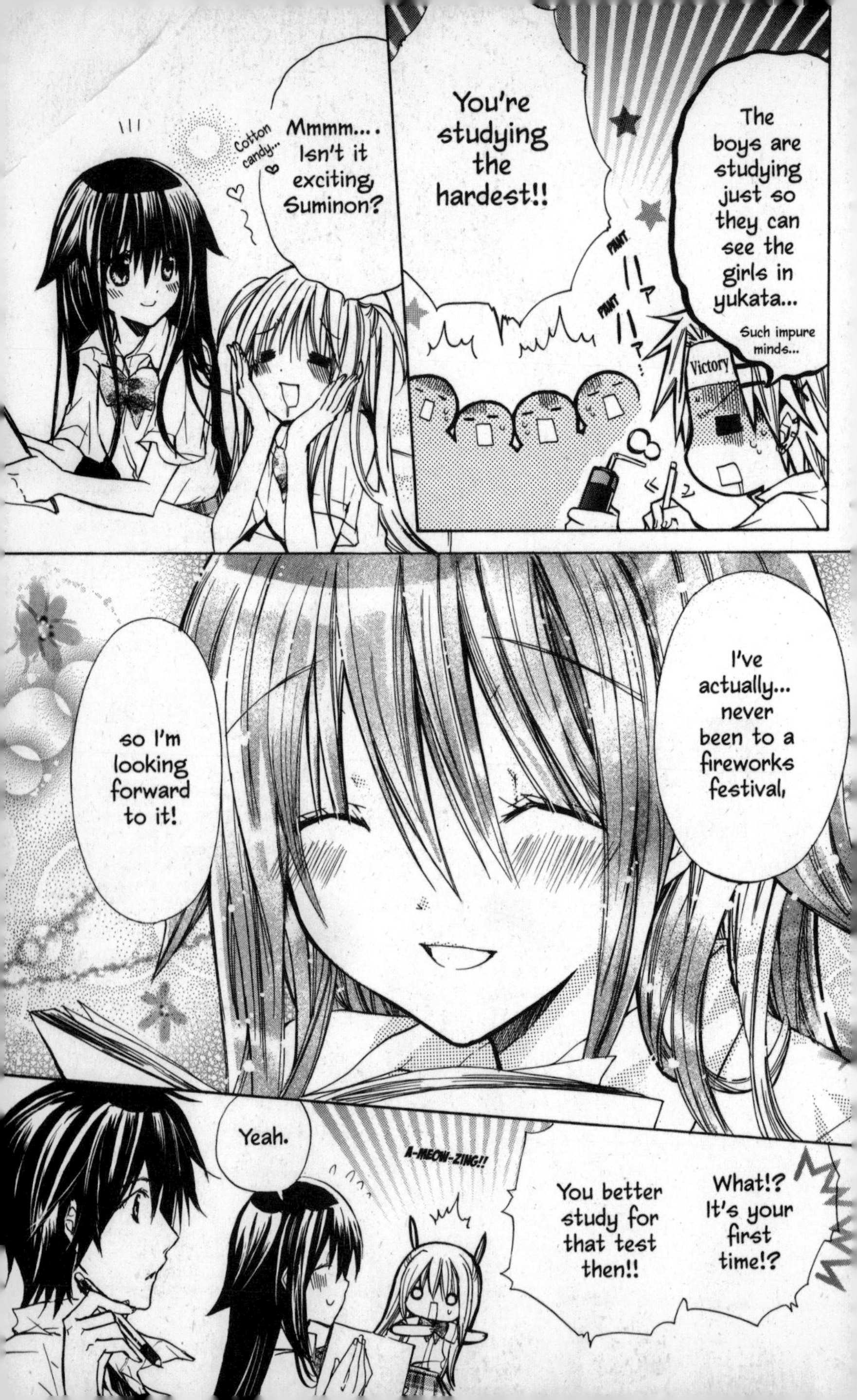
The boys are studying just so they can see the girls in yukata...
You're studying the hardest!!
PANT
PANT
Such impure minds...
Victory
Mmmm.... Isn't it exciting, Suminon?
Cotton candy...
I've actually... never been to a fireworks festival,
so I'm looking forward to it!
What!? It's your first time!?
You better study for that test then!!
A-MEOW-ZING!!
Yeah.

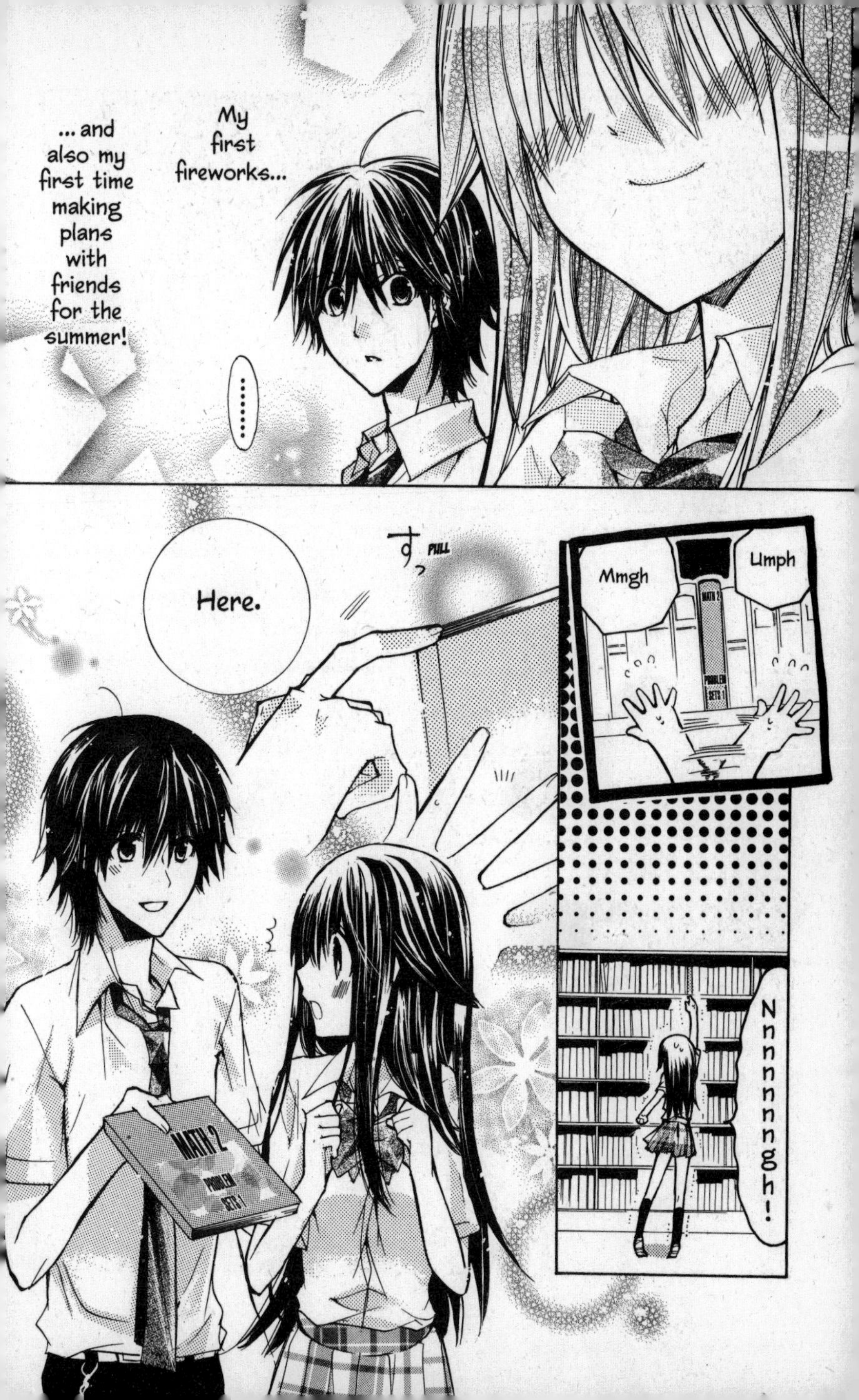
My first fireworks...
... and also my first time making plans with friends for the summer!
......
Umph
Mmgh
Nnnnnngh!
すっ PULL
Here.
MATH 2 PROBLEM SETS 1

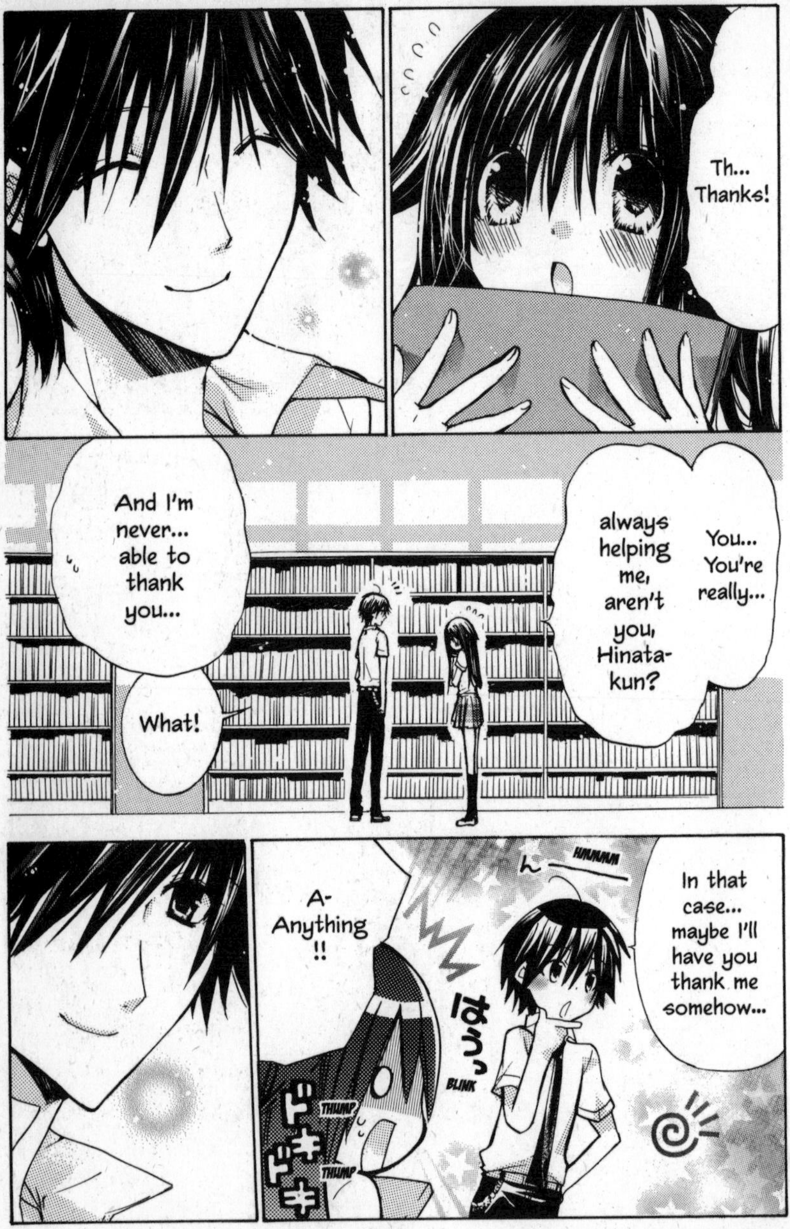
Th... Thanks!
You... You're really...
always helping me, aren't you, Hinata-kun?
And I'm never... able to thank you...
What!
In that case... maybe I'll have you thank me somehow...
ん— HMMMM
はうっ
BLINK
A- Anything !!
ドキドキ
THUMP
THUMP

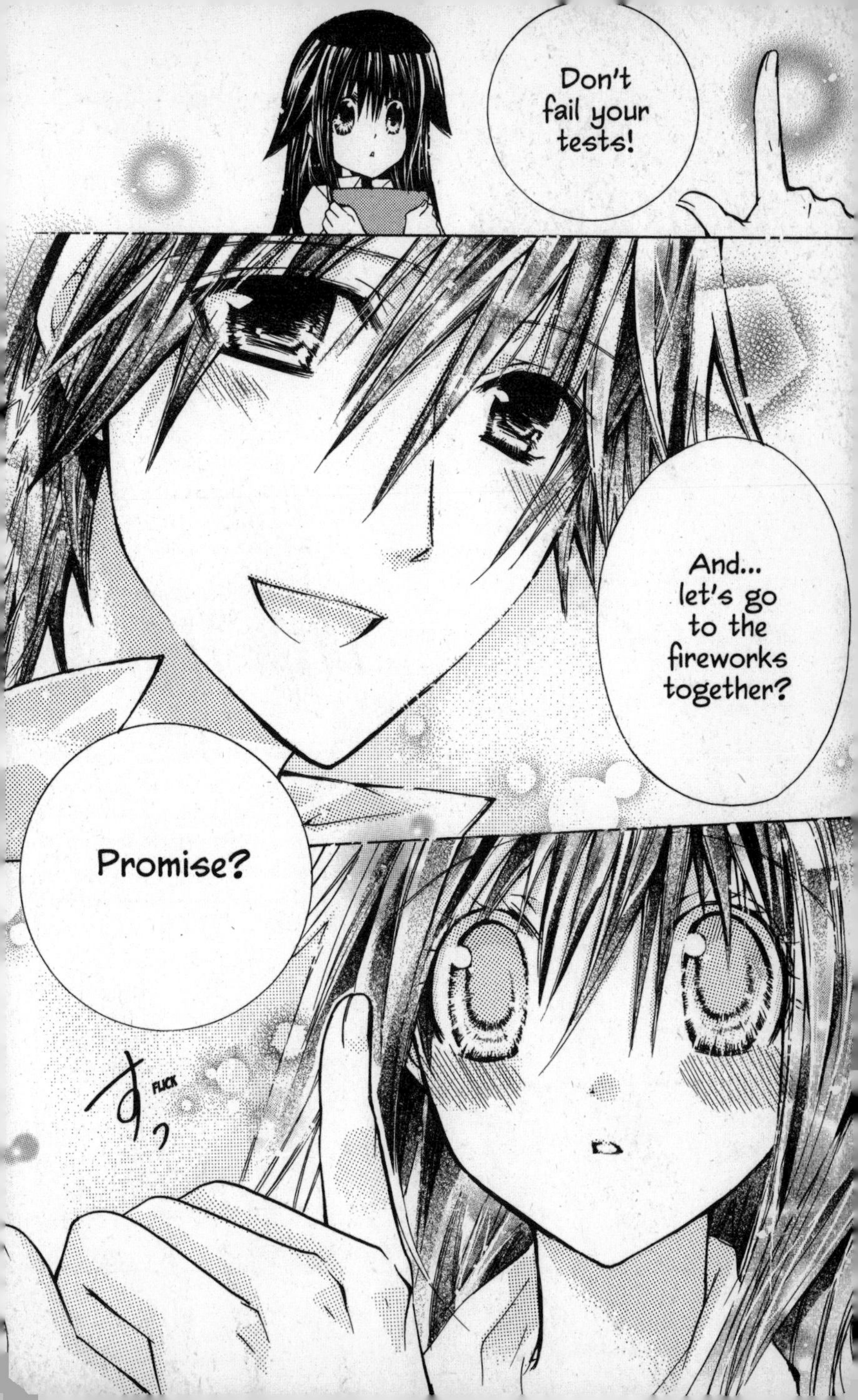
Don't fail your tests!
And... let's go to the fireworks together?
Promise?
すっ
FLICK

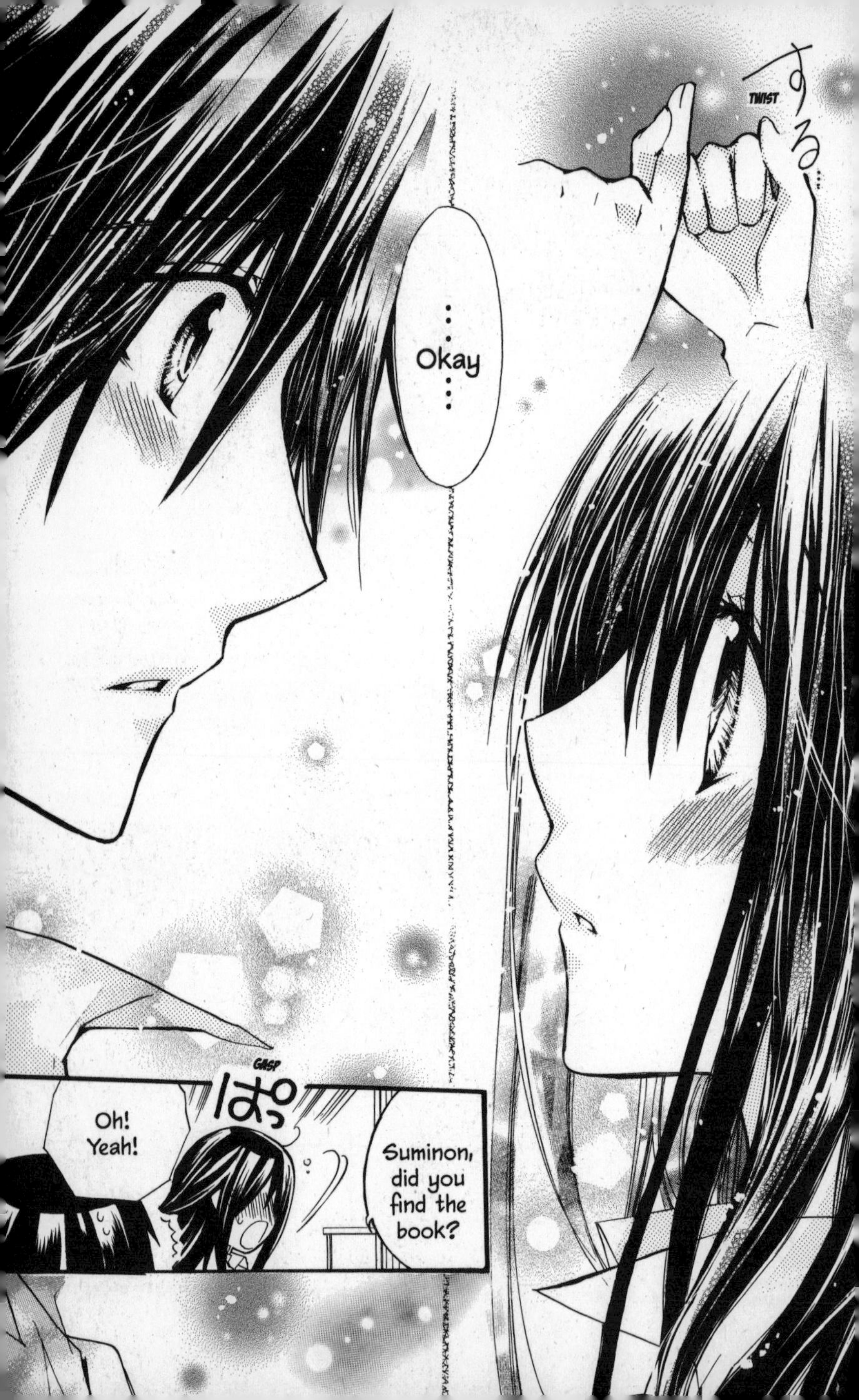
TWIST
する…
...Okay...
Suminon, did you find the book?
GASP
ぱっ
Oh! Yeah!

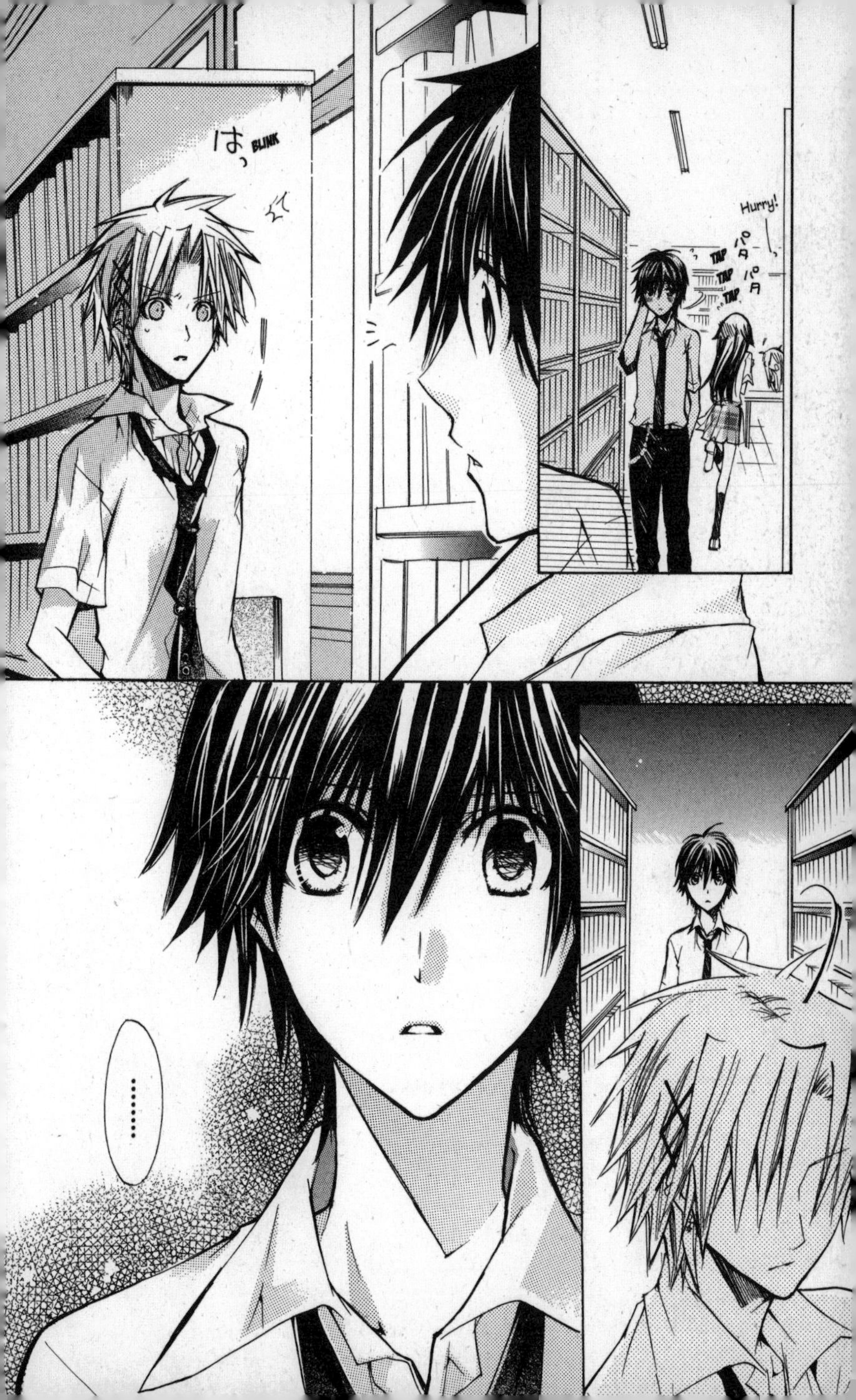
Hurry!
TAP TAP TAP
パタ パタ
は、 BLINK
……

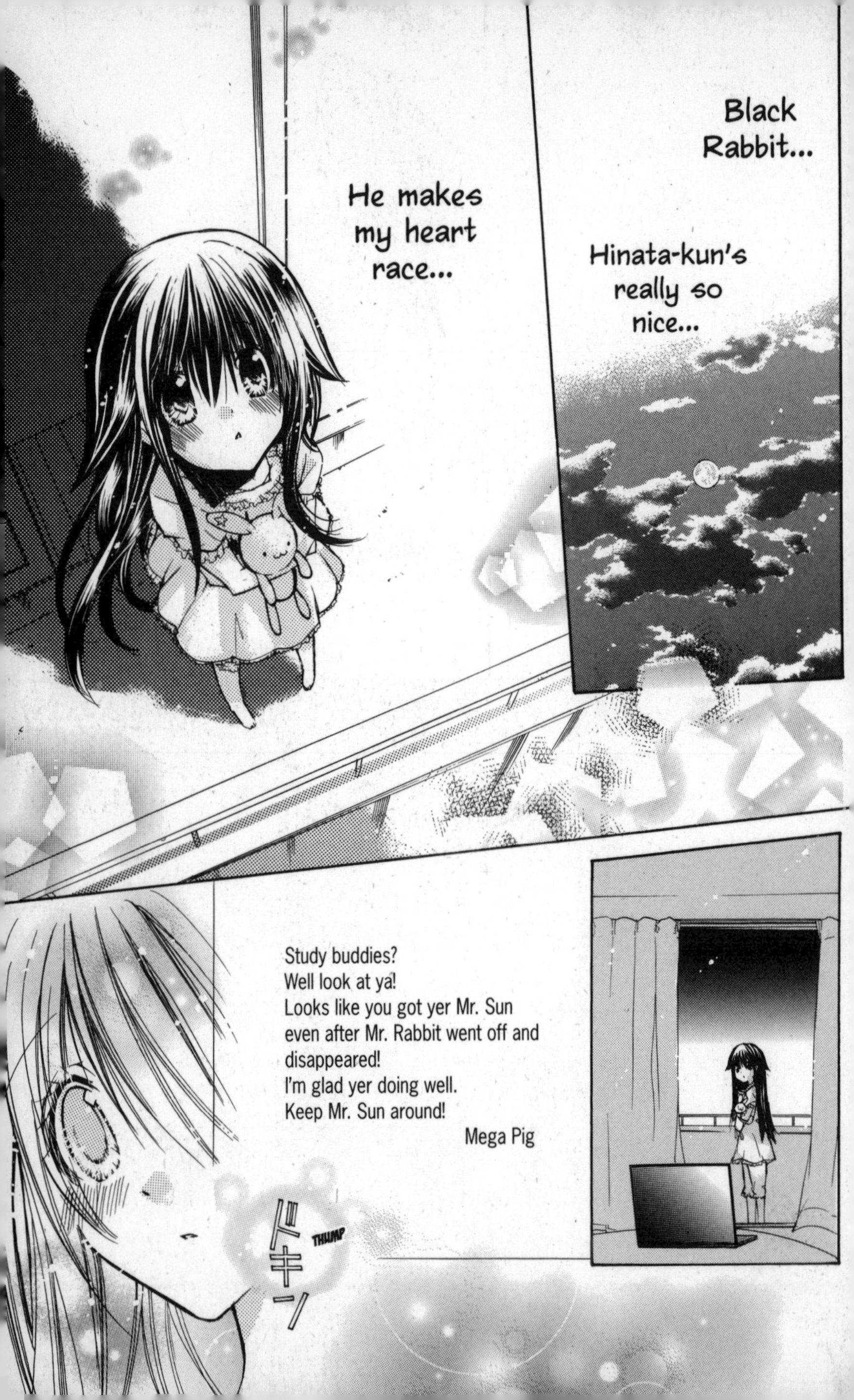
Black Rabbit...
Hinata-kun's really so nice...
He makes my heart race...
Study buddies?
Well look at ya!
Looks like you got yer Mr. Sun even after Mr. Rabbit went off and disappeared!
I'm glad yer doing well.
Keep Mr. Sun around!
Mega Pig
THUMP

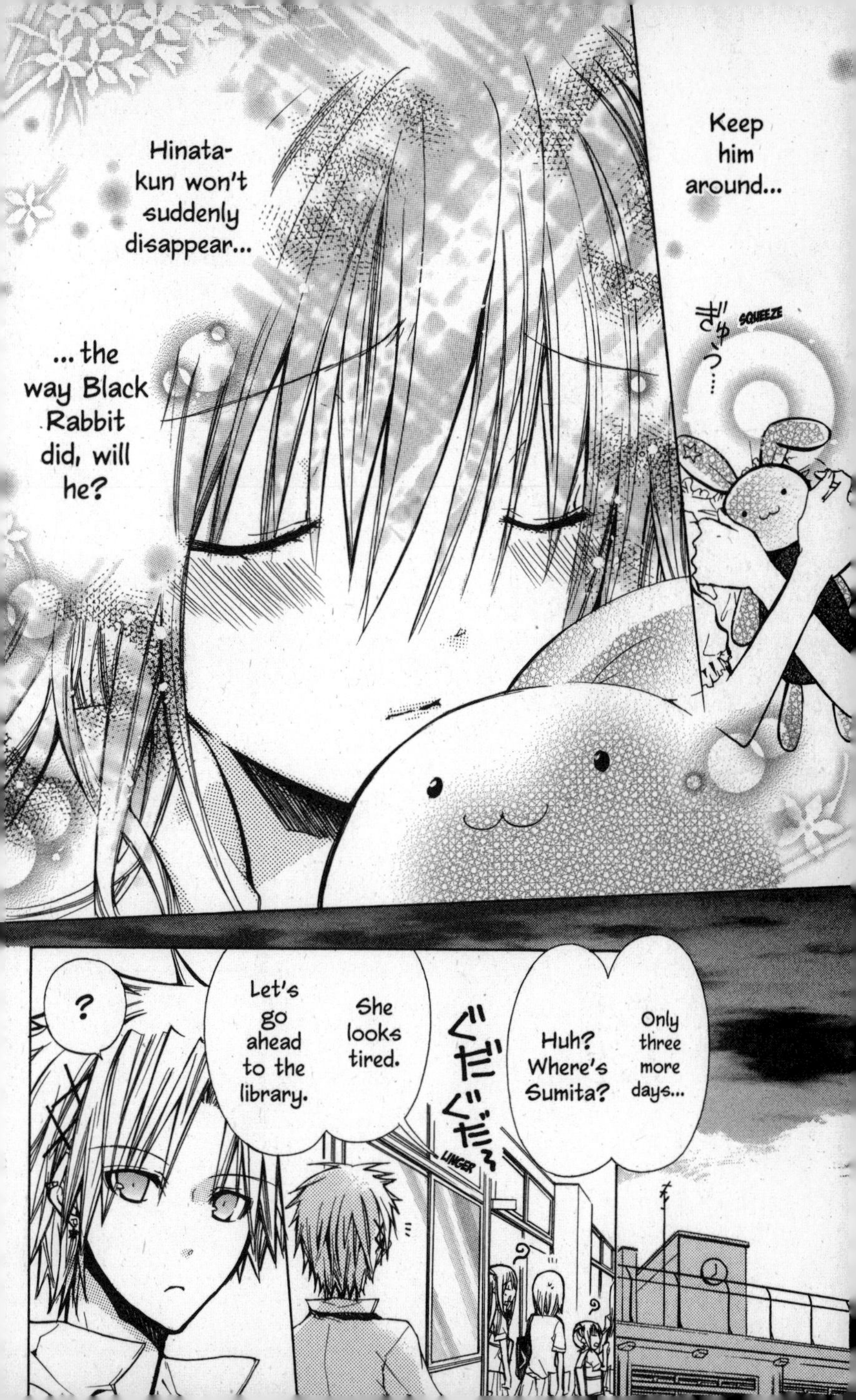
Keep him around...
ぎゅっ…
SQUEEZE
Hinata-kun won't suddenly disappear...
... the way Black Rabbit did, will he?
Only three more days...
Huh? Where's Sumita?
ぐだぐだ~
LINGER
She looks tired.
Let's go ahead to the library.
?

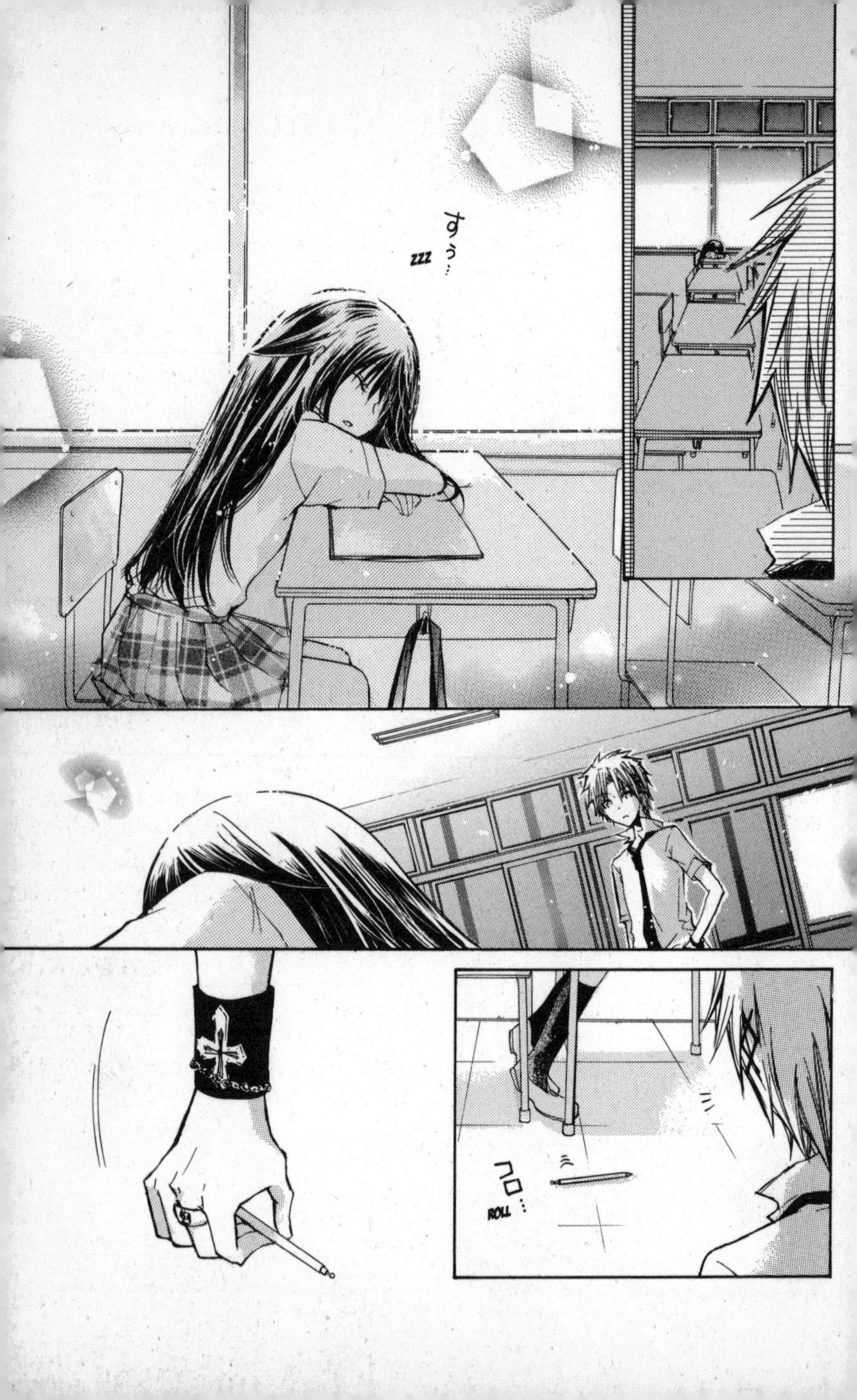
すぅ…
ZZZ
コロ…
ROLL

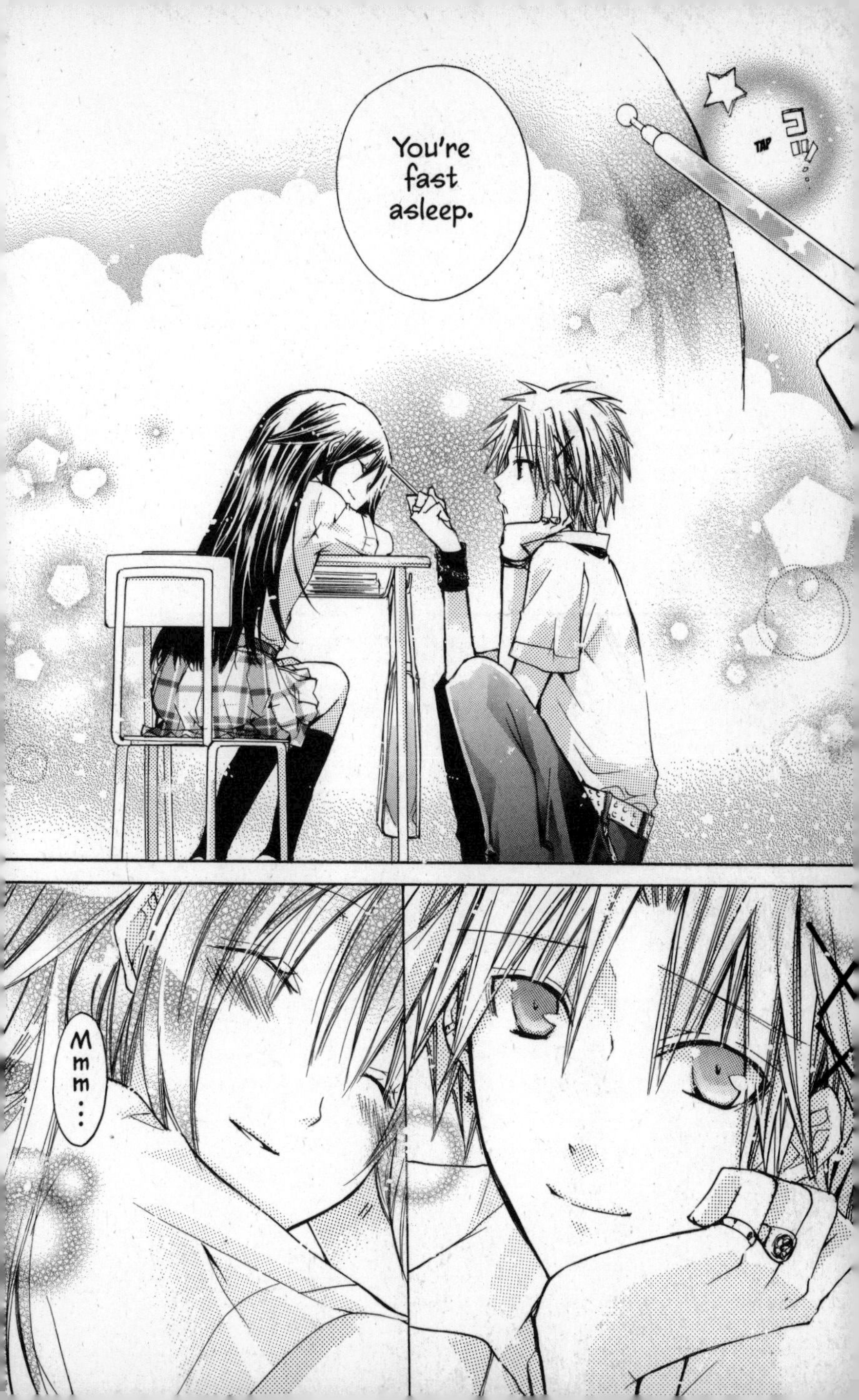
TAP
You're fast asleep.
Mmm...

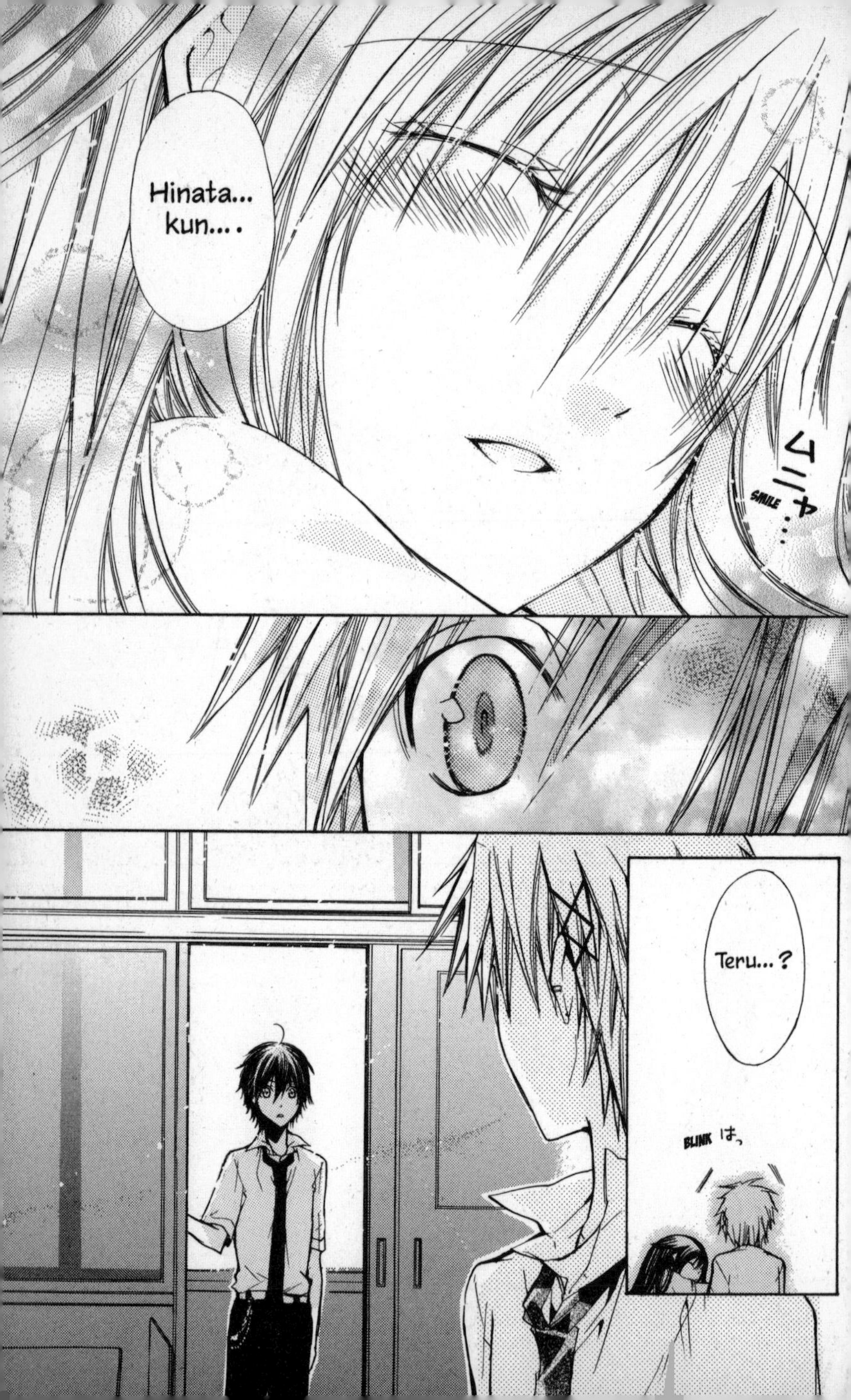
Hinata... kun....
ムニャ...
SMILE
Teru...?
BLINK はっ

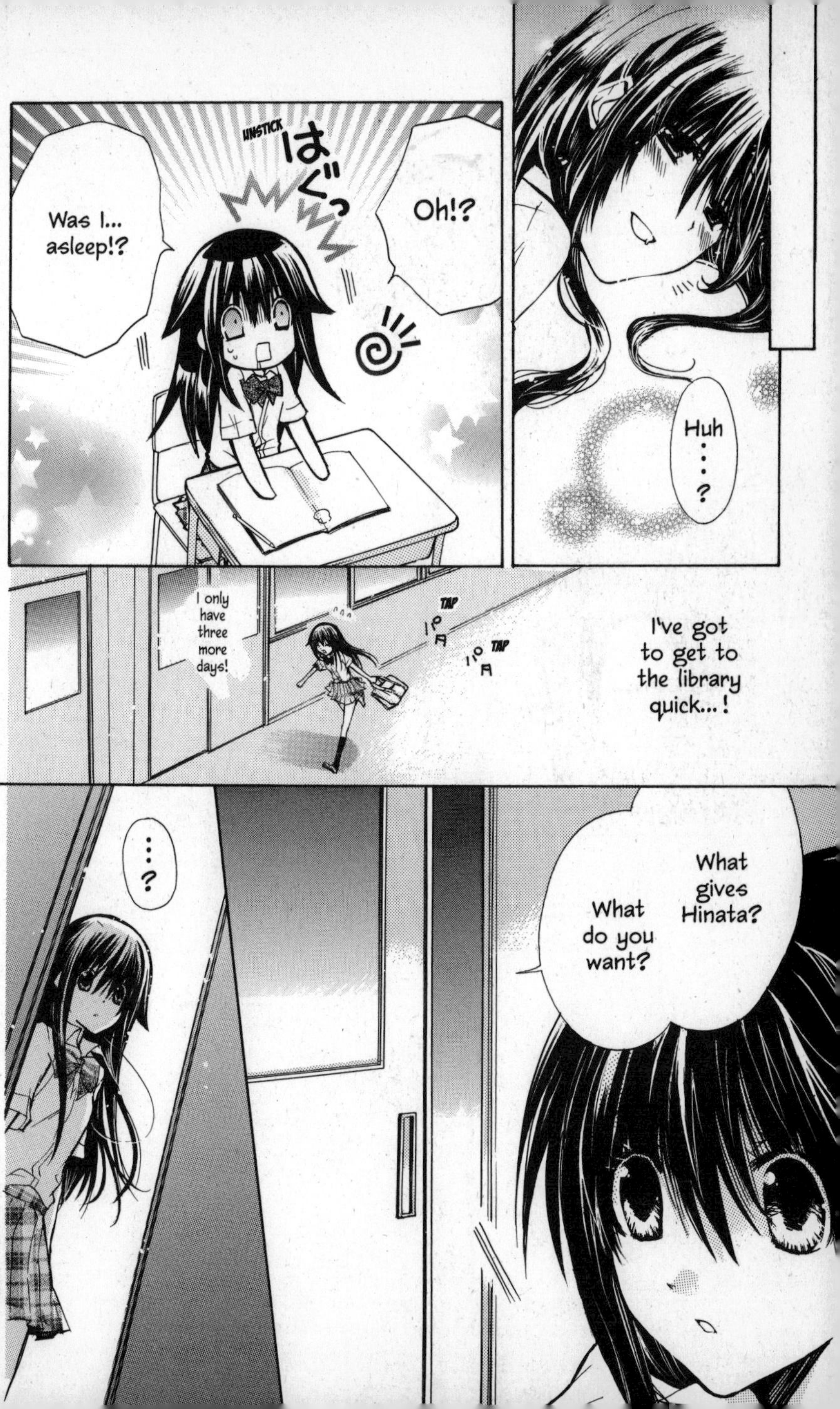
Huh...?
UNSTICK はぐっ
Oh!?
Was I... asleep!?
I've got to get to the library quick...!
TAP パタ
TAP パタ
I only have three more days!
What gives Hinata? What do you want?
...?

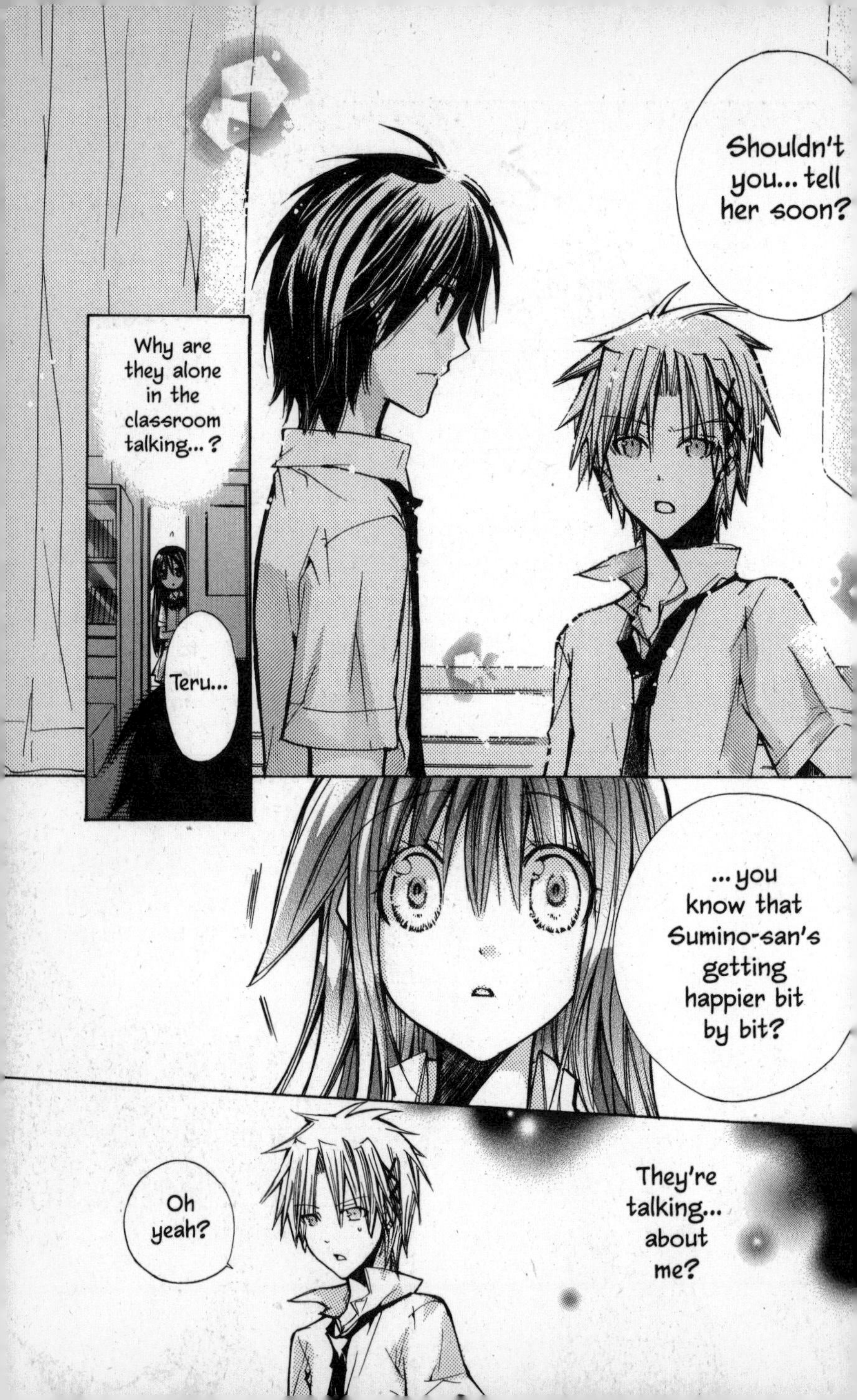
Shouldn't you... tell her soon?
Why are they alone in the classroom talking...?
Teru...
...you know that Sumino-san's getting happier bit by bit?
They're talking... about me?
Oh yeah?

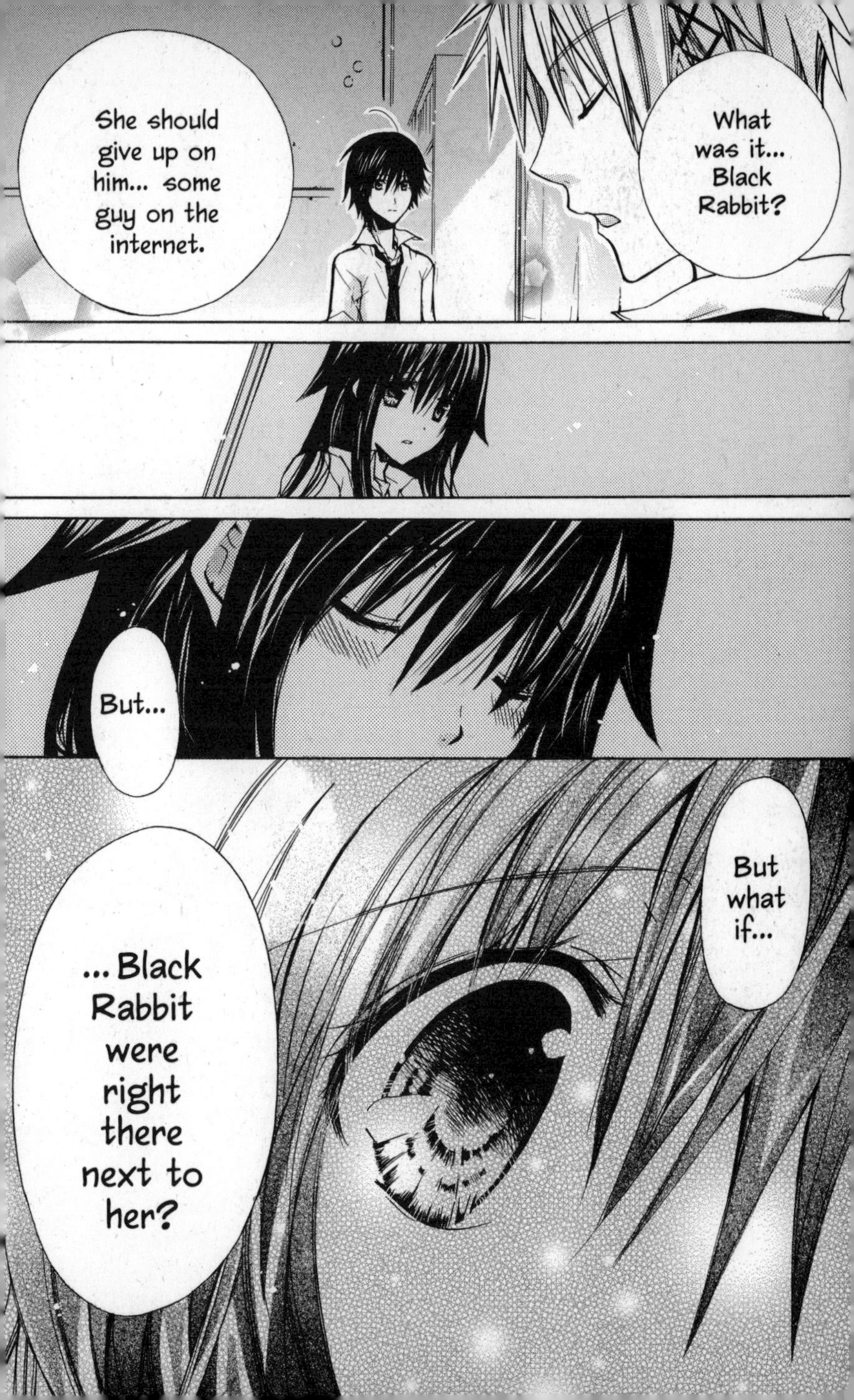
What was it... Black Rabbit?
She should give up on him... some guy on the internet.
But...
But what if...
...Black Rabbit were right there next to her?

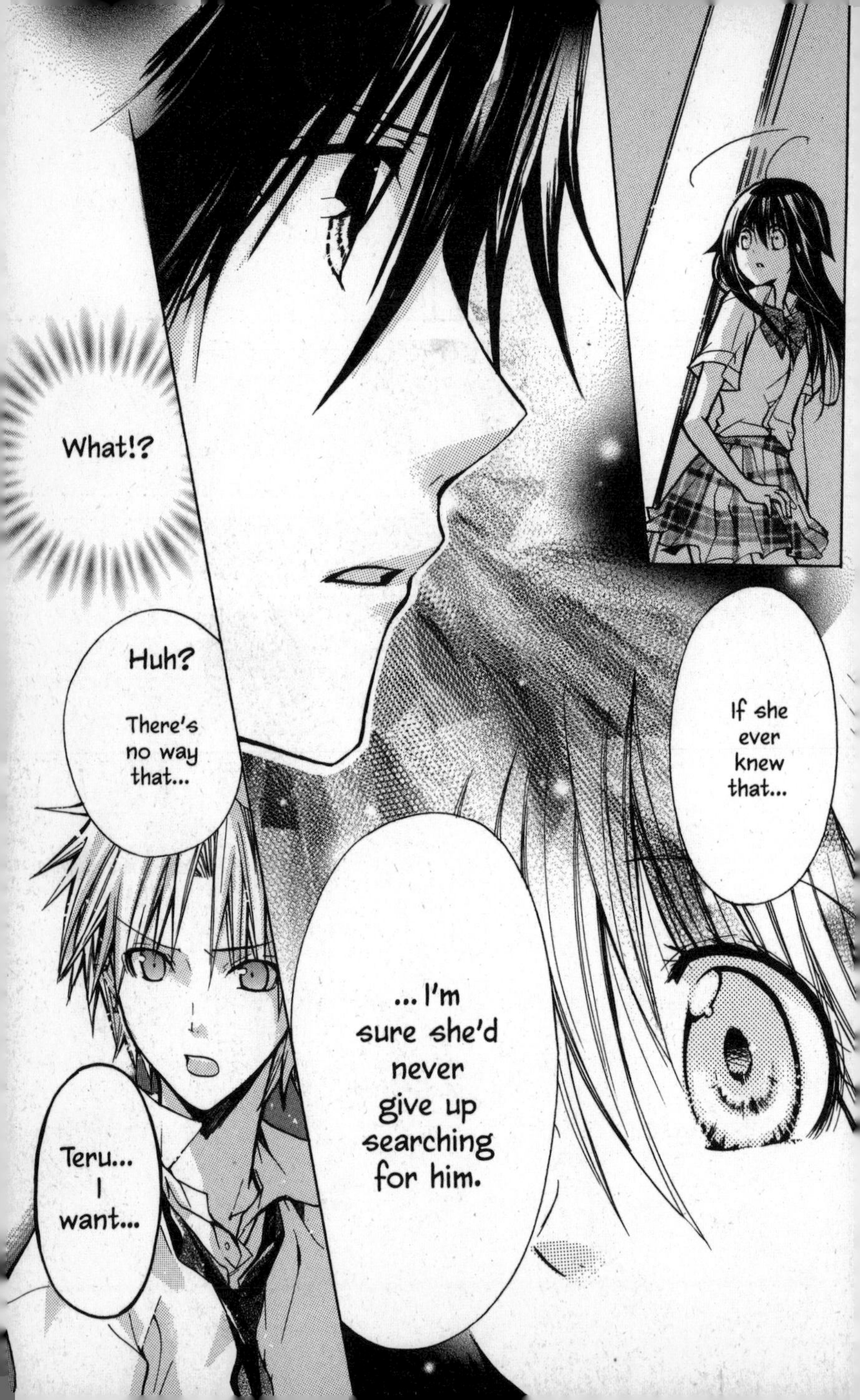

If she ever knew that...
... I'm sure she'd never give up searching for him.
What!?
Huh?
There's no way that...
Teru... I want...

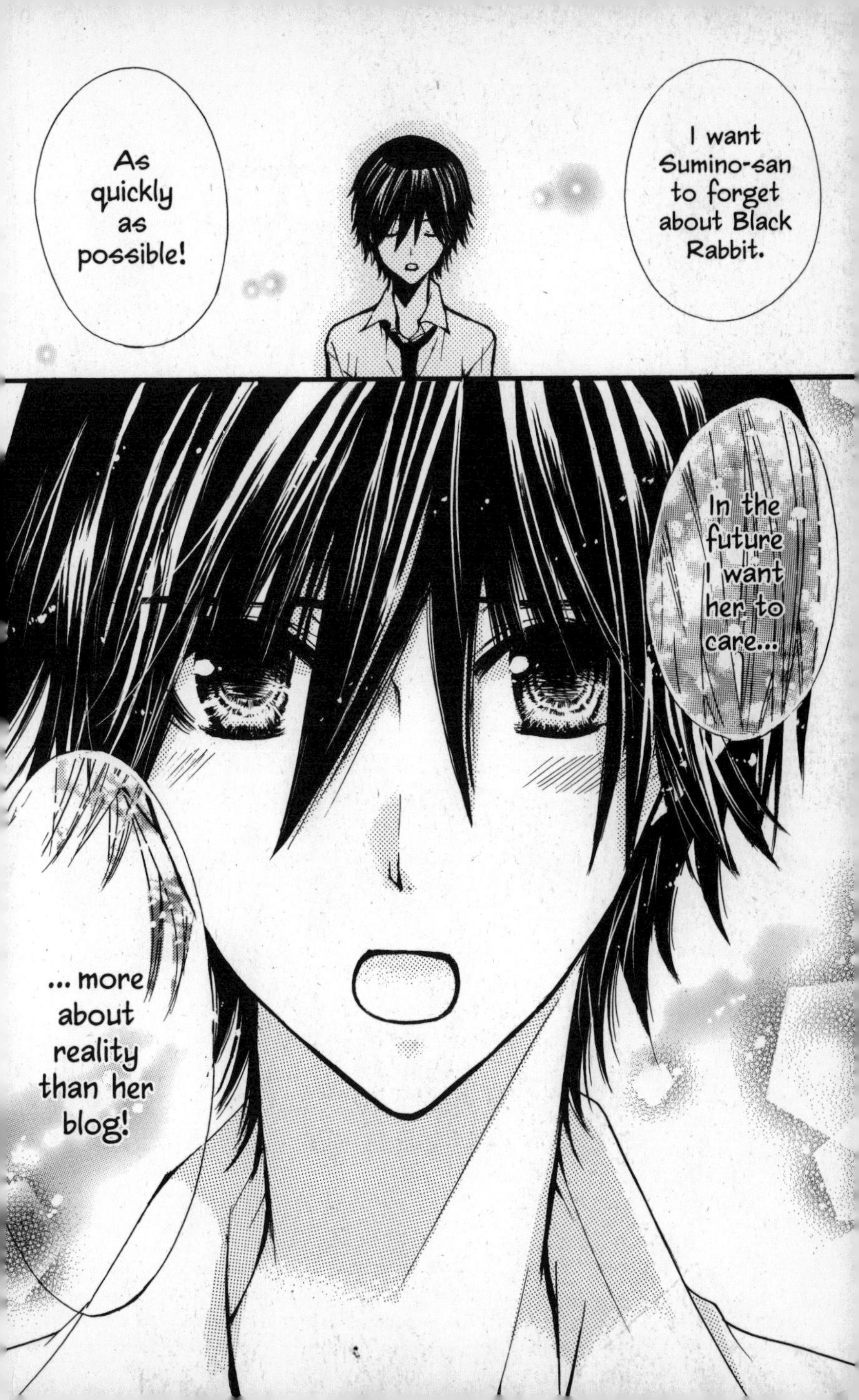
I want Sumino-san to forget about Black Rabbit.
As quickly as possible!
In the future I want her to care...
... more about reality than her blog!

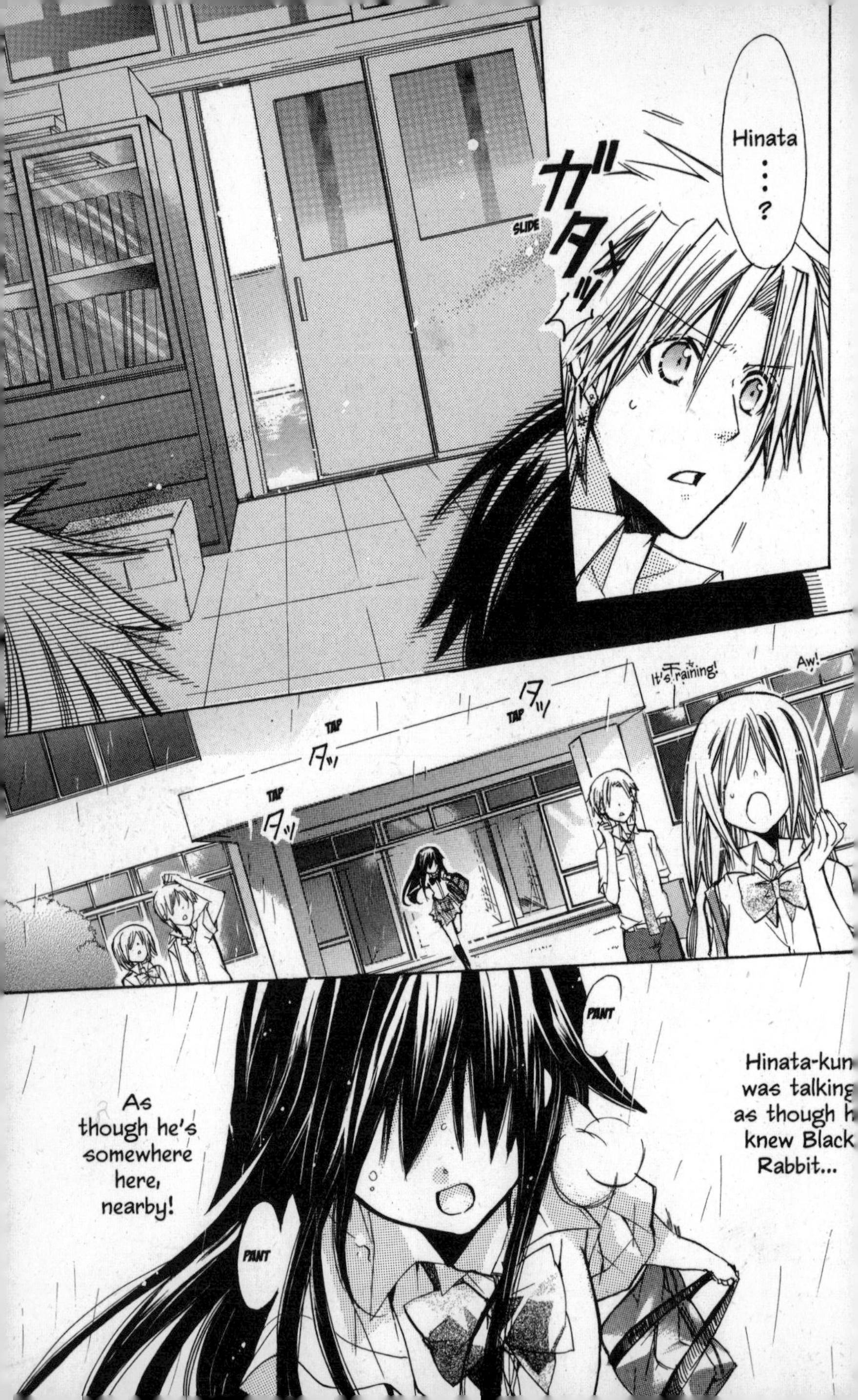
Hinata...?
ガタッ
SLIDE
Aw!
It's raining!
タッ
TAP
タッ
TAP
タッ
TAP
Hinata-kun was talking as though h knew Black Rabbit...
As though he's somewhere here, nearby!
PANT
PANT

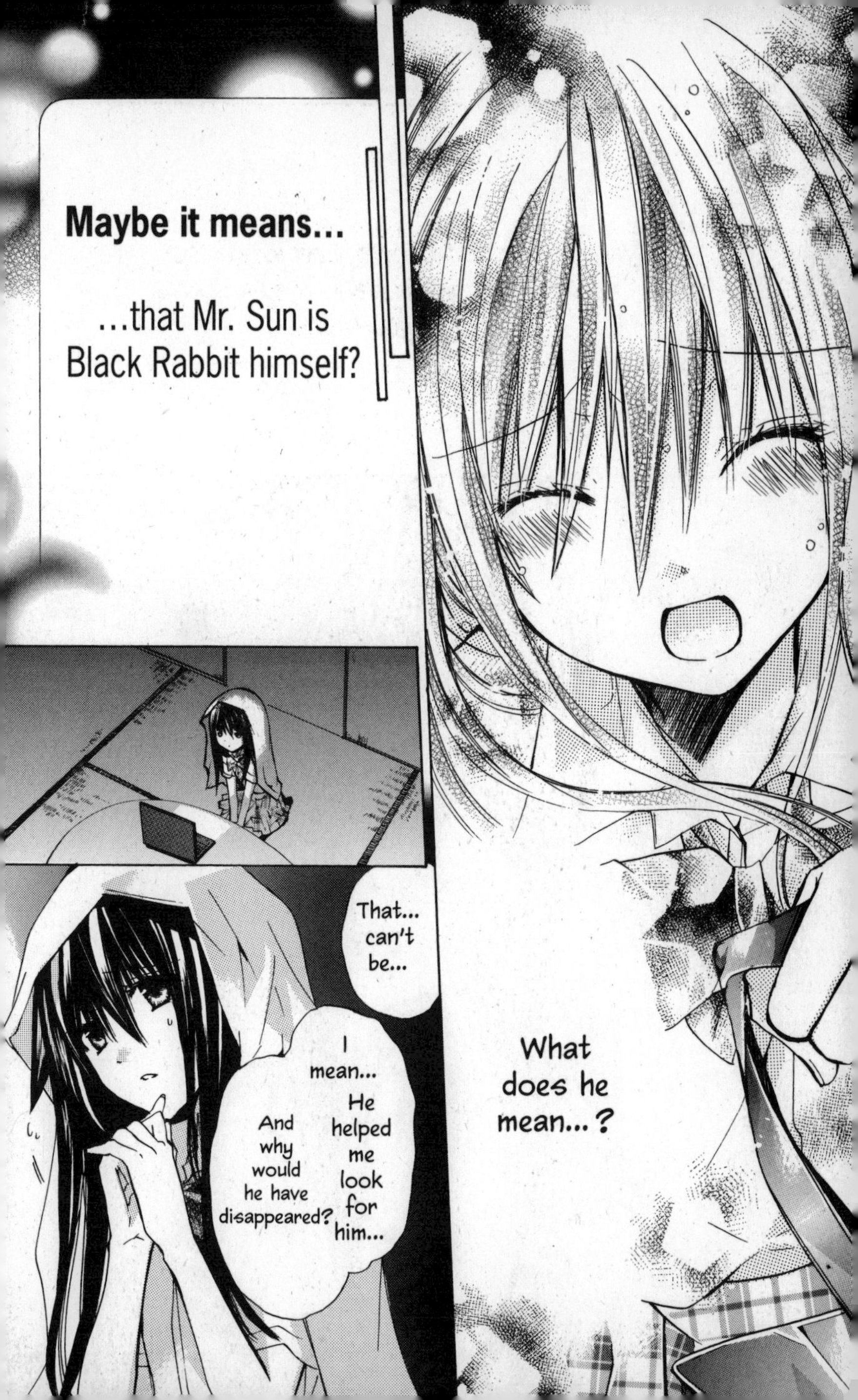

What does he mean...?
Maybe it means...
...that Mr. Sun is Black Rabbit himself?
That... can't be...
I mean... He helped me look for him...
And why would he have disappeared?

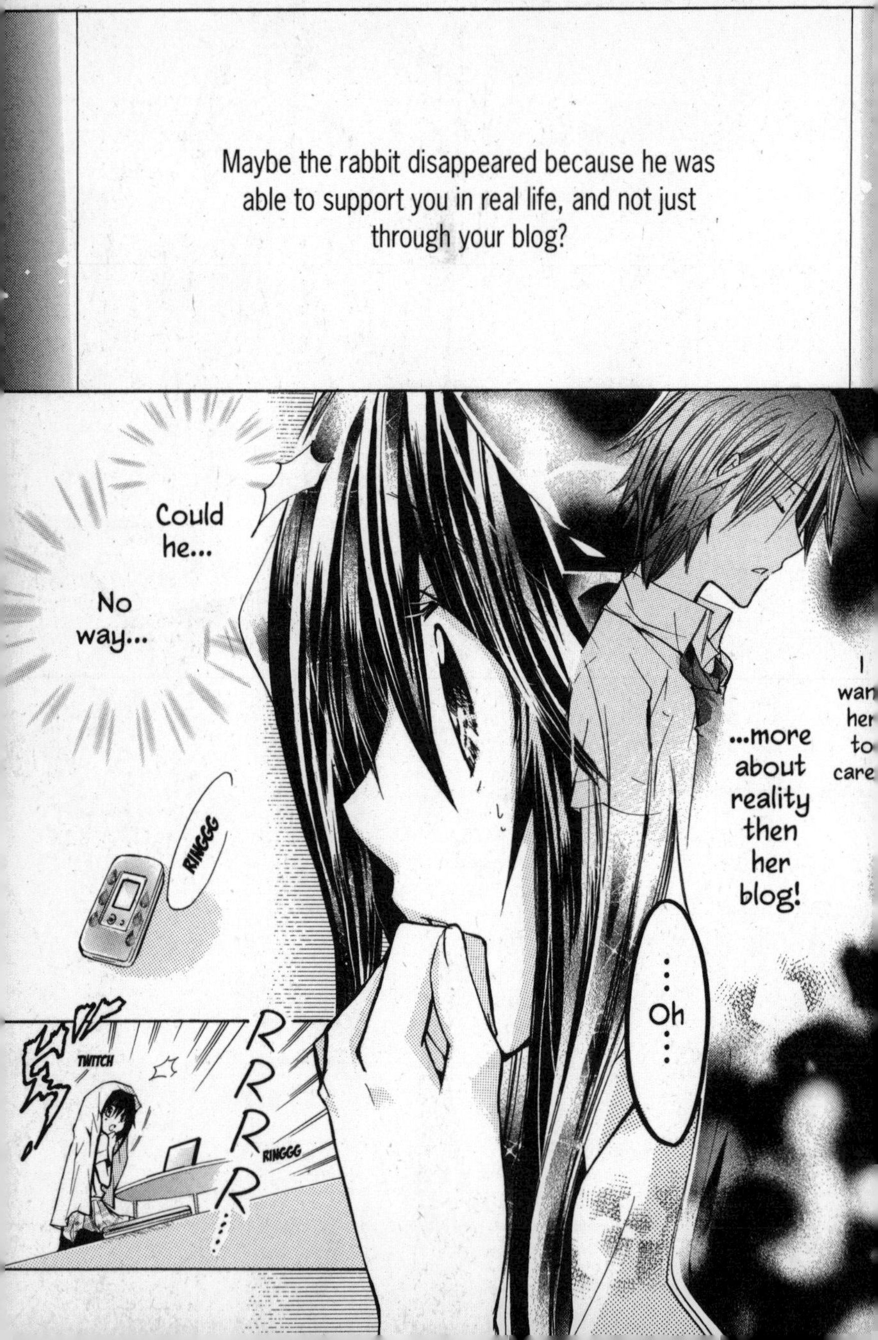
Maybe the rabbit disappeared because he was able to support you in real life, and not just through your blog?
I wan her to care
...more about reality then her blog!
...Oh...
Could he...
No way...
RINGGG
RRRR...
RINGGG
TWITCH

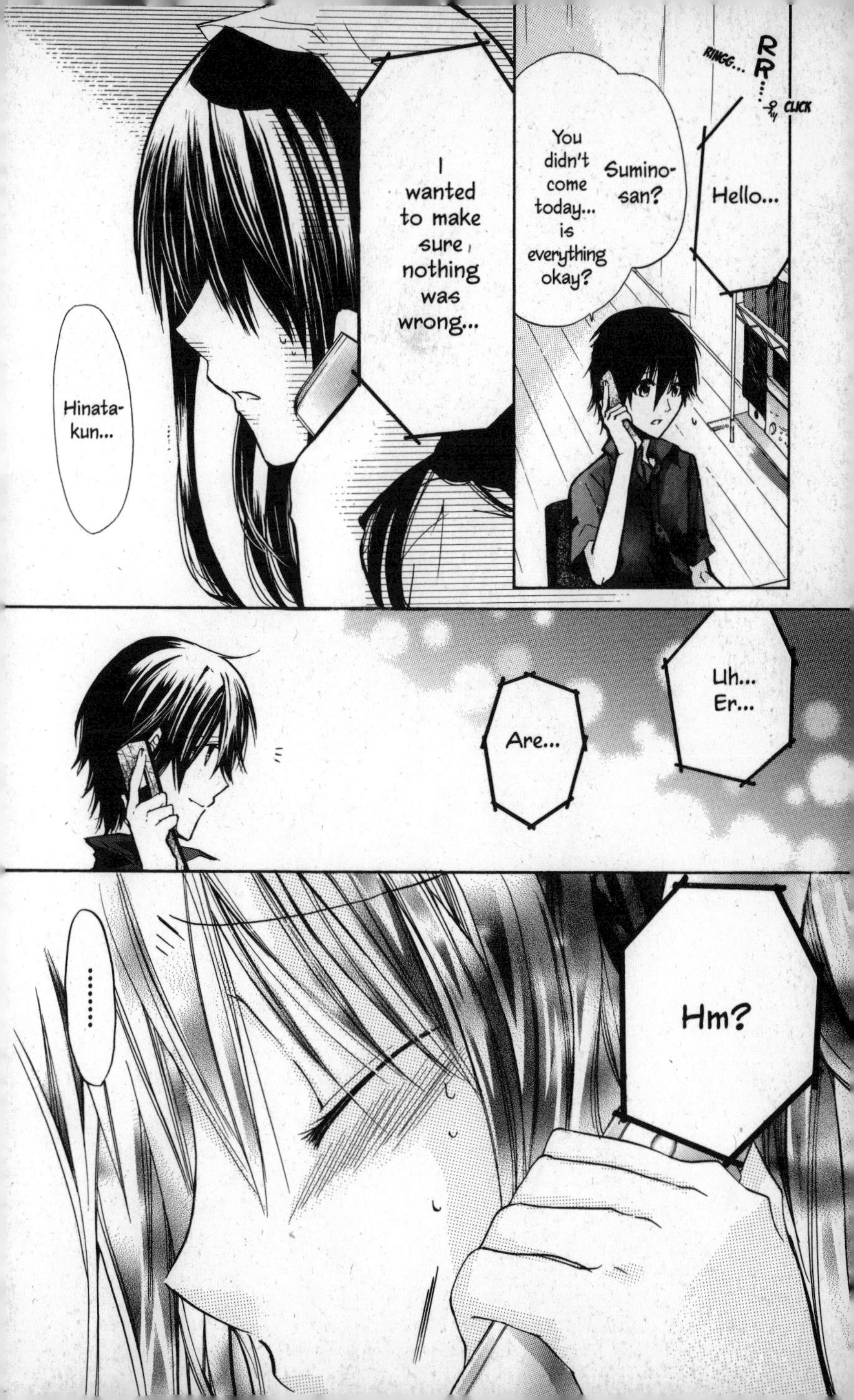
RINGG... RR...
CLICK
Hello...
Sumino-san?
You didn't come today... is everything okay?
I wanted to make sure nothing was wrong...
Hinata-kun...
Uh... Er...
Are...
Hm?
......

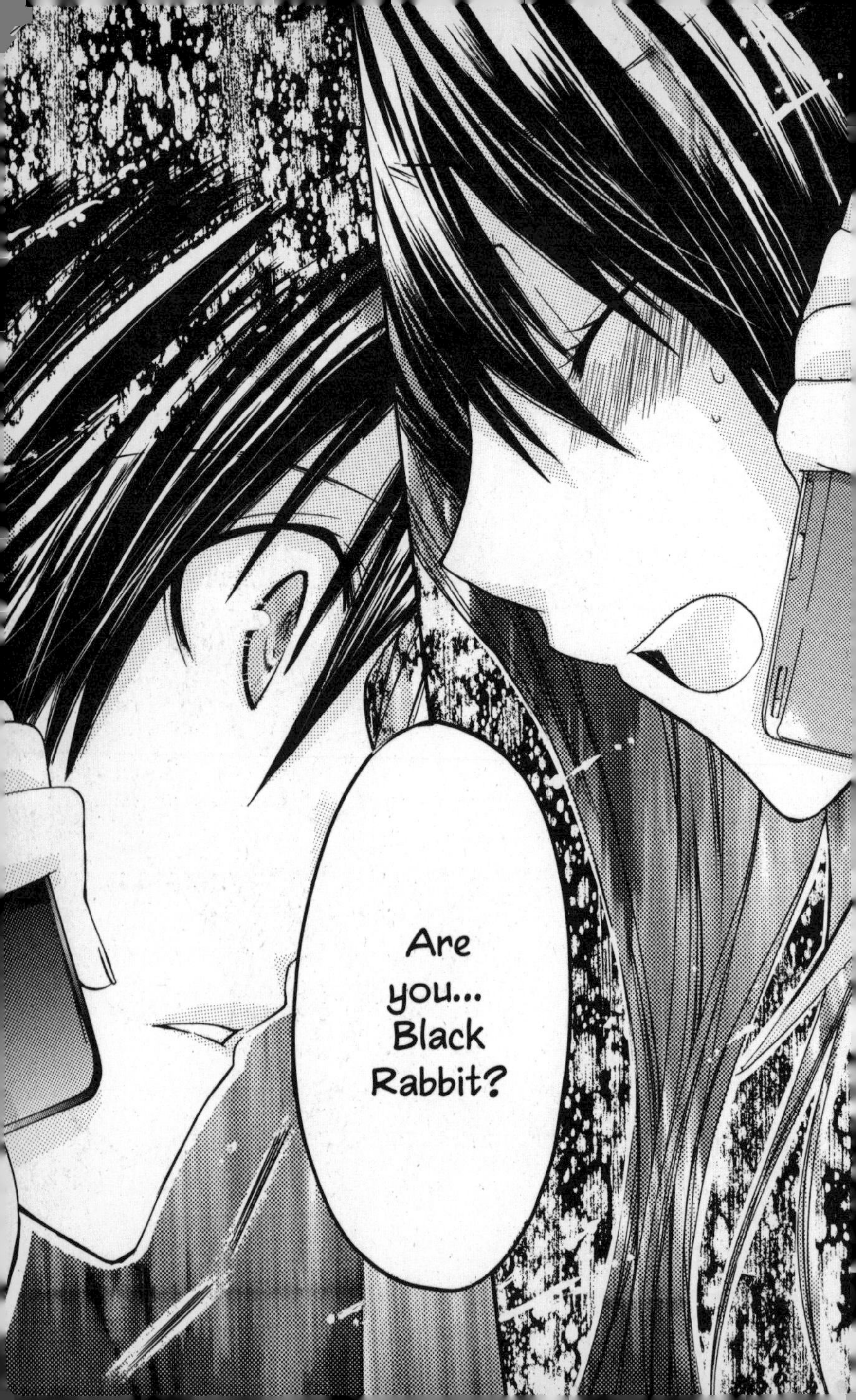
Are you... Black Rabbit?

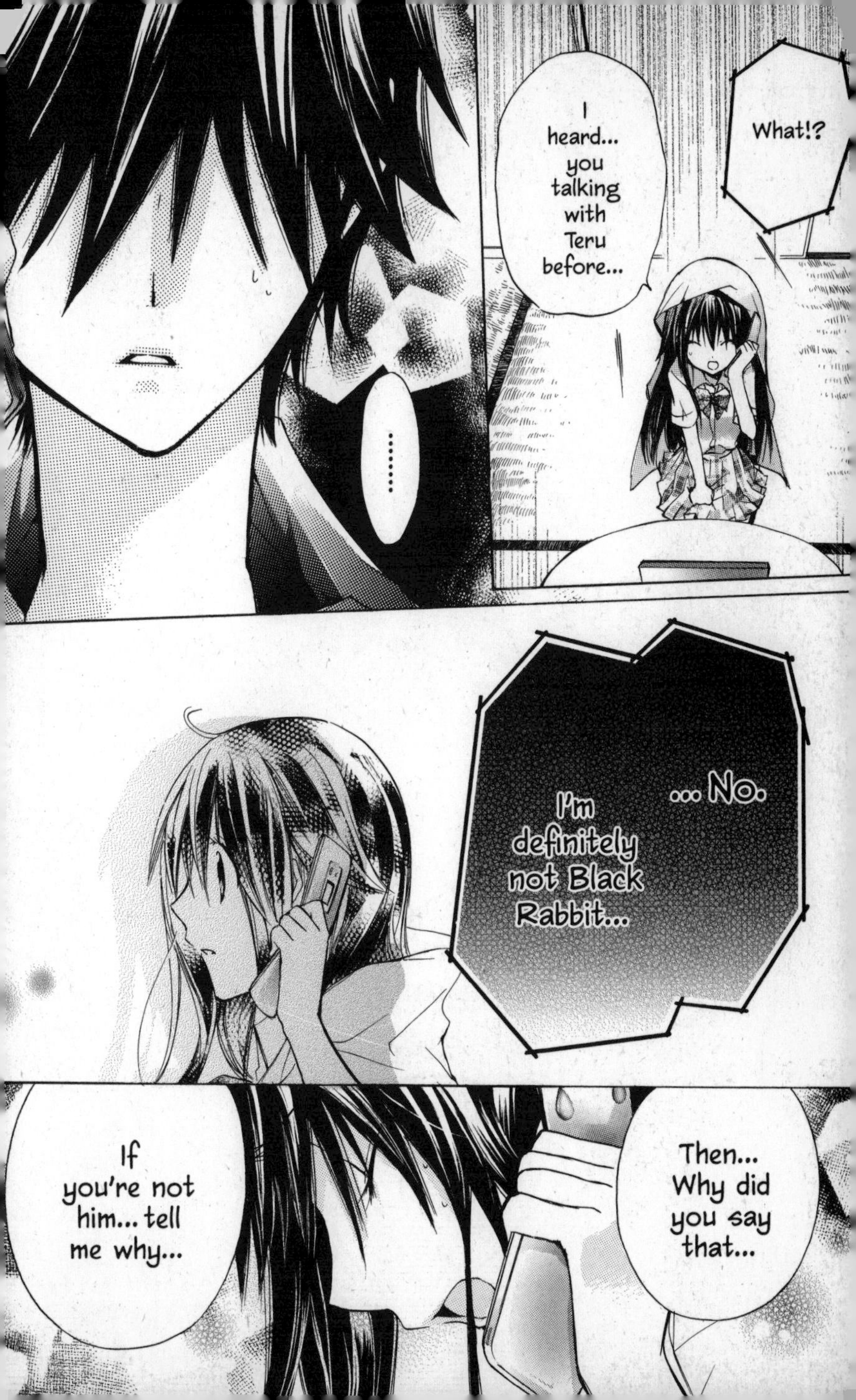
What!?
I heard... you talking with Teru before...
......
... No.
I'm definitely not Black Rabbit...
Then... Why did you say that...
If you're not him... tell me why...

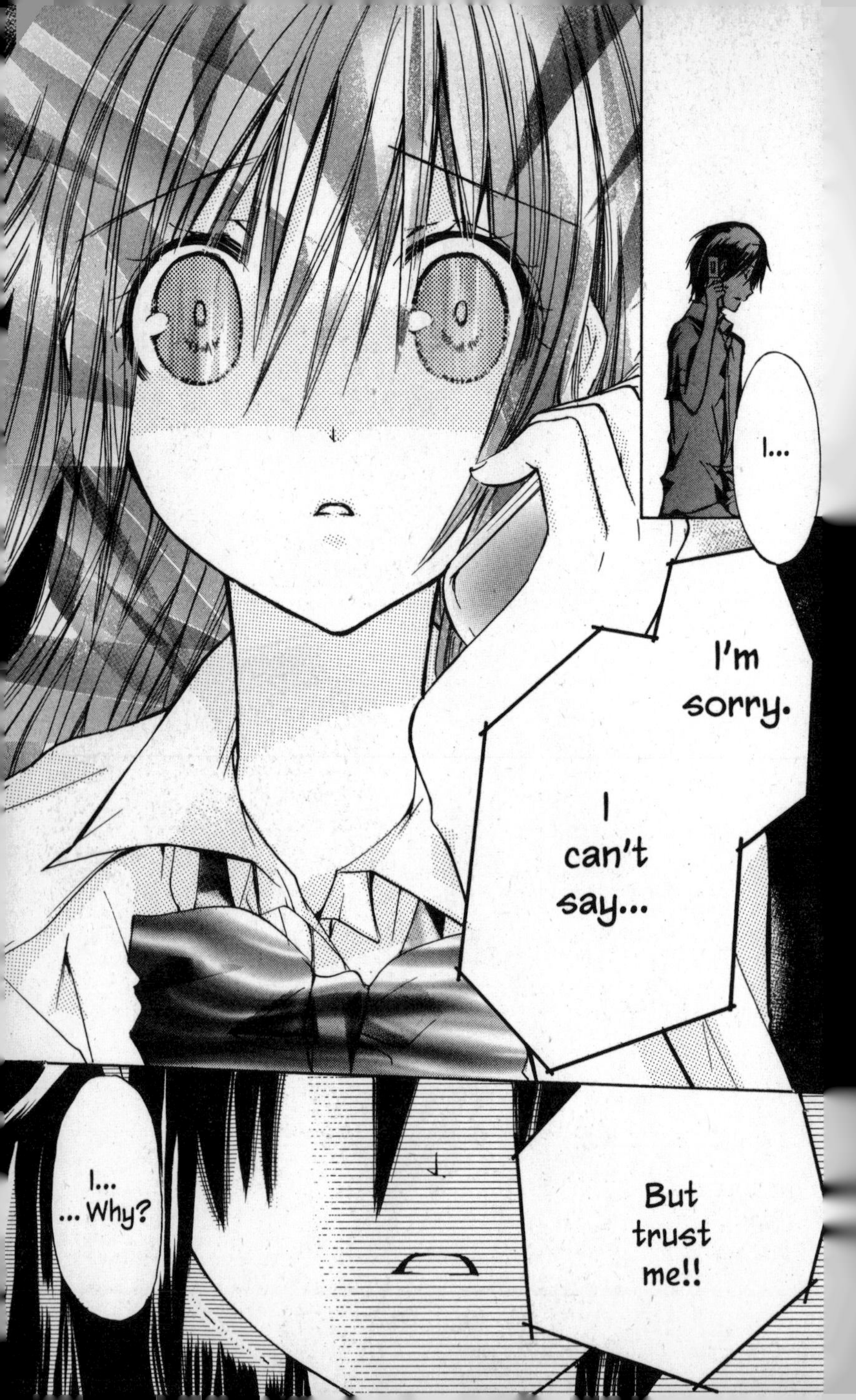
I...
I'm sorry. I can't say...
But trust me!!
I... ...Why?

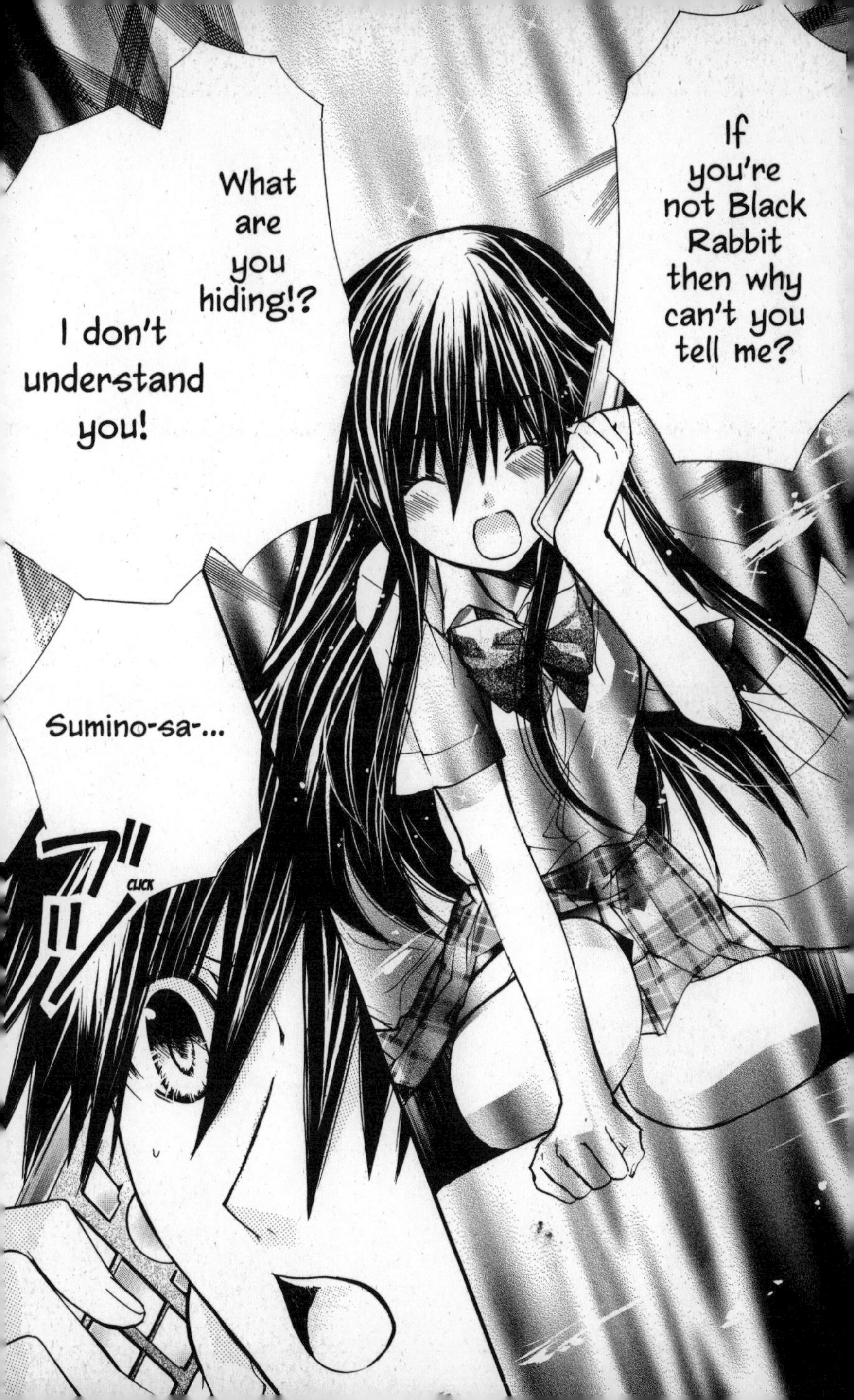
If you're not Black Rabbit then why can't you tell me?
What are you hiding!?
I don't understand you!
Sumino-sa-...
CLICK

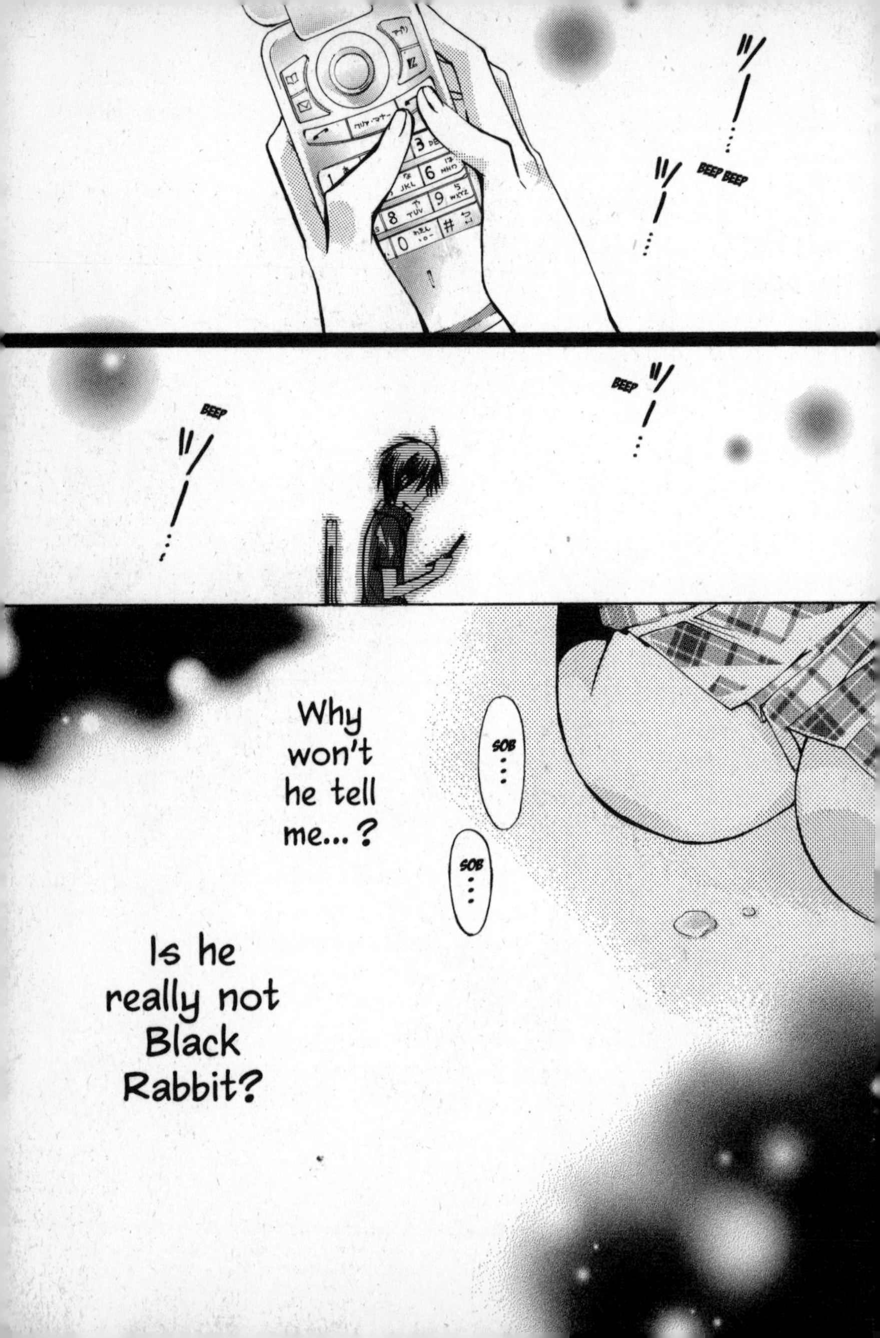

ツー……
BEEP BEEP
ツー……
BEEP
ツー……
BEEP
ツー……
SOB…
SOB…
Why won't he tell me...?
Is he really not Black Rabbit?

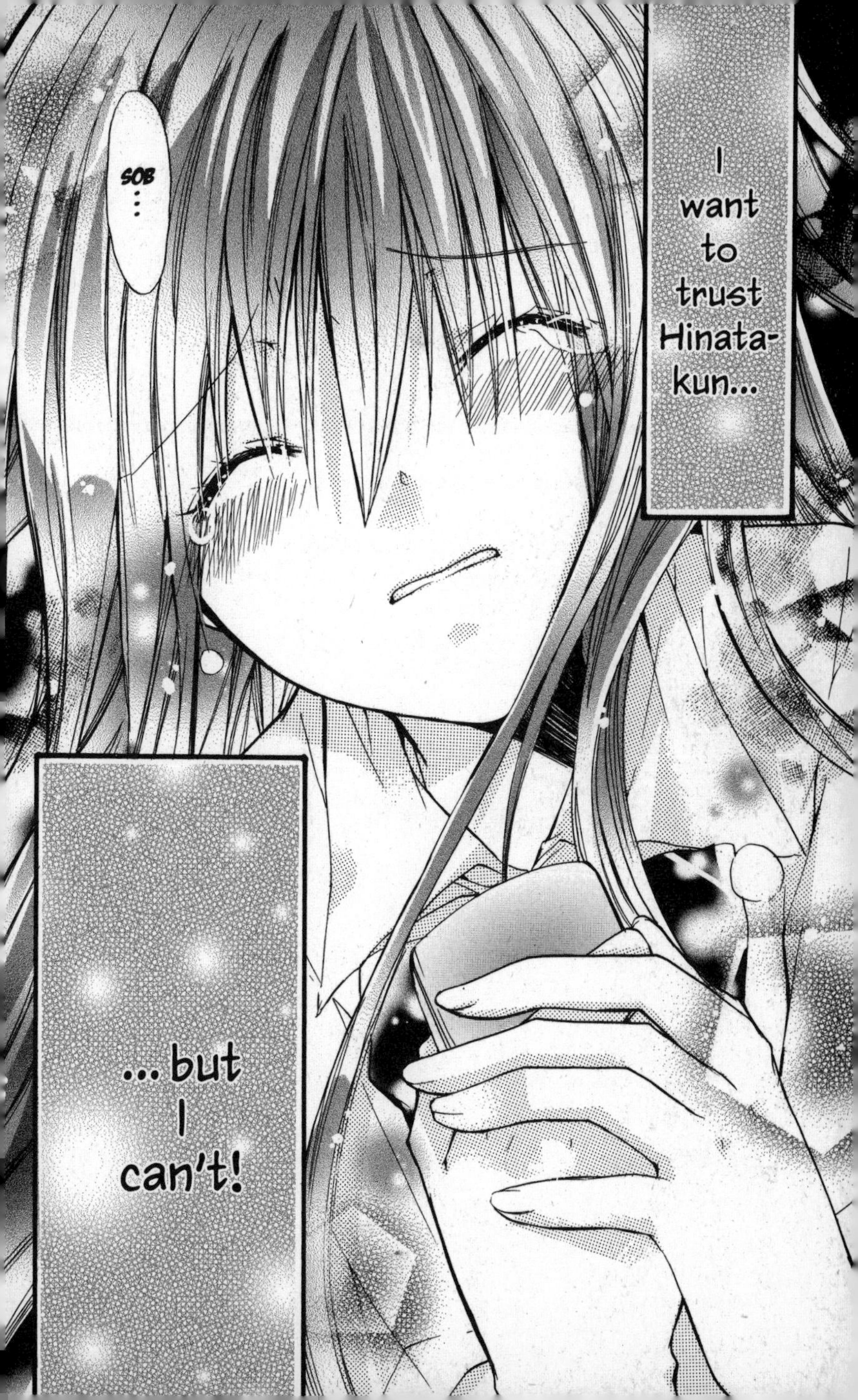
I want to trust Hinata-kun...
SOB...
...but I can't!

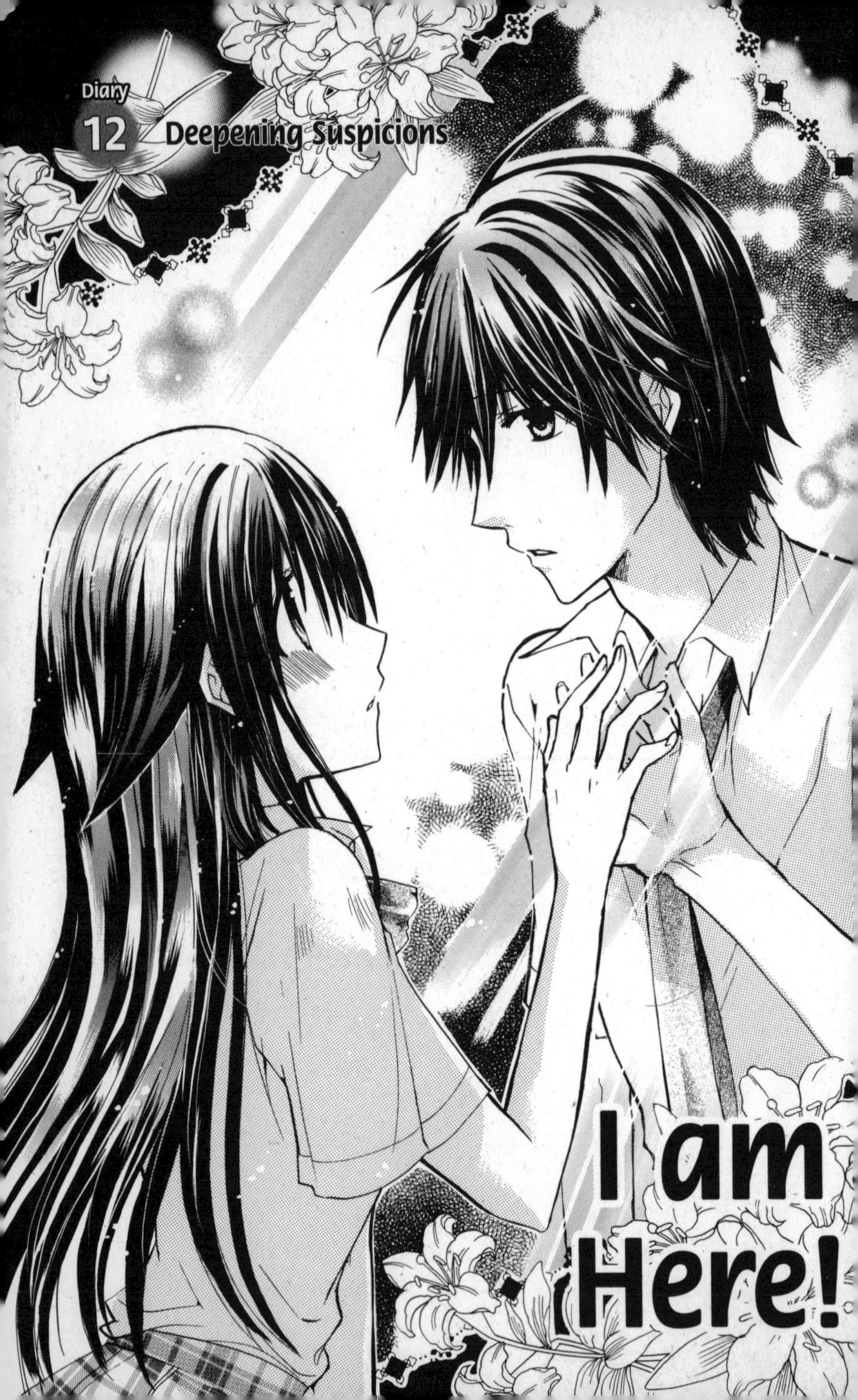
Diary
12 Deepening Suspicions
I am Here!

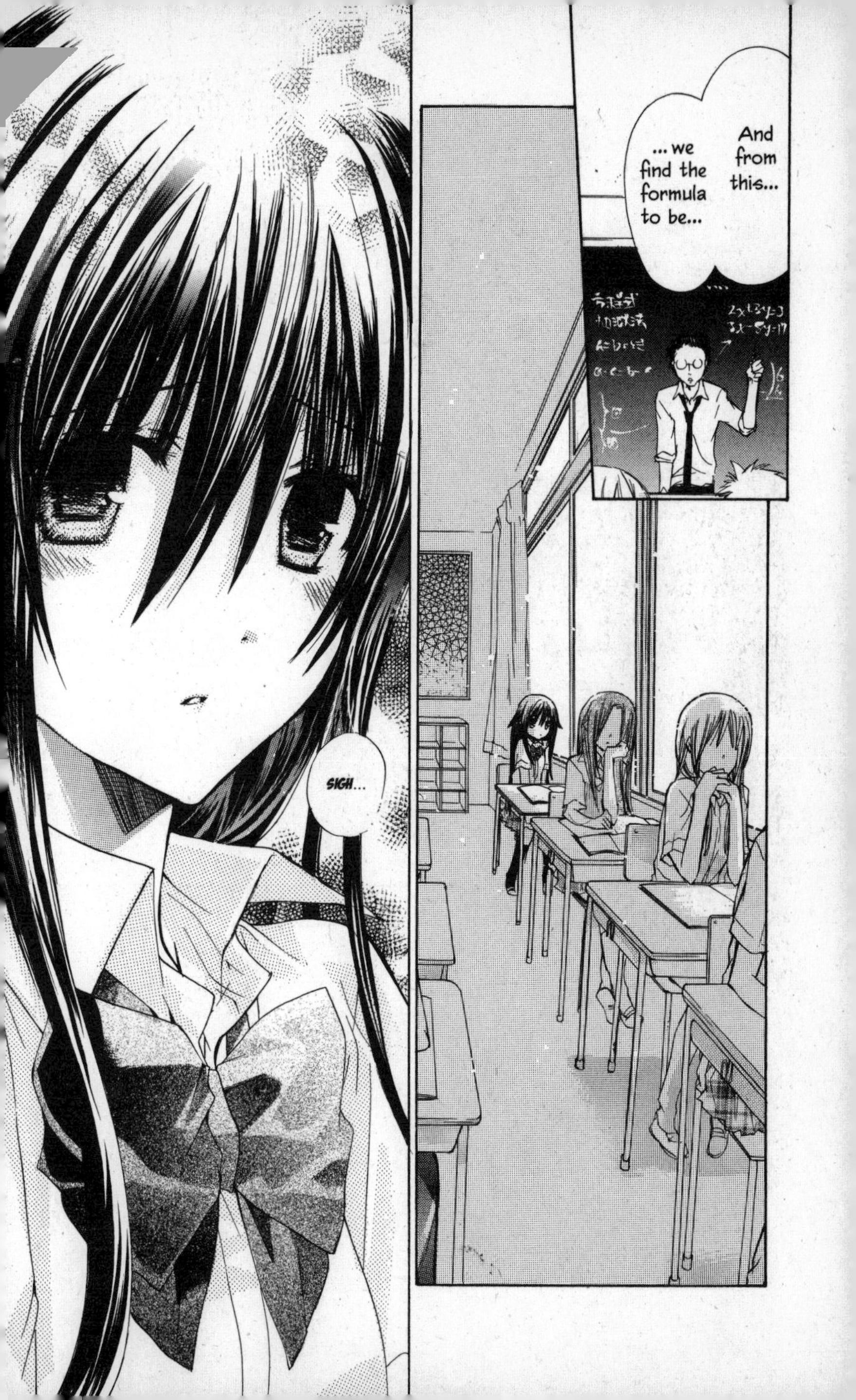
And from this...
...we find the formula to be...
SIGH...

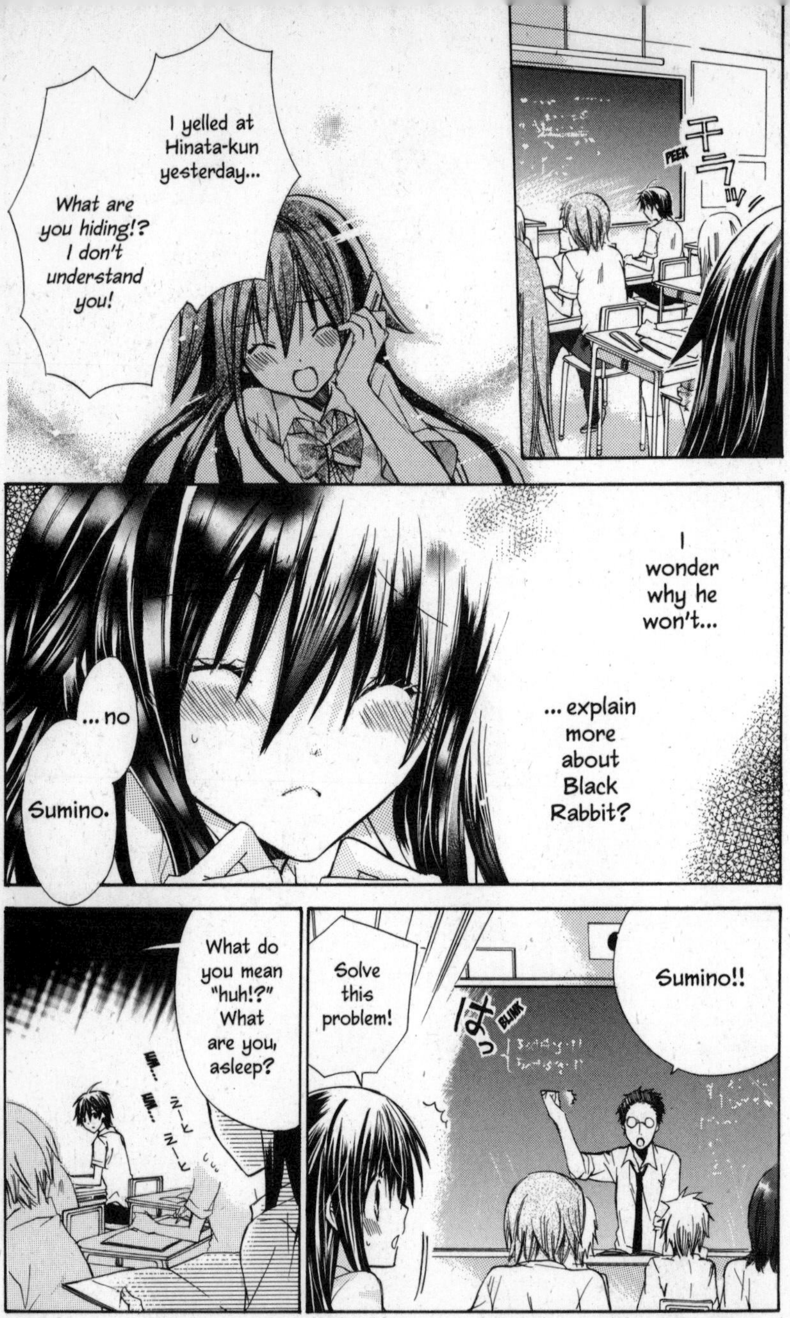
PEEK
I yelled at Hinata-kun yesterday...
What are you hiding!? I don't understand you!
I wonder why he won't...
... explain more about Black Rabbit?
... no
Sumino.
Sumino!!
Solve this problem!
BLINK
What do you mean "huh!?" What are you, asleep?
UM... UM...

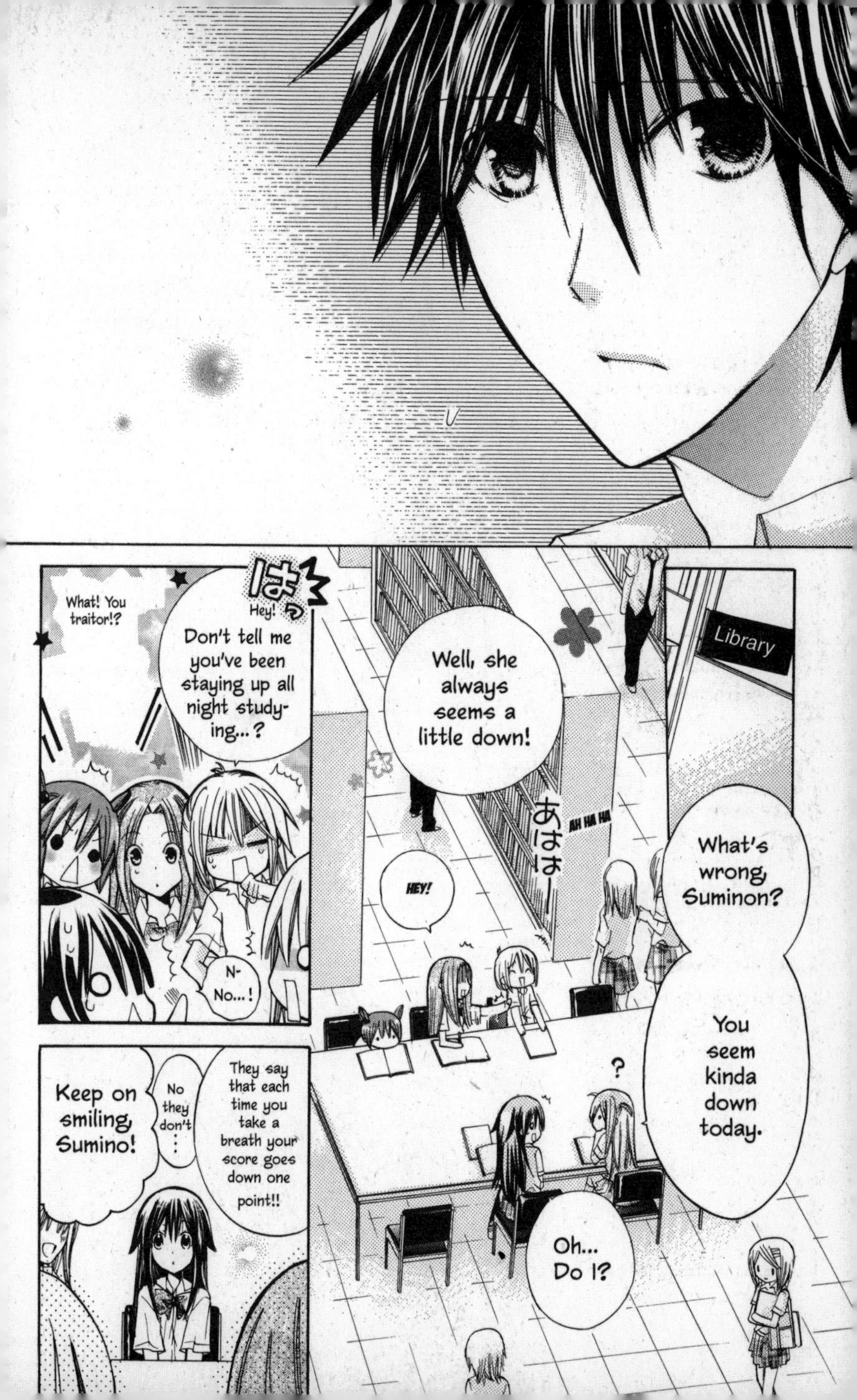

Library
What's wrong, Suminon?
You seem kinda down today.
Well, she always seems a little down!
あははー
AH HA HA
HEY!
Oh... Do I?
はっ
Hey!
Don't tell me you've been staying up all night study-ing...?
What! You traitor!?
N- No...!
They say that each time you take a breath your score goes down one point!!
No they don't...
Keep on smiling, Sumino!

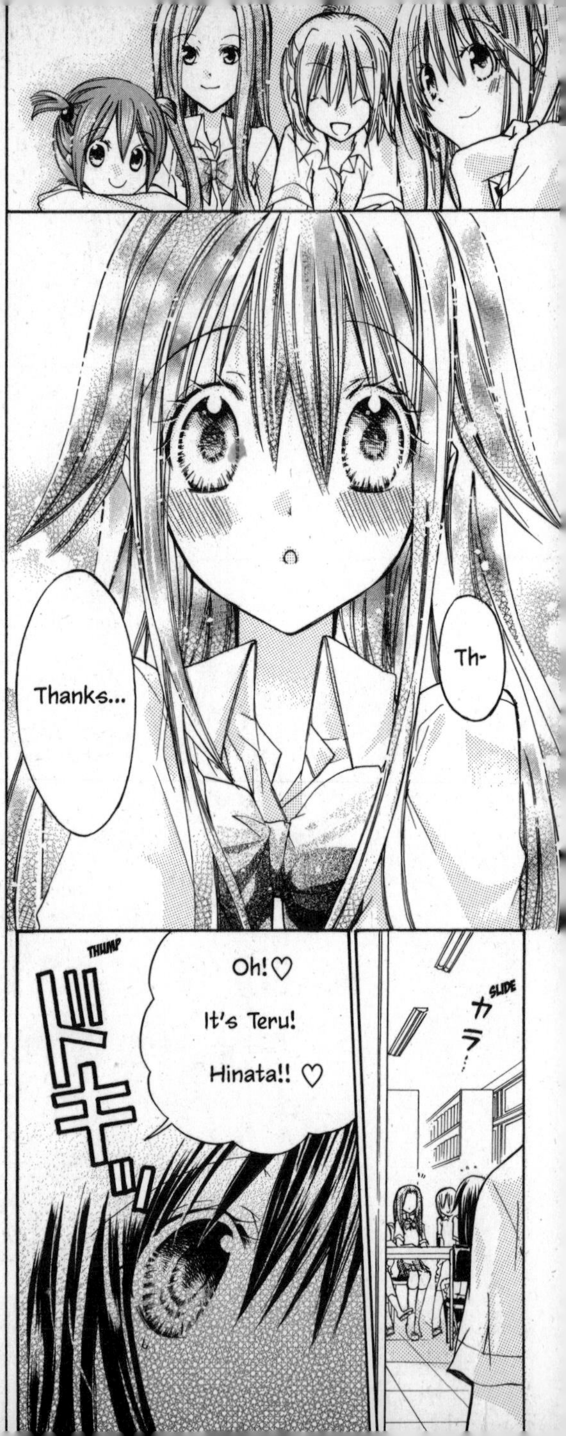
Th-
Thanks...
SLIDE
カラ...
THUMP
Oh!♡
It's Teru!
Hinata!! ♡

The Adventures of Mahimahi 4

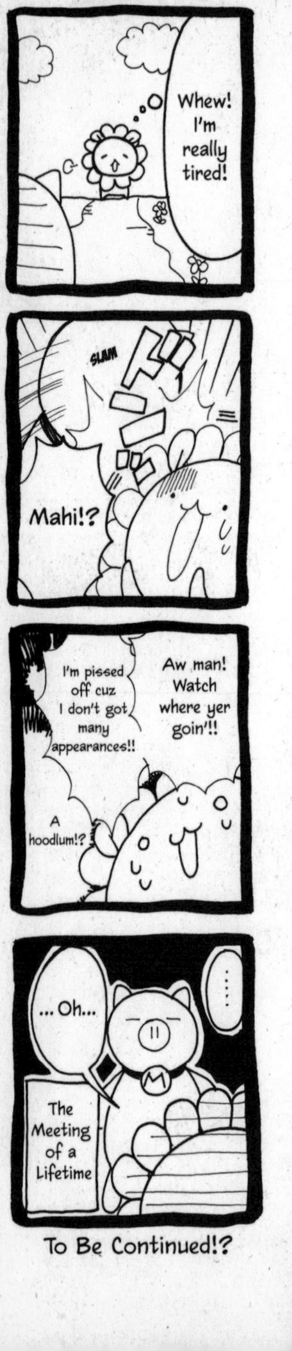
Whew! I'm really tired!
SLAM
Mahi!?
Aw man! Watch where yer goin'!!
I'm pissed off cuz I don't got many appearances!!
A hoodlum!?
......
...Oh...
The Meeting of a Lifetime

To Be Continued!?

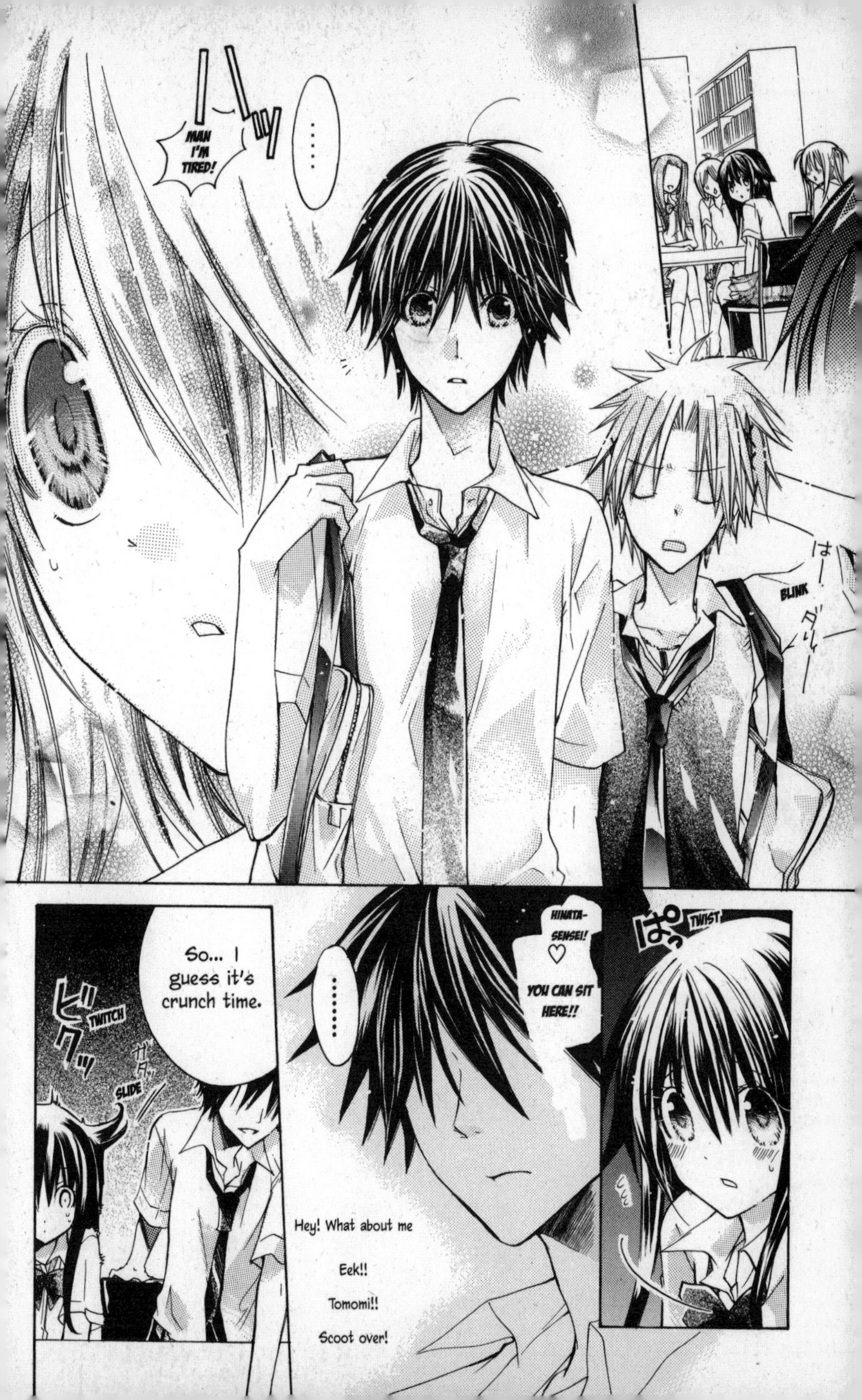

BLINK
MAN I'M TIRED!
......
TWIST
HINATA-SENSEI! ♡
YOU CAN SIT HERE!!
....
Hey! What about me
Eek!!
Tomomi!!
Scoot over!
So... I guess it's crunch time.
TWITCH
SLIDE

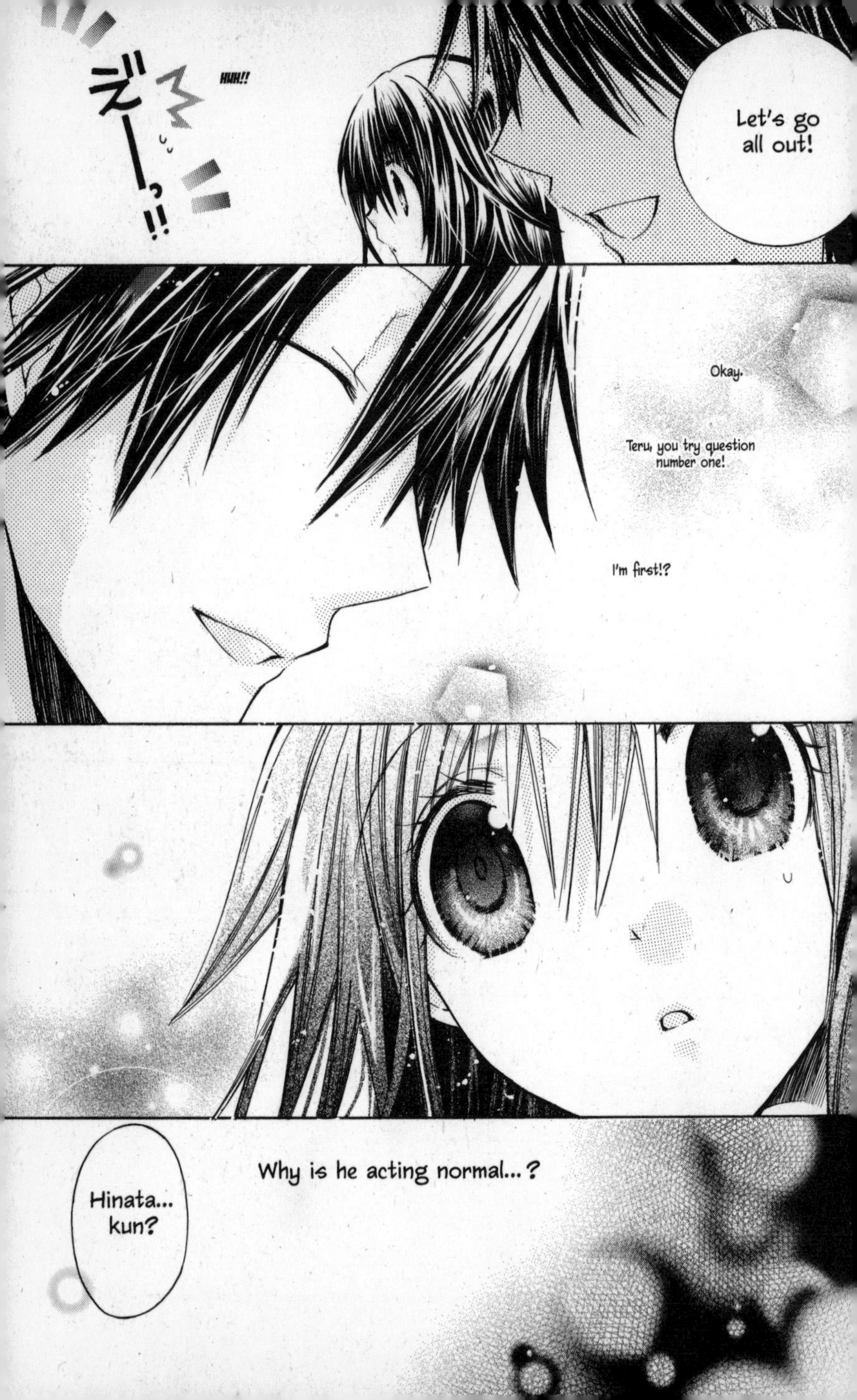

Let's go all out!
HUH!!
えーっ!!
Okay.
Teru, you try question number one!
I'm first!?
Why is he acting normal...?
Hinata... kun?

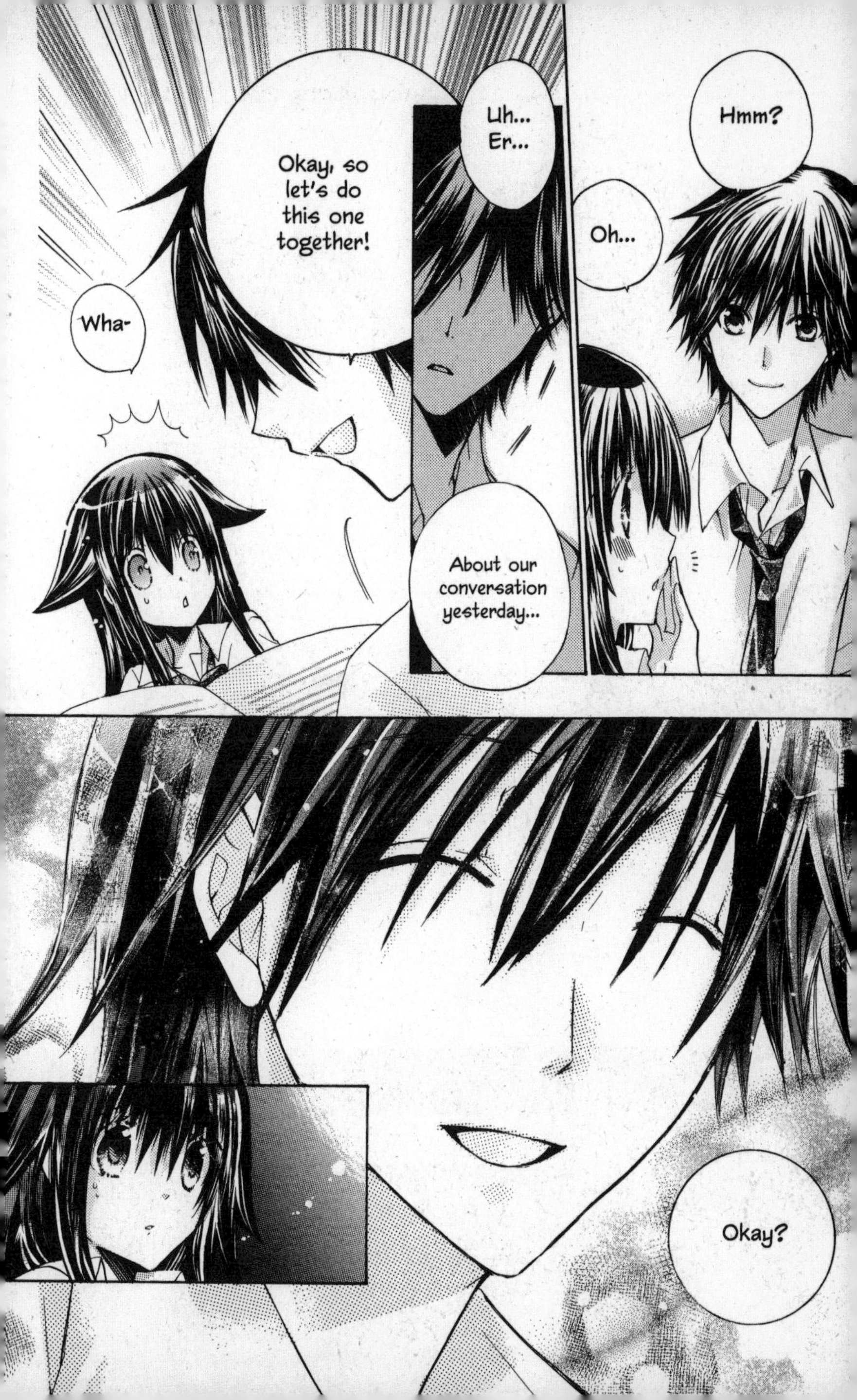
Hmm?
Oh...
Uh... Er...
About our conversation yesterday...
Okay, so let's do this one together!
Wha-
Okay?

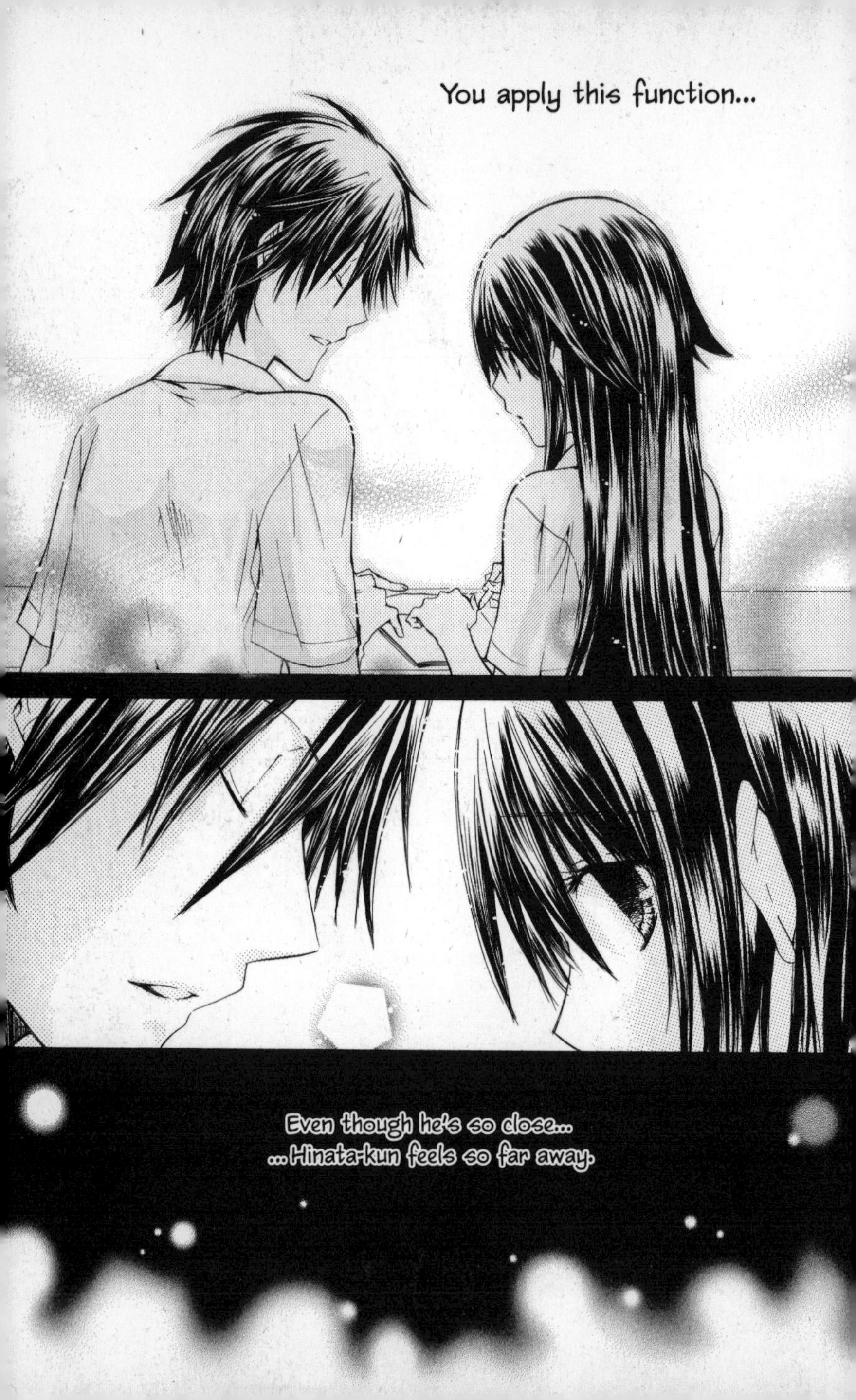
You apply this function...
Even though he's so close...
...Hinata-kun feels so far away.

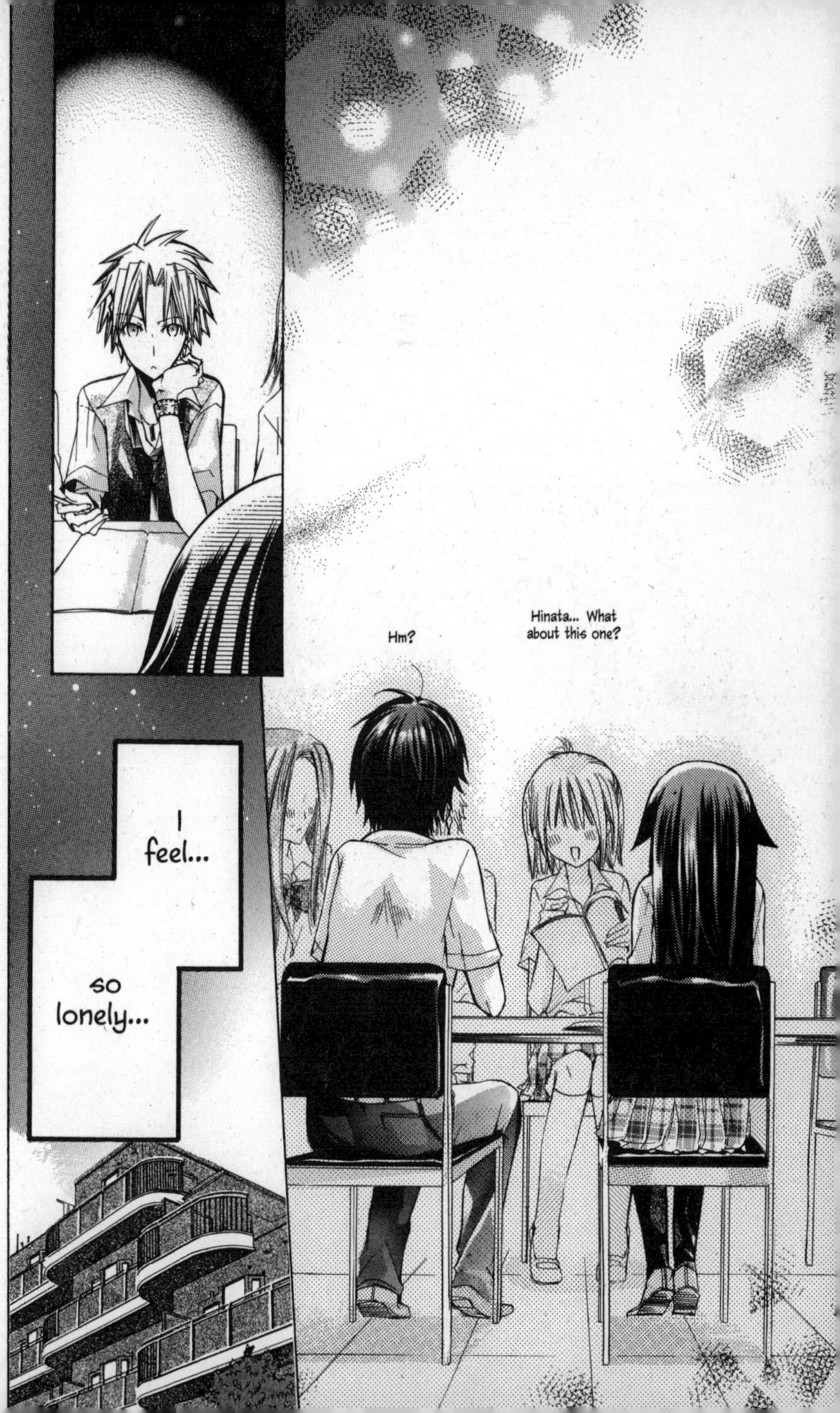
Hinata... What about this one?
Hm?
I feel...
so lonely...

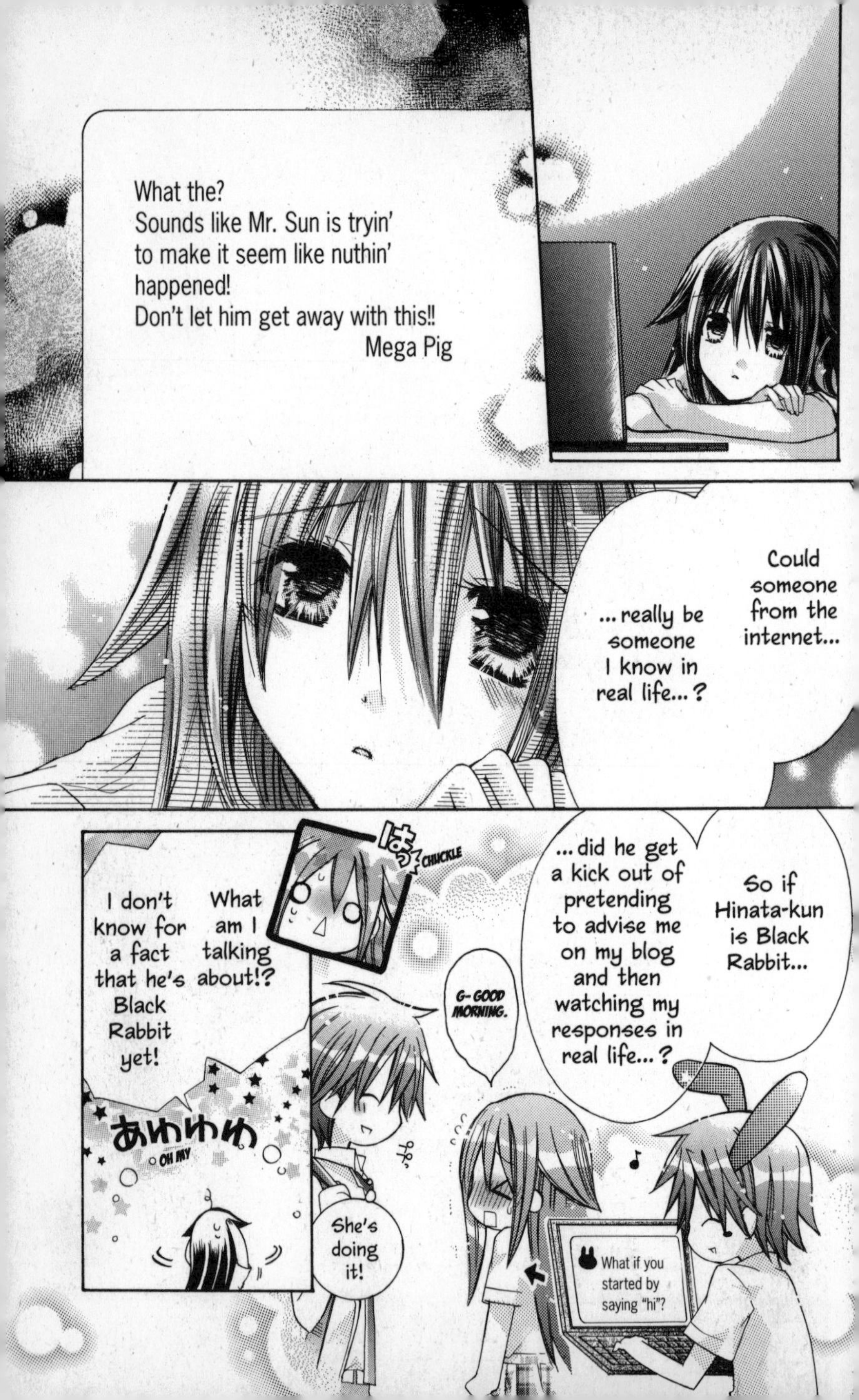
What the?
Sounds like Mr. Sun is tryin' to make it seem like nuthin' happened!
Don't let him get away with this!!
Mega Pig
Could someone from the internet...
...really be someone I know in real life...?
So if Hinata-kun is Black Rabbit...
...did he get a kick out of pretending to advise me on my blog and then watching my responses in real life...?
What if you started by saying "hi"?
G-GOOD MORNING.
She's doing it!
はっ CHUCKLE
What am I talking about!?
I don't know for a fact that he's Black Rabbit yet!
あわわわ OH MY

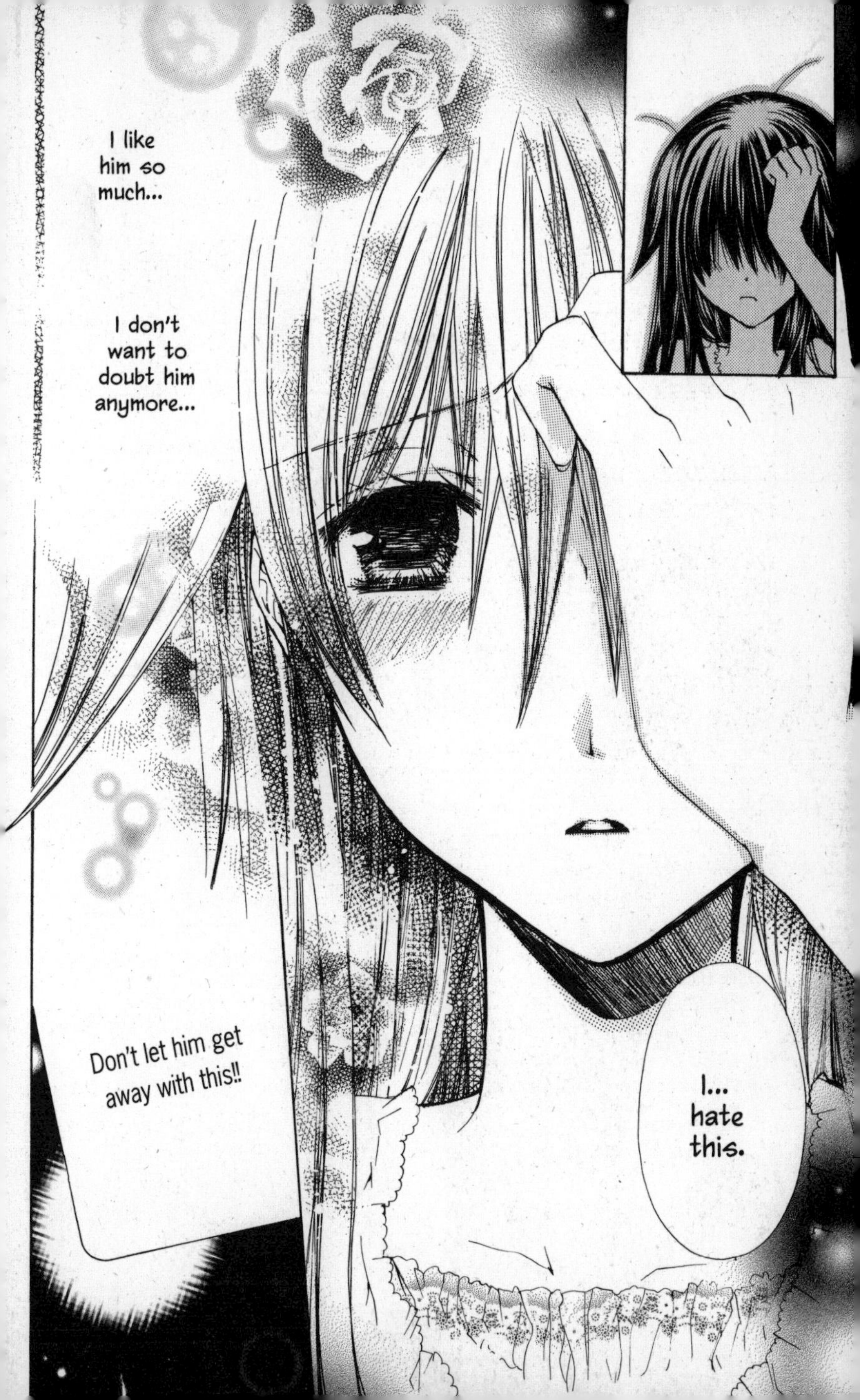
I like him so much...
I don't want to doubt him anymore...
I... hate this.
Don't let him get away with this!!

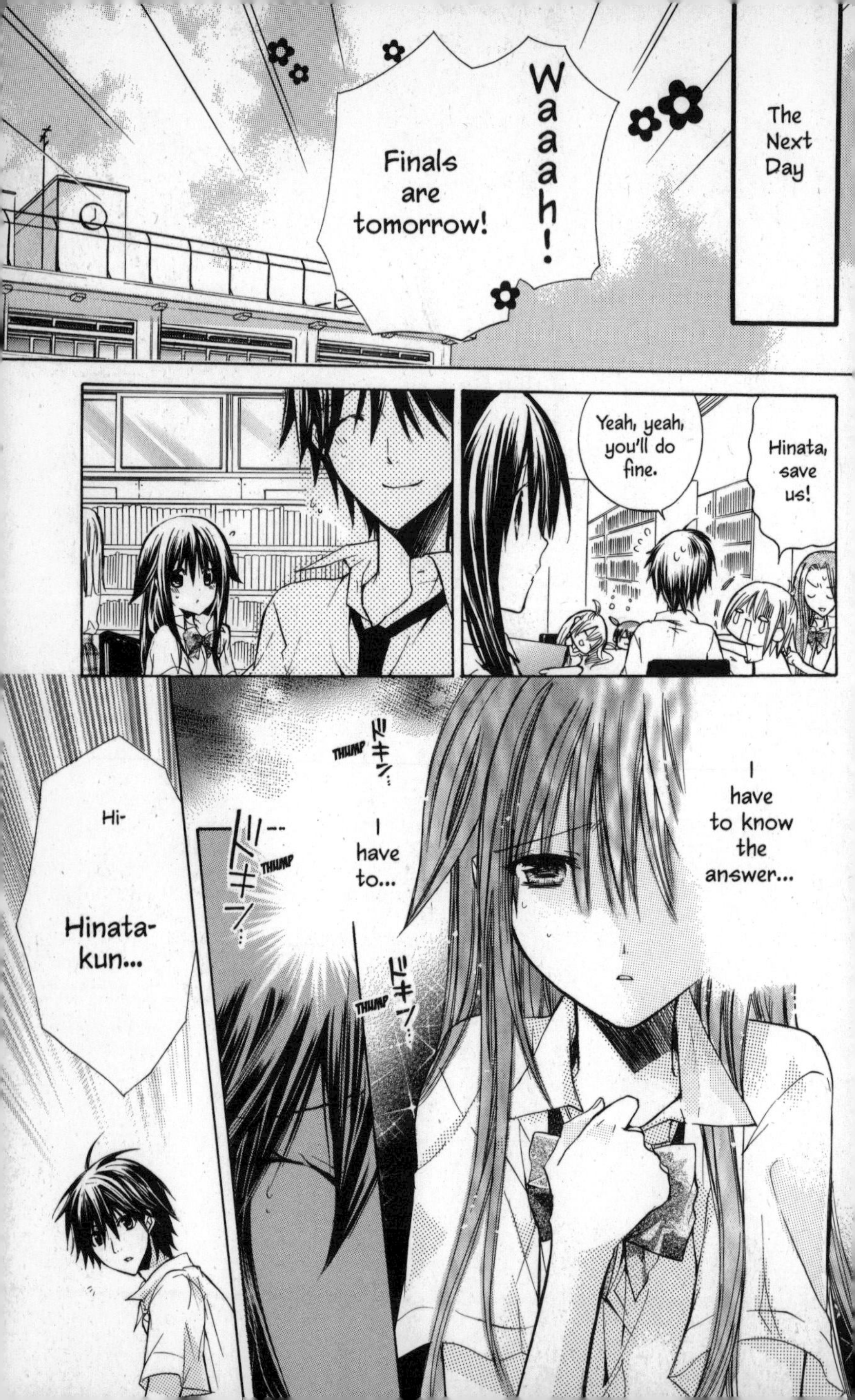
The Next Day
Waaah!
Finals are tomorrow!
Hinata, save us!
Yeah, yeah, you'll do fine.
I have to know the answer...
THUMP ドキン…
I have to...
THUMP ドキン…
THUMP ドキン…
Hi-
Hinata-kun...

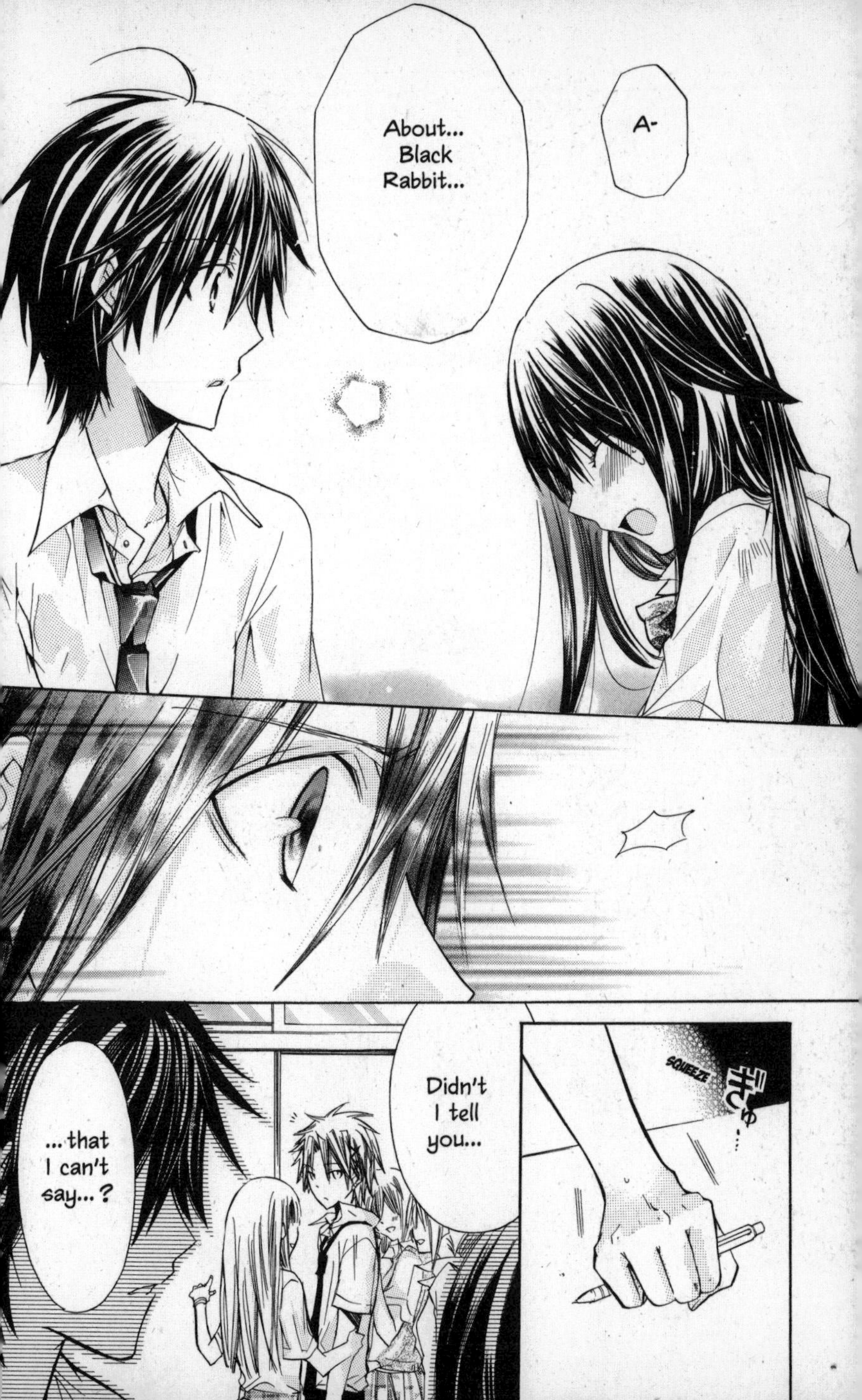
A-
About... Black Rabbit...
SQUEEZE
ぎゅ…
Didn't I tell you...
... that I can't say...?

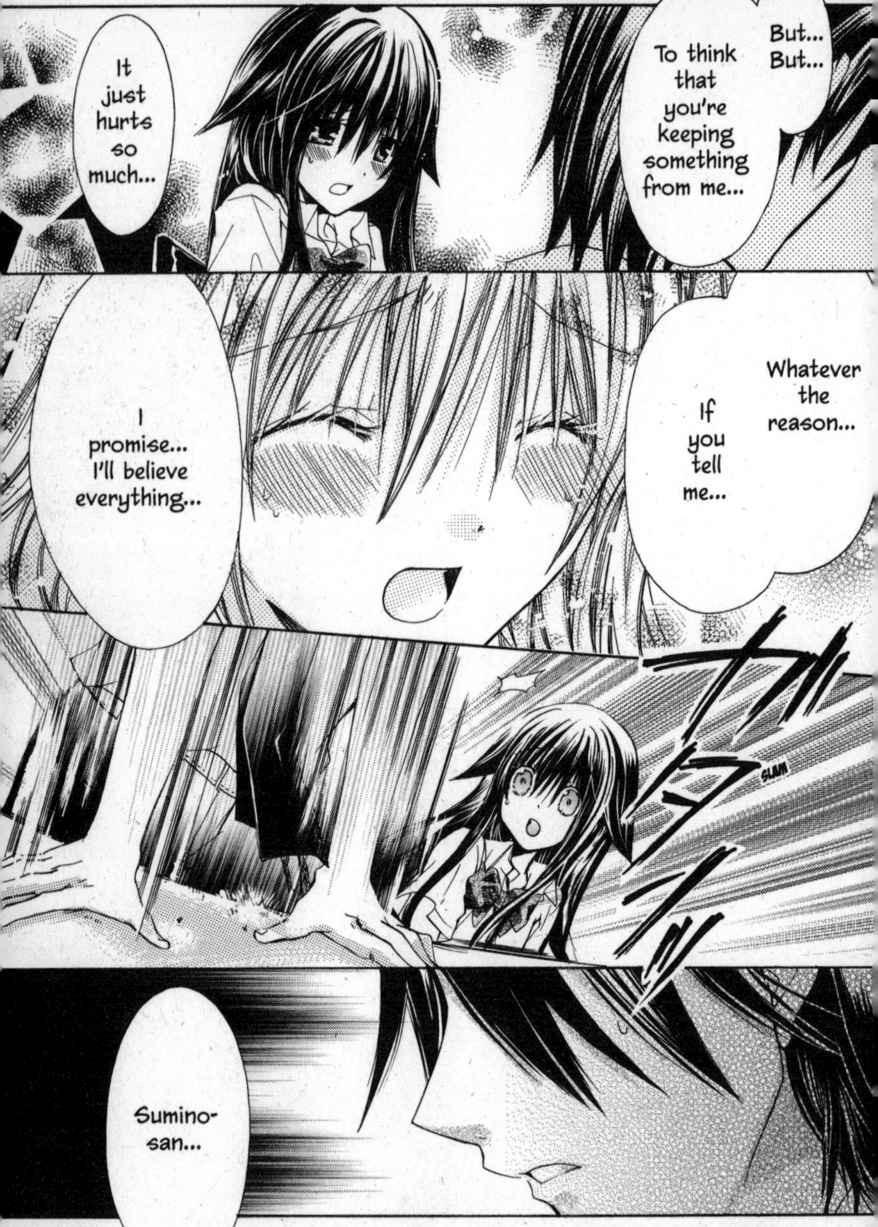
But... But...
To think that you're keeping something from me...
It just hurts so much...
Whatever the reason...
If you tell me...
I promise... I'll believe everything...
SLAM
Sumino-san...

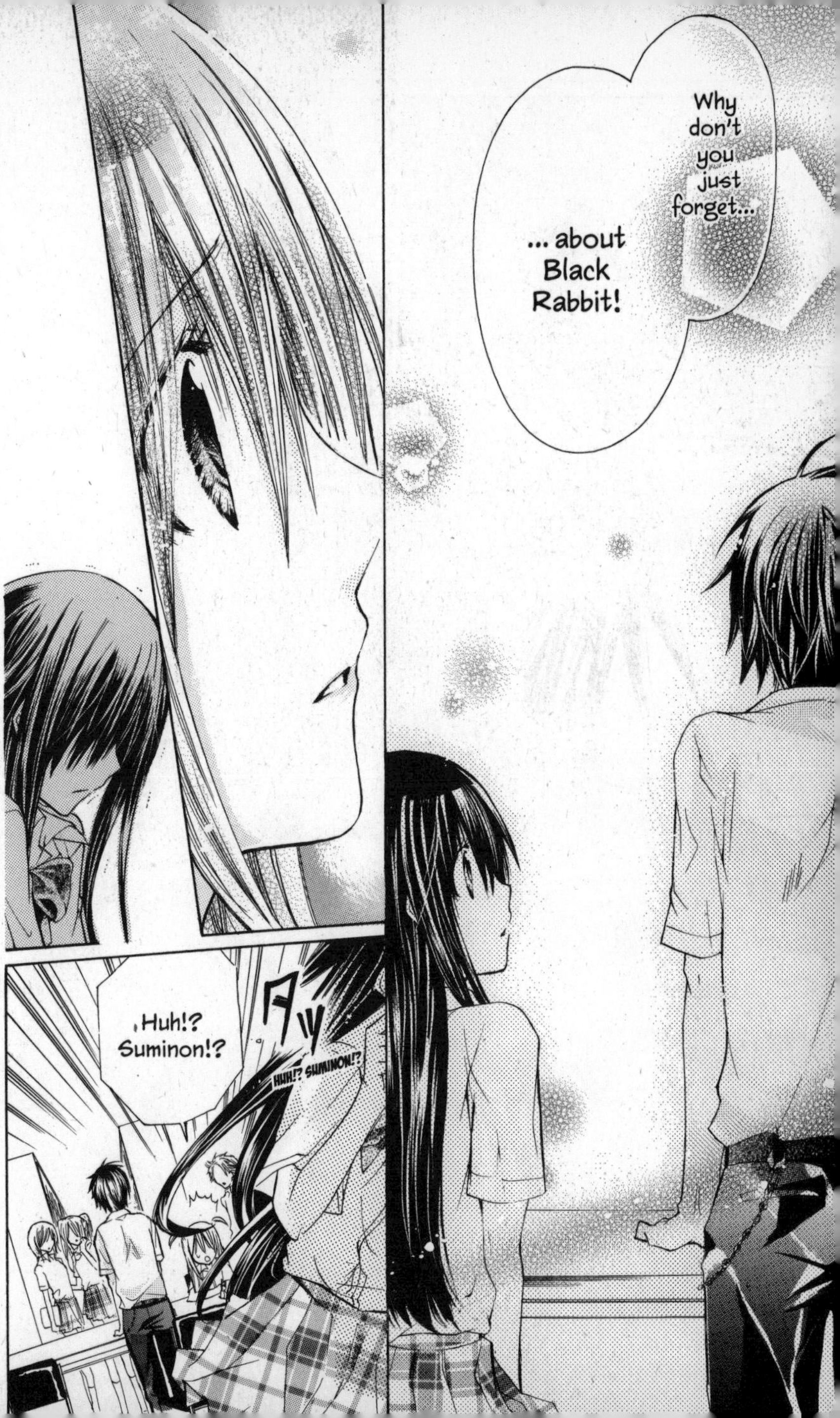
Why don't you just forget...
... about Black Rabbit!
Huh!? Suminon!?
タッ
HUH!? SUMINON!?

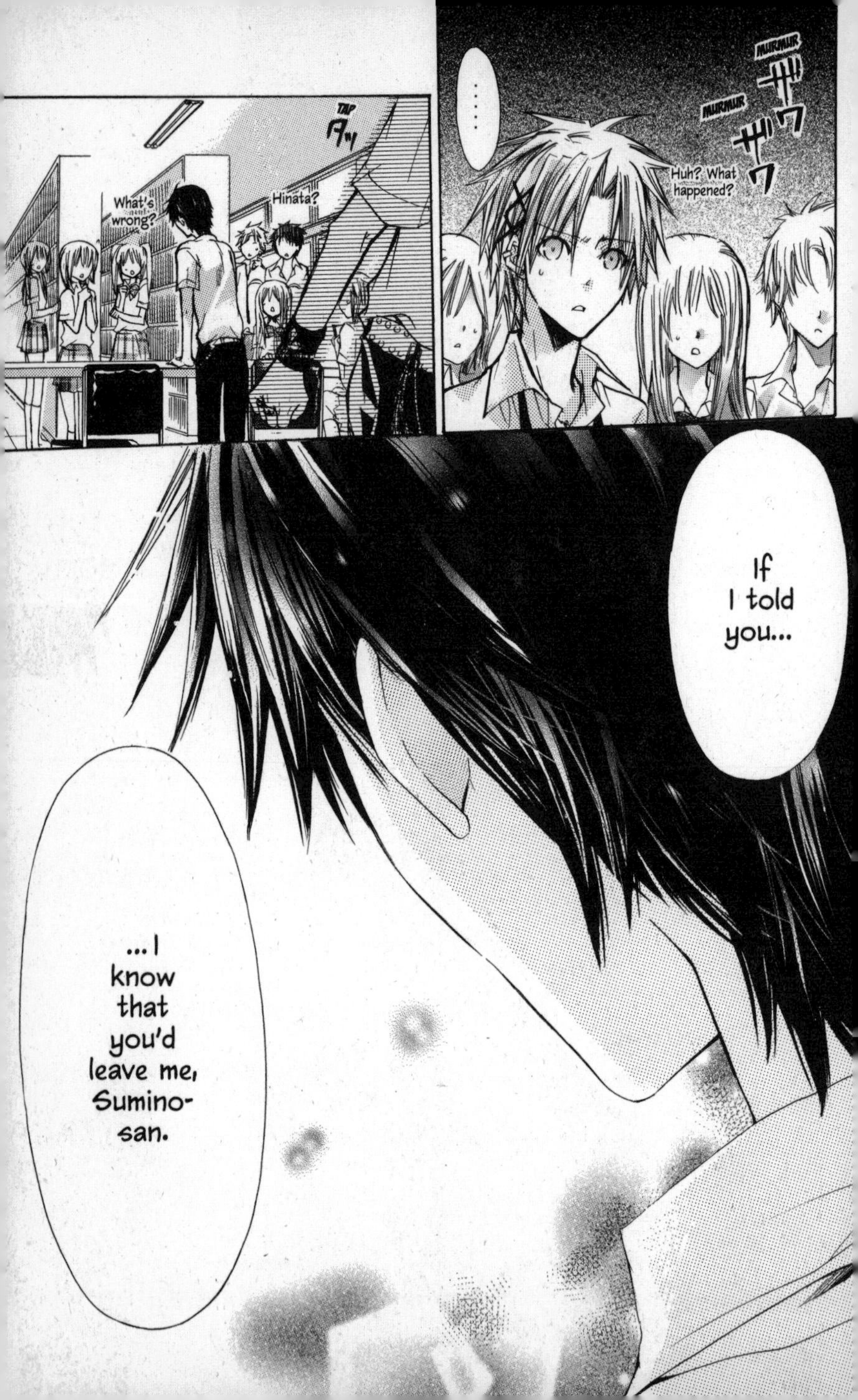
......
MURMUR
ザワ
MURMUR
ザワ
Huh? What happened?
TAP
タッ
Hinata?
What's wrong?
If I told you...
...I know that you'd leave me, Sumino-san.

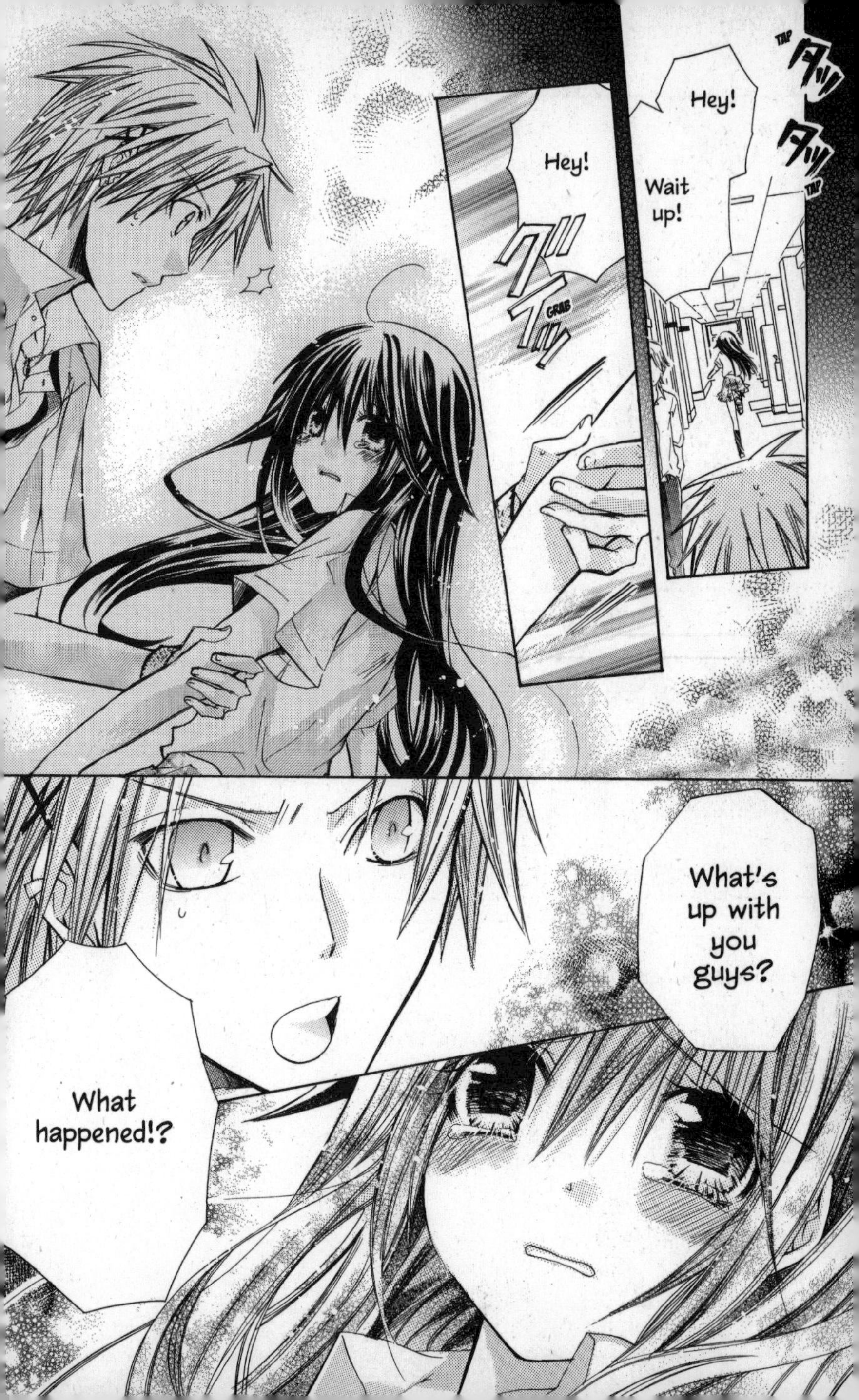
TAP
タッ
タッ
TAP
Hey!
Wait up!
Hey!
グイッ
GRAB
What's up with you guys?
What happened!?

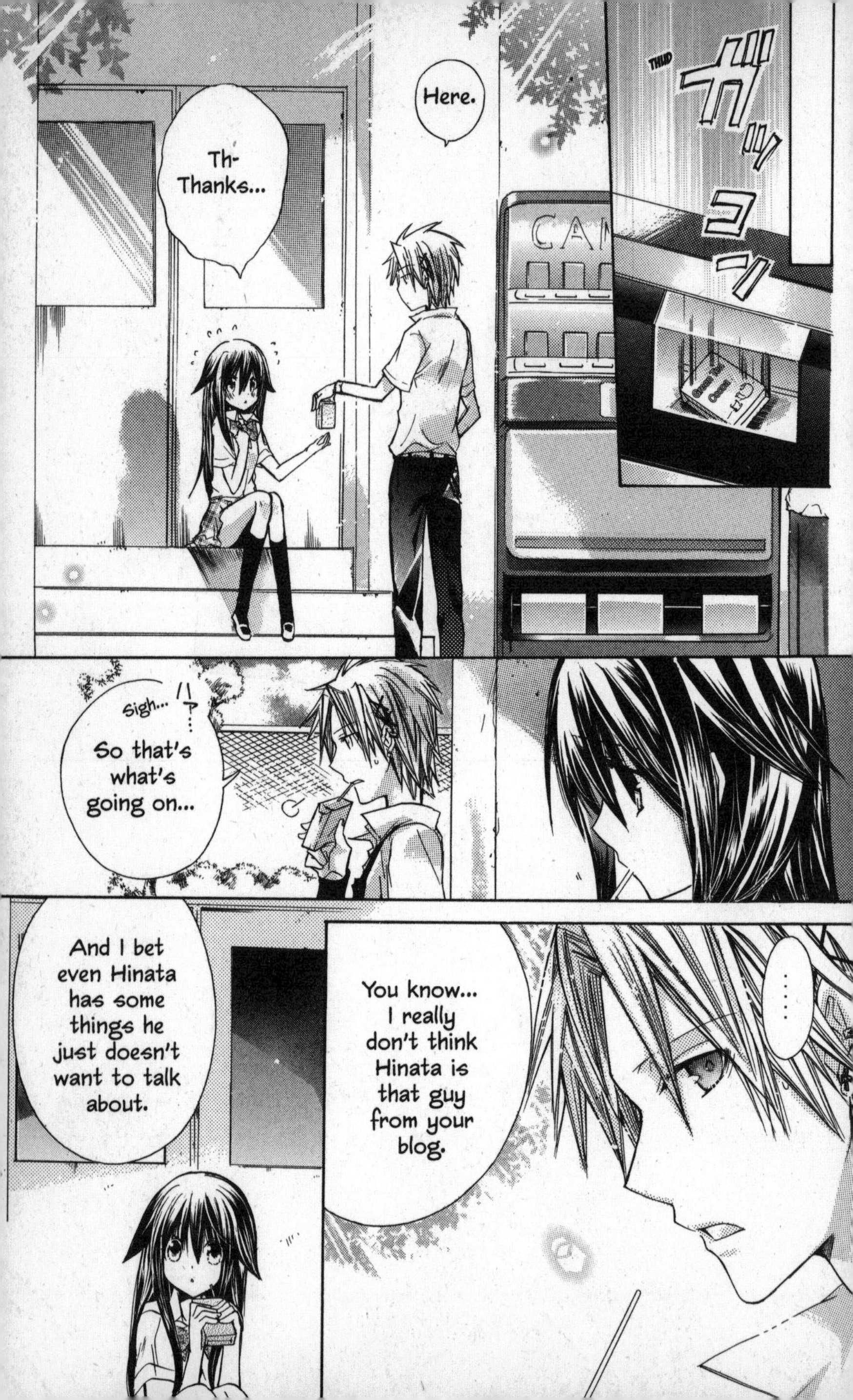
THUD
ガッコン
Here.
Th- Thanks...
Sigh... ハァ…
So that's what's going on...
.....
You know... I really don't think Hinata is that guy from your blog.
And I bet even Hinata has some things he just doesn't want to talk about.

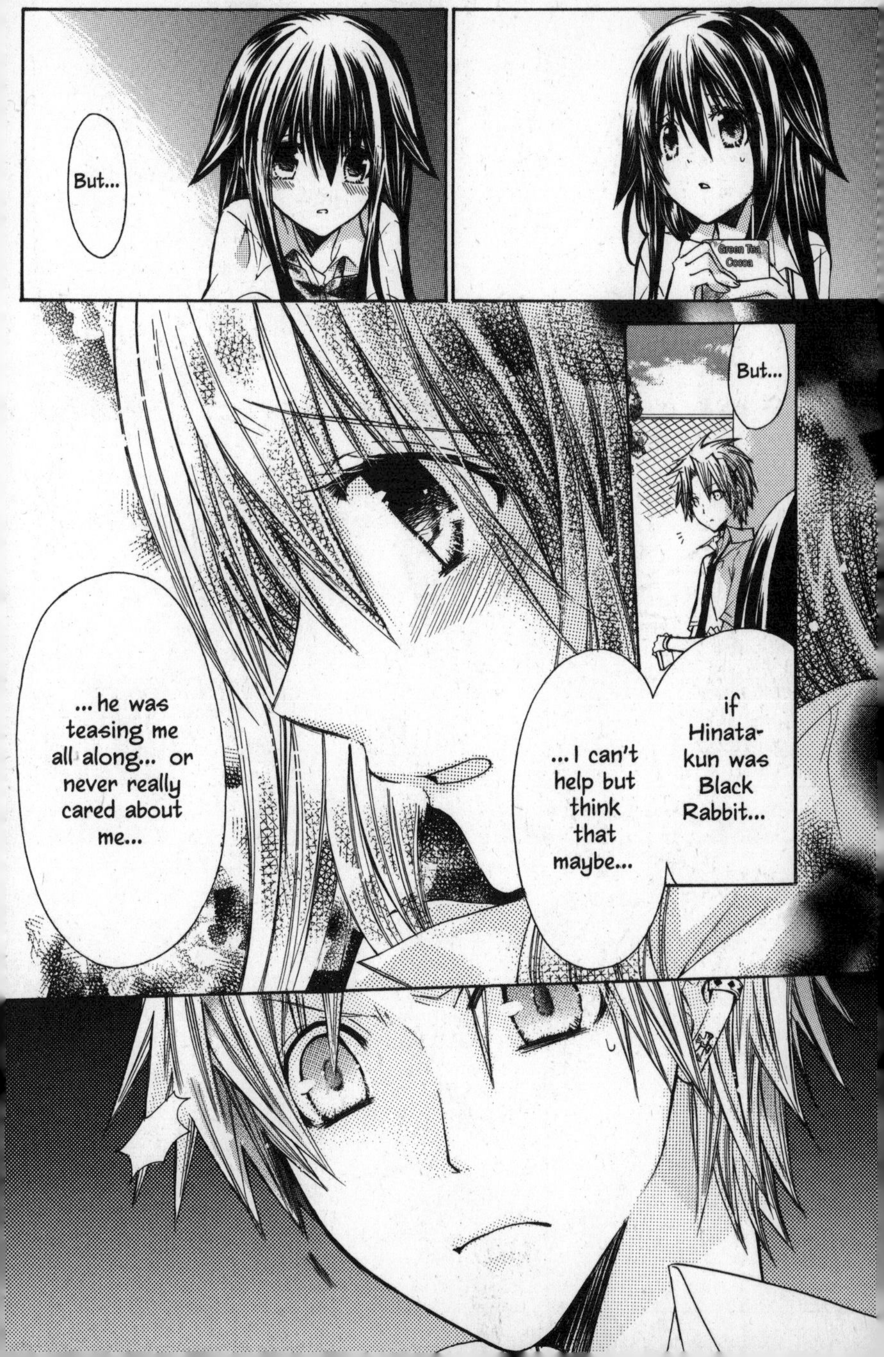
Green Tea Cocoa
But...
But...
if Hinata-kun was Black Rabbit...
...I can't help but think that maybe...
...he was teasing me all along... or never really cared about me...

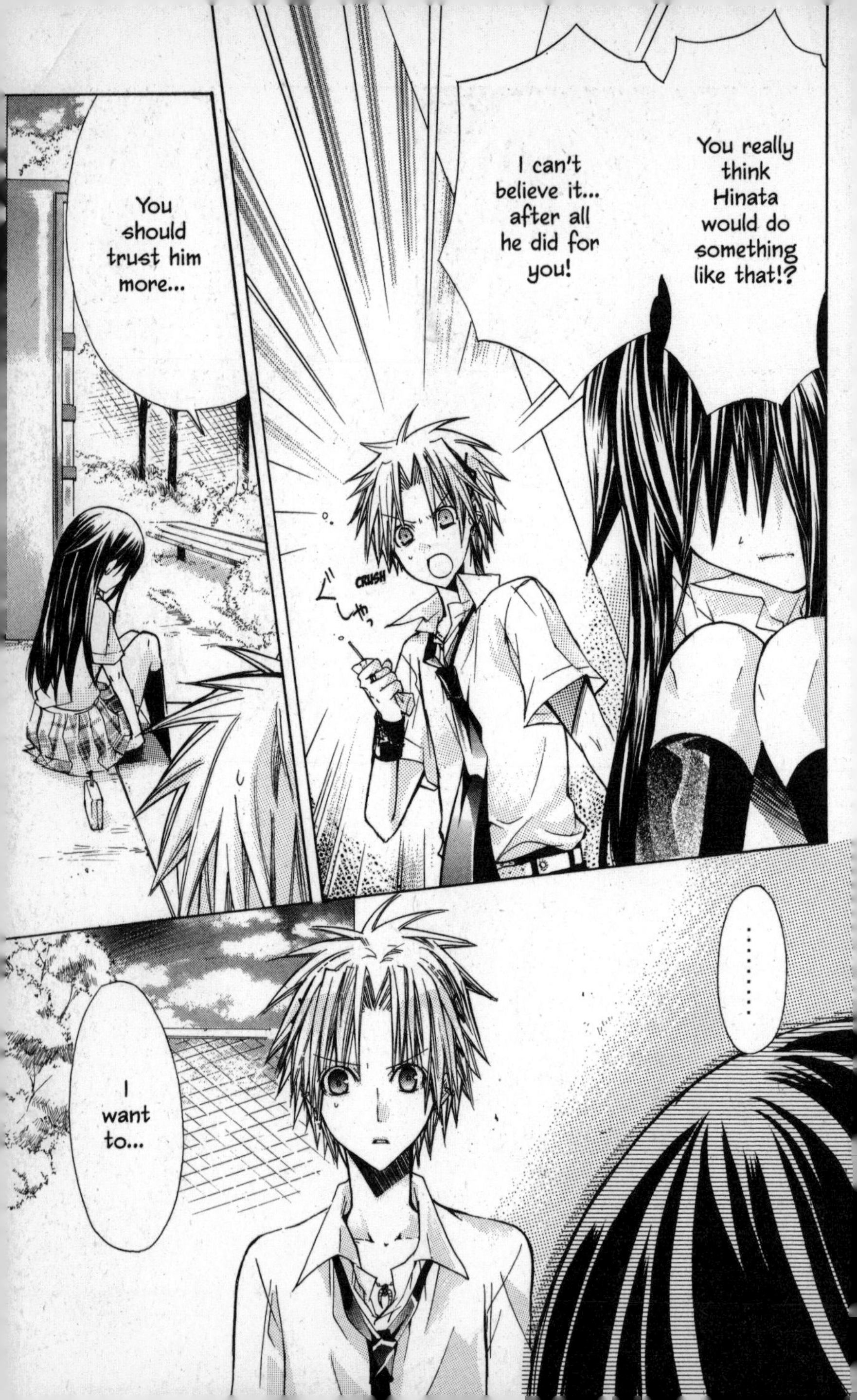
You really think Hinata would do something like that!?
I can't believe it... after all he did for you!
CRUSH
You should trust him more...
....
I want to...

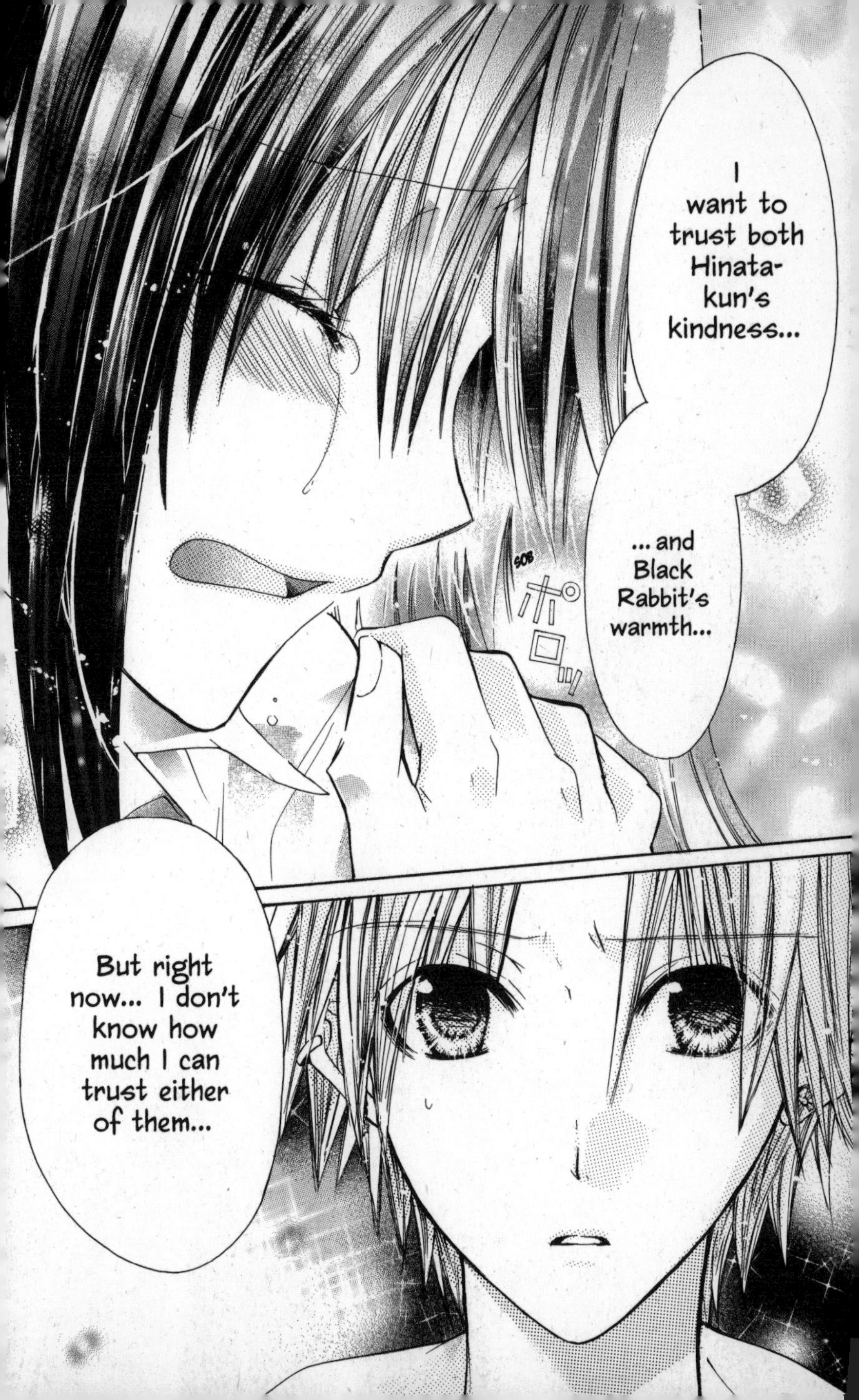
I want to trust both Hinata-kun's kindness...
... and Black Rabbit's warmth...
SOB
ポロッ
But right now... I don't know how much I can trust either of them...

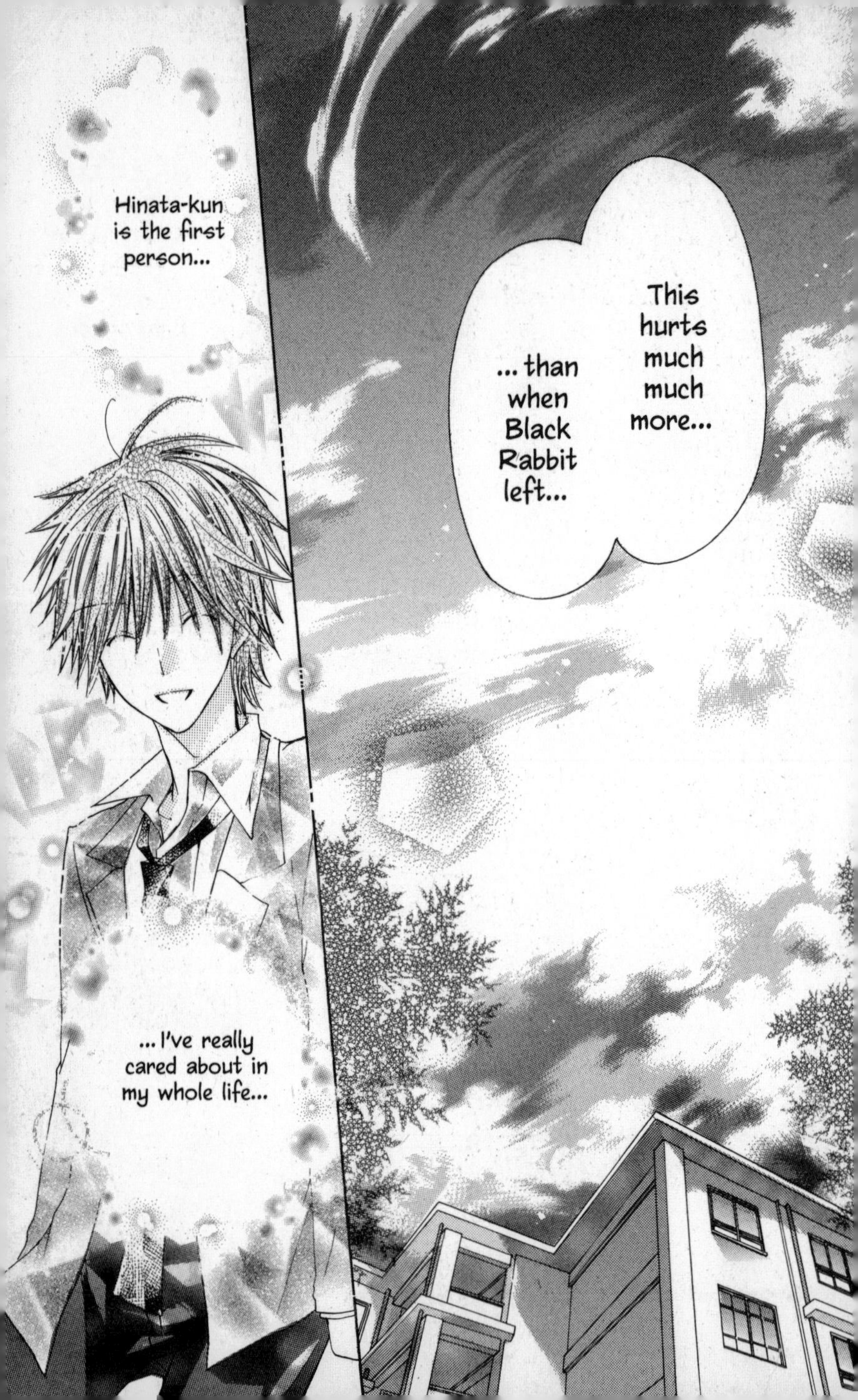
This hurts much much more...
... than when Black Rabbit left...
Hinata-kun is the first person...
... I've really cared about in my whole life...

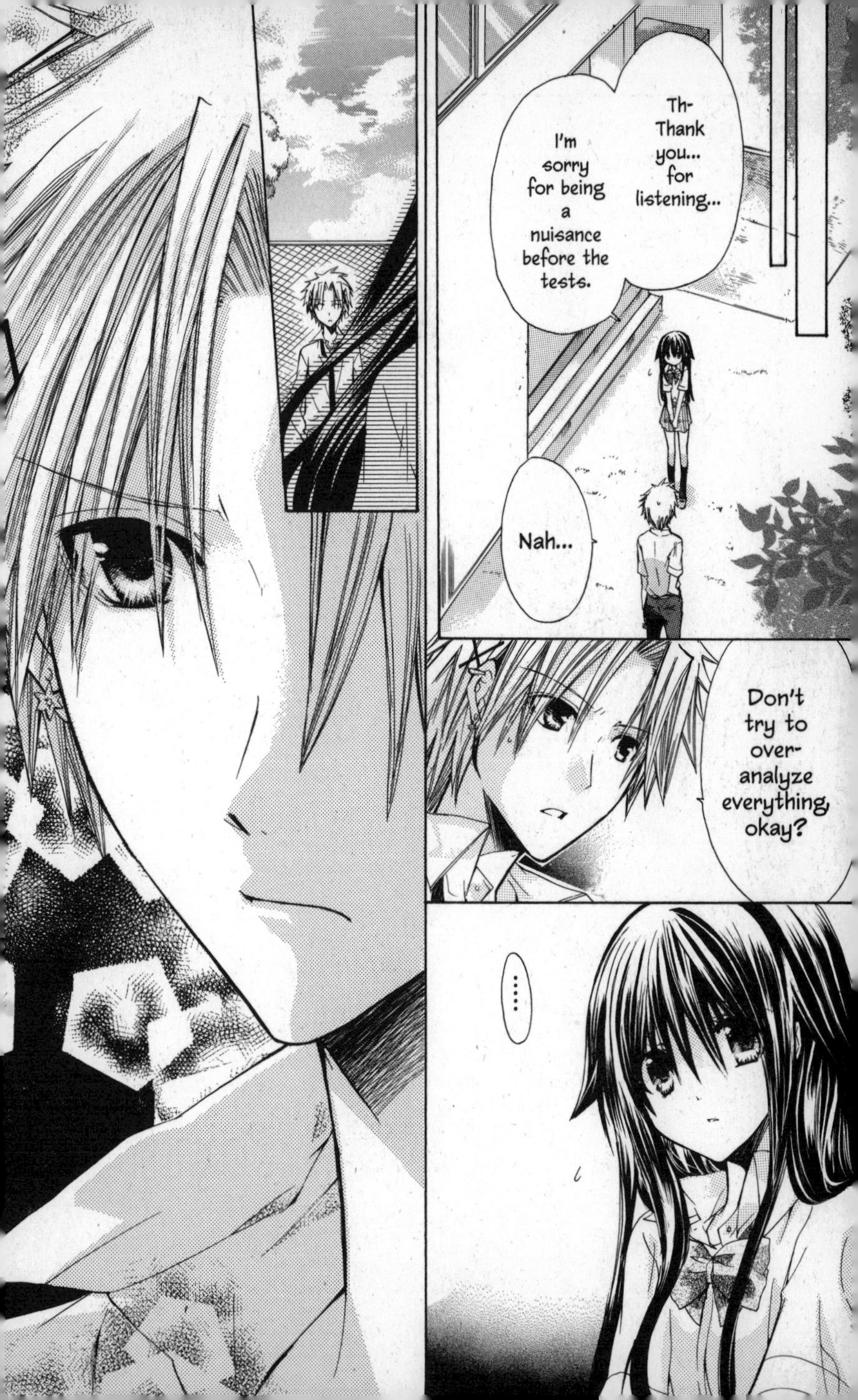
Th- Thank you... for listening...
I'm sorry for being a nuisance before the tests.
Nah...
Don't try to over-analyze everything, okay?
......

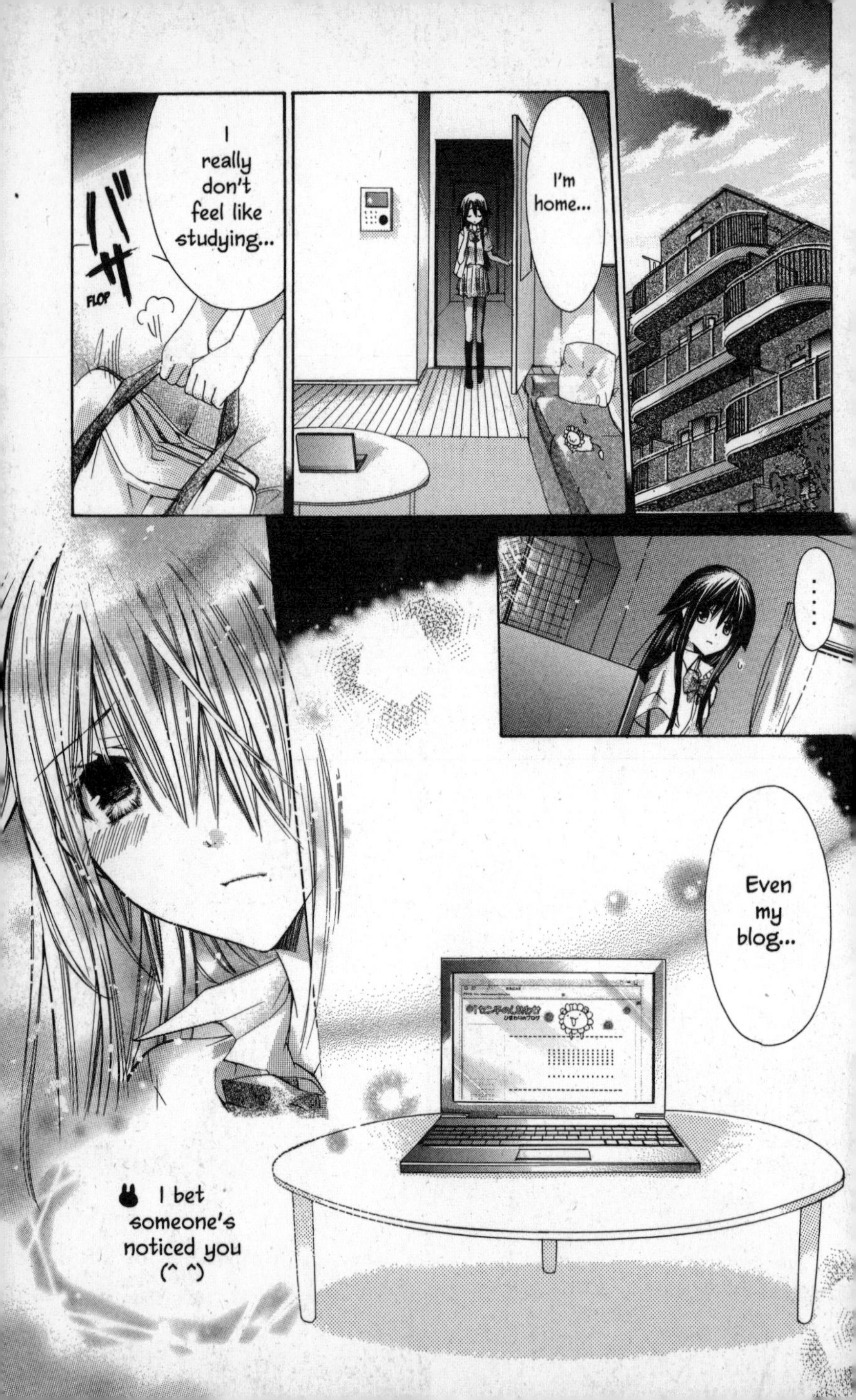
I'm home...
I really don't feel like studying...
バサ
FLOP
......
Even my blog...
I bet someone's noticed you (^ ^)

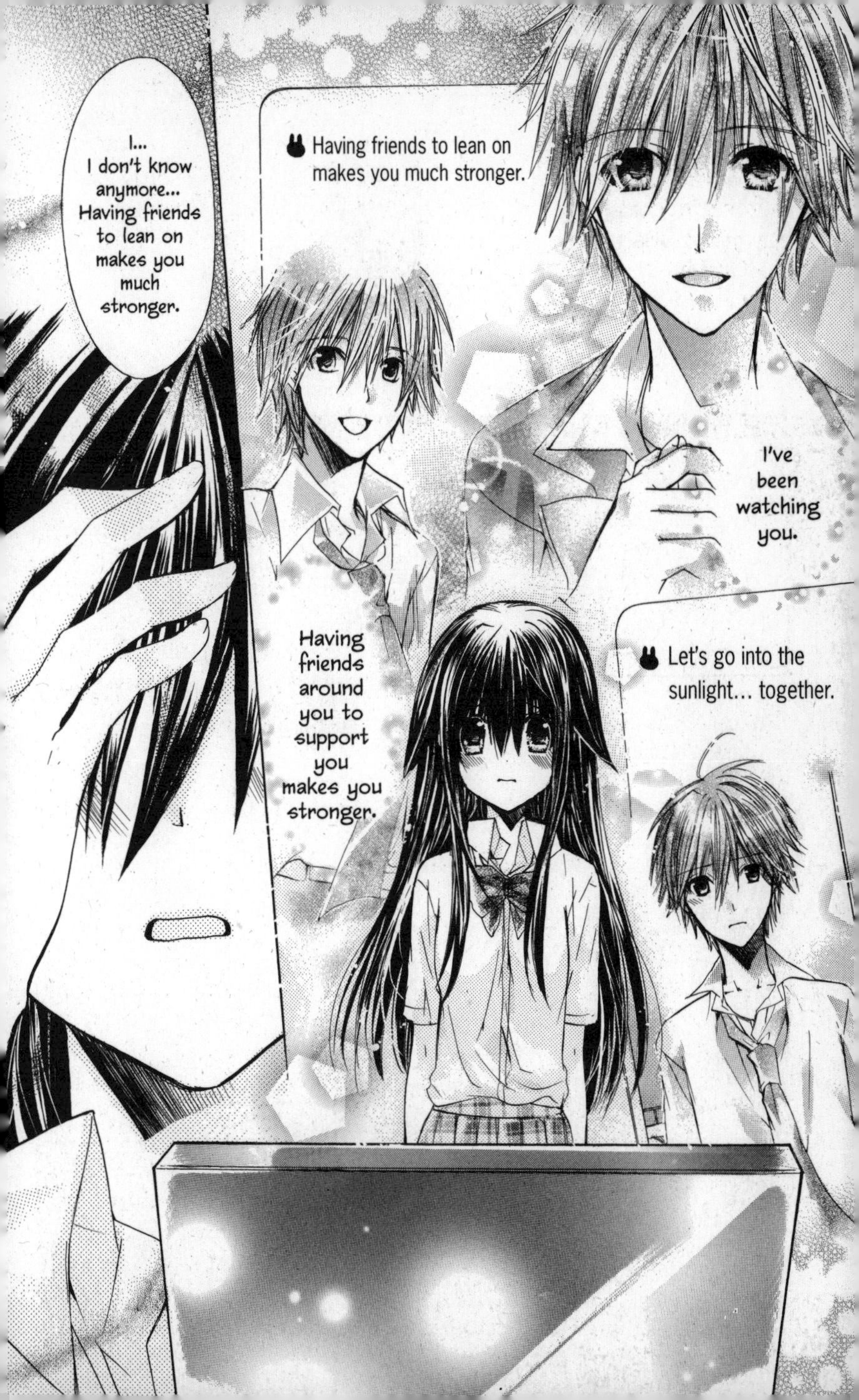
Having friends to lean on makes you much stronger.
I've been watching you.
Let's go into the sunlight... together.
Having friends around you to support you makes you stronger.
I... I don't know anymore... Having friends to lean on makes you much stronger.

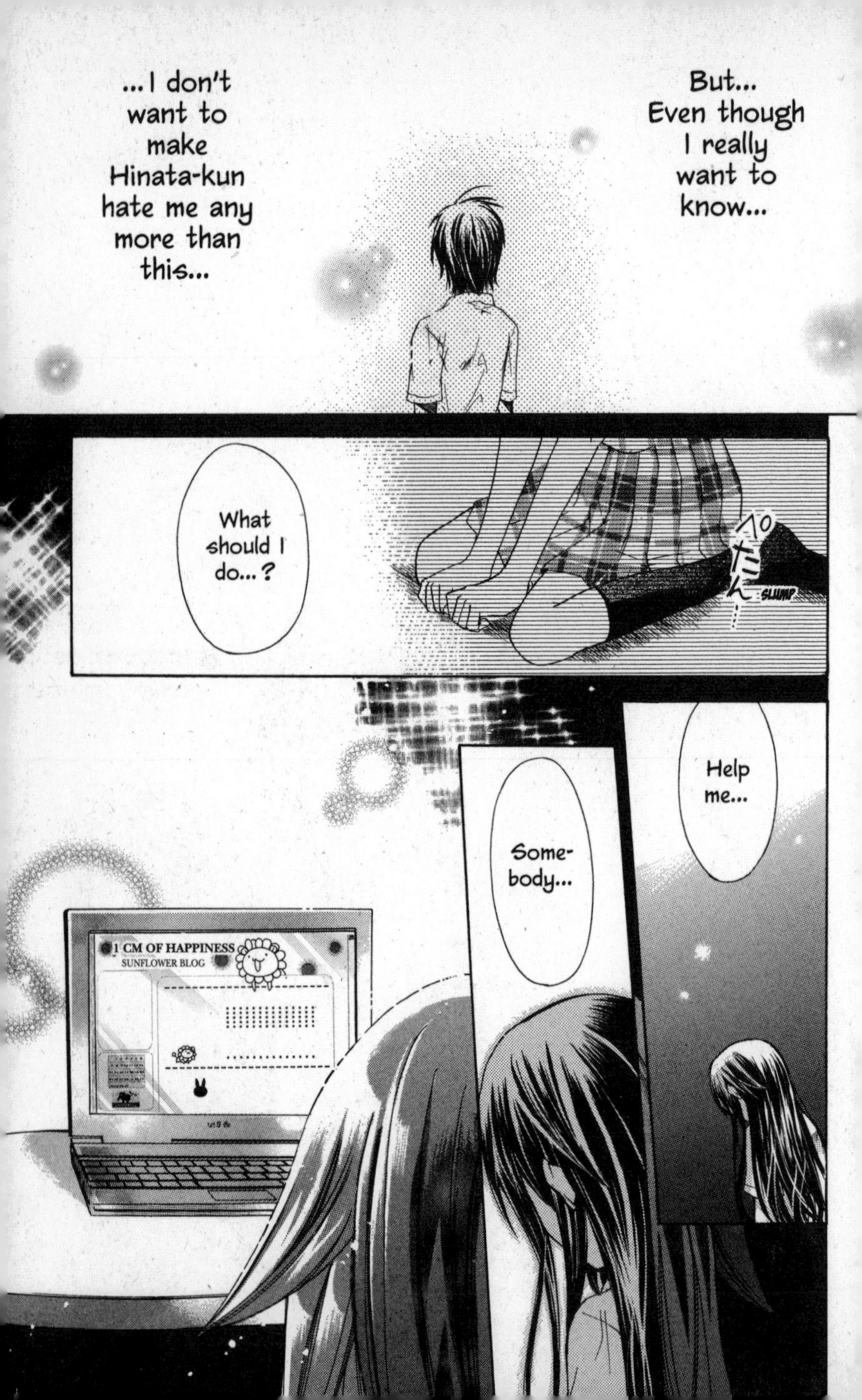
But... Even though I really want to know...
...I don't want to make Hinata-kun hate me any more than this...
What should I do...?
へたん
SLUMP
Help me...
Some-body...
1 CM OF HAPPINESS
SUNFLOWER BLOG

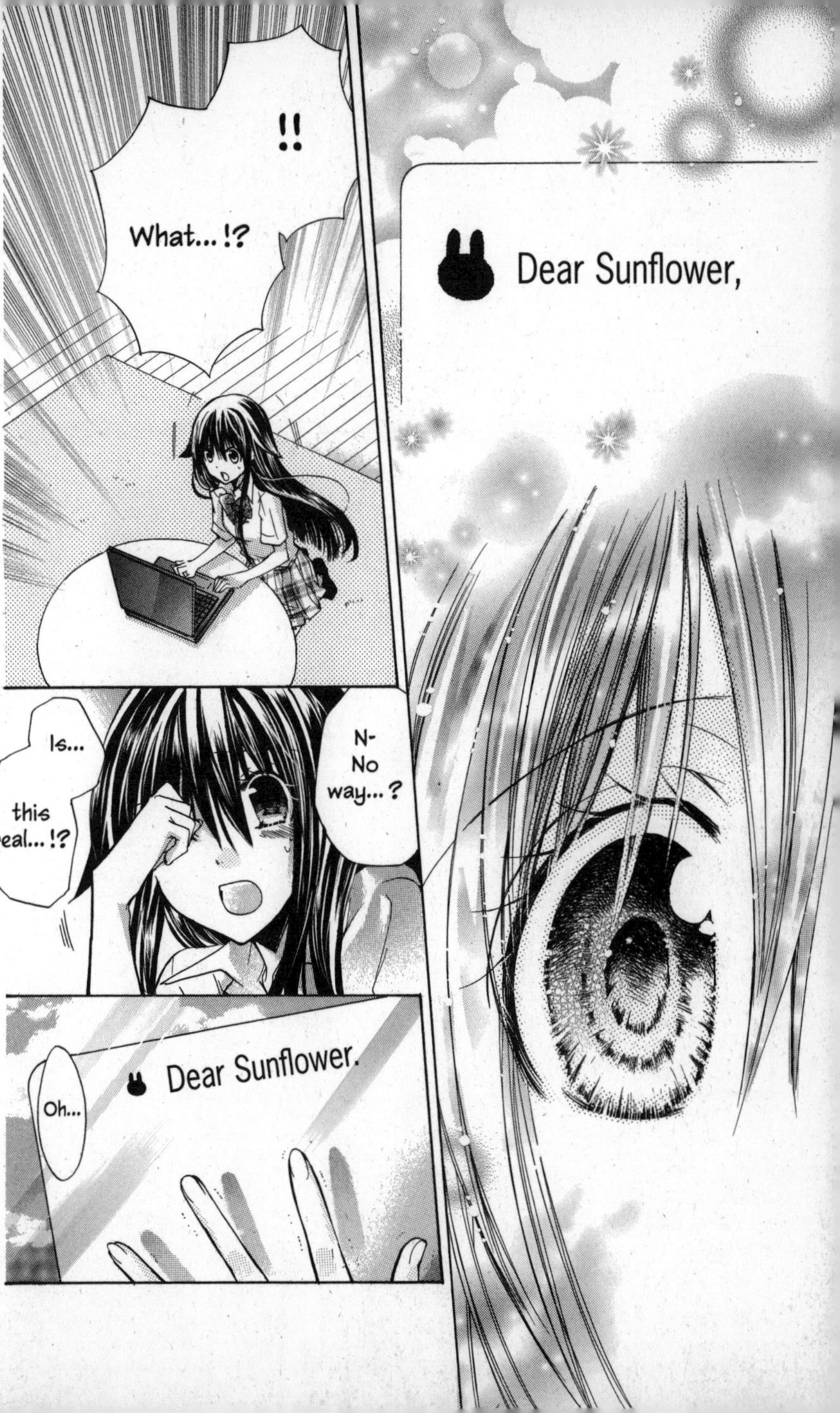

Dear Sunflower,
!!
What...!?
N-
No
way...?
Is...
this
real...!?
Dear Sunflower.
Oh...

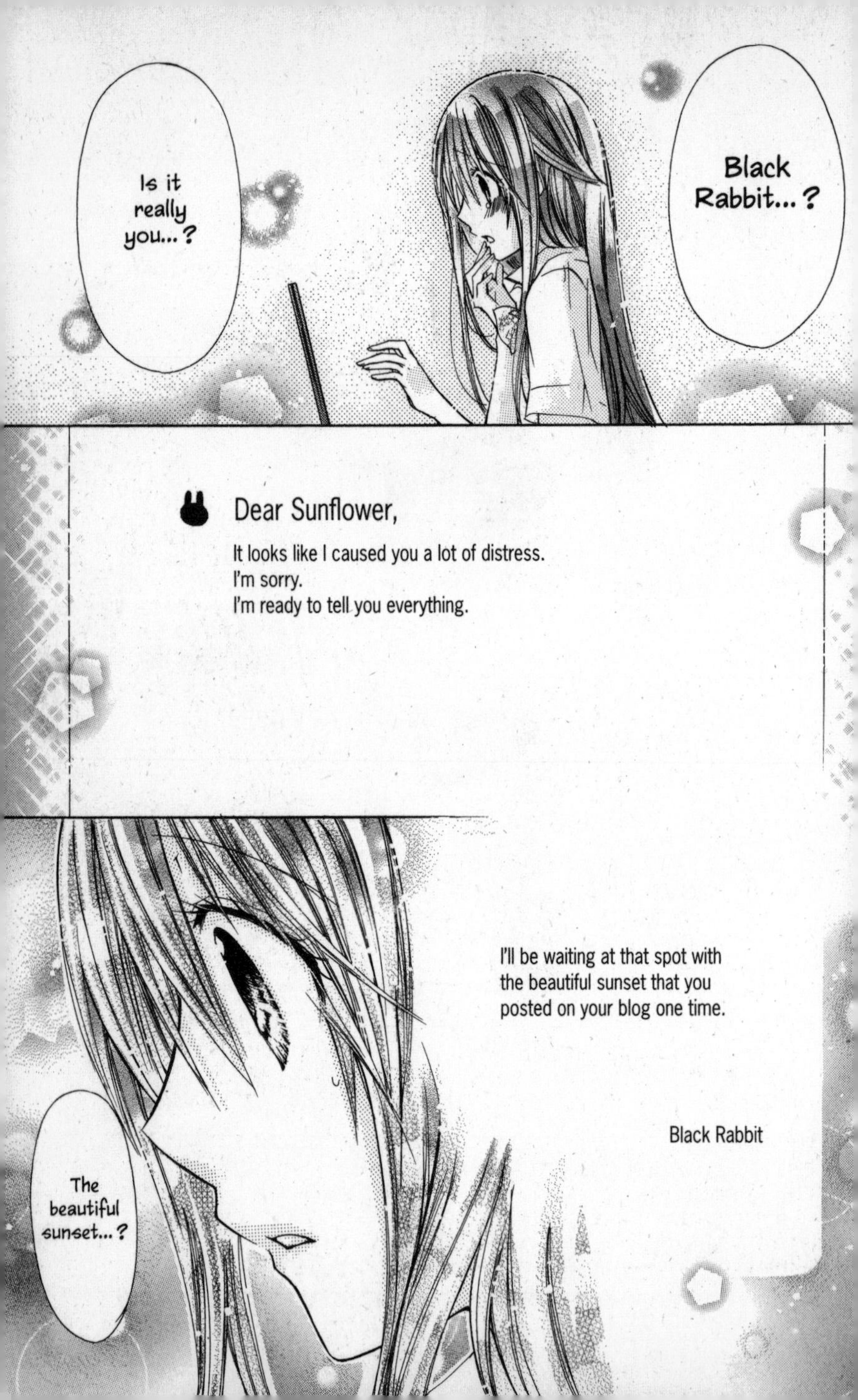

Black Rabbit...?
Is it really you...?
Dear Sunflower,
It looks like I caused you a lot of distress.
I'm sorry.
I'm ready to tell you everything.
I'll be waiting at that spot with the beautiful sunset that you posted on your blog one time.
Black Rabbit
The beautiful sunset...?

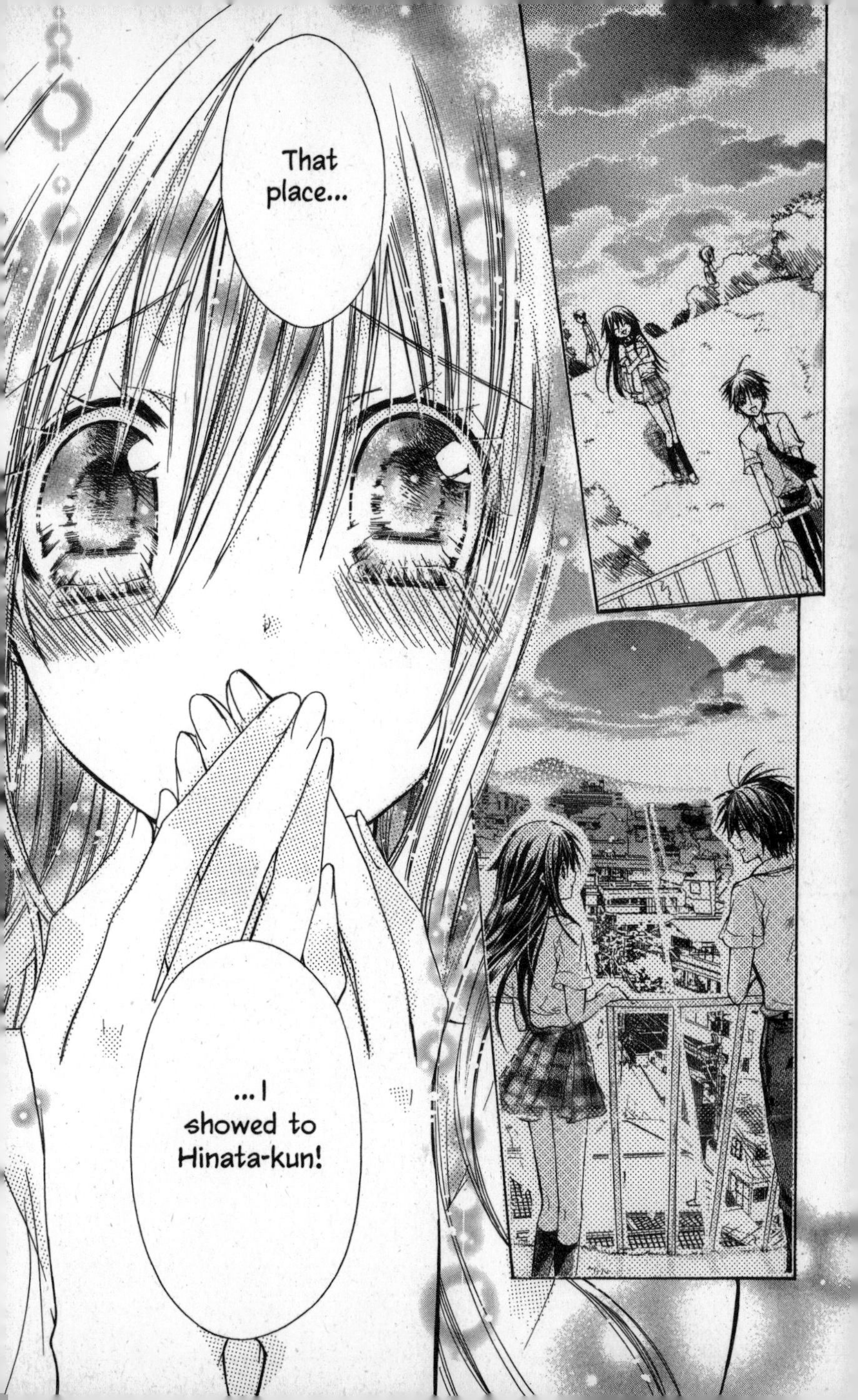
That place...
...I showed to Hinata-kun!

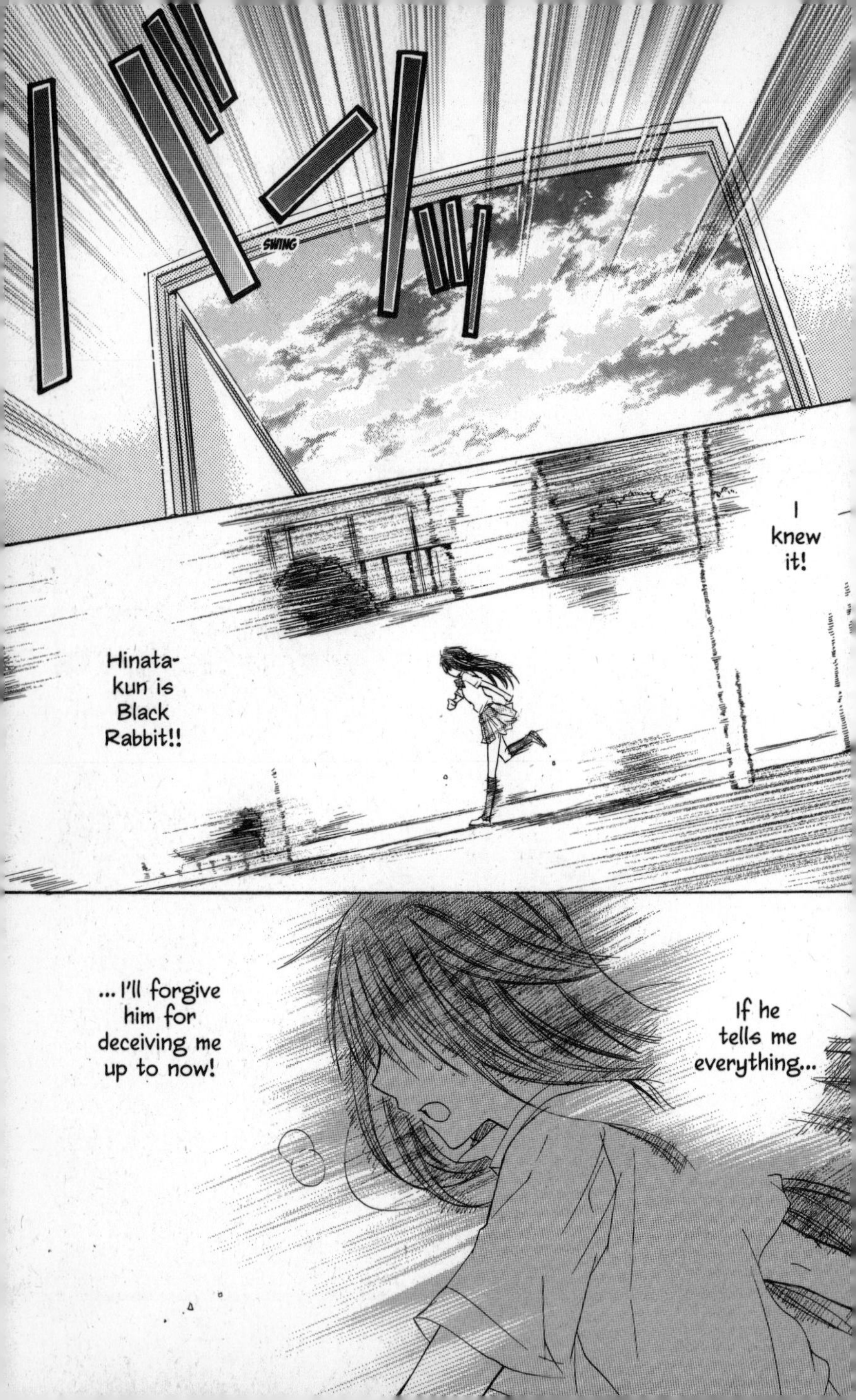
SWING
I knew it!
Hinata-kun is Black Rabbit!!
If he tells me everything...
...I'll forgive him for deceiving me up to now!

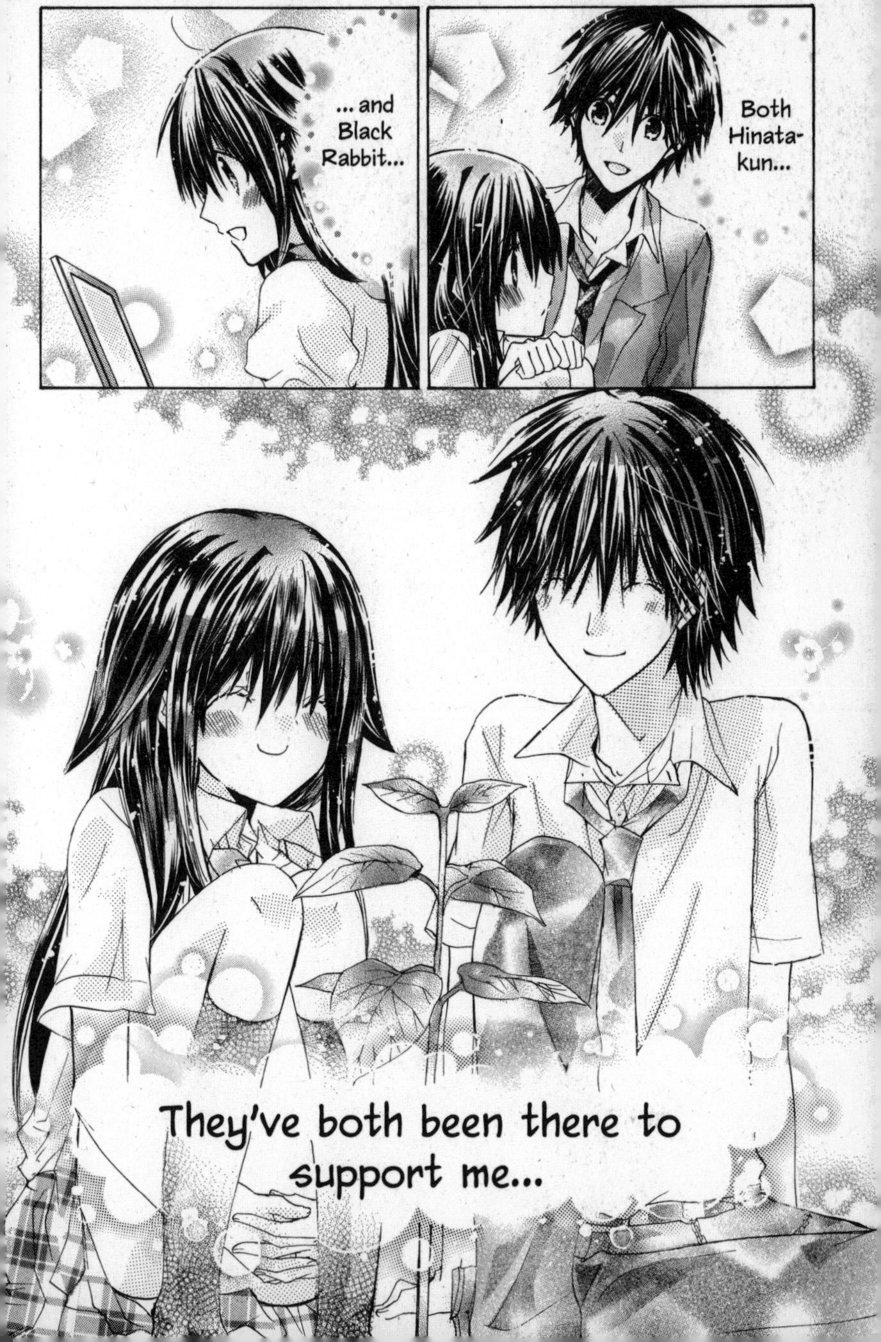
Both Hinata-kun...
...and Black Rabbit...
They've both been there to support me...

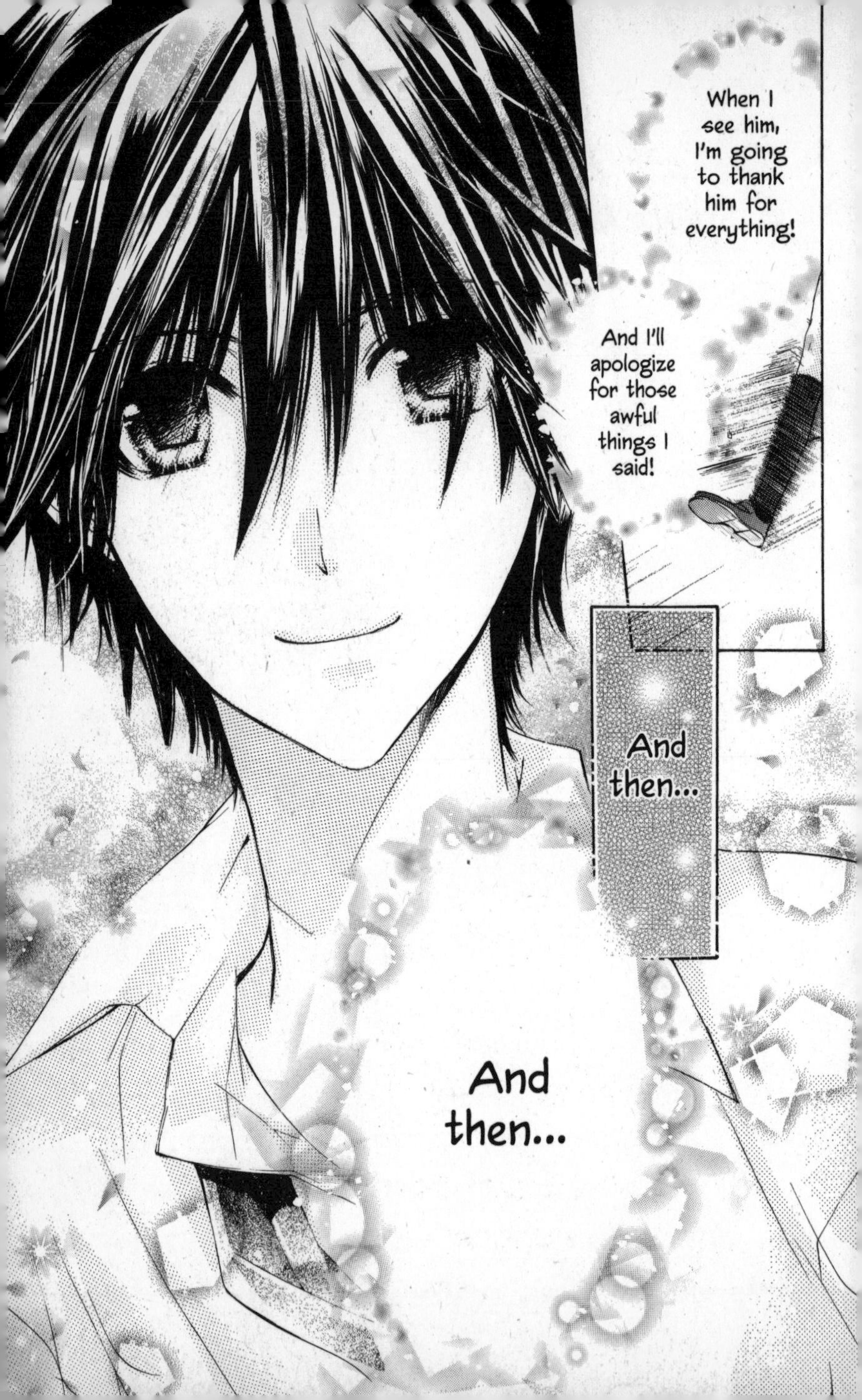
When I see him, I'm going to thank him for everything!
And I'll apologize for those awful things I said!
And then...
And then...

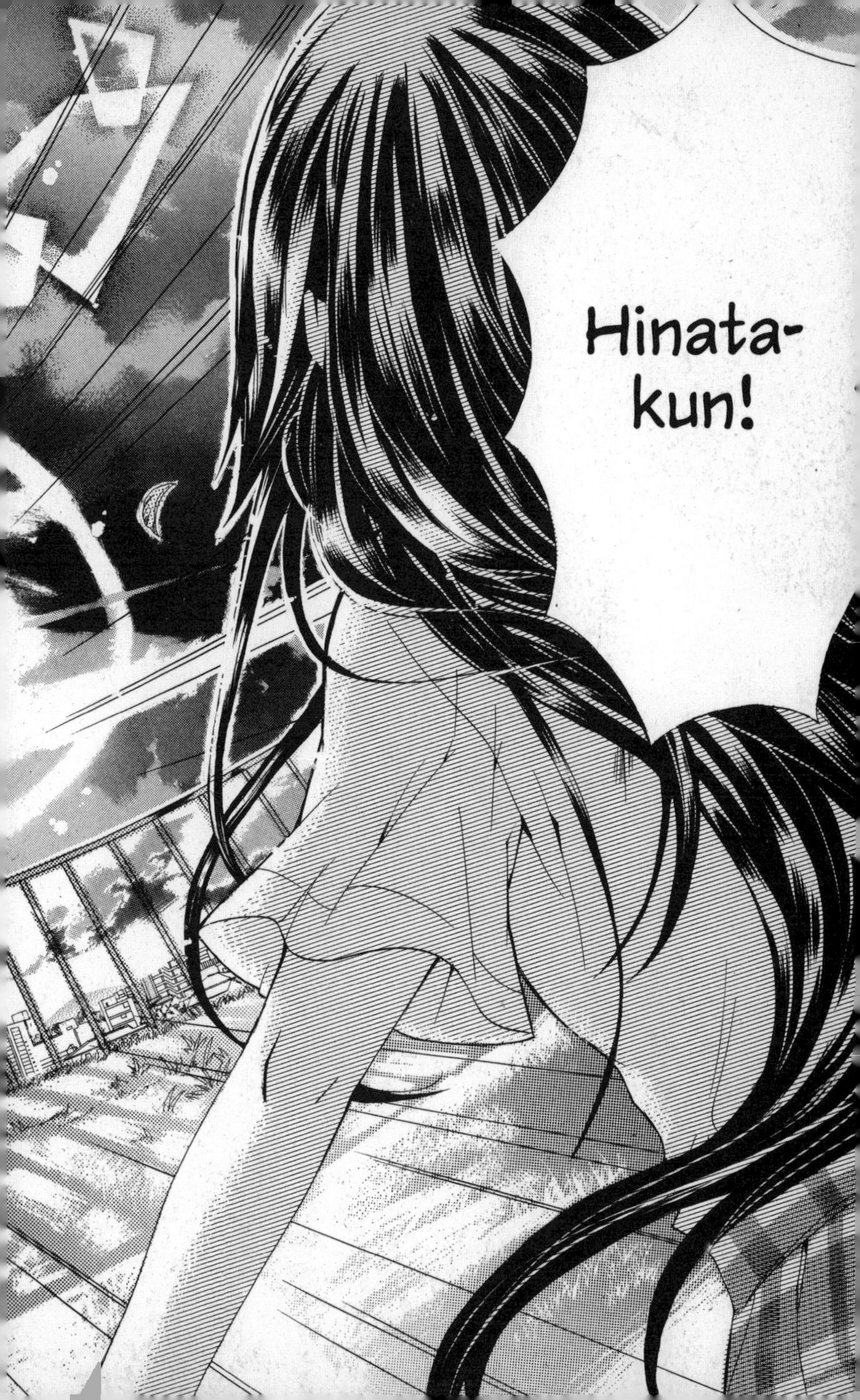
Hinata-kun!

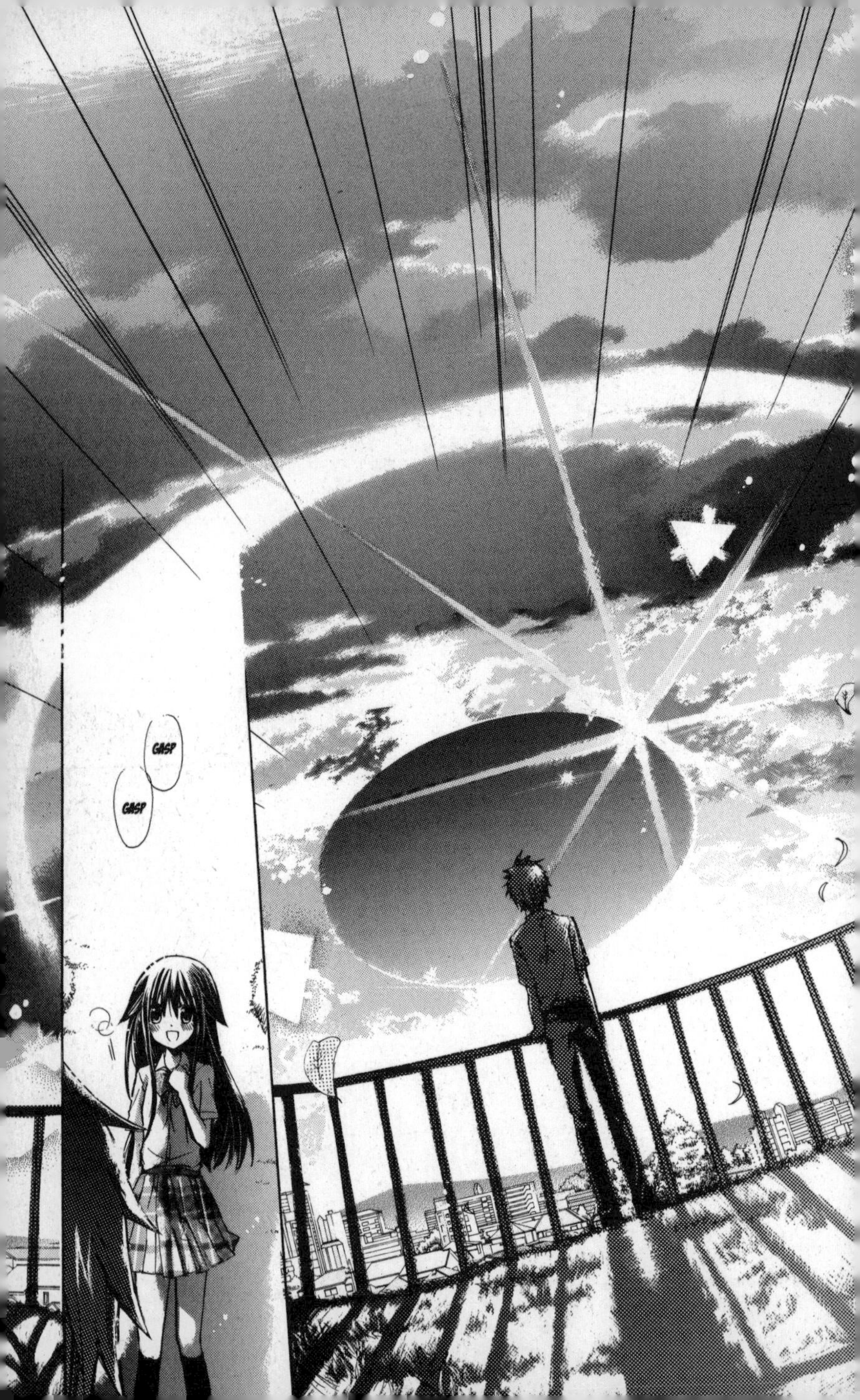
GASP
GASP

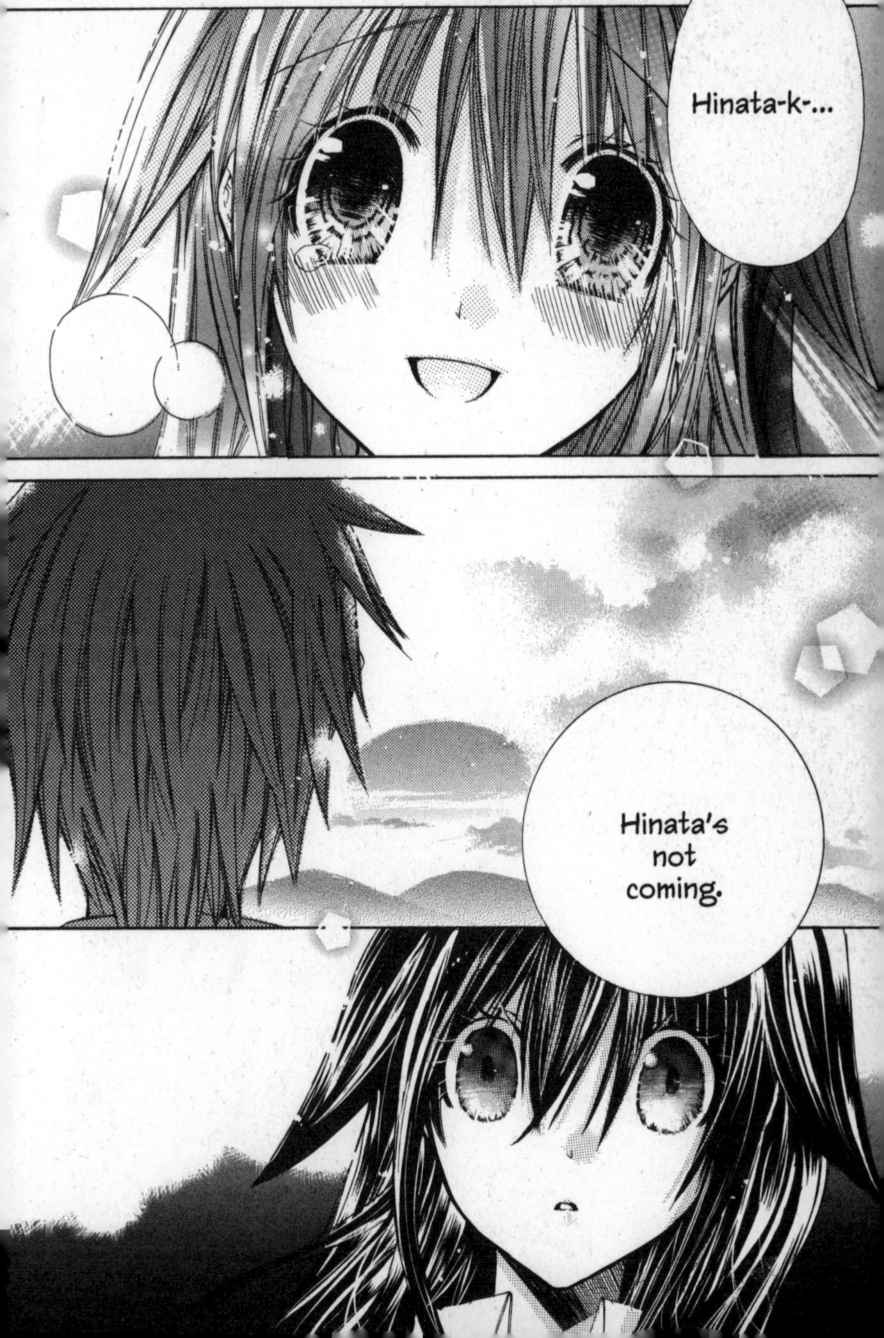
Hinata-k-...
Hinata's not coming.

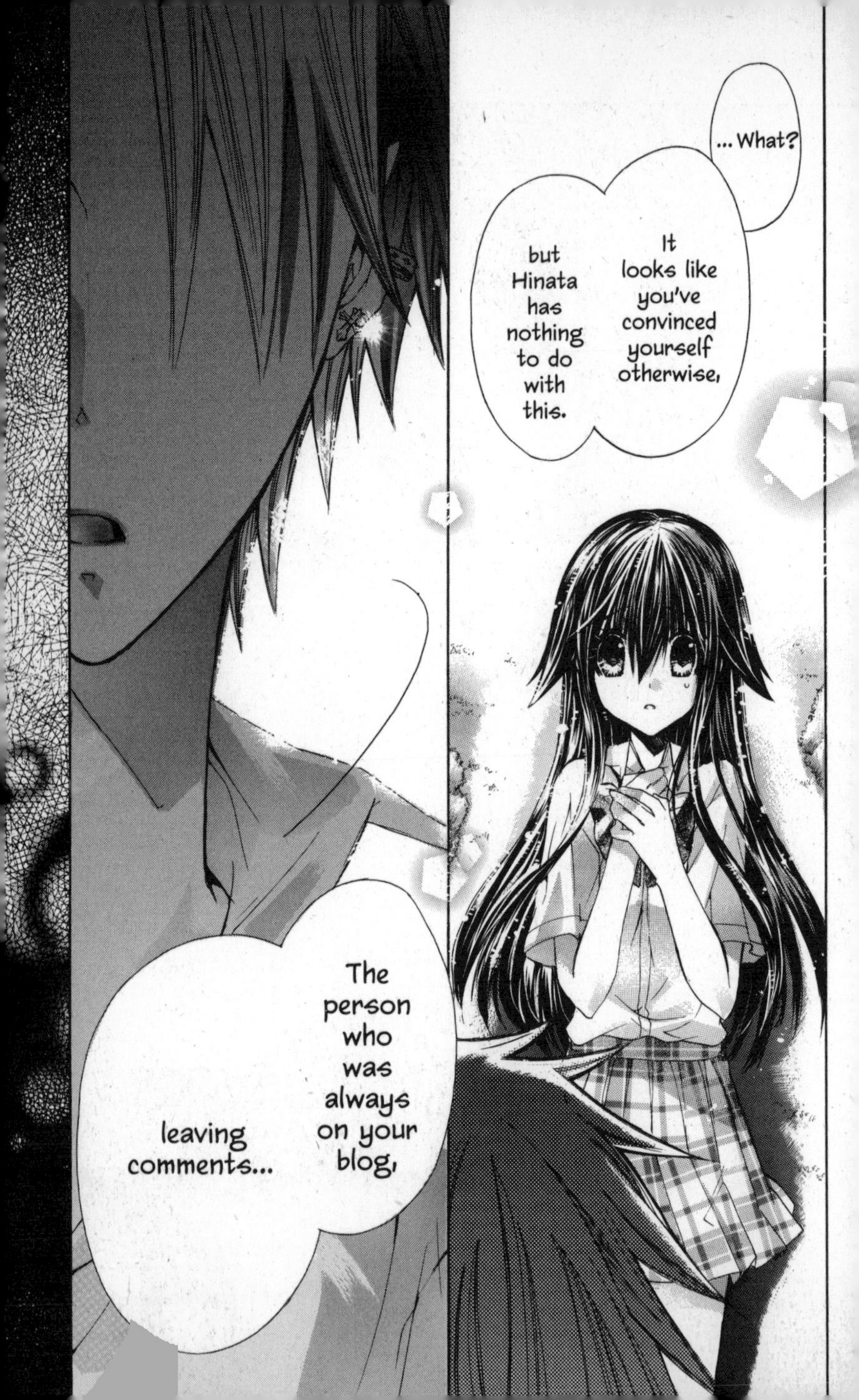
...What?
It looks like you've convinced yourself otherwise, but Hinata has nothing to do with this.
The person who was always on your blog, leaving comments...

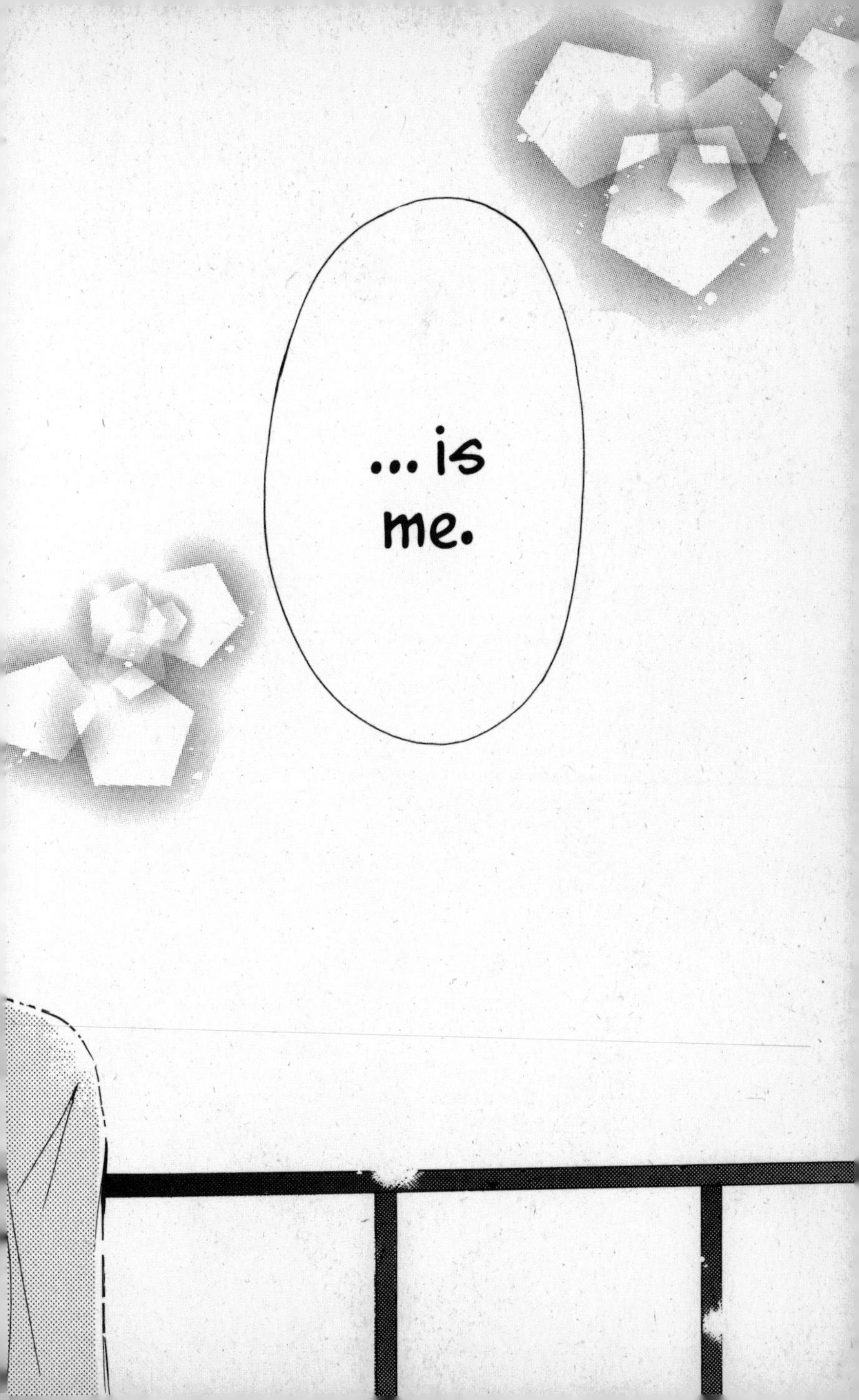
...is me.

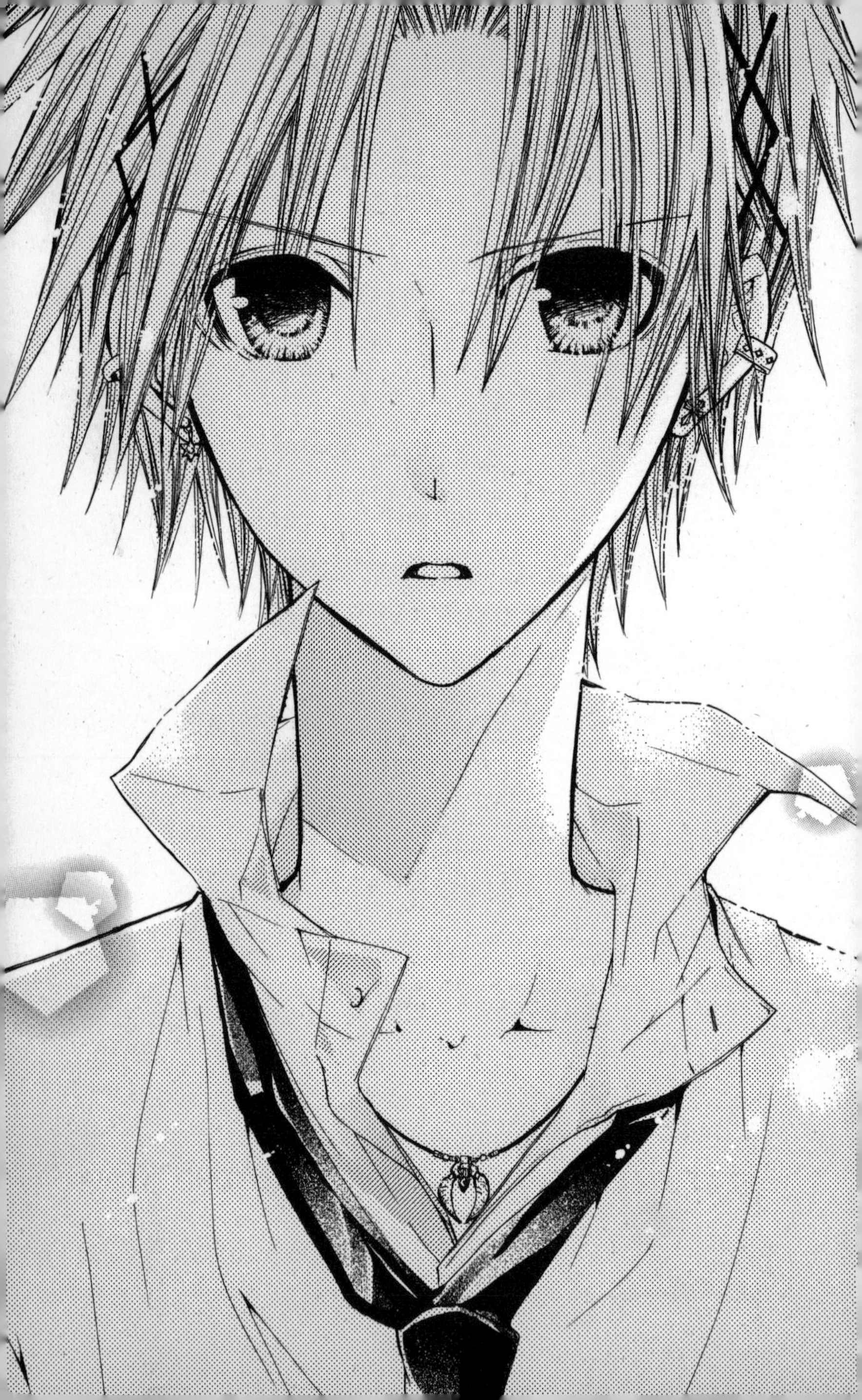

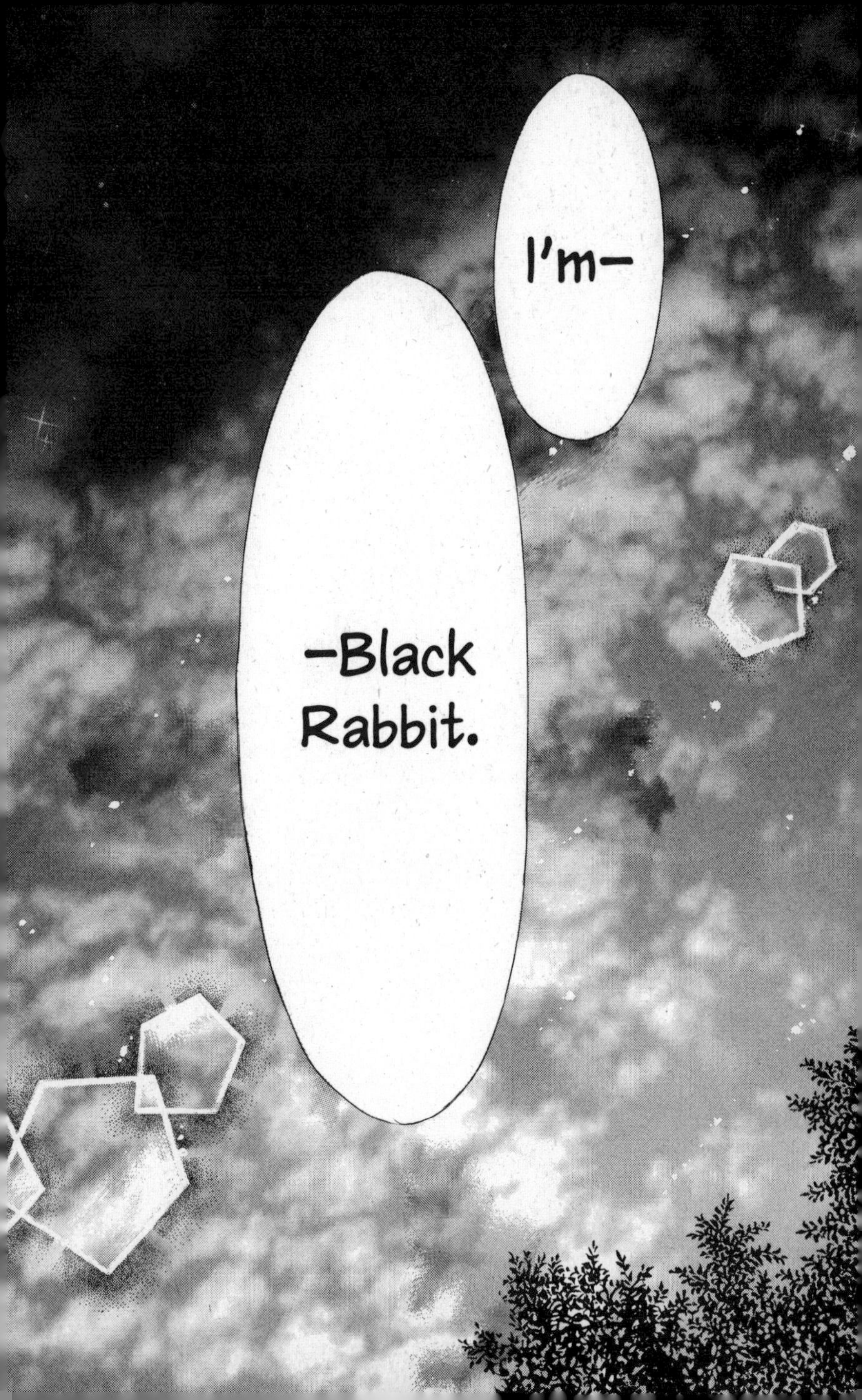
I'm—
—Black Rabbit.

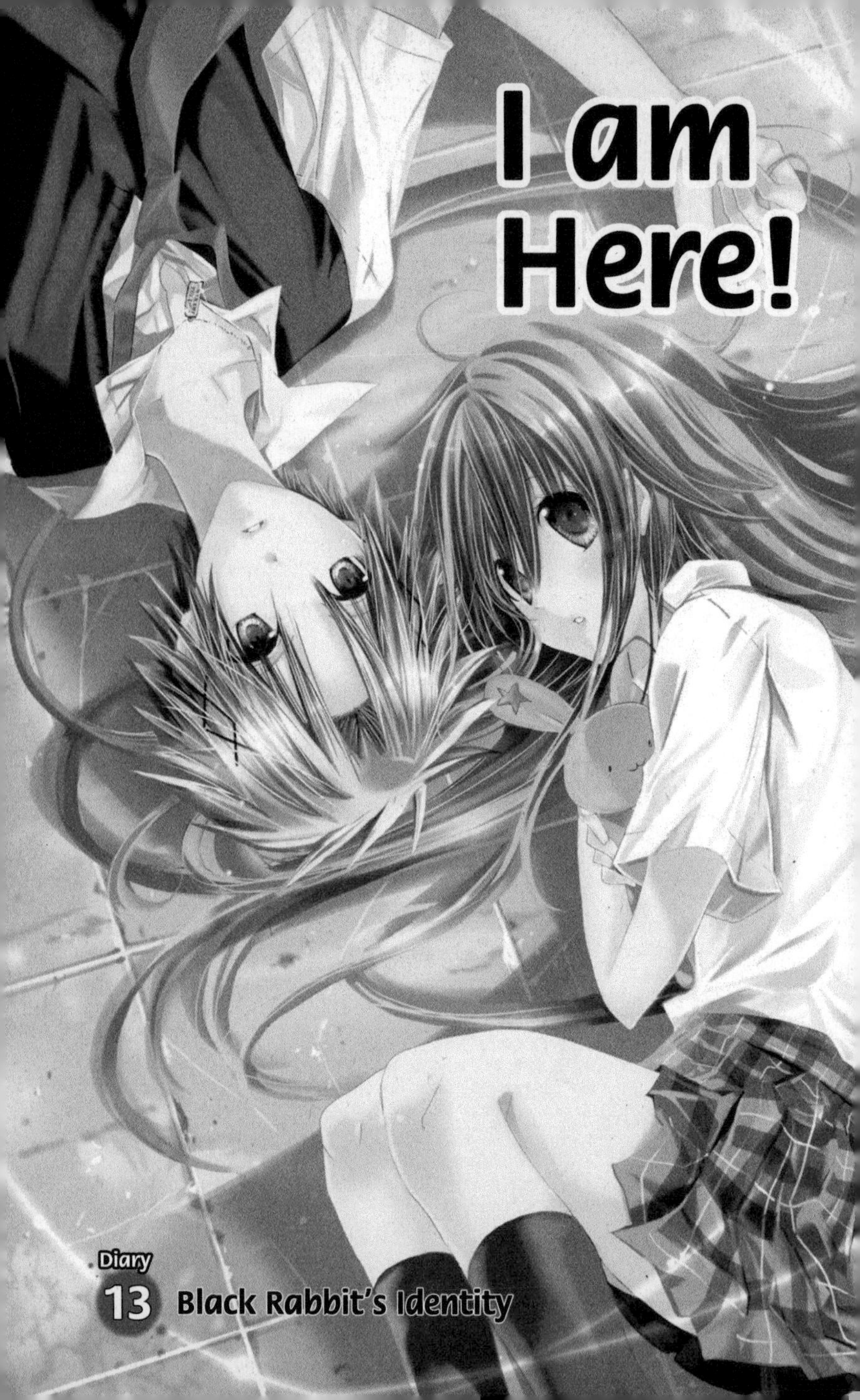
I am Here!
Diary 13 Black Rabbit's Identity

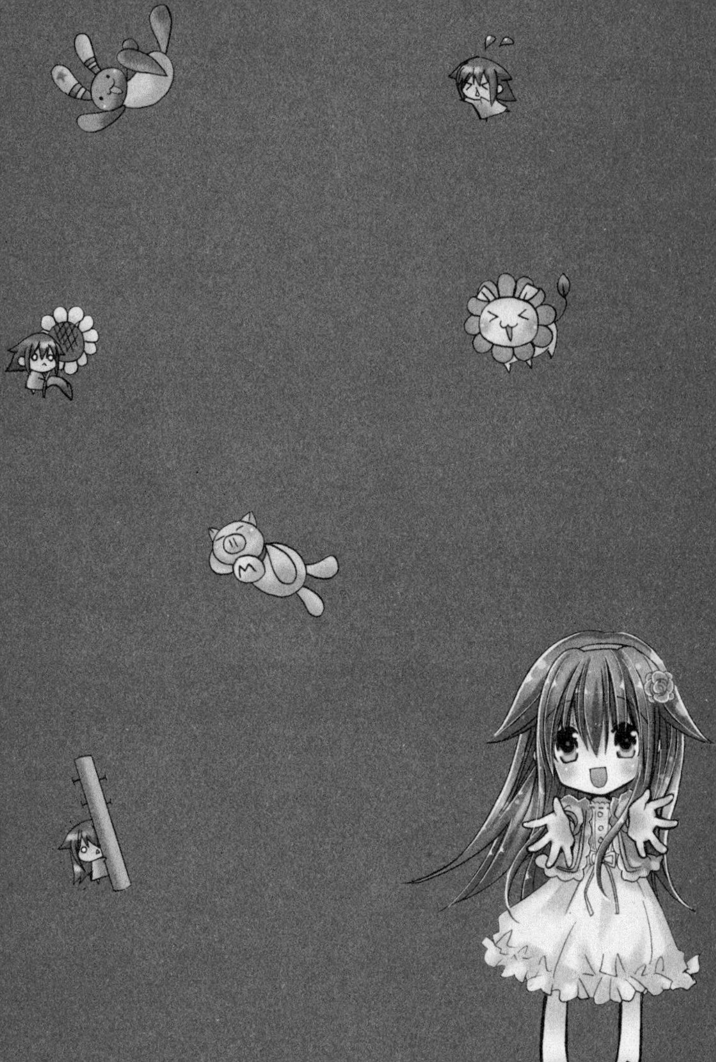

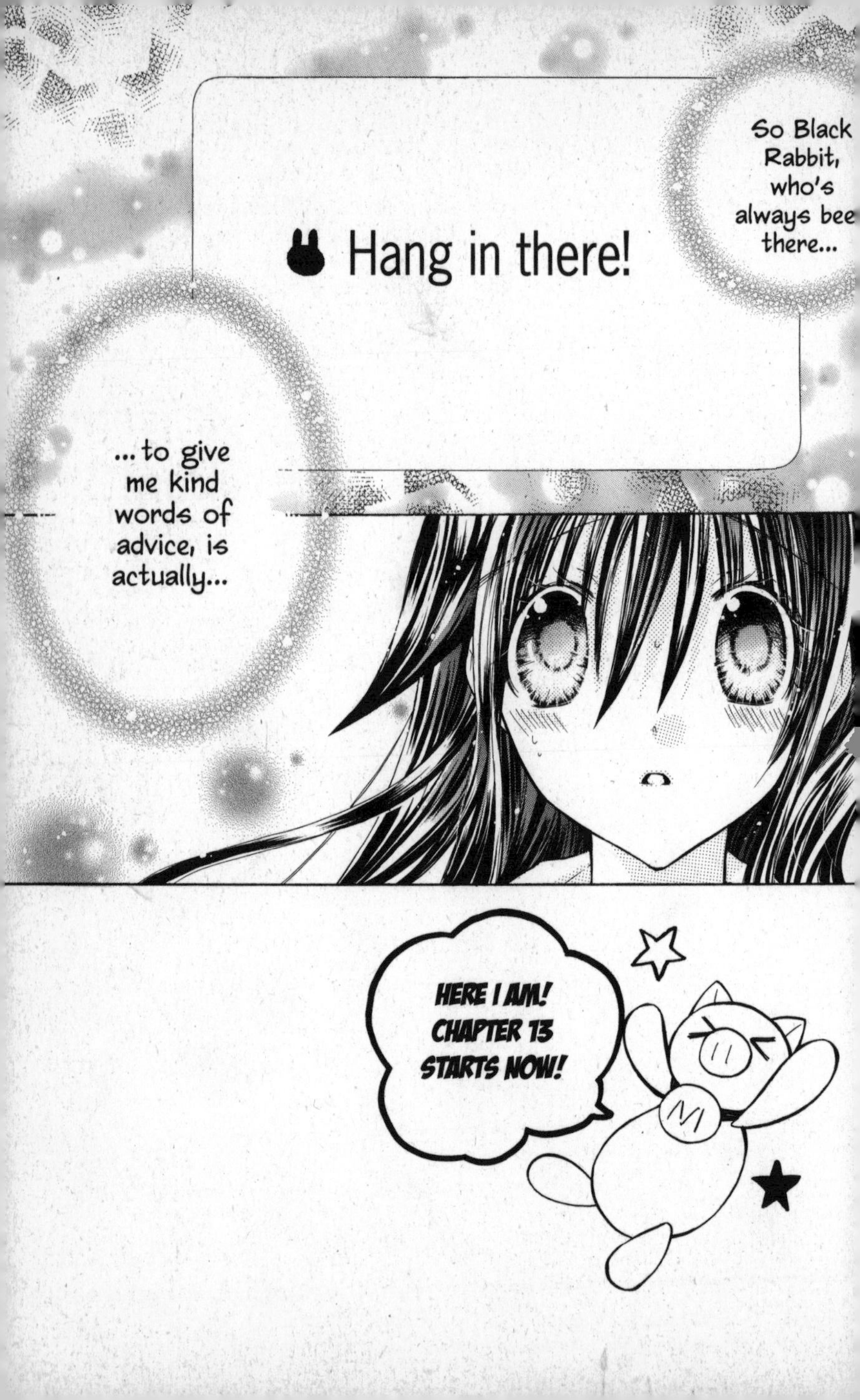
So Black Rabbit, who's always bee there...
Hang in there!
...to give me kind words of advice, is actually...
HERE I AM! CHAPTER 13 STARTS NOW!

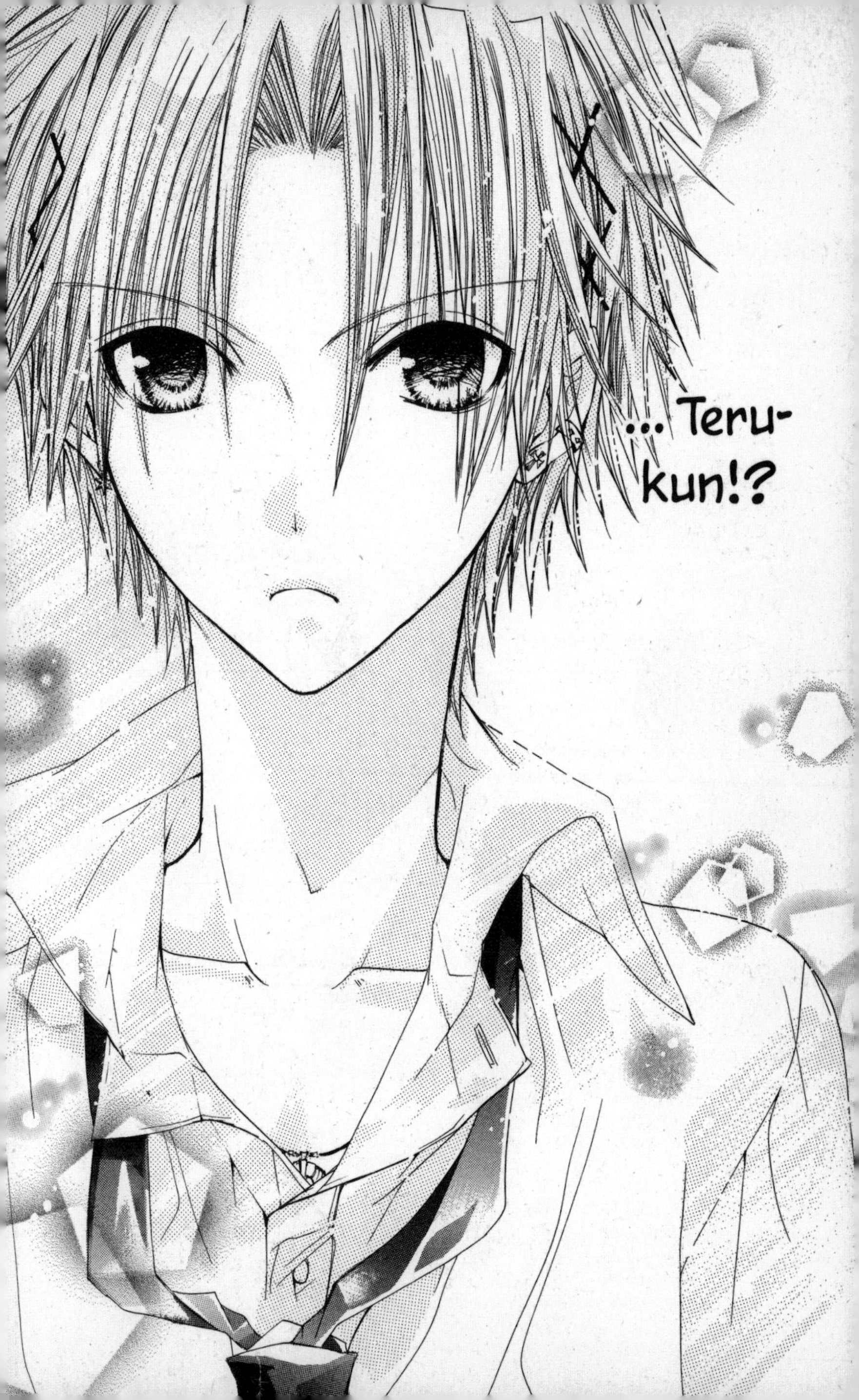
... Teru-kun!?

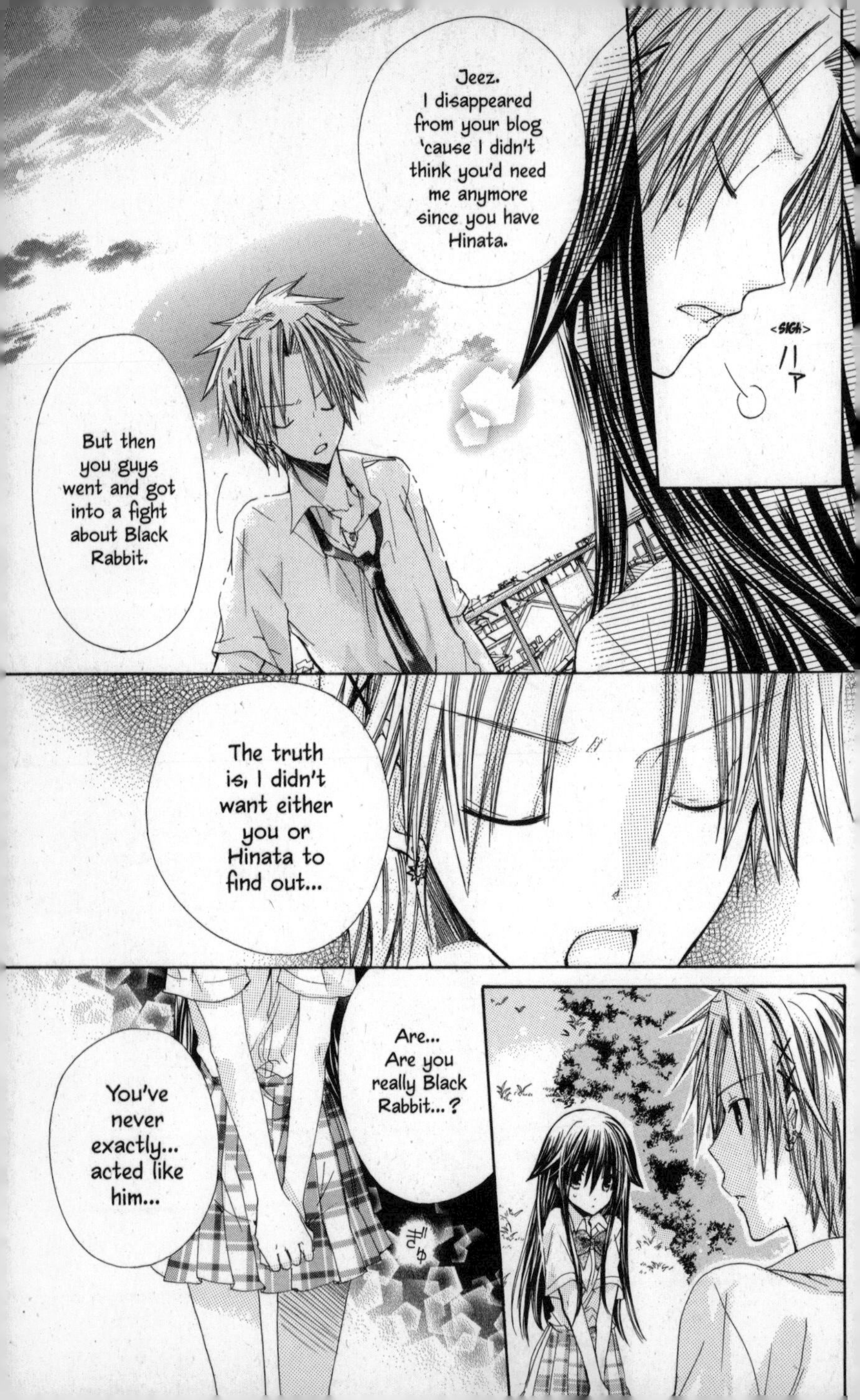
<SIGH>
ハァ
Jeez. I disappeared from your blog 'cause I didn't think you'd need me anymore since you have Hinata.
But then you guys went and got into a fight about Black Rabbit.
The truth is, I didn't want either you or Hinata to find out...
Are... Are you really Black Rabbit...?
You've never exactly... acted like him...

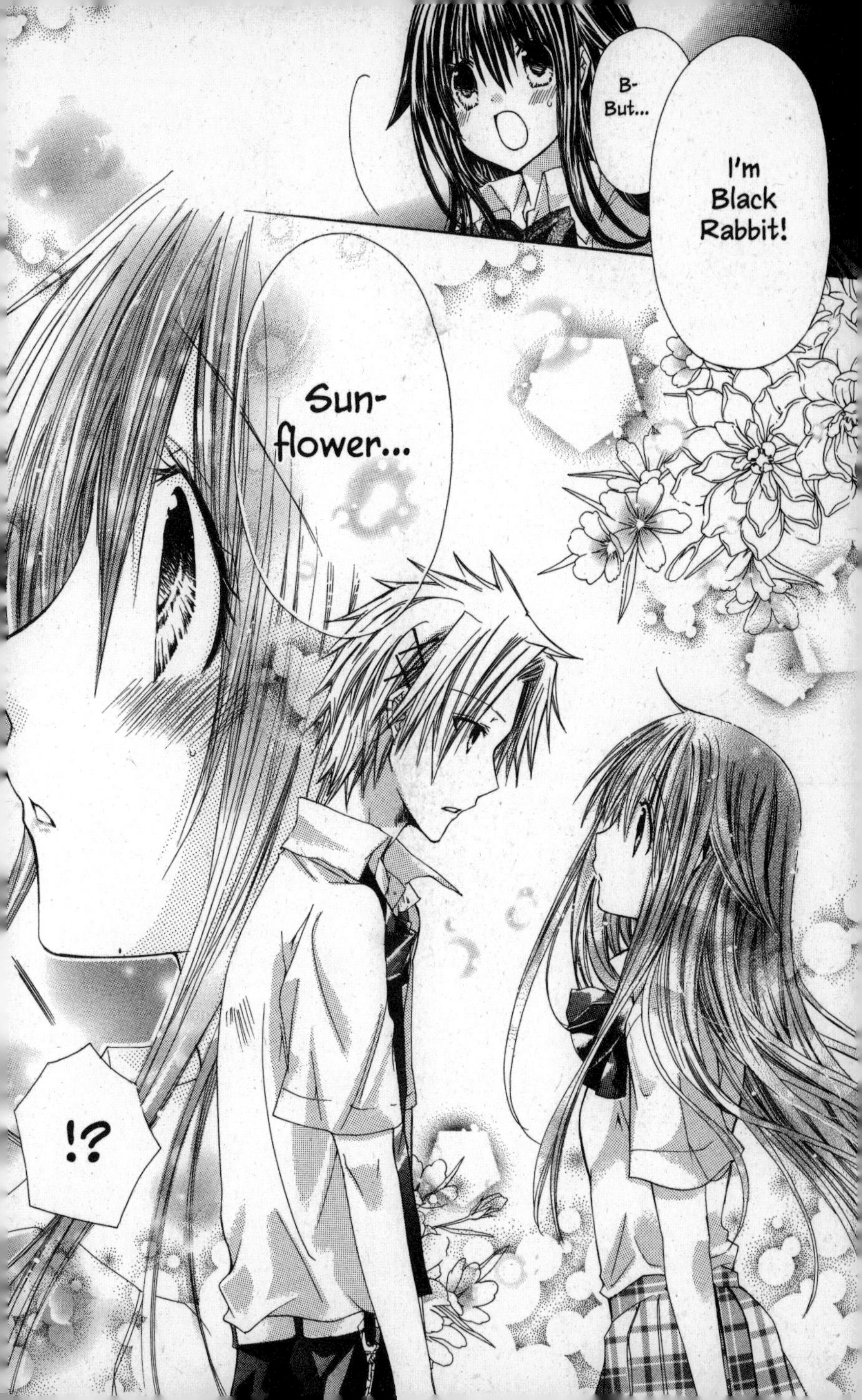
B-But...
I'm Black Rabbit!
Sun-flower...
!?

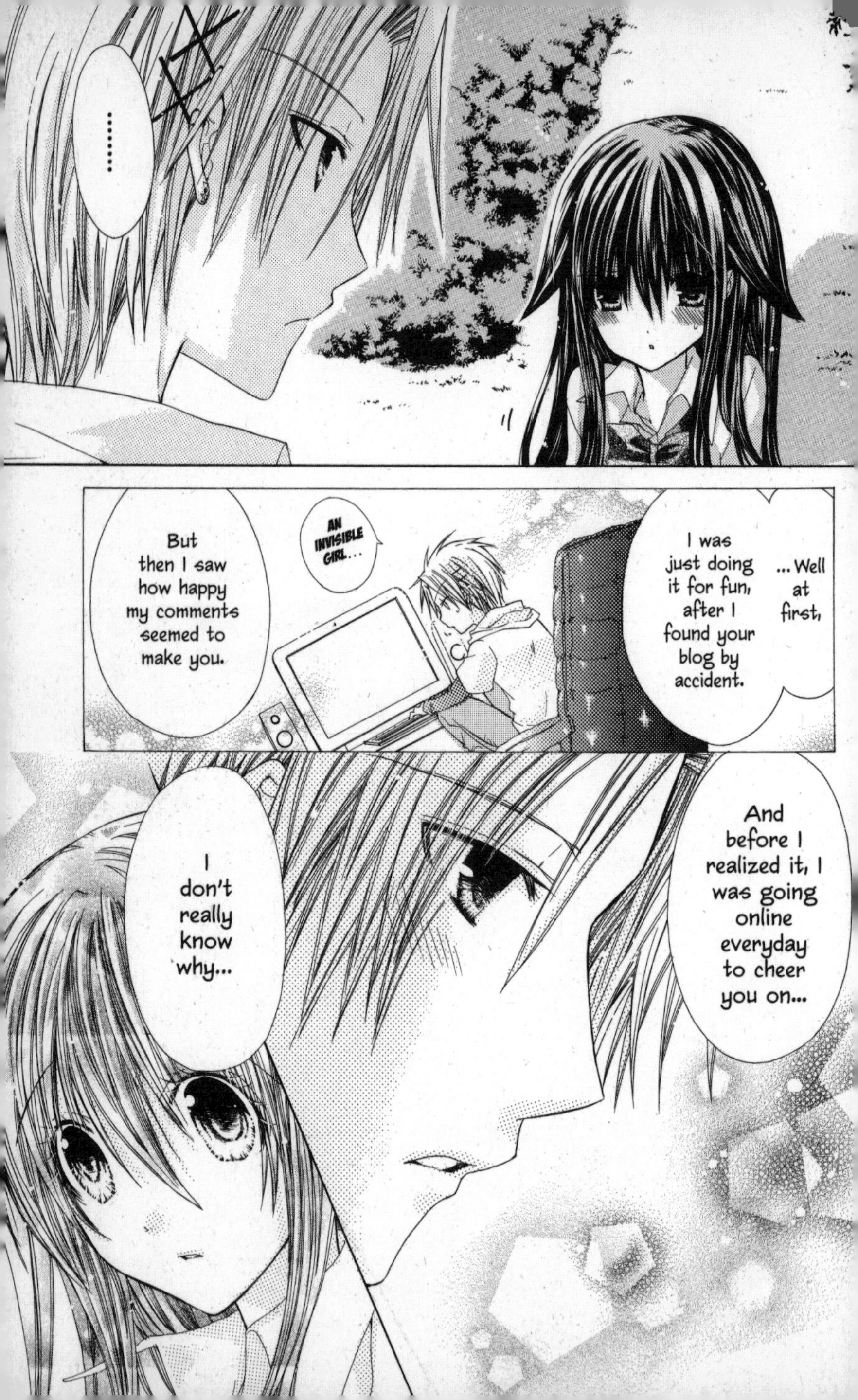
......
...Well at first,
I was just doing it for fun, after I found your blog by accident.
AN INVISIBLE GIRL...
But then I saw how happy my comments seemed to make you.
And before I realized it, I was going online everyday to cheer you on...
I don't really know why...

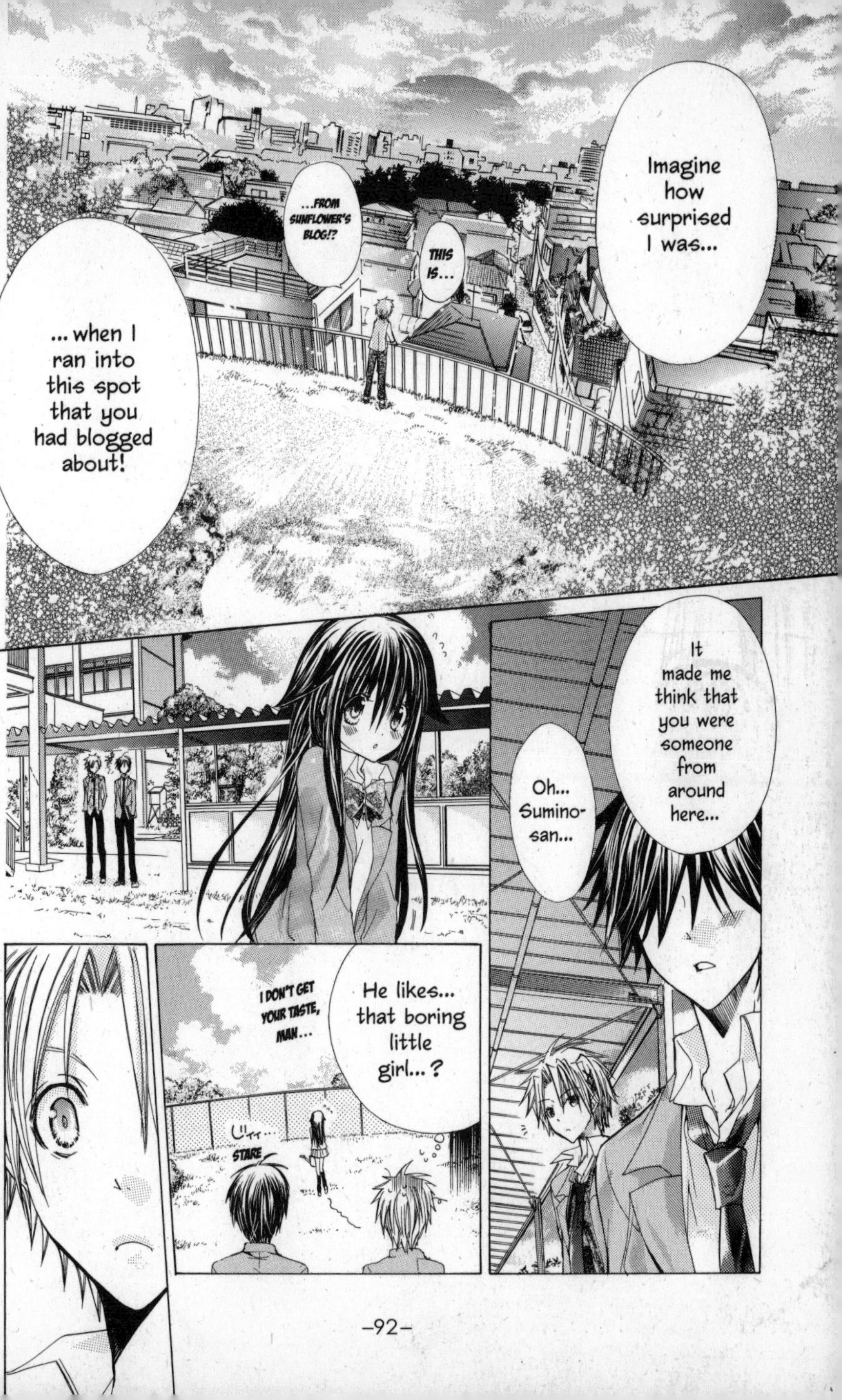
Imagine how surprised I was...
THIS IS...
...FROM SUNFLOWER'S BLOG!?
...when I ran into this spot that you had blogged about!
It made me think that you were someone from around here...
Oh... Sumino-san...
He likes... that boring little girl...?
I DON'T GET YOUR TASTE, MAN...
じーー...
STARE

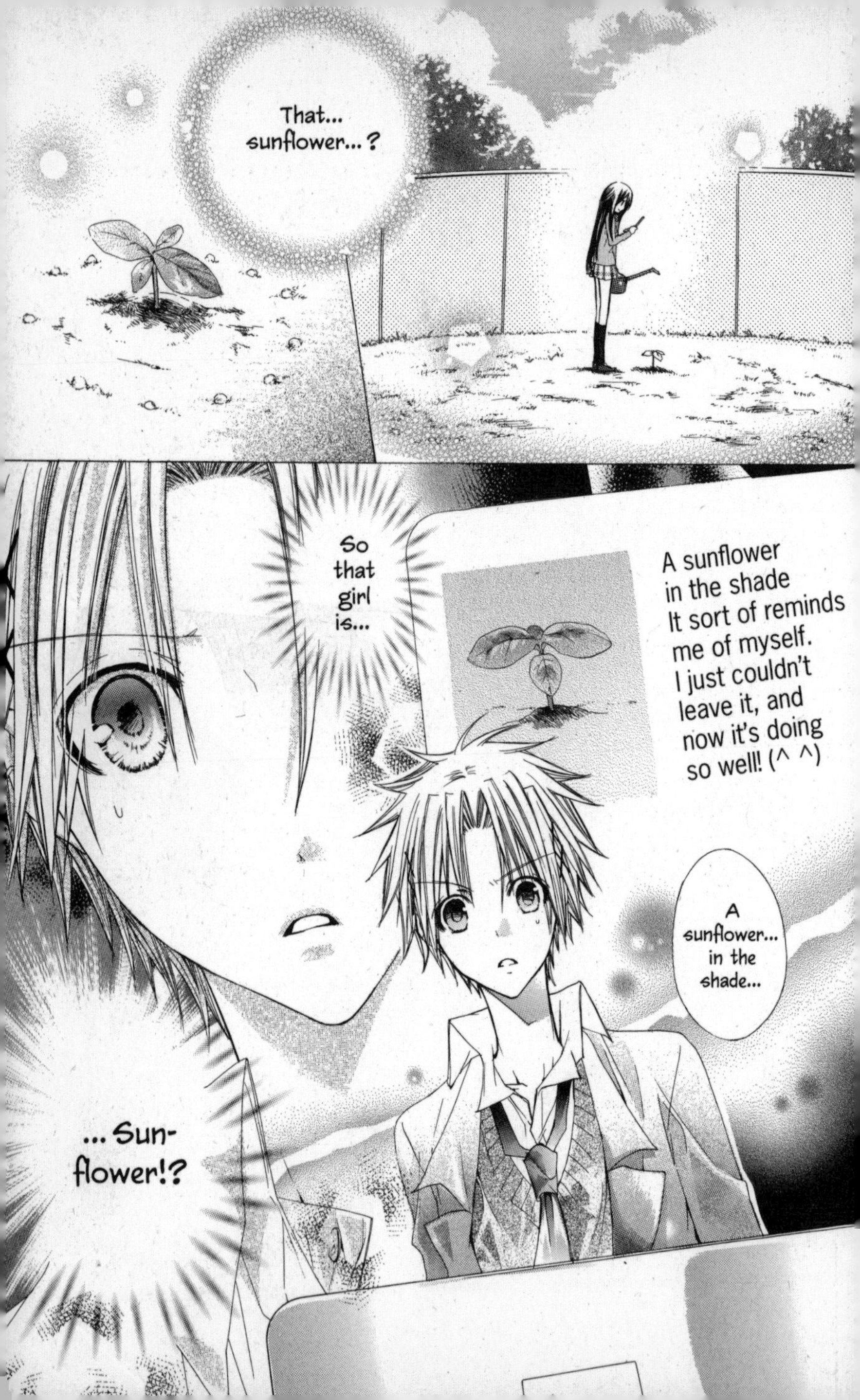
That... sunflower...?
A sunflower in the shade It sort of reminds me of myself. I just couldn't leave it, and now it's doing so well! (^ ^)
So that girl is...
A sunflower... in the shade...
... Sun-flower!?

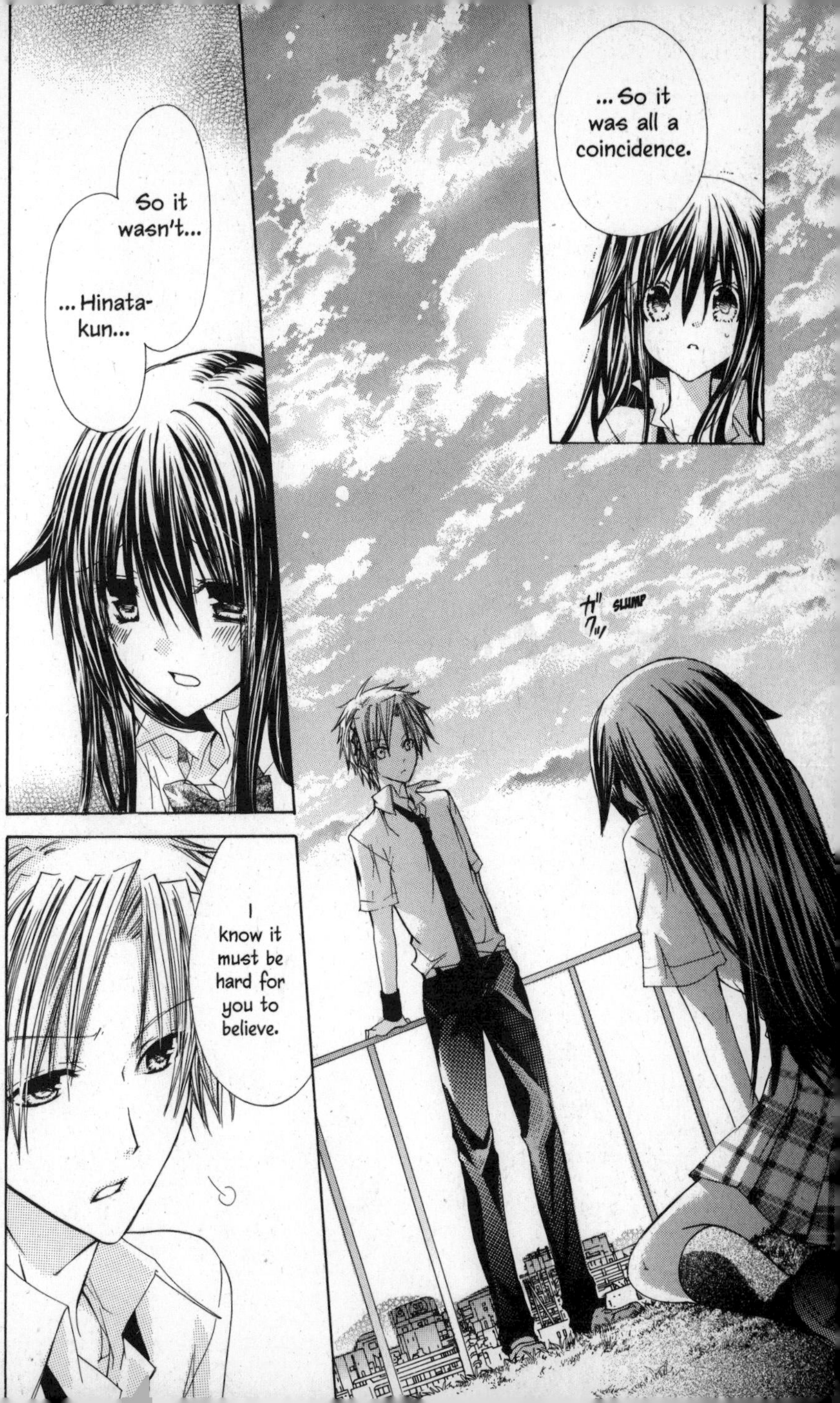
...So it was all a coincidence.
SLUMP
So it wasn't...
...Hinata-kun...
I know it must be hard for you to believe.

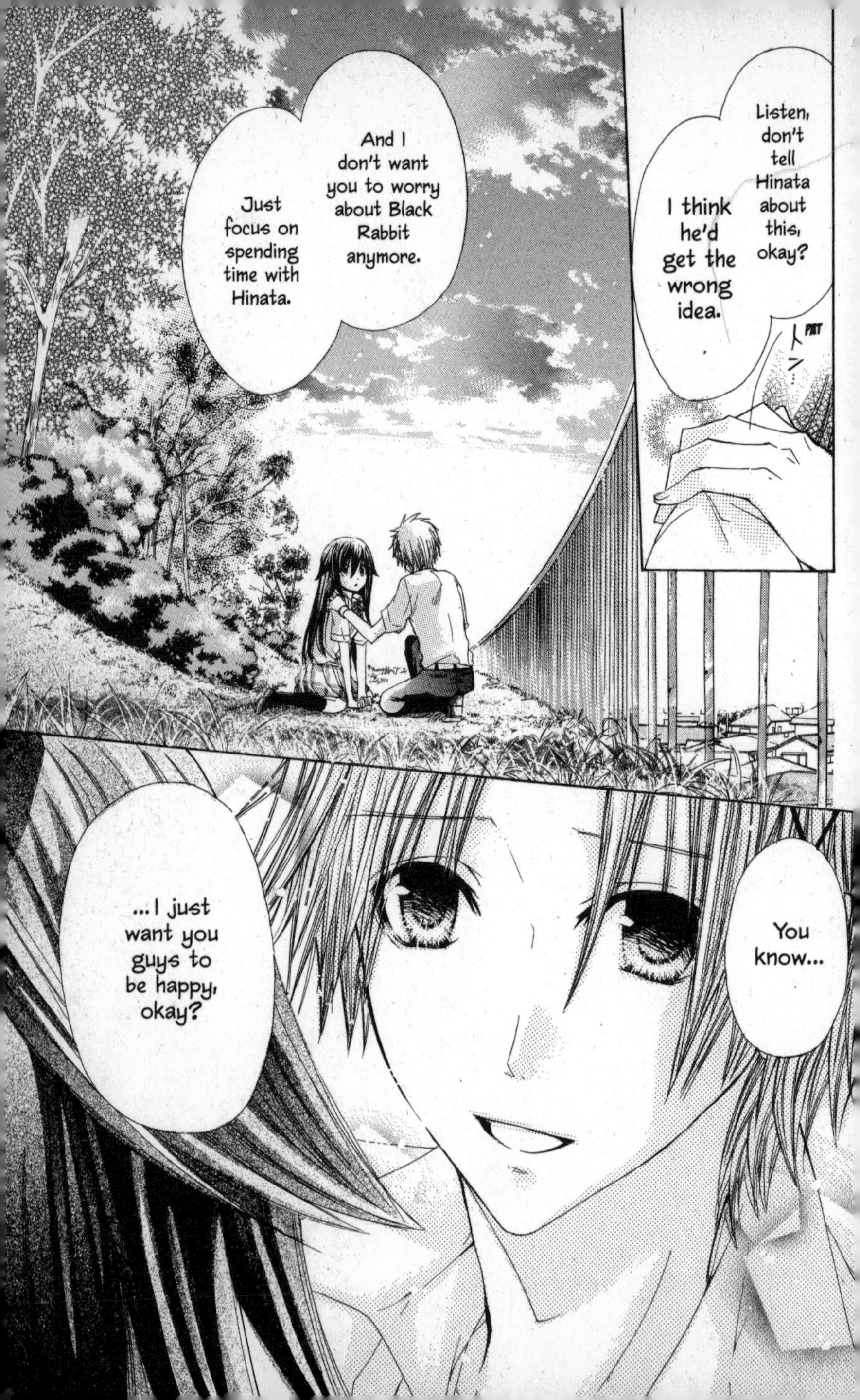
Listen, don't tell Hinata about this, okay?
I think he'd get the wrong idea.
PAT
And I don't want you to worry about Black Rabbit anymore.
Just focus on spending time with Hinata.
You know...
...I just want you guys to be happy, okay?

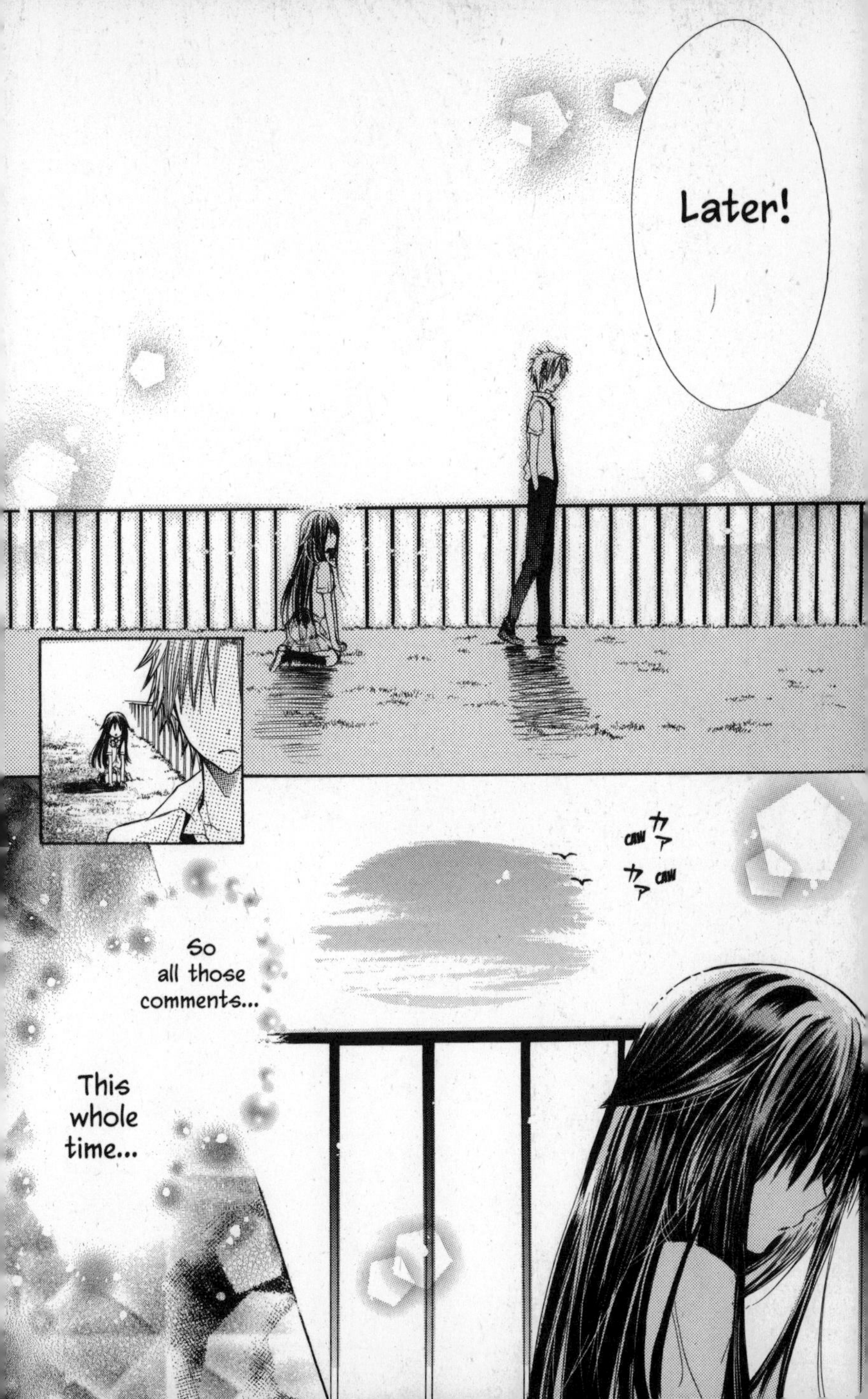
Later!
CAW カァ
カァ CAW
So all those comments...
This whole time...

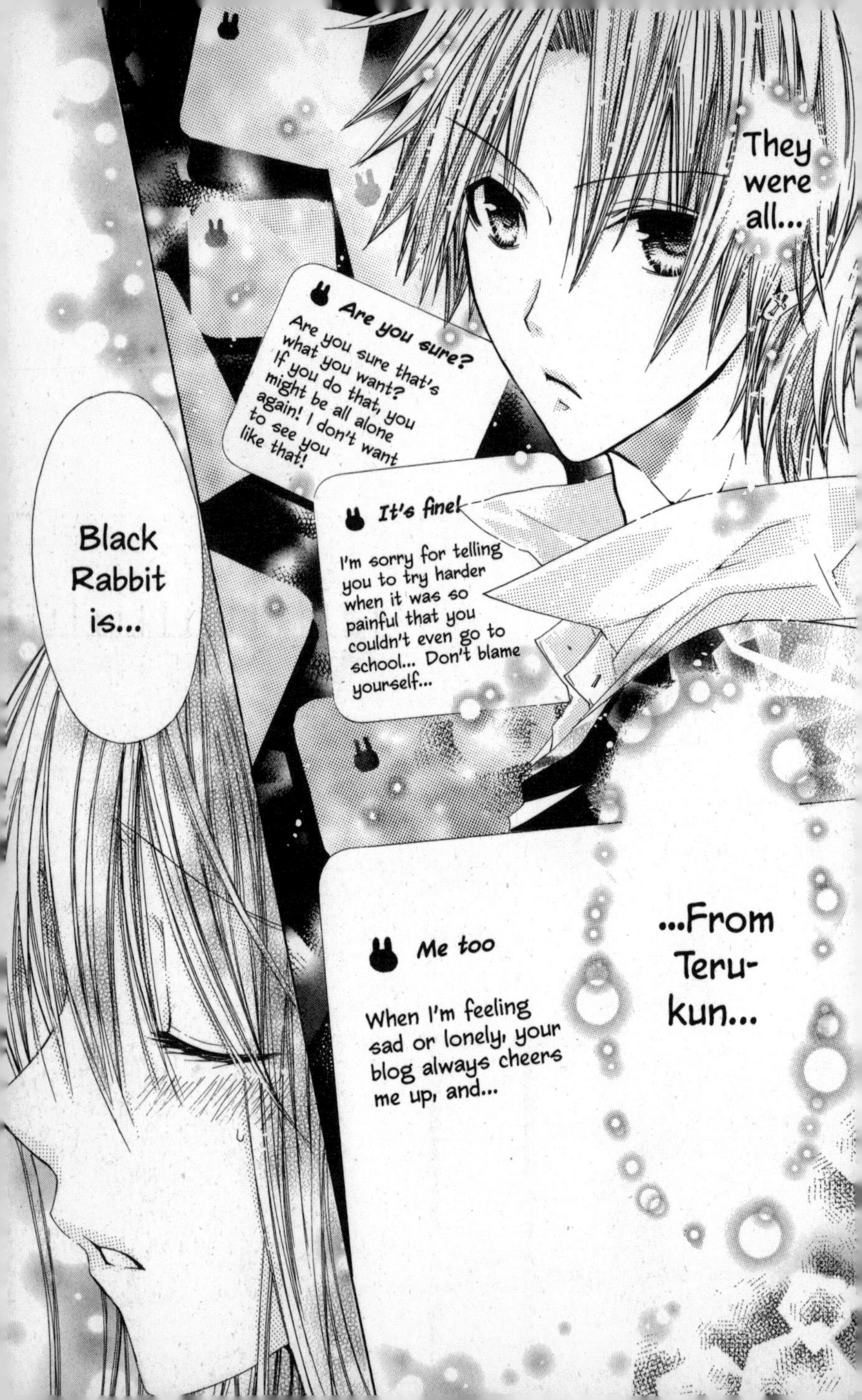
They were all...
Are you sure?
Are you sure that's what you want? If you do that, you might be all alone again! I don't want to see you like that!
It's fine!
I'm sorry for telling you to try harder when it was so painful that you couldn't even go to school... Don't blame yourself...
Black Rabbit is...
...From Teru-kun...
Me too
When I'm feeling sad or lonely, your blog always cheers me up, and...

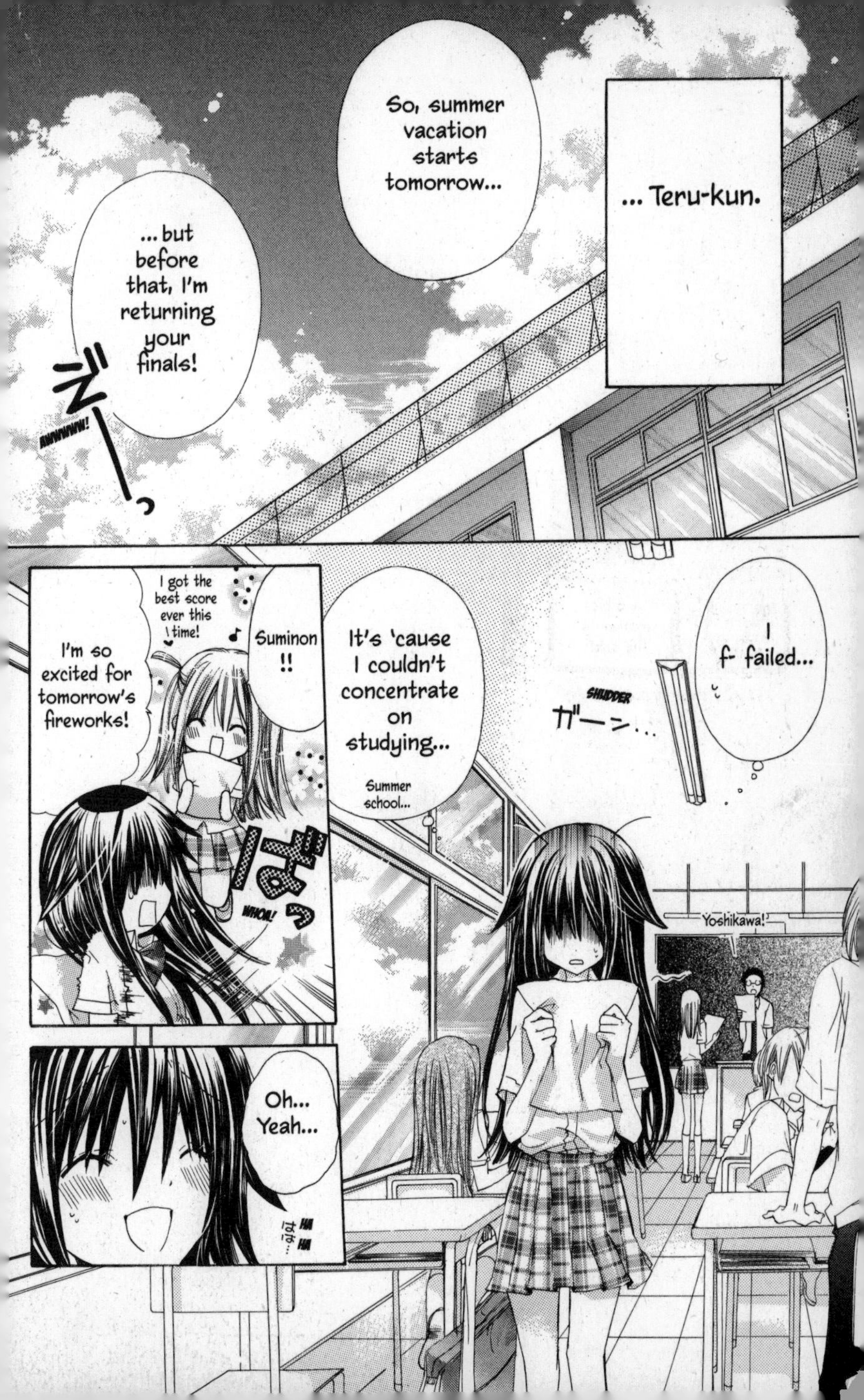

... Teru-kun.
So, summer vacation starts tomorrow...
... but before that, I'm returning your finals!
AWWWWW!
ズーッ
I f- failed...
SHUDDER
ガーン...
It's 'cause I couldn't concentrate on studying...
Summer school...
Yoshikawa!
Suminon !!
I got the best score ever this time!
I'm so excited for tomorrow's fireworks!
ばっ
WHOA!
Oh... Yeah...
HA HA
はは...

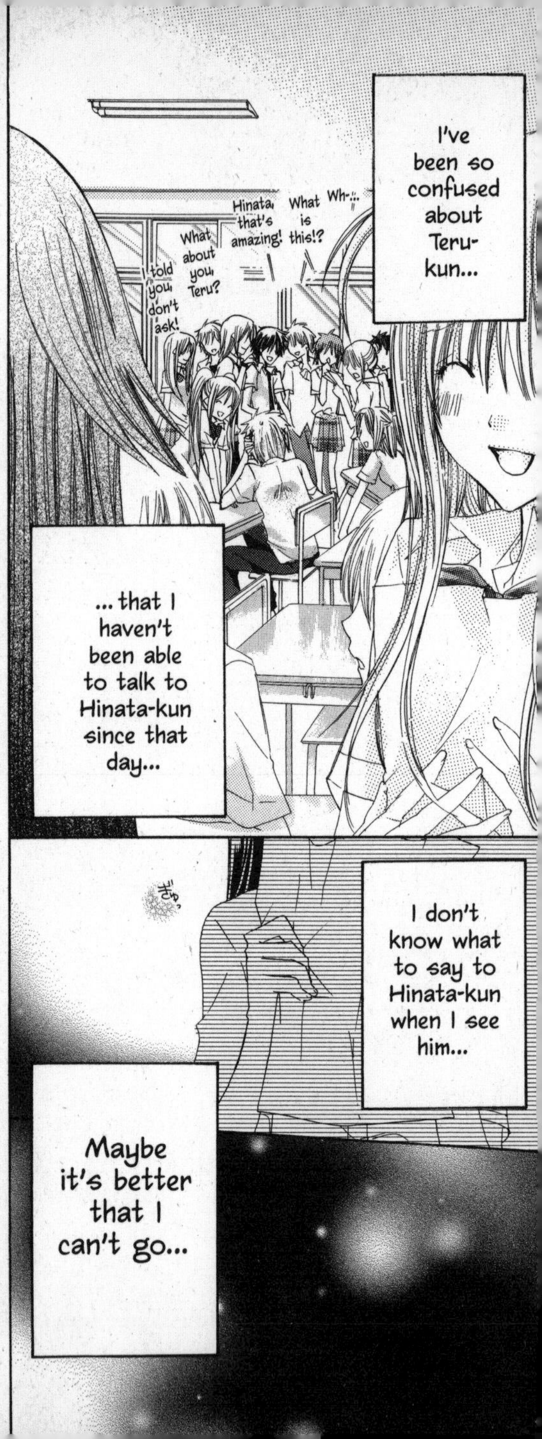

I've been so confused about Teru-kun...
Wh-...
What is this!?
Hinata, that's amazing!
What about you, Teru?
I told you, don't ask!
... that I haven't been able to talk to Hinata-kun since that day...
I don't know what to say to Hinata-kun when I see him...
Maybe it's better that I can't go...

Once when I was hanging out with my friend.

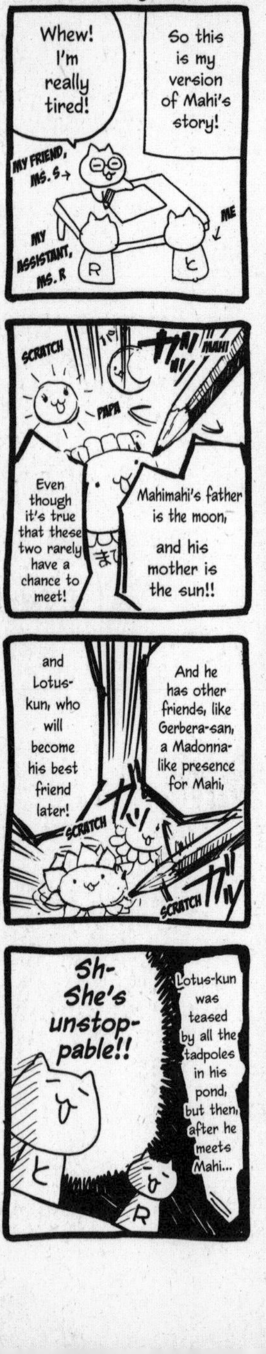

So this is my version of Mahi's story!
Whew! I'm really tired!
MY FRIEND, MS. S
ME
MY ASSISTANT, MS. R
SCRATCH
MAHI
PAPA
Mahimahi's father is the moon, and his mother is the sun!!
Even though it's true that these two rarely have a chance to meet!
And he has other friends, like Gerbera-san, a Madonna-like presence for Mahi,
and Lotus-kun, who will become his best friend later!
SCRATCH
SCRATCH
Lotus-kun was teased by all the tadpoles in his pond, but then, after he meets Mahi...
Sh-She's unstoppable!!

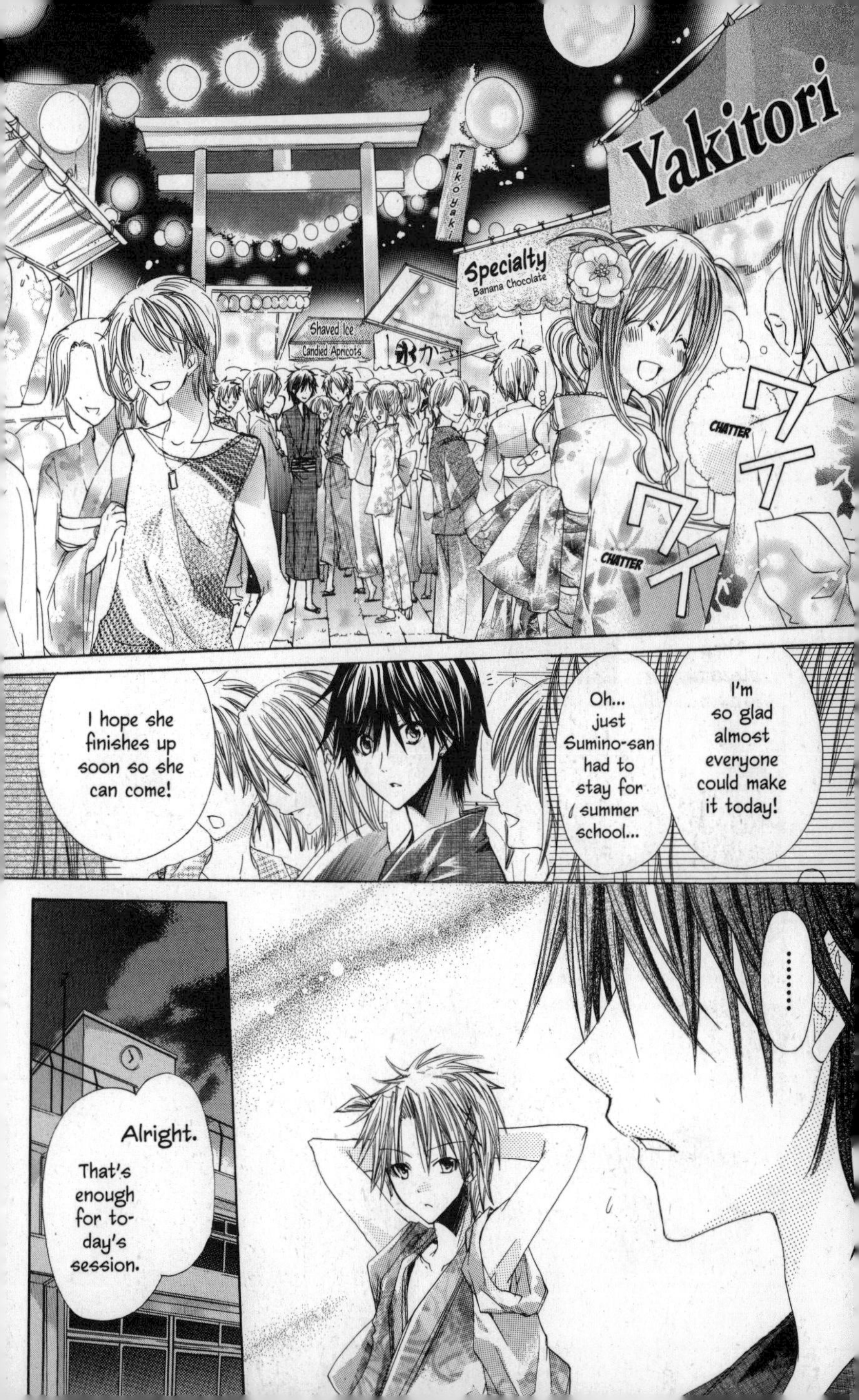
Yakitori
Takoyaki
Specialty
Banana Chocolate
Shaved Ice
Candied Apricots
ワイ
CHATTER
ワイ
CHATTER
I'm so glad almost everyone could make it today!
Oh... just Sumino-san had to stay for summer school...
I hope she finishes up soon so she can come!
......
Alright.
That's enough for to-day's session.

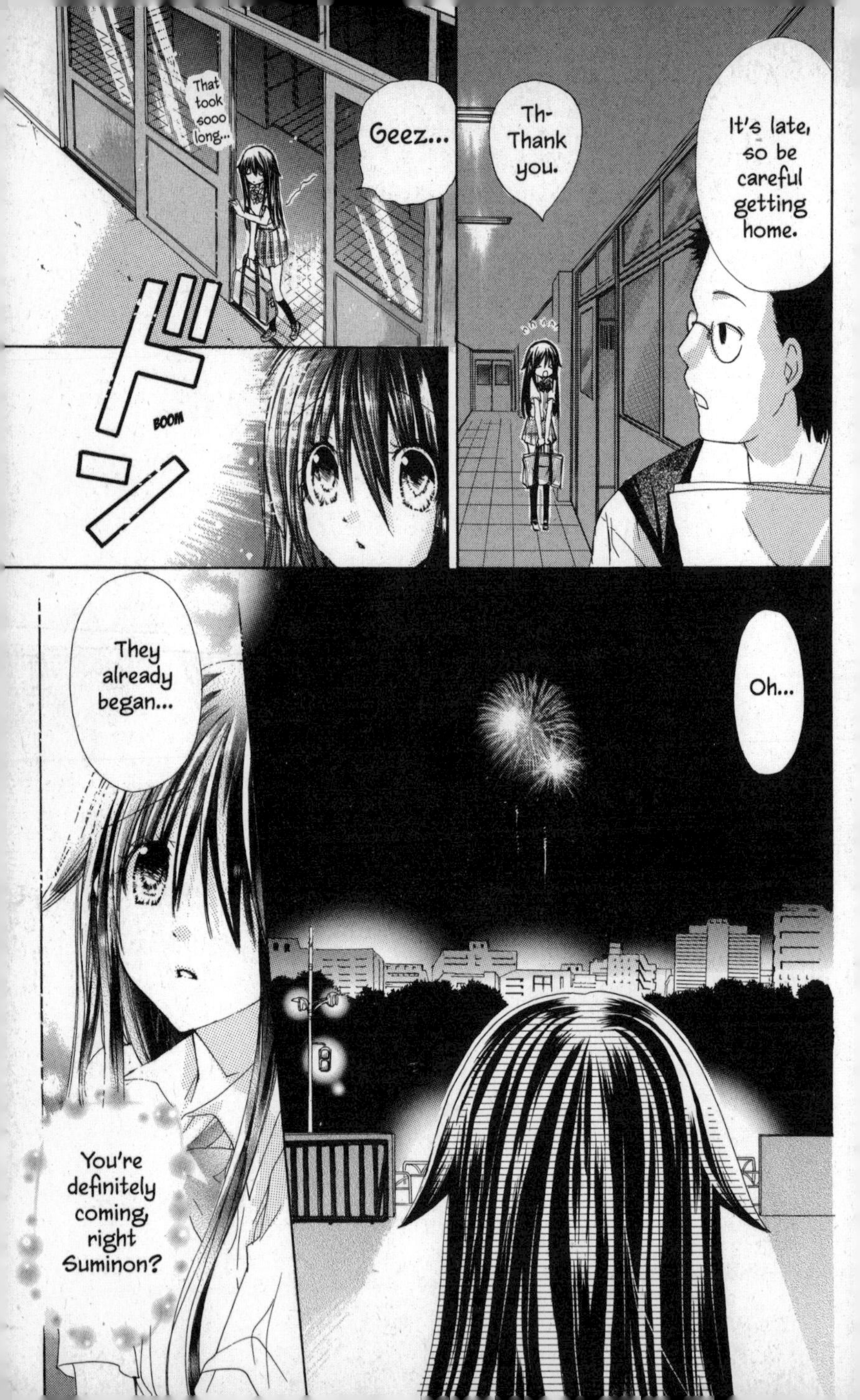
It's late, so be careful getting home.
Th- Thank you.
Geez...
That took sooo long...
ドーン
BOOM
Oh...
They already began...
You're definitely coming, right Suminon?

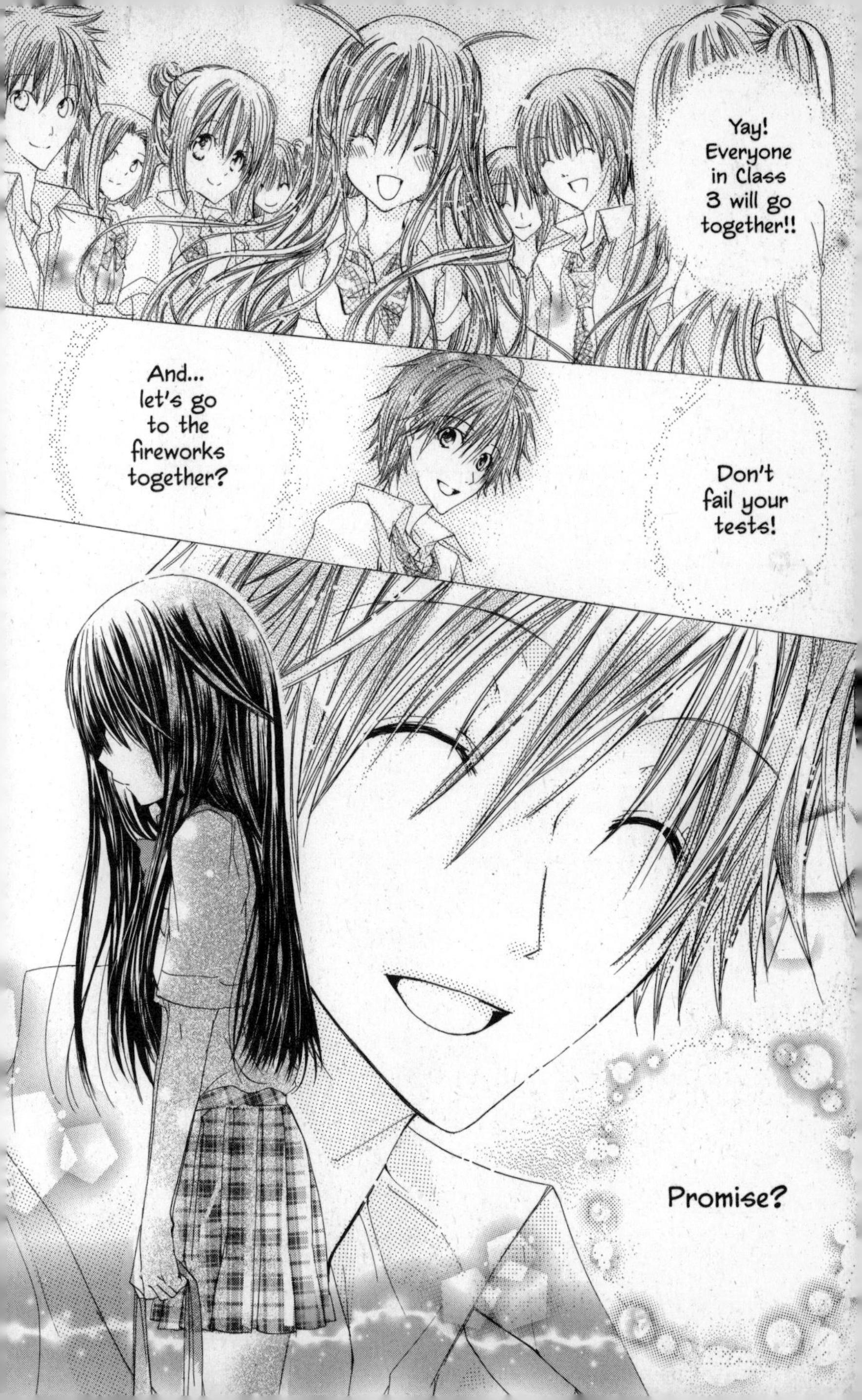
Yay! Everyone in Class 3 will go together!!
Don't fail your tests!
And... let's go to the fireworks together?
Promise?

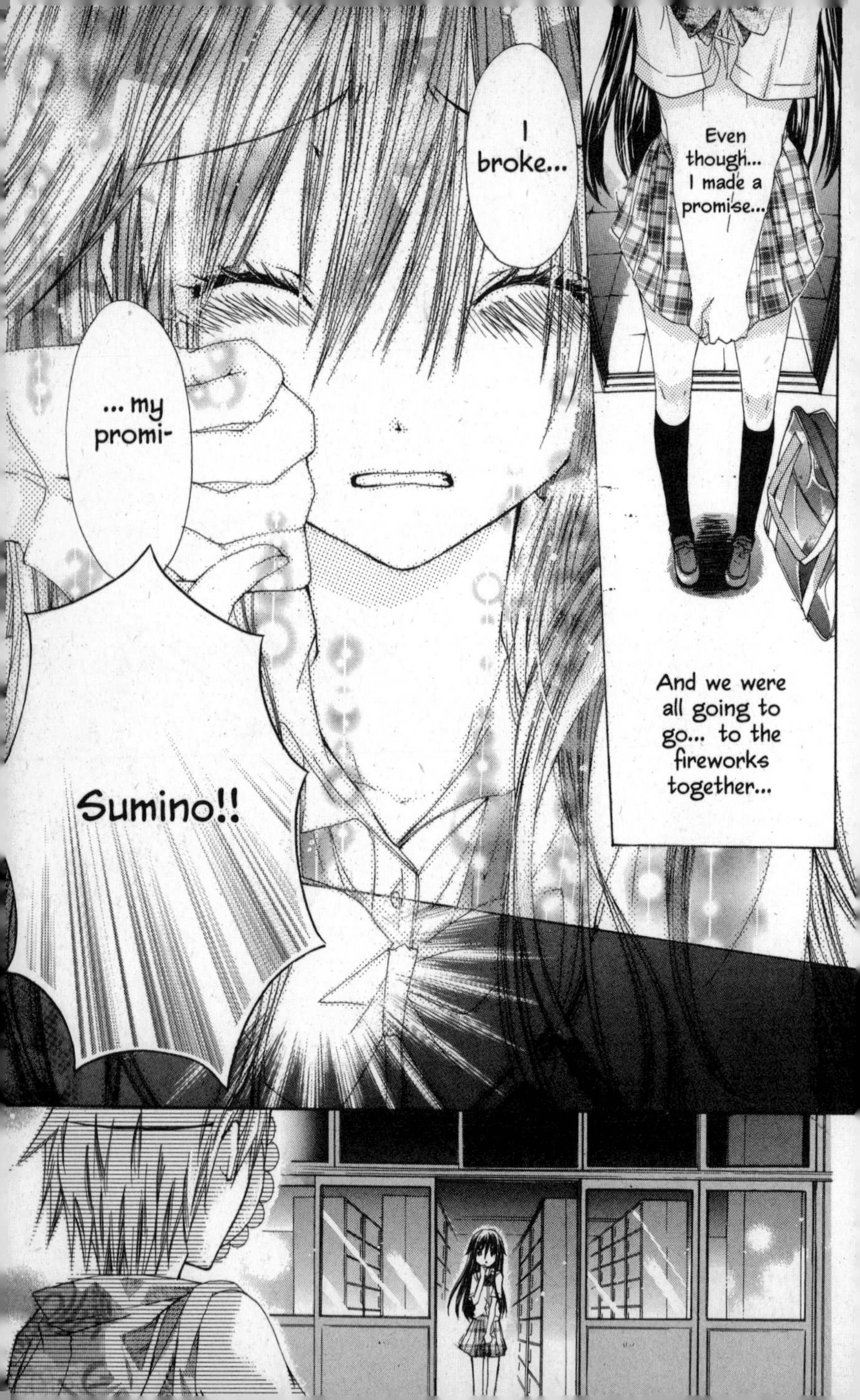
Even though... I made a promise...
And we were all going to go... to the fireworks together...
I broke...
... my promi-
Sumino!!

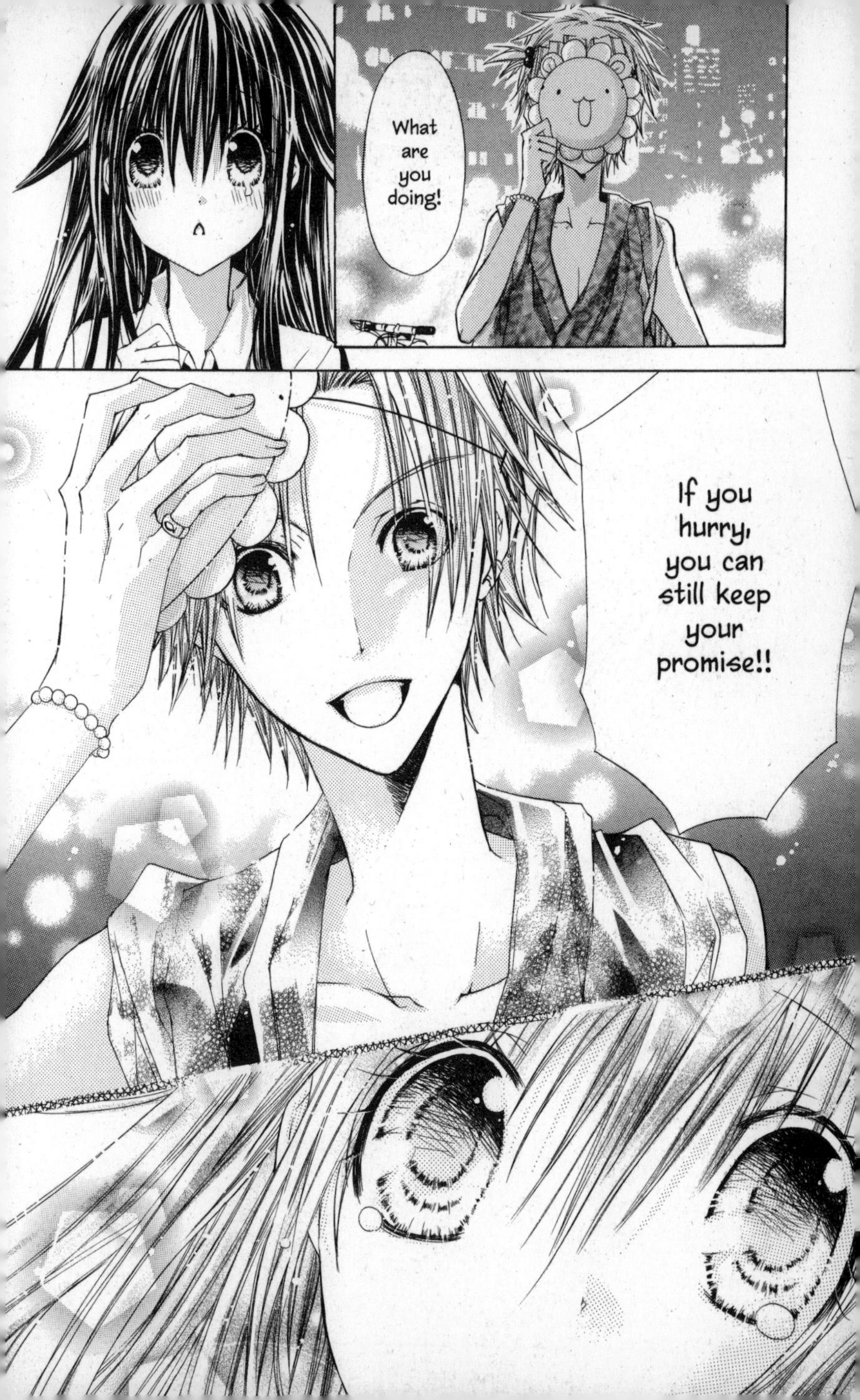
What are you doing!
If you hurry, you can still keep your promise!!

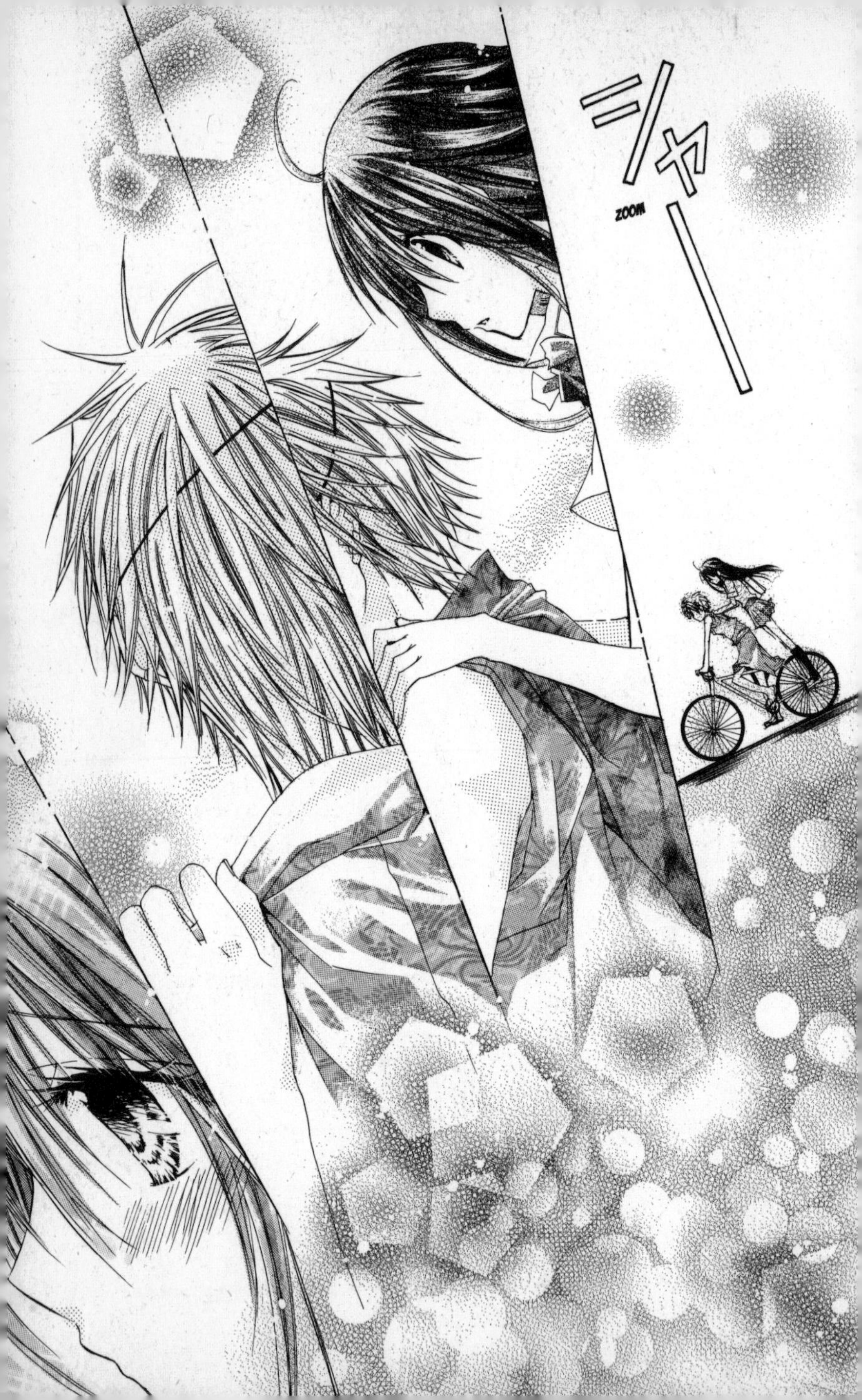
シャー
ZOOM

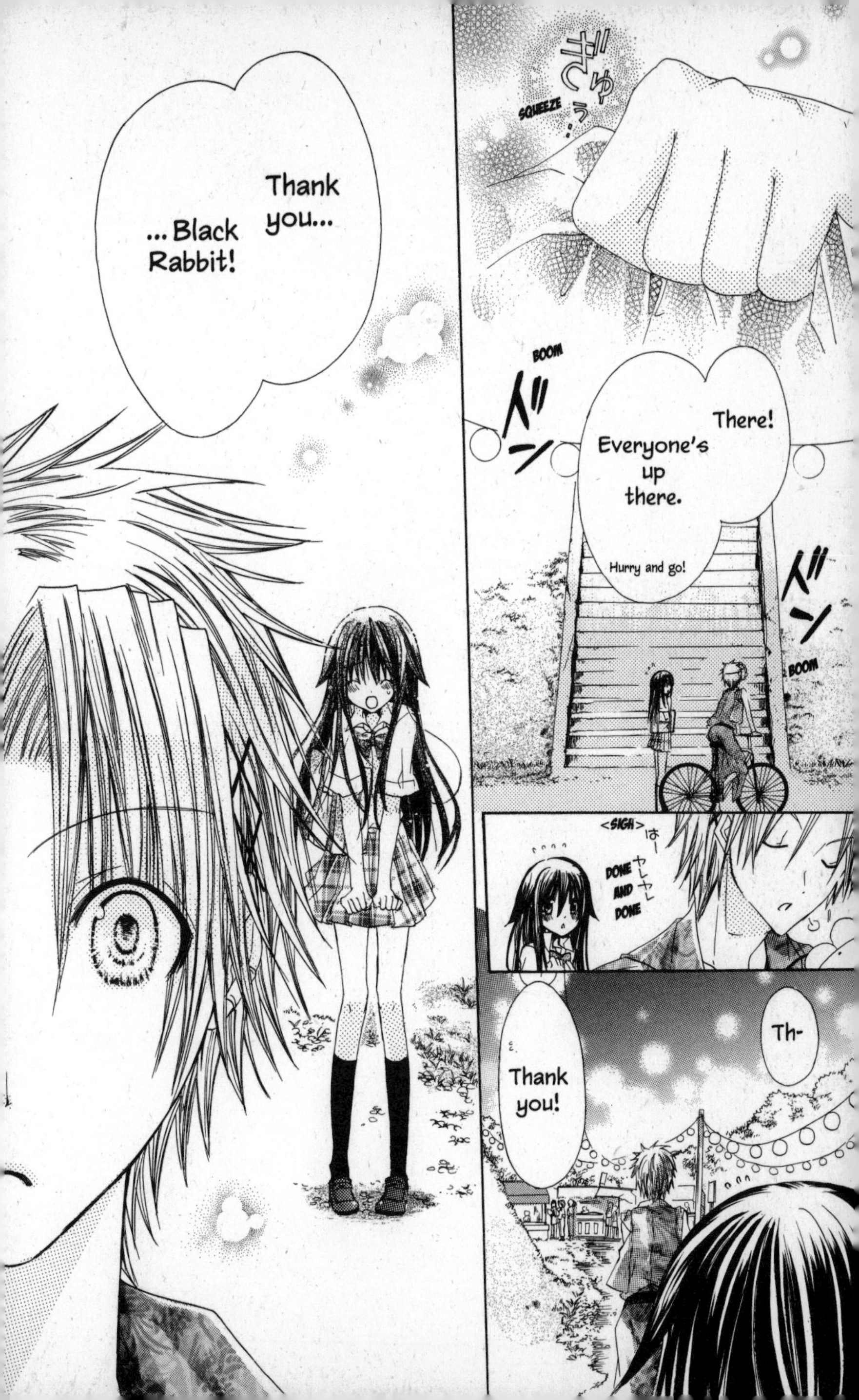

ぎゅう…
SQUEEZE
BOOM
There! Everyone's up there.
Hurry and go!
BOOM
<SIGH>
はー
DONE AND DONE
ヤレヤレ
Th-
Thank you!
Thank you...
...Black Rabbit!

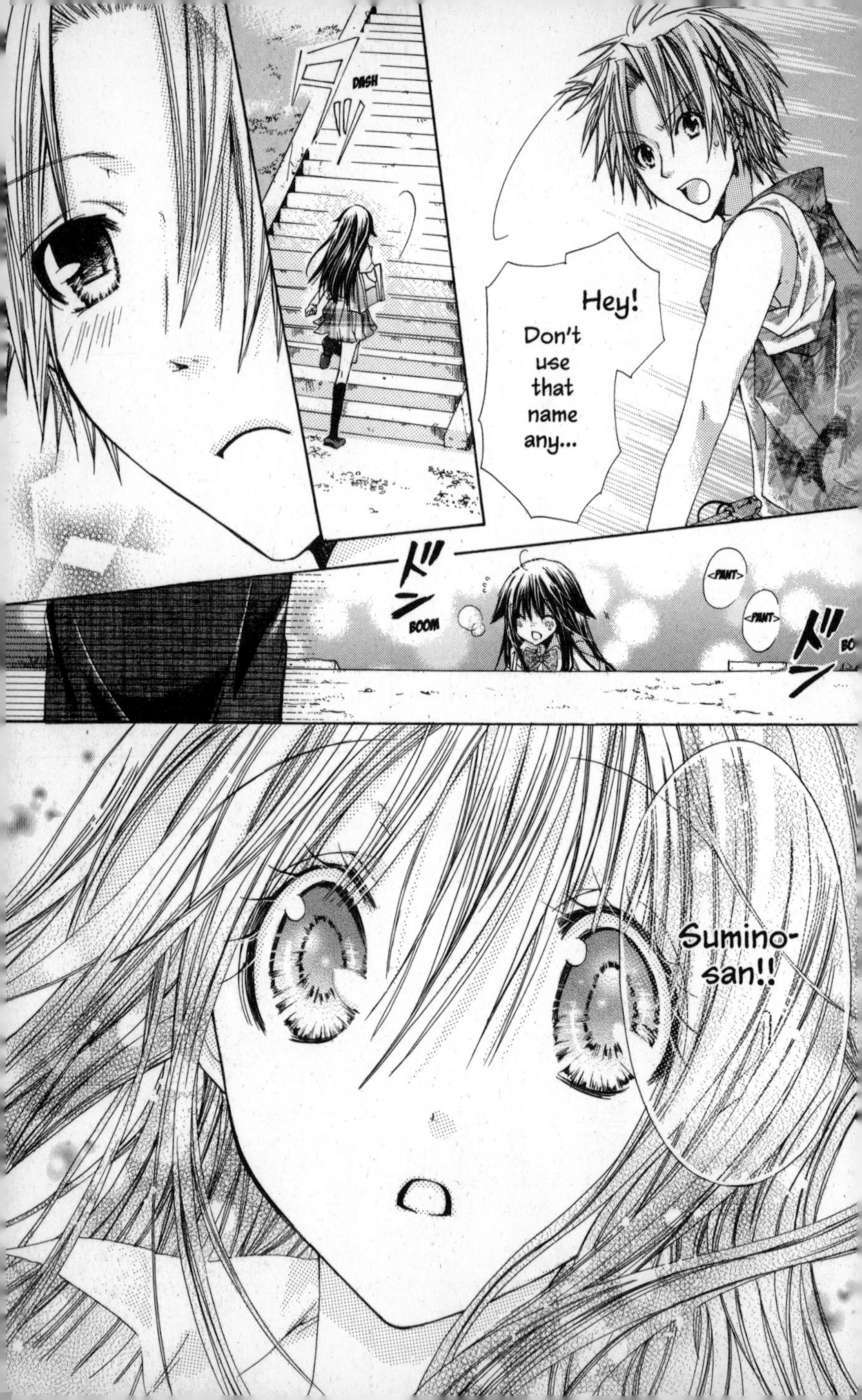

Hey!
Don't use that name any...
DASH
<PANT>
<PANT>
BOOM
Sumino-san!!

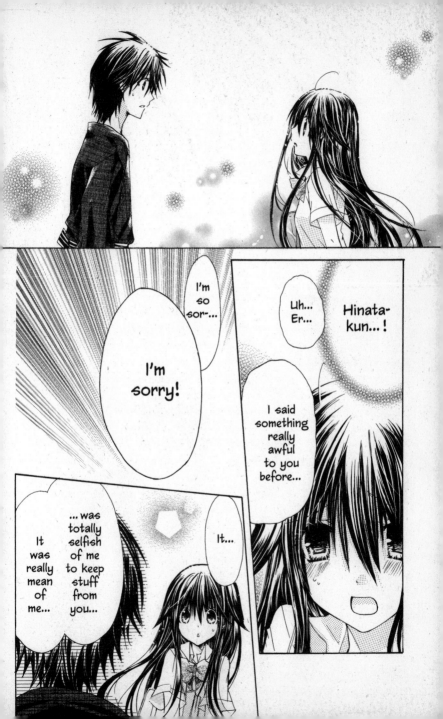

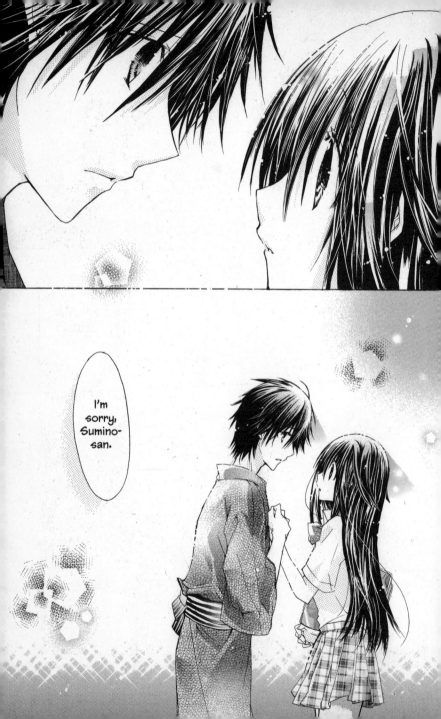

I'm sorry, Sumino-san.

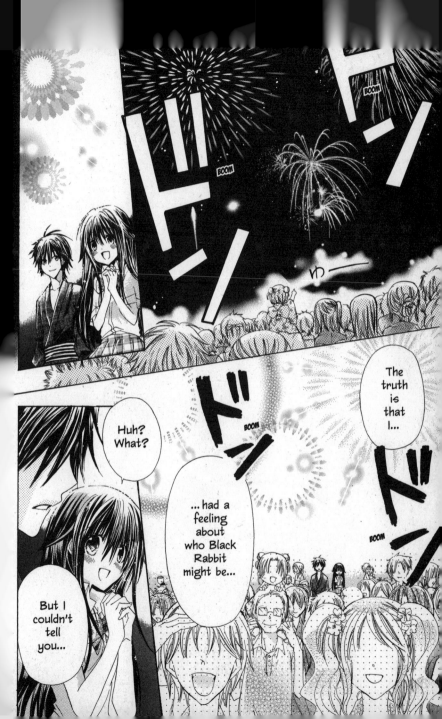

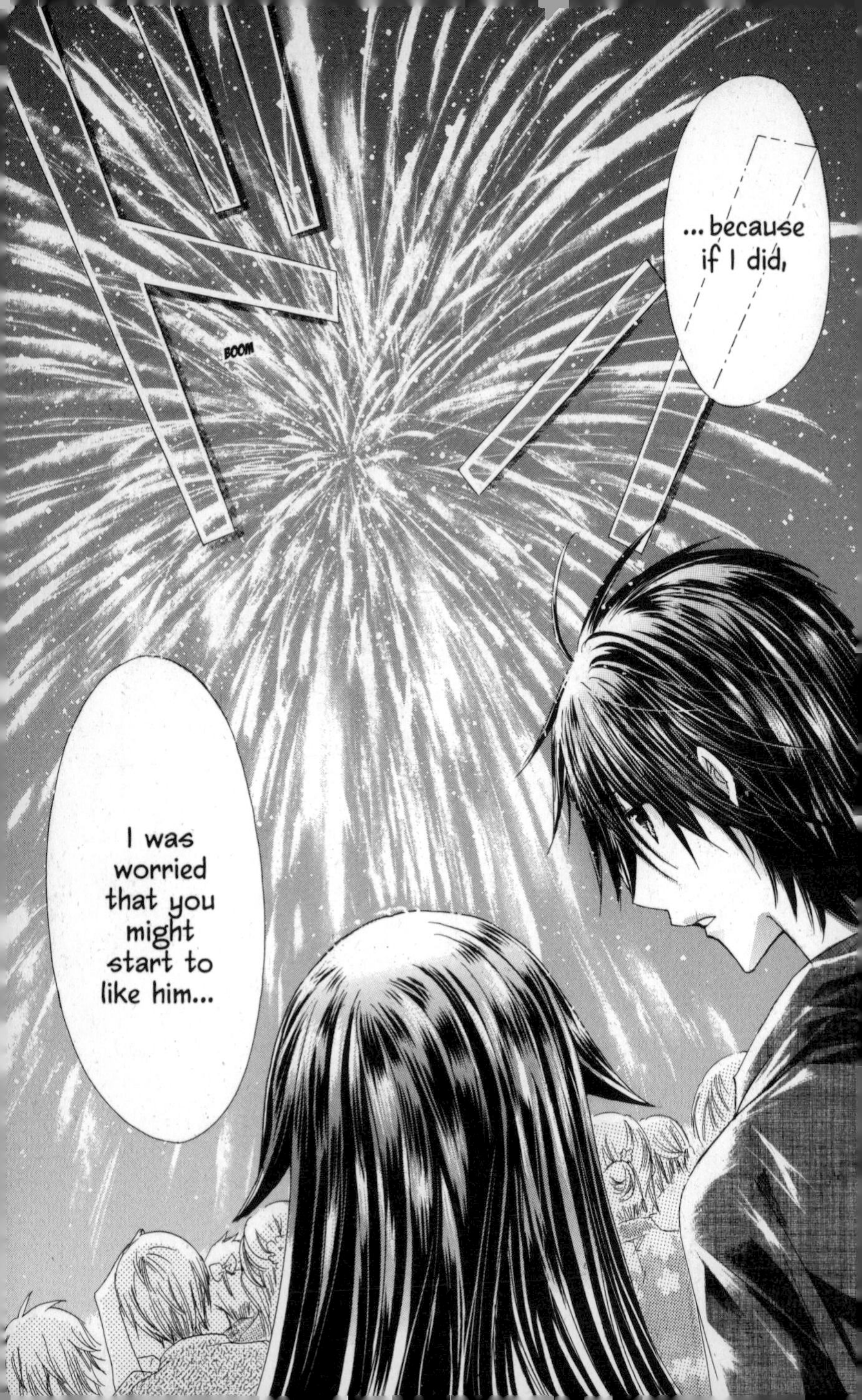
...because if I did,
BOOM
I was worried that you might start to like him...

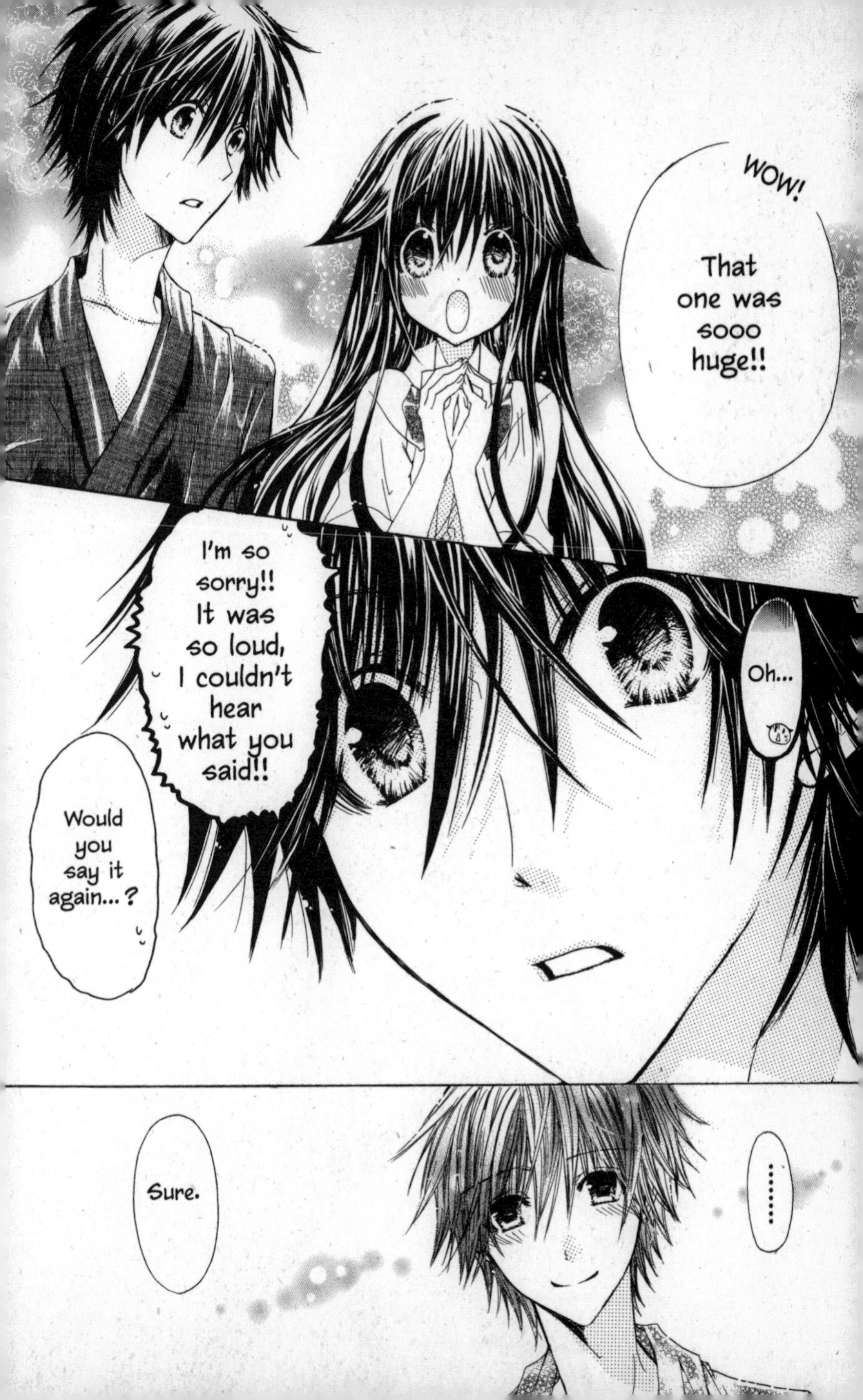
WOW!
That one was sooo huge!!
Oh...
I'm so sorry!! It was so loud, I couldn't hear what you said!!
Would you say it again...?
......
Sure.

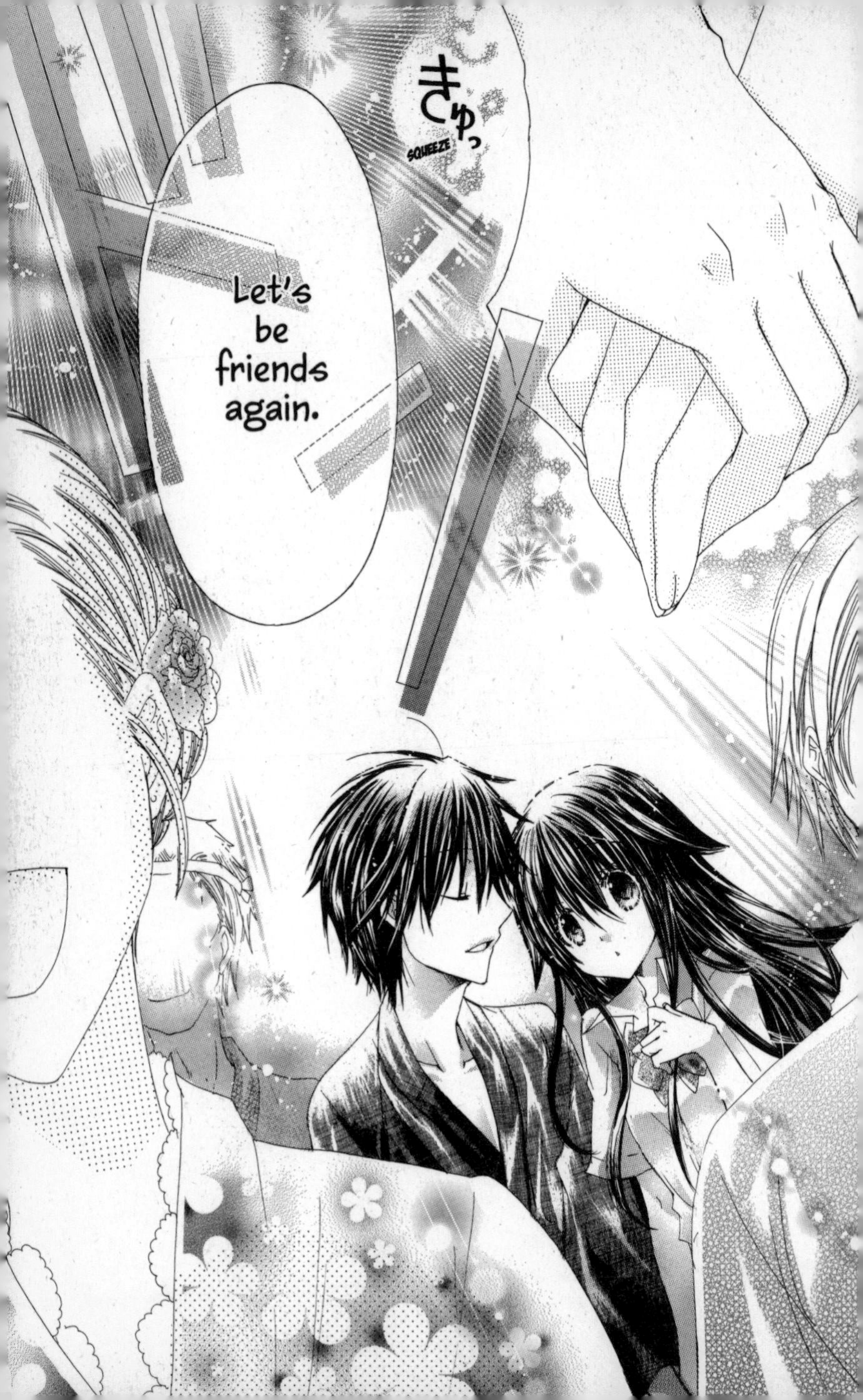
きゅっ
SQUEEZE
Let's be friends again.

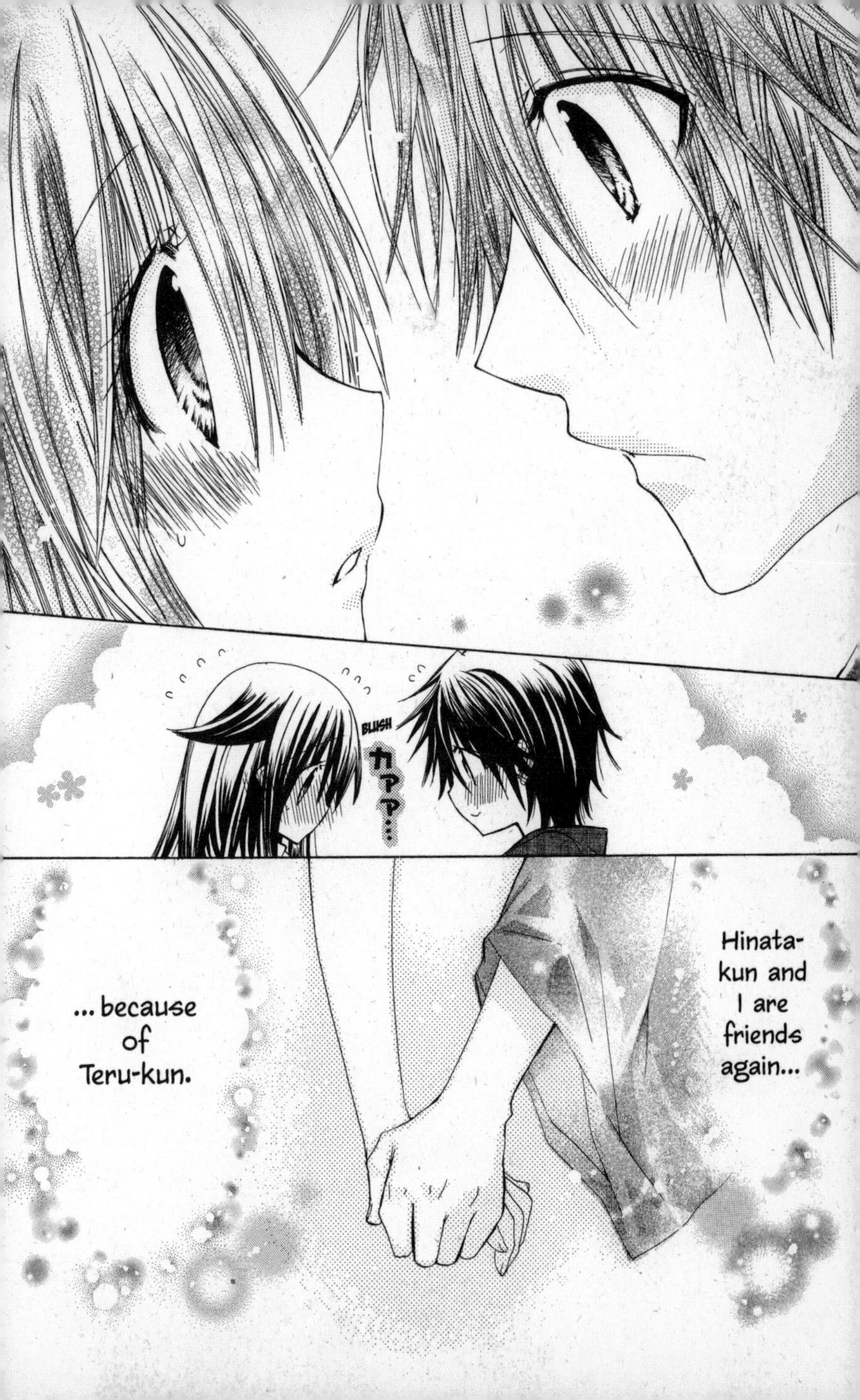
BLUSH
カァァ…
Hinata-kun and I are friends again...
...because of Teru-kun.

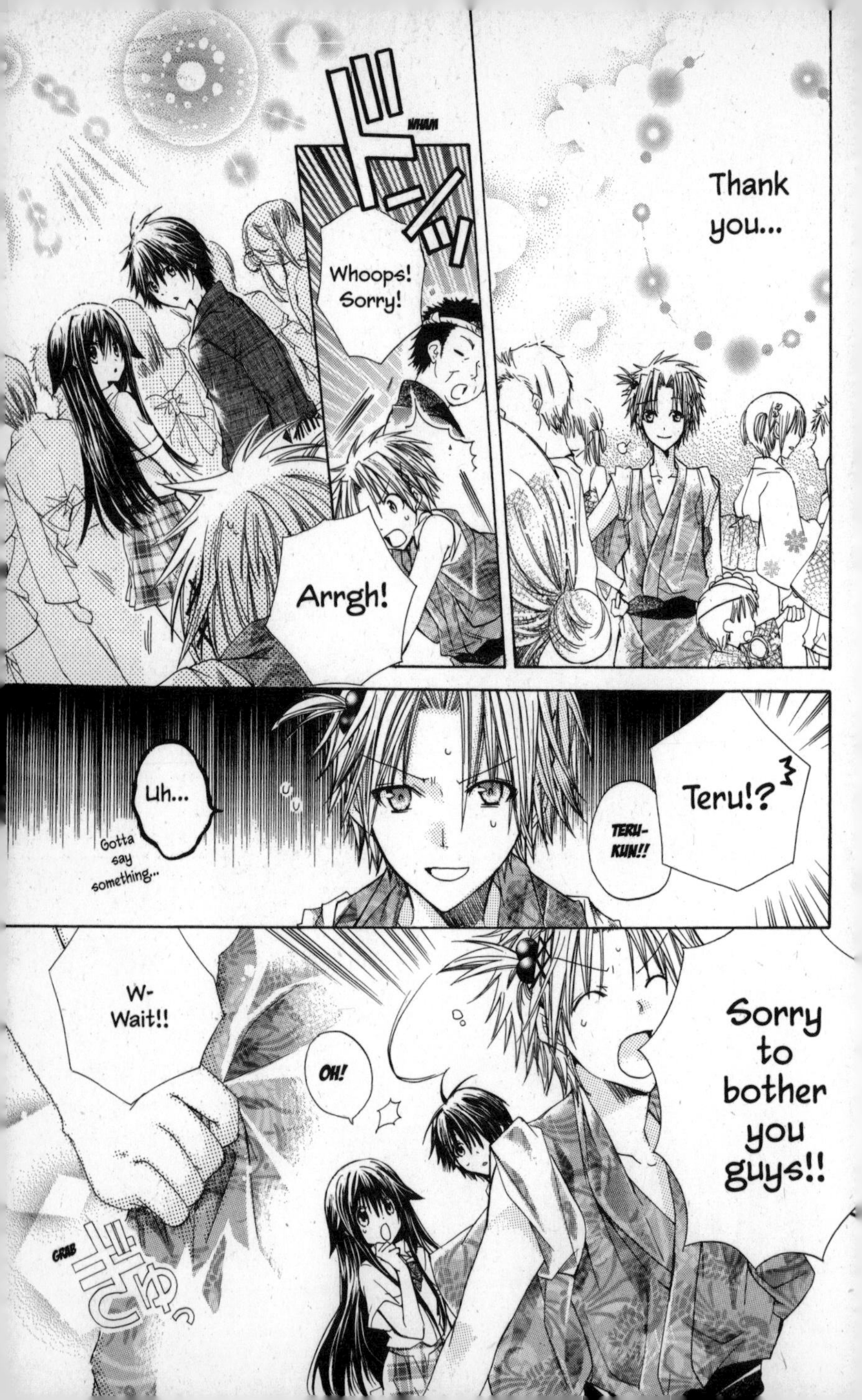

Thank you...
WHAM
Whoops! Sorry!
Arrgh!
Teru!?
TERU-KUN!!
Uh...
Gotta say something...
Sorry to bother you guys!!
OH!
W- Wait!!
GRAB

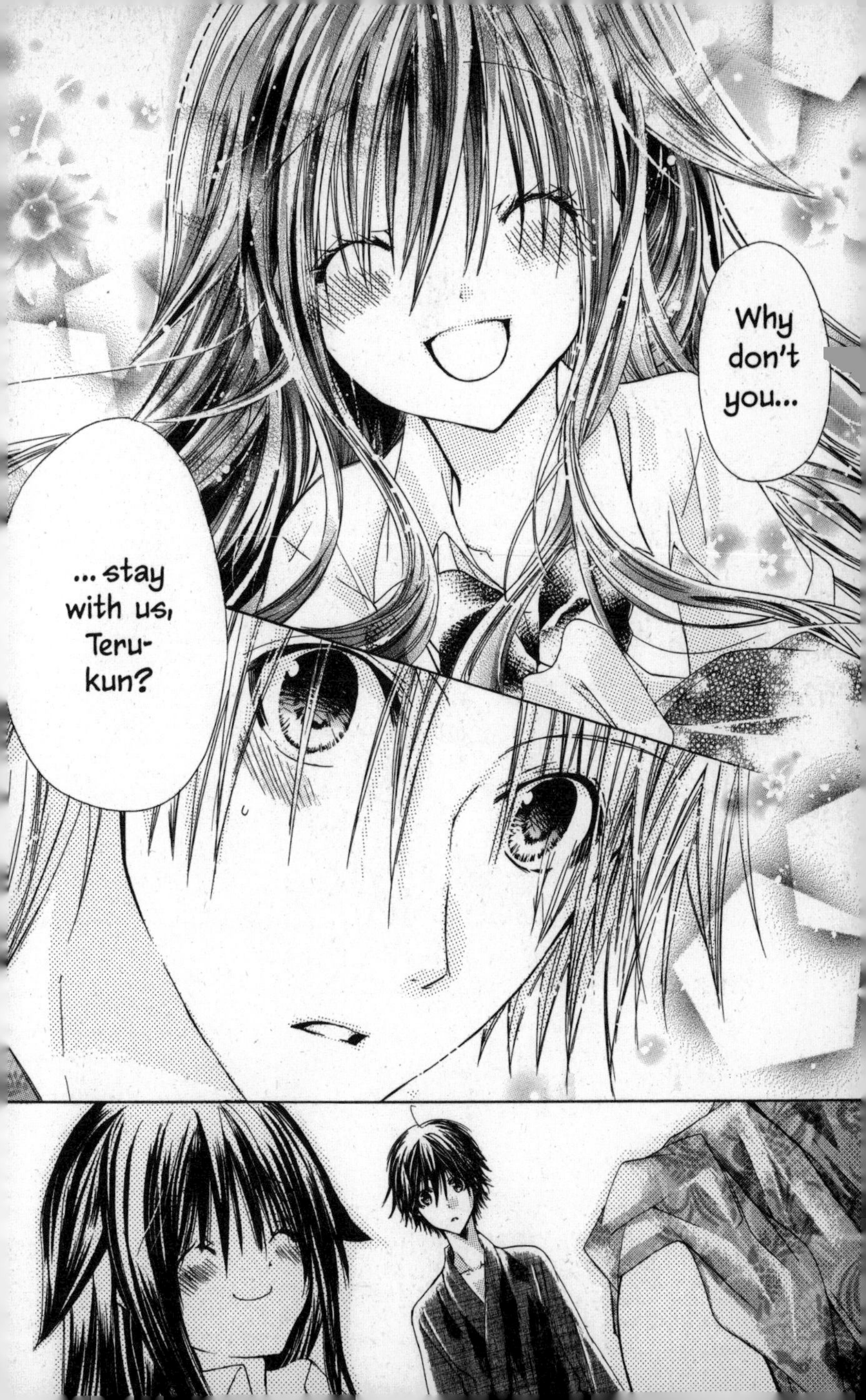
Why don't you...
... stay with us, Teru-kun?

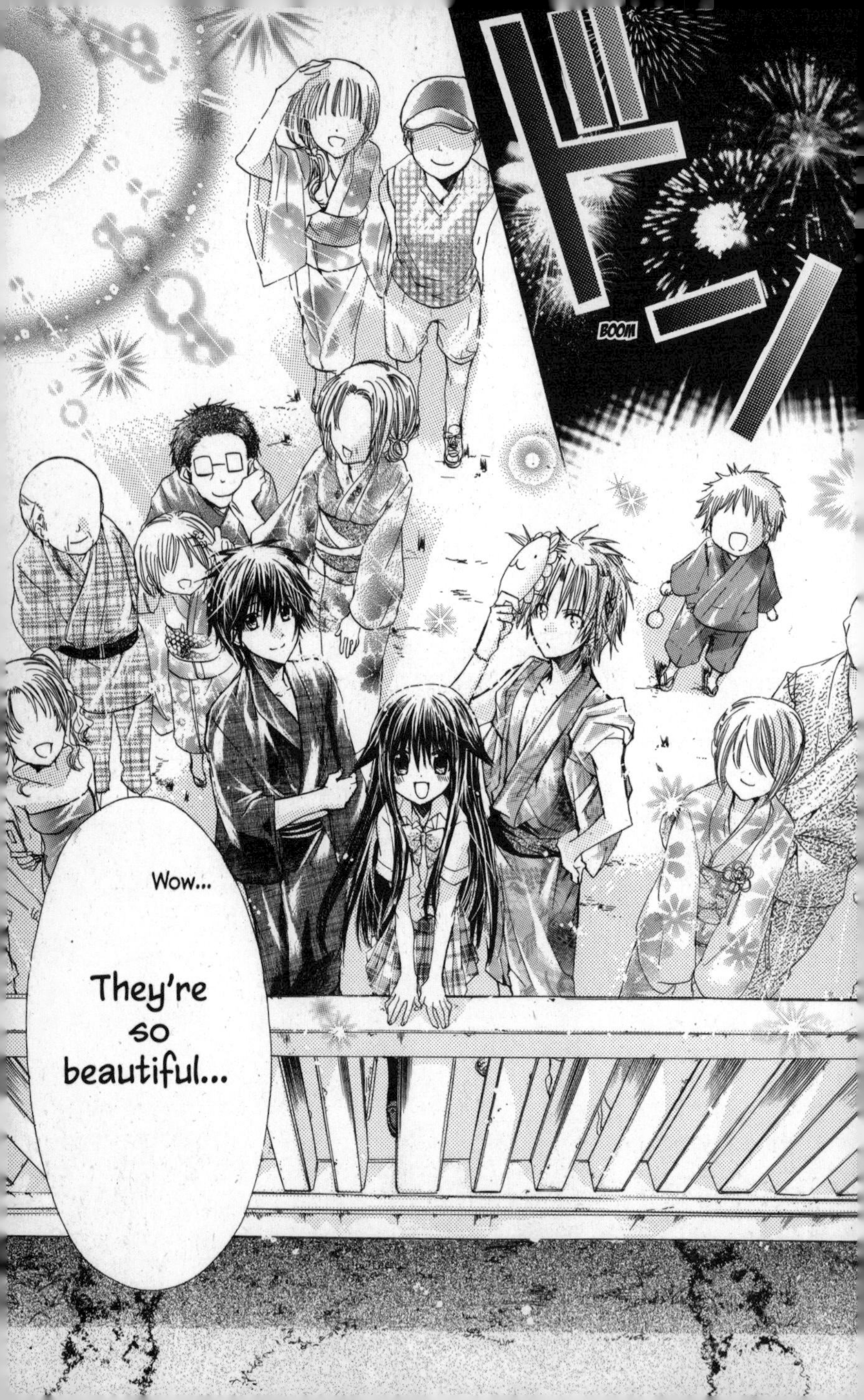
ドーン
BOOM
Wow...
They're so beautiful...

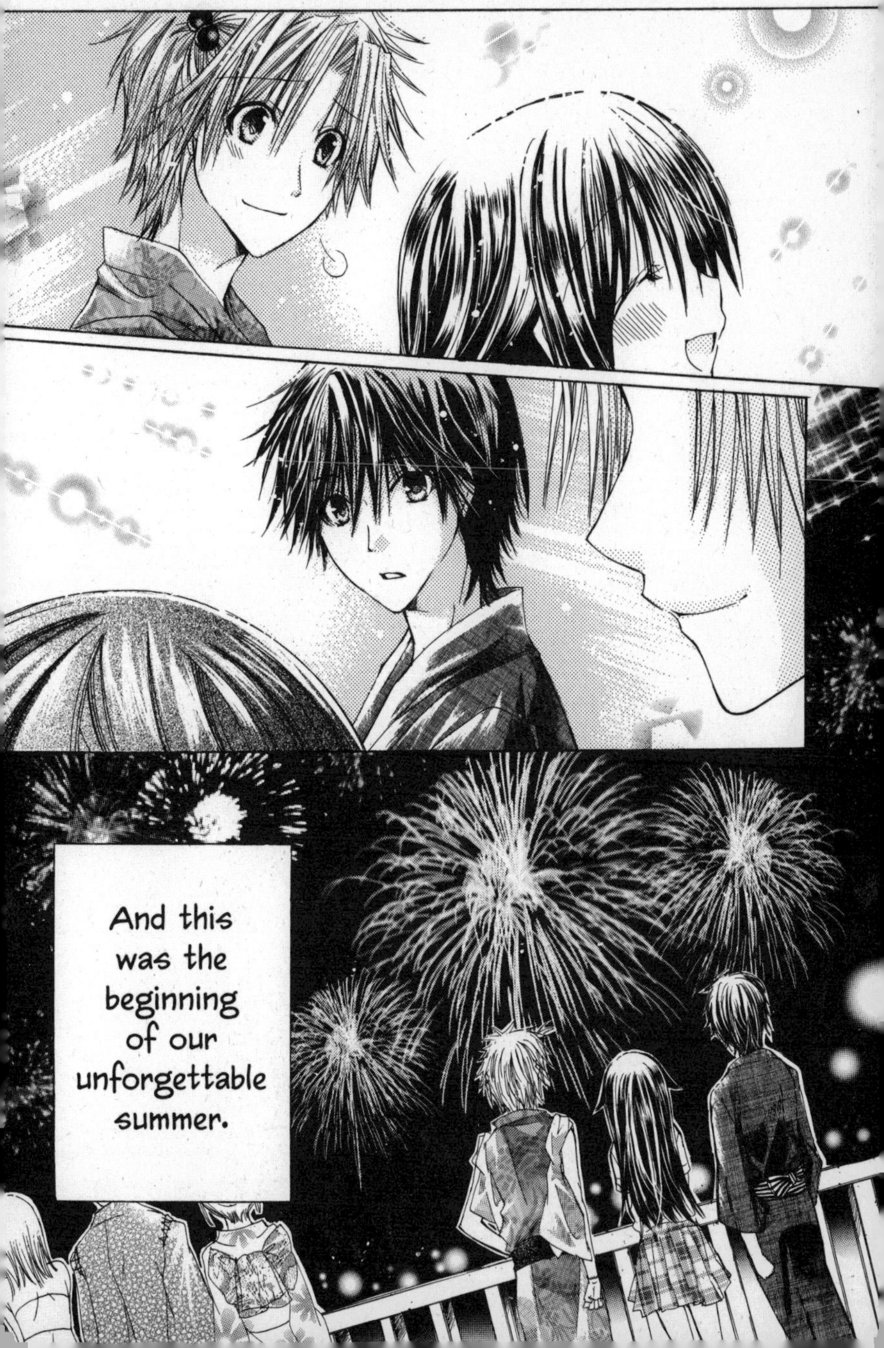
And this was the beginning of our unforgettable summer.

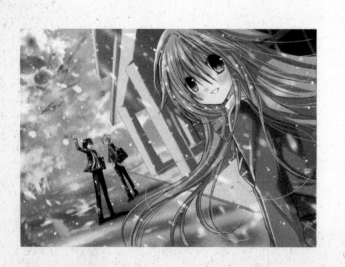

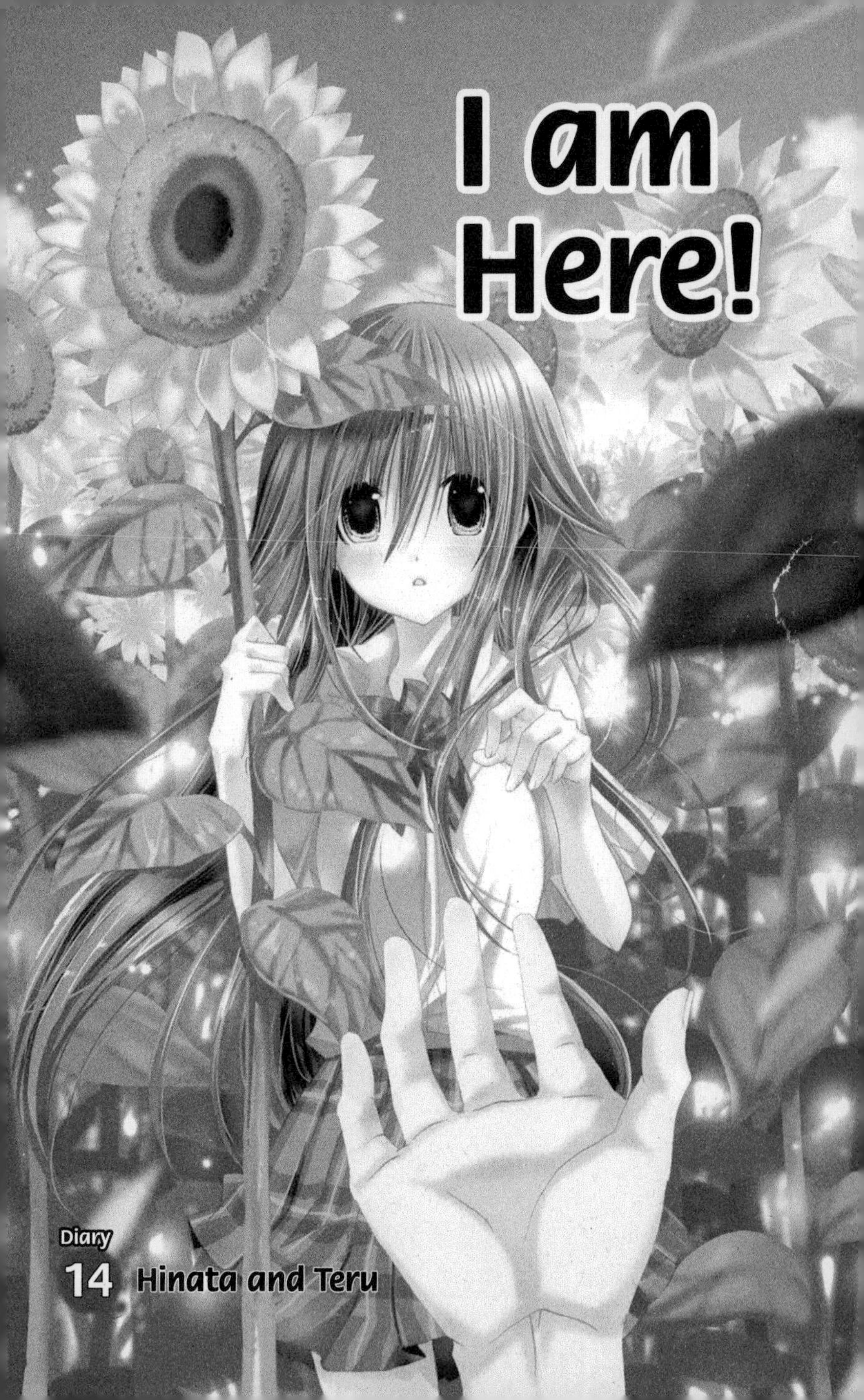
I am Here!
Diary
14 Hinata and Teru

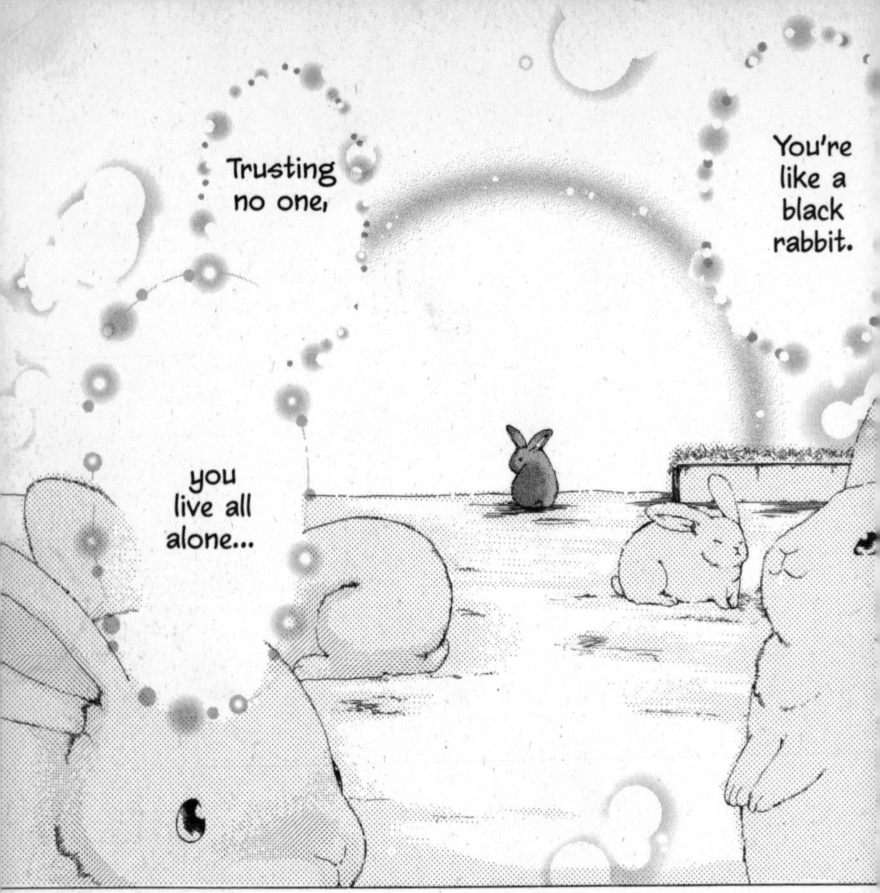
You're like a black rabbit.
Trusting no one,
you live all alone...

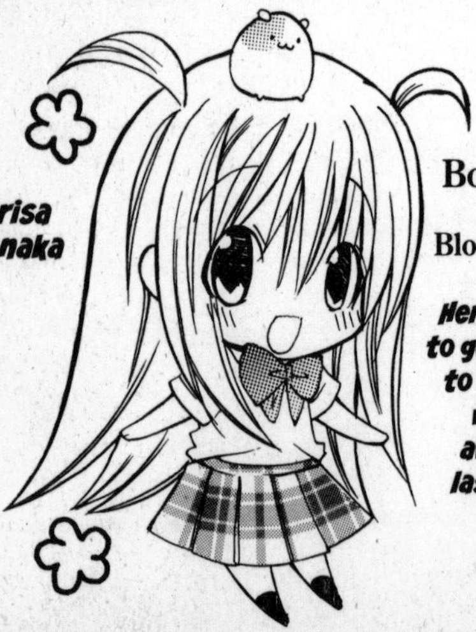

Arisa Tanaka

Born 6/6

Blood type O

Her dream is to get married to someone with an awesome last name.

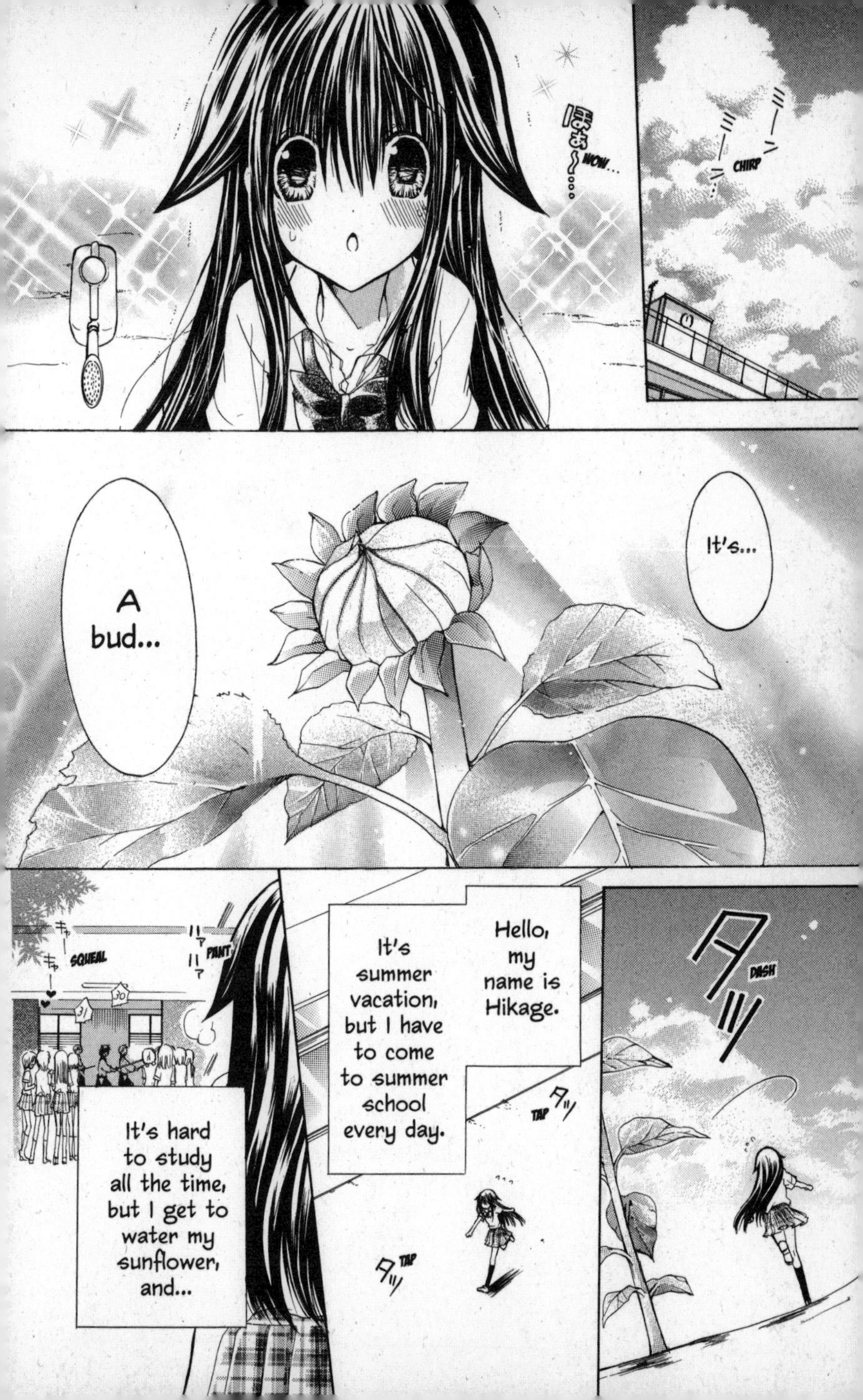
CHIRP
WOW...
It's...
A bud...
DASH
Hello, my name is Hikage.
It's summer vacation, but I have to come to summer school every day.
TAP
TAP
PANT
SQUEAL
It's hard to study all the time, but I get to water my sunflower, and...

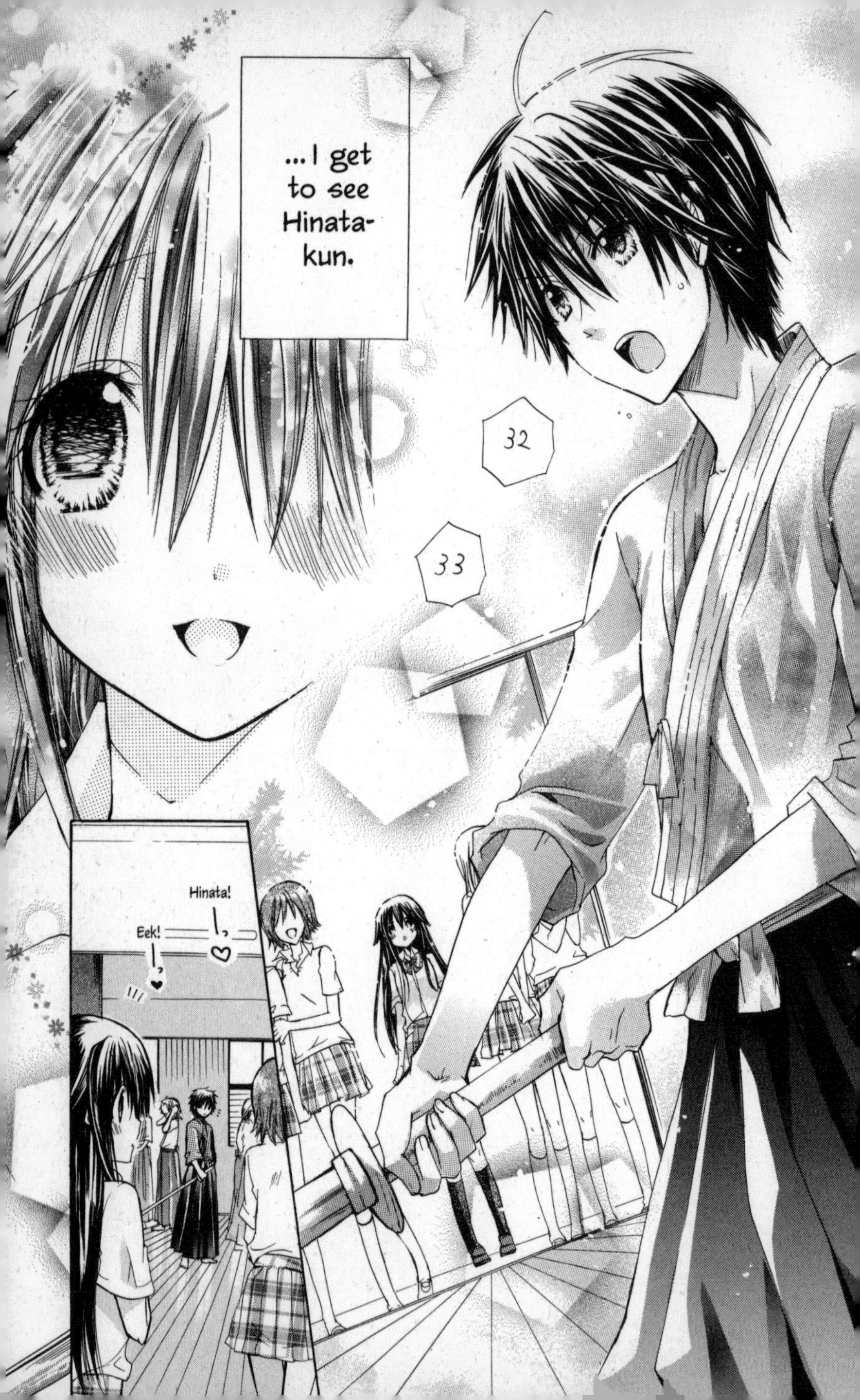
...I get to see Hinata-kun.
32
33
Hinata!
Eek!

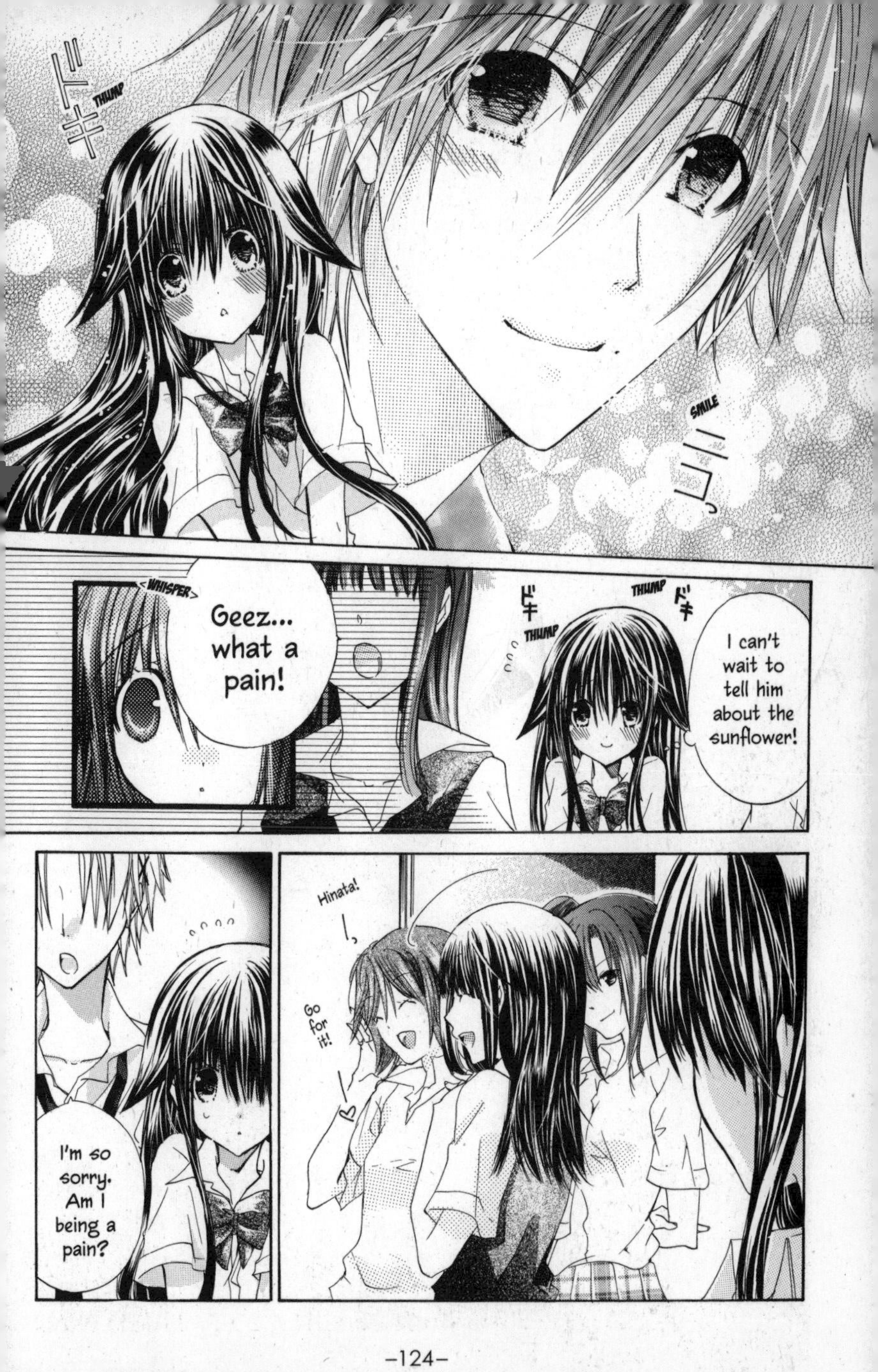
SMILE
ニコッ
THUMP
ドキ
THUMP ドキ
THUMP ドキ
I can't wait to tell him about the sunflower!
<WHISPER>
Geez... what a pain!
Hinata!
Go for it!
I'm so sorry. Am I being a pain?

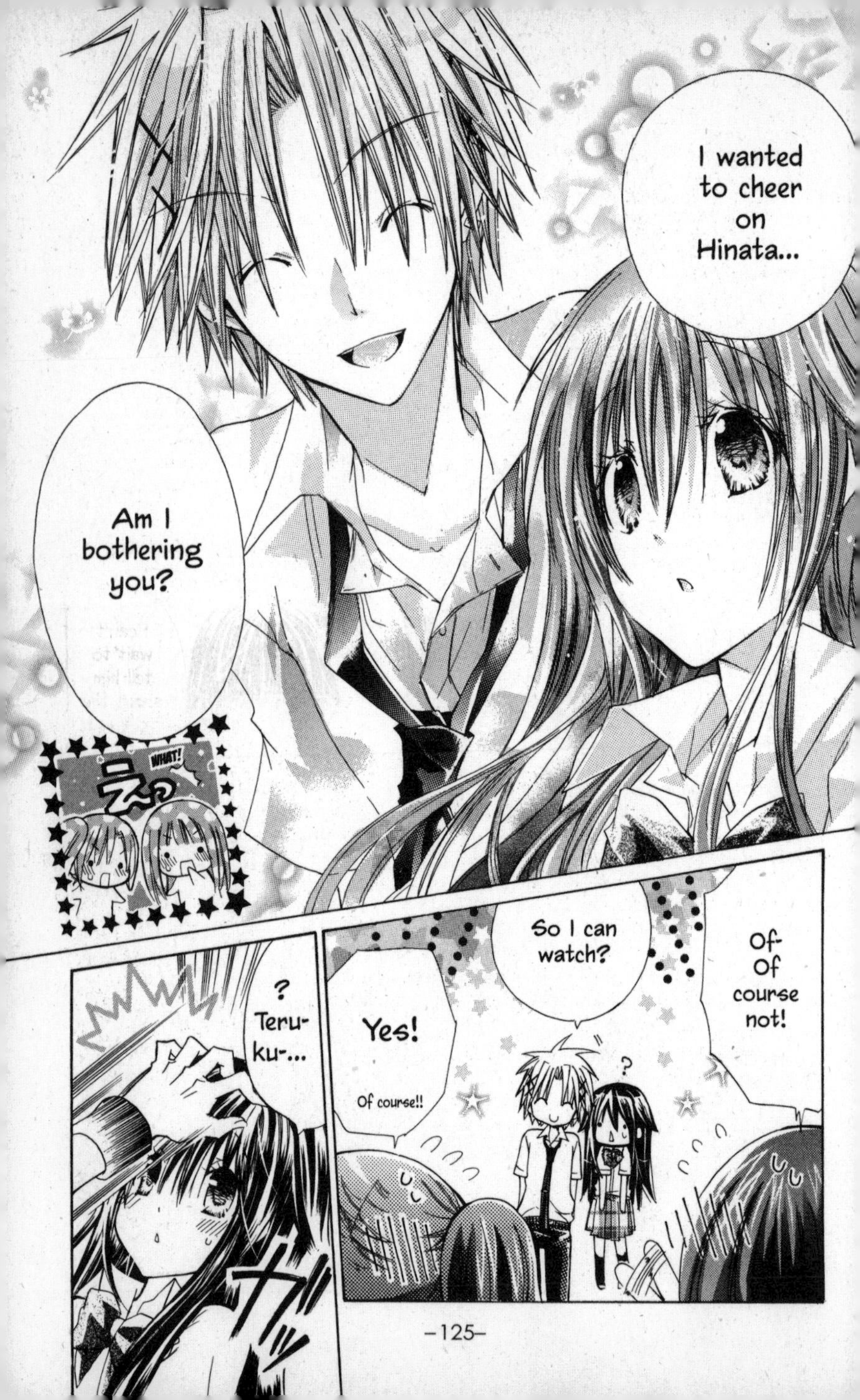
I wanted to cheer on Hinata...
Am I bothering you?
えっ
WHAT!
Of- Of course not!
So I can watch?
Yes!
Of course!!
? Teru-ku-...

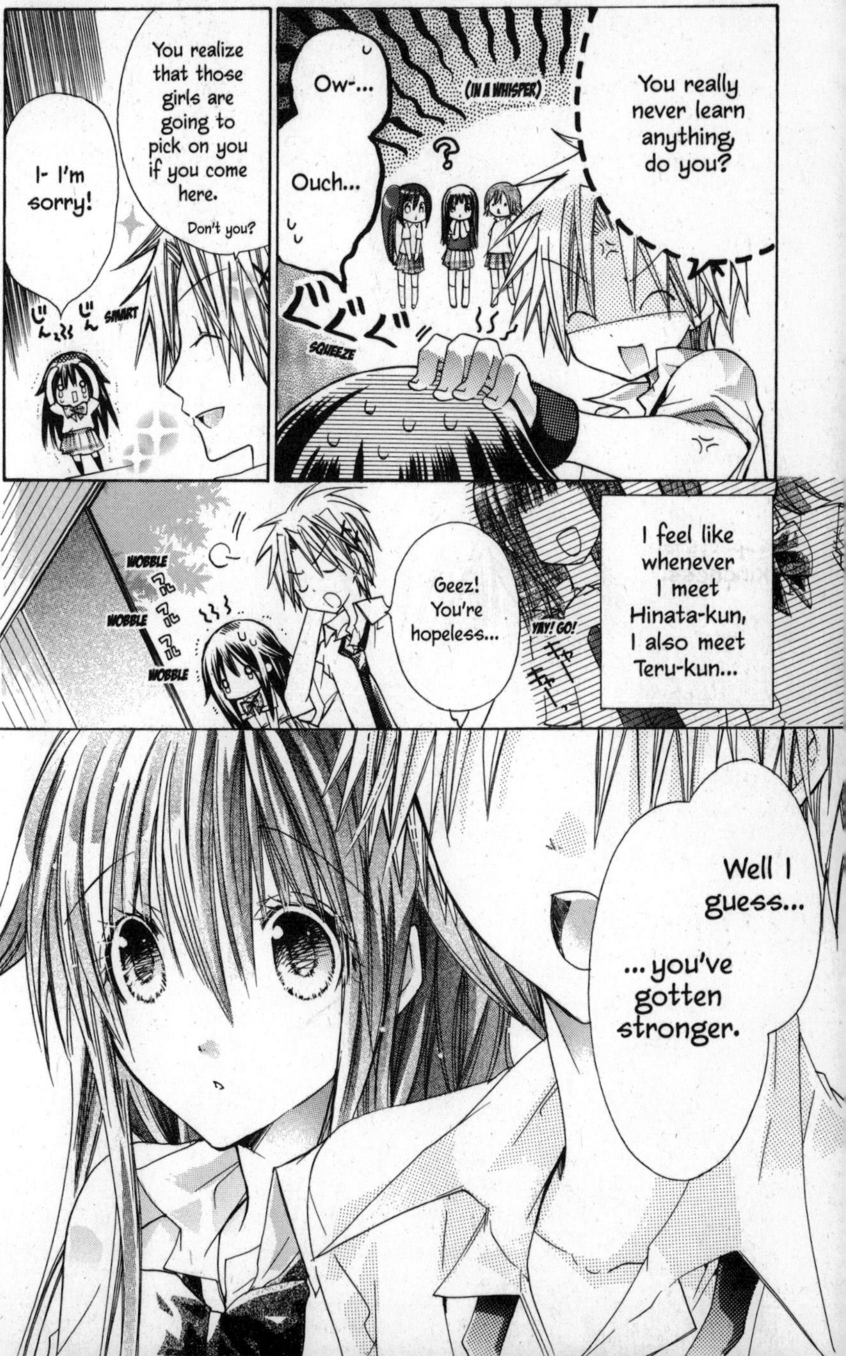
(IN A WHISPER)
You really never learn anything, do you?
Ow-...
Ouch...
ぐぐぐ
SQUEEZE
You realize that those girls are going to pick on you if you come here.
Don't you?
I- I'm sorry!
じんじん
SMART
I feel like whenever I meet Hinata-kun, I also meet Teru-kun...
YAY! GO!
キャーキャー
Geez! You're hopeless...
WOBBLE
WOBBLE
WOBBLE
Well I guess...
...you've gotten stronger.

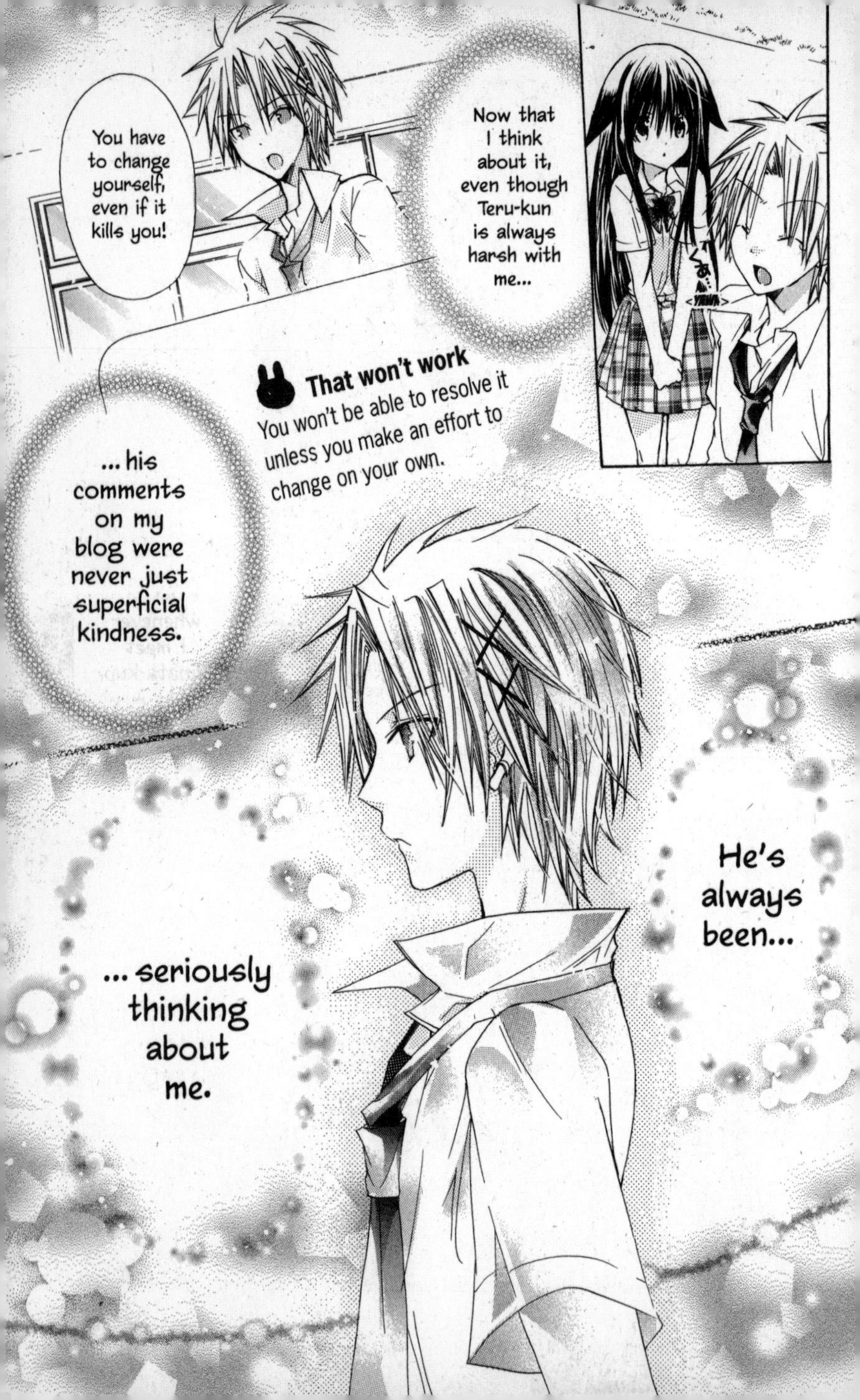
Now that I think about it, even though Teru-kun is always harsh with me...
You have to change yourself, even if it kills you!
That won't work
You won't be able to resolve it unless you make an effort to change on your own.
...his comments on my blog were never just superficial kindness.
He's always been...
...seriously thinking about me.

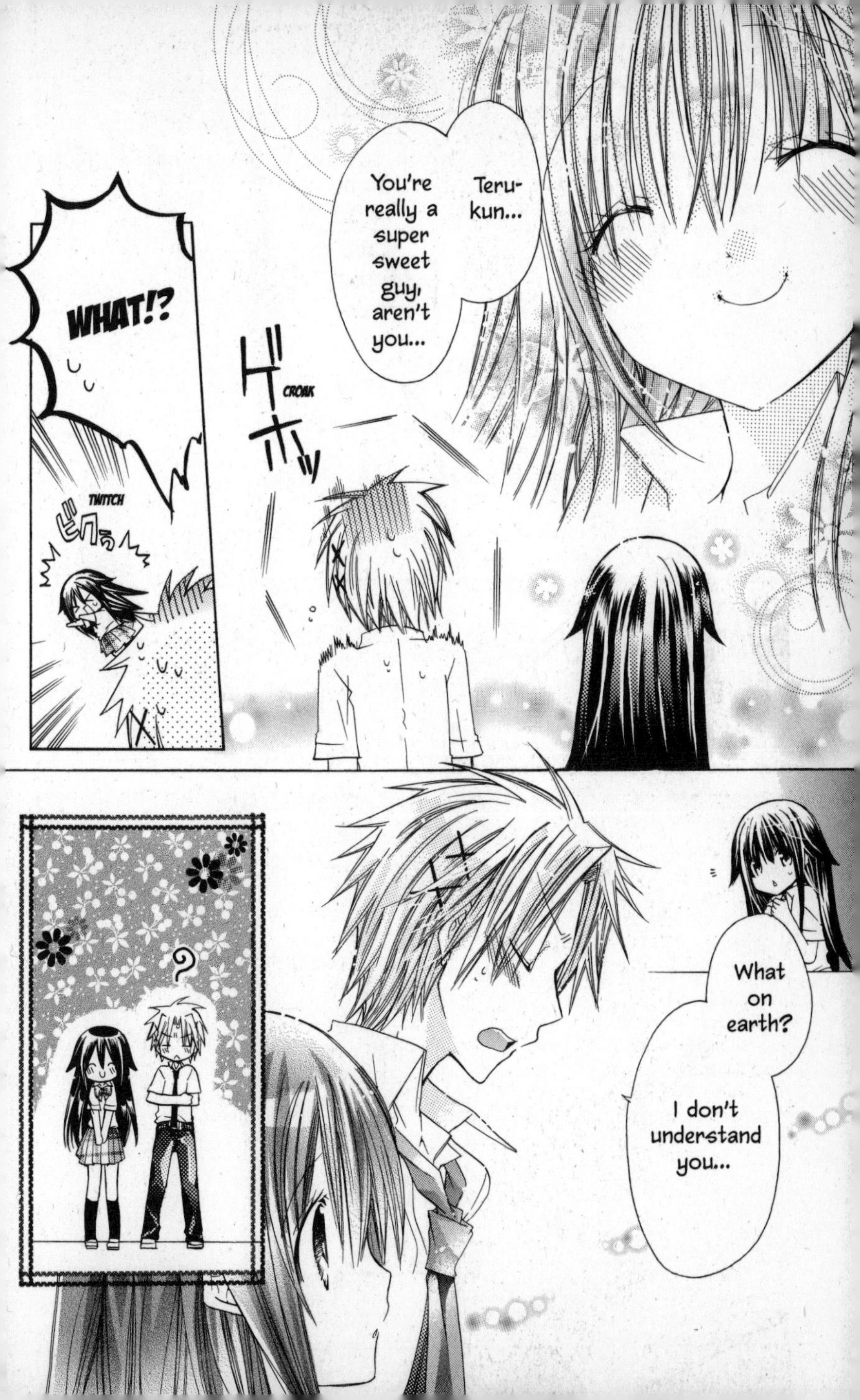
Teru-kun...
You're really a super sweet guy, aren't you...
CROAK
WHAT!?
TWITCH
What on earth?
I don't understand you...
?

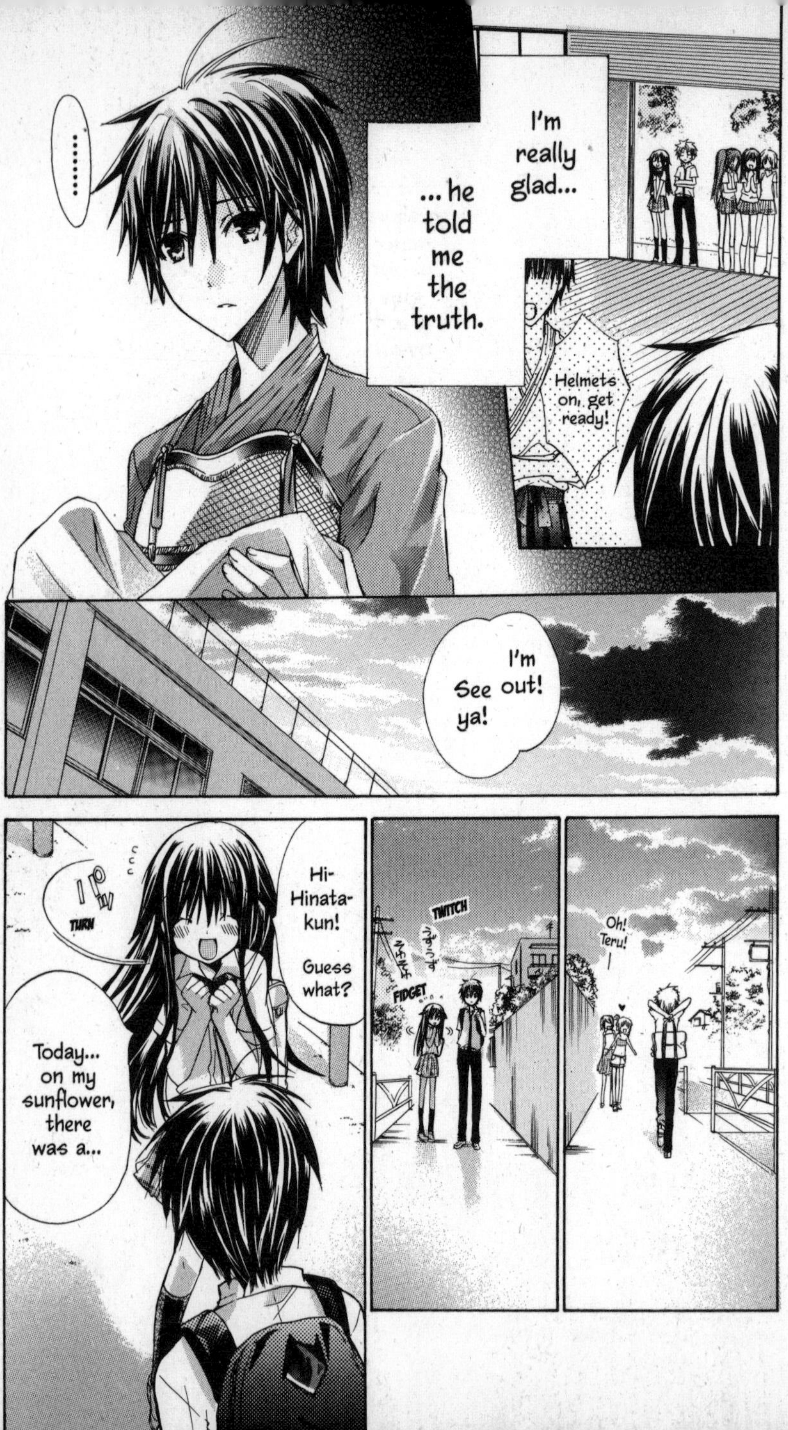

I'm really glad...
... he told me the truth.
Helmets on, get ready!
......
I'm out!
See ya!
Oh! Teru!
TWITCH
FIDGET
TURN
Hi- Hinata-kun!
Guess what?
Today... on my sunflower, there was a...

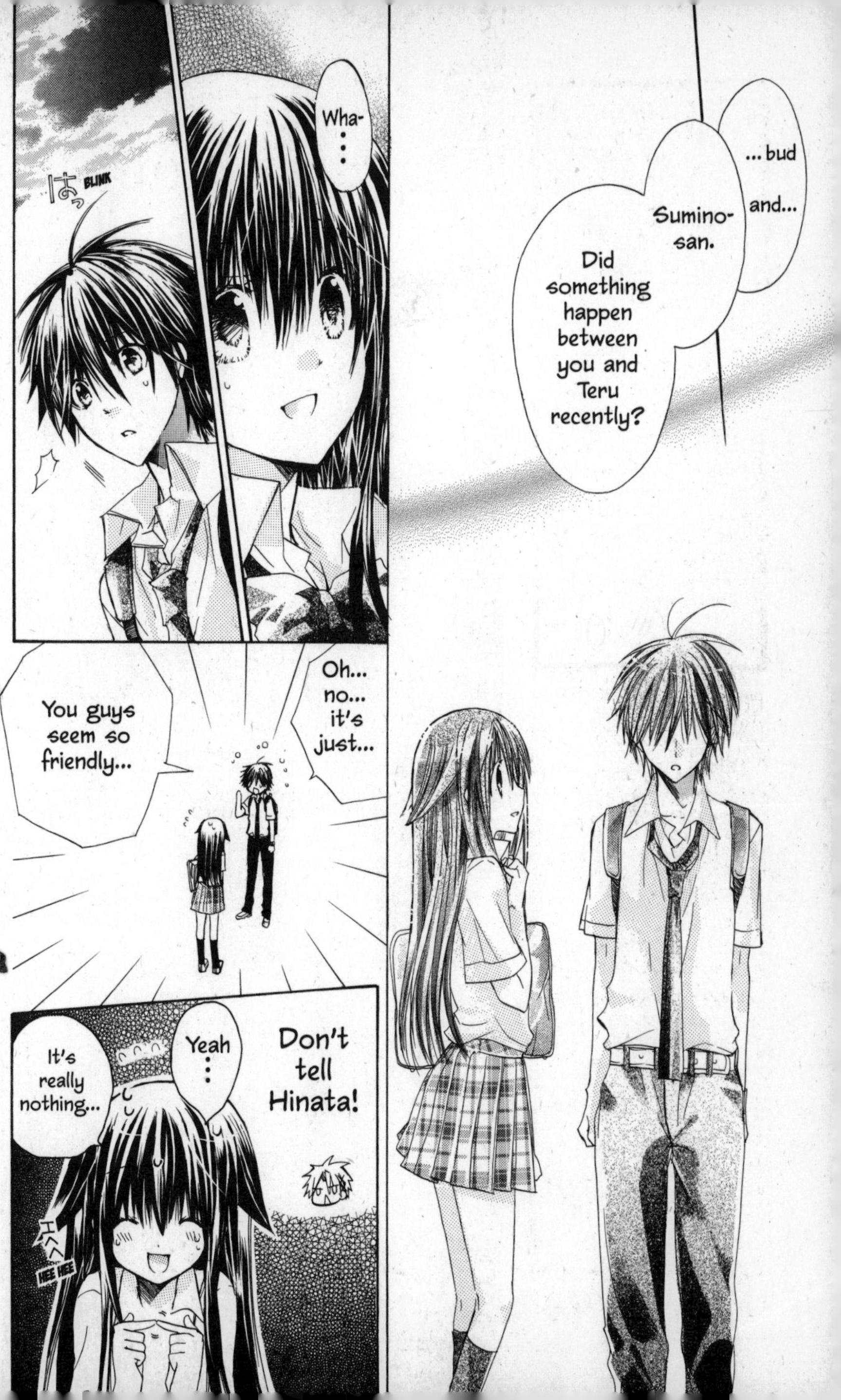

... bud and...
Sumino-san.
Did something happen between you and Teru recently?
Wha-...
はっ BLINK
Oh... no... it's just...
You guys seem so friendly...
Don't tell Hinata!
Yeah...
It's really nothing...
エヘヘ HEE HEE

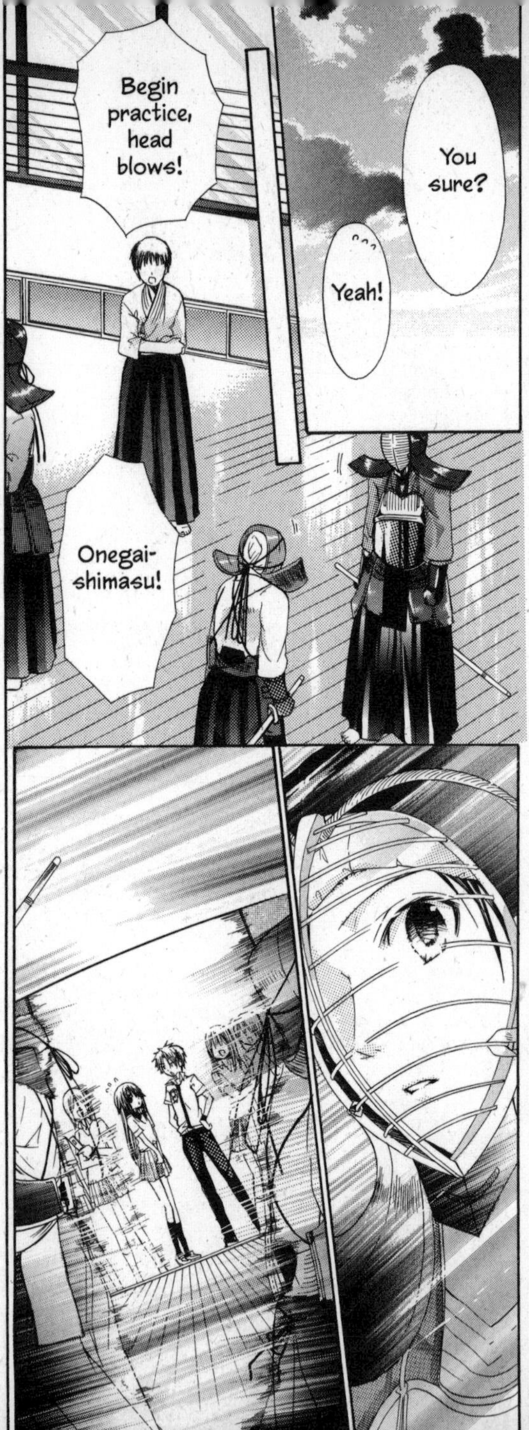
You sure?
Yeah!
Begin practice, head blows!
Onegai-shimasu!

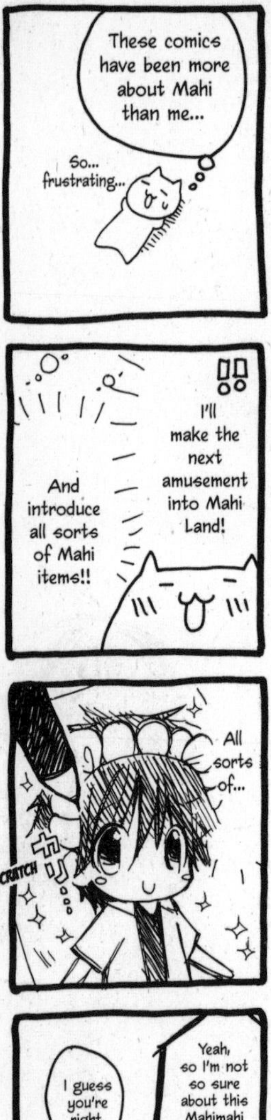
These comics have been more about Mahi than me...
So... frustrating...
!!
I'll make the next amusement into Mahi Land!
And introduce all sorts of Mahi items!!
All sorts of...
SCRATCH
Yeah, so I'm not so sure about this Mahimahi headband.
EDITOR
I guess you're right.

So I snuck it onto Hikage instead.

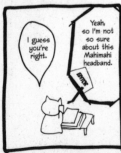

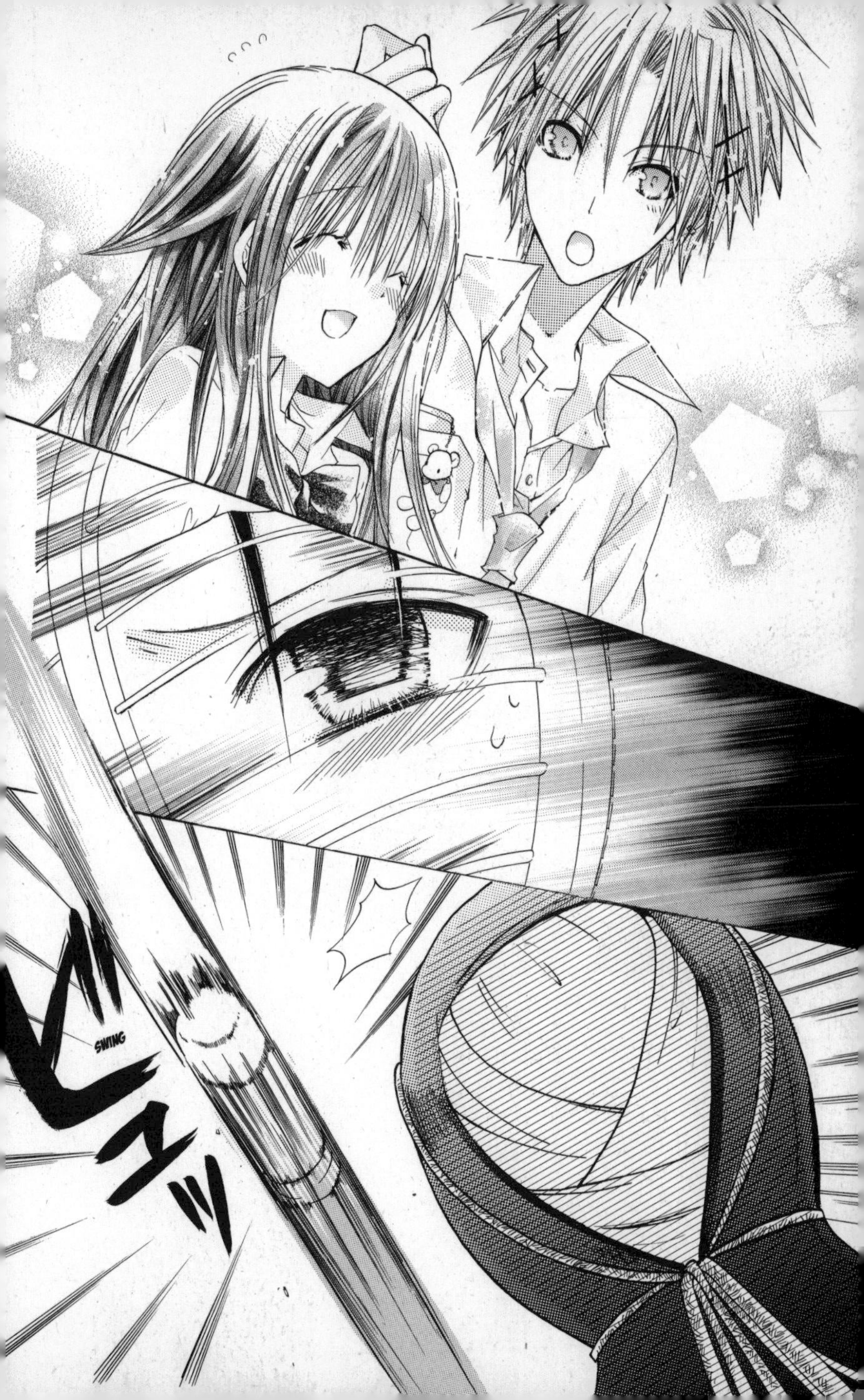
SWING

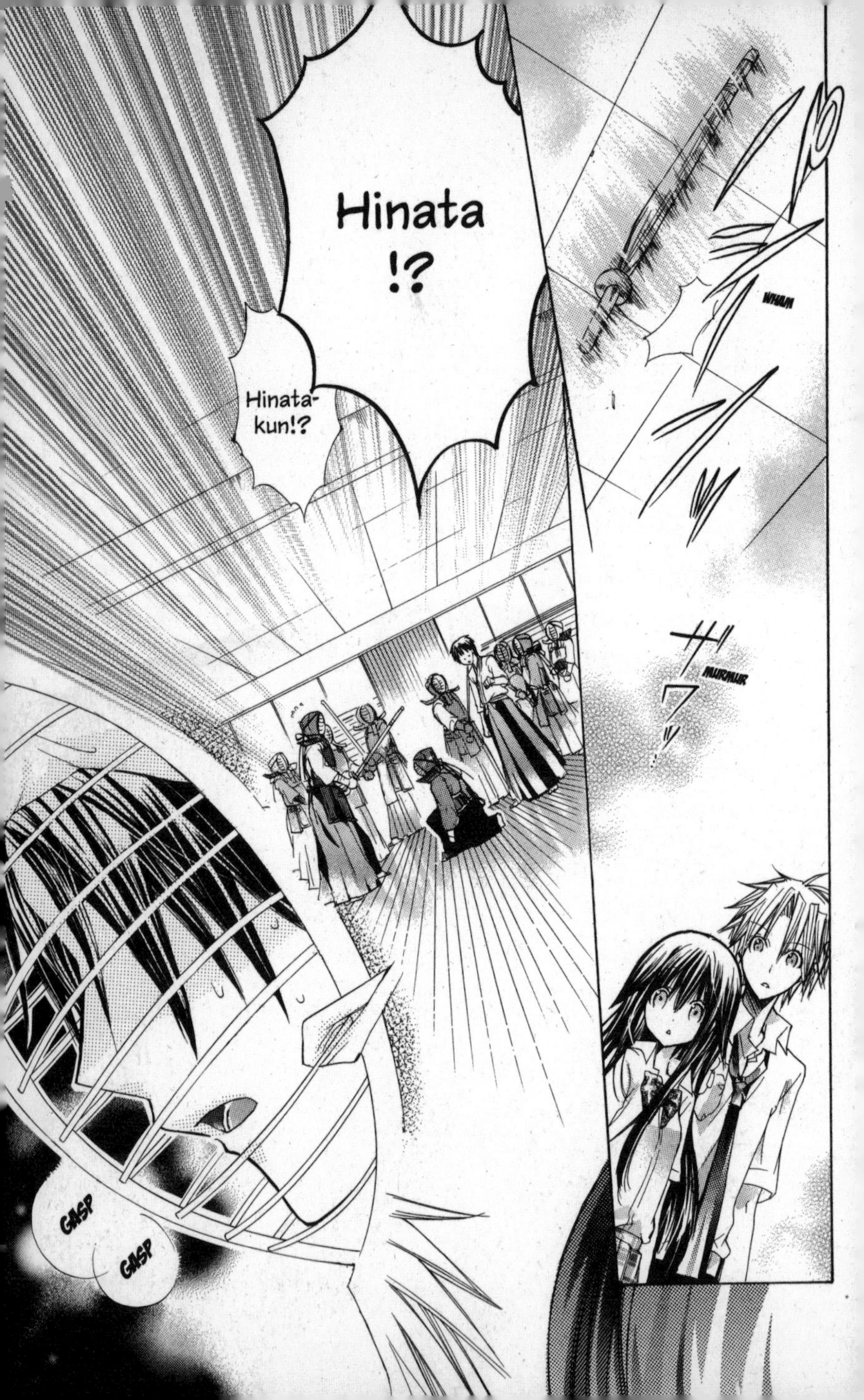
WHAM
MURMUR
Hinata !?
Hinata-kun!?
GASP
GASP

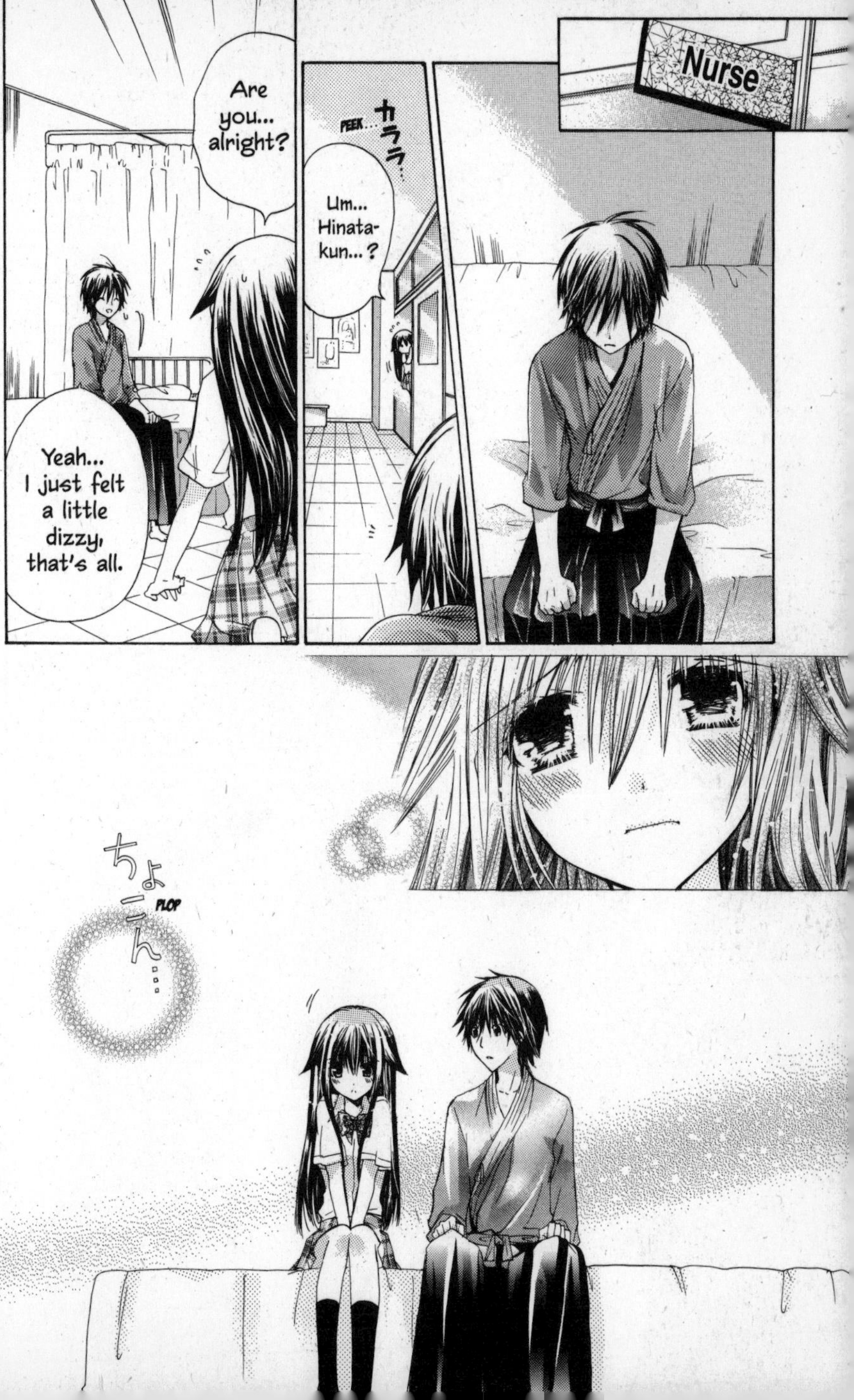
Nurse
カララ
PEEK...
Um... Hinata-kun...?
Are you... alright?
Yeah... I just felt a little dizzy, that's all.
ちょこん...
PLOP

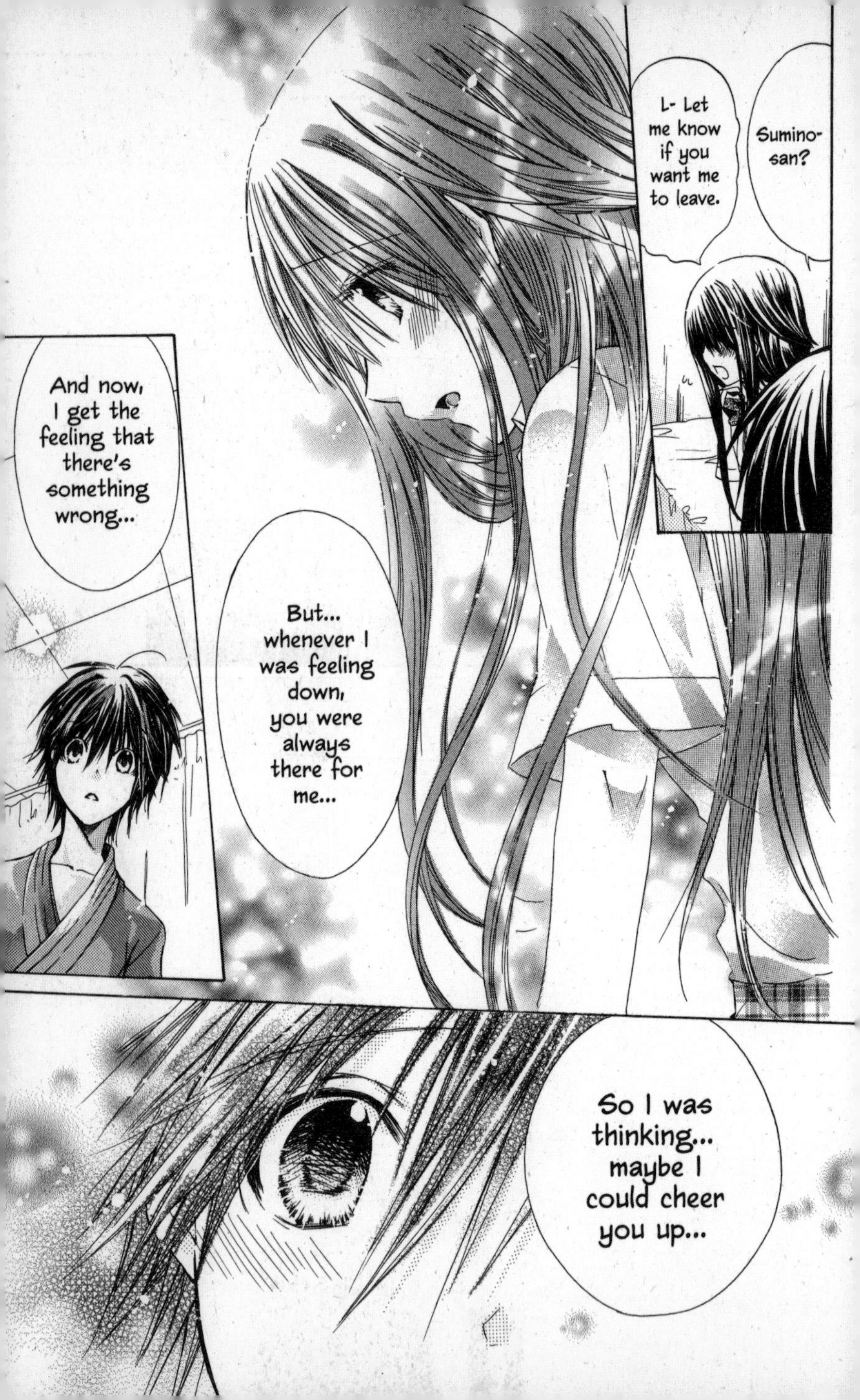
Sumino-san?
L- Let me know if you want me to leave.
But... whenever I was feeling down, you were always there for me...
And now, I get the feeling that there's something wrong...
So I was thinking... maybe I could cheer you up...

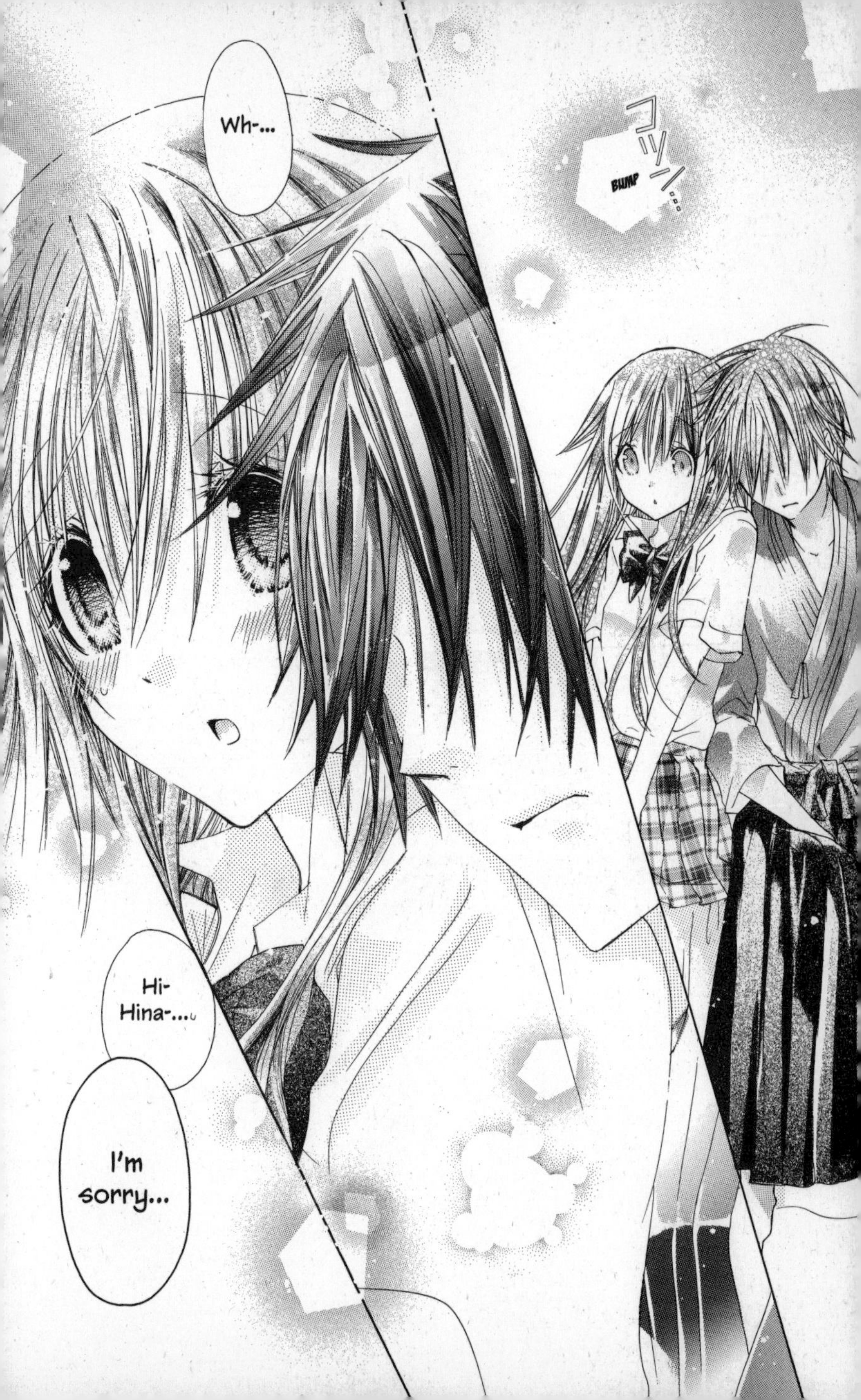
コツン…
BUMP
Wh-...
Hi-
Hina-...
I'm
sorry...

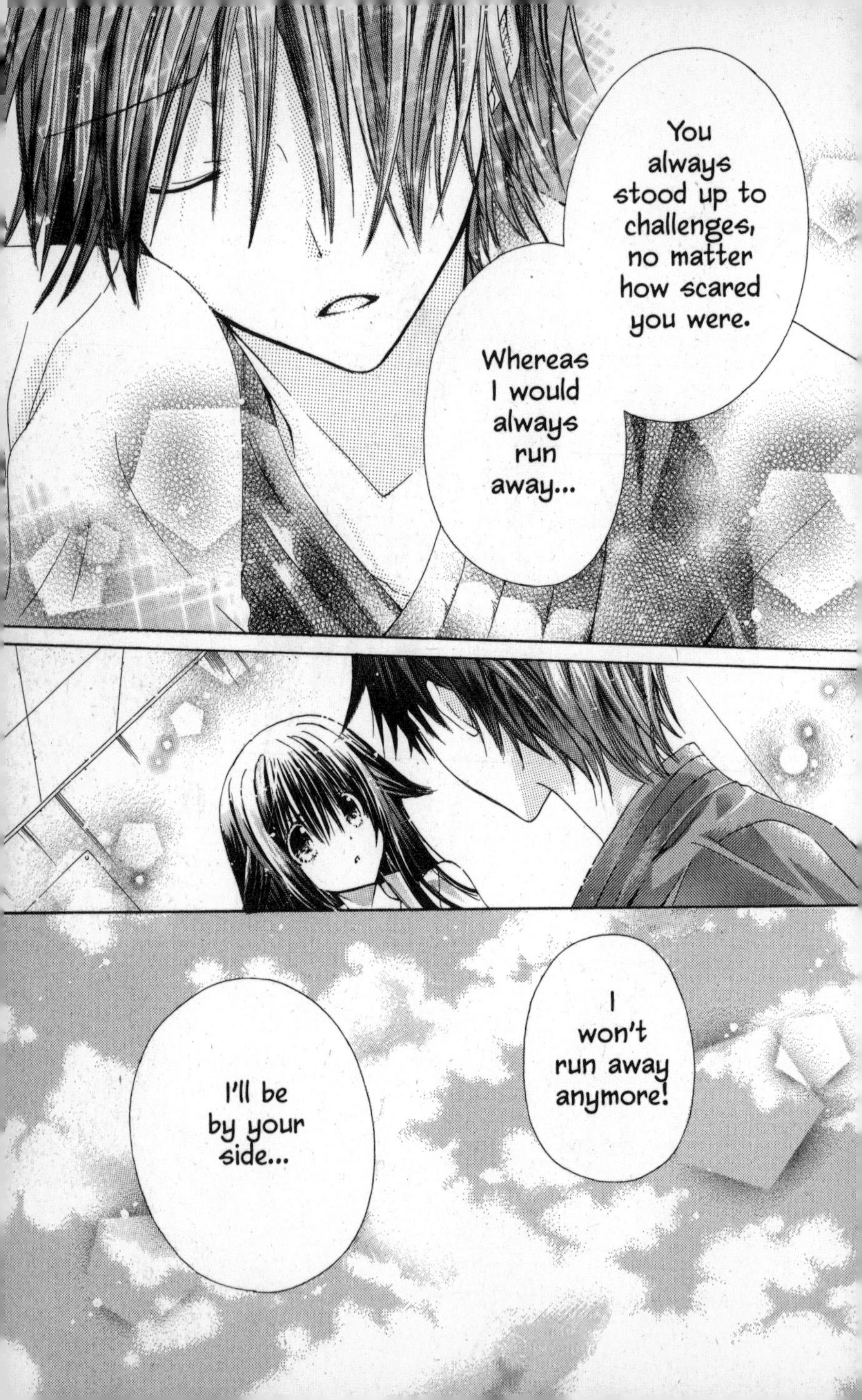
You always stood up to challenges, no matter how scared you were.
Whereas I would always run away...
I won't run away anymore!
I'll be by your side...

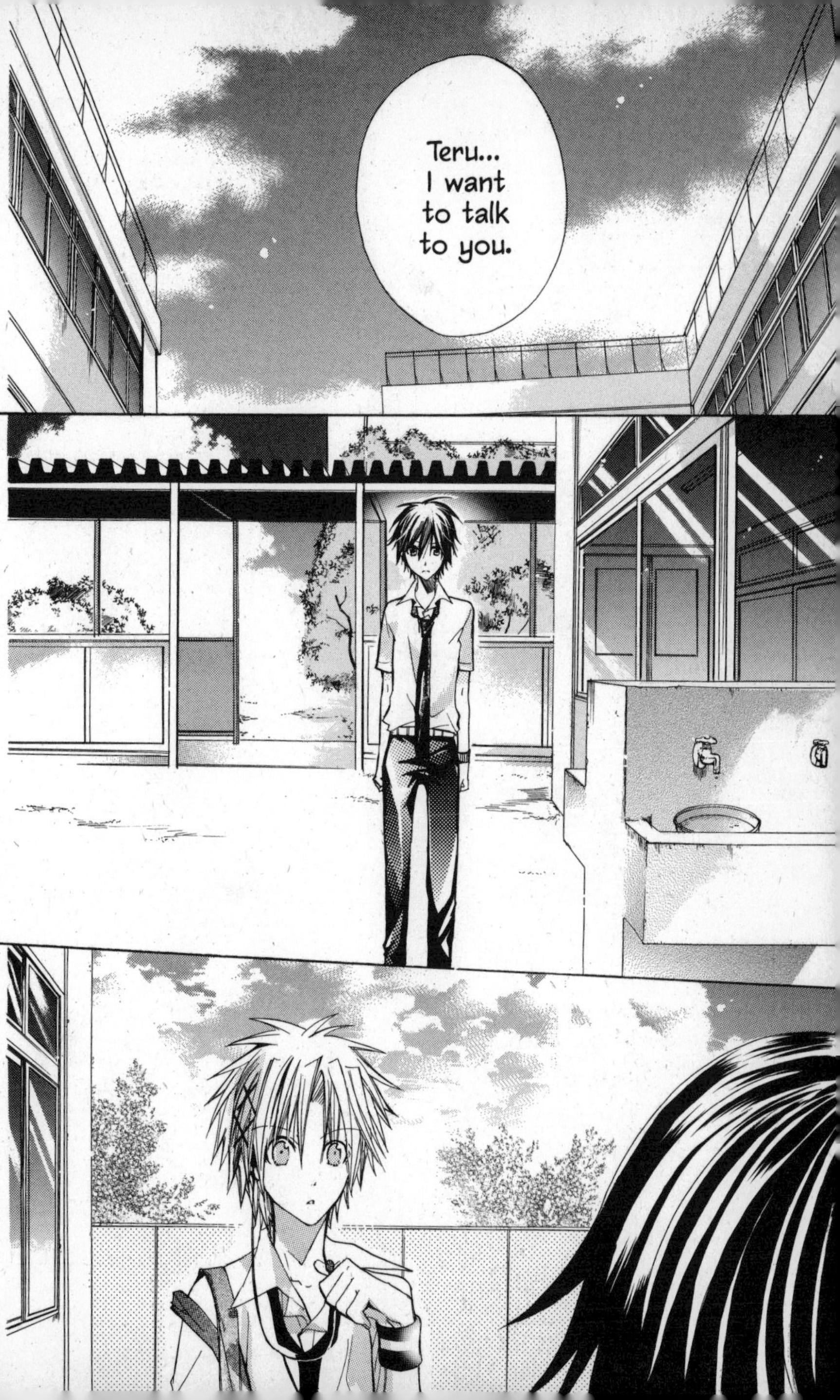
Teru...
I want
to talk
to you.

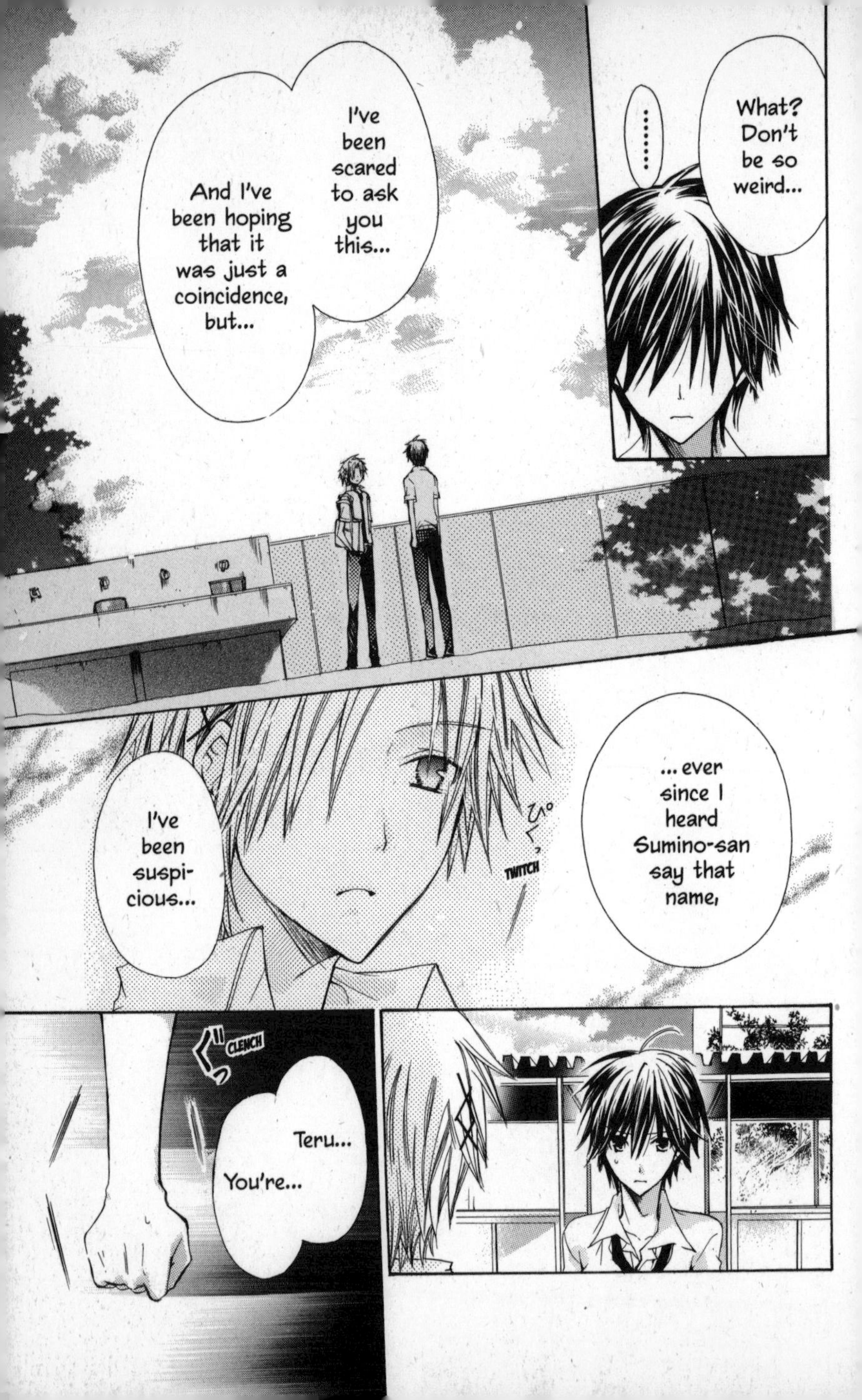
What? Don't be so weird...
......
I've been scared to ask you this...
And I've been hoping that it was just a coincidence, but...
... ever since I heard Sumino-san say that name,
TWITCH
I've been suspicious...
CLENCH
Teru... You're...

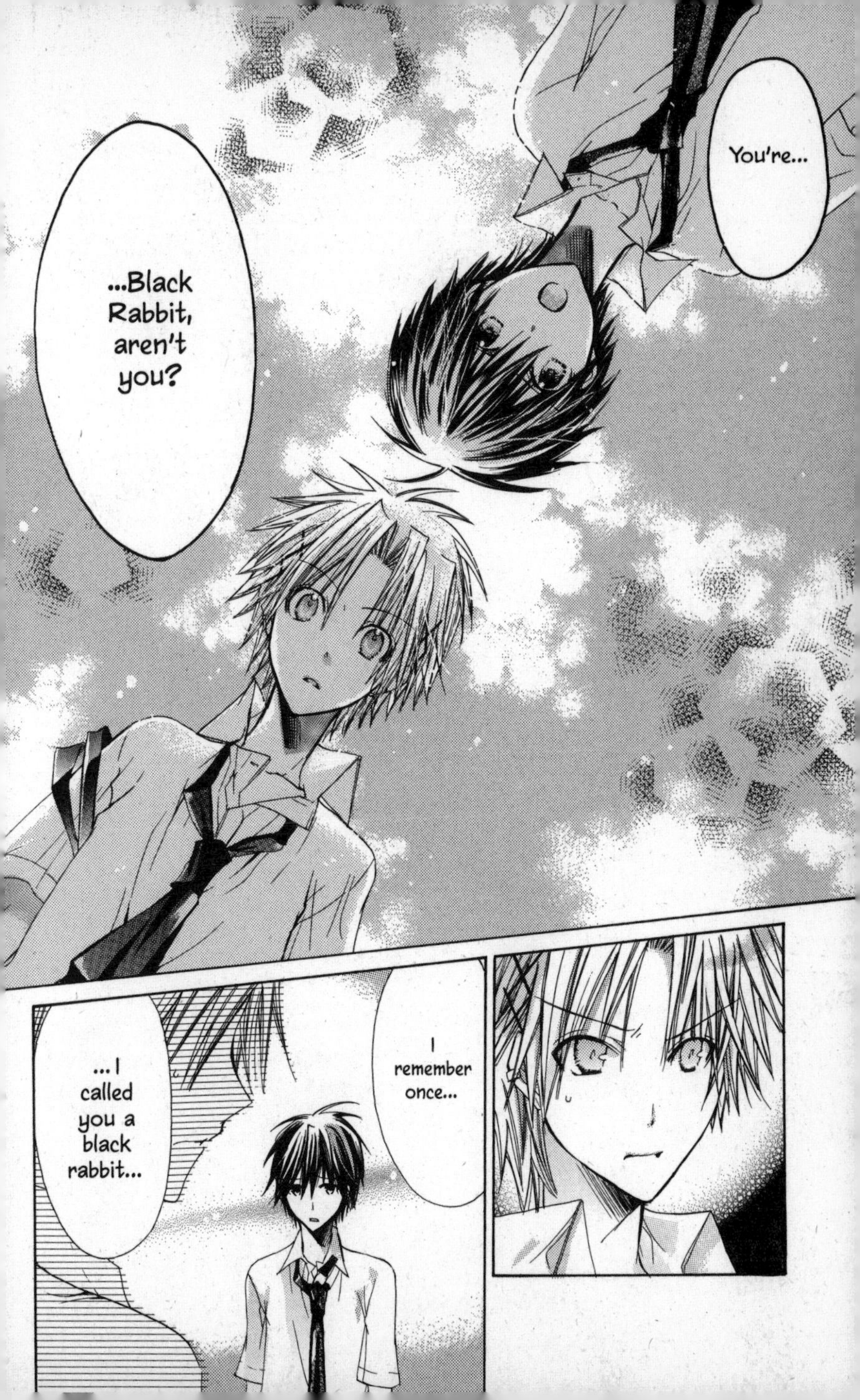
You're...
...Black Rabbit, aren't you?
I remember once...
...I called you a black rabbit...

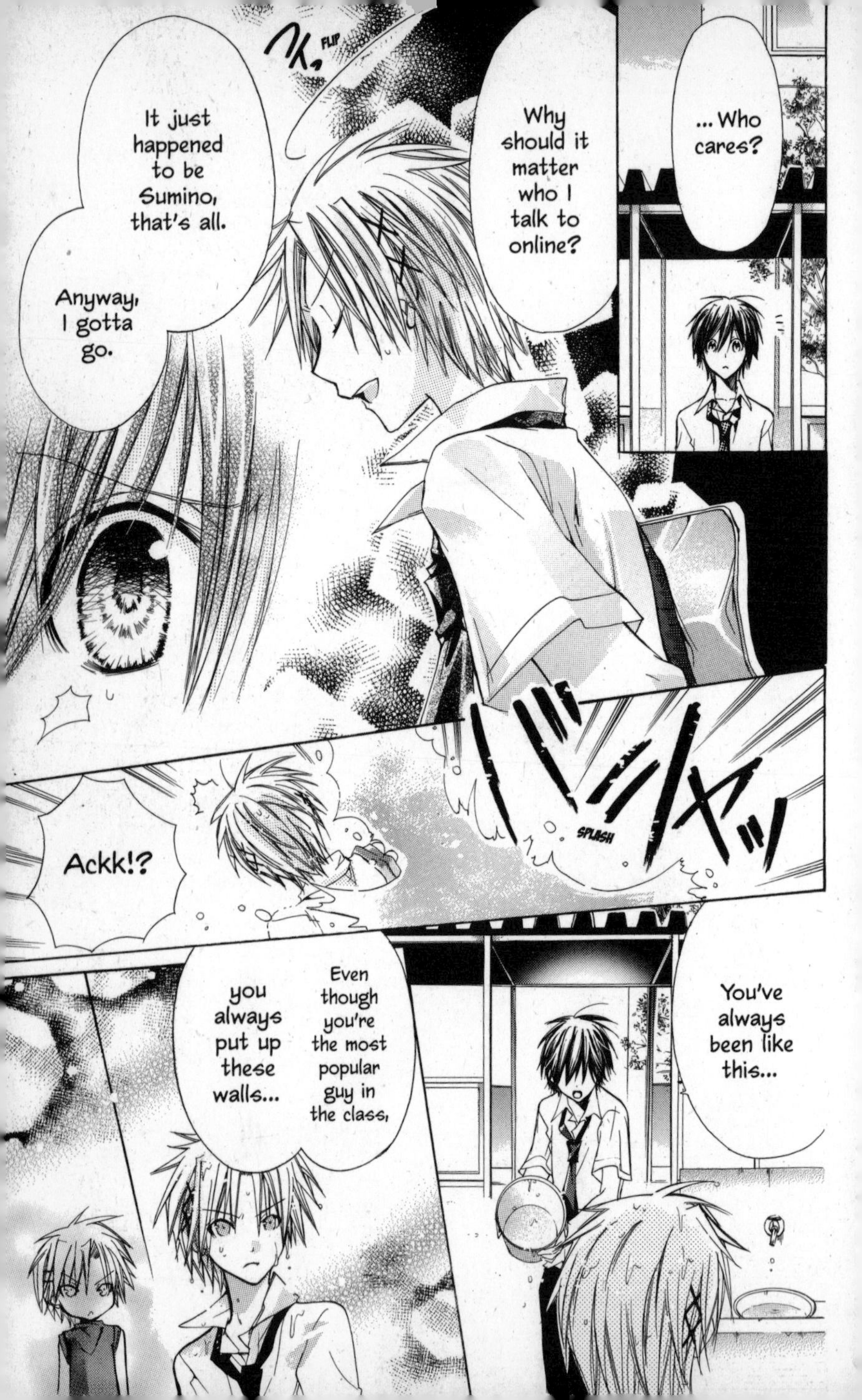
...Who cares?
Why should it matter who I talk to online?
FLIP
It just happened to be Sumino, that's all.
Anyway, I gotta go.
SPLASH
Ackk!?
You've always been like this...
Even though you're the most popular guy in the class,
you always put up these walls...

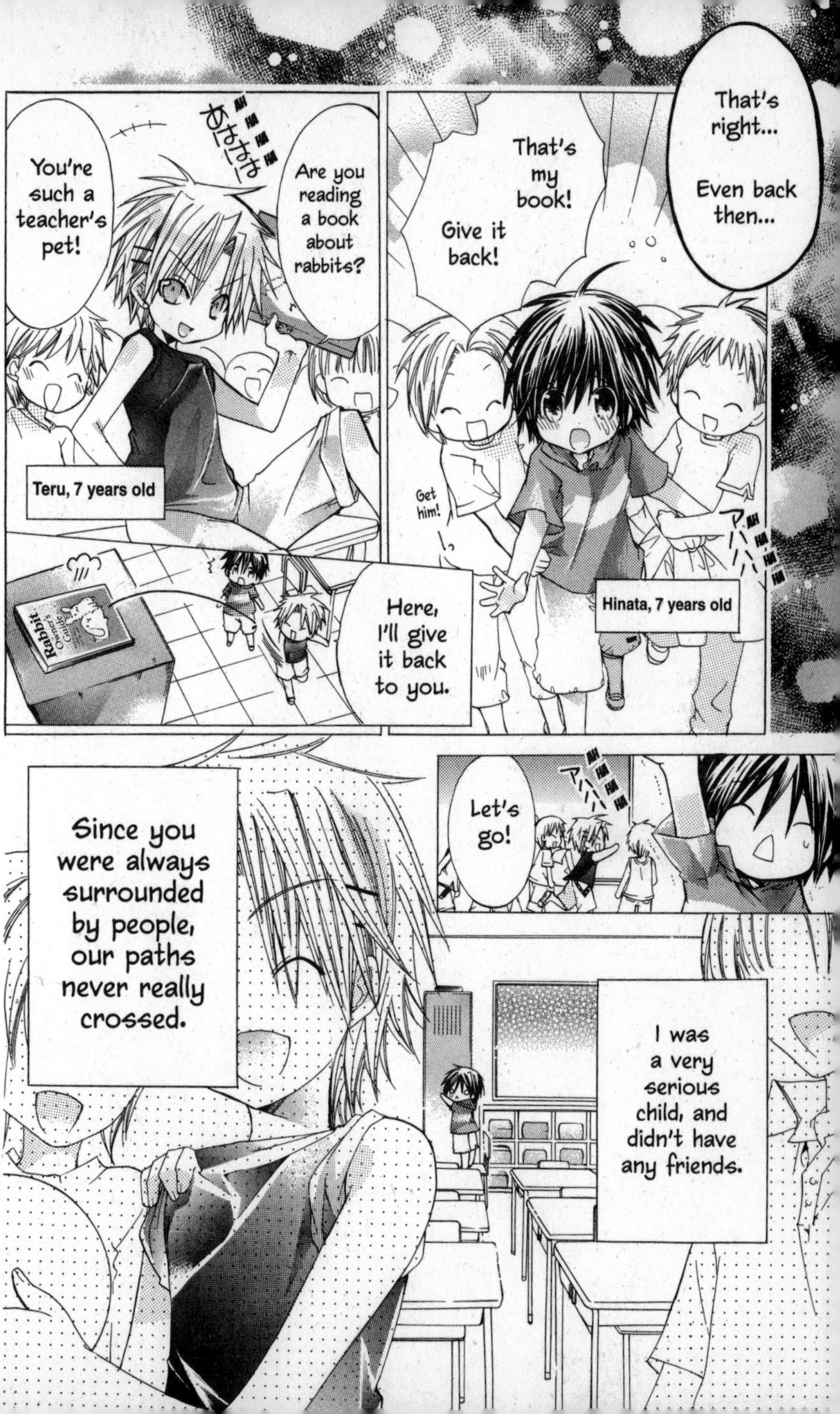
That's right...
Even back then...
That's my book!
Give it back!
Get him!
アハハ AH HA HA HA
Hinata, 7 years old
Are you reading a book about rabbits?
あははは AH HA HA HA
You're such a teacher's pet!
Teru, 7 years old
Rabbit Owner's Guide
Here, I'll give it back to you.
アハハ AH HA HA HA
Let's go!
I was a very serious child, and didn't have any friends.
Since you were always surrounded by people, our paths never really crossed.

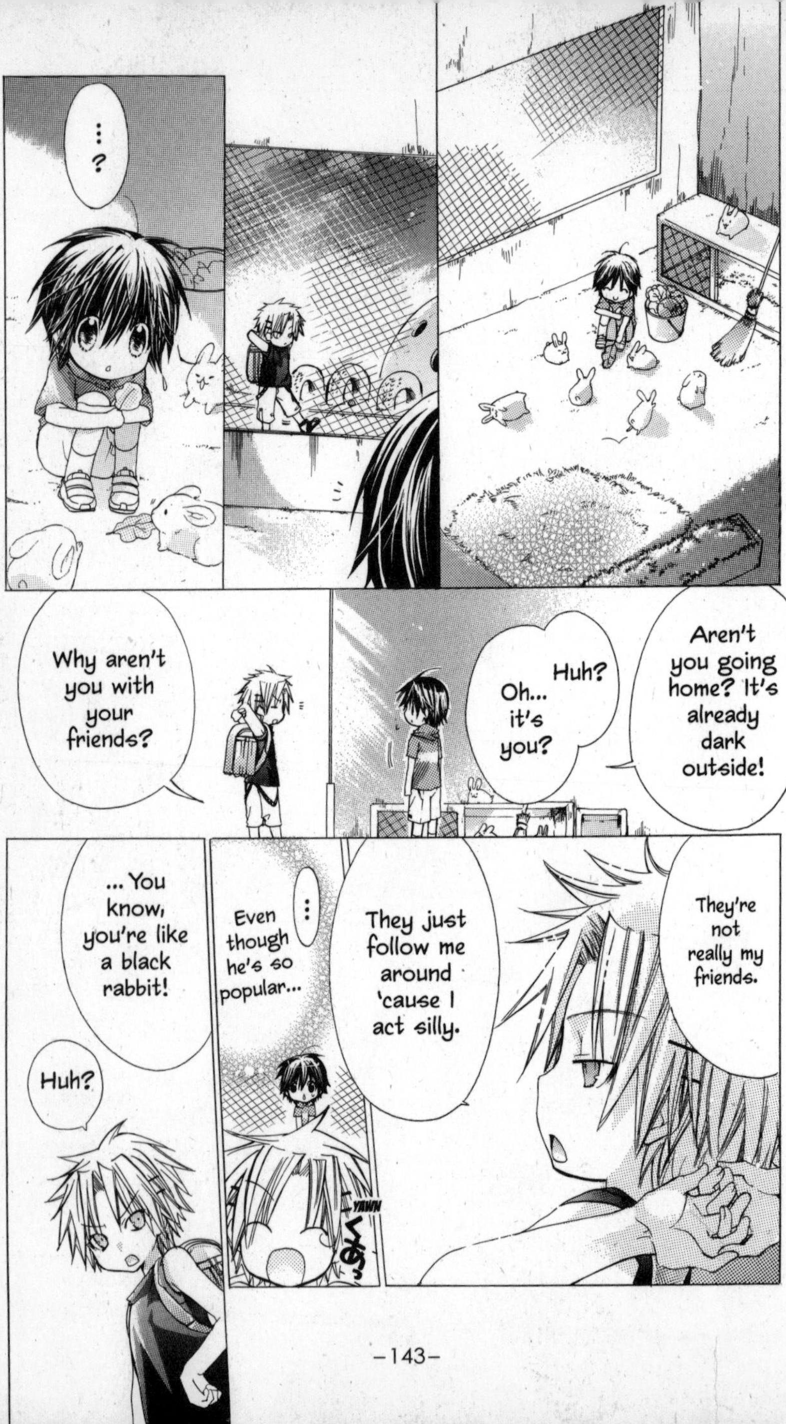
…?
Aren't you going home? It's already dark outside!
Huh?
Oh… it's you?
Why aren't you with your friends?
They're not really my friends.
They just follow me around 'cause I act silly.
…
Even though he's so popular…
YAWN
…You know, you're like a black rabbit!
Huh?

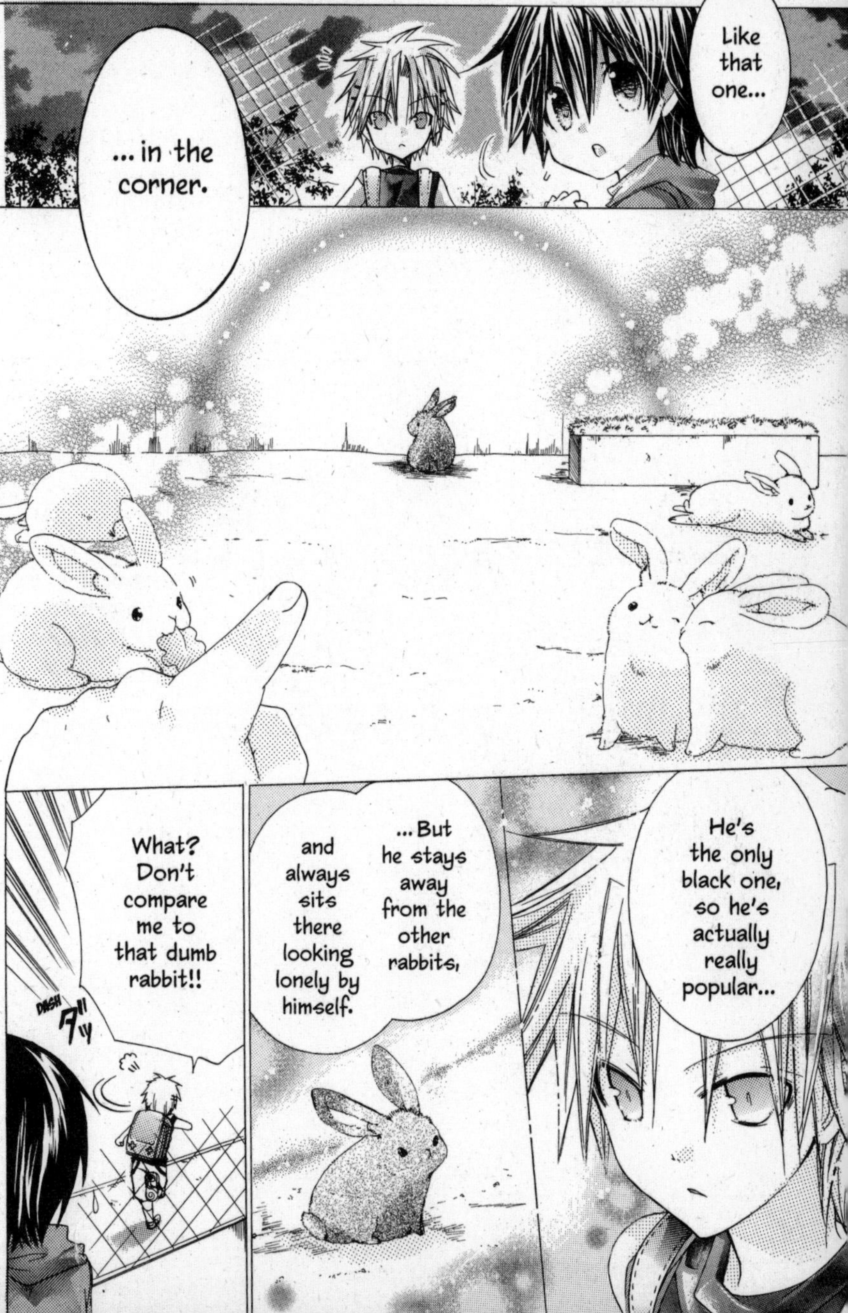
Like that one...
...in the corner.
He's the only black one, so he's actually really popular...
...But he stays away from the other rabbits,
and always sits there looking lonely by himself.
What? Don't compare me to that dumb rabbit!!
DASH

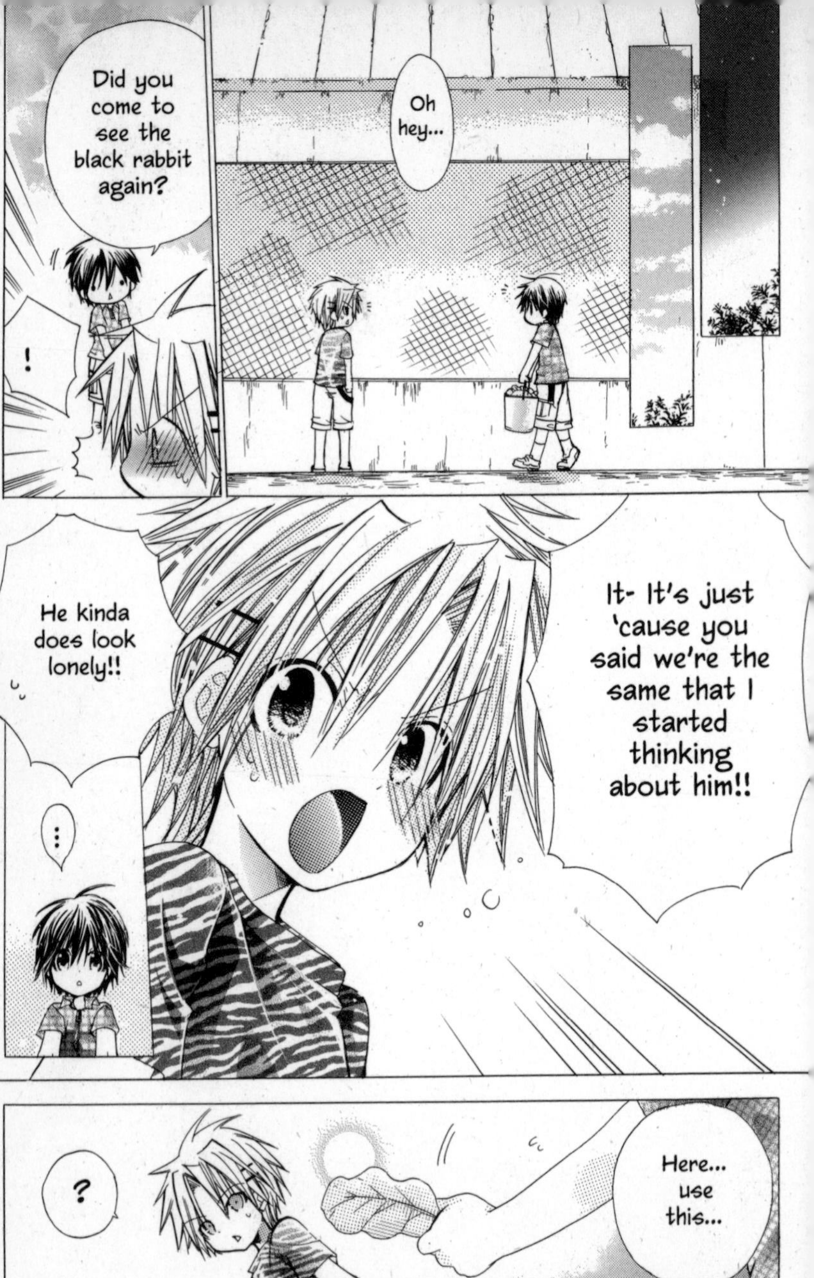
Oh hey...
Did you come to see the black rabbit again?
!
It- It's just 'cause you said we're the same that I started thinking about him!!
He kinda does look lonely!!
...
Here... use this...
?

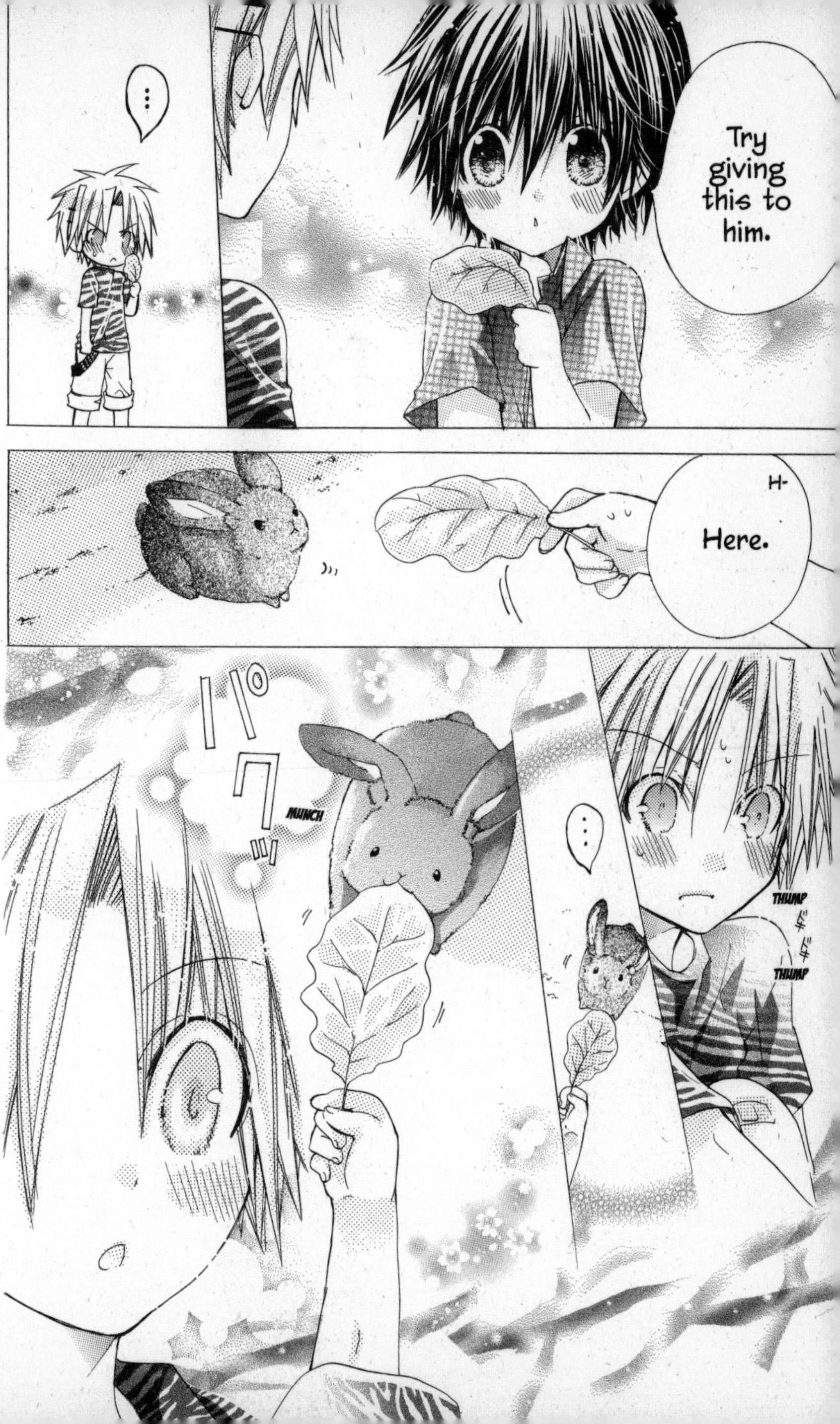

Try giving this to him.
…
H-
Here.
…
THUMP
THUMP
パク
MUNCH

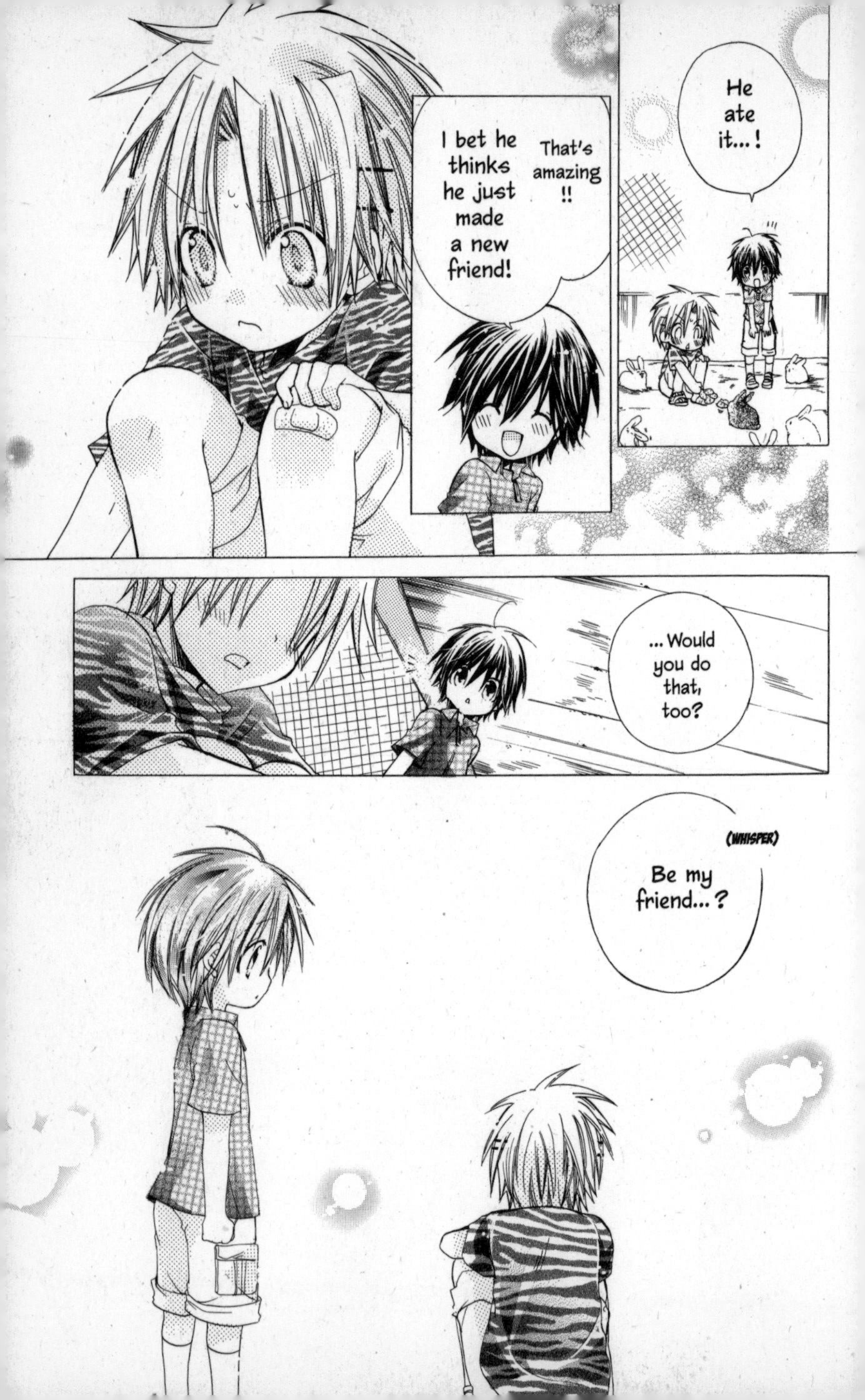
He ate it...!
That's amazing!!
I bet he thinks he just made a new friend!
...Would you do that, too?
(WHISPER)
Be my friend...?

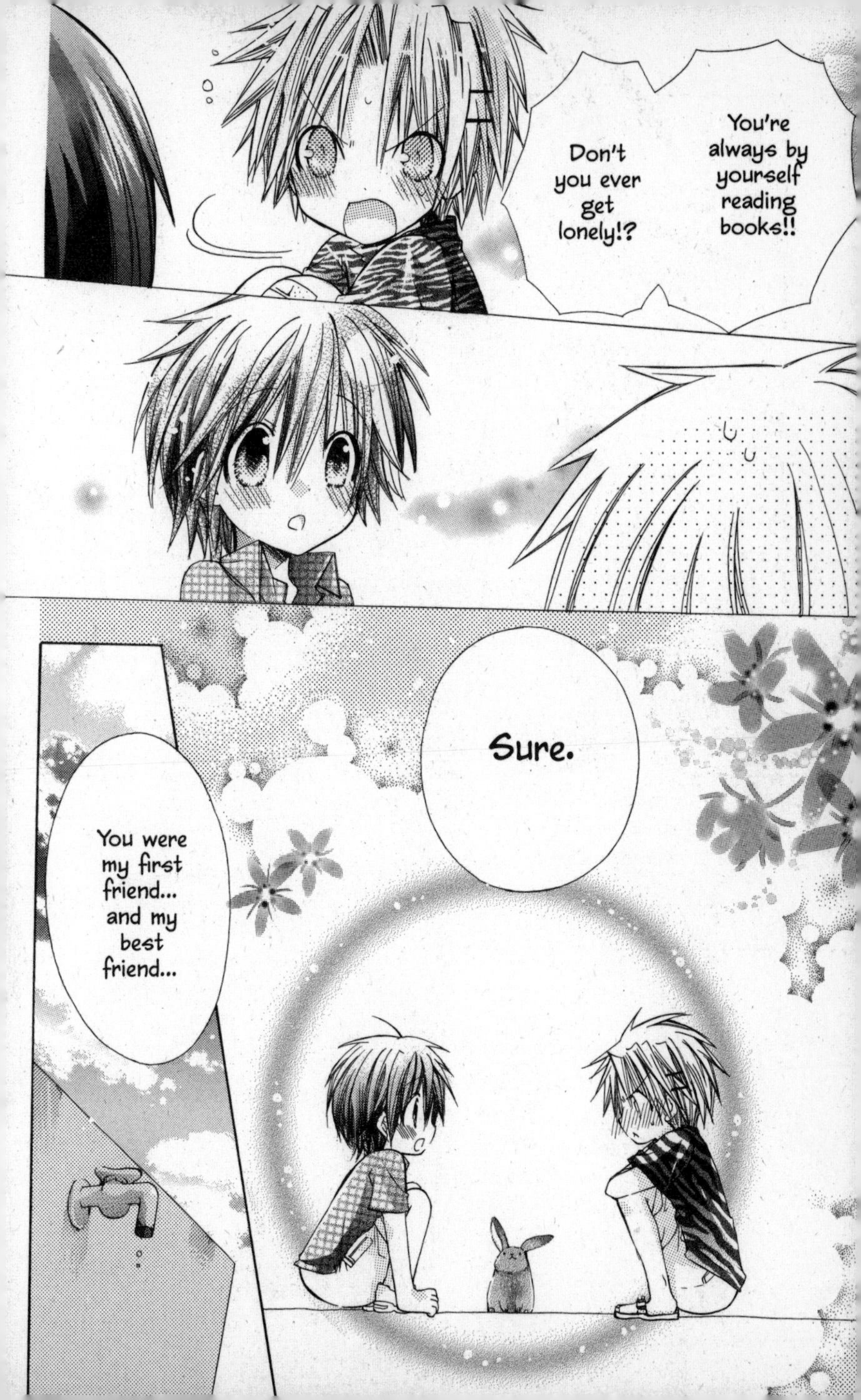

You're always by yourself reading books!!
Don't you ever get lonely!?
Sure.
You were my first friend... and my best friend...

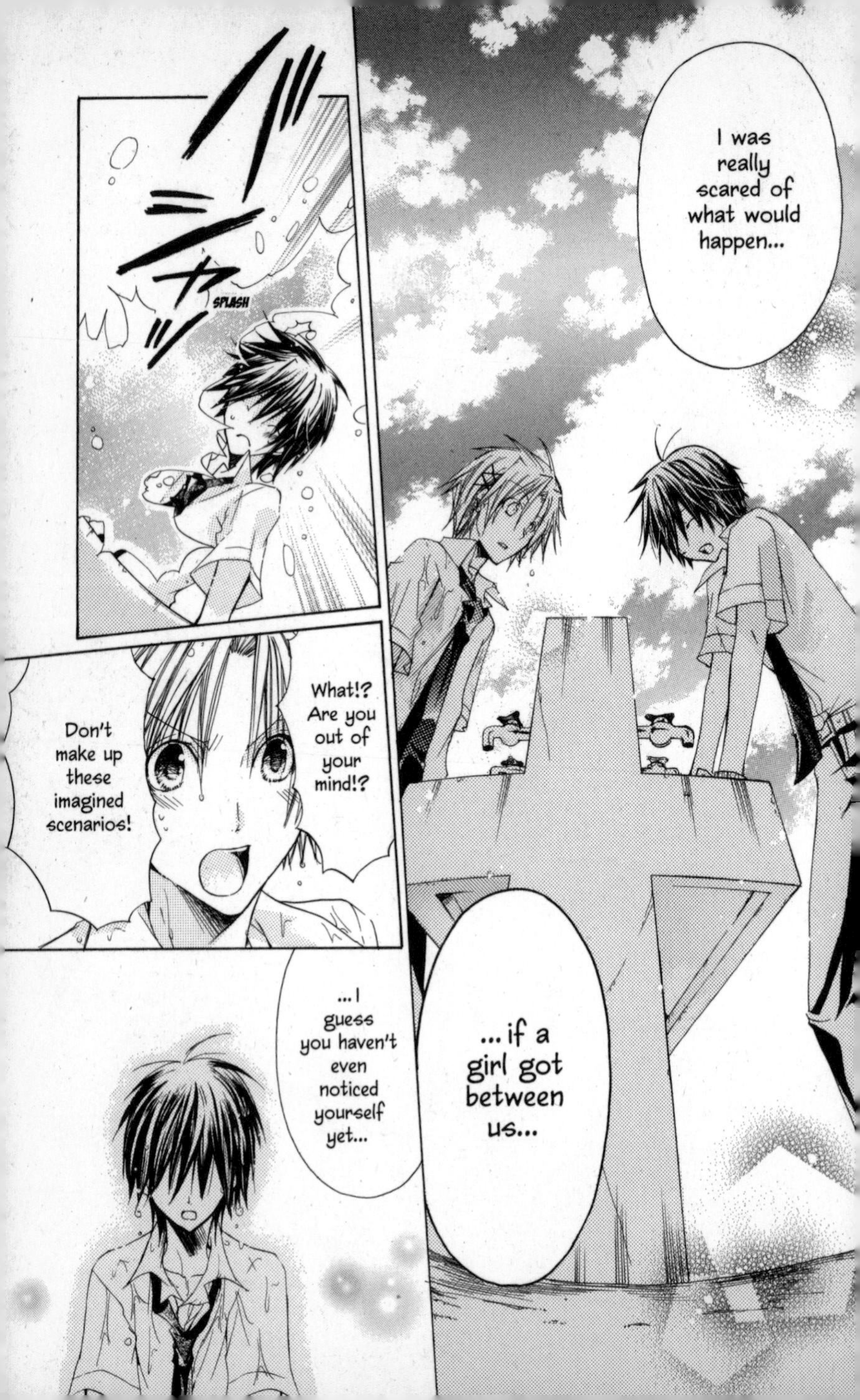

I was really scared of what would happen...
...if a girl got between us...
SPLASH
What!? Are you out of your mind!?
Don't make up these imagined scenarios!
...I guess you haven't even noticed yourself yet...

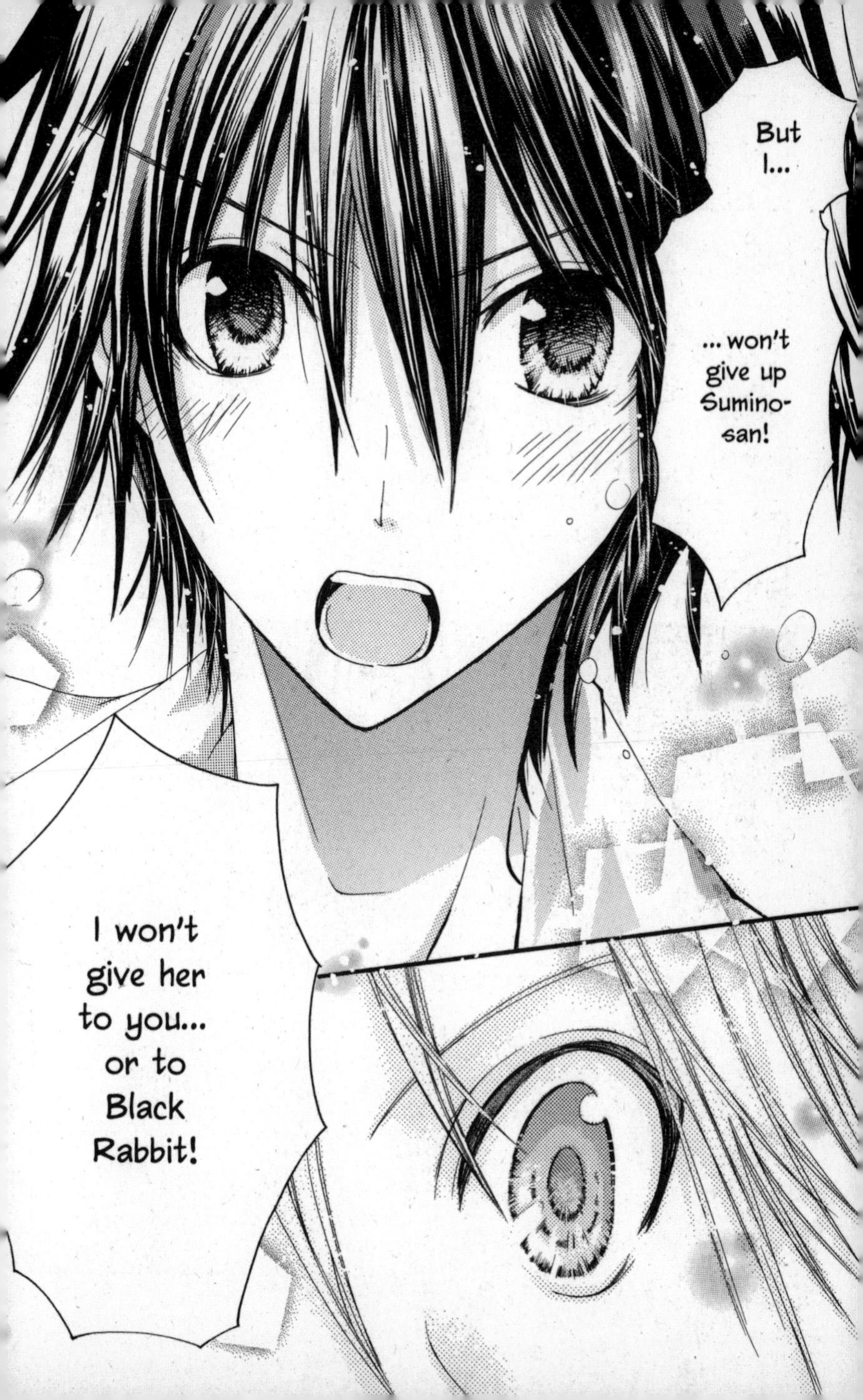
But I...
...won't give up Sumino-san!
I won't give her to you... or to Black Rabbit!

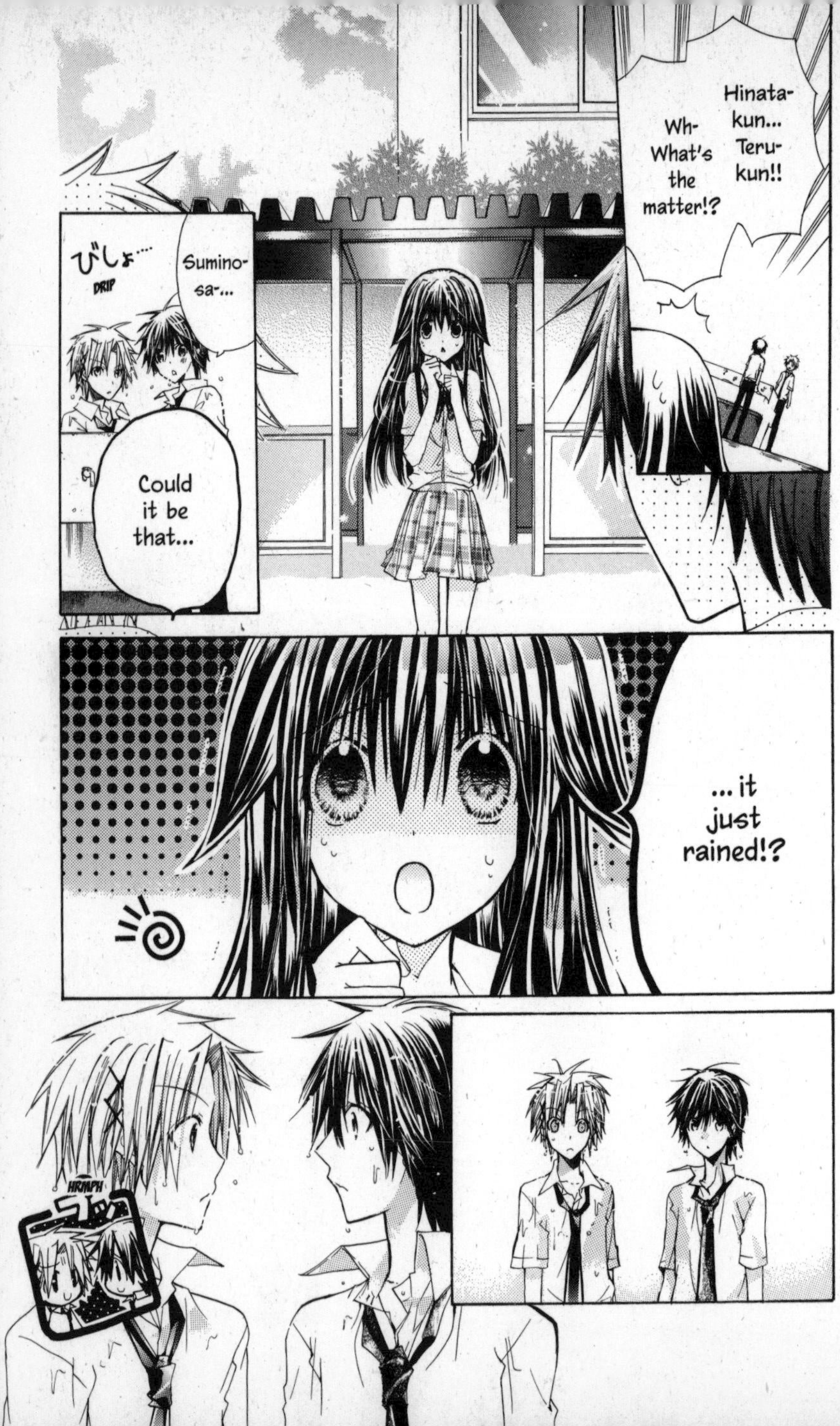
Hinata-kun... Teru-kun!!
Wh- What's the matter!?
Sumino-sa-...
びしょ…
DRIP
Could it be that...
... it just rained!?
HRMPH

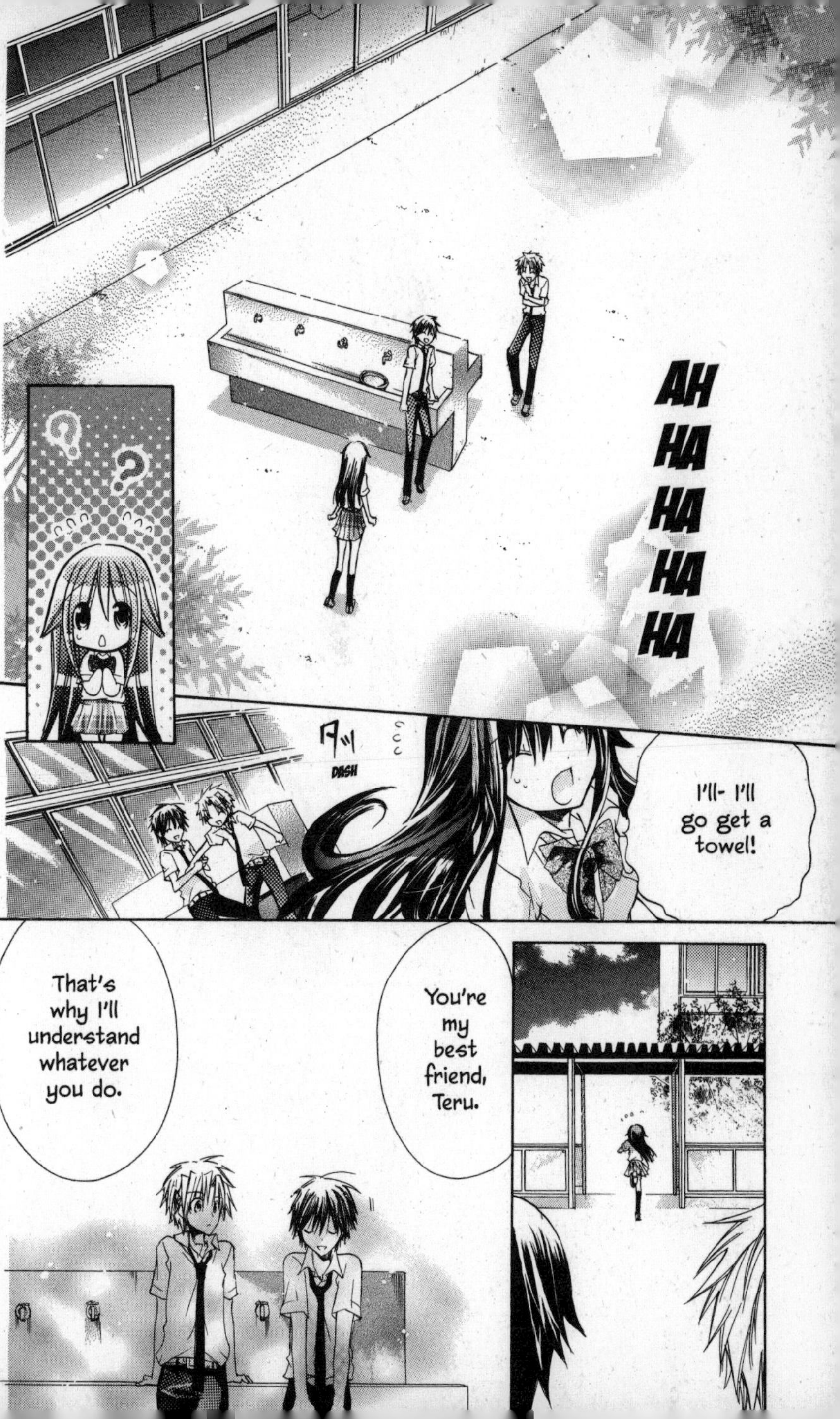
AH HA HA HA HA
I'll- I'll go get a towel!
タッ
DASH
You're my best friend, Teru.
That's why I'll understand whatever you do.

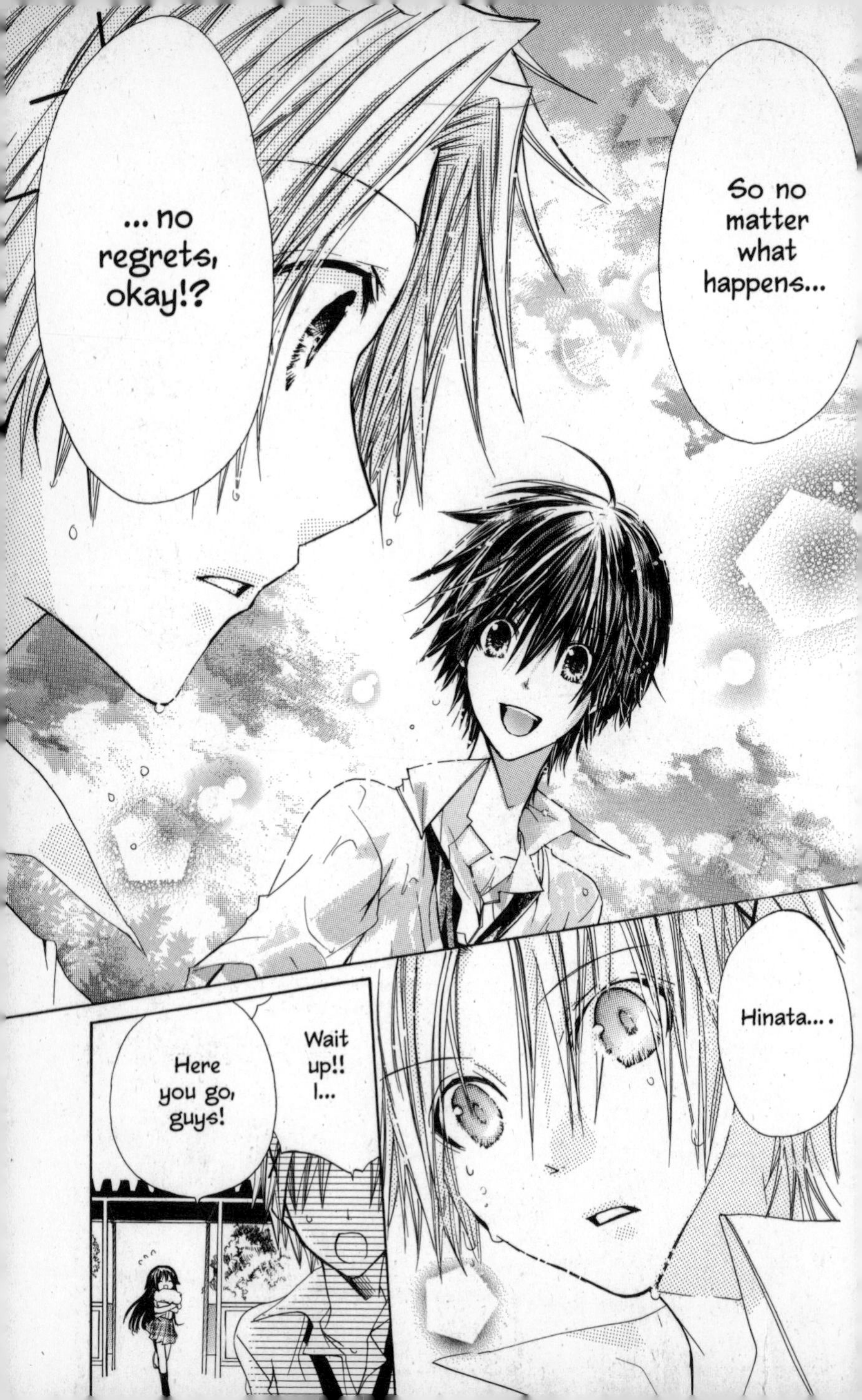
So no matter what happens...
... no regrets, okay!?
Hinata....
Wait up!! I...
Here you go, guys!

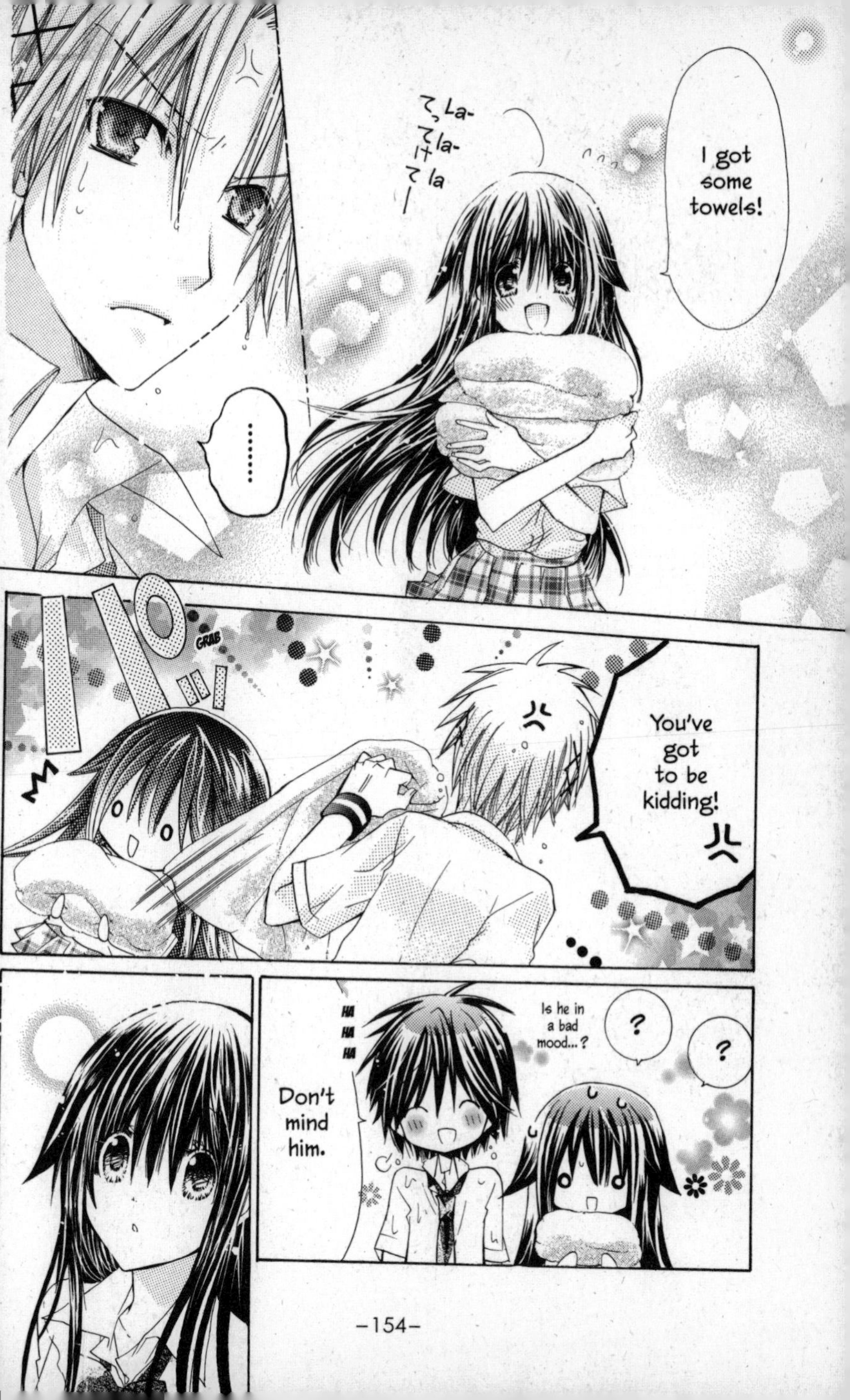
I got some towels!
てってけてー
La- la- la
......
You've got to be kidding!
GRAB
Is he in a bad mood...?
?
?
HA HA HA
Don't mind him.

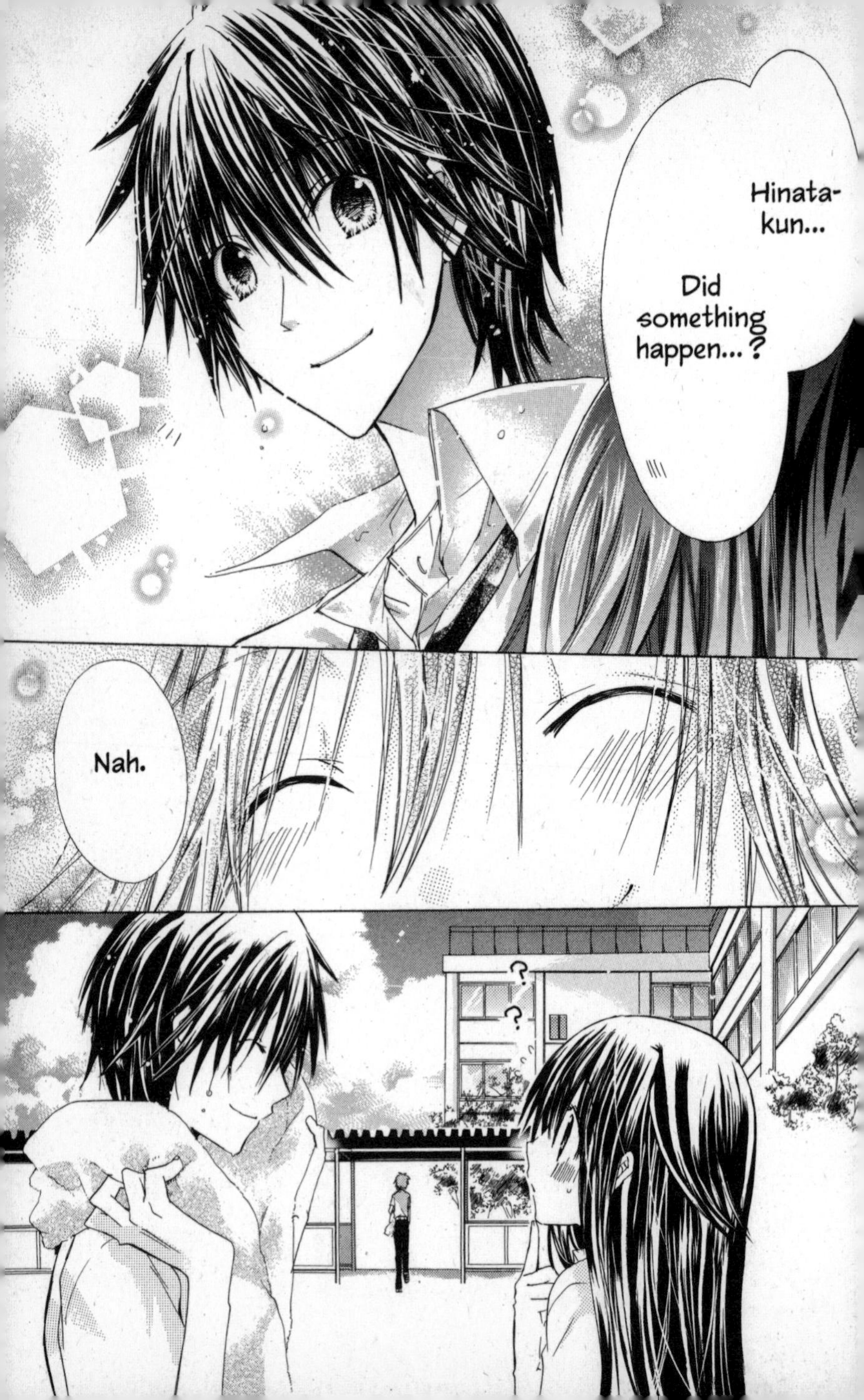
Hinata-kun...
Did something happen...?
Nah.

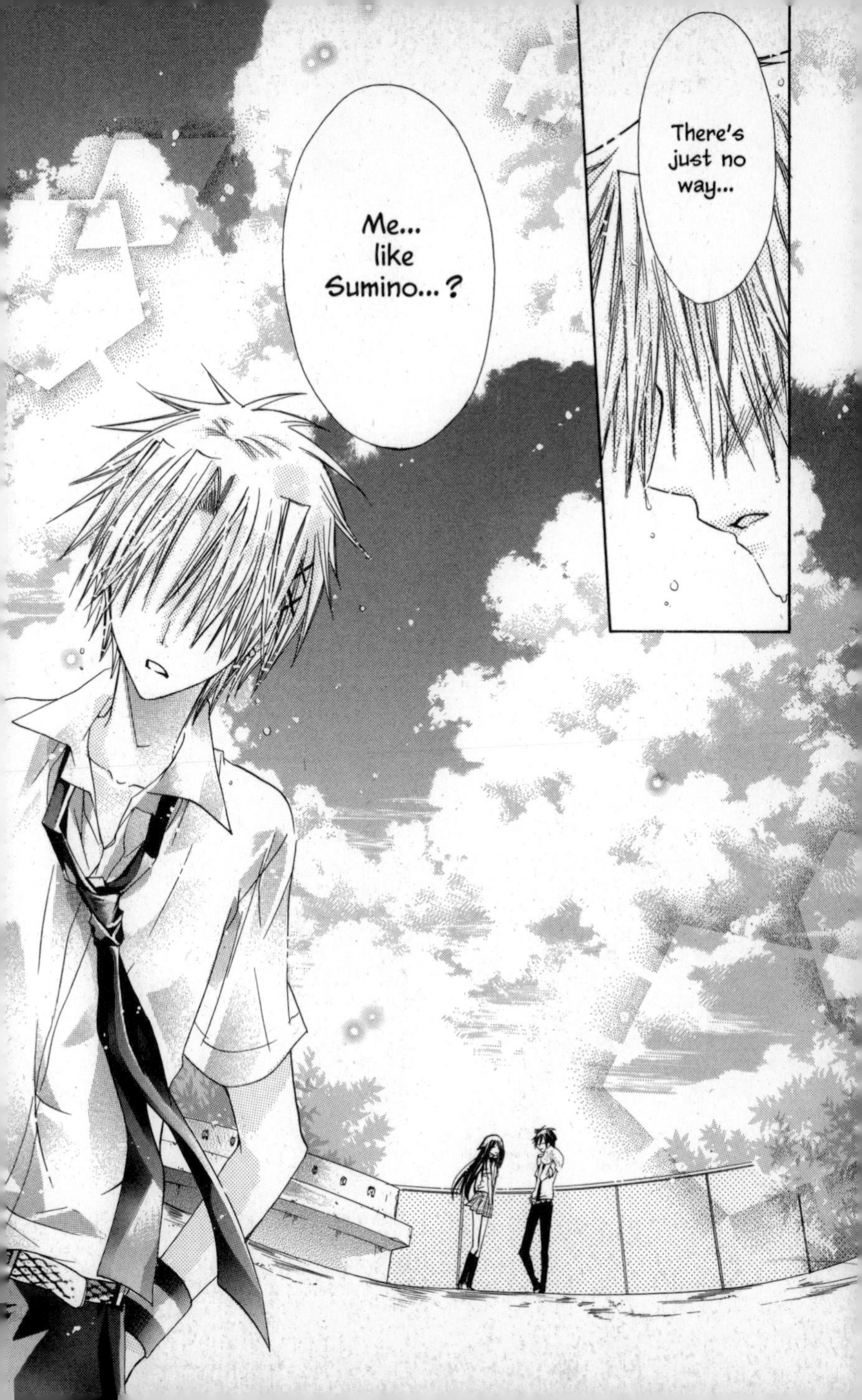
There's just no way...
Me... like Sumino...?

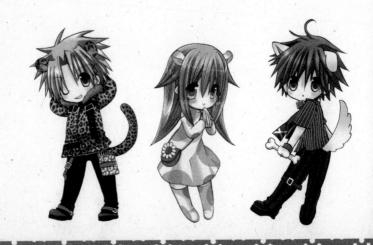

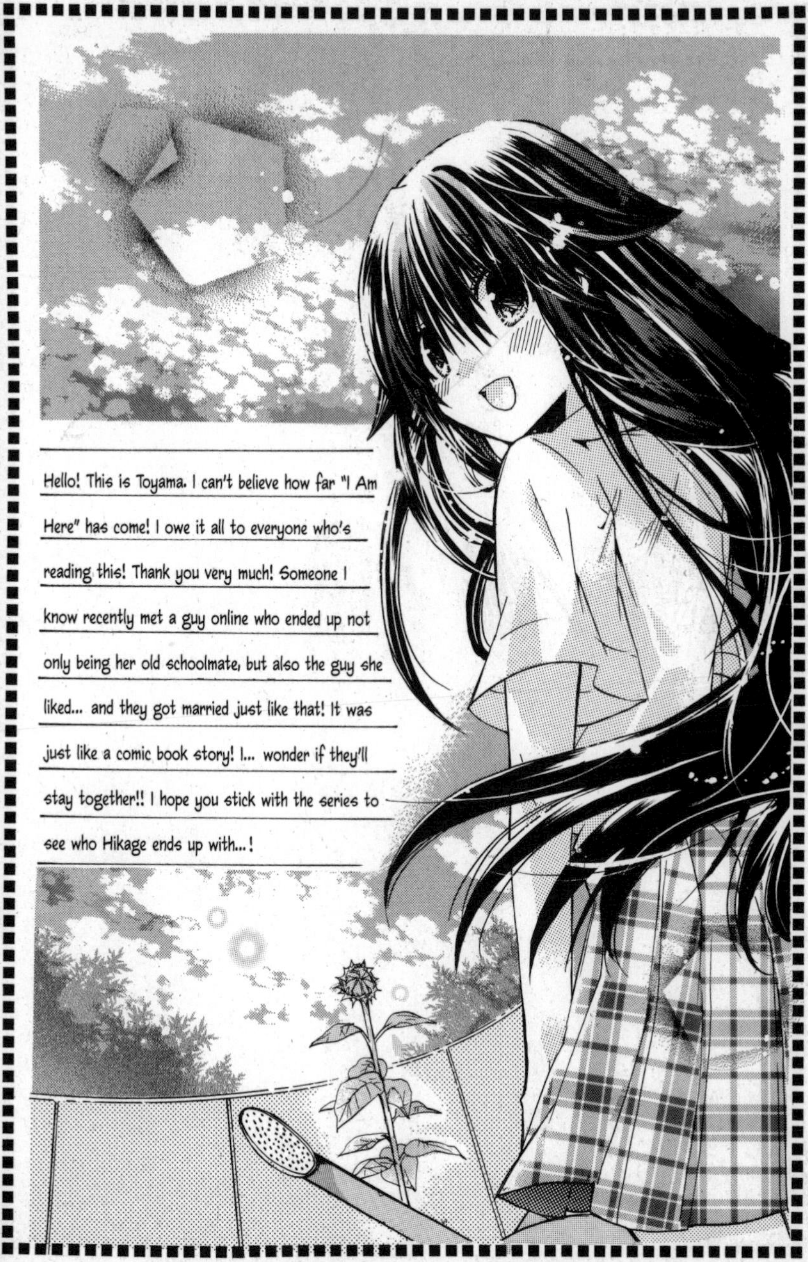
Hello! This is Toyama. I can't believe how far "I Am Here" has come! I owe it all to everyone who's reading this! Thank you very much! Someone I know recently met a guy online who ended up not only being her old schoolmate, but also the guy she liked... and they got married just like that! It was just like a comic book story! I... wonder if they'll stay together!! I hope you stick with the series to see who Hikage ends up with...!

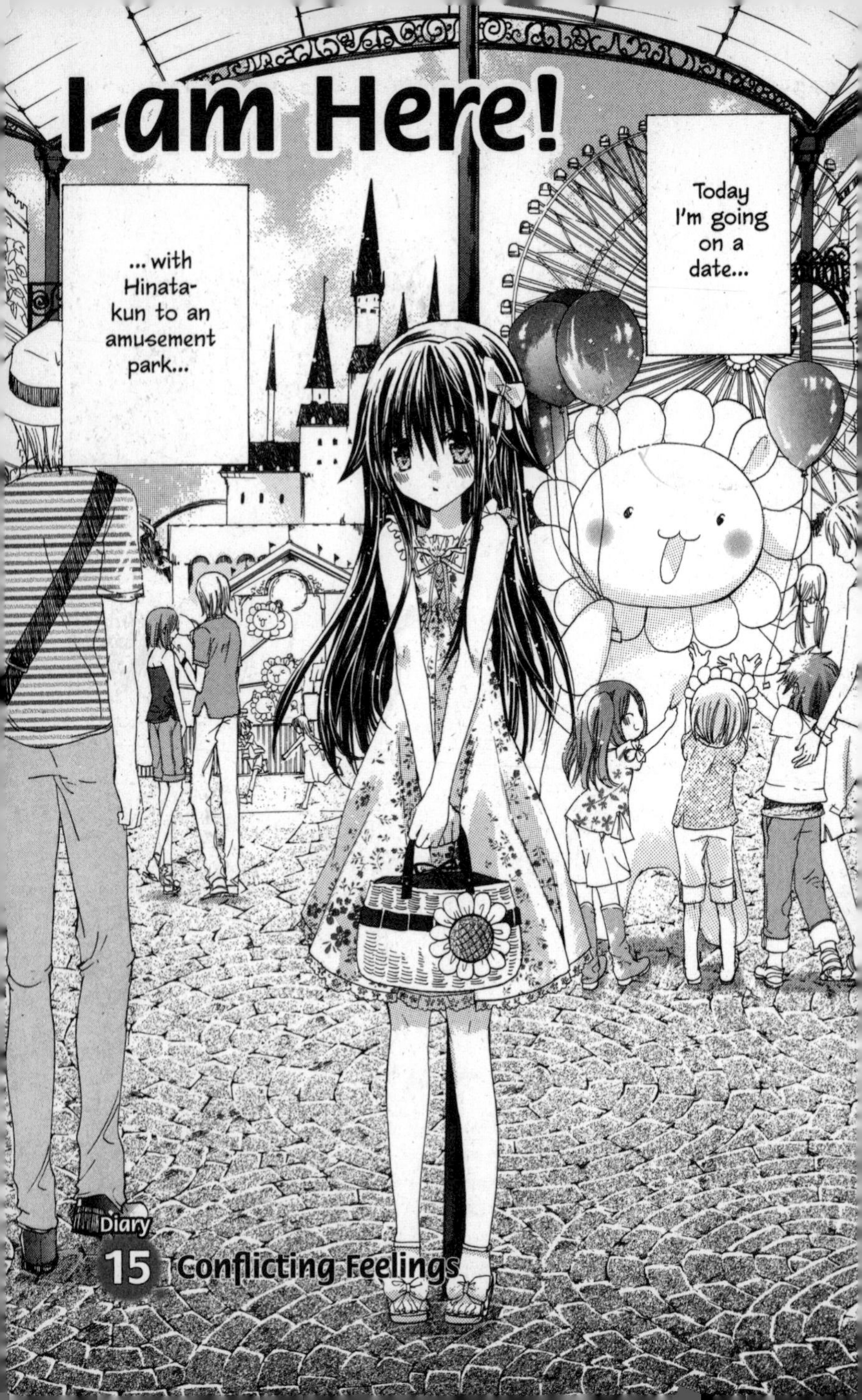
I am Here!
Today I'm going on a date...
... with Hinata-kun to an amusement park...
Diary 15 Conflicting Feelings

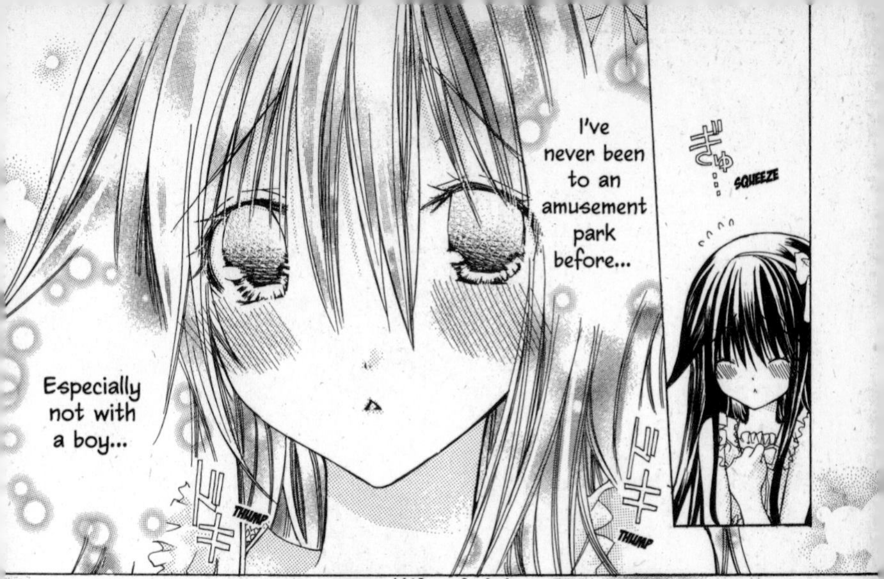
ぎゅ…
SQUEEZE
I've never been to an amusement park before...
Especially not with a boy...
ドキ
THUMP
ドキ
THUMP

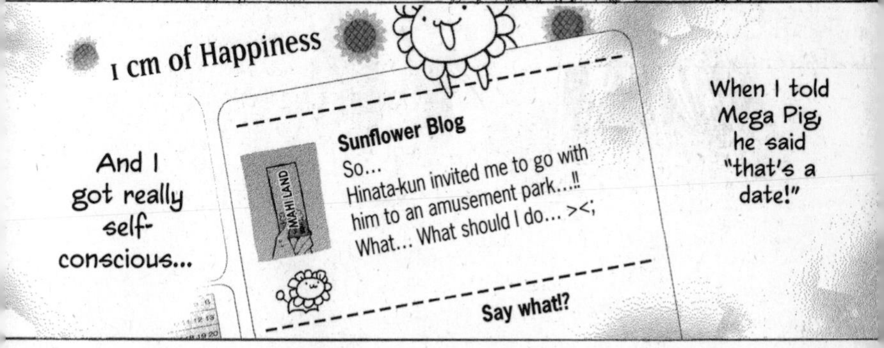
When I told Mega Pig, he said "that's a date!"
1 cm of Happiness
Sunflower Blog
MAHI LAND
So...
Hinata-kun invited me to go with him to an amusement park...!!
What... What should I do... ><;
Say what!?
And I got really self-conscious...

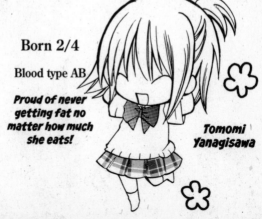

Born 2/4

Blood type AB

Proud of never getting fat no matter how much she eats!

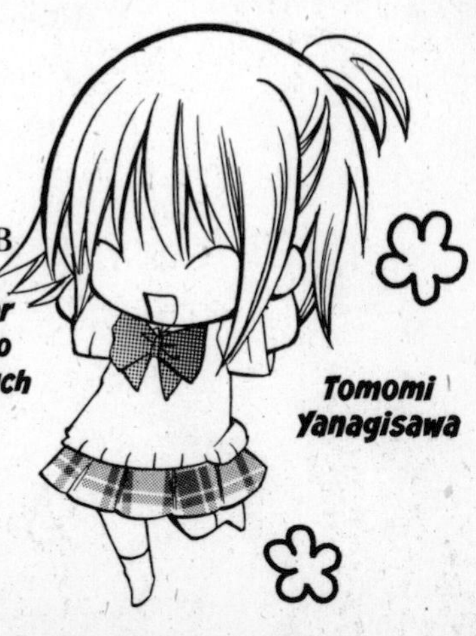

Tomomi Yanagisawa

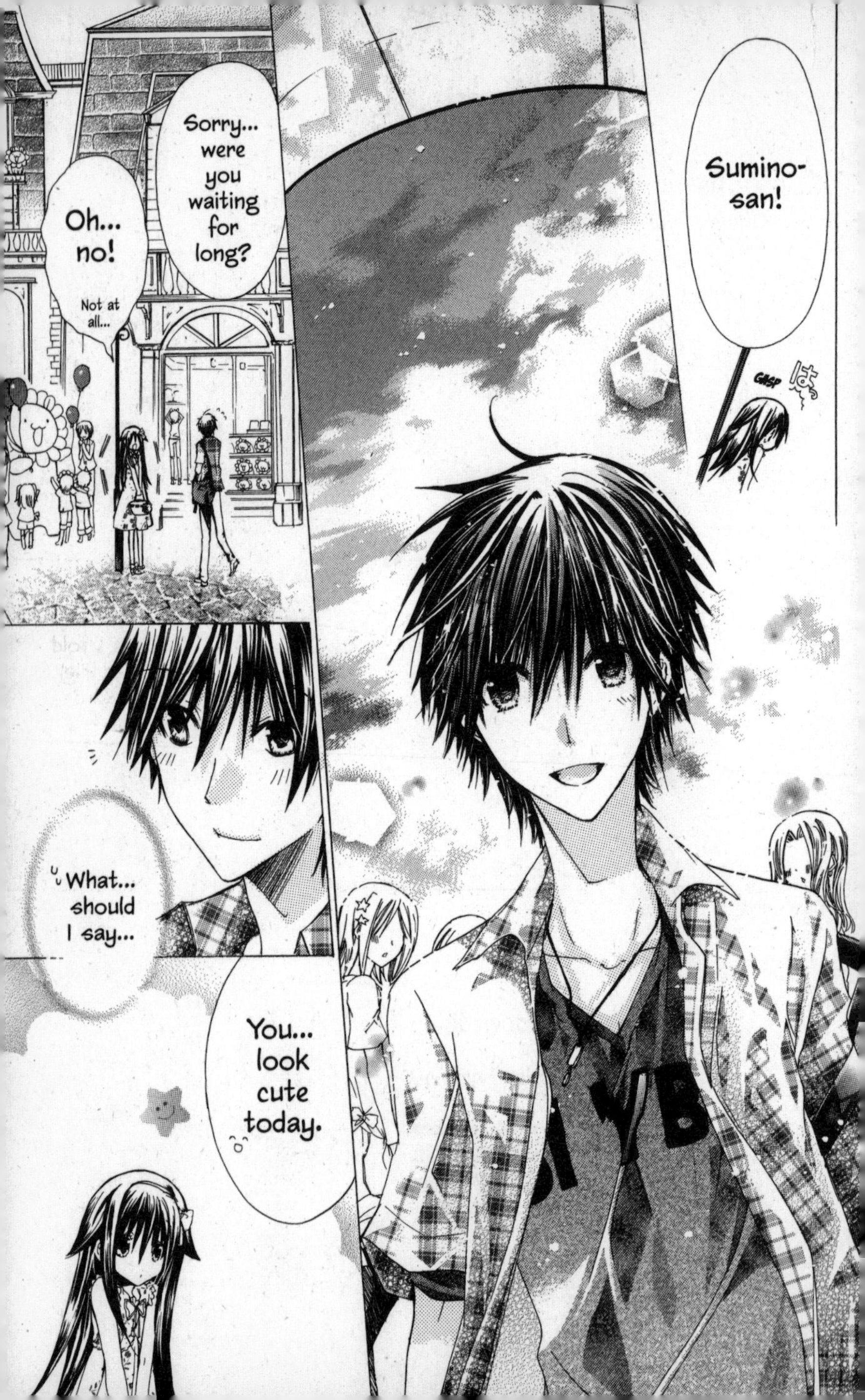

Sumino-san!
GASP
はっ
Sorry... were you waiting for long?
Oh... no!
Not at all...
What... should I say...
You... look cute today.

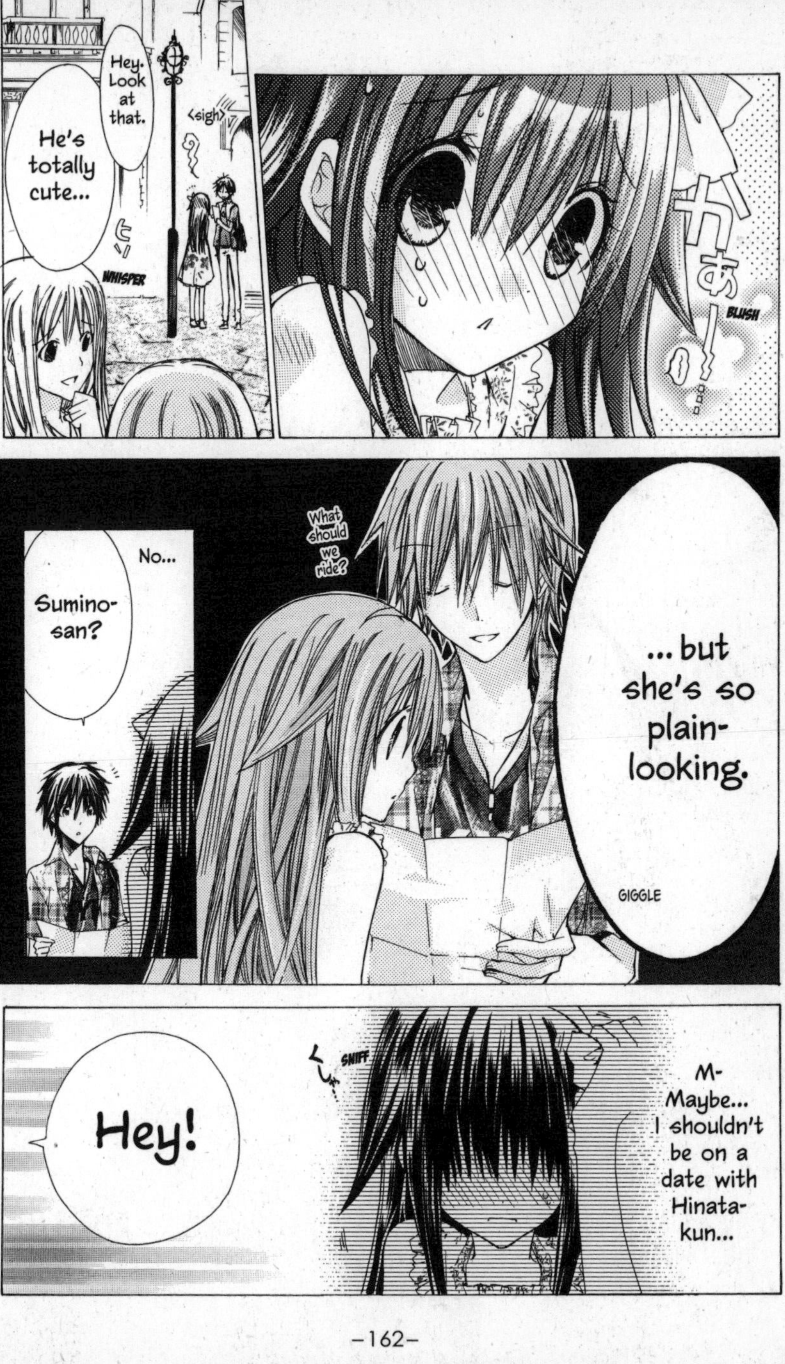
BLUSH
Hey. Look at that.
He's totally cute...
<sigh>
WHISPER
...but she's so plain-looking.
GIGGLE
What should we ride?
No...
Sumino-san?
M-Maybe... I shouldn't be on a date with Hinata-kun...
SNIFF
Hey!

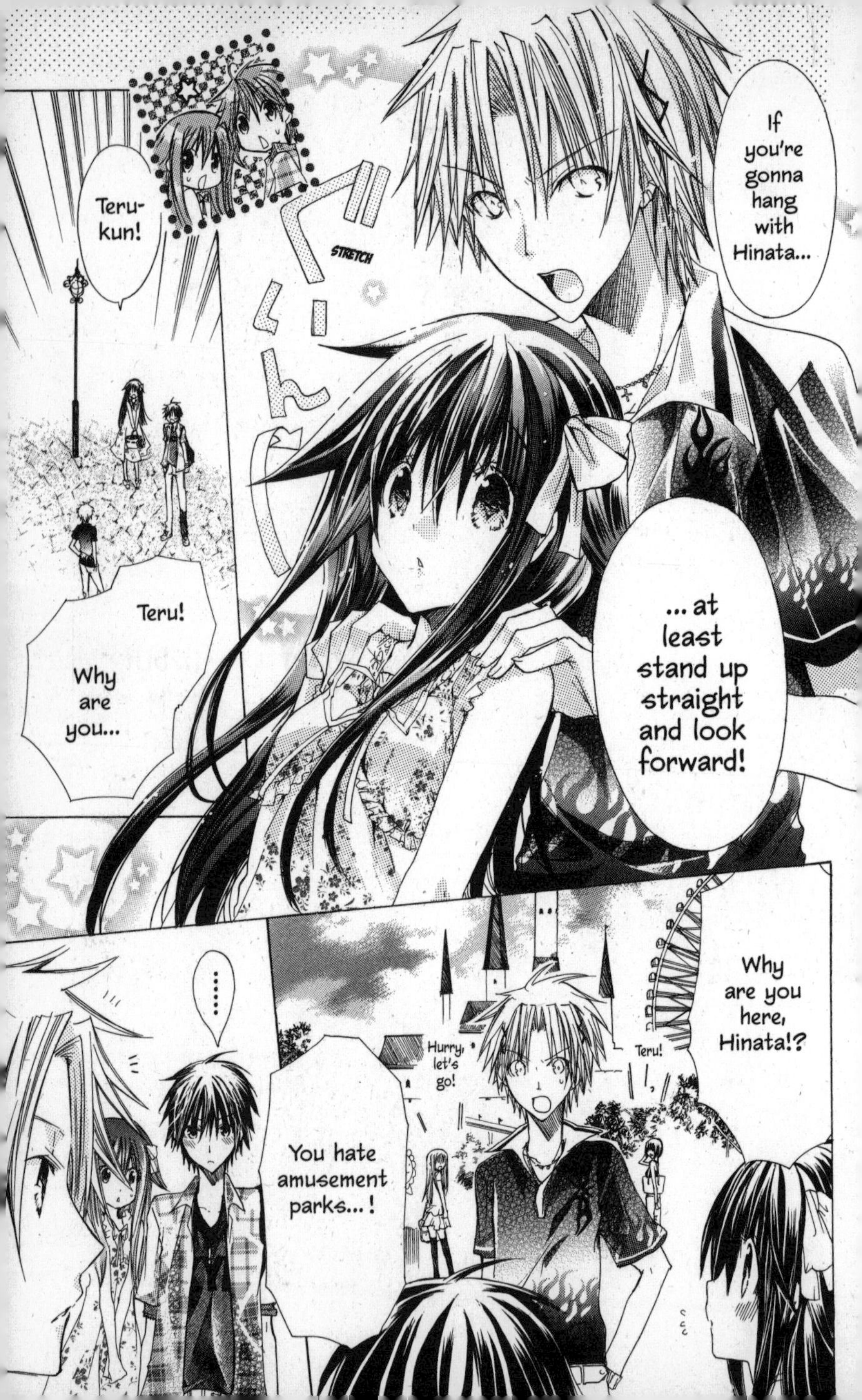

If you're gonna hang with Hinata...
STRETCH
... at least stand up straight and look forward!
Teru-kun!
Teru!
Why are you...
Why are you here, Hinata!?
Teru!
Hurry, let's go!
You hate amusement parks...!
......

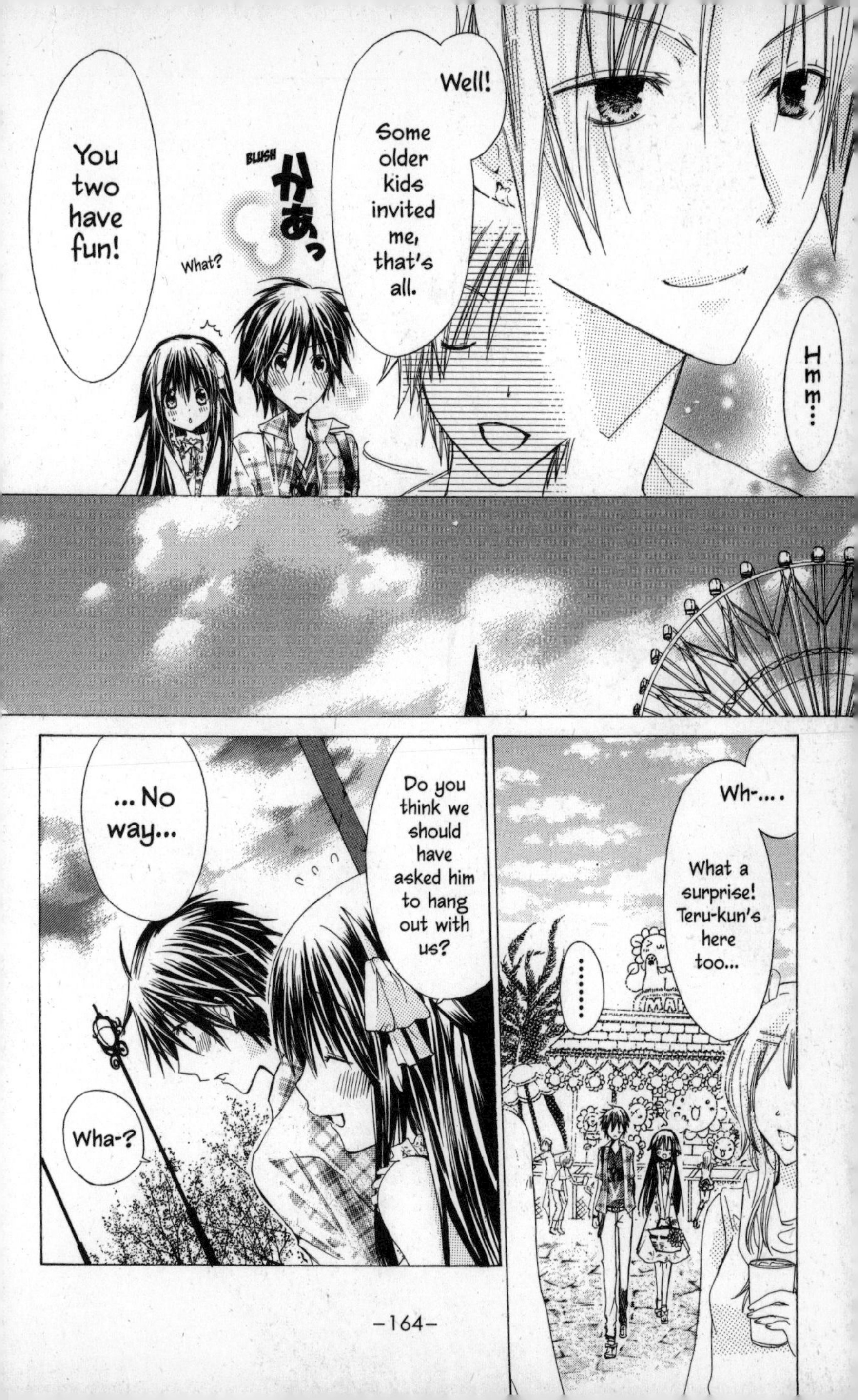
Hmm...
Well!
Some older kids invited me, that's all.
BLUSH
かあっ
What?
You two have fun!
Wh-....
What a surprise! Teru-kun's here too...
......
Do you think we should have asked him to hang out with us?
... No way...
Wha-?

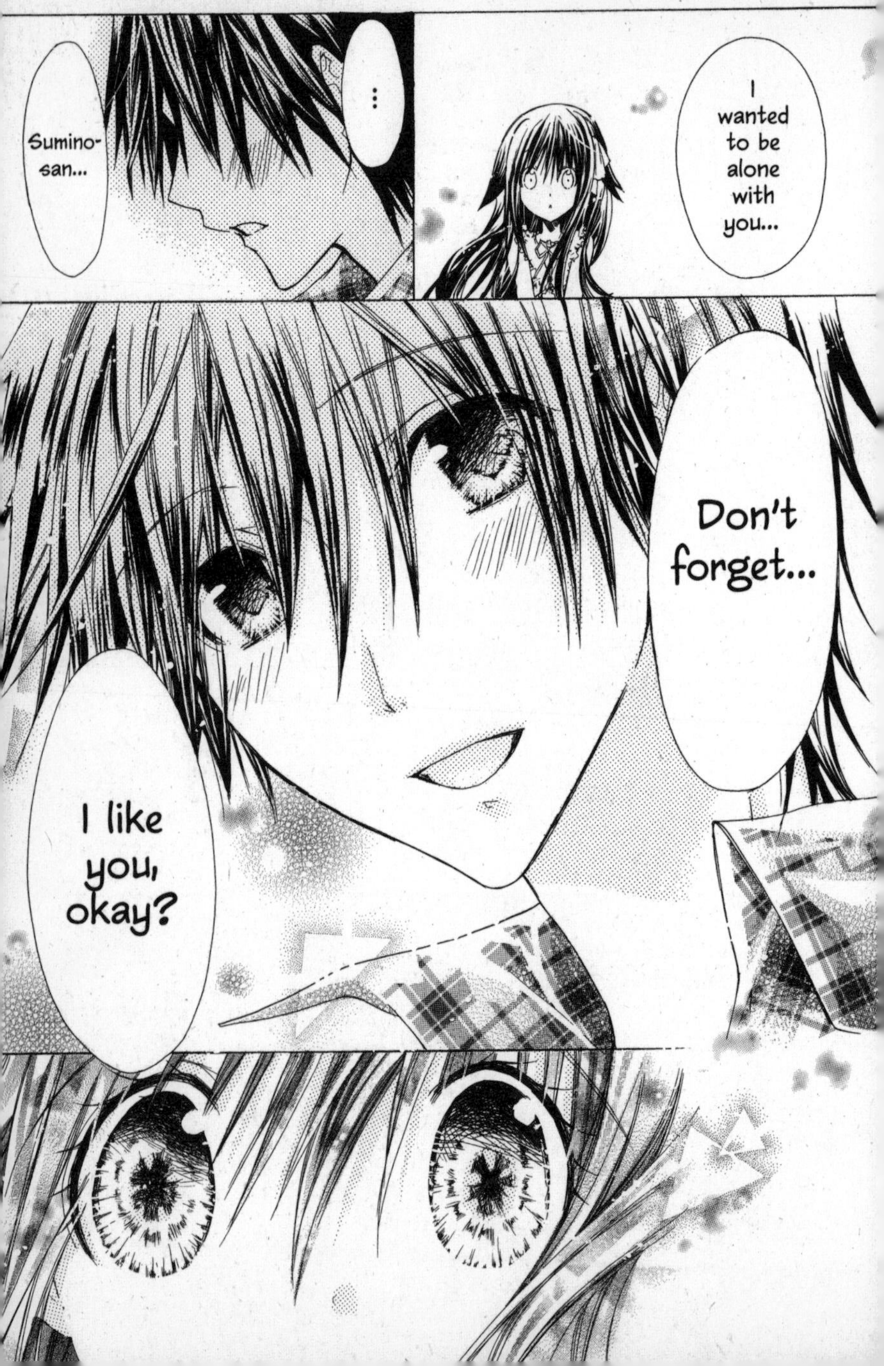
I wanted to be alone with you...
...
Sumino-san...
Don't forget...
I like you, okay?

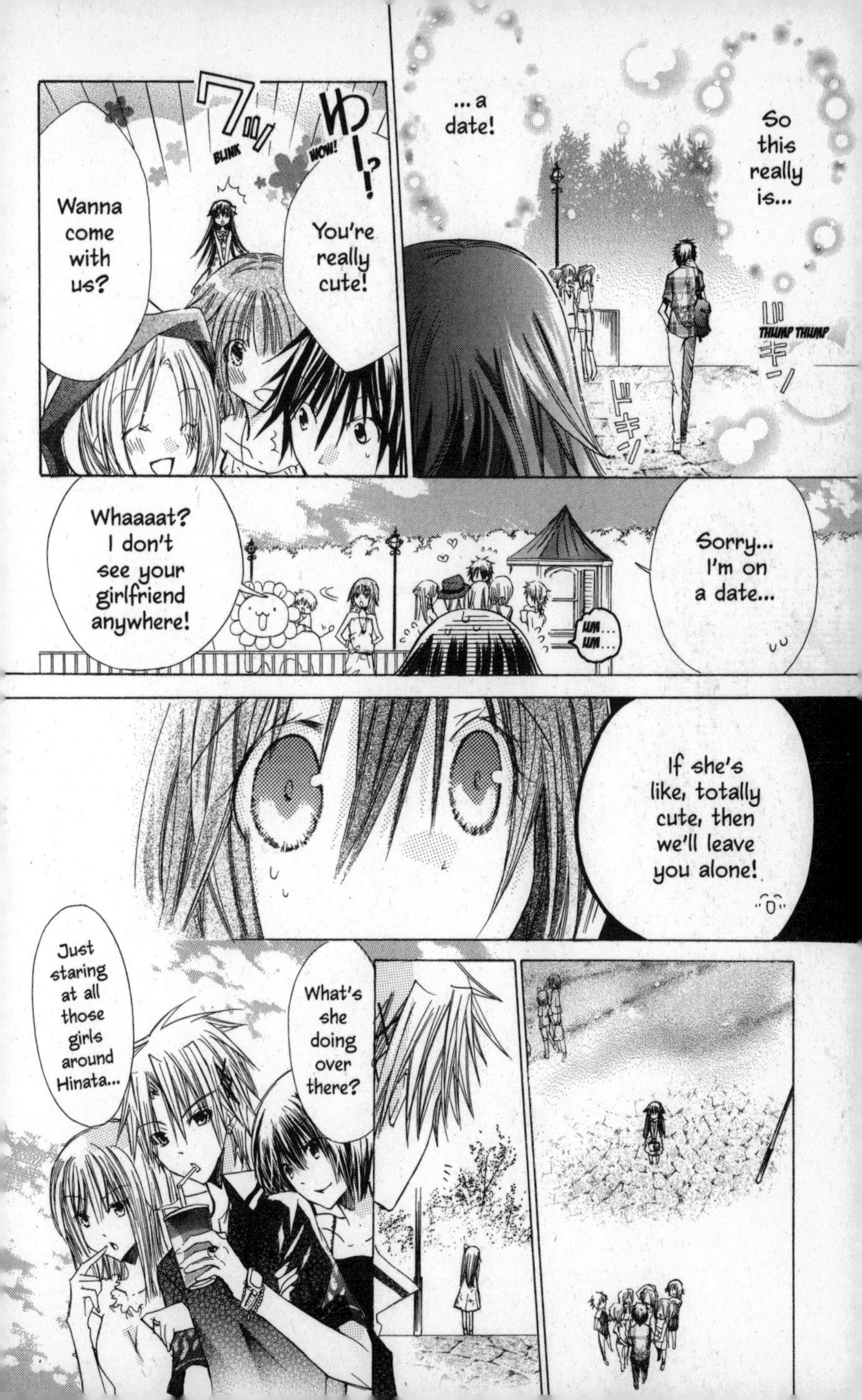

So this really is...
... a date!
THUMP THUMP
WOW!
BLINK
You're really cute!
Wanna come with us?
Sorry... I'm on a date...
UM... UM...
Whaaaat? I don't see your girlfriend anywhere!
If she's like, totally cute, then we'll leave you alone!
What's she doing over there?
Just staring at all those girls around Hinata...

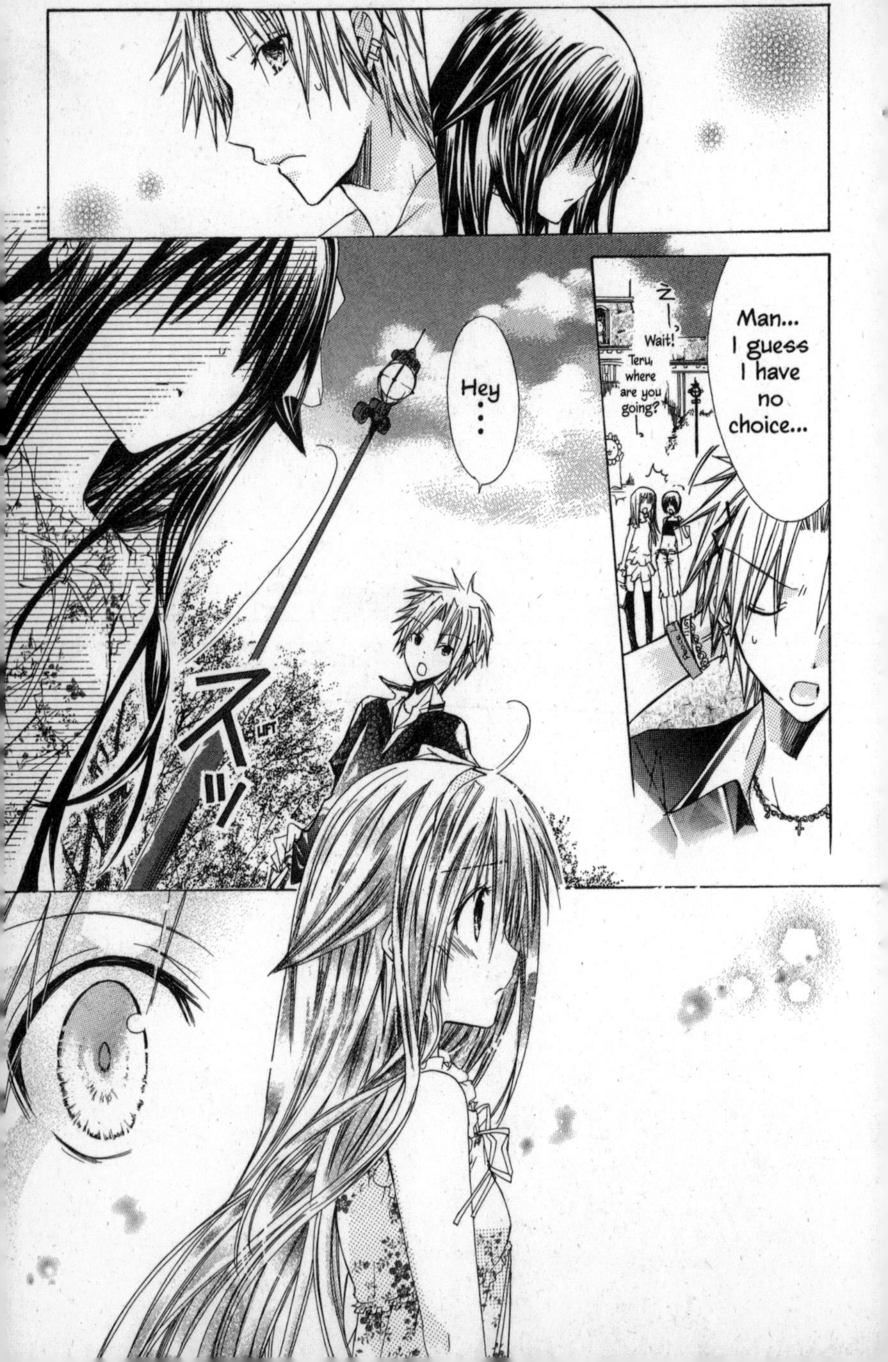
Man... I guess I have no choice...
Wait! Teru, where are you going?
Hey...
LIFT

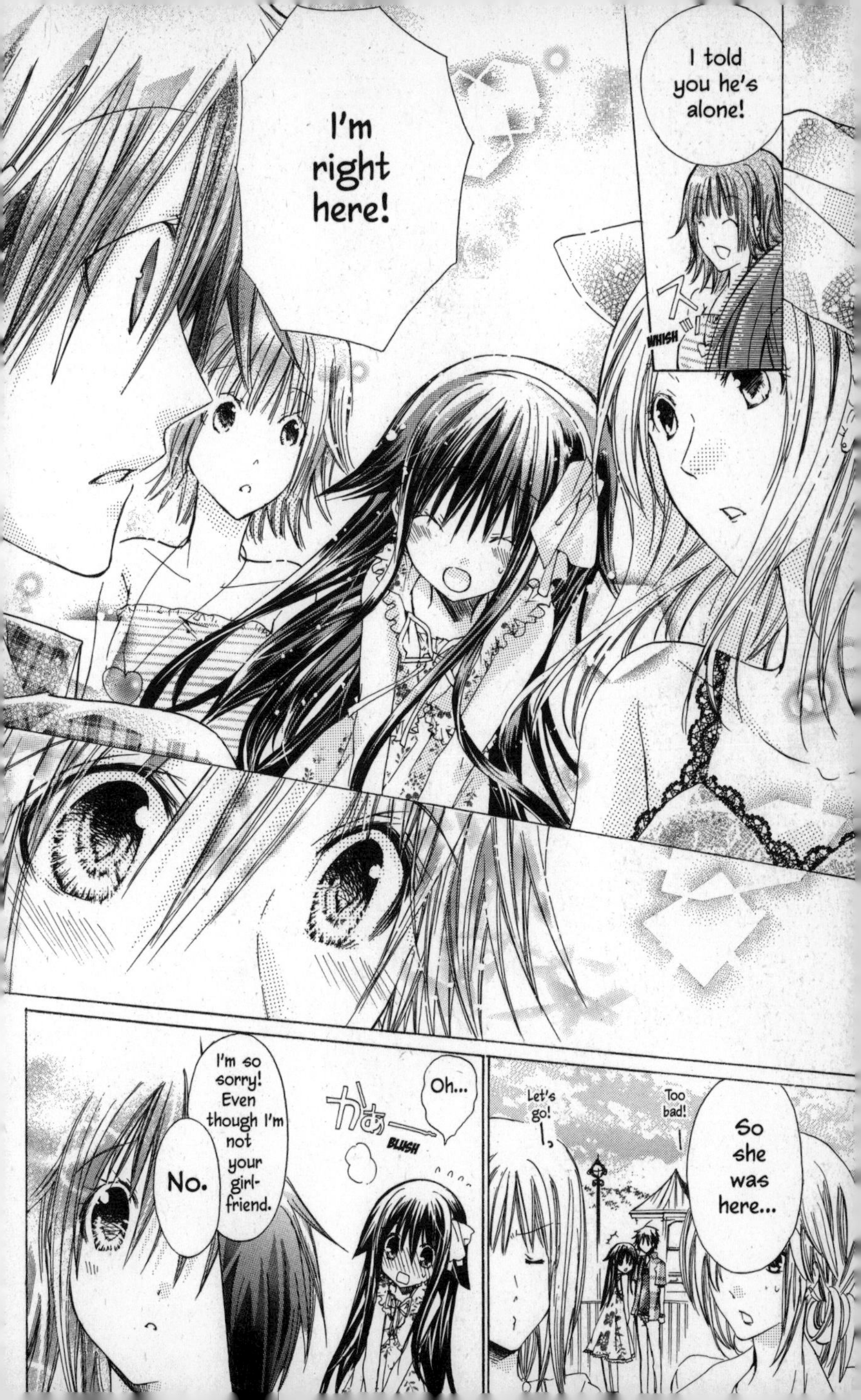
I told you he's alone!
WHISH
I'm right here!
So she was here...
Too bad!
Let's go!
Oh...
BLUSH
I'm so sorry! Even though I'm not your girlfriend.
No.

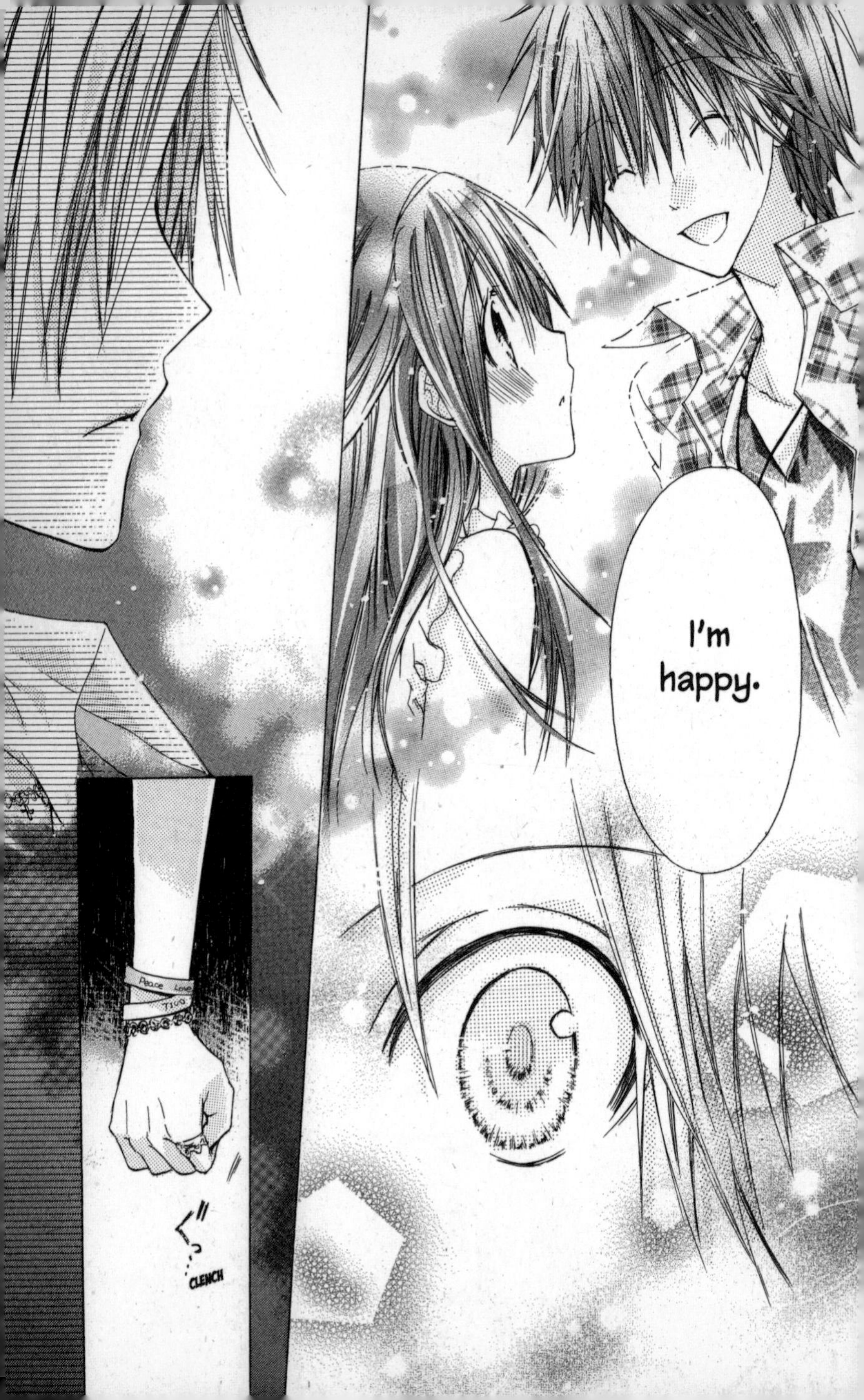
I'm happy.
Peace Love
CLENCH

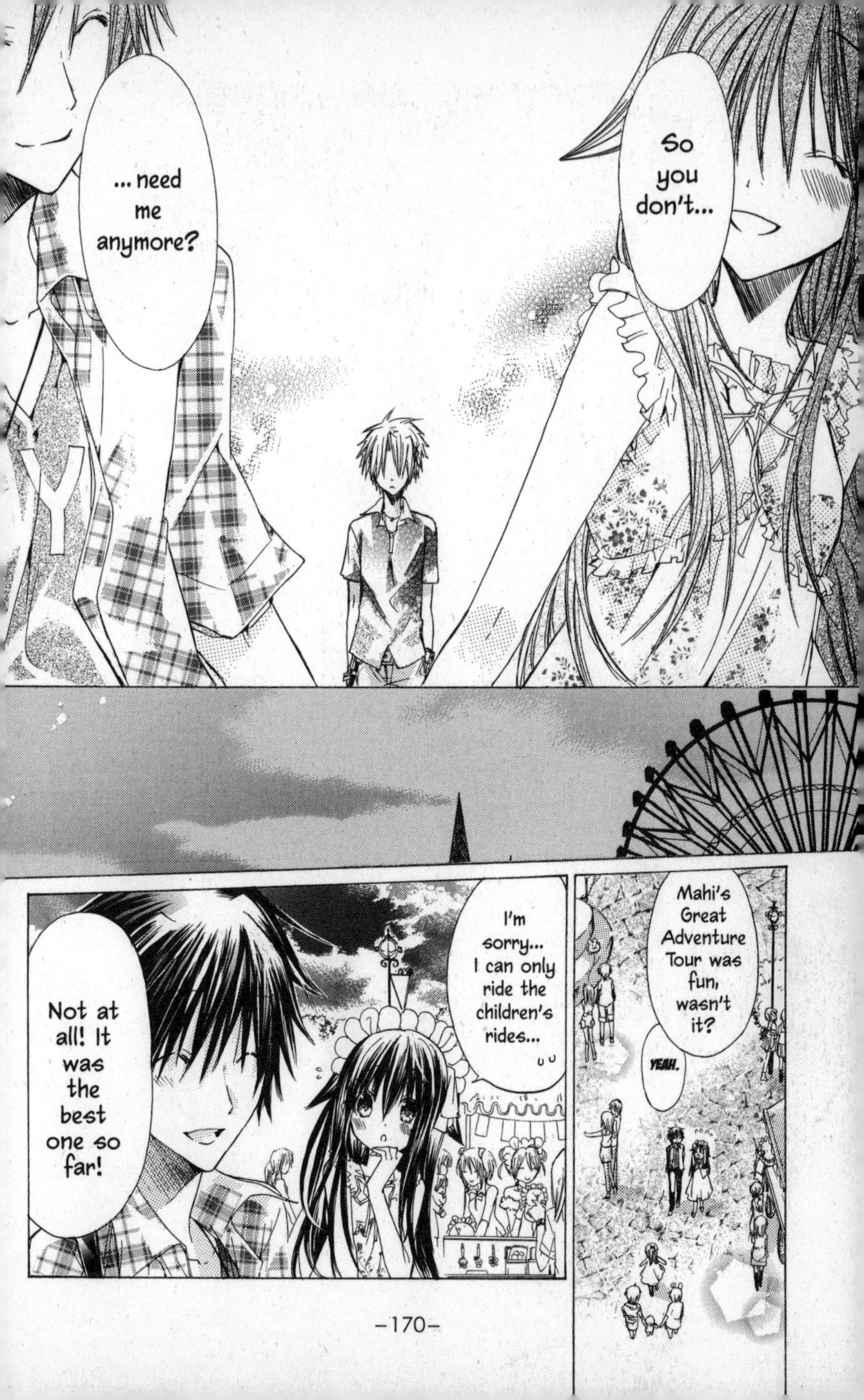
So you don't...
...need me anymore?
Mahi's Great Adventure Tour was fun, wasn't it?
YEAH.
I'm sorry... I can only ride the children's rides...
Not at all! It was the best one so far!

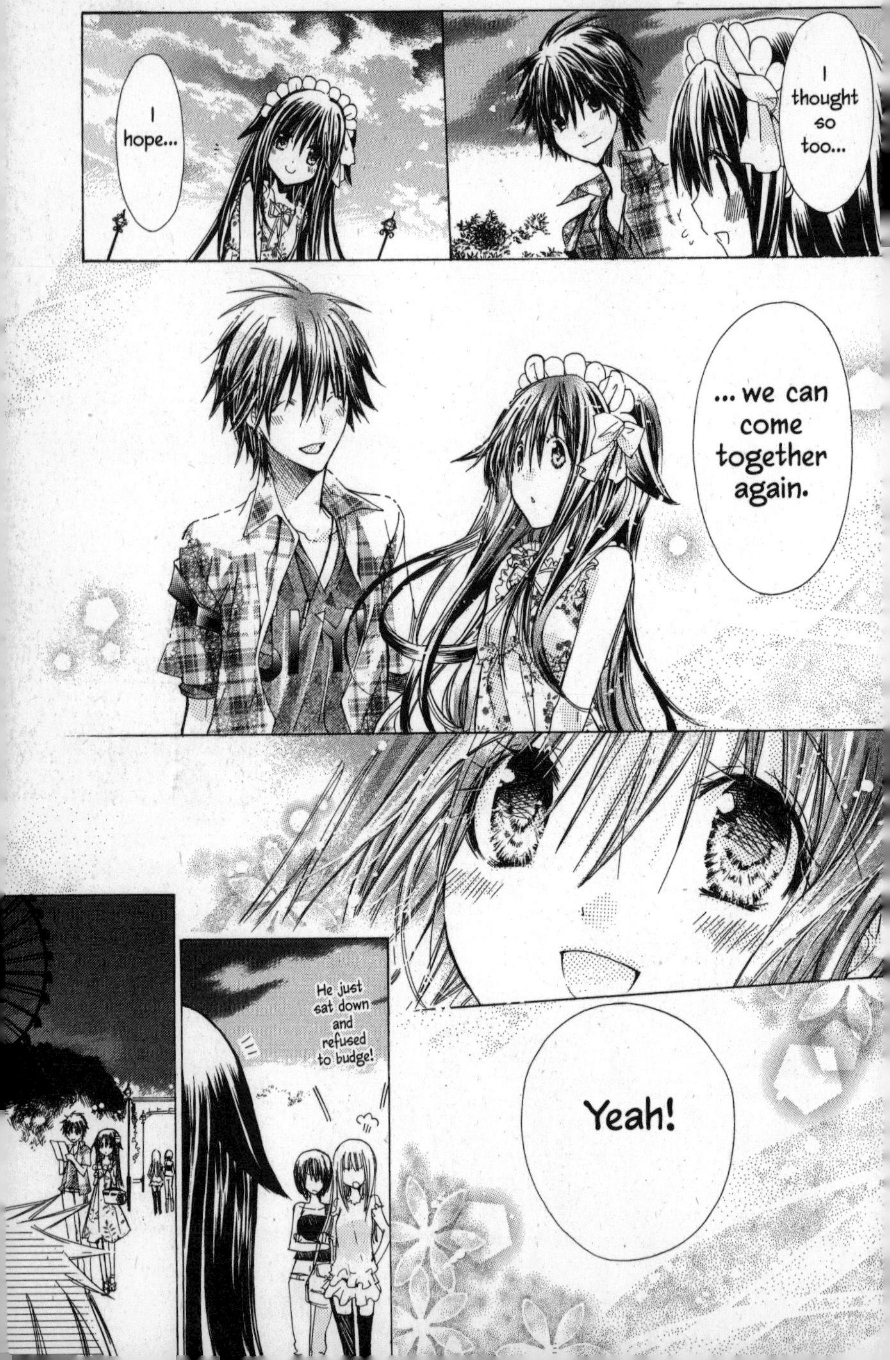
I thought so too...
I hope...
... we can come together again.
Yeah!
He just sat down and refused to budge!

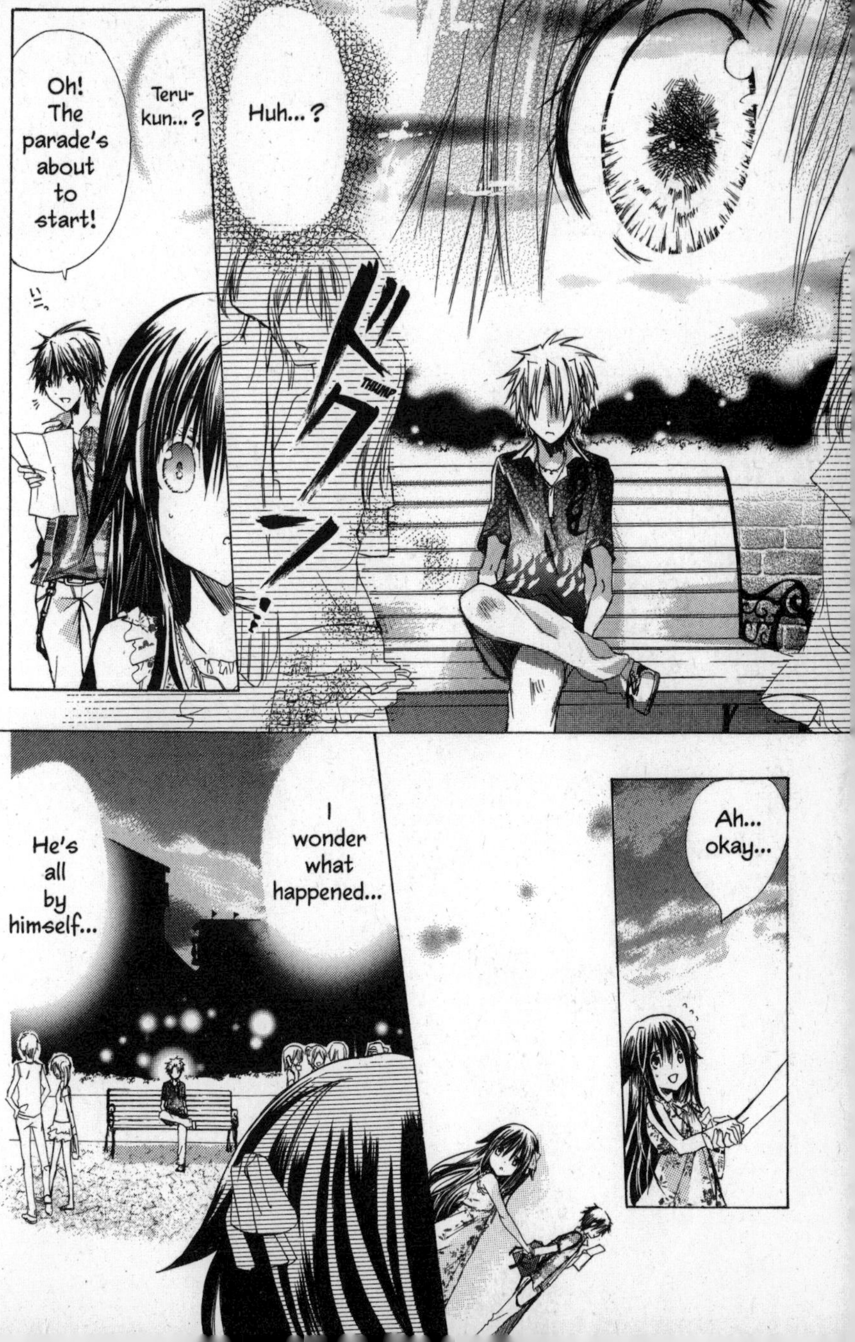
Huh...?
Teru-kun...?
THUMP
Oh! The parade's about to start!
Ah... okay...
I wonder what happened...
He's all by himself...

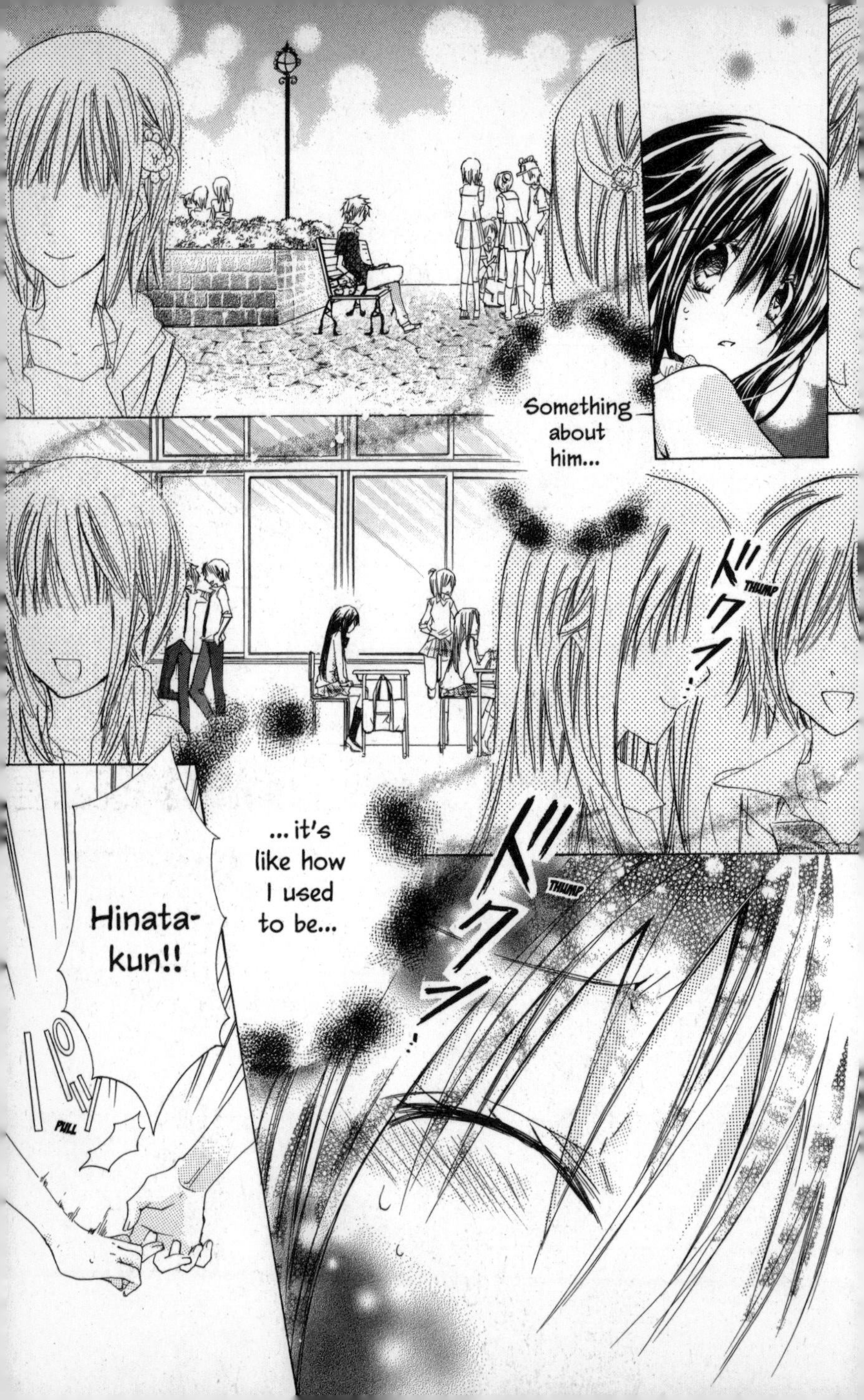
Something about him...
ドクン
THUMP
ドクン
THUMP
... it's like how I used to be...
Hinata-kun!!
PULL

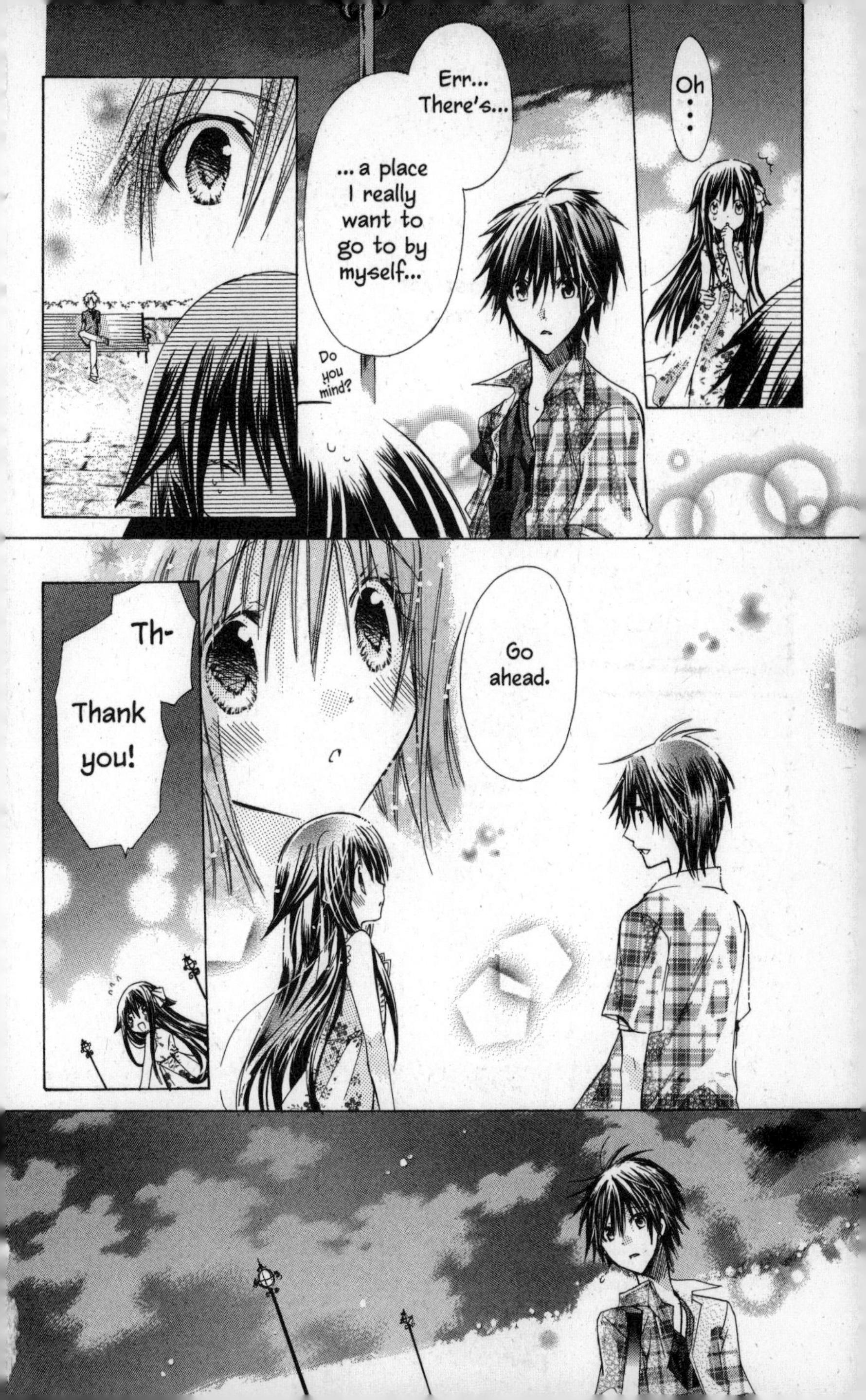
Oh...
Err... There's...
... a place I really want to go to by myself...
Do you mind?
Go ahead.
Th- Thank you!

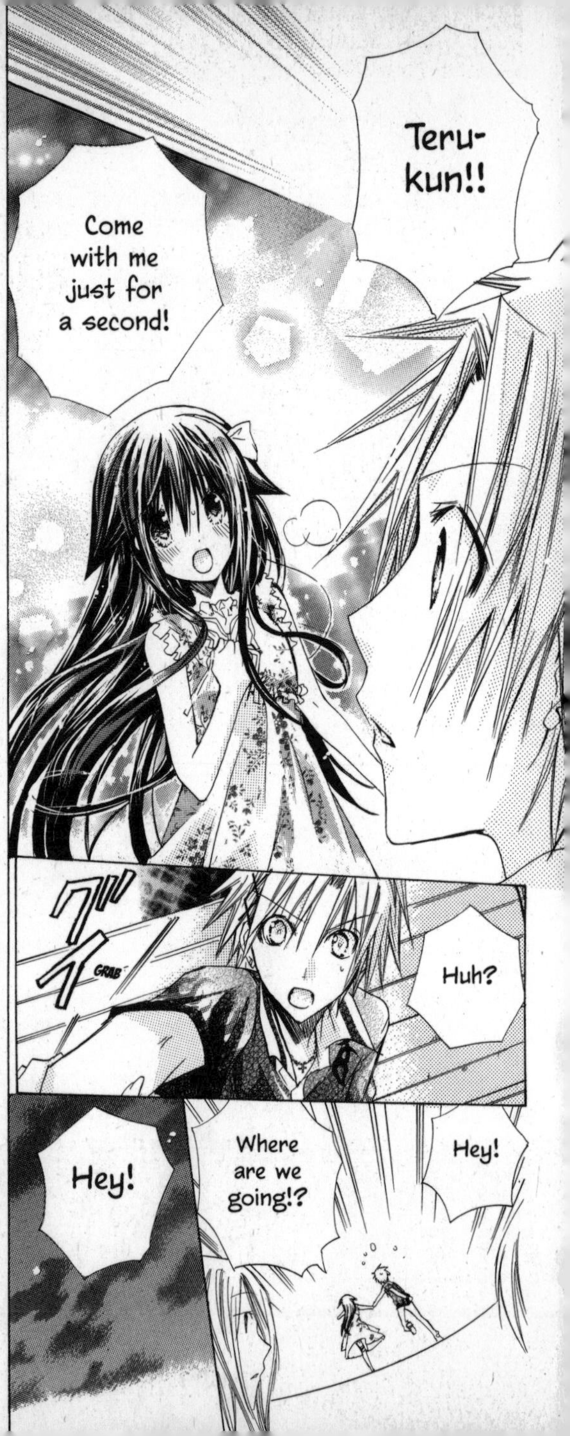
Teru-kun!!
Come with me just for a second!
GRAB
Huh?
Hey!
Where are we going!?
Hey!

I went to a signing event.

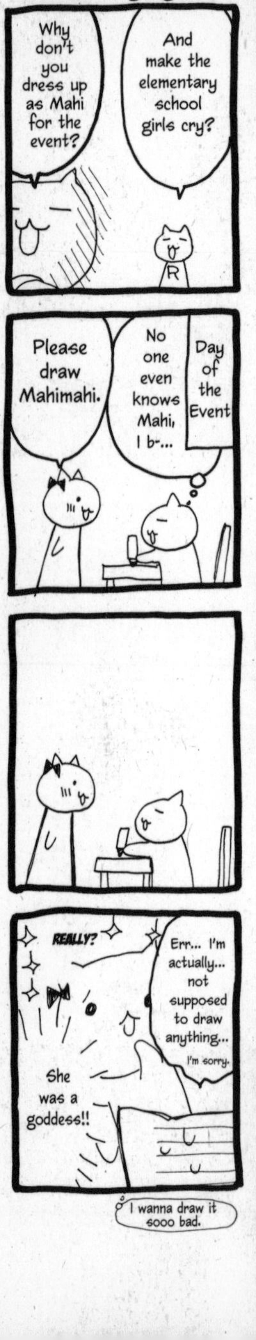
And make the elementary school girls cry?
Why don't you dress up as Mahi for the event?
Day of the Event
No one even knows Mahi, I b-...
Please draw Mahimahi.
Err... I'm actually... not supposed to draw anything...
I'm sorry.
REALLY?
She was a goddess!!
I wanna draw it sooo bad.

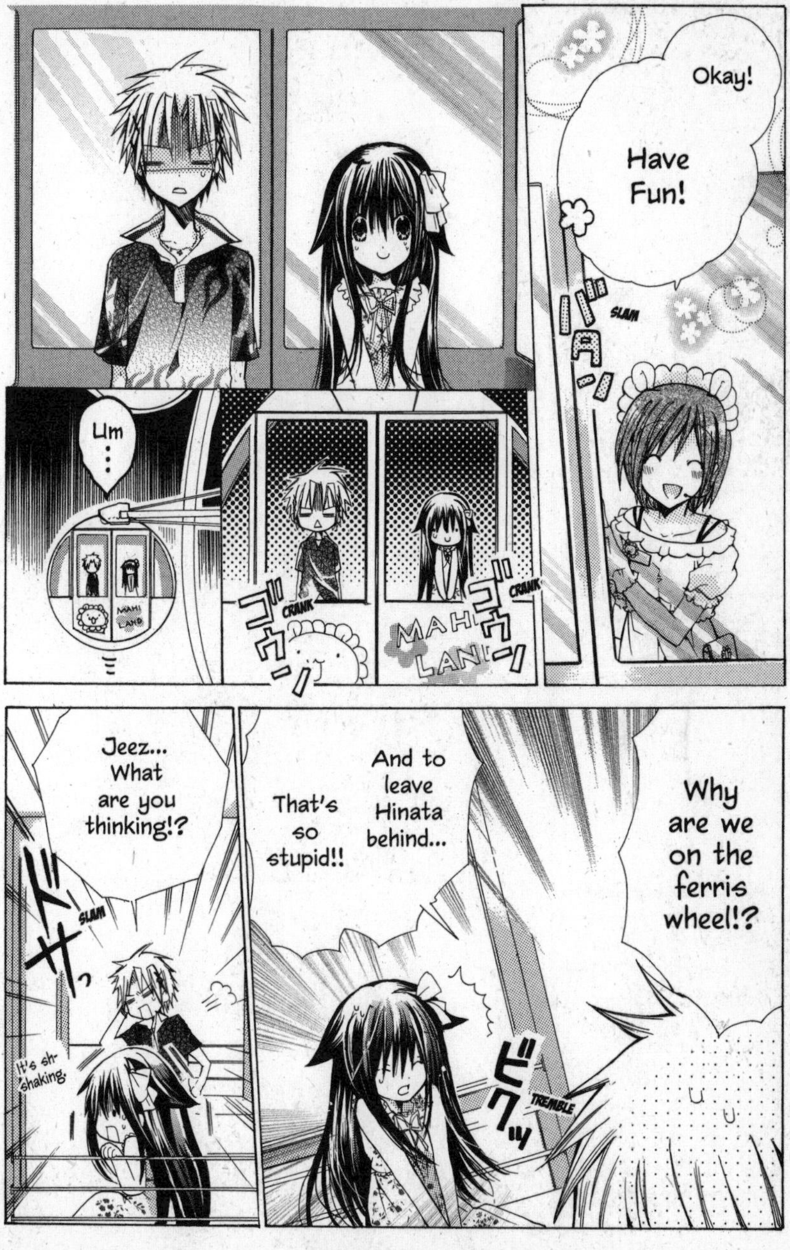
Okay!
Have Fun!
SLAM
CRANK
CRANK
Um...
MAHI LAND
Why are we on the ferris wheel!?
And to leave Hinata behind...
That's so stupid!!
TREMBLE
Jeez... What are you thinking!?
SLAM
It's sh-shaking.

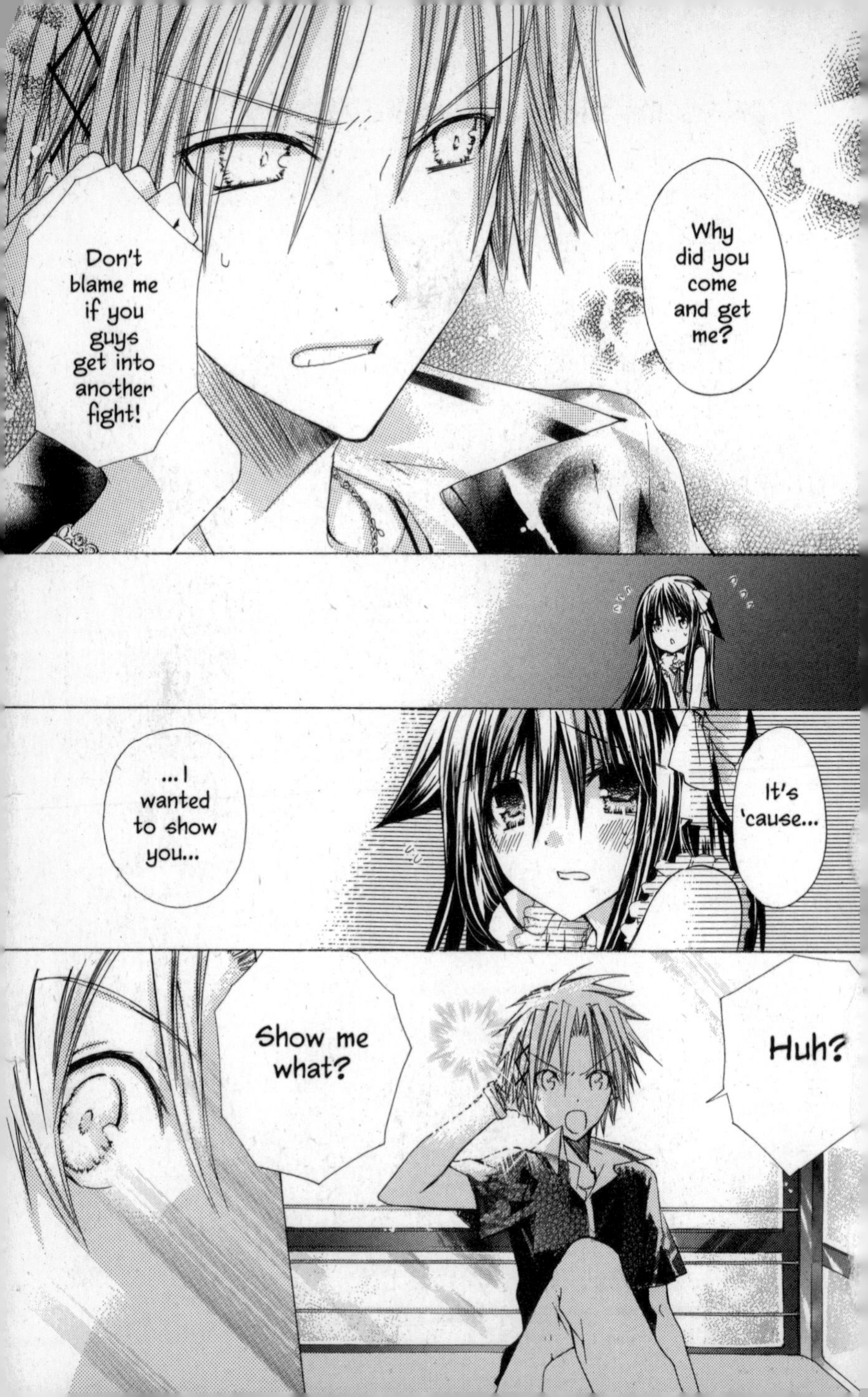
Why did you come and get me?
Don't blame me if you guys get into another fight!
It's 'cause...
...I wanted to show you...
Huh?
Show me what?

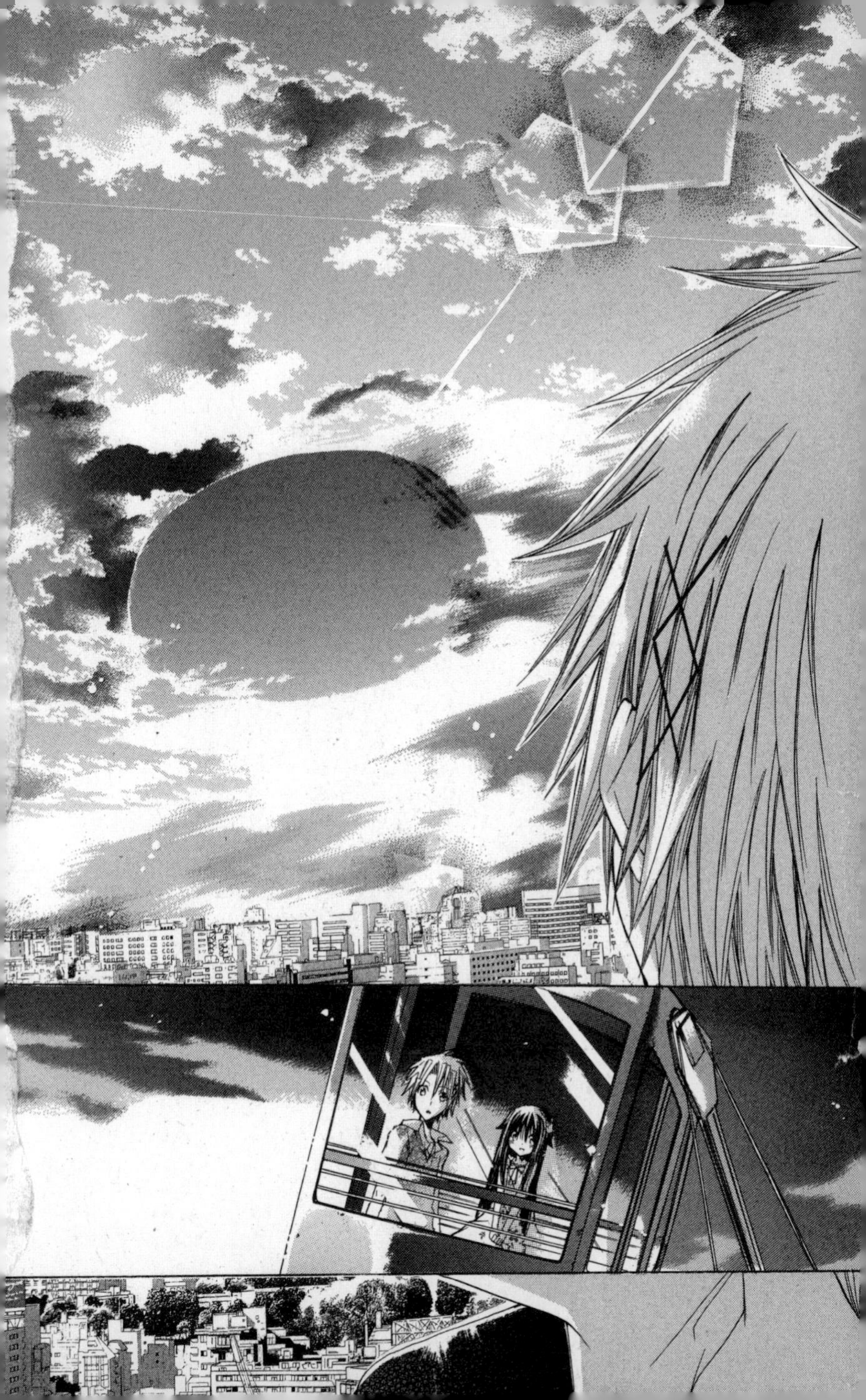

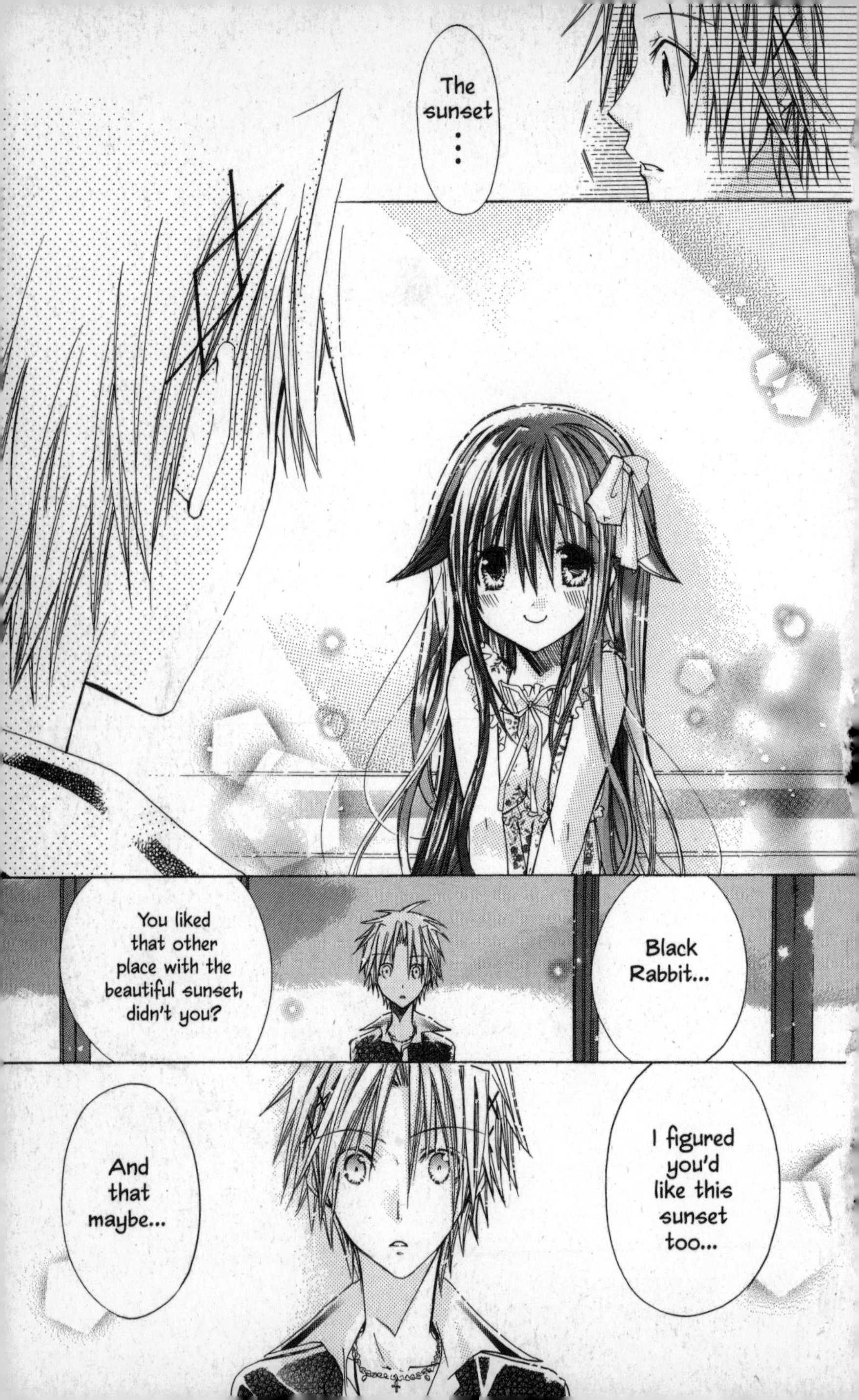
The sunset...
Black Rabbit...
You liked that other place with the beautiful sunset, didn't you?
I figured you'd like this sunset too...
And that maybe...

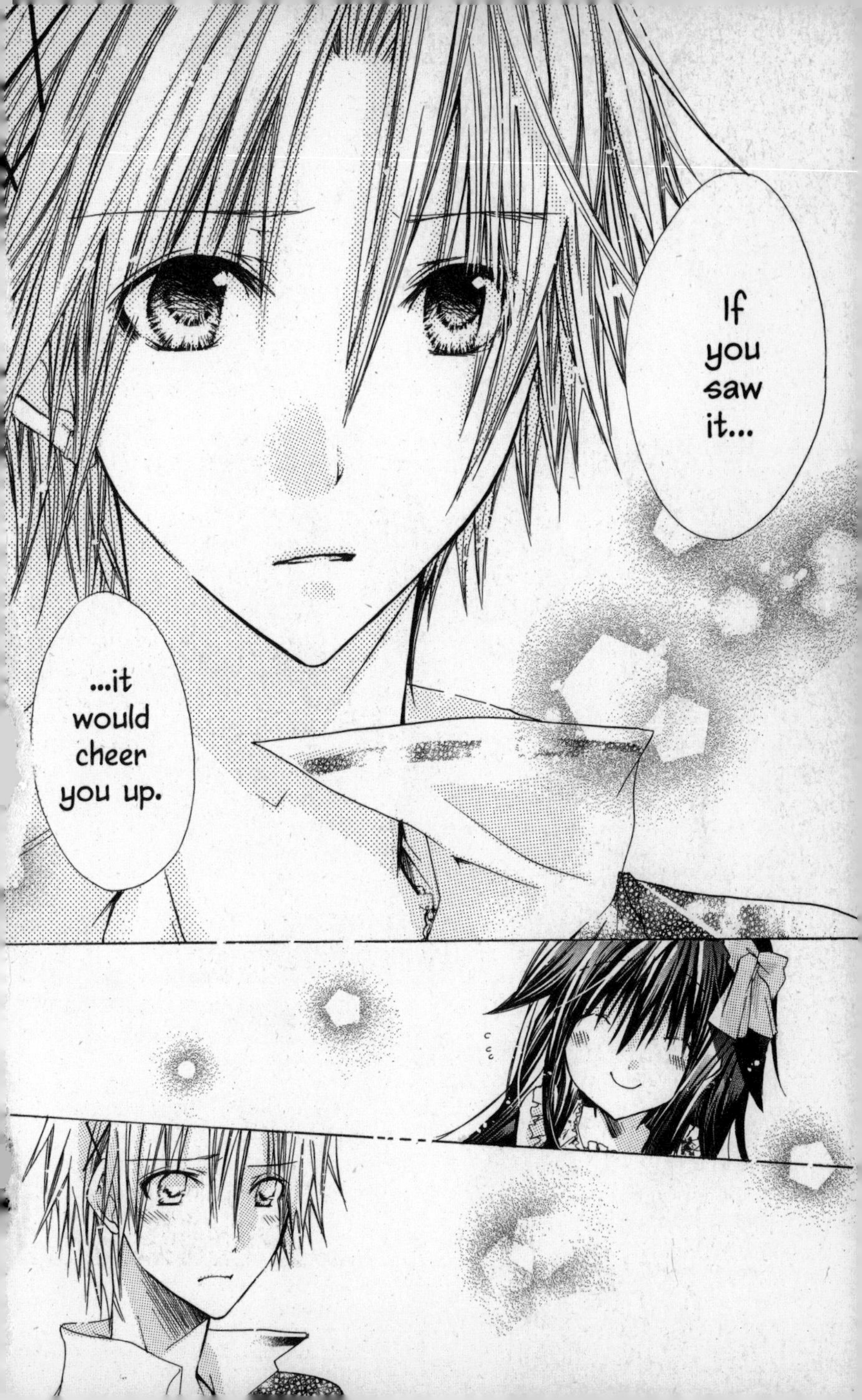
If you saw it...
...it would cheer you up.

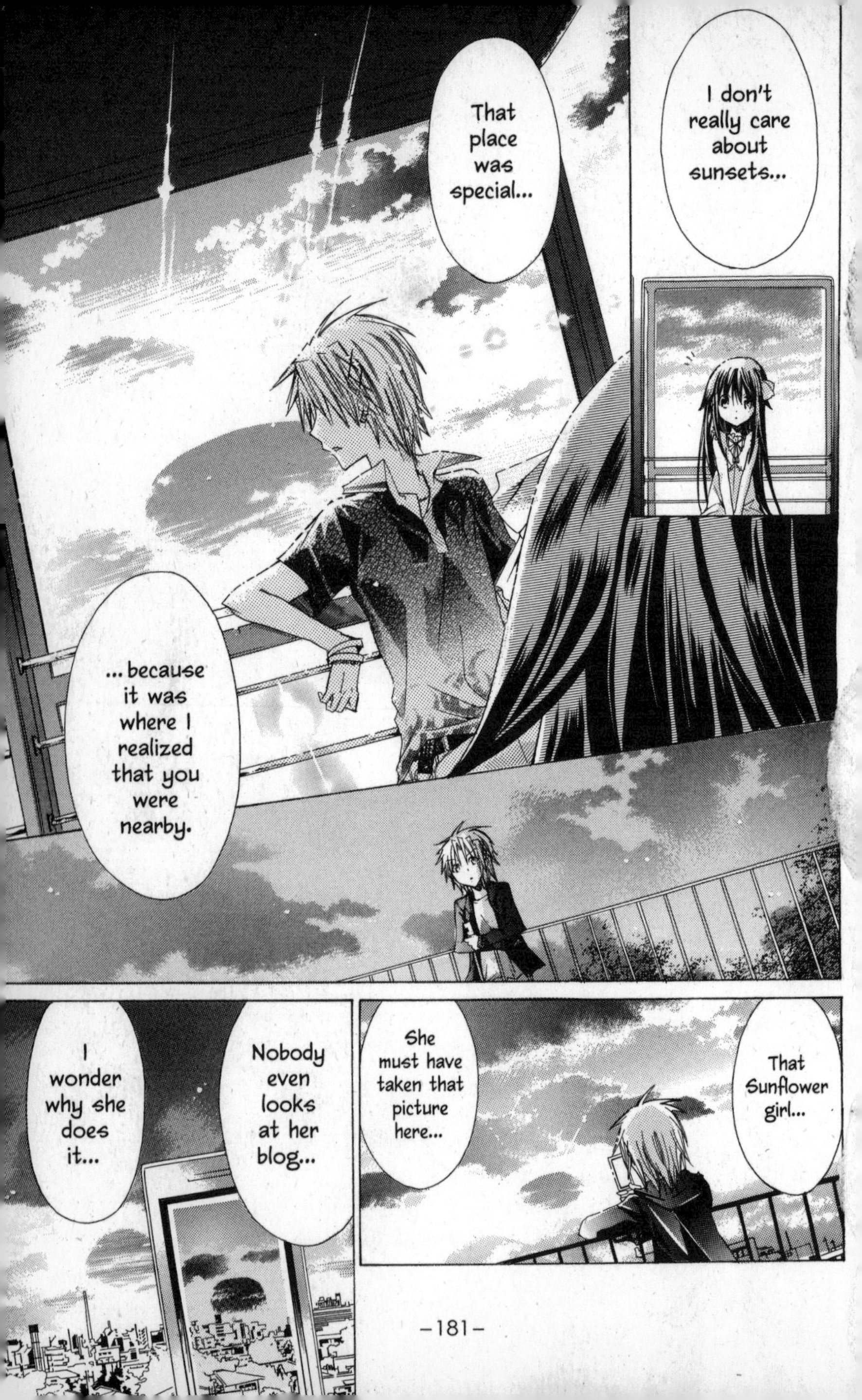
I don't really care about sunsets...
That place was special...
...because it was where I realized that you were nearby.
That Sunflower girl...
She must have taken that picture here...
Nobody even looks at her blog...
I wonder why she does it...

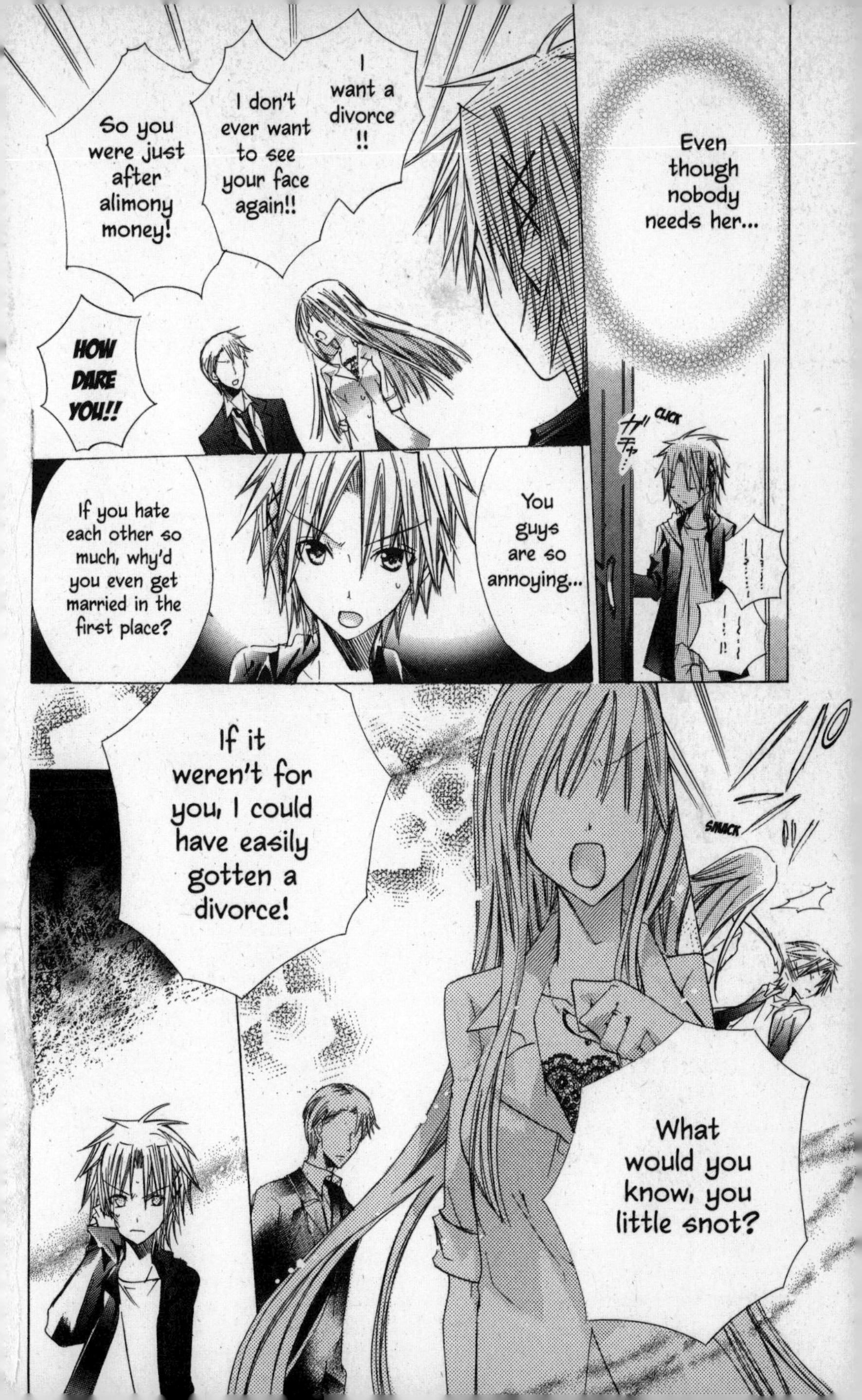
Even though nobody needs her...
CLICK
I want a divorce!!
I don't ever want to see your face again!!
So you were just after alimony money!
HOW DARE YOU!!
You guys are so annoying...
If you hate each other so much, why'd you even get married in the first place?
SMACK
If it weren't for you, I could have easily gotten a divorce!
What would you know, you little snot?

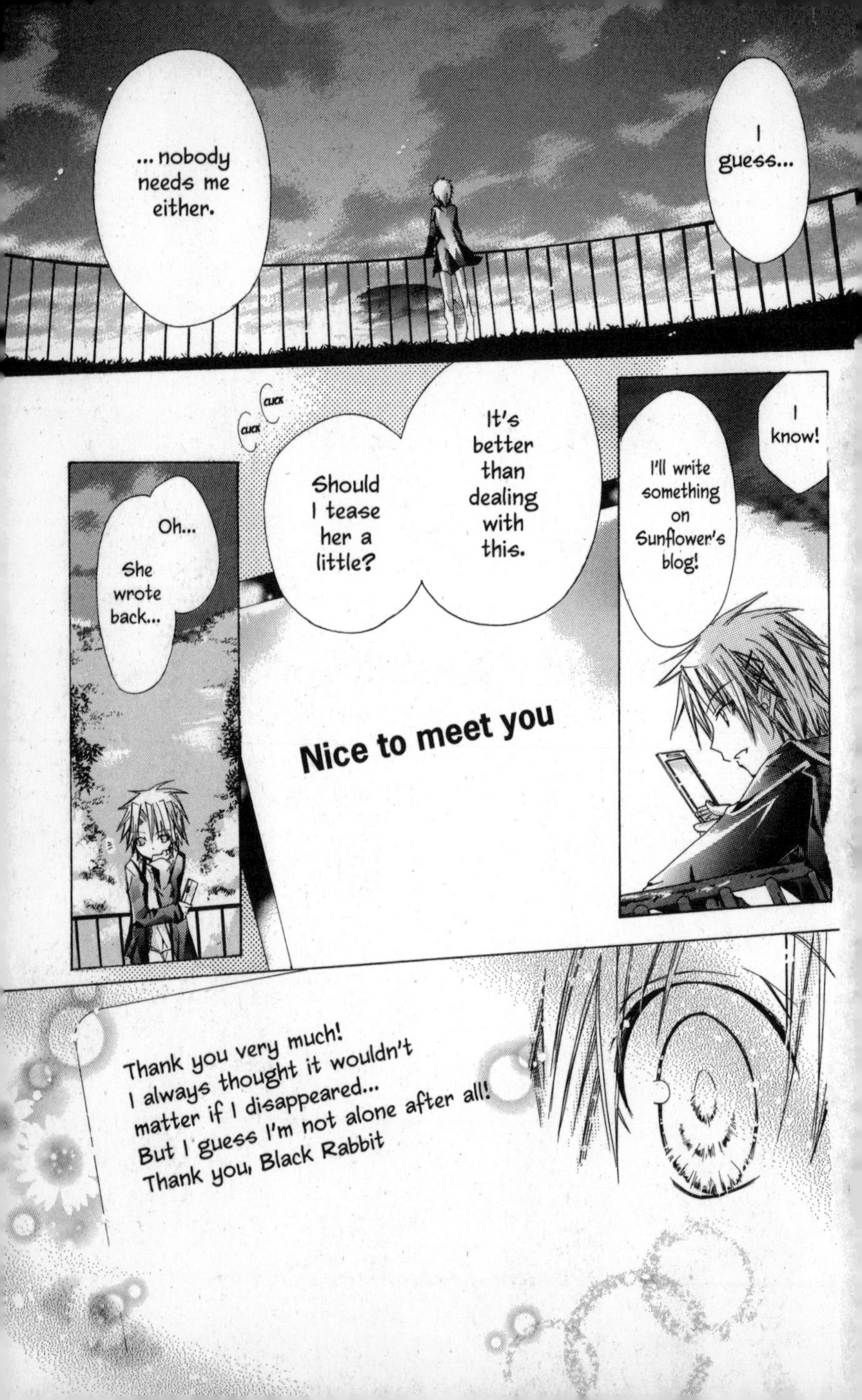
I guess...
... nobody needs me either.
I know!
I'll write something on Sunflower's blog!
It's better than dealing with this.
Should I tease her a little?
CLICK
CLICK
Nice to meet you
Oh...
She wrote back...
Thank you very much!
I always thought it wouldn't
matter if I disappeared...
But I guess I'm not alone after all!
Thank you, Black Rabbit

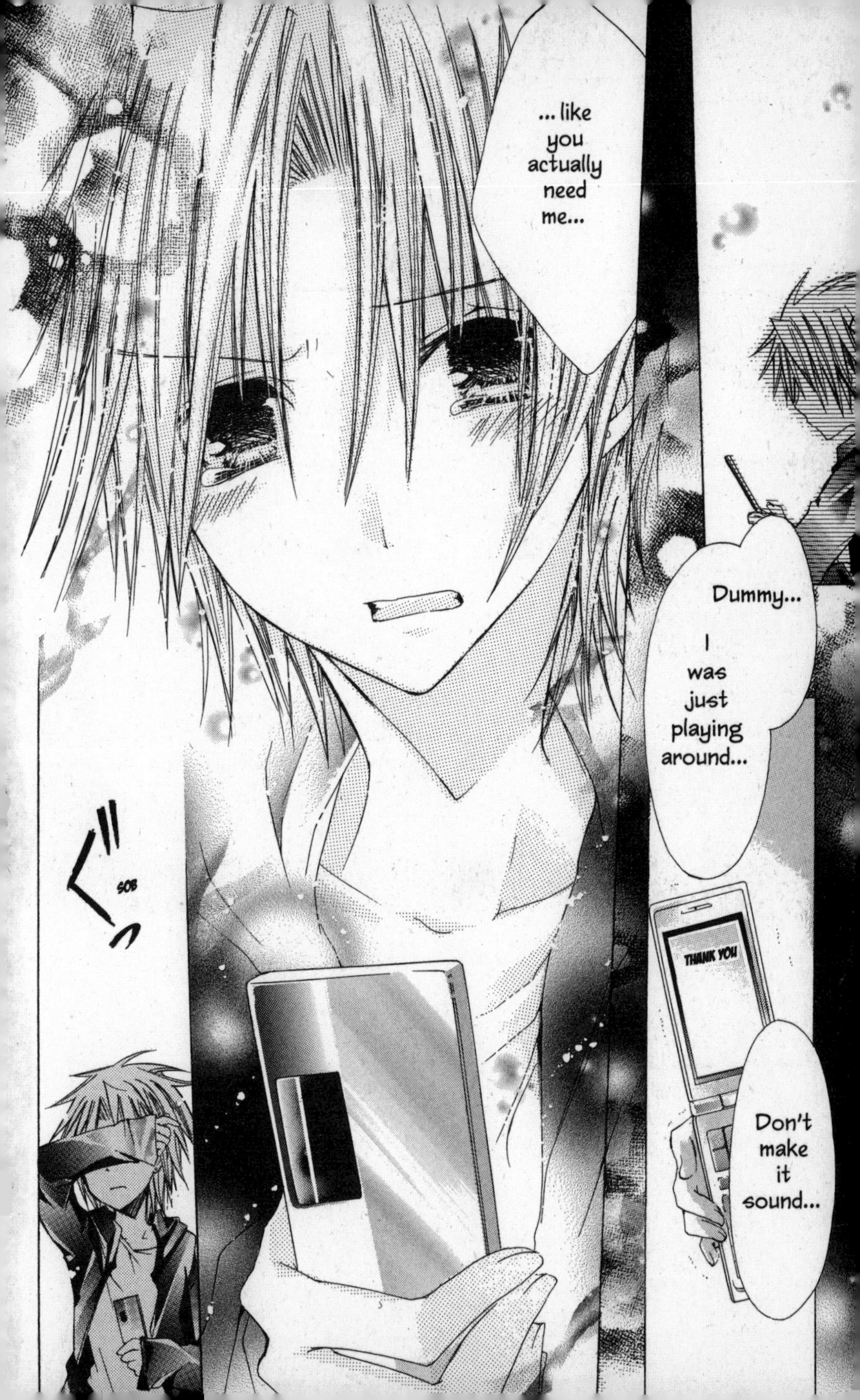
Dummy... I was just playing around...
THANK YOU
Don't make it sound...
... like you actually need me...
SOB

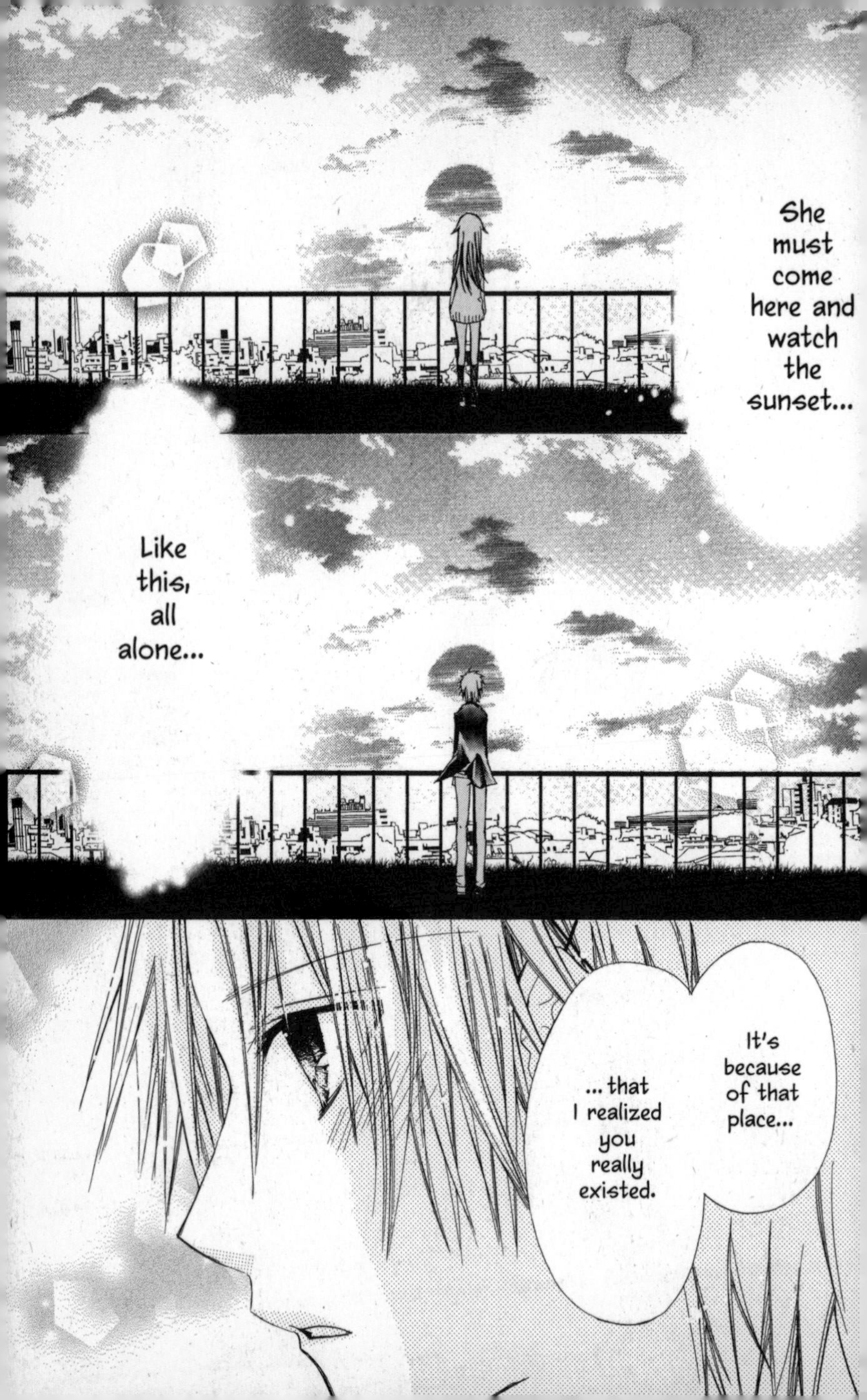
She must come here and watch the sunset...
Like this, all alone...
It's because of that place...
...that I realized you really existed.

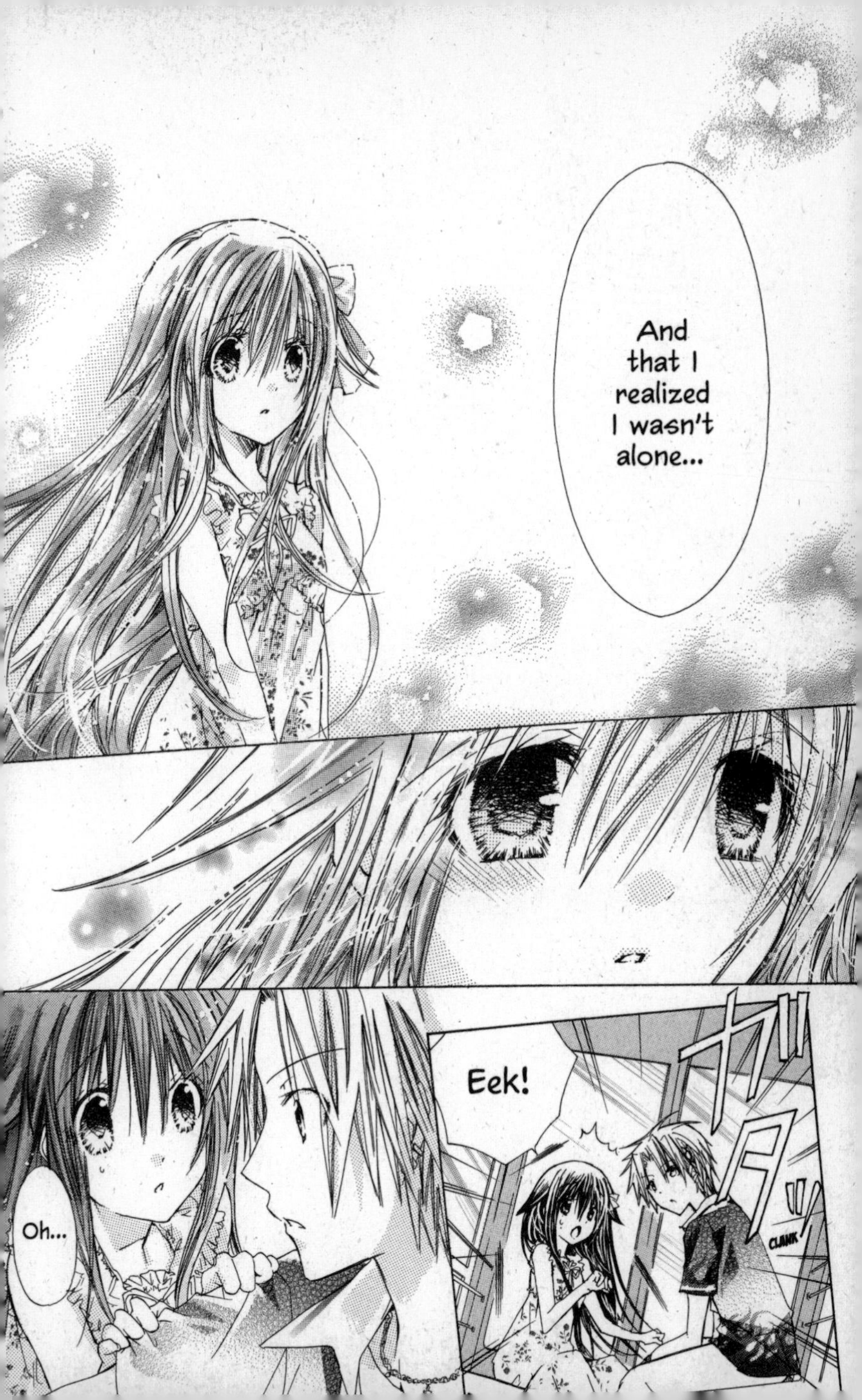
And that I realized I wasn't alone...
Eek!
CLANK
Oh...

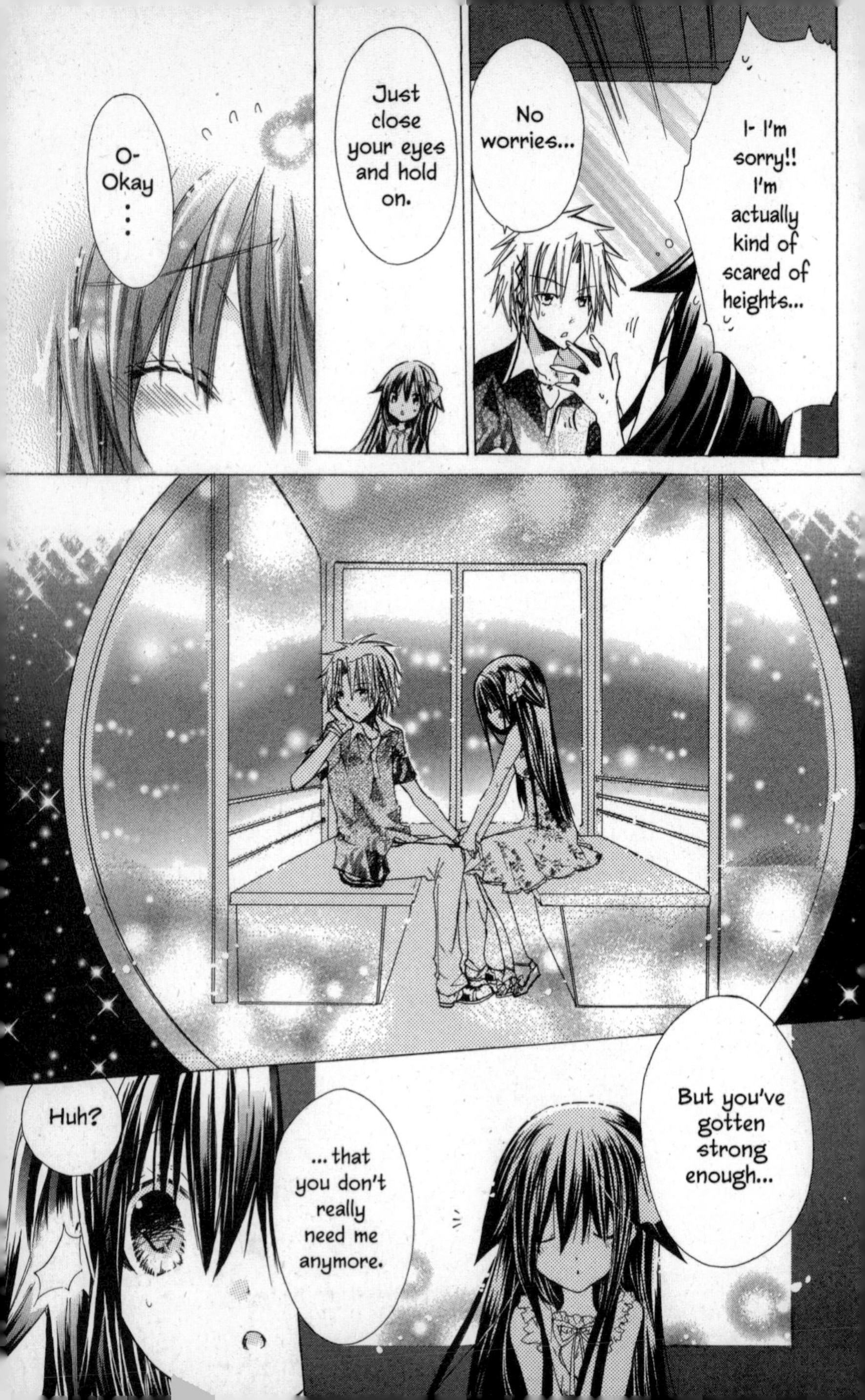
I- I'm sorry!! I'm actually kind of scared of heights...
No worries...
Just close your eyes and hold on.
O- Okay ...
But you've gotten strong enough...
... that you don't really need me anymore.
Huh?

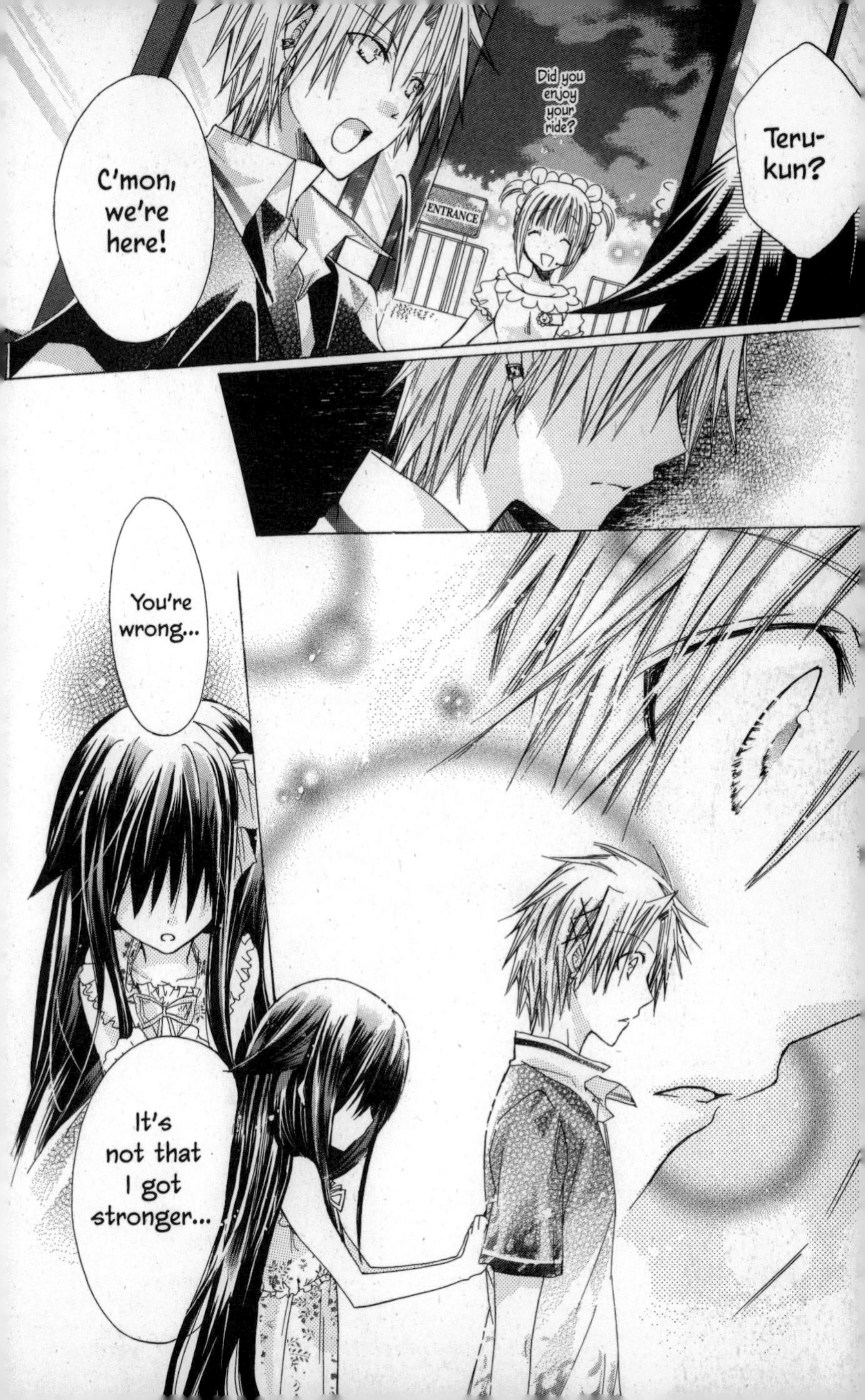
Teru-kun?
Did you enjoy your ride?
ENTRANCE
C'mon, we're here!
You're wrong...
It's not that I got stronger...

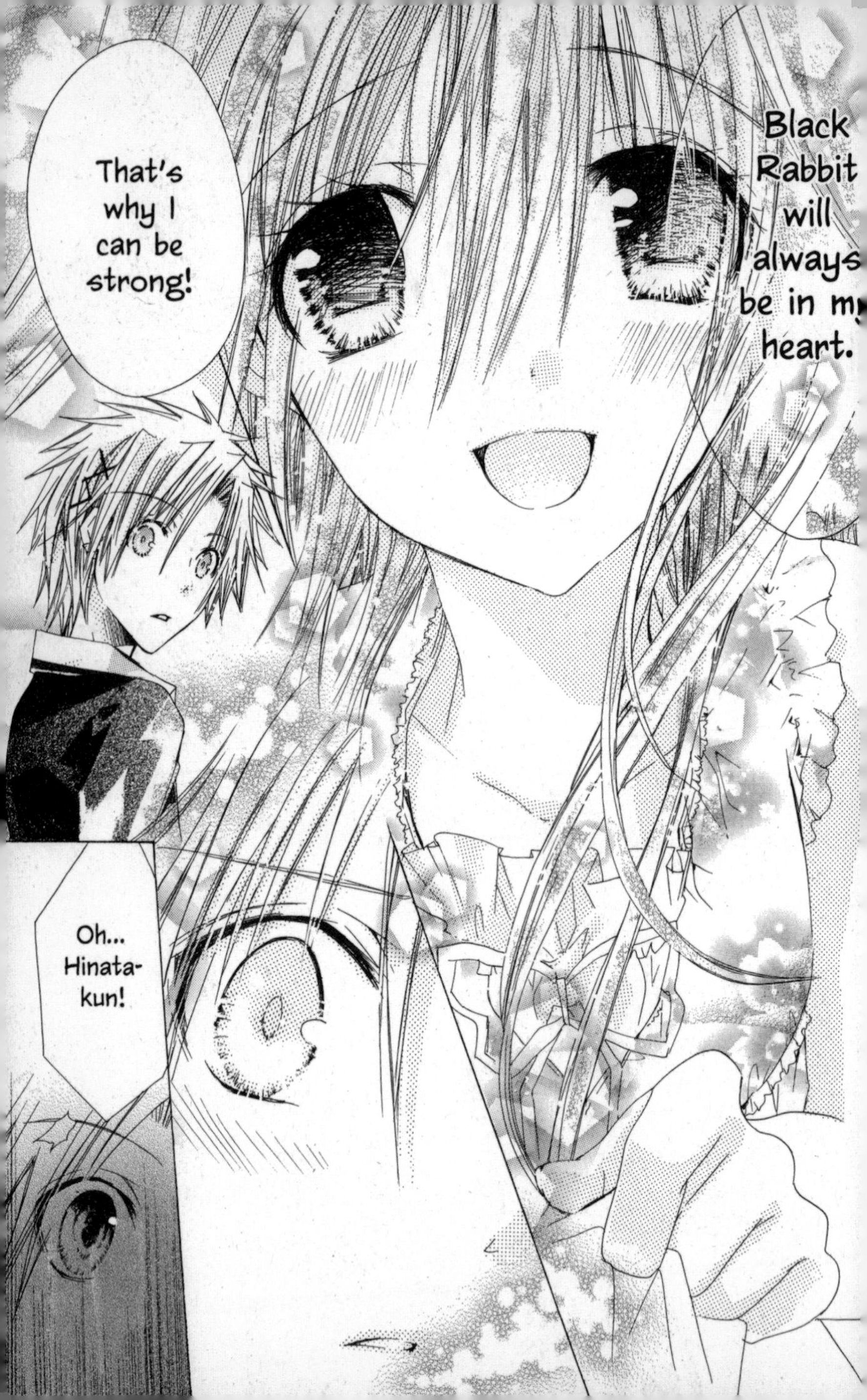
Black Rabbit will always be in my heart.
That's why I can be strong!
Oh... Hinata-kun!

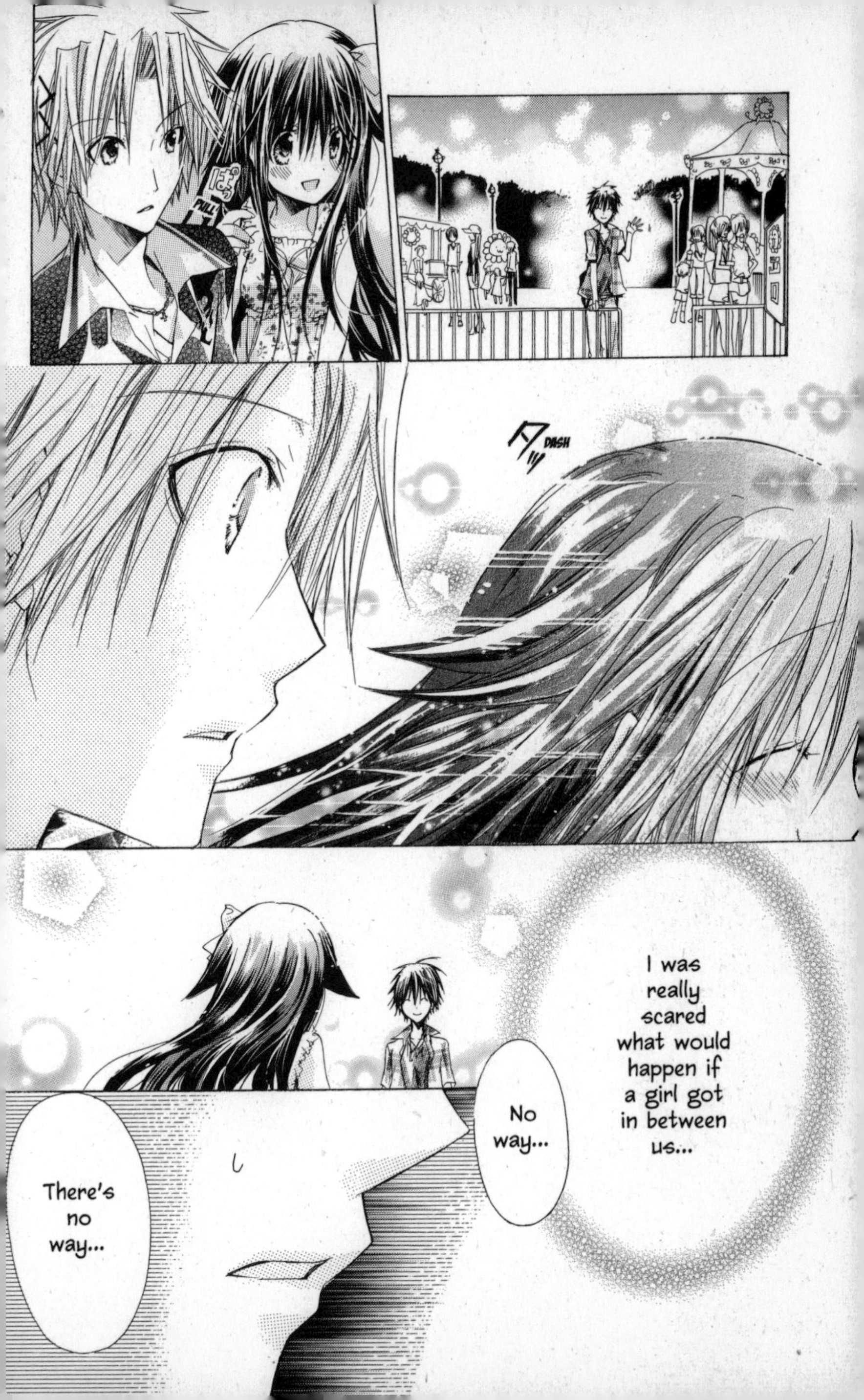
ぱっ PULL
タッ DASH
I was really scared what would happen if a girl got in between us...
No way...
There's no way...

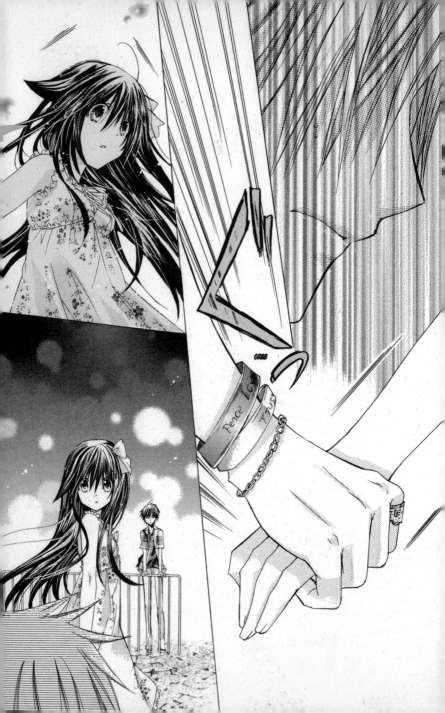

GRAB

Peace Love Trust

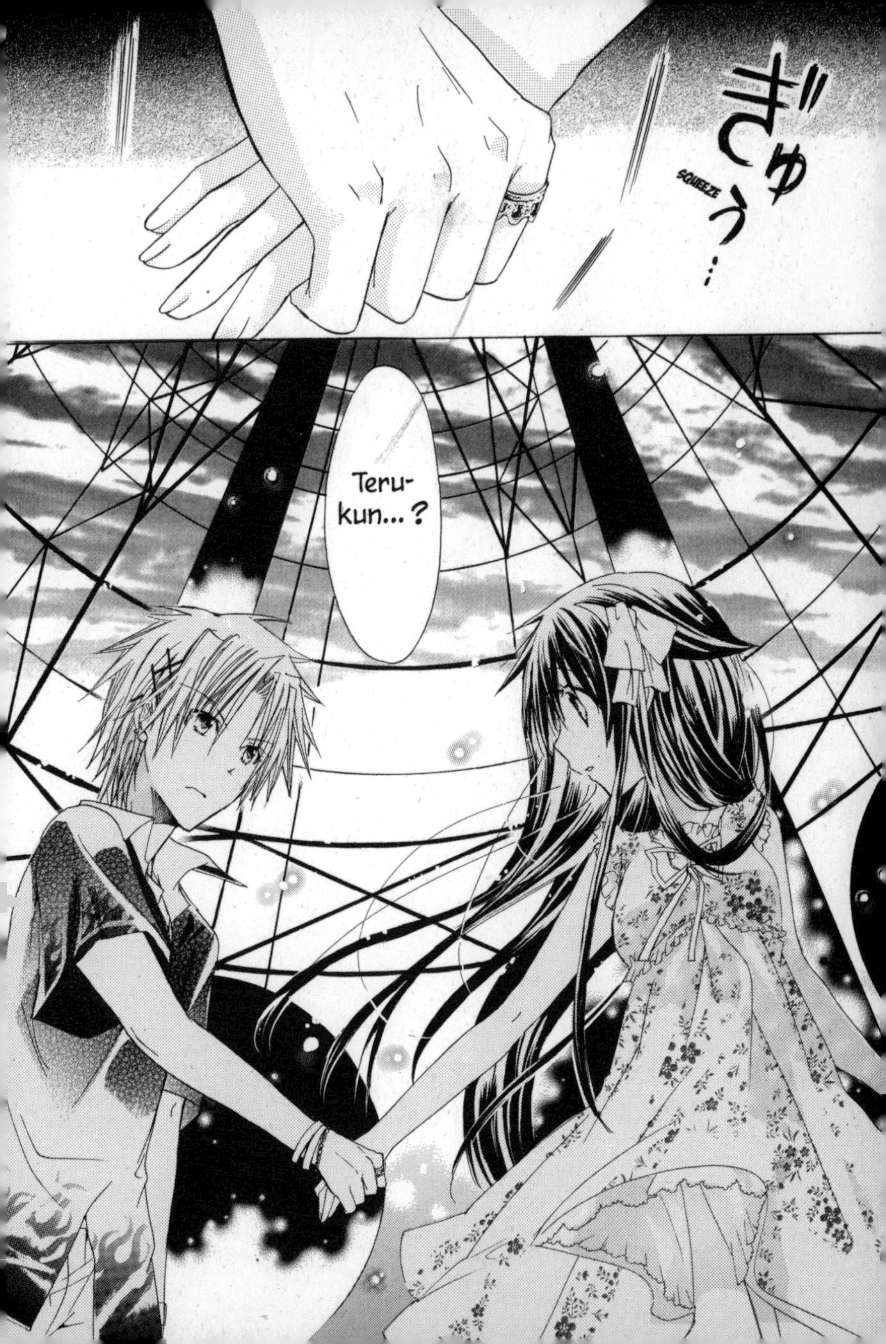
ぎゅう…
SQUEEZE
Teru-kun...?

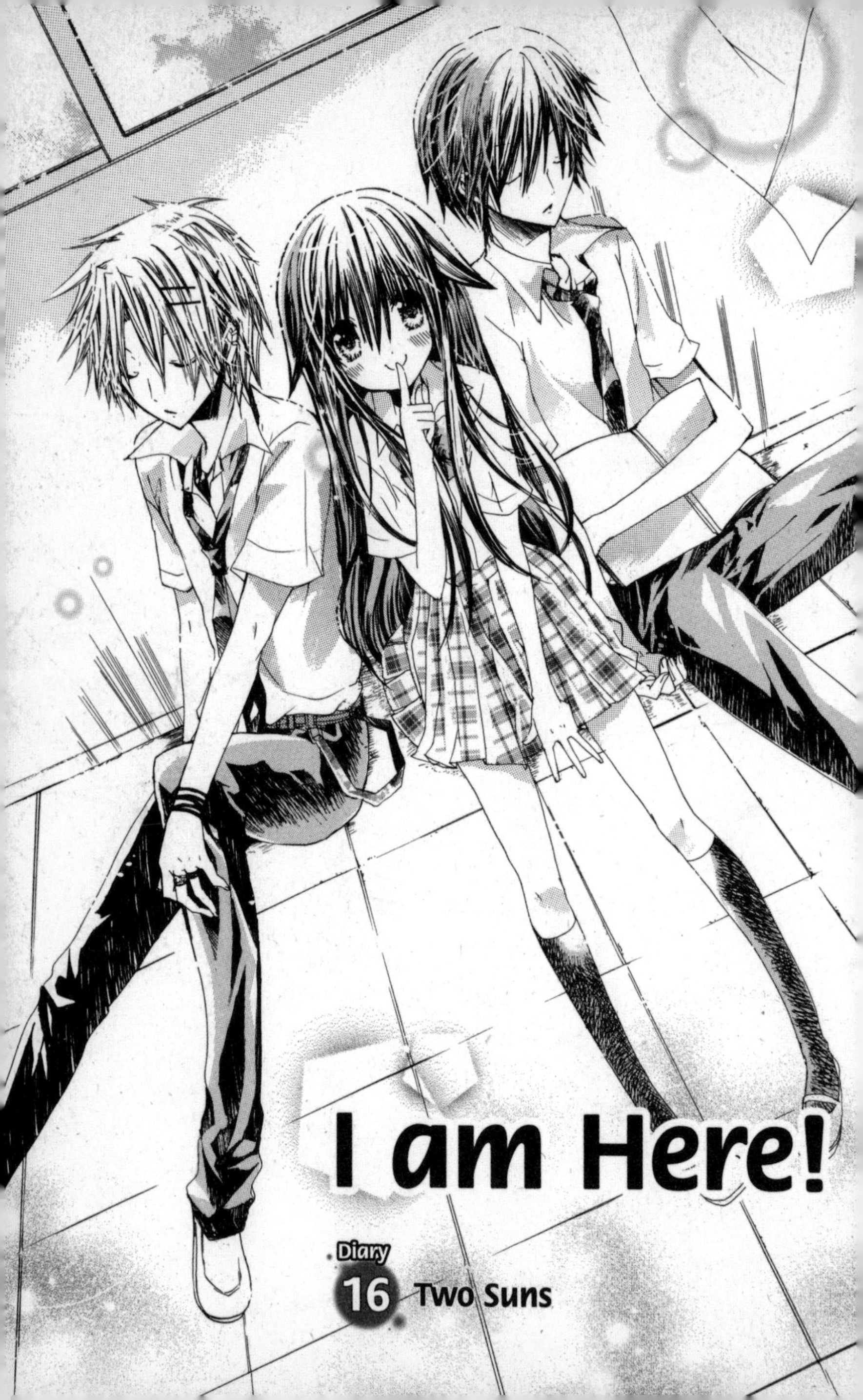
I am Here!
Diary
16 Two Suns

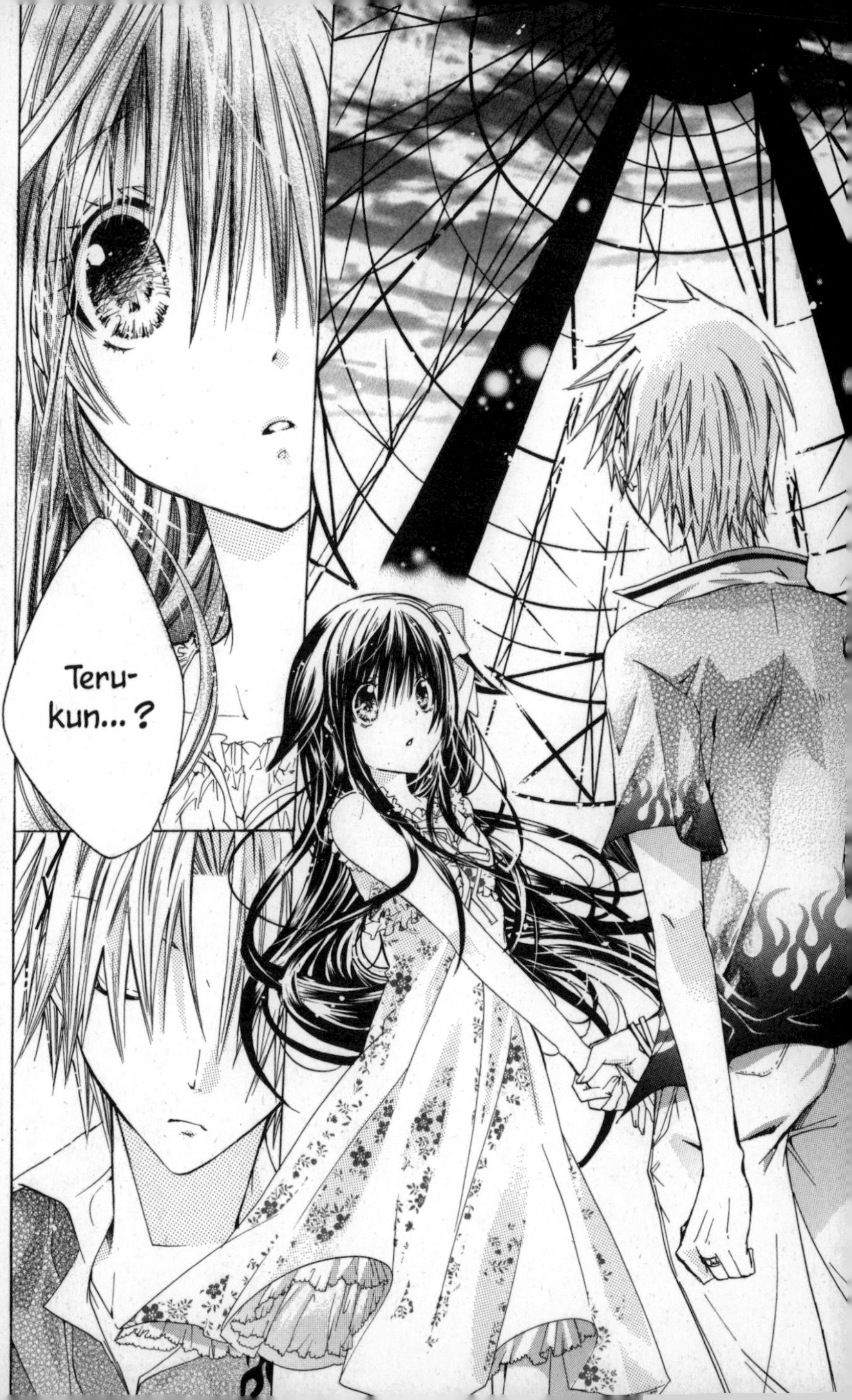
Teru-kun...?

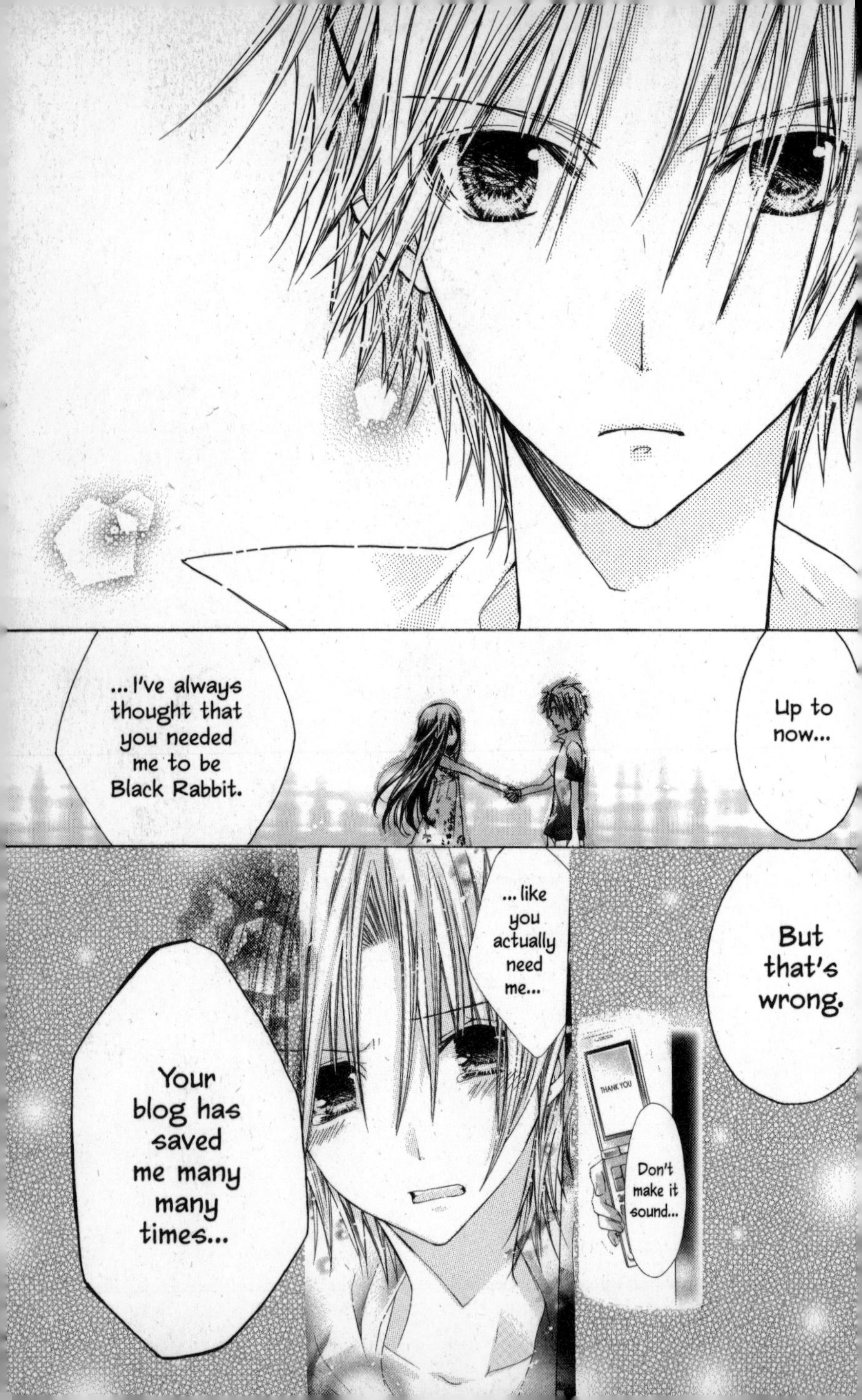
Up to now...
...I've always thought that you needed me to be Black Rabbit.
But that's wrong.
THANK YOU
Don't make it sound...
...like you actually need me...
Your blog has saved me many many times...

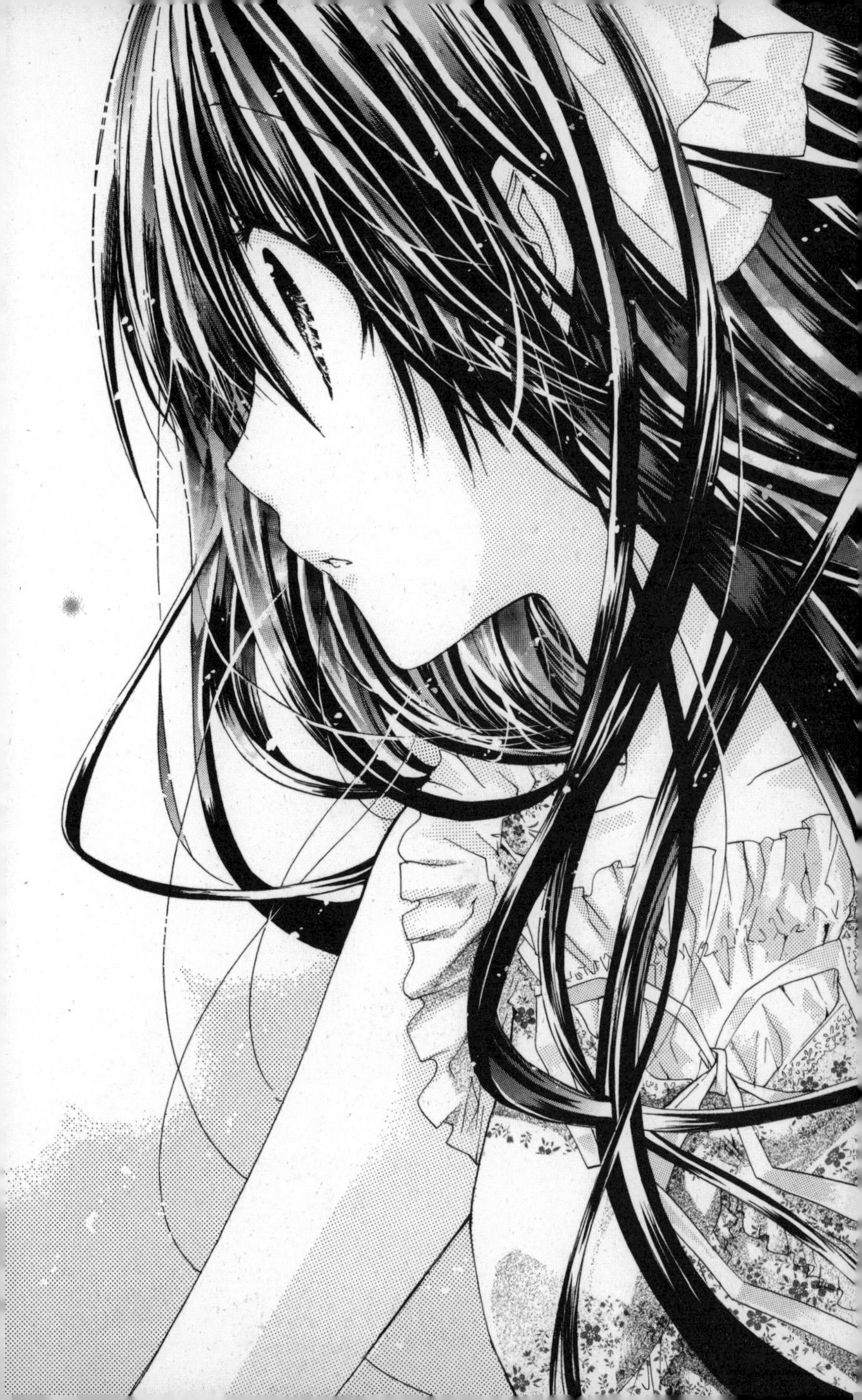

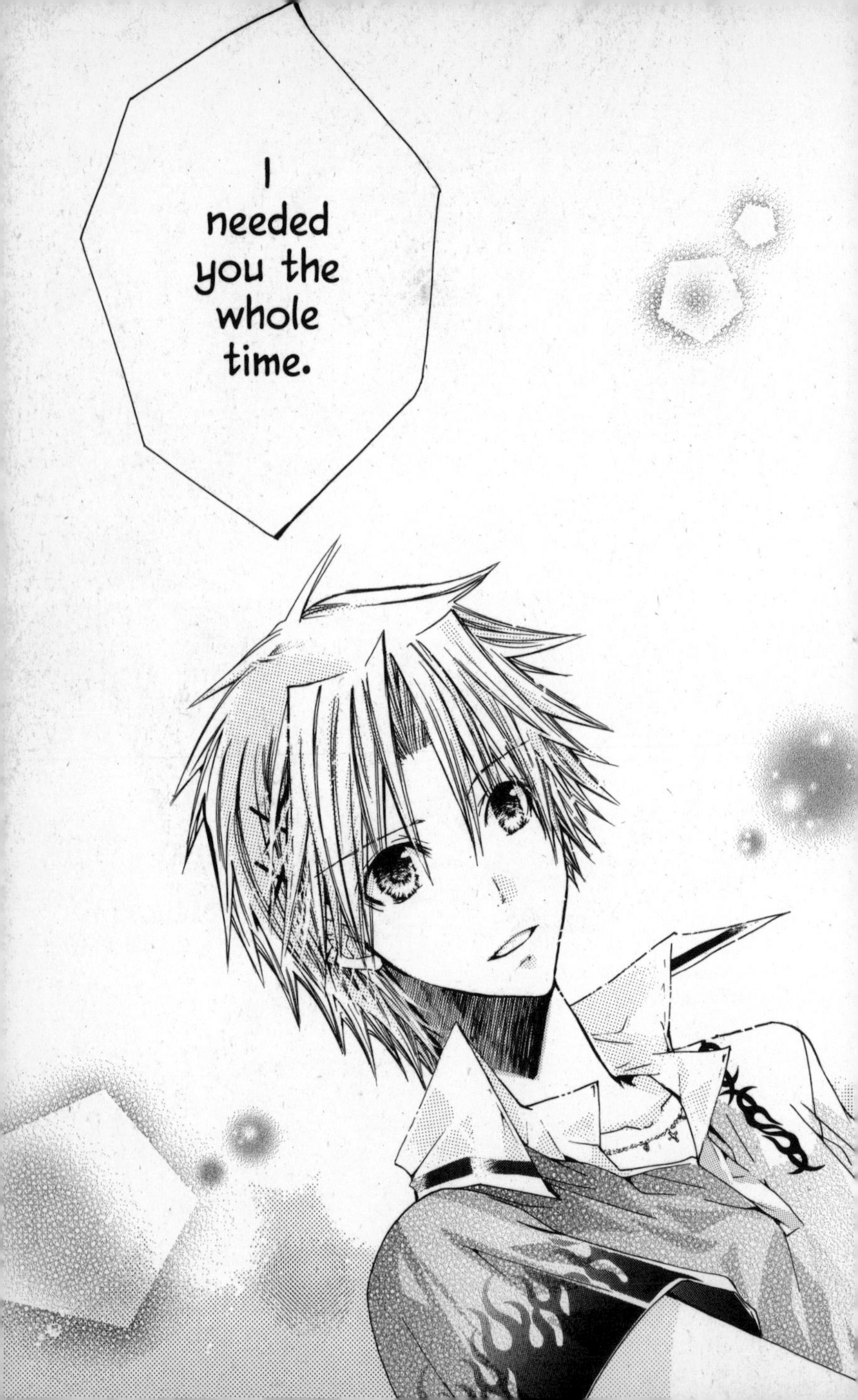
I needed you the whole time.

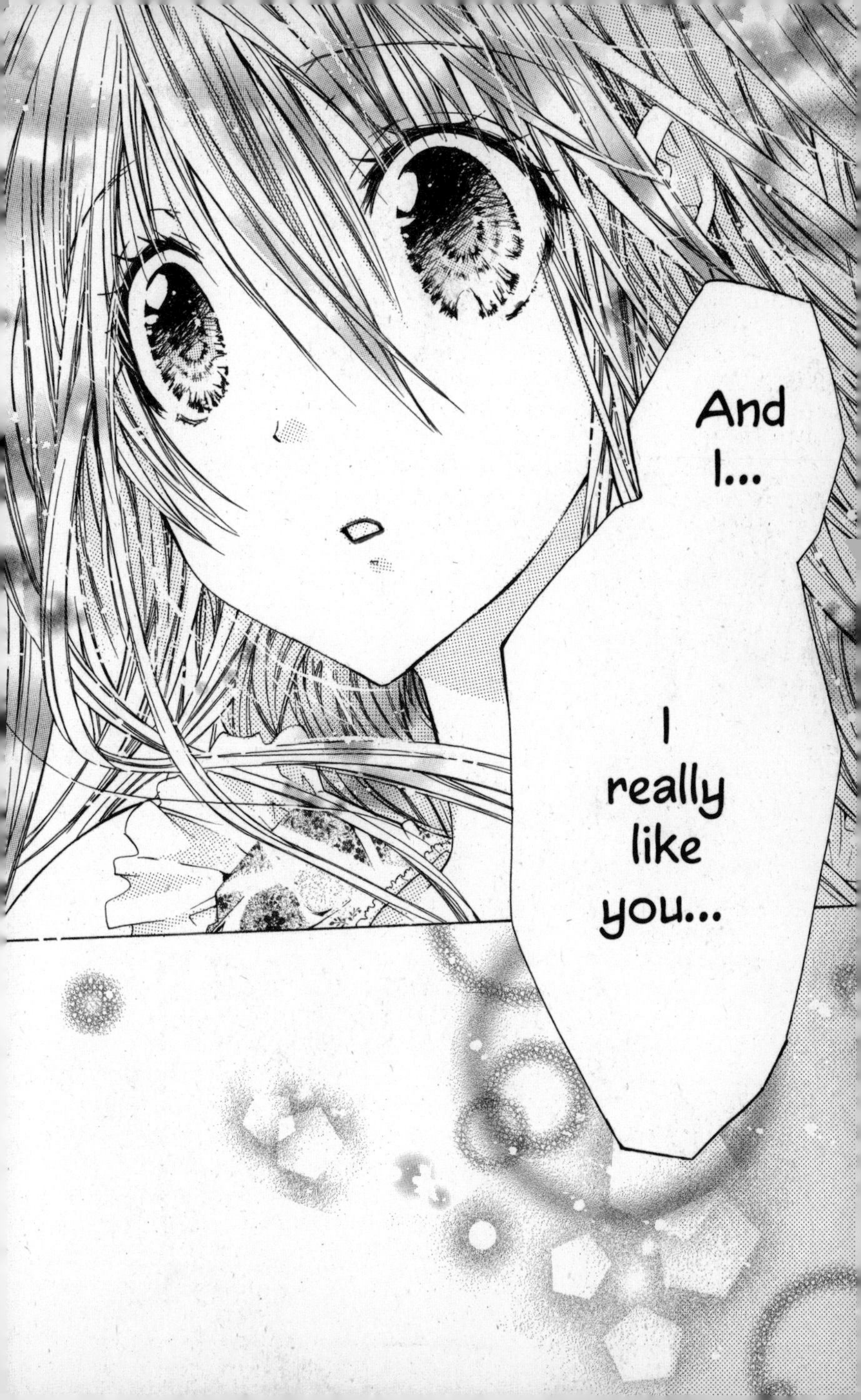
And I...
I really like you...

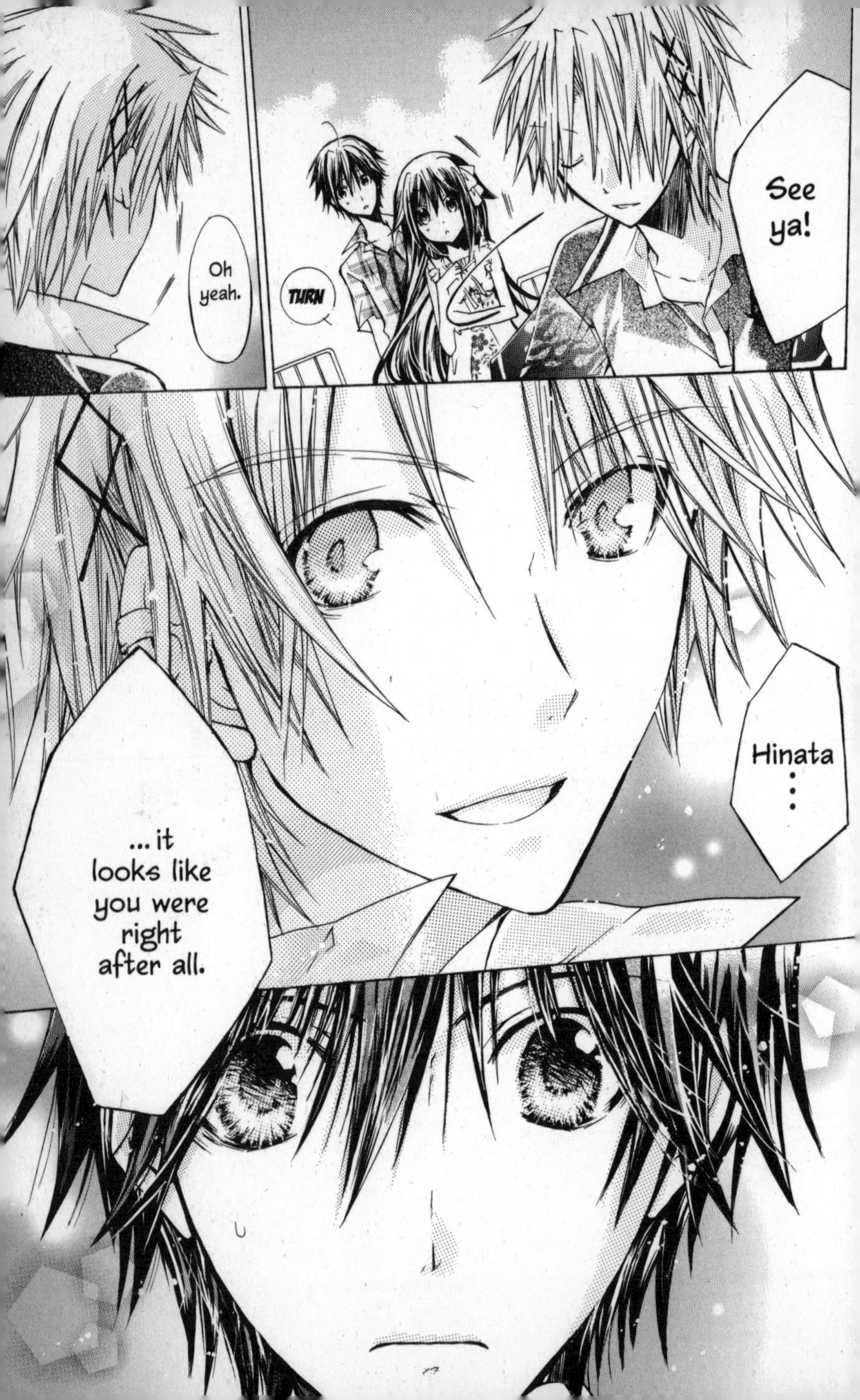
See ya!
TURN
Oh yeah.
Hinata...
...it looks like you were right after all.

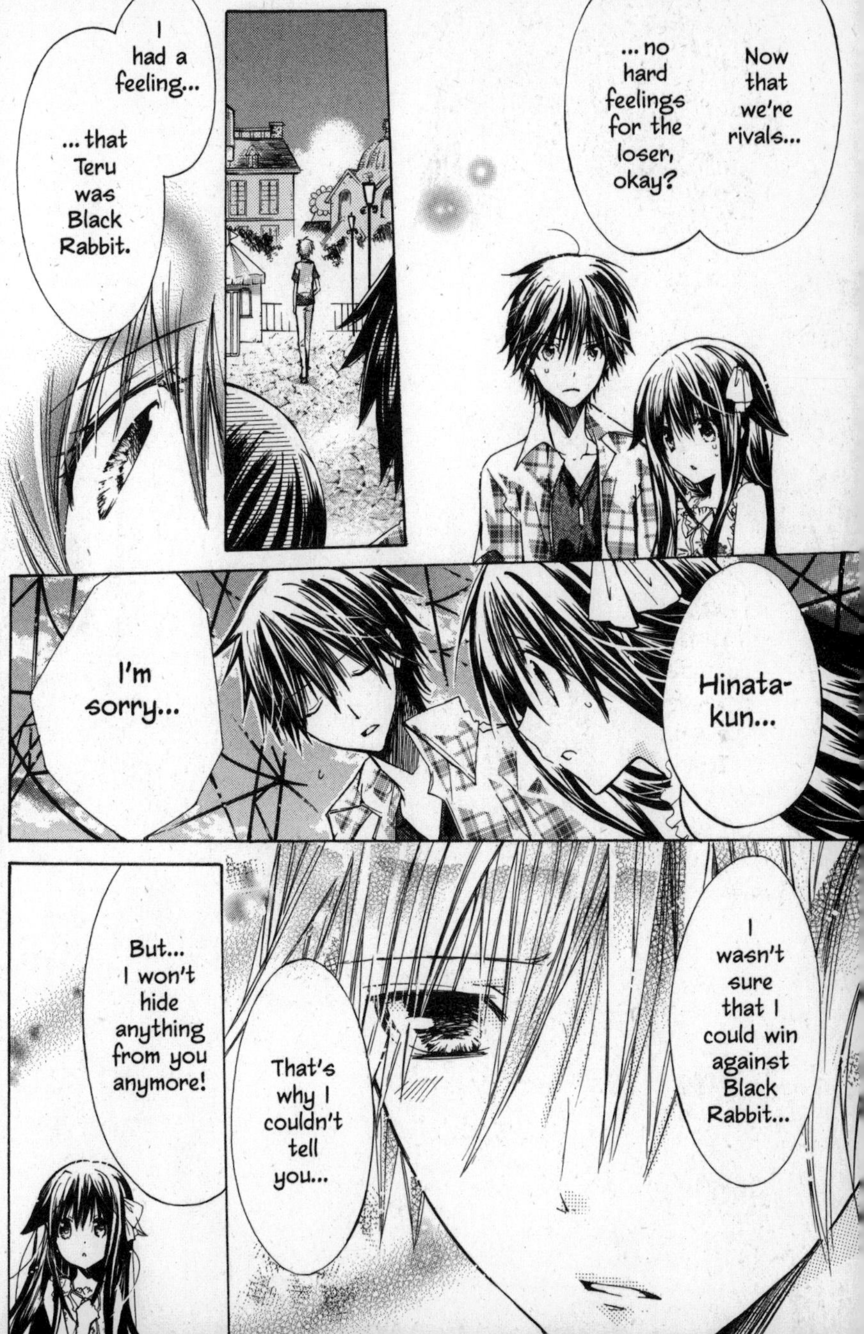

Now that we're rivals...
...no hard feelings for the loser, okay?
I had a feeling...
...that Teru was Black Rabbit.
Hinata-kun...
I'm sorry...
I wasn't sure that I could win against Black Rabbit...
That's why I couldn't tell you...
But... I won't hide anything from you anymore!

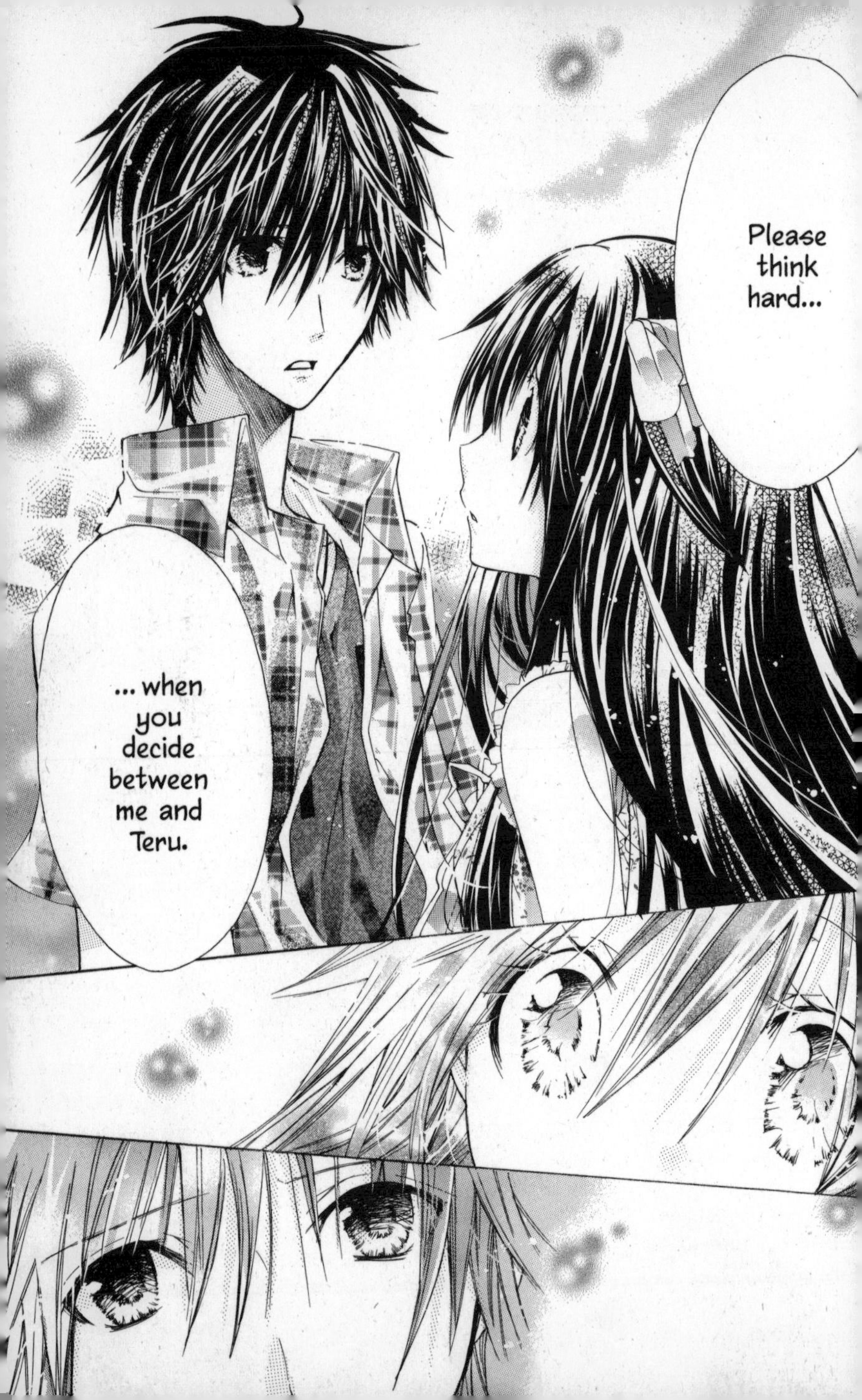
Please think hard...
... when you decide between me and Teru.

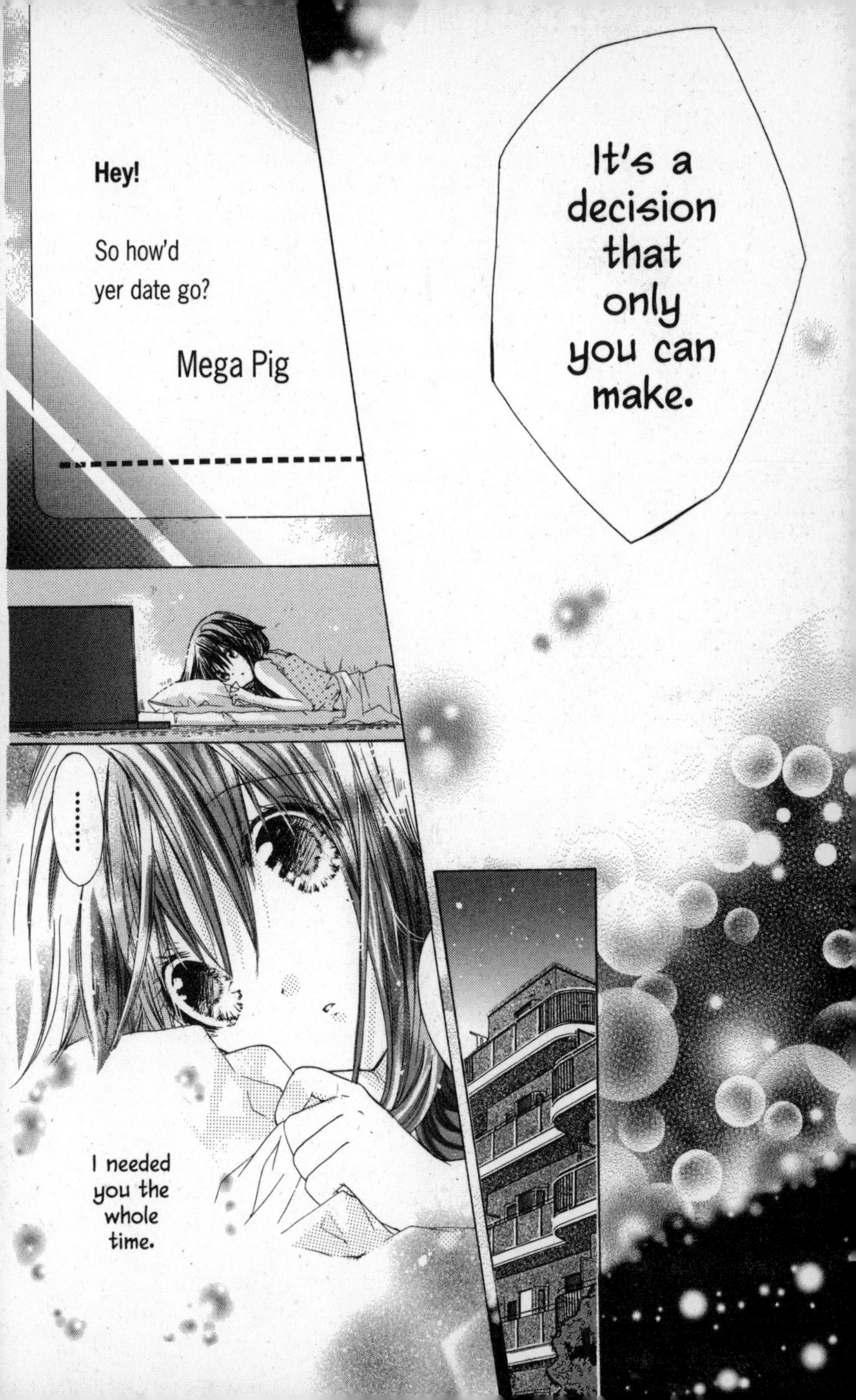
It's a decision that only you can make.
Hey!
So how'd yer date go?
Mega Pig
......
I needed you the whole time.

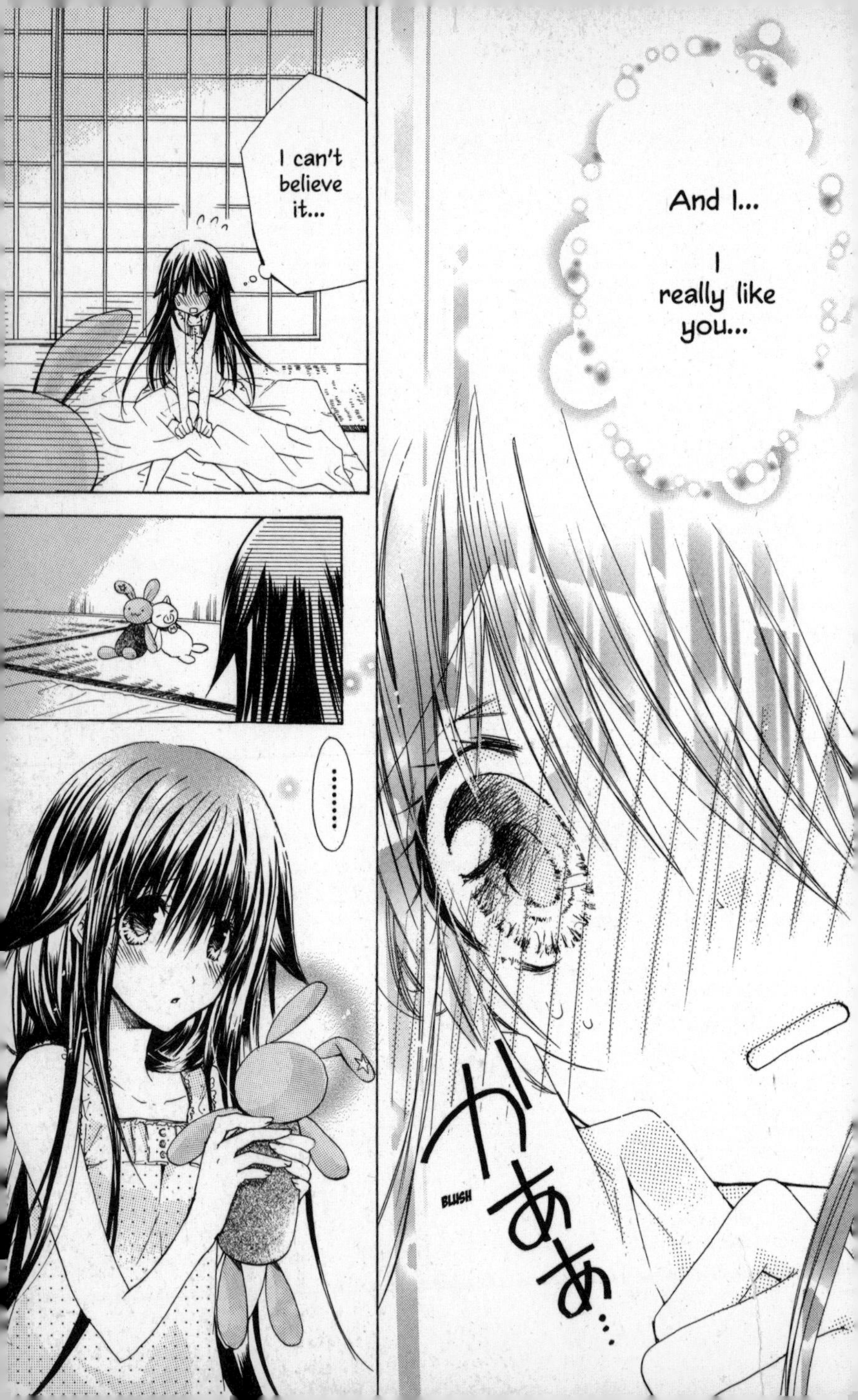
And I...
I really like you...
かあぁ…
BLUSH
I can't believe it...
....

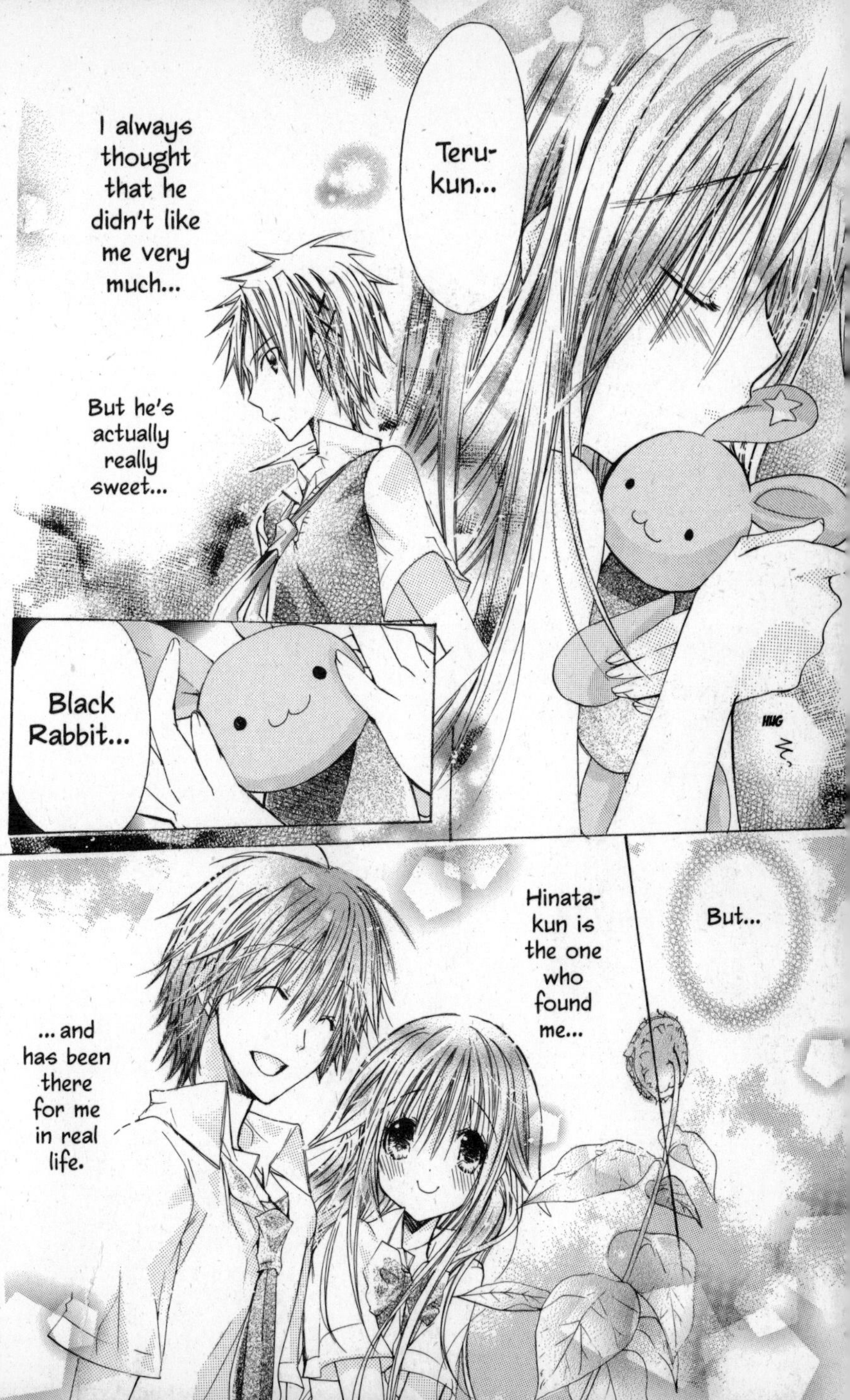
Teru-kun...
HUG
I always thought that he didn't like me very much...
But he's actually really sweet...
Black Rabbit...
But...
Hinata-kun is the one who found me...
... and has been there for me in real life.

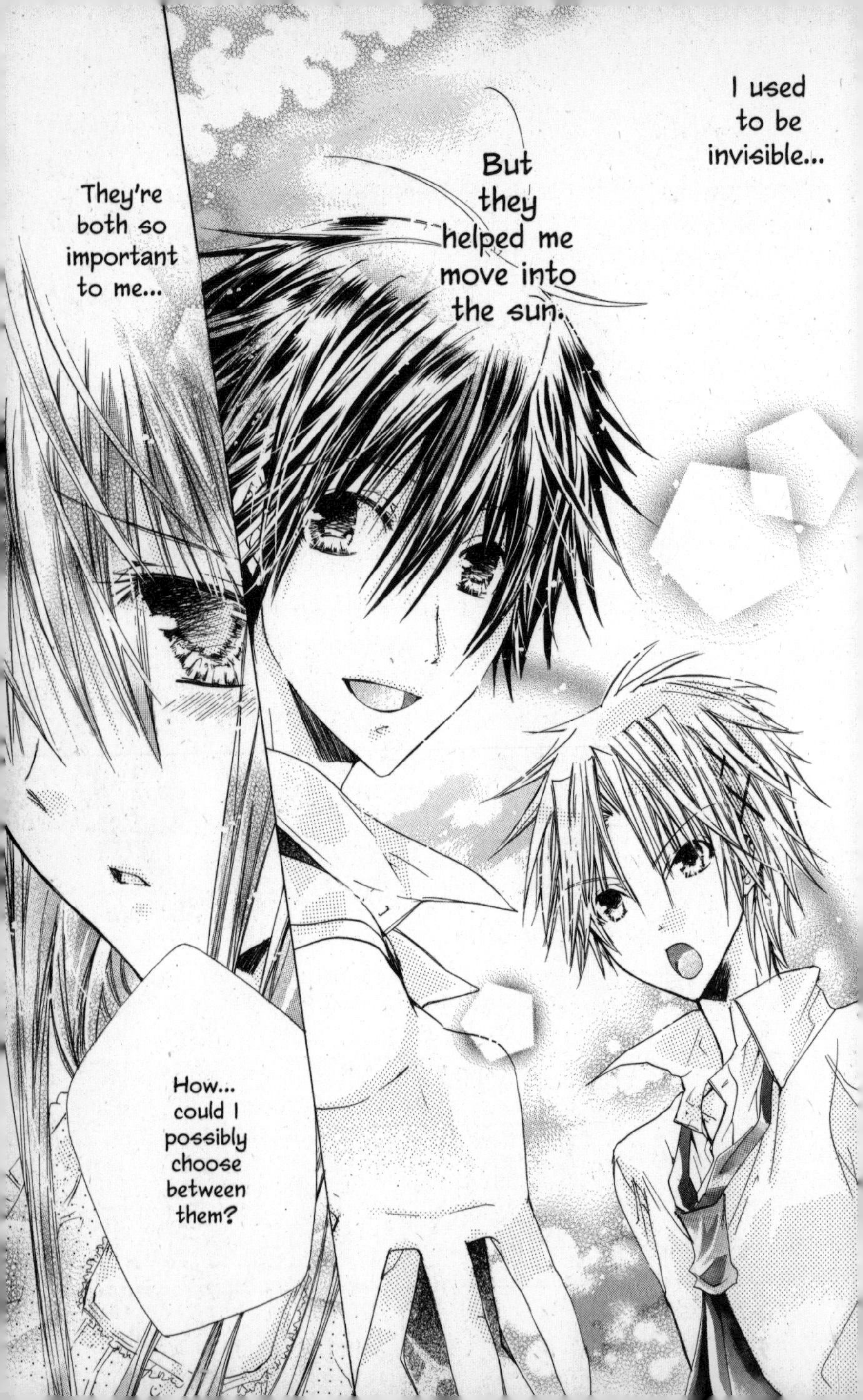
I used to be invisible...
But they helped me move into the sun.
They're both so important to me...
How... could I possibly choose between them?

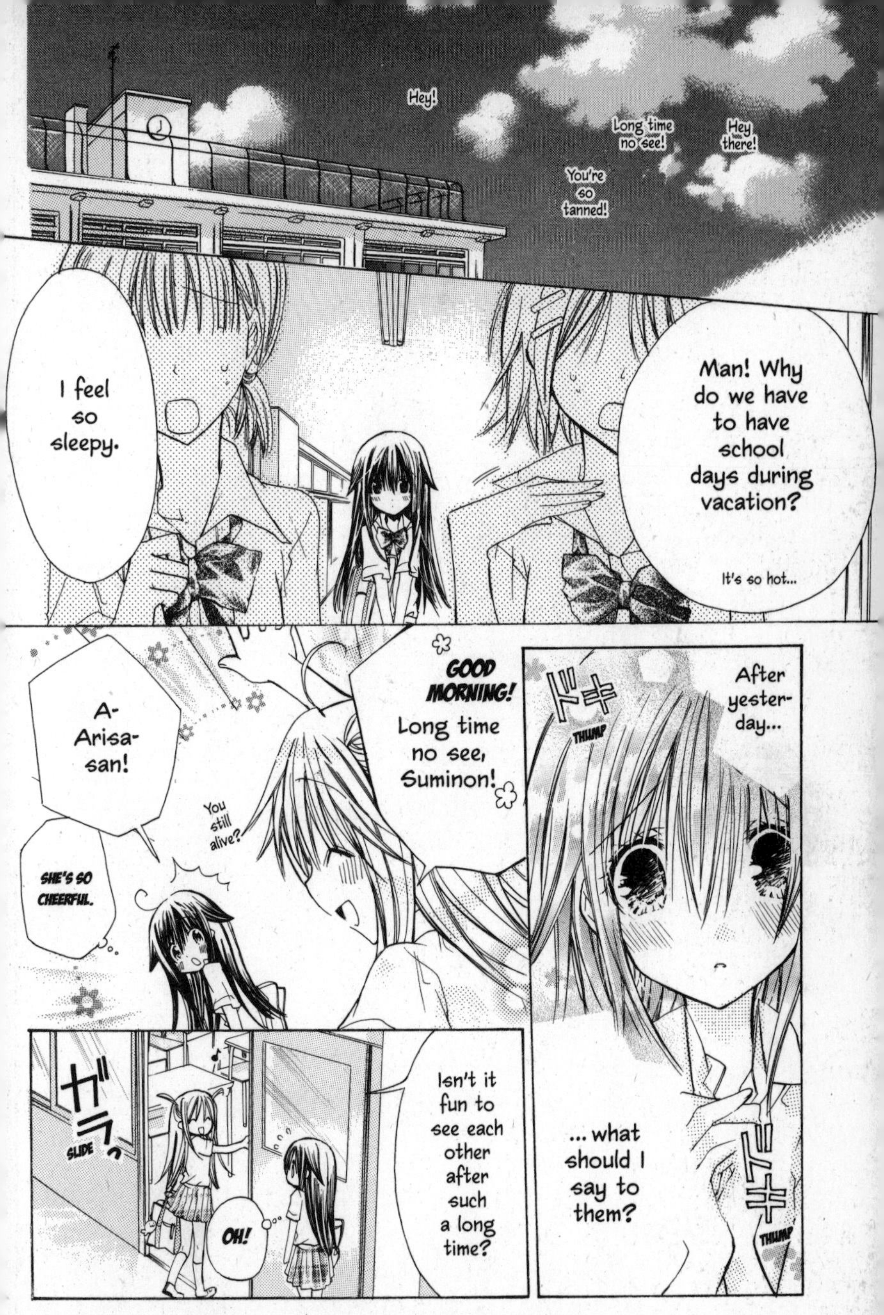
Hey there!
Long time no see!
You're so tanned!
Hey!
Man! Why do we have to have school days during vacation?
It's so hot...
I feel so sleepy.
After yester-day...
ドキ
THUMP
... what should I say to them?
ドキ
THUMP
GOOD MORNING! Long time no see, Suminon!
You still alive?
A-Arisa-san!
SHE'S SO CHEERFUL.
Isn't it fun to see each other after such a long time?
OH!
ガラ
SLIDE

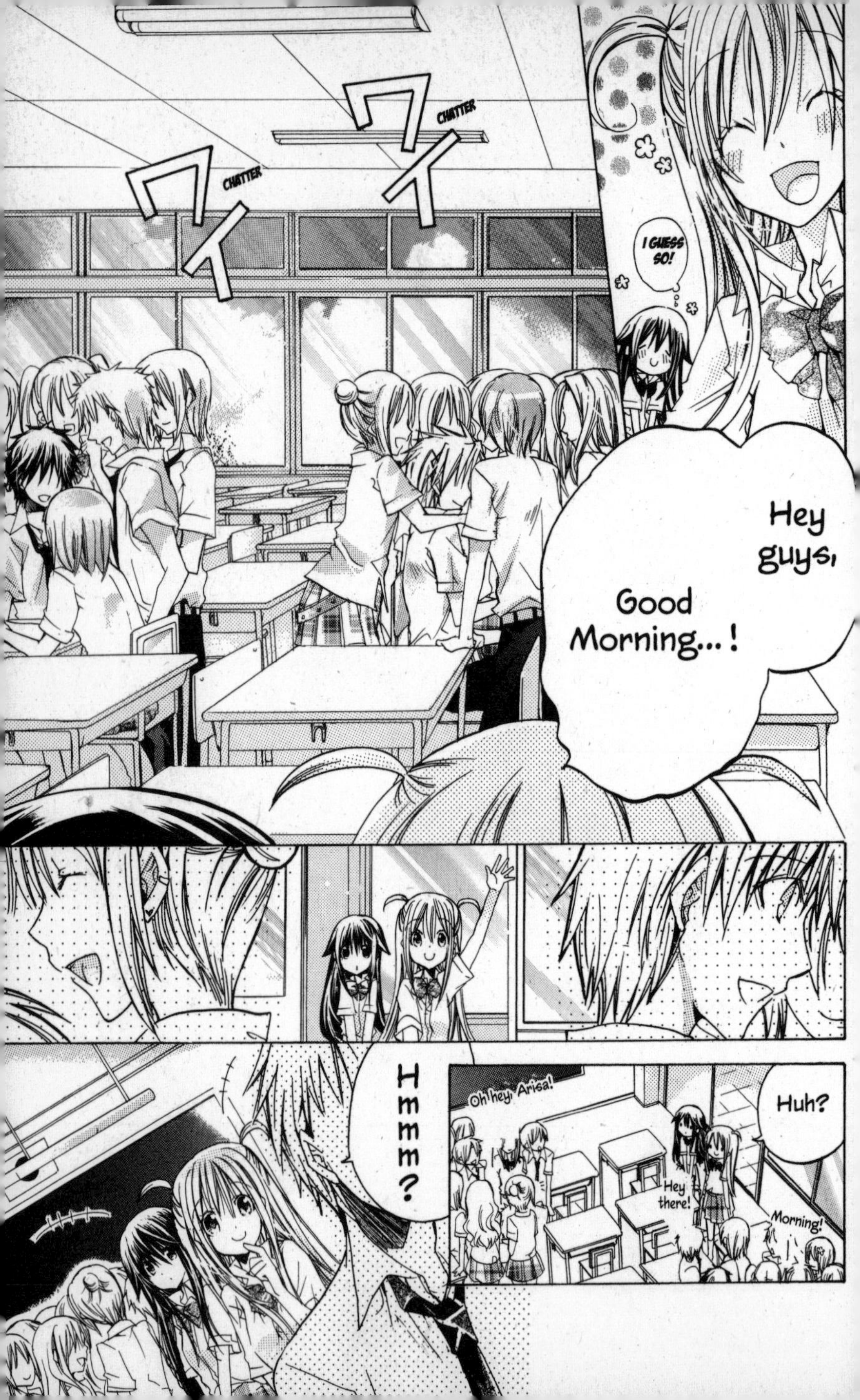

I GUESS SO!
CHATTER
CHATTER
Hey guys,
Good Morning...!
Huh?
Oh hey, Arisa!
Hey there!
Morning!
Hmmm?

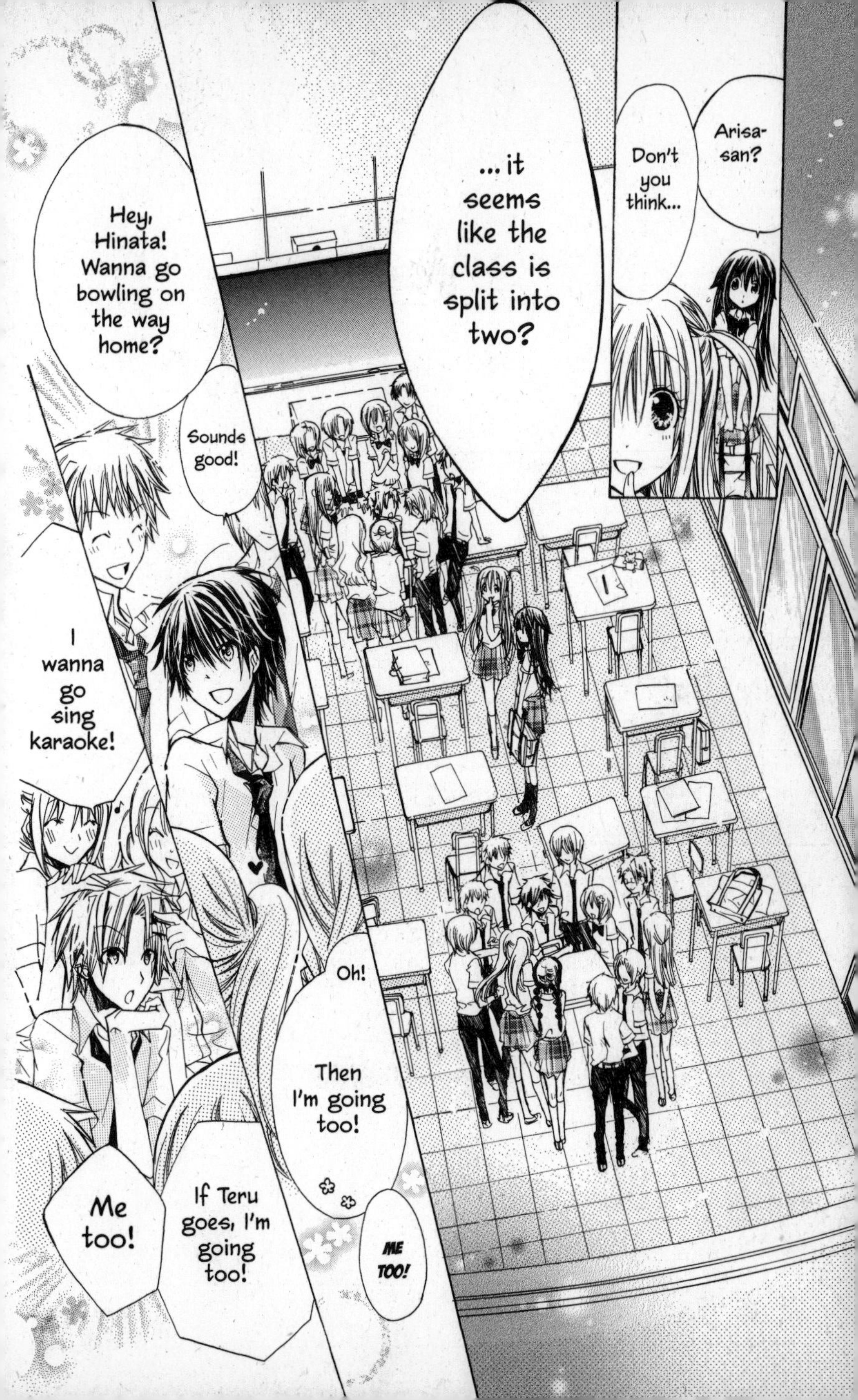
Arisa-san?
Don't you think...
... it seems like the class is split into two?
Hey, Hinata! Wanna go bowling on the way home?
Sounds good!
I wanna go sing karaoke!
Oh!
Then I'm going too!
ME TOO!
If Teru goes, I'm going too!
Me too!

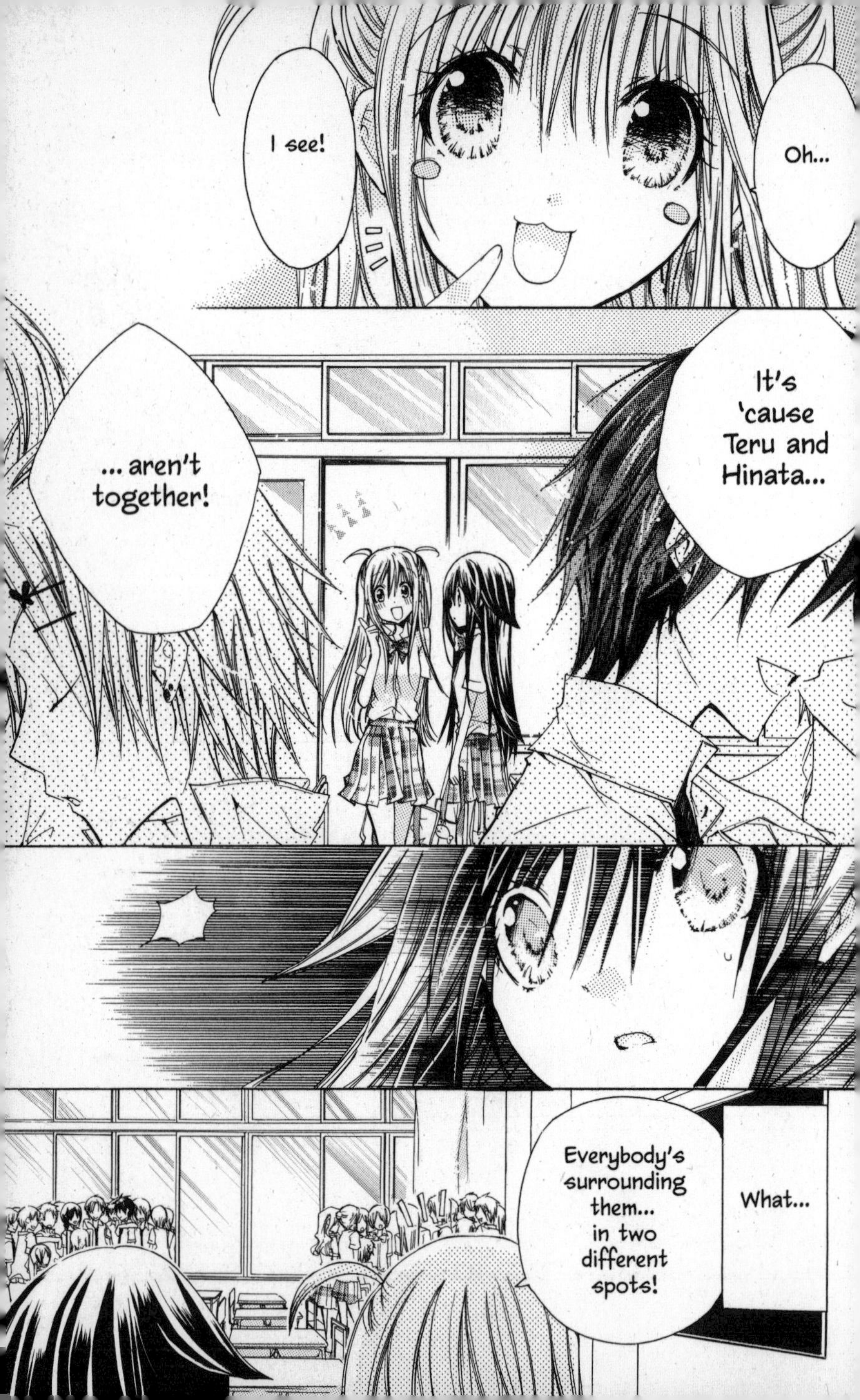
Oh...
I see!
It's 'cause Teru and Hinata...
... aren't together!
What...
Everybody's surrounding them... in two different spots!

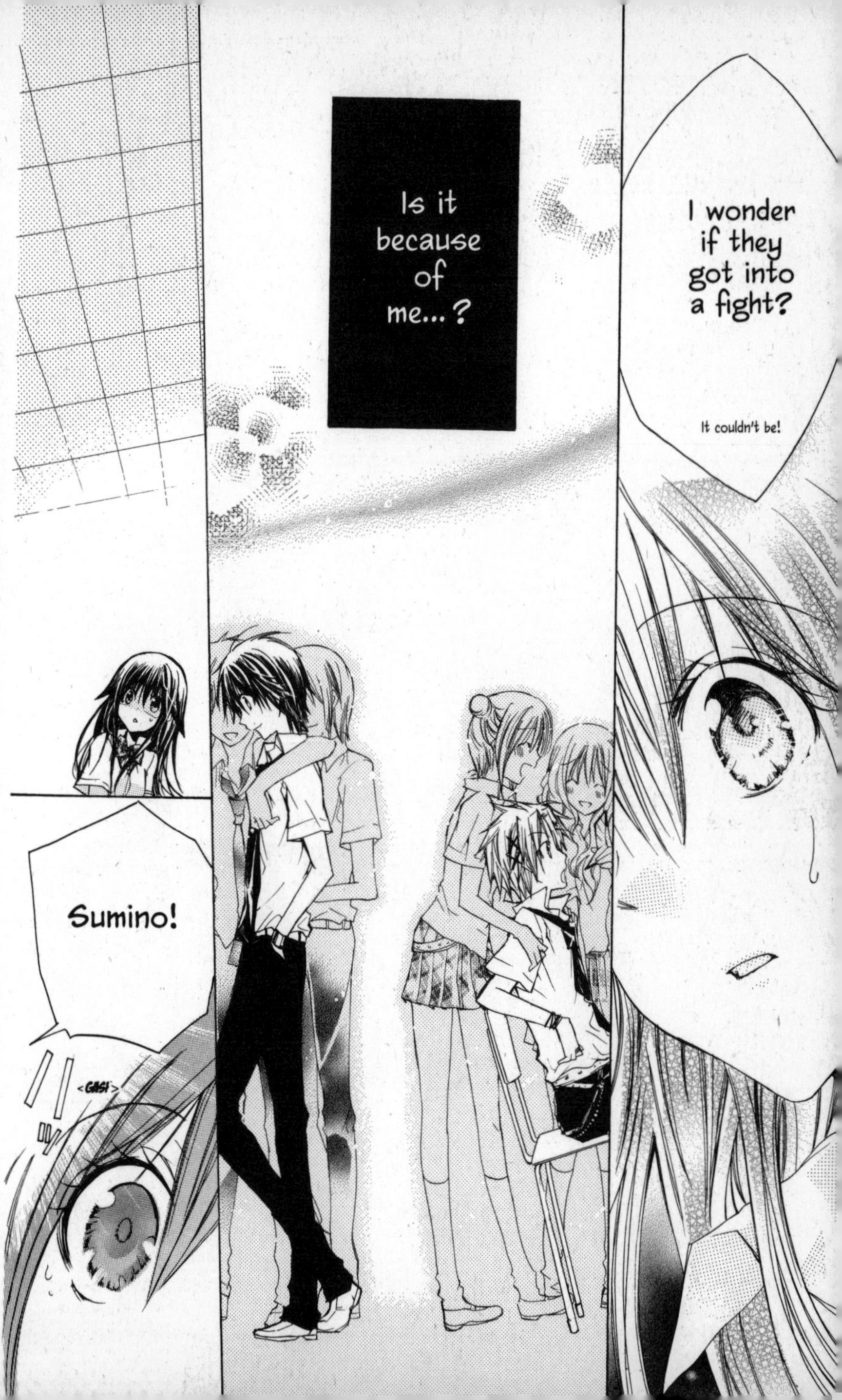

I wonder if they got into a fight?
It couldn't be!
Is it because of me...?
Sumino!
<GASI>

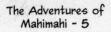

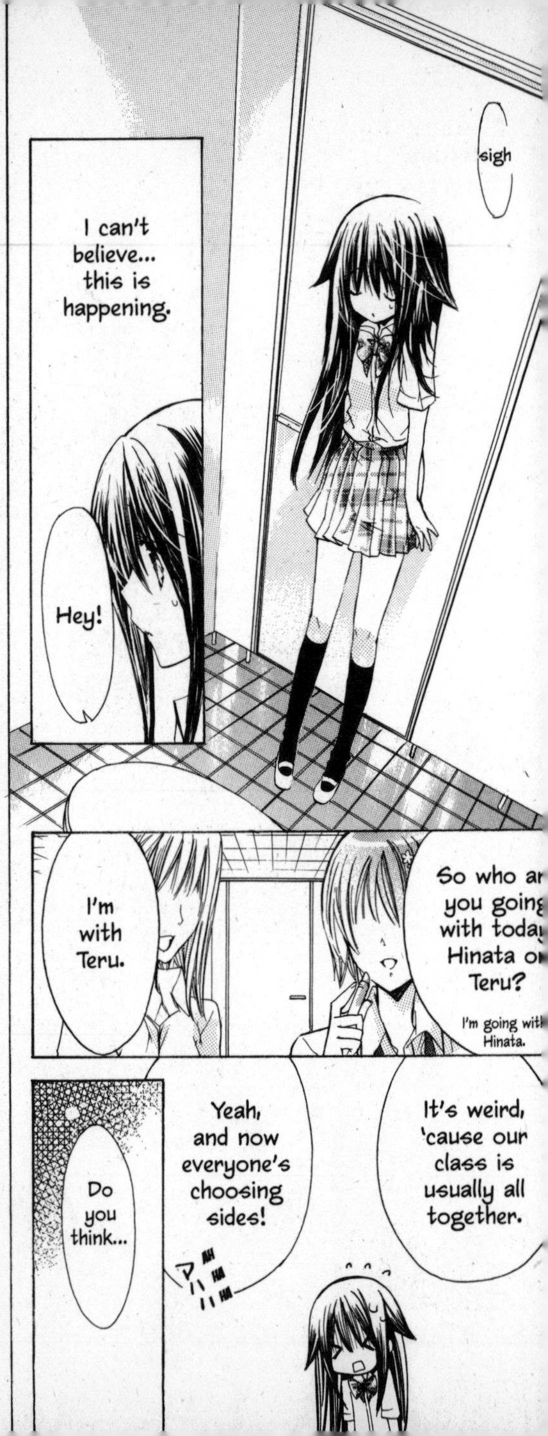
sigh
I can't believe... this is happening.
Hey!
So who ar you going with toda Hinata o Teru?
I'm going wit Hinata.
I'm with Teru.
It's weird, 'cause our class is usually all together.
Yeah, and now everyone's choosing sides!
AH HA HA
Do you think...

The Adventures of Mahimahi - 5

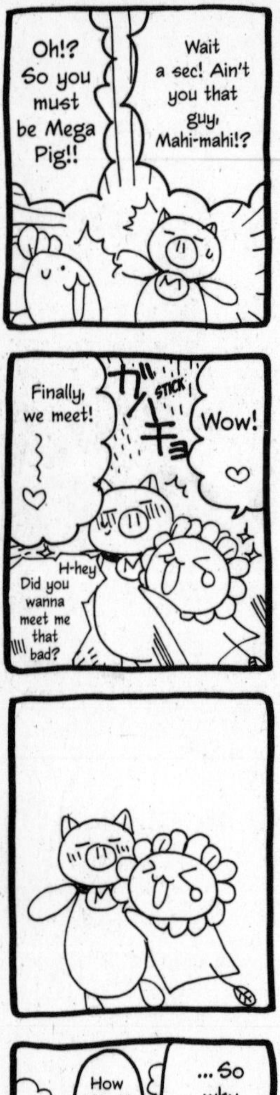
Wait a sec! Ain't you that guy, Mahi-mahi!?
Oh!? So you must be Mega Pig!!
Wow!
STICK
Finally, we meet!
H-hey Did you wanna meet me that bad?
...So why was I looking for you again?
How should I know, silly?
Mahimahi-kun just realized something very important.

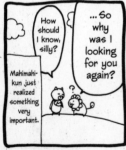

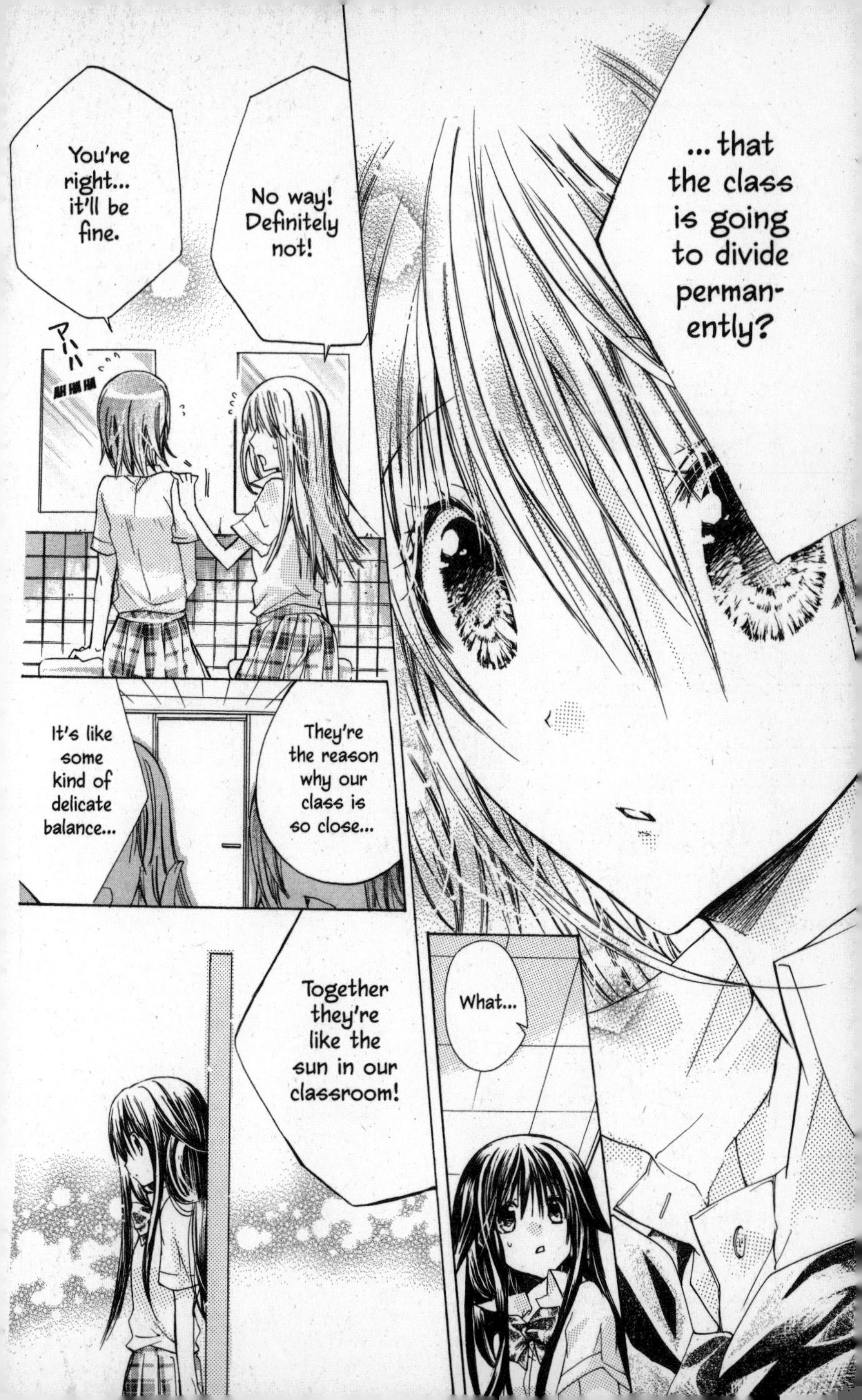
... that the class is going to divide perman-ently?
No way! Definitely not!
You're right... it'll be fine.
アハハ
AH HA HA
They're the reason why our class is so close...
It's like some kind of delicate balance...
What...
Together they're like the sun in our classroom!

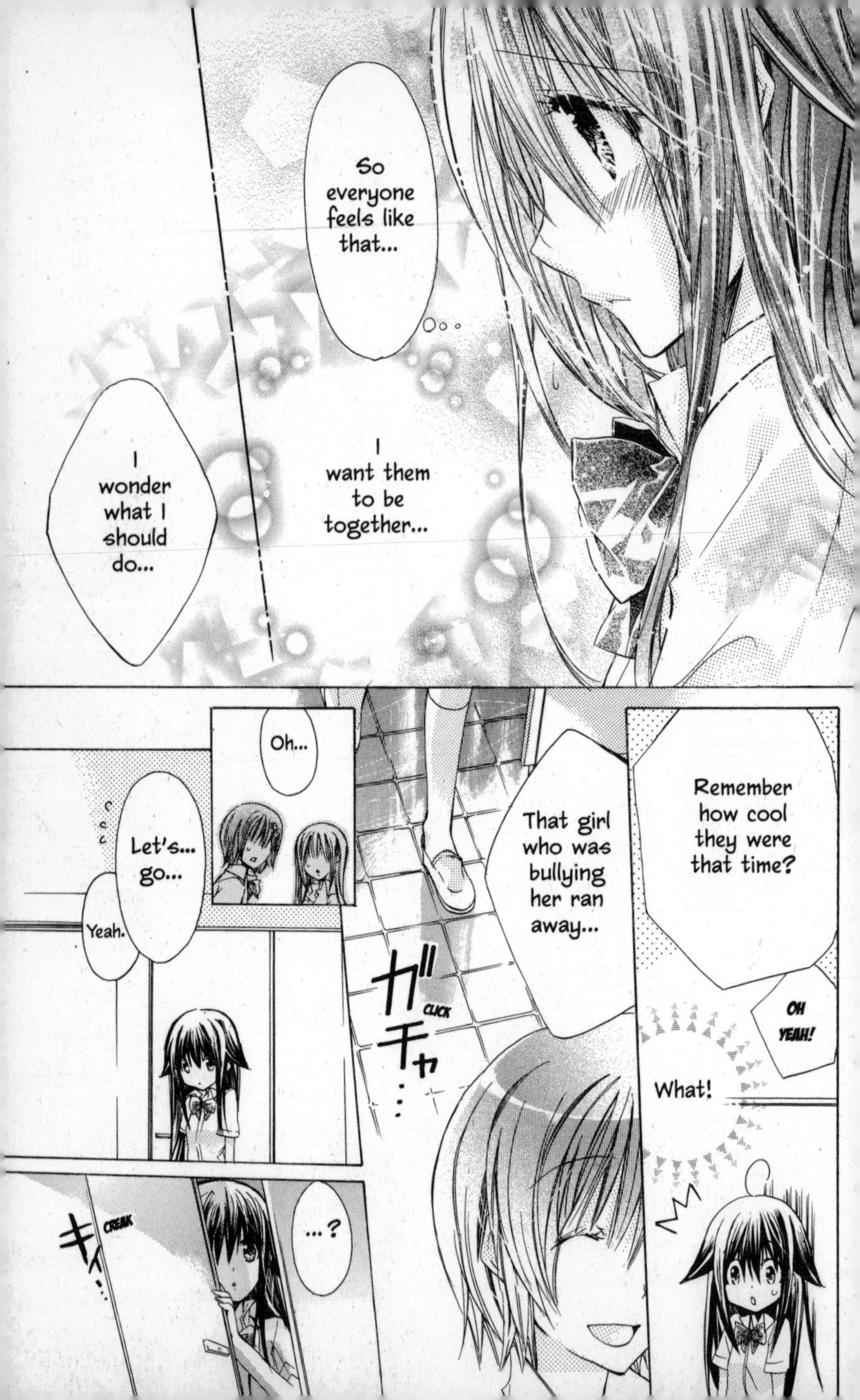

So everyone feels like that...
I want them to be together...
I wonder what I should do...
Remember how cool they were that time?
That girl who was bullying her ran away...
OH YEAH!
What!
ガチャ...
CLICK
Oh...
Let's... go...
Yeah.
...?
キィ...
CREAK

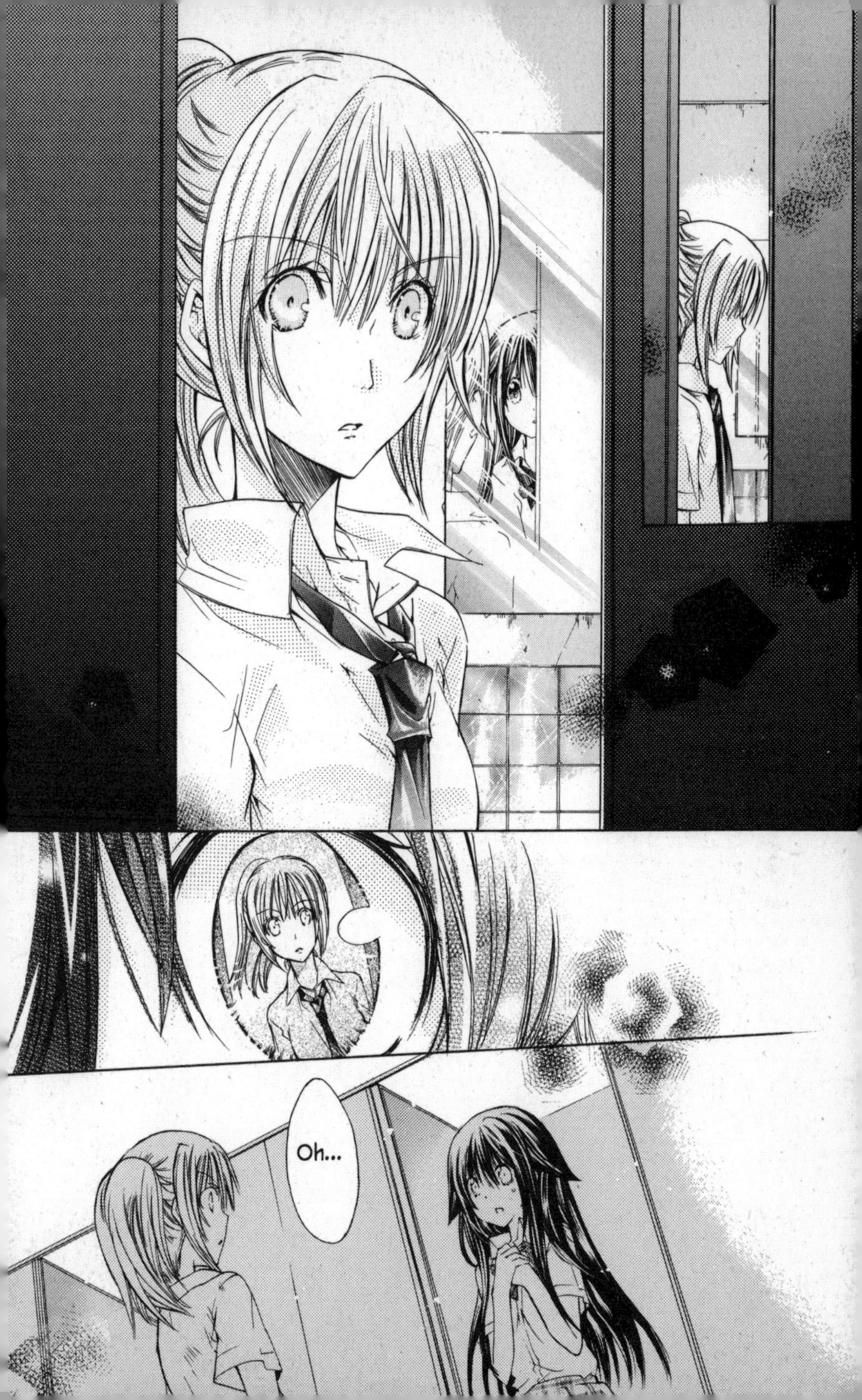
Oh...

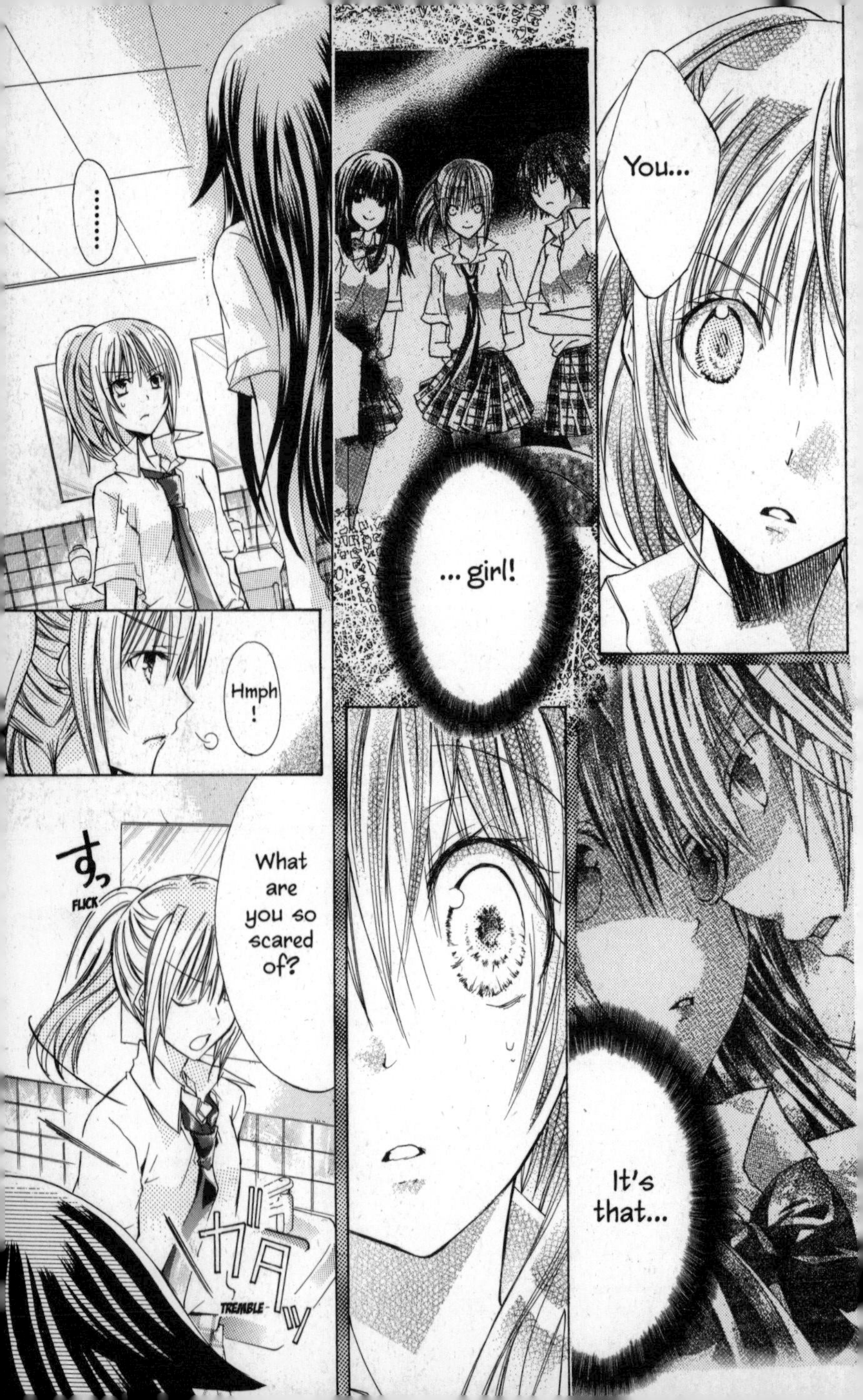
You...
... girl!
It's that...
......
Hmph!
What are you so scared of?
すっ
FLICK
TREMBLE

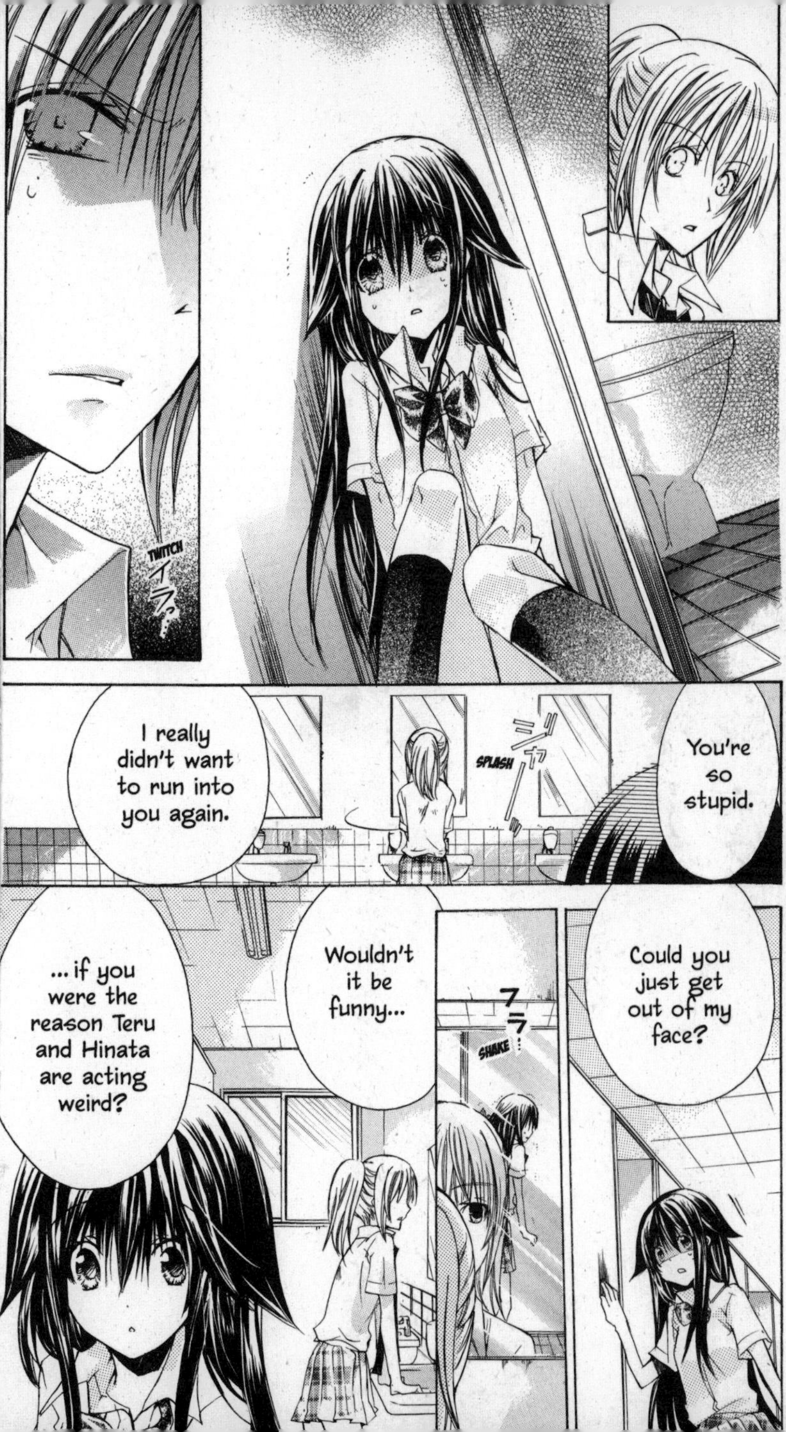

TWITCH
イラッ
You're so stupid.
SPLASH
I really didn't want to run into you again.
Could you just get out of my face?
SHAKE
Wouldn't it be funny...
... if you were the reason Teru and Hinata are acting weird?

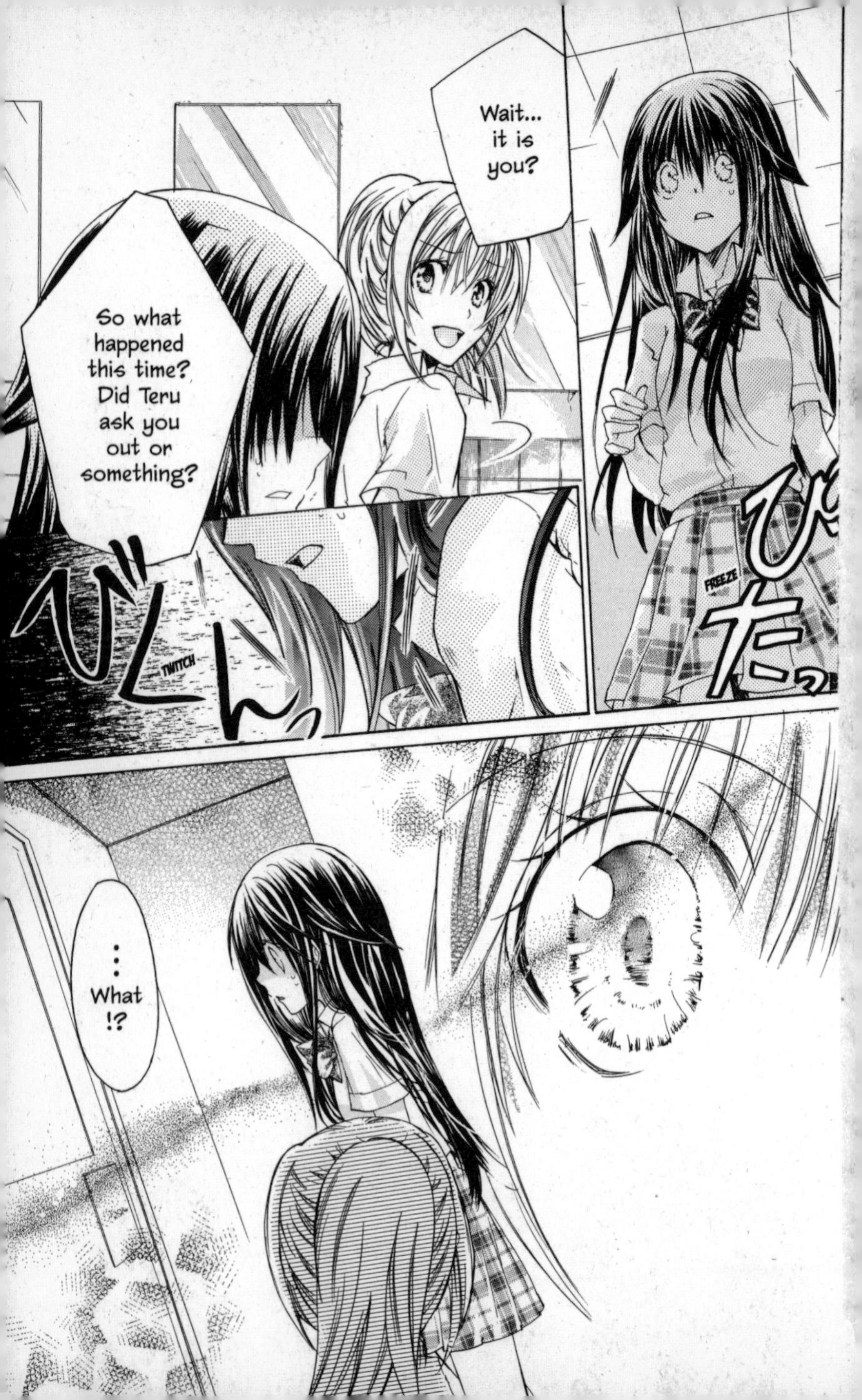
ぴたっ
FREEZE
Wait... it is you?
So what happened this time? Did Teru ask you out or something?
びくん
TWITCH
...What!?

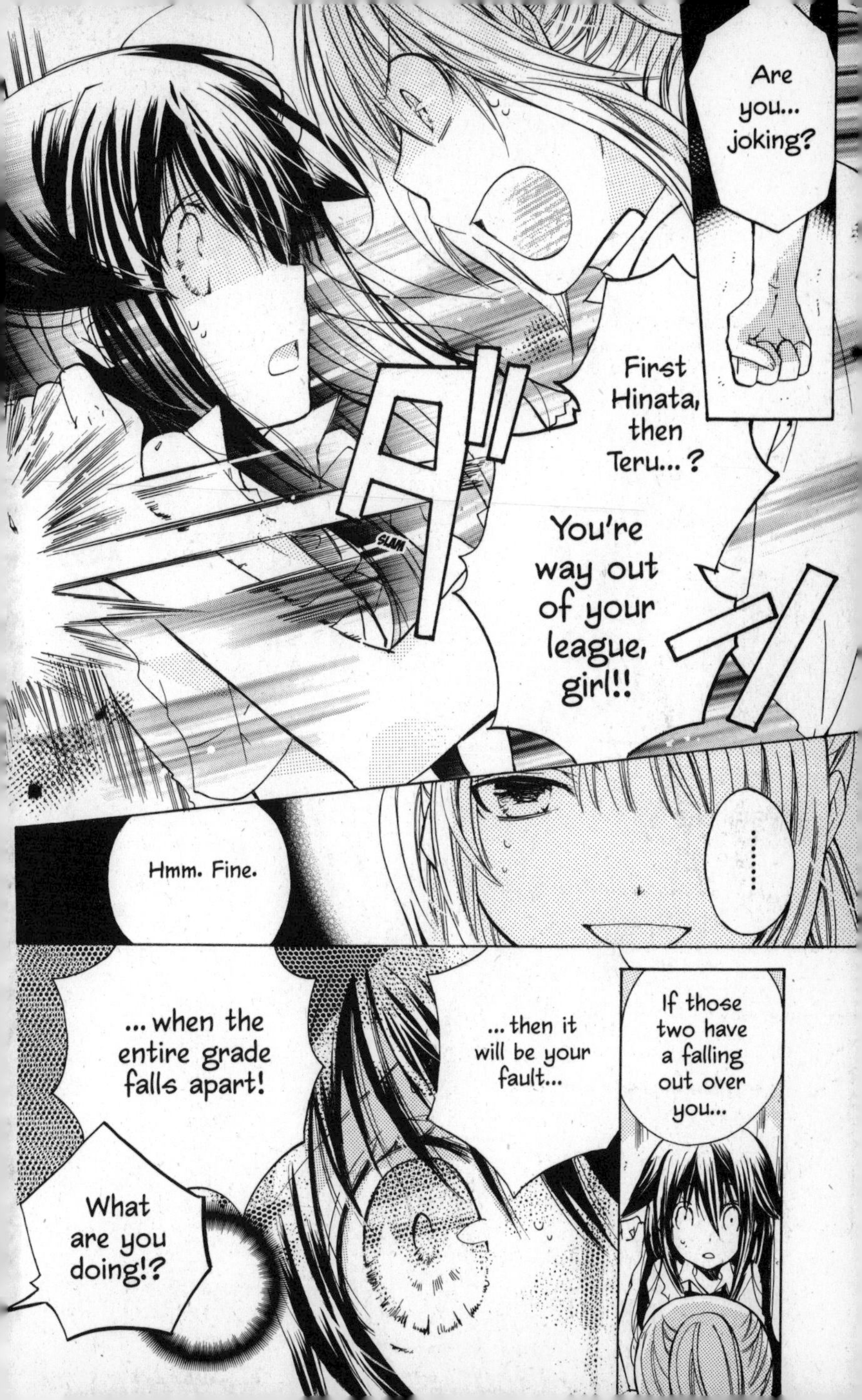
Are you... joking?
First Hinata, then Teru...?
You're way out of your league, girl!!
SLAM
......
Hmm. Fine.
If those two have a falling out over you...
...then it will be your fault...
...when the entire grade falls apart!
What are you doing!?

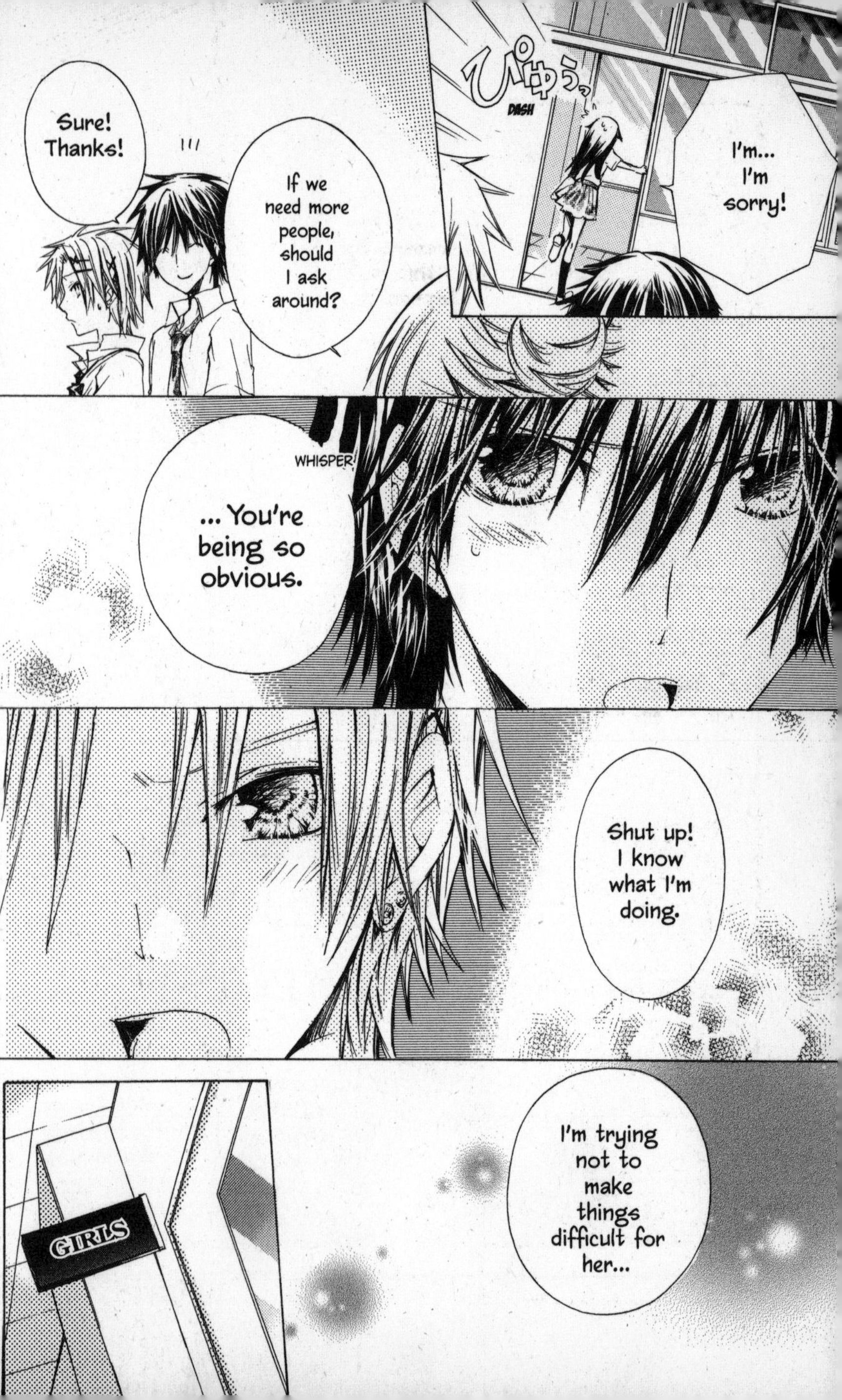
ぴゅうっ
DASH
I'm... I'm sorry!
If we need more people, should I ask around?
Sure! Thanks!
WHISPER
... You're being so obvious.
Shut up! I know what I'm doing.
I'm trying not to make things difficult for her...
GIRLS

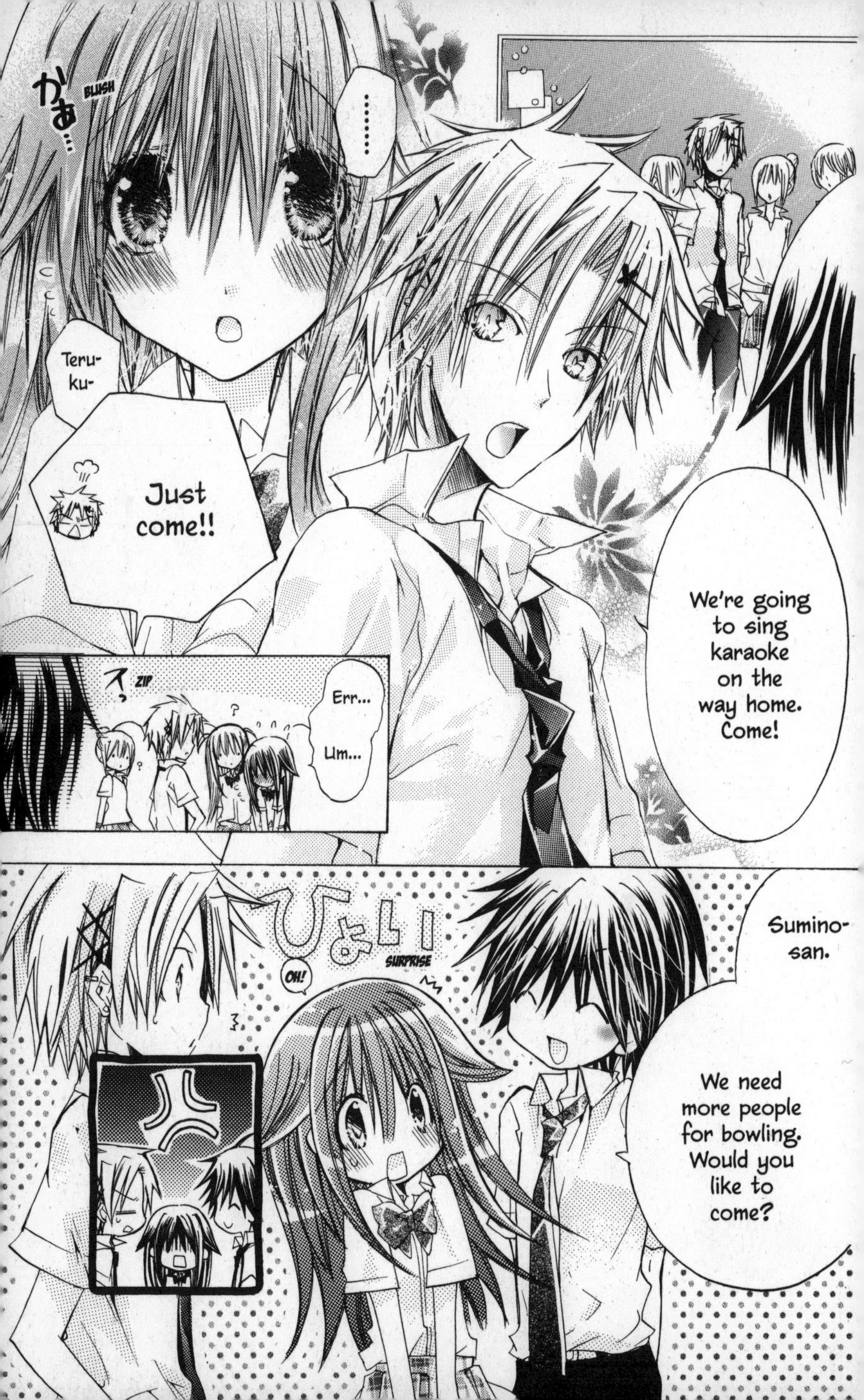
We're going to sing karaoke on the way home. Come!
......
かぁ...
BLUSH
Teru-ku-
Just come!!
ZIP
Err...
Um...
Sumino-san.
We need more people for bowling. Would you like to come?
SURPRISE
OH!

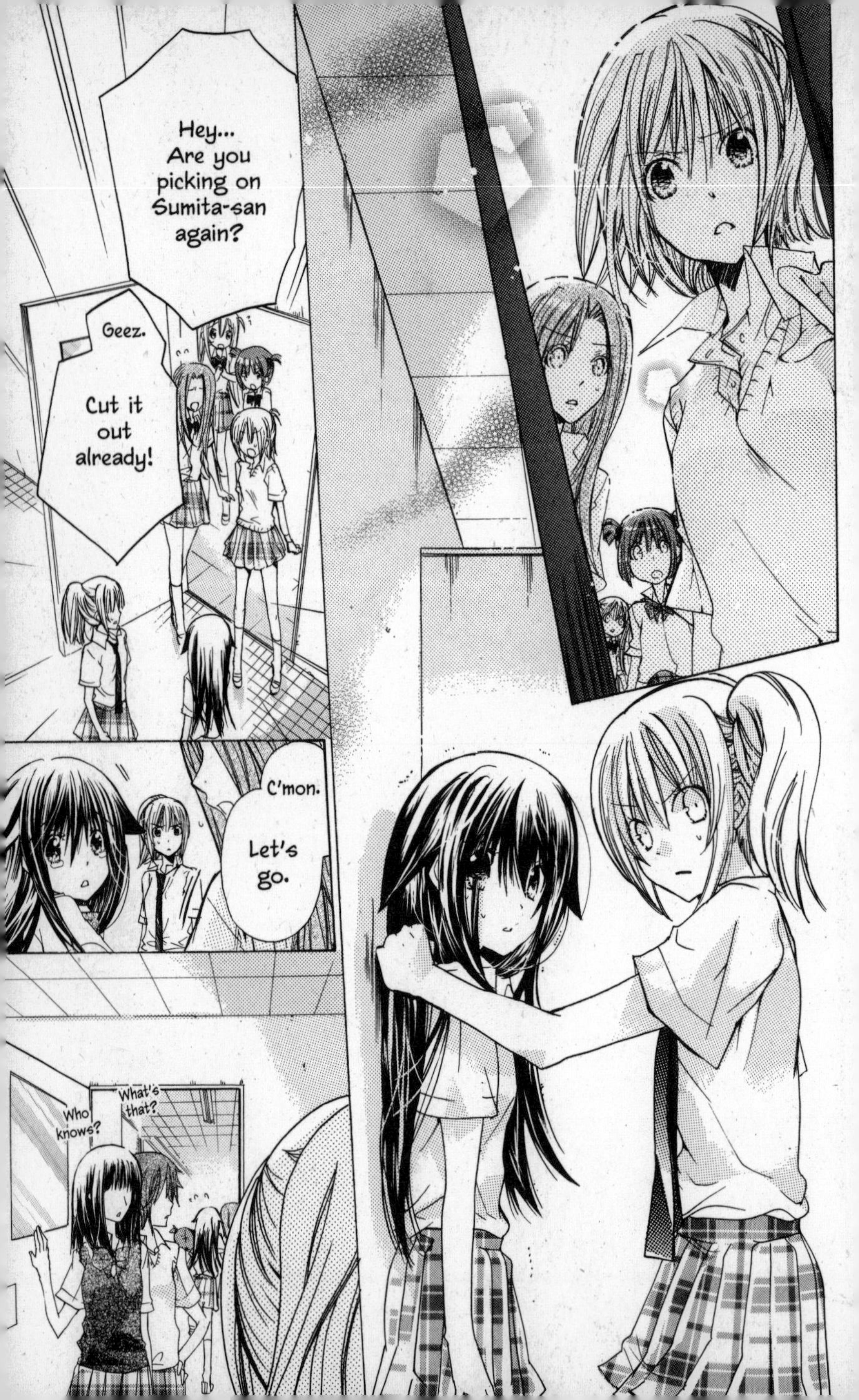

Hey... Are you picking on Sumita-san again?
Geez.
Cut it out already!
C'mon.
Let's go.
What's that?
Who knows?

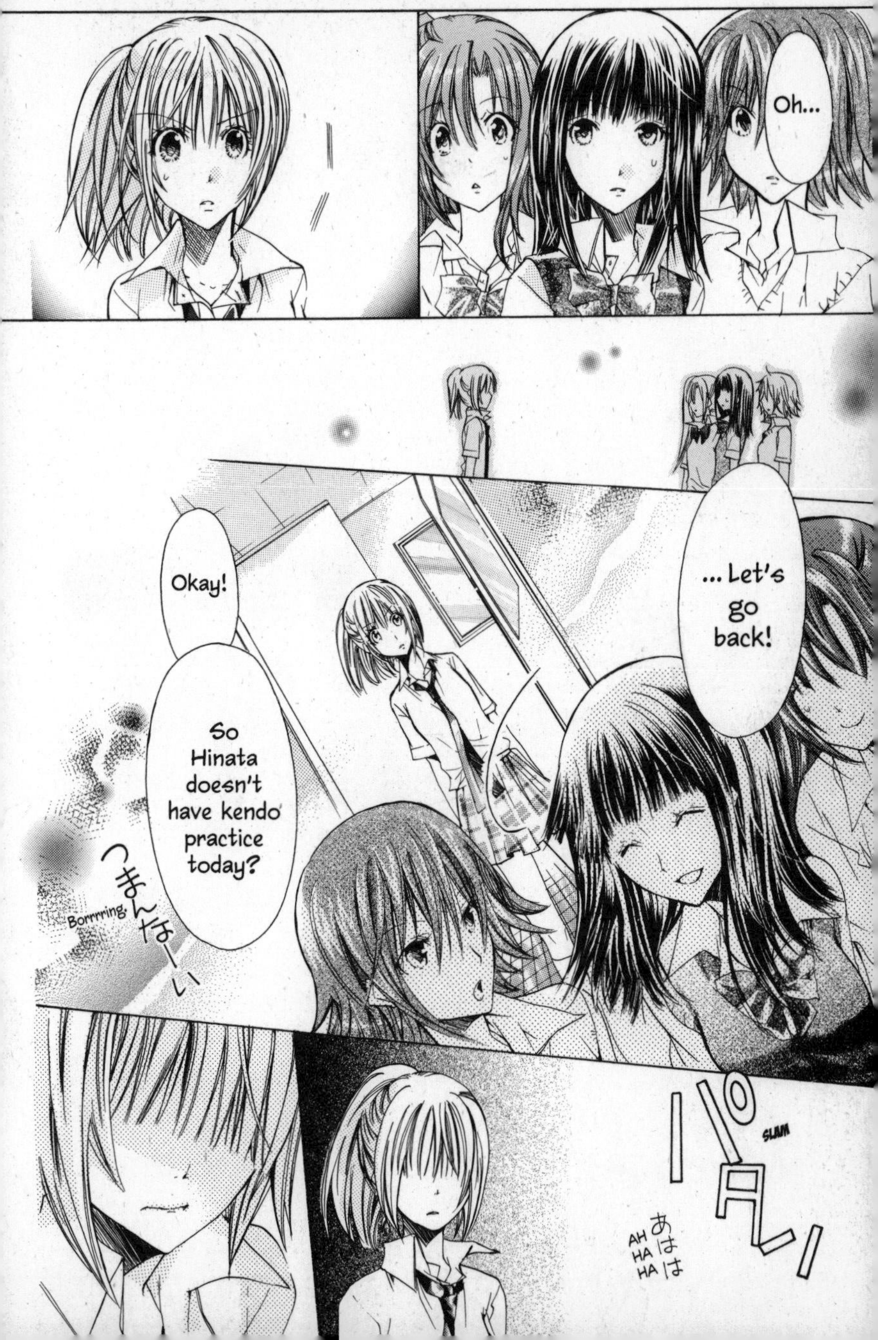
Oh...
... Let's go back!
Okay!
So Hinata doesn't have kendo practice today?
つまんなーい
Borrrring.
パタ
SLAM
あはは
AH HA HA

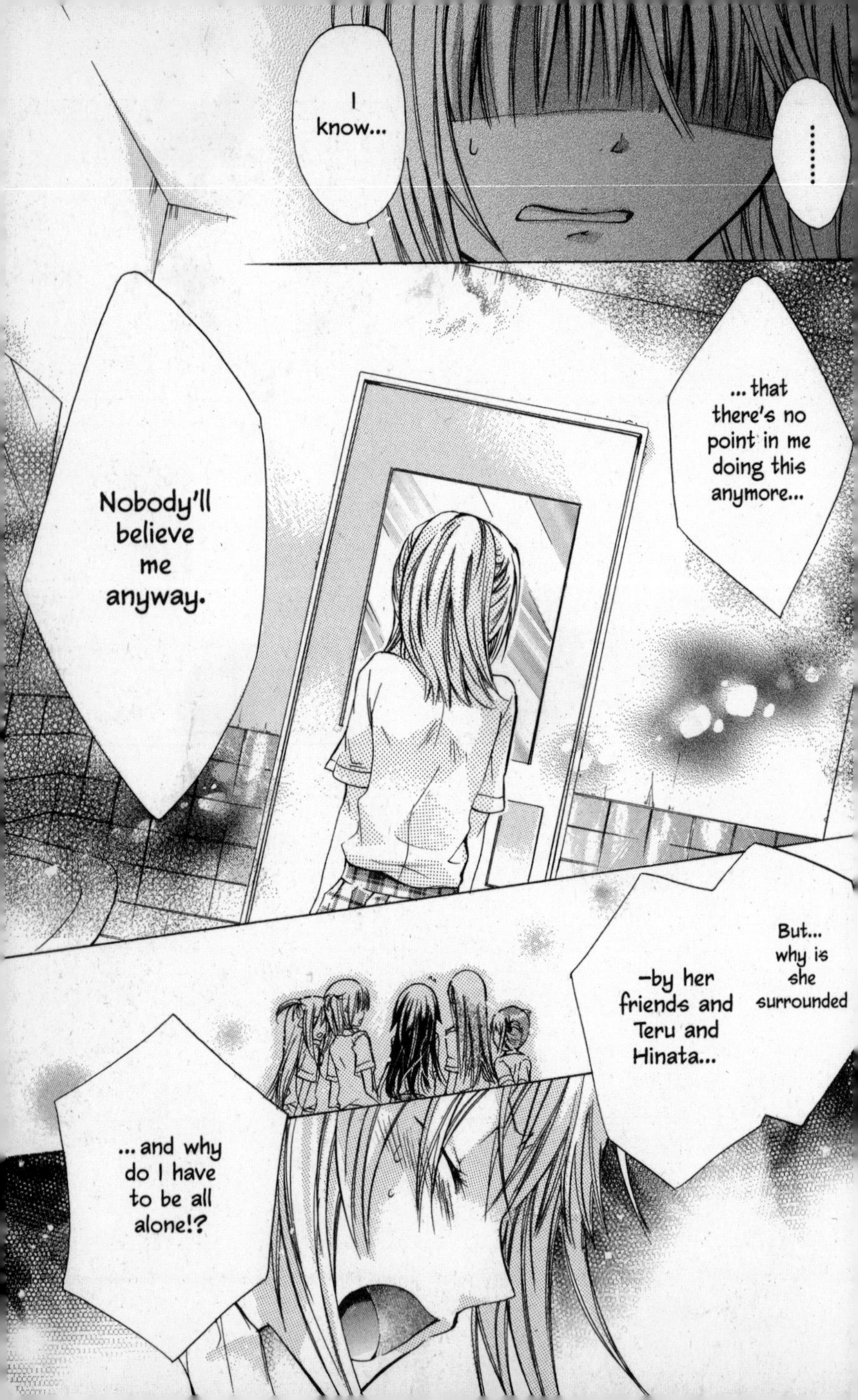
......
I know...
...that there's no point in me doing this anymore...
Nobody'll believe me anyway.
But... why is she surrounded
–by her friends and Teru and Hinata...
...and why do I have to be all alone!?

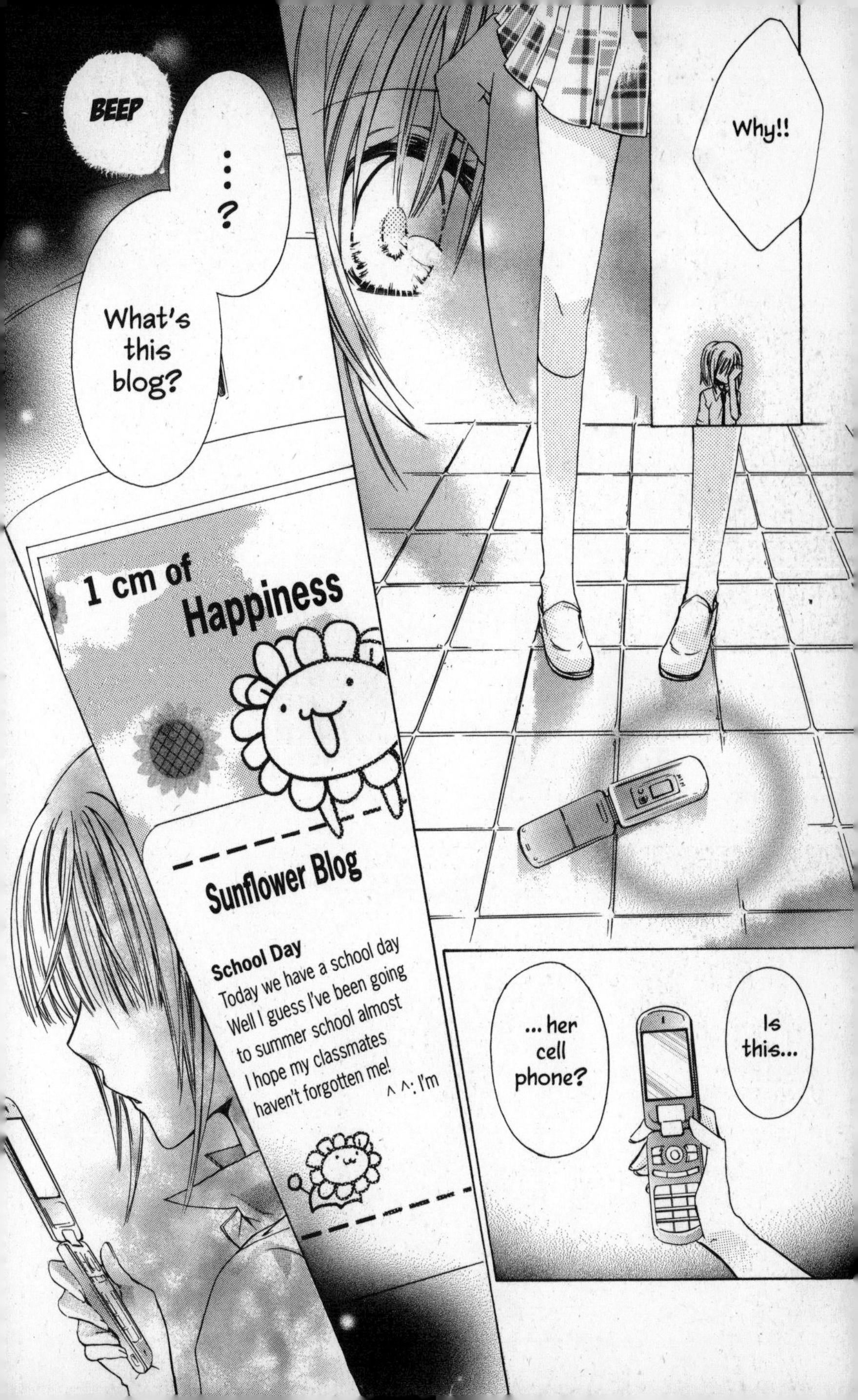
Why!!
Is this...
... her cell phone?
BEEP
...?
What's this blog?
1 cm of Happiness
Sunflower Blog
School Day
Today we have a school day
Well I guess I've been going
to summer school almost
I hope my classmates
haven't forgotten me!
^ ^; I'm

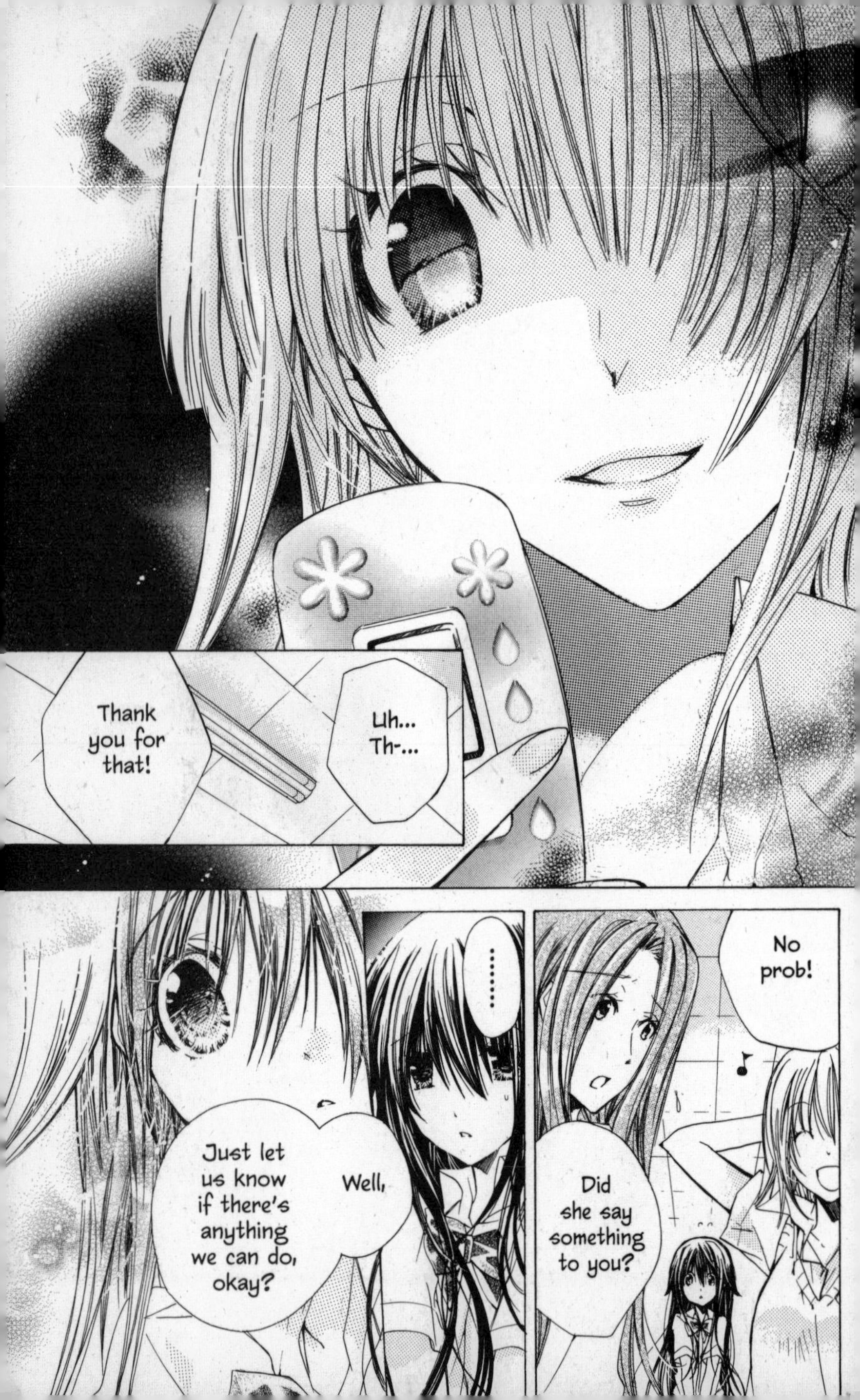
Uh... Th-...
Thank you for that!
No prob!
Did she say something to you?
......
Well,
Just let us know if there's anything we can do, okay?

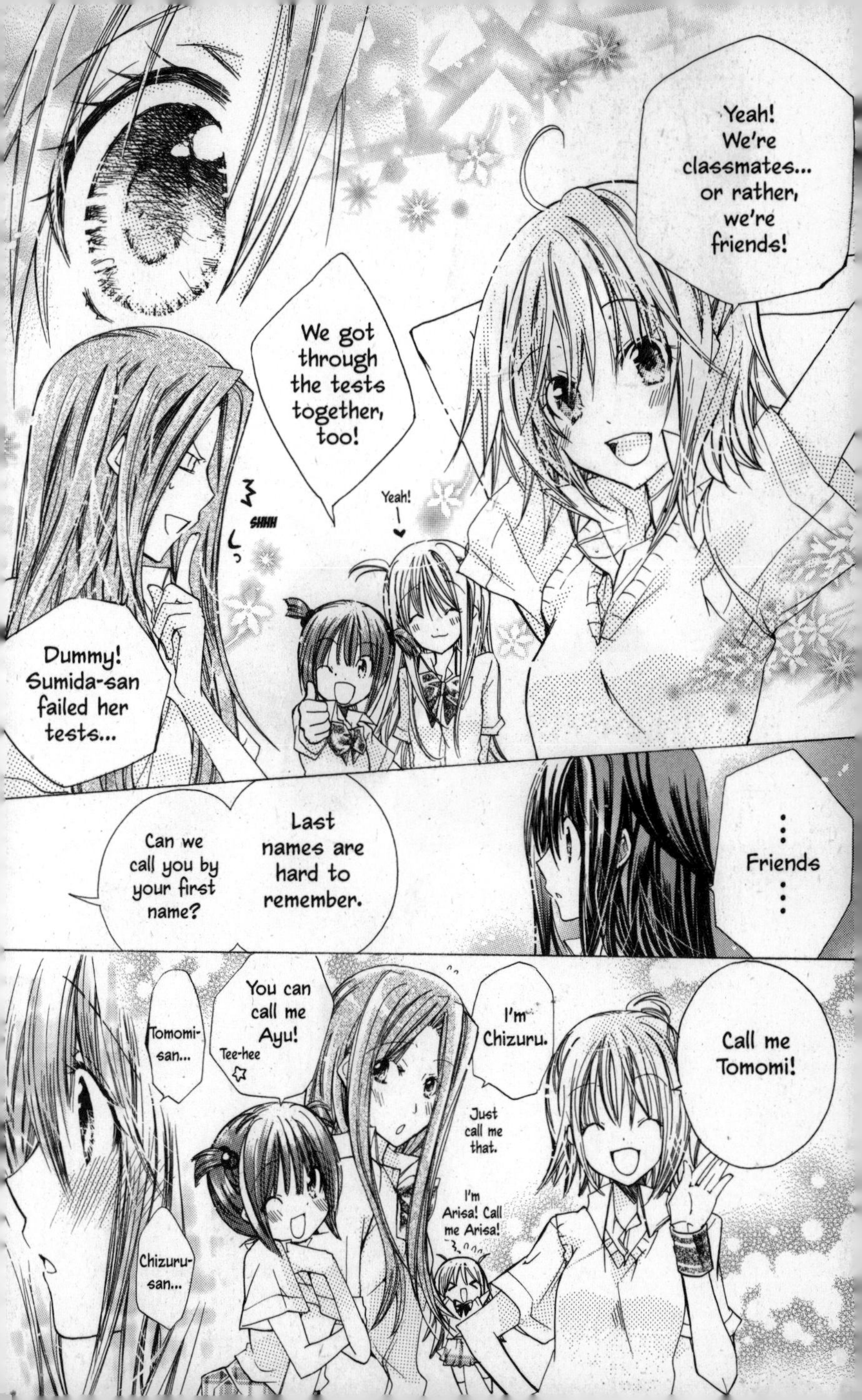

Yeah! We're classmates... or rather, we're friends!
We got through the tests together, too!
Yeah!
SHHH
Dummy! Sumida-san failed her tests...
... Friends ...
Last names are hard to remember.
Can we call you by your first name?
Call me Tomomi!
I'm Chizuru.
Just call me that.
I'm Arisa! Call me Arisa!
You can call me Ayu!
Tee-hee
Tomomi-san...
Chizuru-san...

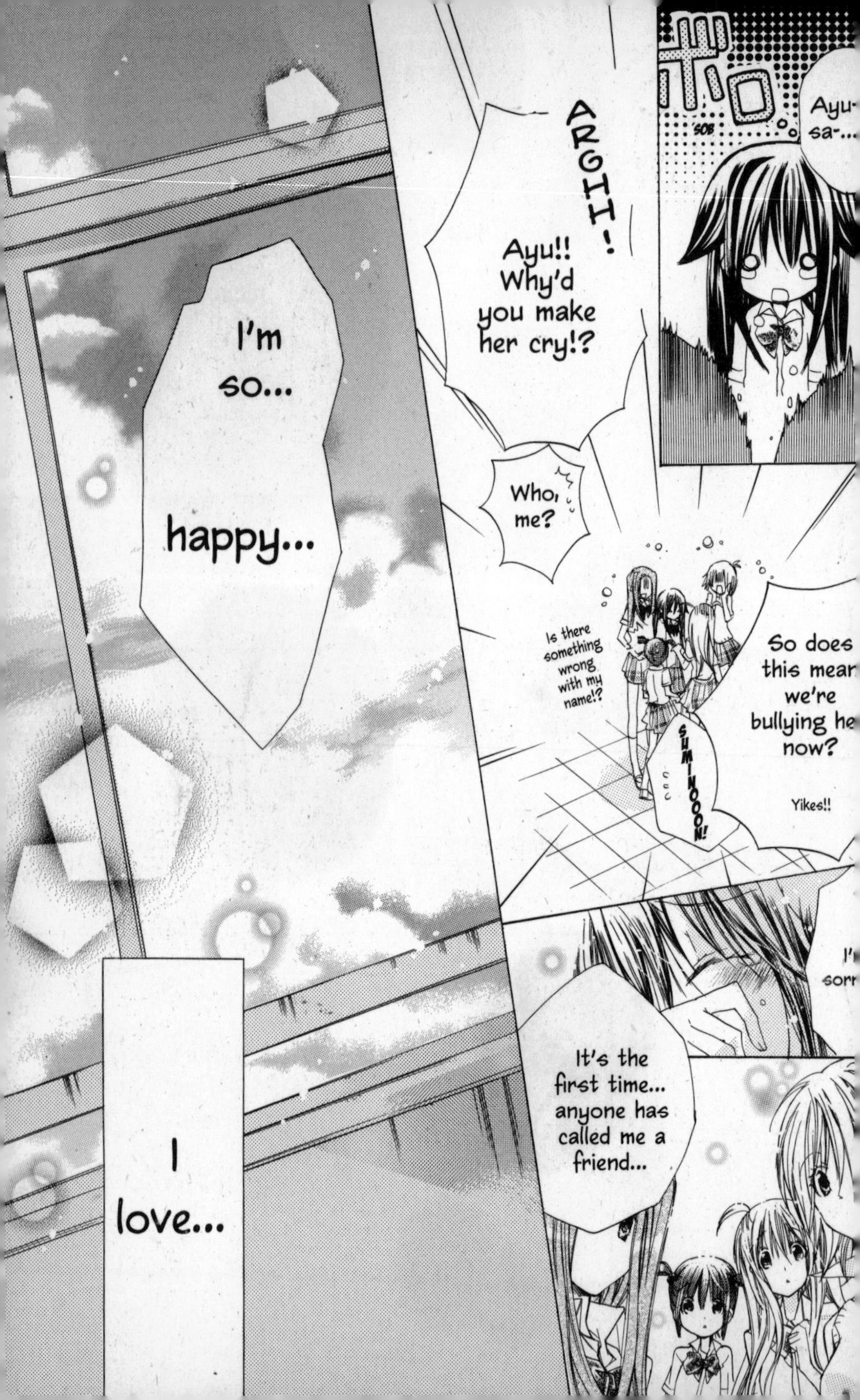
SOB
Ayu-sa-...
ARGHH!
Ayu!! Why'd you make her cry!?
Who, me?
So does this mean we're bullying he now?
Yikes!!
SUMINOOON!
Is there something wrong with my name!?
It's the first time... anyone has called me a friend...
I'm so...
happy...
I love...

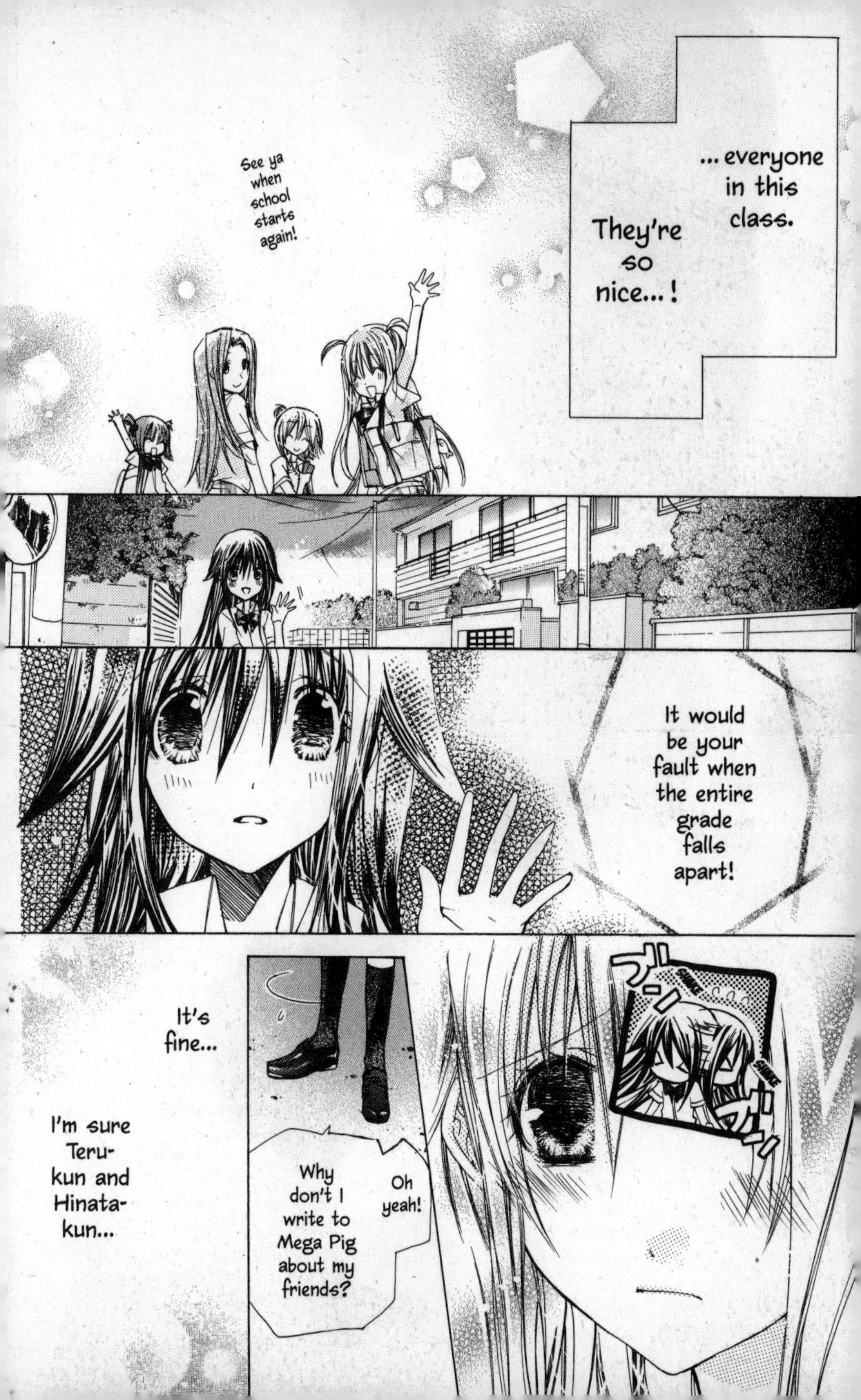

...everyone in this class.
They're so nice...!
See ya when school starts again!
It would be your fault when the entire grade falls apart!
SHAKE
SHAKE
Oh yeah!
Why don't I write to Mega Pig about my friends?
It's fine...
I'm sure Teru-kun and Hinata-kun...

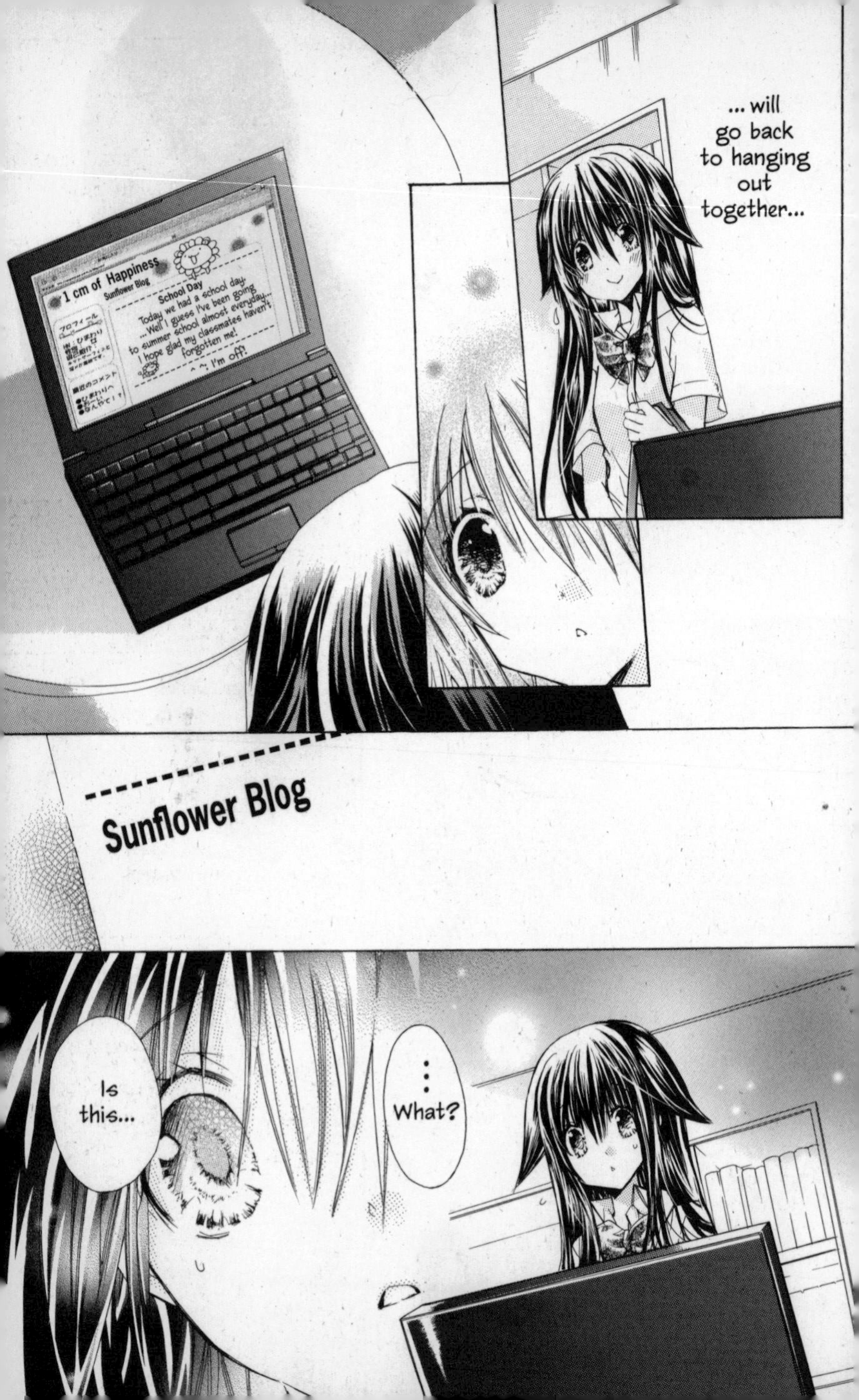

... will go back to hanging out together...
1 cm of Happiness
Sunflower Blog
School Day
Today we had a school day.
...Well I guess I've been going to summer school almost everyday...
I hope glad my classmates haven't forgotten me!
^ ^; I'm off!
Sunflower Blog
... What?
Is this...

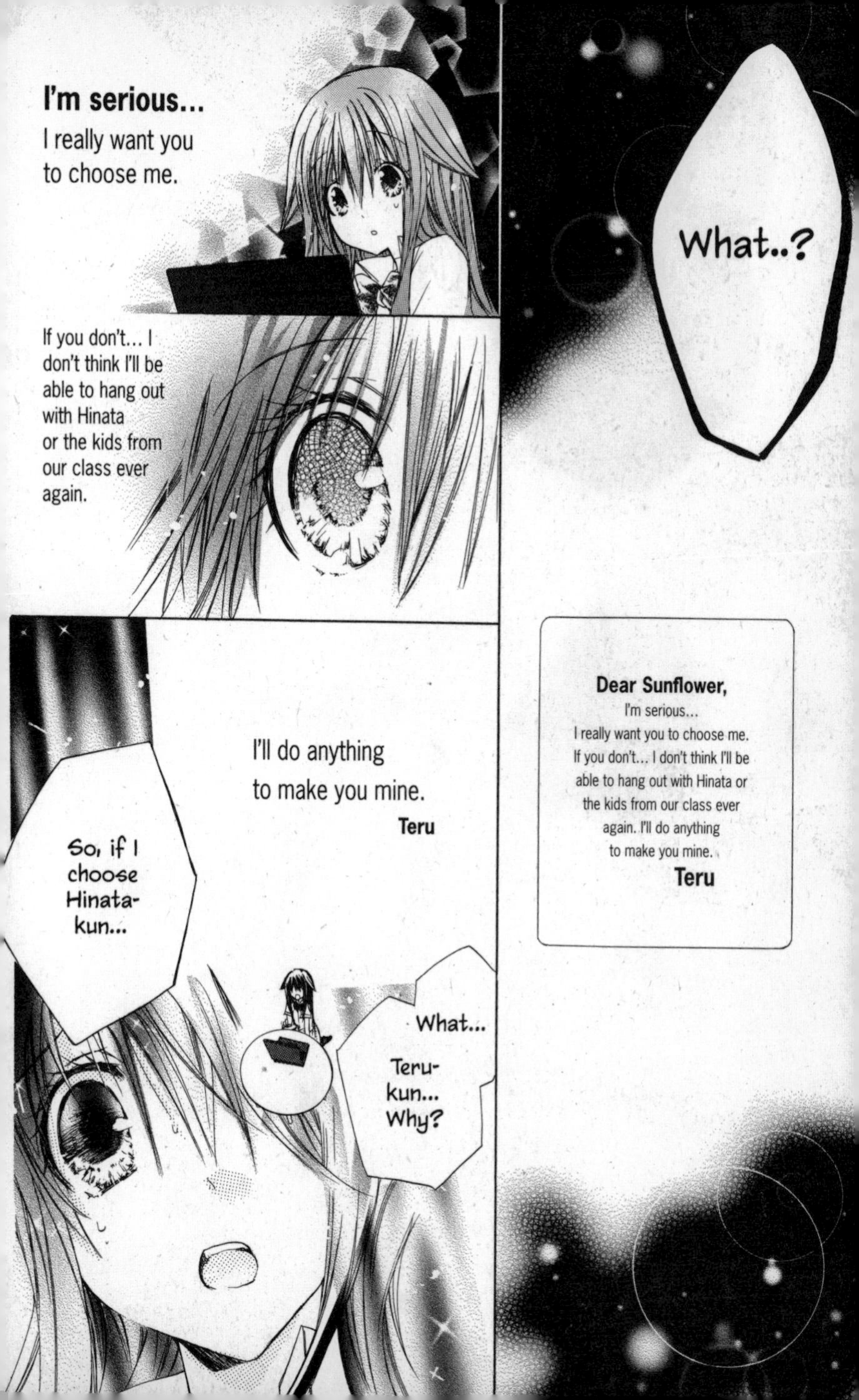
What..?
Dear Sunflower,
I'm serious...
I really want you to choose me.
If you don't... I don't think I'll be able to hang out with Hinata or the kids from our class ever again. I'll do anything to make you mine.
Teru
I'm serious...
I really want you to choose me.
If you don't... I don't think I'll be able to hang out with Hinata or the kids from our class ever again.
I'll do anything to make you mine.
Teru
So, if I choose Hinata-kun...
What...
Teru-kun... Why?

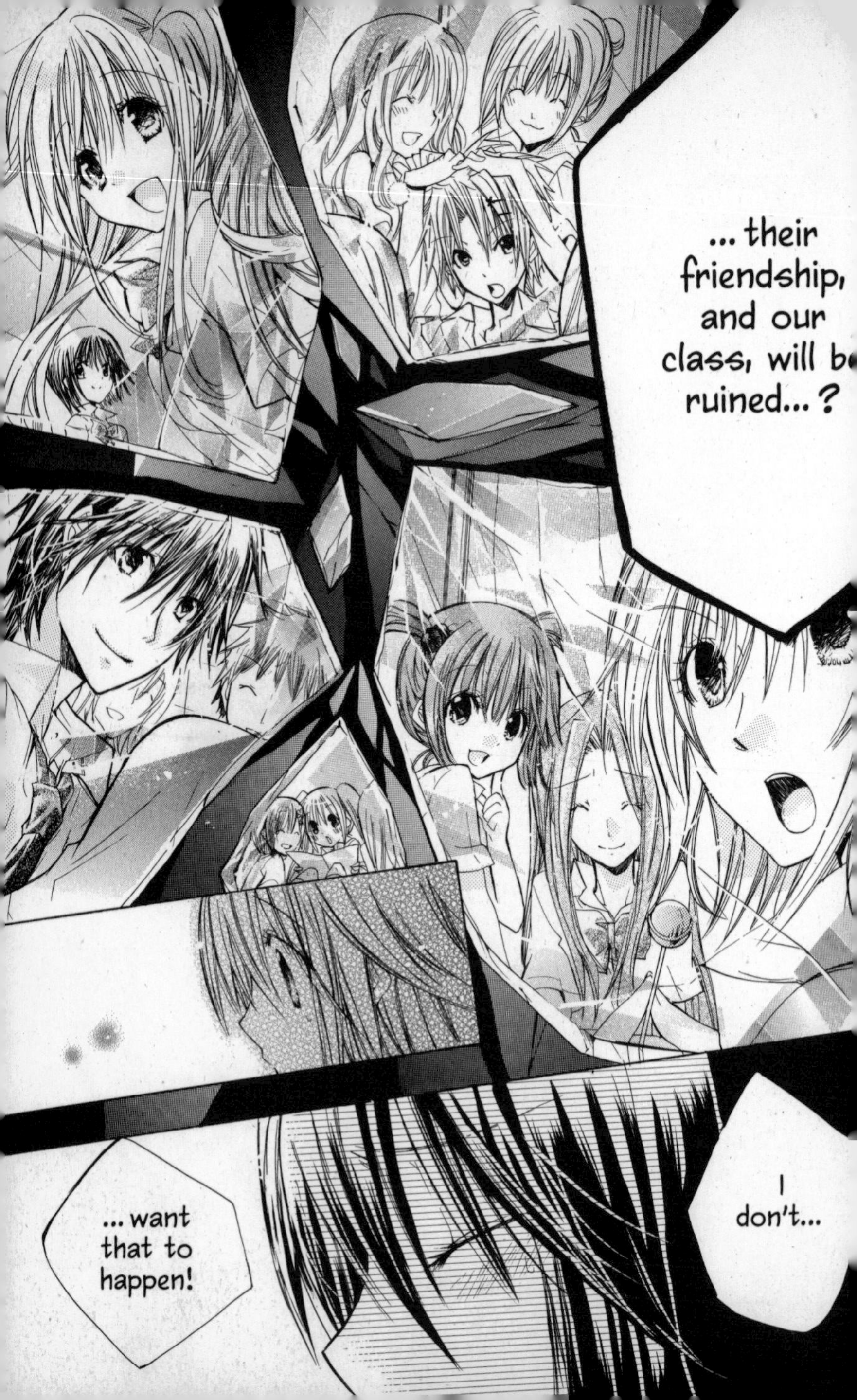
... their friendship, and our class, will be ruined...?
I don't...
... want that to happen!

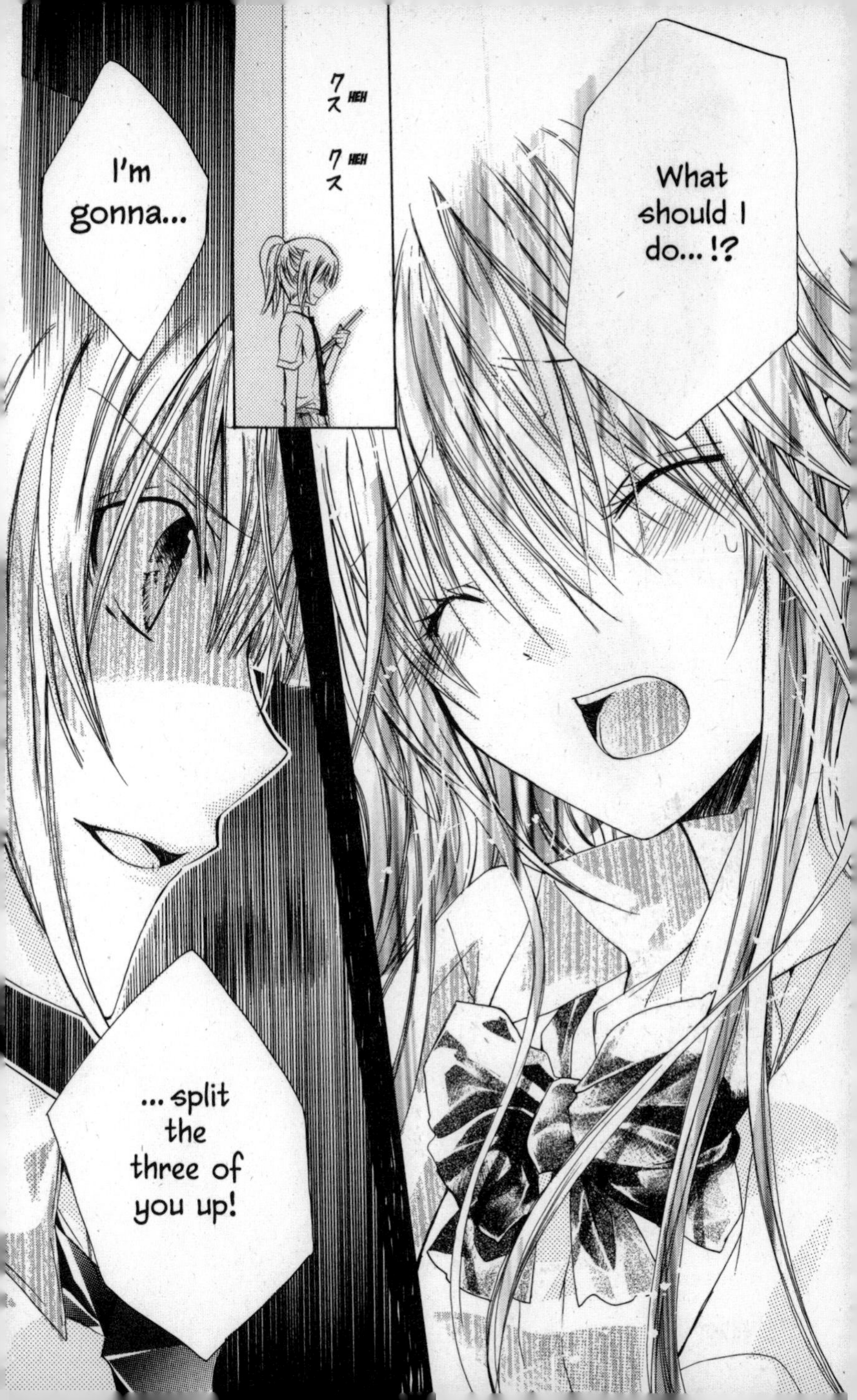
What should I do...!?
クス HEH
クス HEH
I'm gonna...
... split the three of you up!

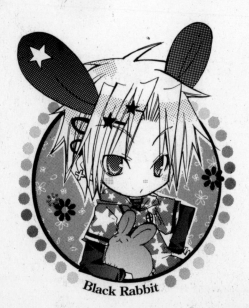

Black Rabbit

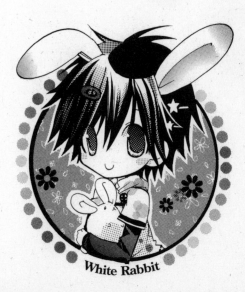

White Rabbit

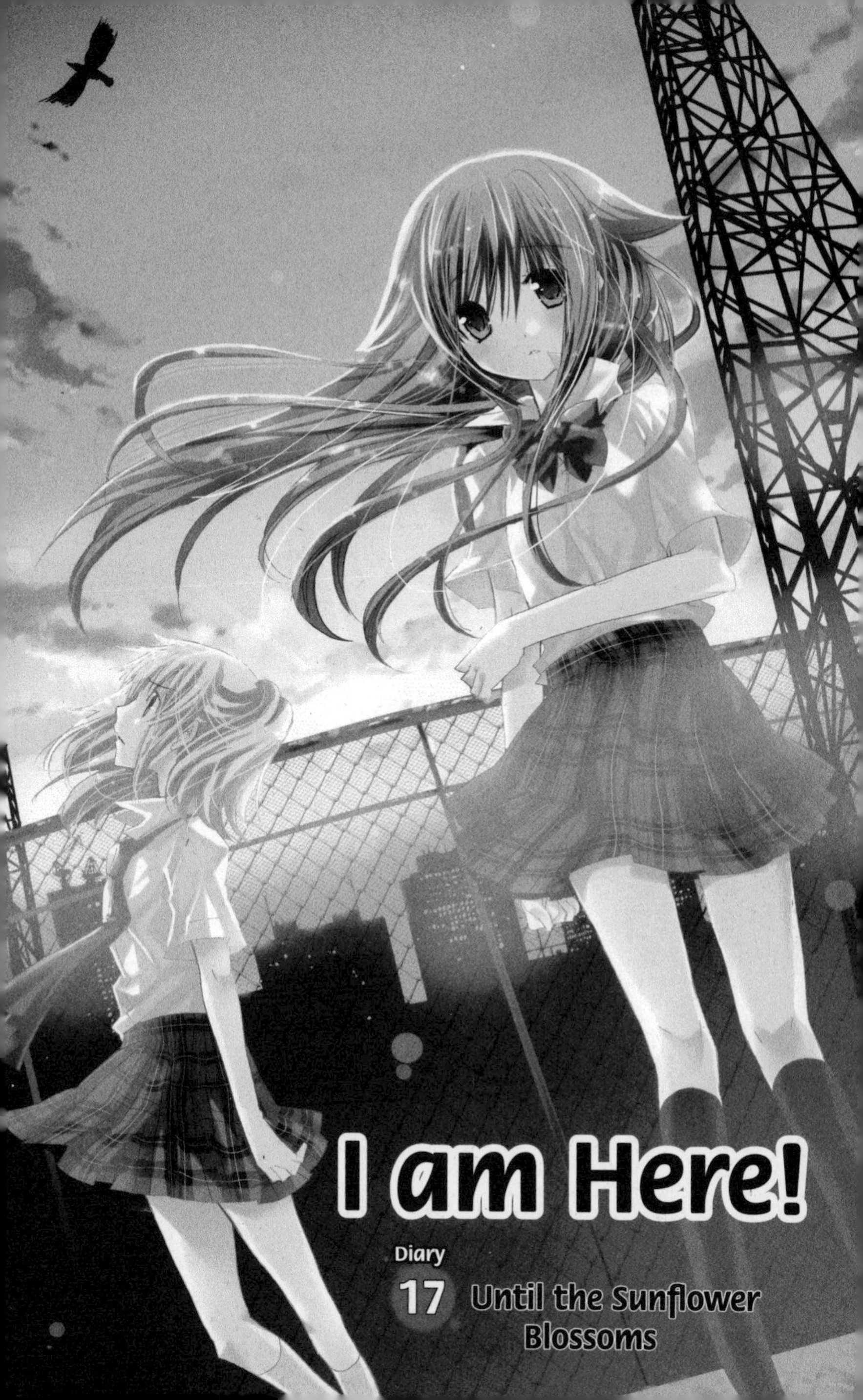
I am Here!
Diary
17
Until the Sunflower Blossoms

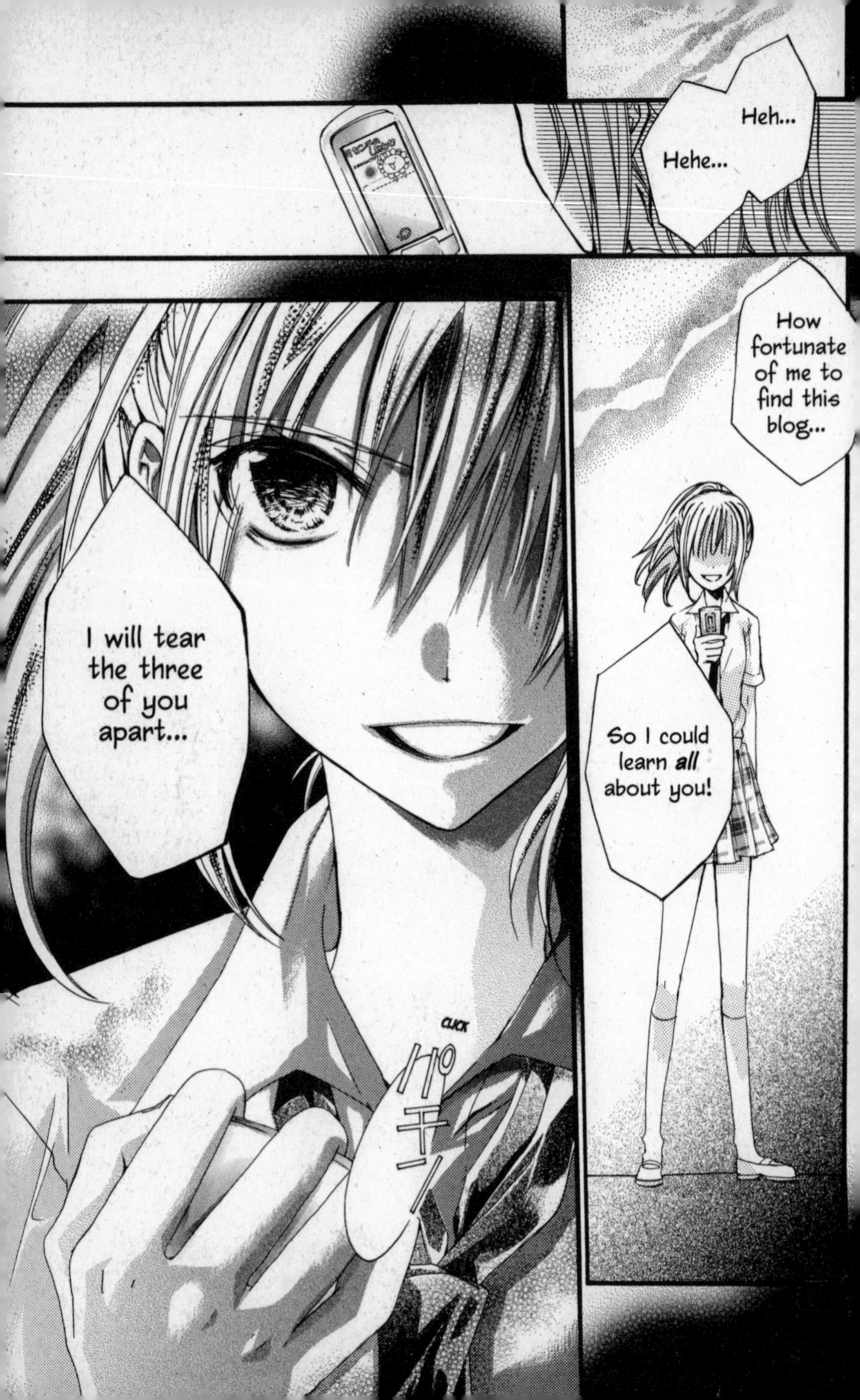
Heh...
Hehe...
How fortunate of me to find this blog...
So I could learn all about you!
I will tear the three of you apart...
CLICK

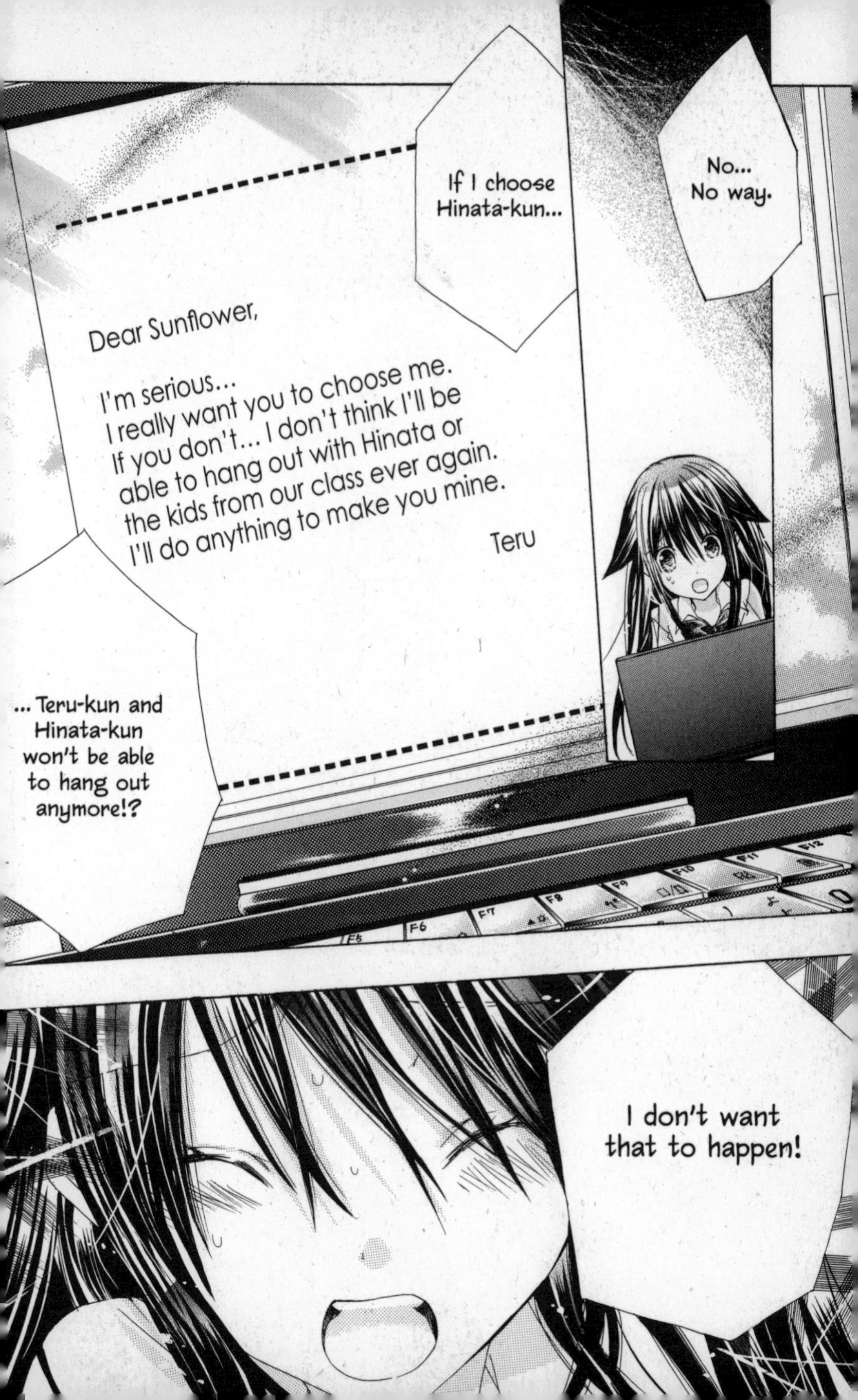
No... No way.
If I choose Hinata-kun...
Dear Sunflower,
I'm serious...
I really want you to choose me.
If you don't... I don't think I'll be able to hang out with Hinata or the kids from our class ever again.
I'll do anything to make you mine.
Teru
... Teru-kun and Hinata-kun won't be able to hang out anymore!?
I don't want that to happen!

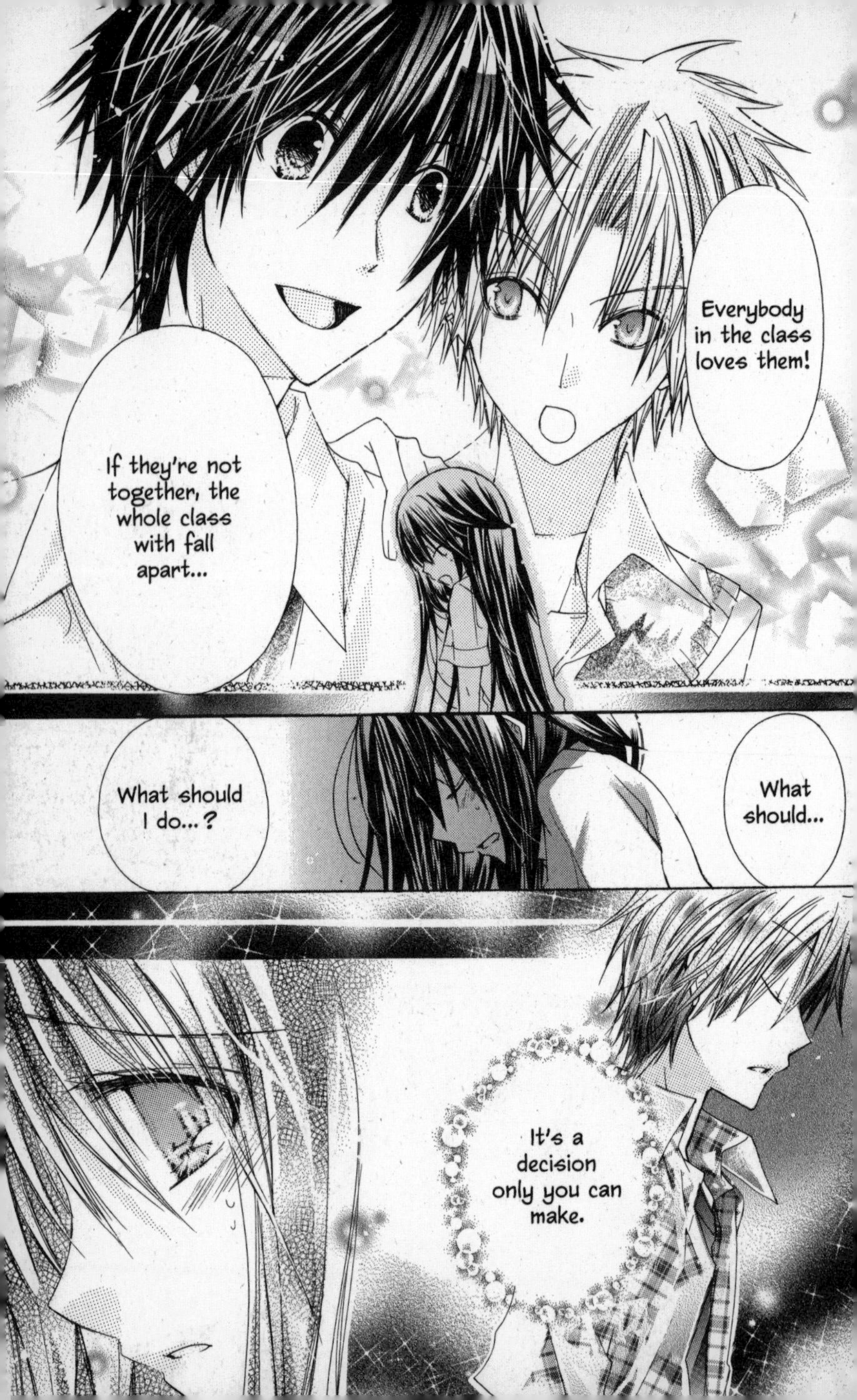
Everybody in the class loves them!
If they're not together, the whole class with fall apart...
What should...
What should I do...?
It's a decision only you can make.

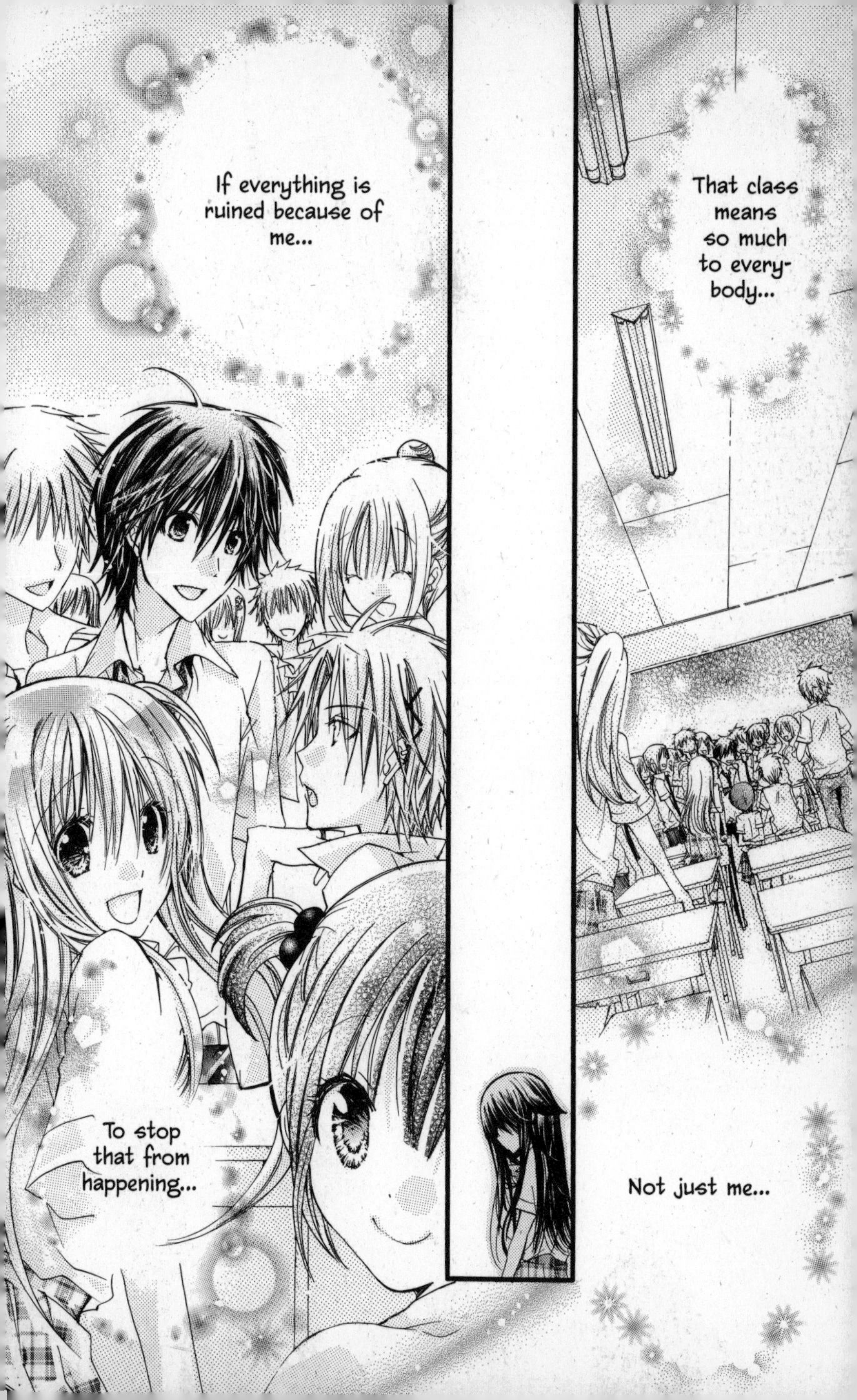
That class means so much to every-body...
Not just me...
If everything is ruined because of me...
To stop that from happening...

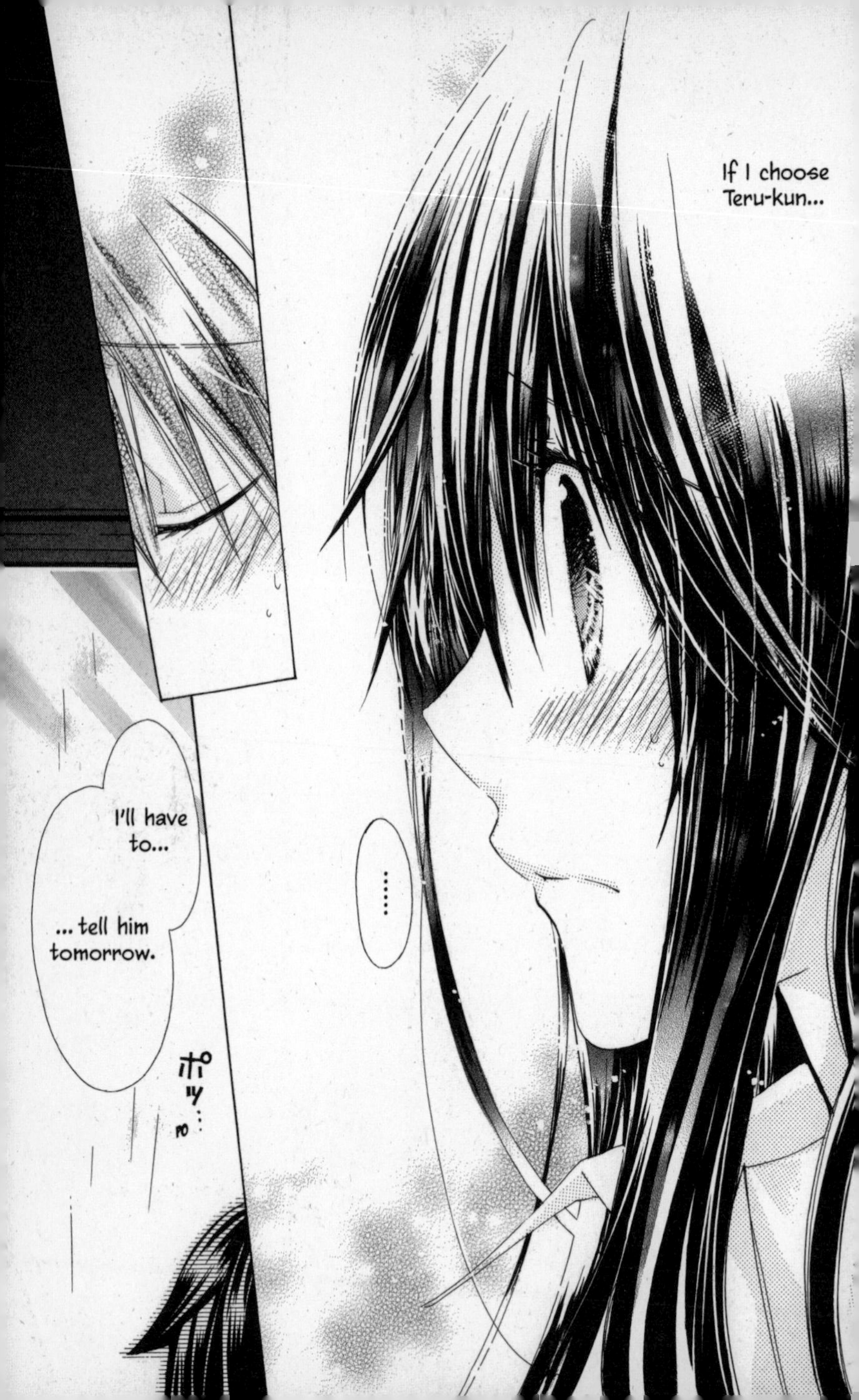
If I choose Teru-kun...
......
I'll have to...
... tell him tomorrow.
ポッ...
PO

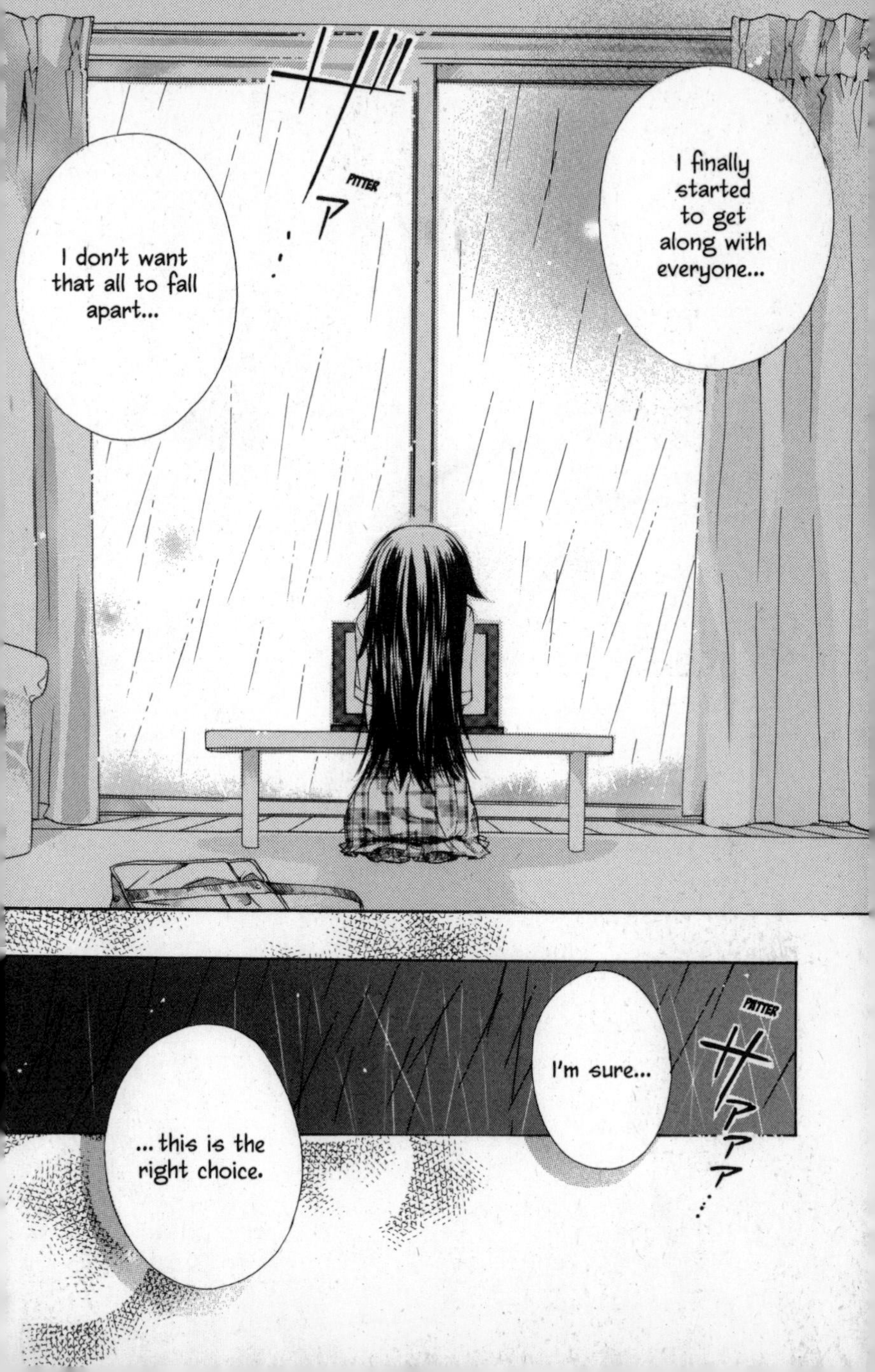
PITTER
I finally started to get along with everyone...
I don't want that all to fall apart...
PITTER
I'm sure...
...this is the right choice.

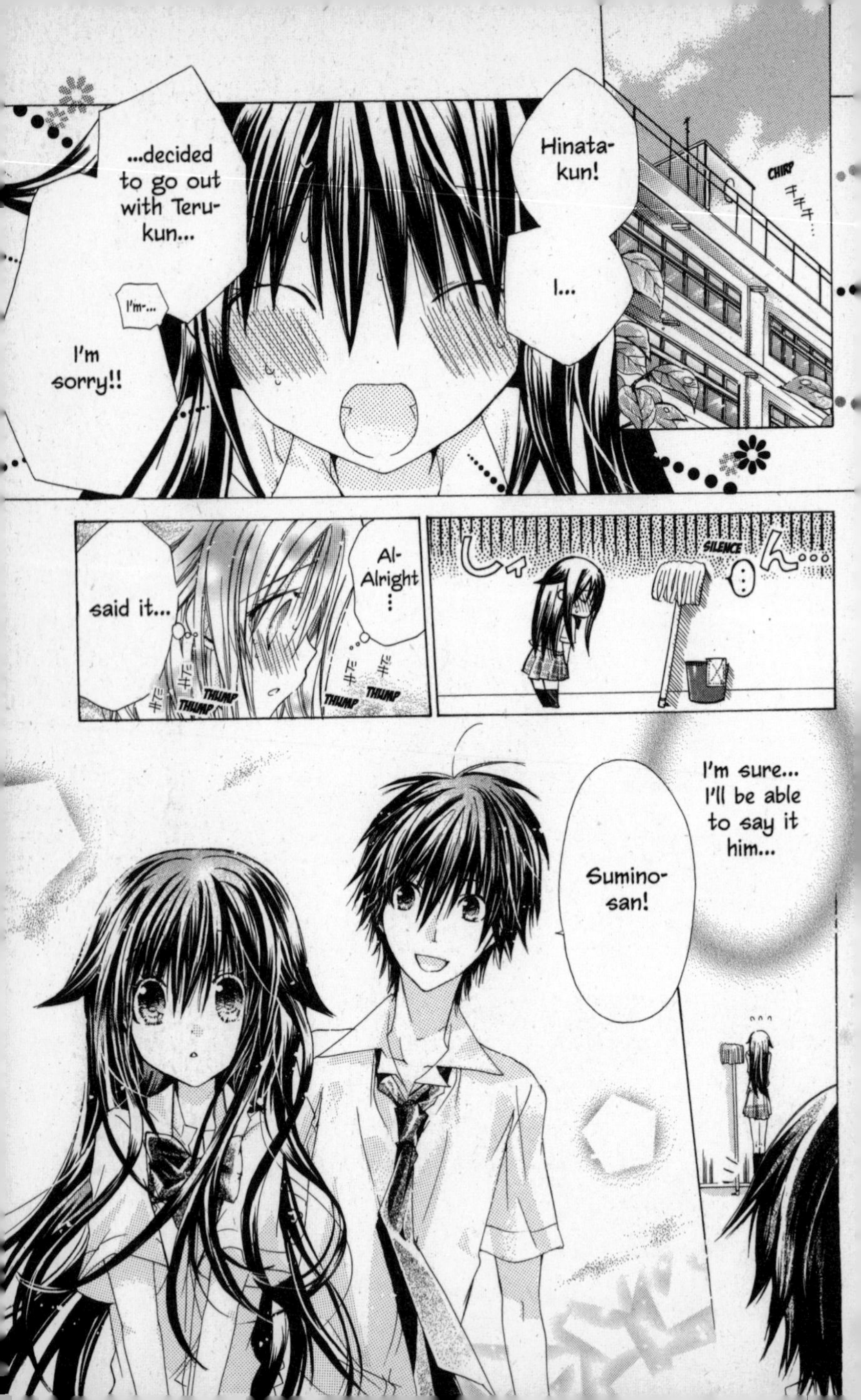
CHIRP
チチチ…
Hinata-kun!
I...
...decided to go out with Teru-kun...
I'm-...
I'm sorry!!
SILENCE
しィん…
…
Al-Alright…
said it...
THUMP
ドキ
THUMP
ドキ
THUMP
ドキ
THUMP
ドキ
I'm sure... I'll be able to say it him...
Sumino-san!

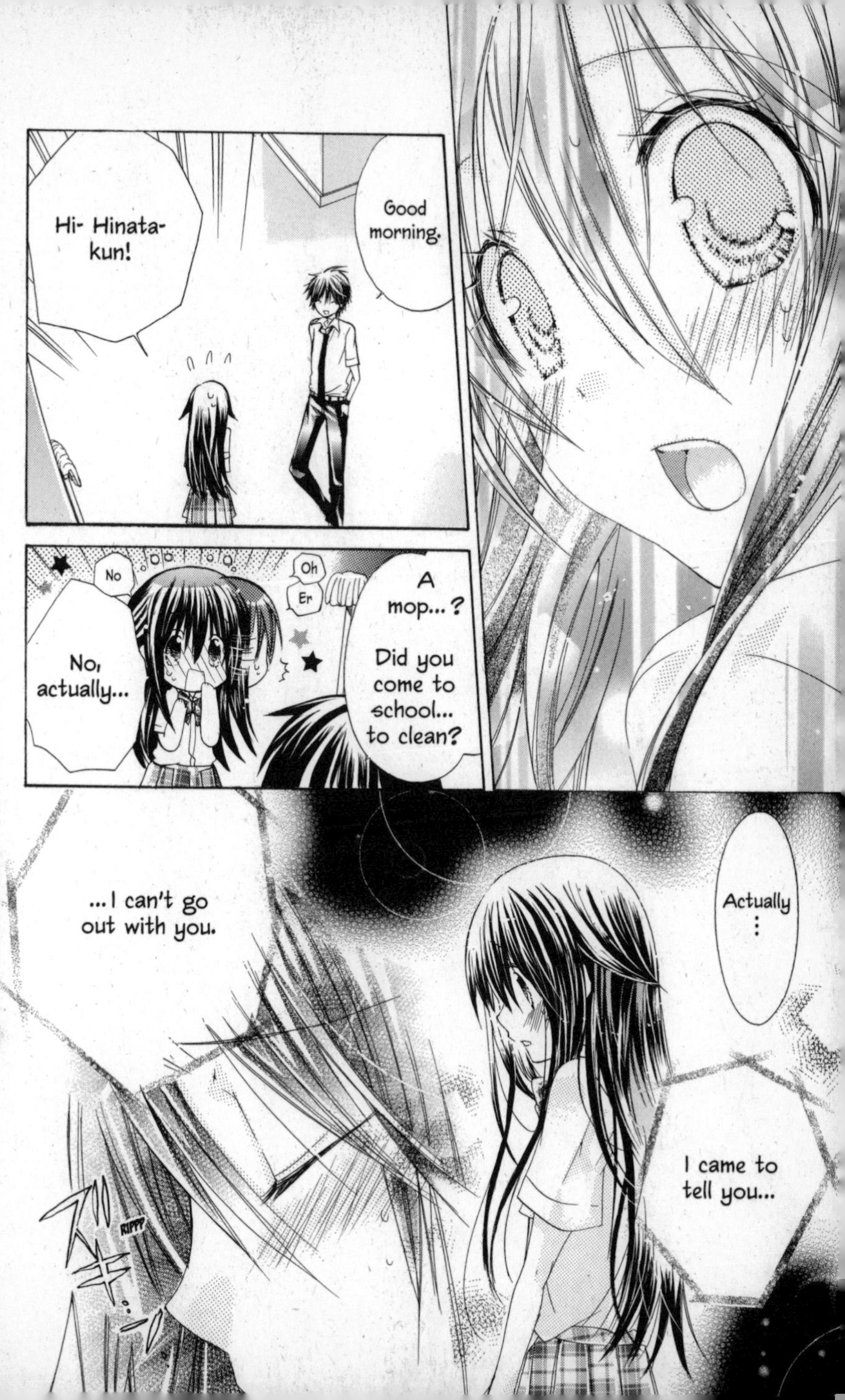
Good morning.
Hi- Hinata-kun!
A mop...?
Did you come to school... to clean?
Oh
Er
No
No, actually...
Actually...
I came to tell you...
...I can't go out with you.
RIPPP

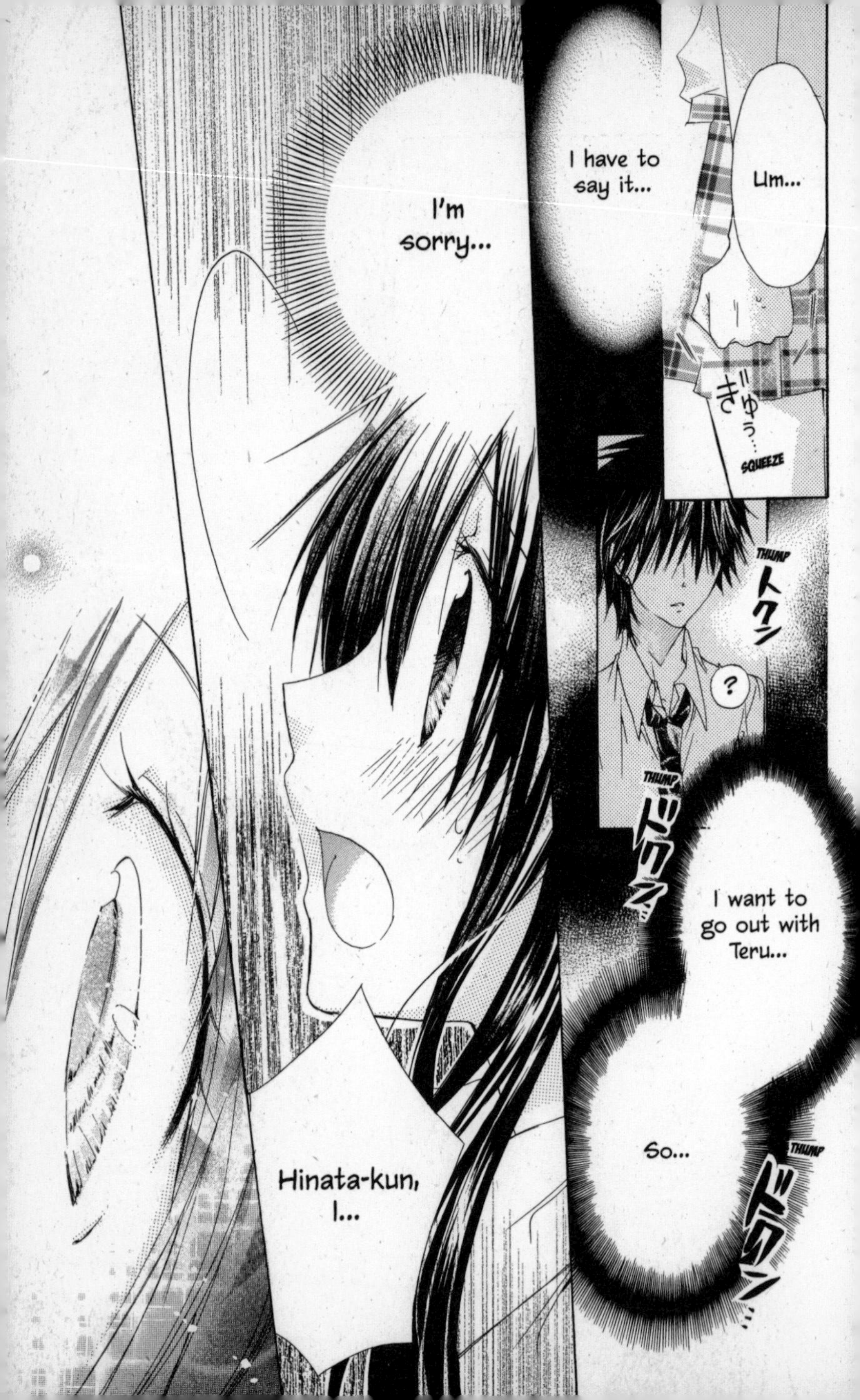

Um...
ぎゅう...
SQUEEZE
I have to say it...
THUMP
トクン
?
THUMP
ドクン
I want to go out with Teru...
So...
THUMP
ドクン
I'm sorry...
Hinata-kun, I...

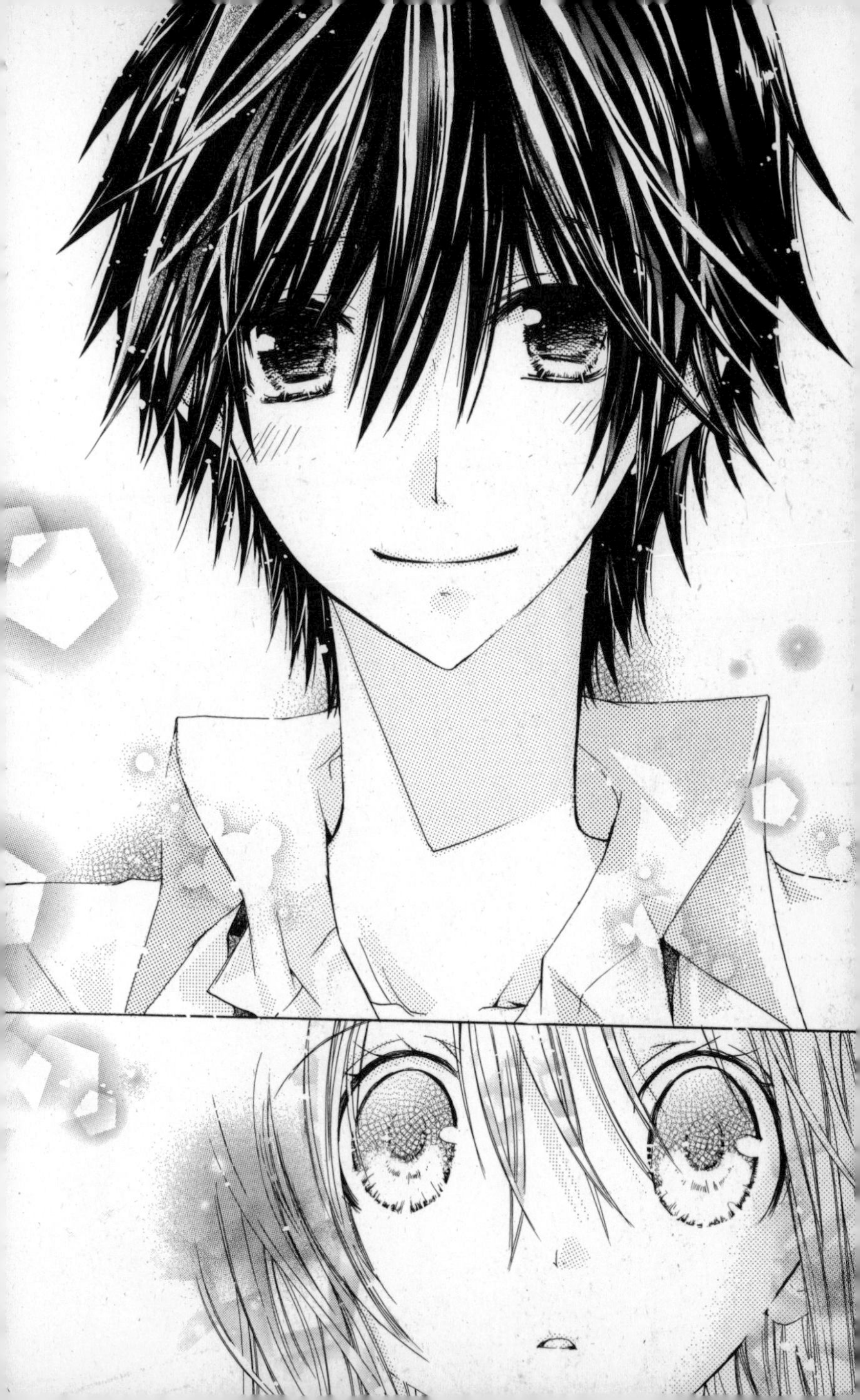

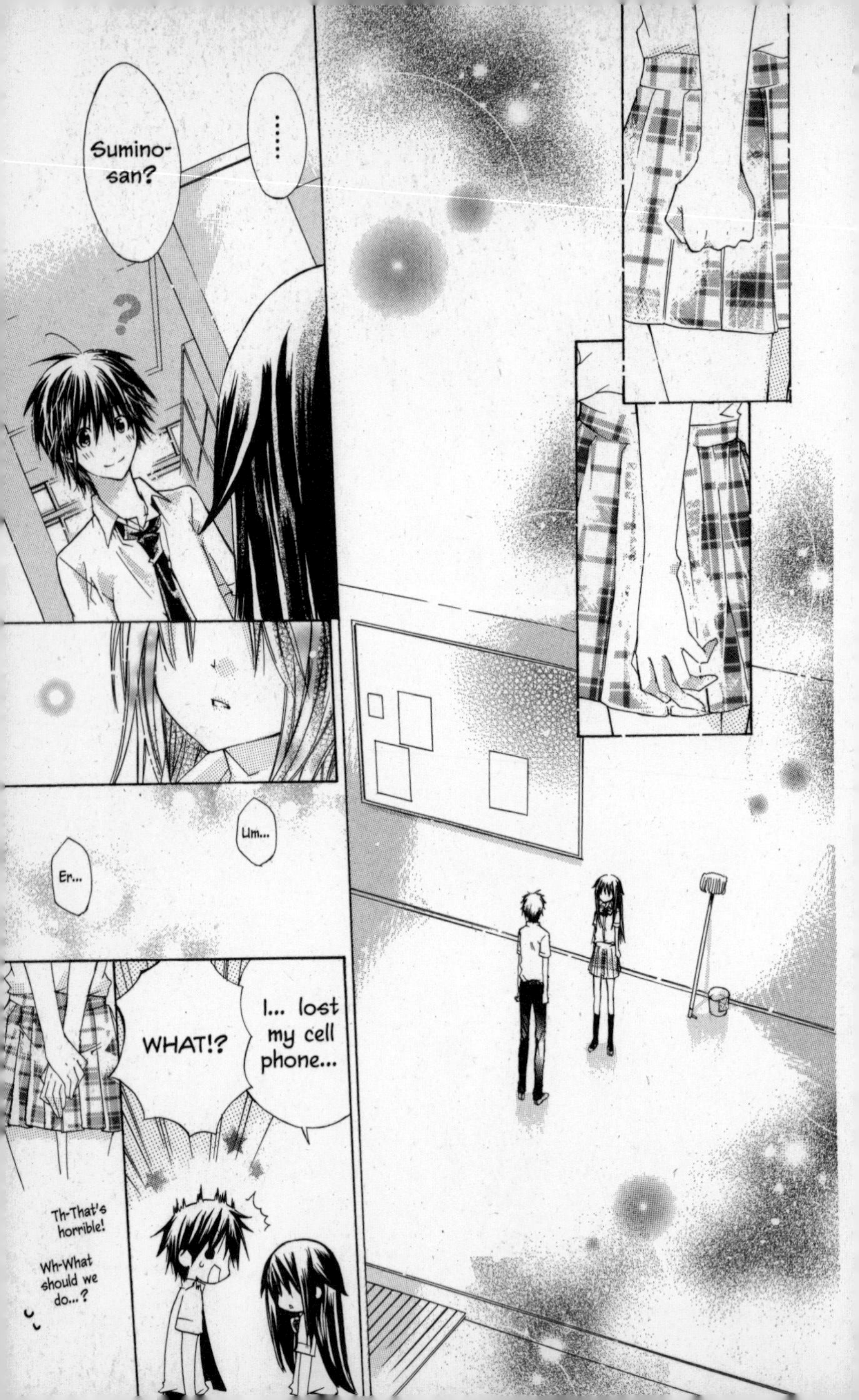
……
Sumino-san?
Um...
Er...
I... lost my cell phone...
WHAT!?
Th-That's horrible!
Wh-What should we do...?

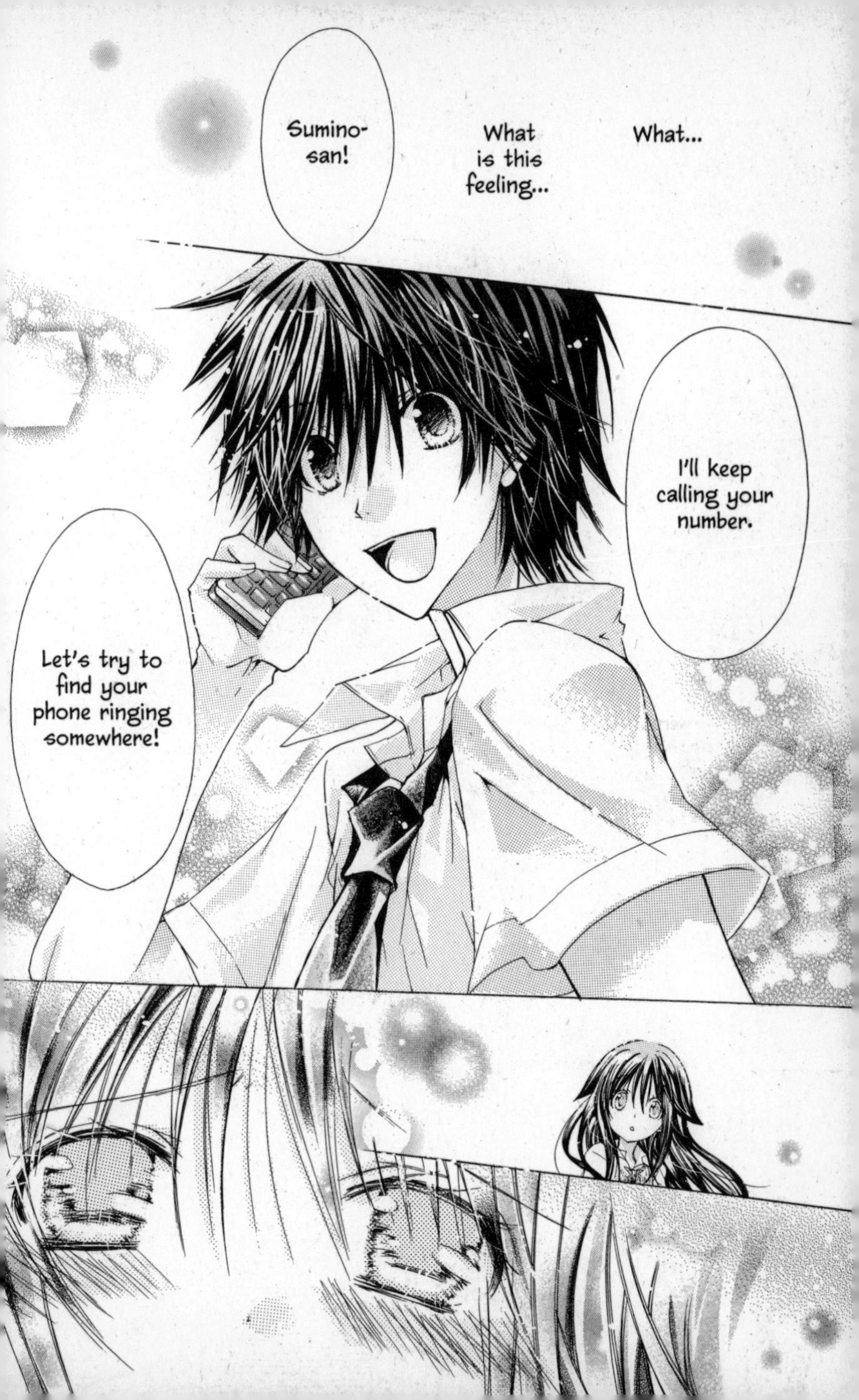
What...
What is this feeling...
Sumino-san!
I'll keep calling your number.
Let's try to find your phone ringing somewhere!

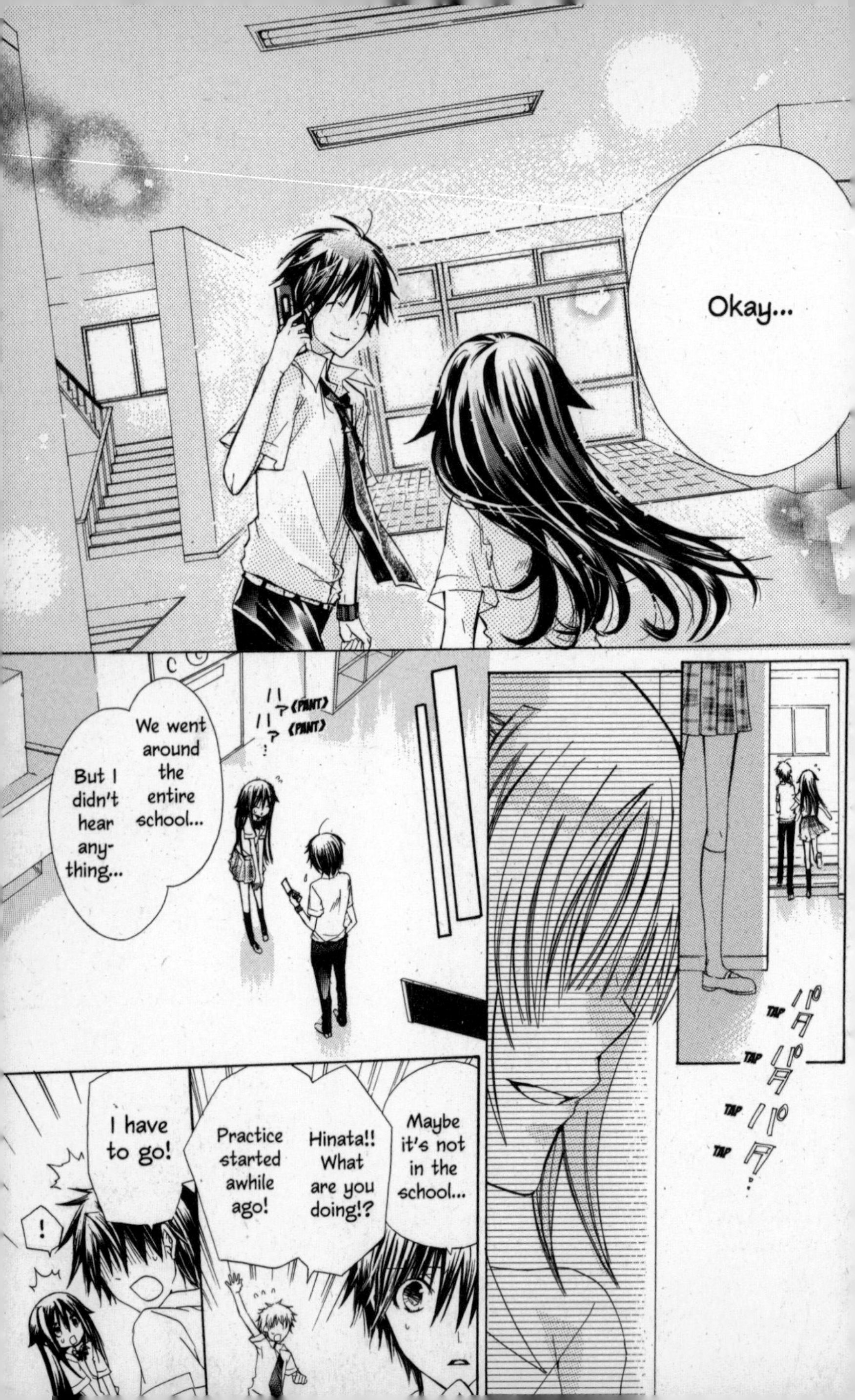
Okay...
TAP
TAP
TAP
TAP
(PANT)
(PANT)
We went around the entire school...
But I didn't hear anything...
Maybe it's not in the school...
Hinata!! What are you doing!?
Practice started awhile ago!
I have to go!
!

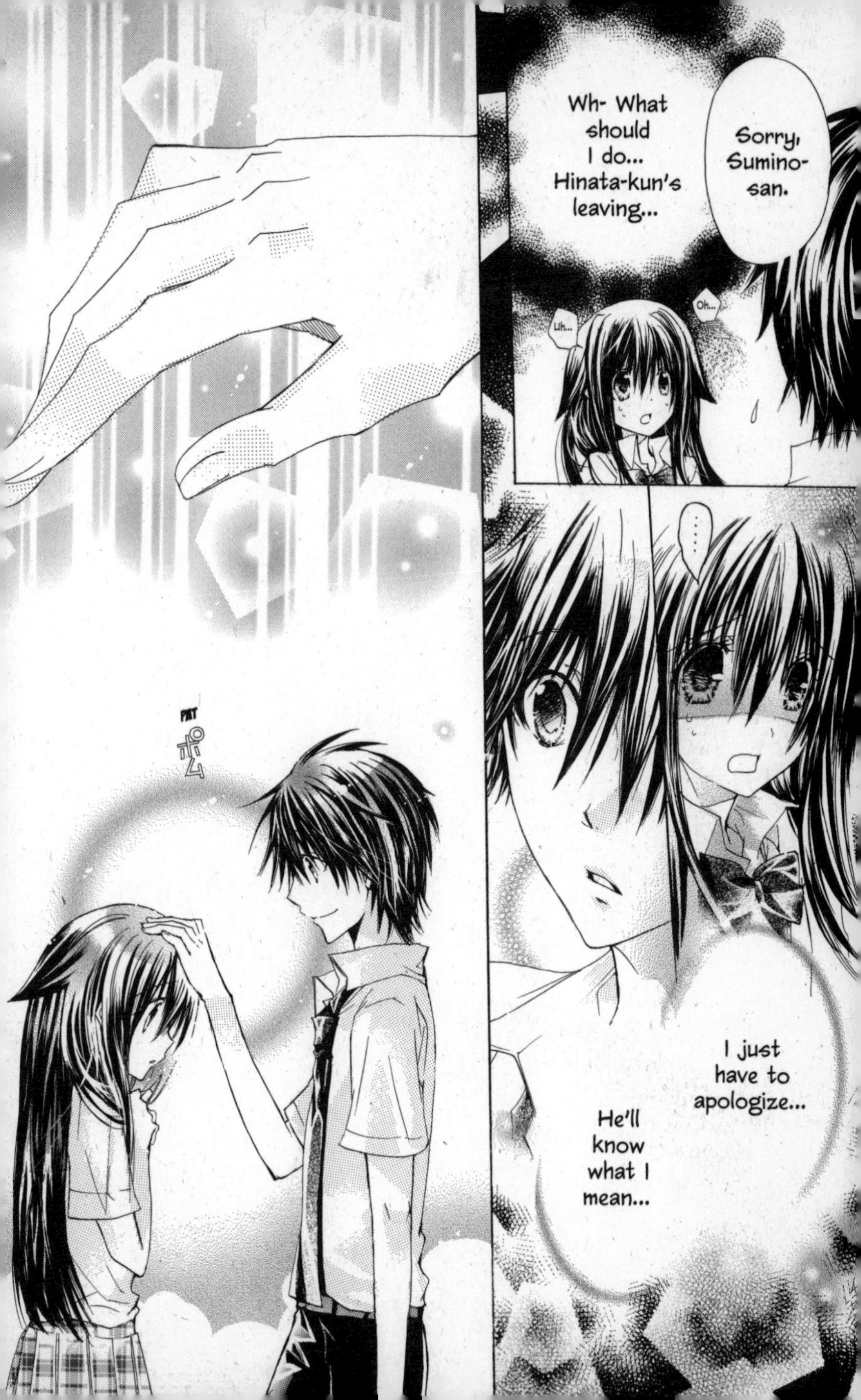
Sorry, Sumino-san.
Wh- What should I do... Hinata-kun's leaving...
Oh...
Uh...
......
I just have to apologize...
He'll know what I mean...
PAT
ポム

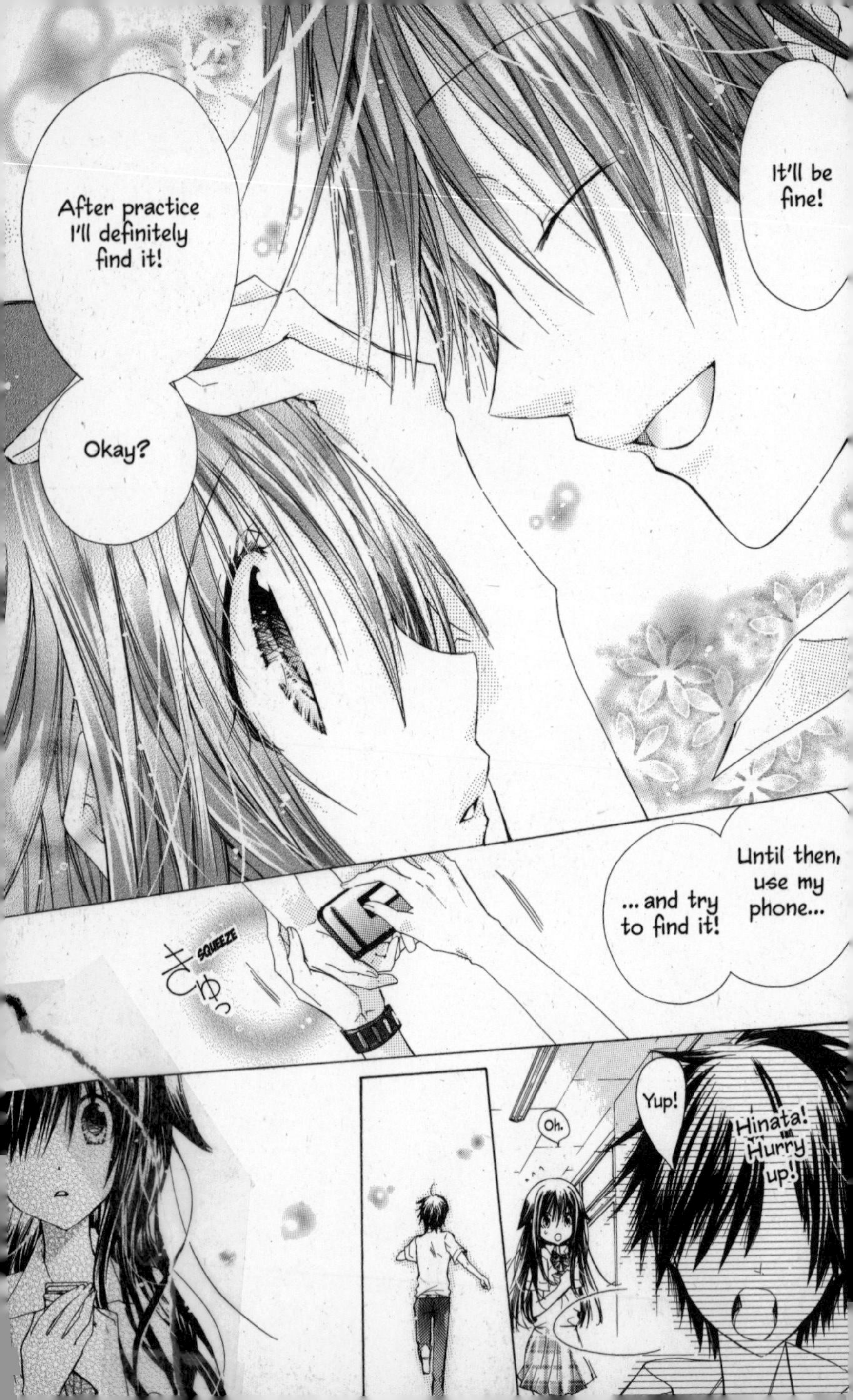
It'll be fine!
After practice I'll definitely find it!
Okay?
Until then, use my phone...
...and try to find it!
SQUEEZE
きゅっ
Hinata! Hurry up!
Yup!
Oh.

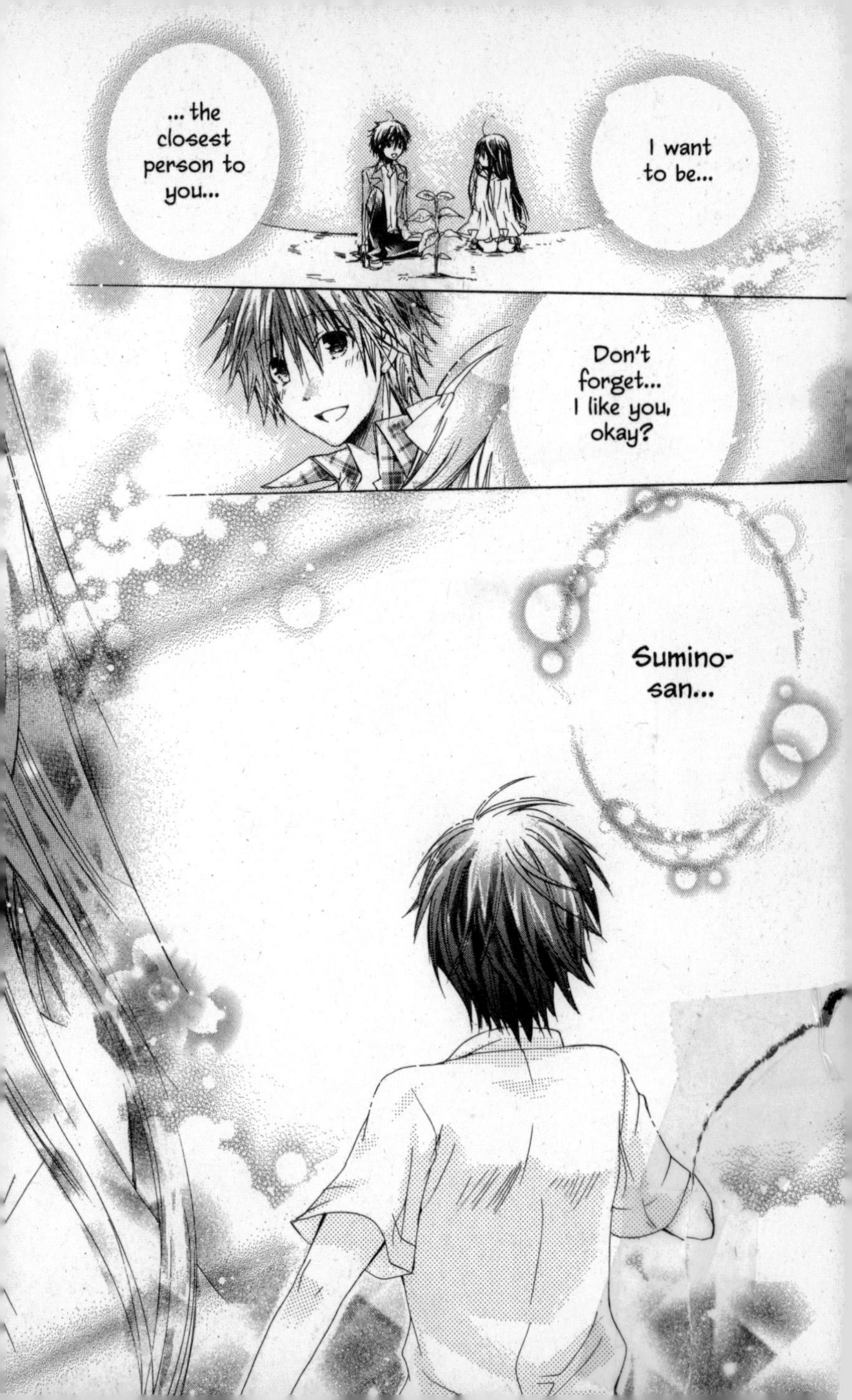
I want to be...
... the closest person to you...
Don't forget... I like you, okay?
Sumino-san...

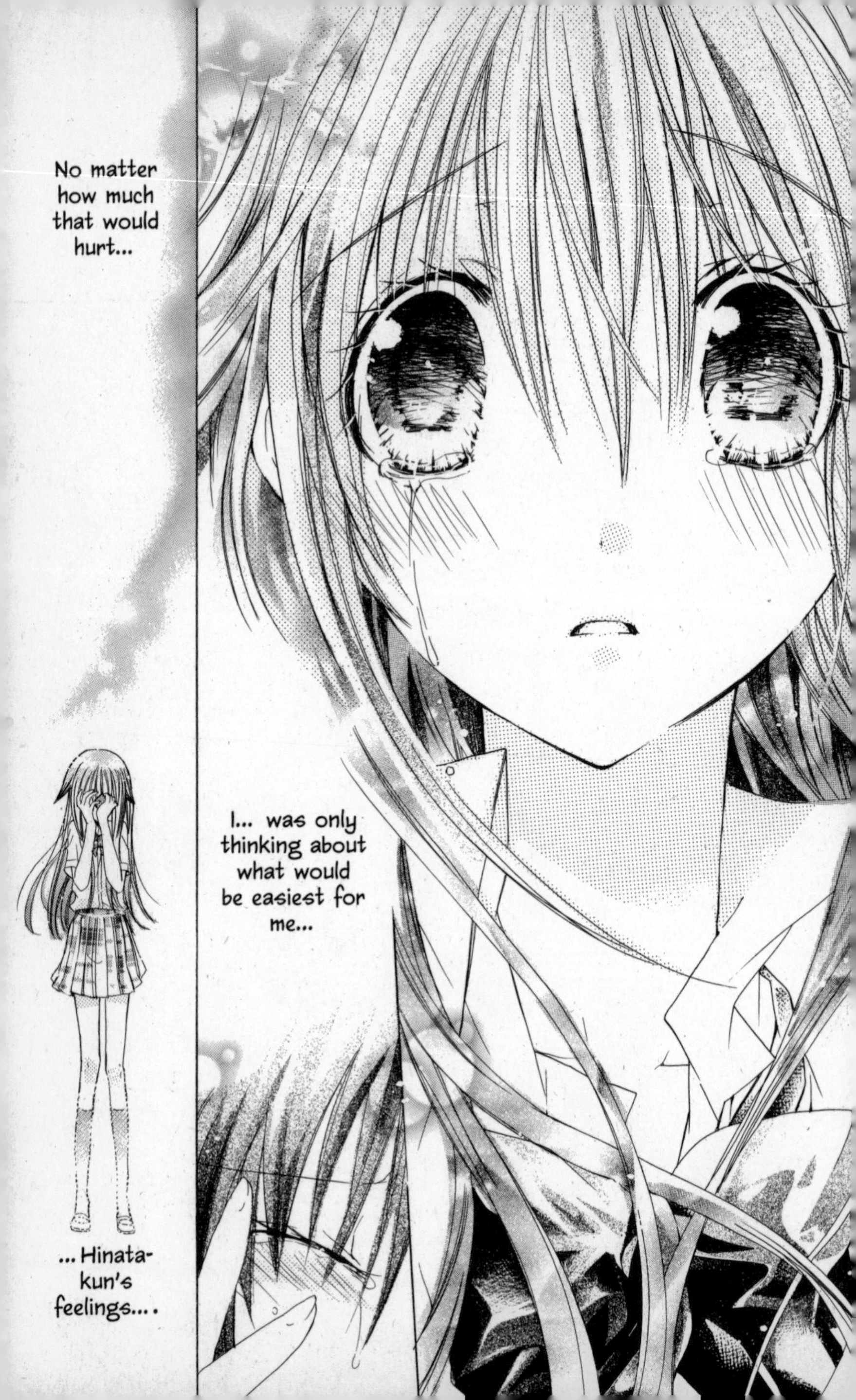
I... was only thinking about what would be easiest for me...
No matter how much that would hurt...
...Hinata-kun's feelings....

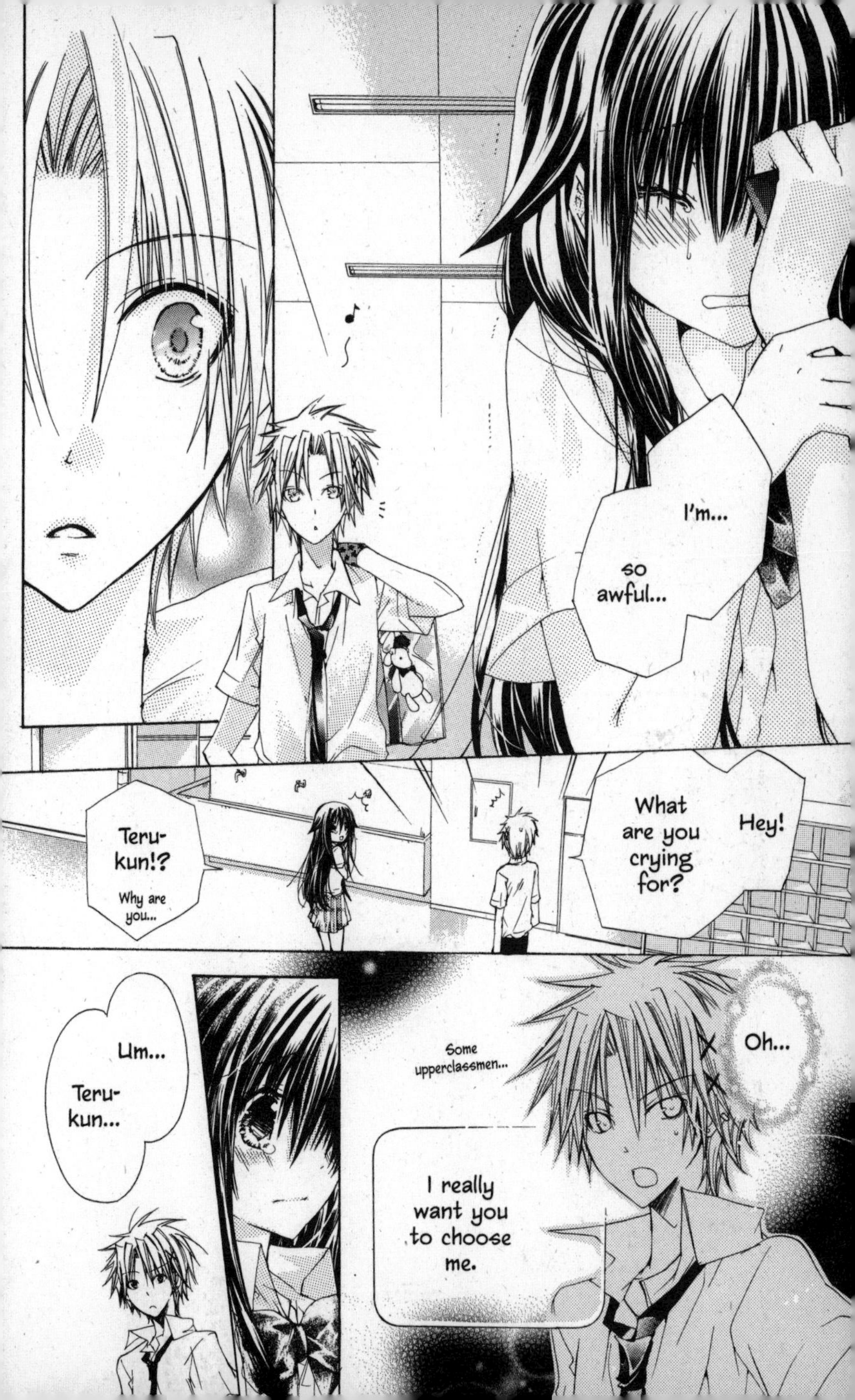
I'm... so awful...
Hey! What are you crying for?
Teru-kun!? Why are you...
Oh...
Some upperclassmen...
I really want you to choose me.
Um... Teru-kun...

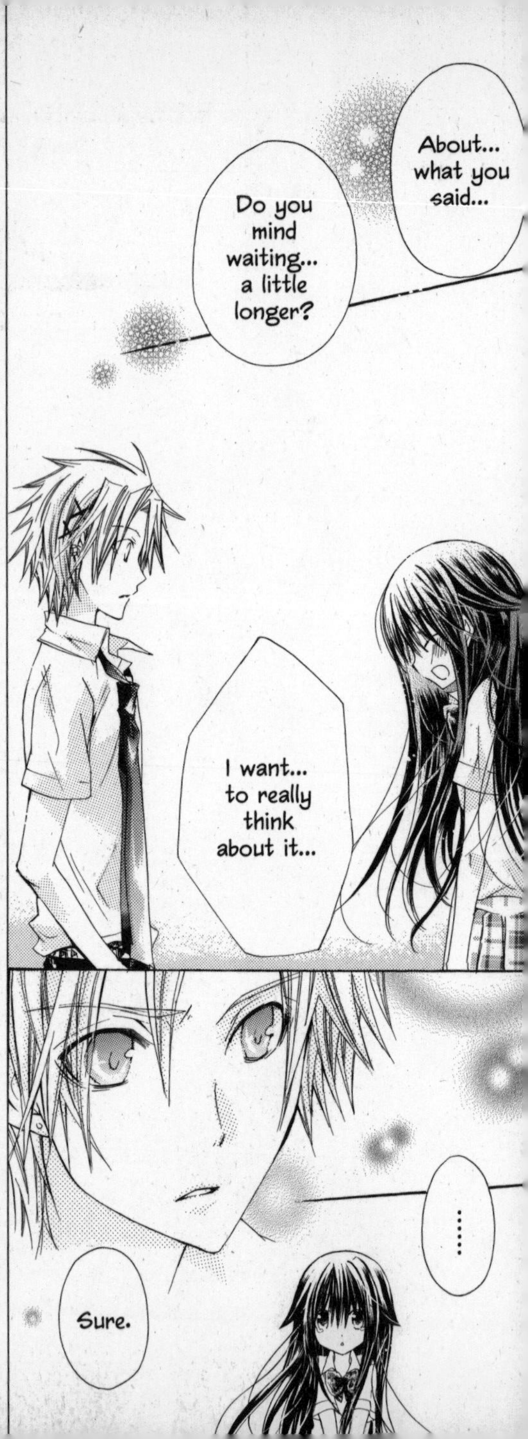
About... what you said...
Do you mind waiting... a little longer?
I want... to really think about it...
......
Sure.

The Adventures of Mahimahi - 6

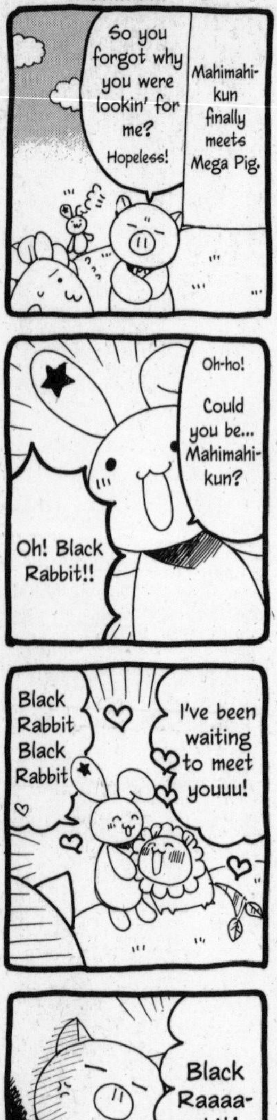
Mahimahi-kun finally meets Mega Pig.
So you forgot why you were lookin' for me? Hopeless!
Oh-ho! Could you be... Mahimahi-kun?
Oh! Black Rabbit!!
I've been waiting to meet youuu!
Black Rabbit Black Rabbit
Black Raaaa-abit!
GLARE
For some reason, he's jealous.

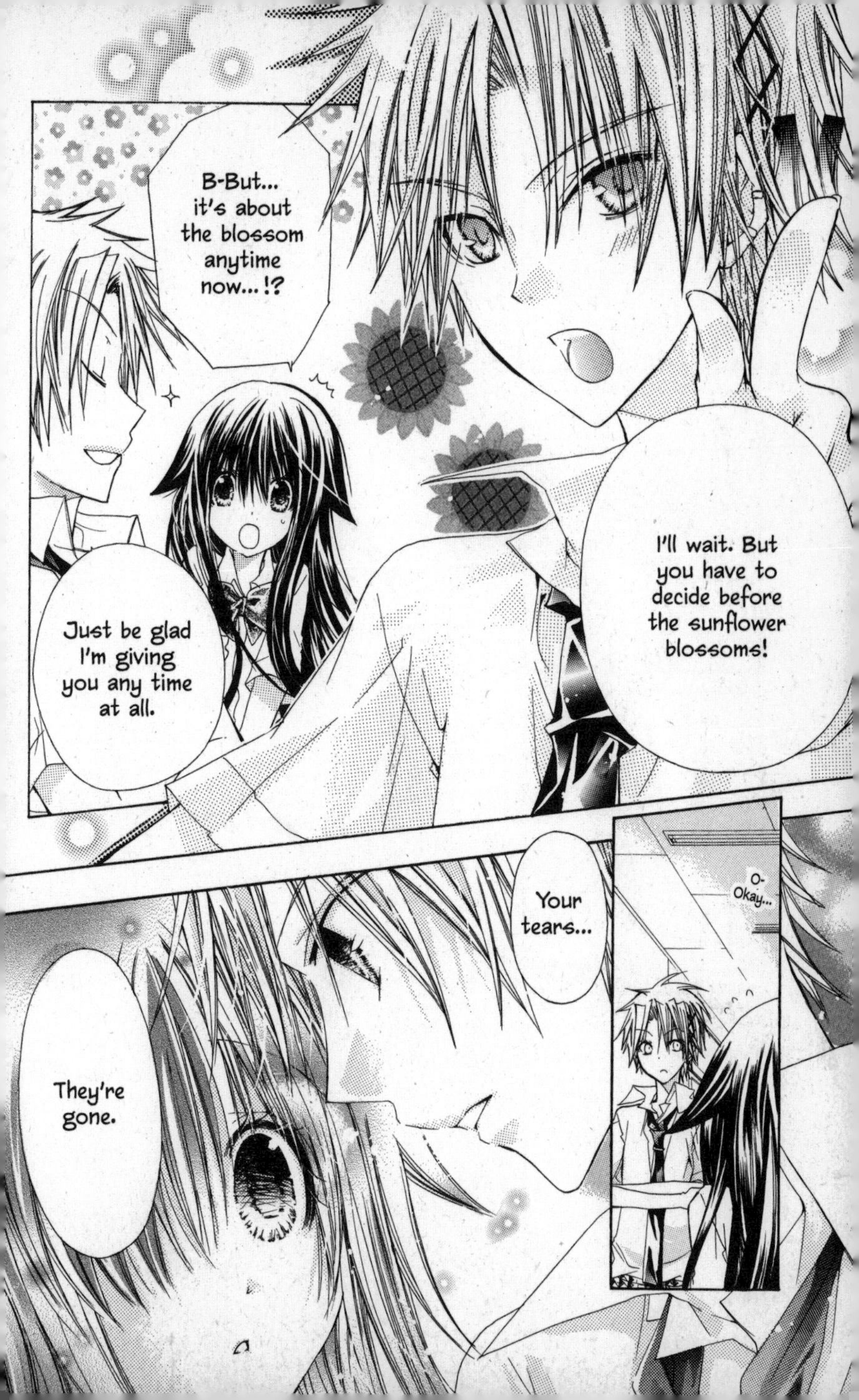
I'll wait. But you have to decide before the sunflower blossoms!
B-But... it's about the blossom anytime now...!?
Just be glad I'm giving you any time at all.
O-Okay...
Your tears...
They're gone.

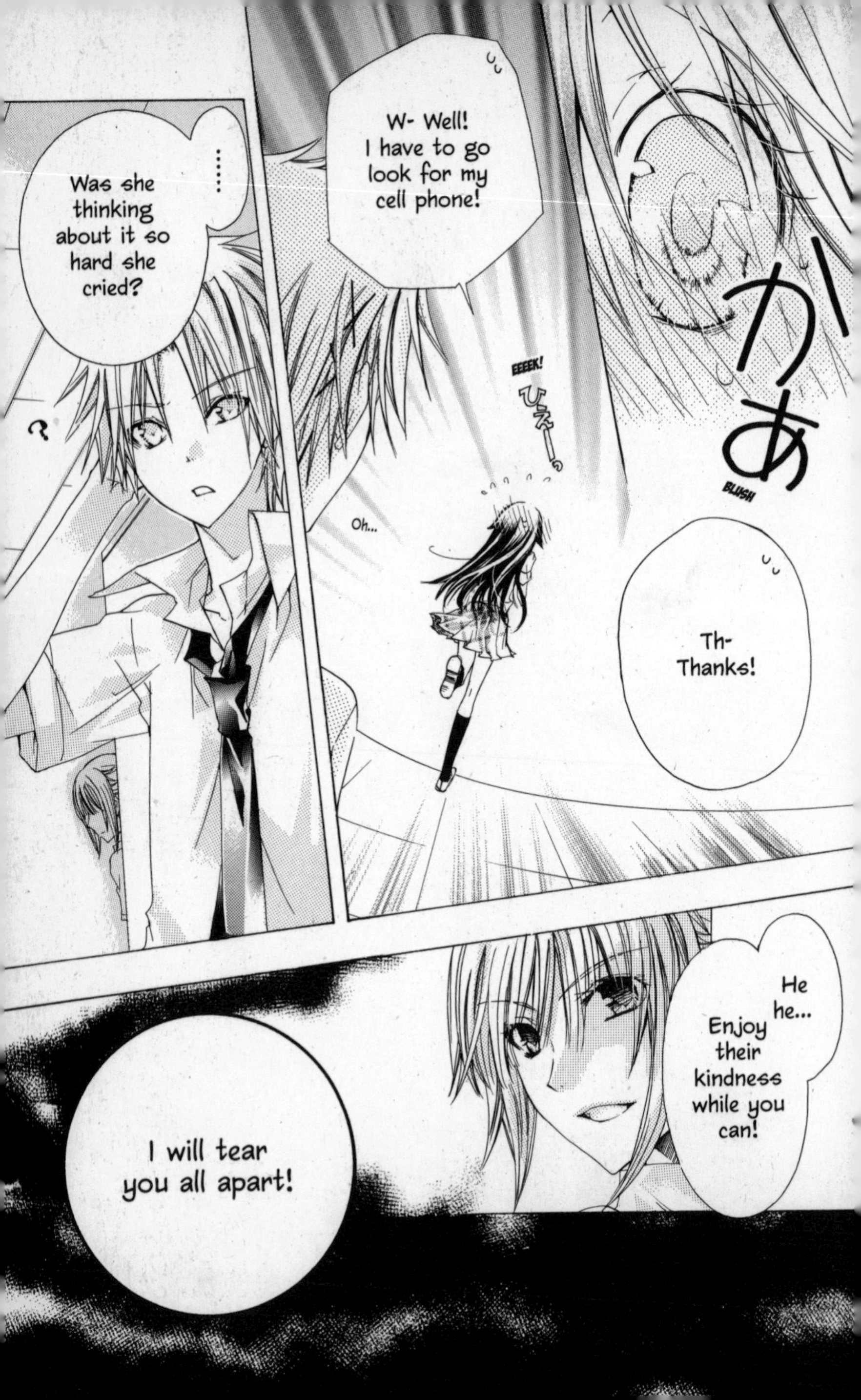
かぁ
BLUSH
Th- Thanks!
W- Well! I have to go look for my cell phone!
EEEEK!
ひえ～
Oh...
......
Was she thinking about it so hard she cried?
?
He he... Enjoy their kindness while you can!
I will tear you all apart!

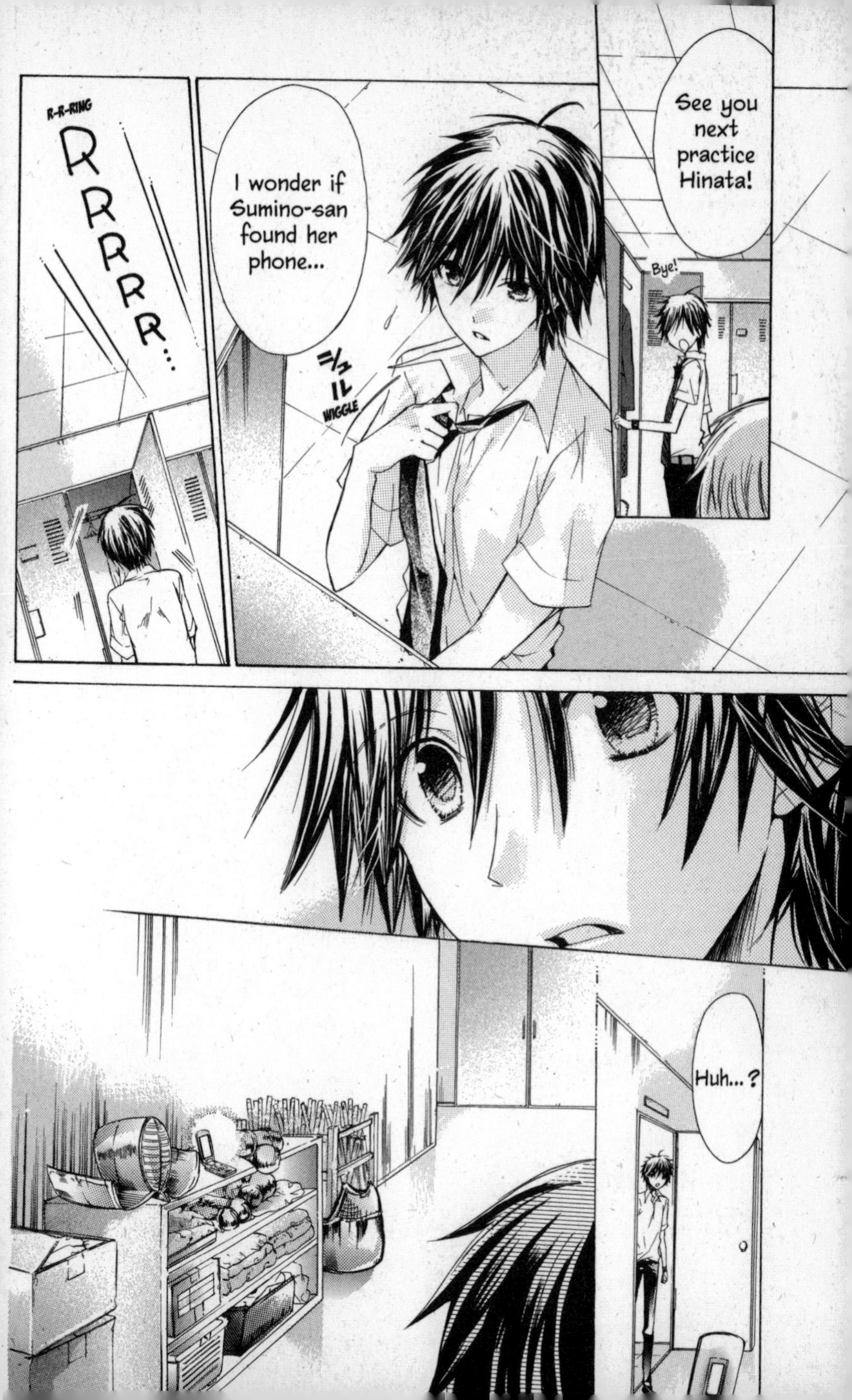
See you next practice Hinata!
Bye!
I wonder if Sumino-san found her phone...
シュル
WIGGLE
R-R-RING
RRRRR...
Huh...?

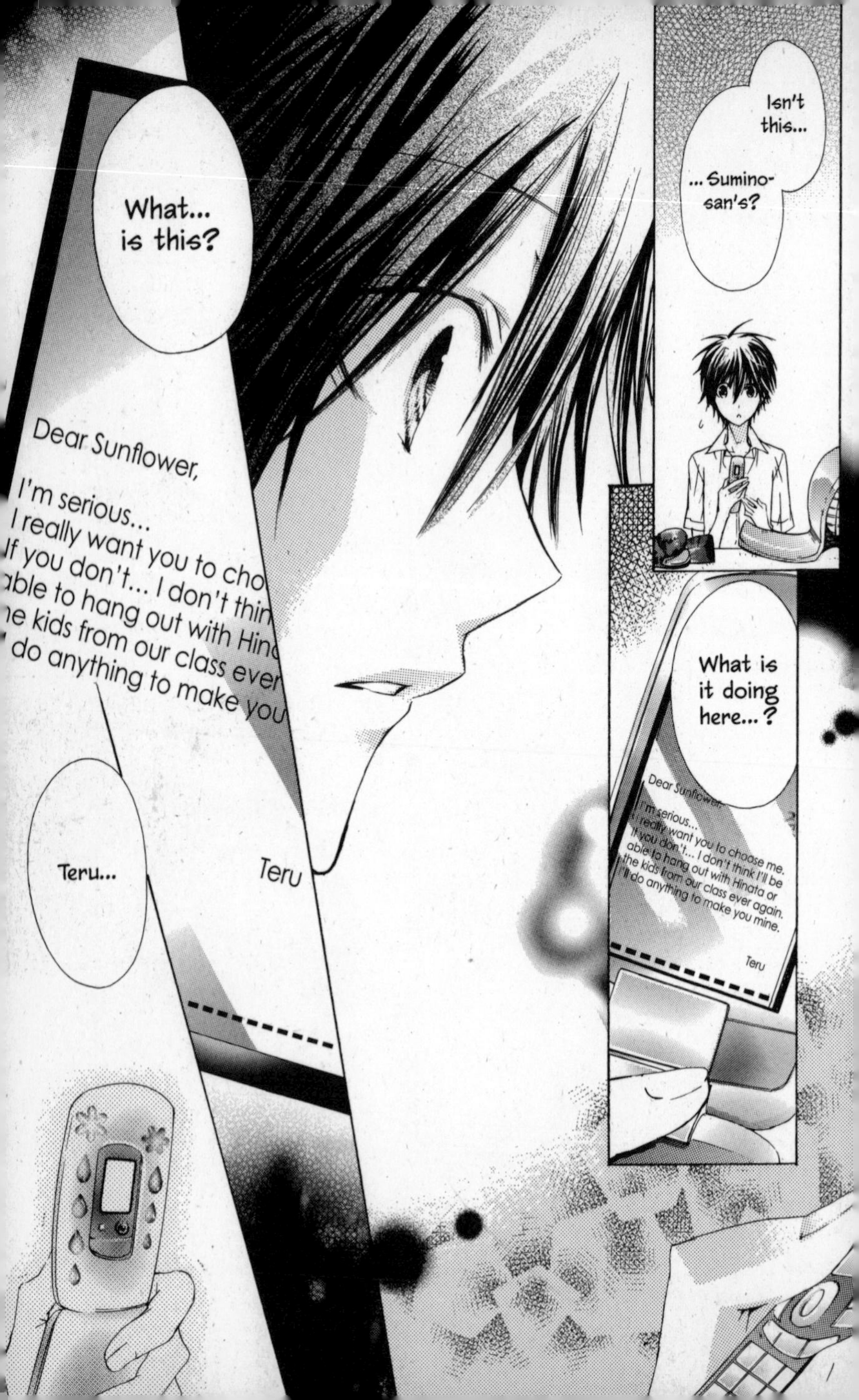
Isn't this...
...Sumino-san's?
What is it doing here...?
Dear Sunflower,
I'm serious...
I really want you to choose me.
If you don't... I don't think I'll be able to hang out with Hinata or the kids from our class ever again.
I'll do anything to make you mine.
Teru
What... is this?
Dear Sunflower,
I'm serious...
I really want you to cho
If you don't... I don't thin
able to hang out with Hin
he kids from our class ever
do anything to make you
Teru
Teru...

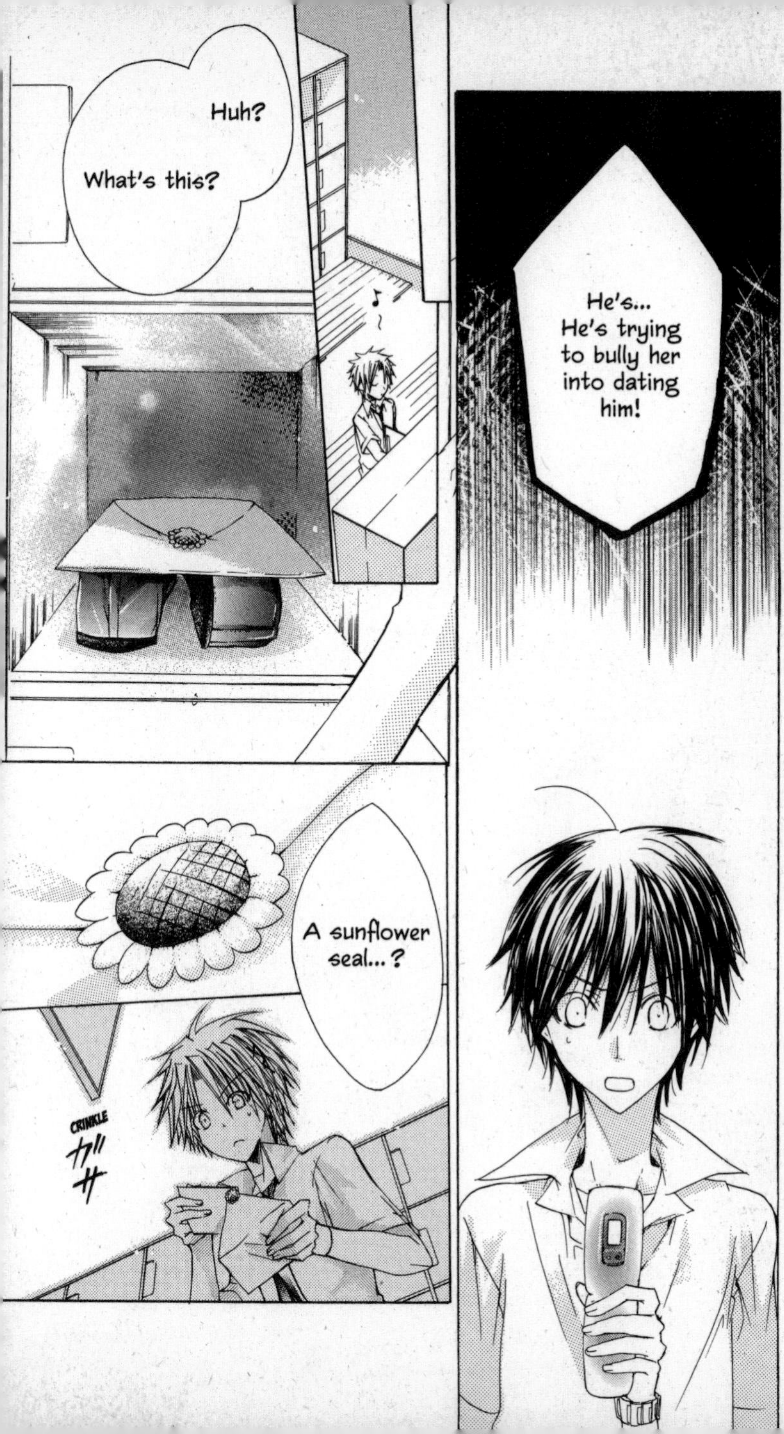
He's... He's trying to bully her into dating him!
Huh?
What's this?
A sunflower seal...?
CRINKLE

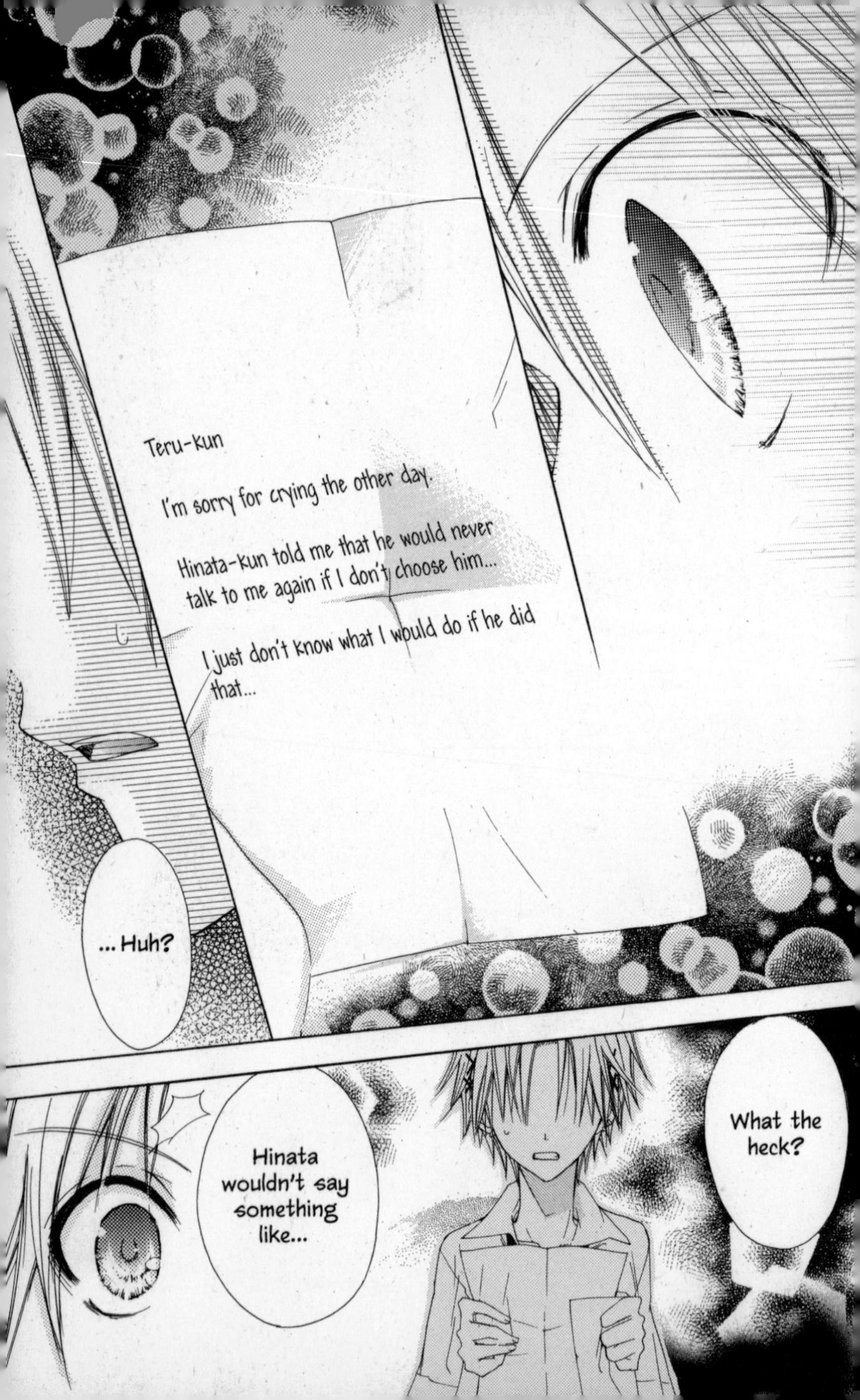
Teru-kun
I'm sorry for crying the other day.
Hinata-kun told me that he would never talk to me again if I don't choose him...
I just don't know what I would do if he did that...
...Huh?
What the heck?
Hinata wouldn't say something like...

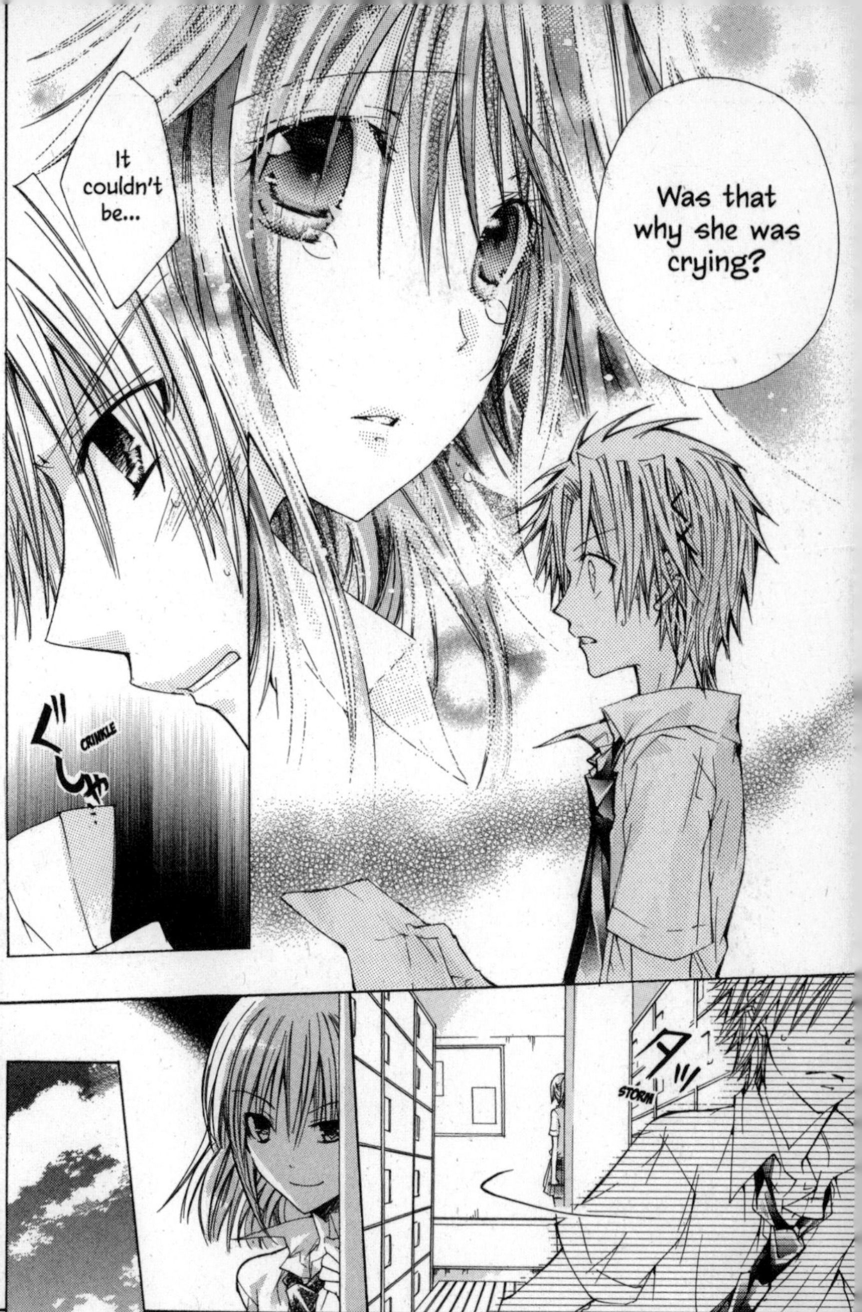
Was that why she was crying?
It couldn't be...
CRINKLE
STORM

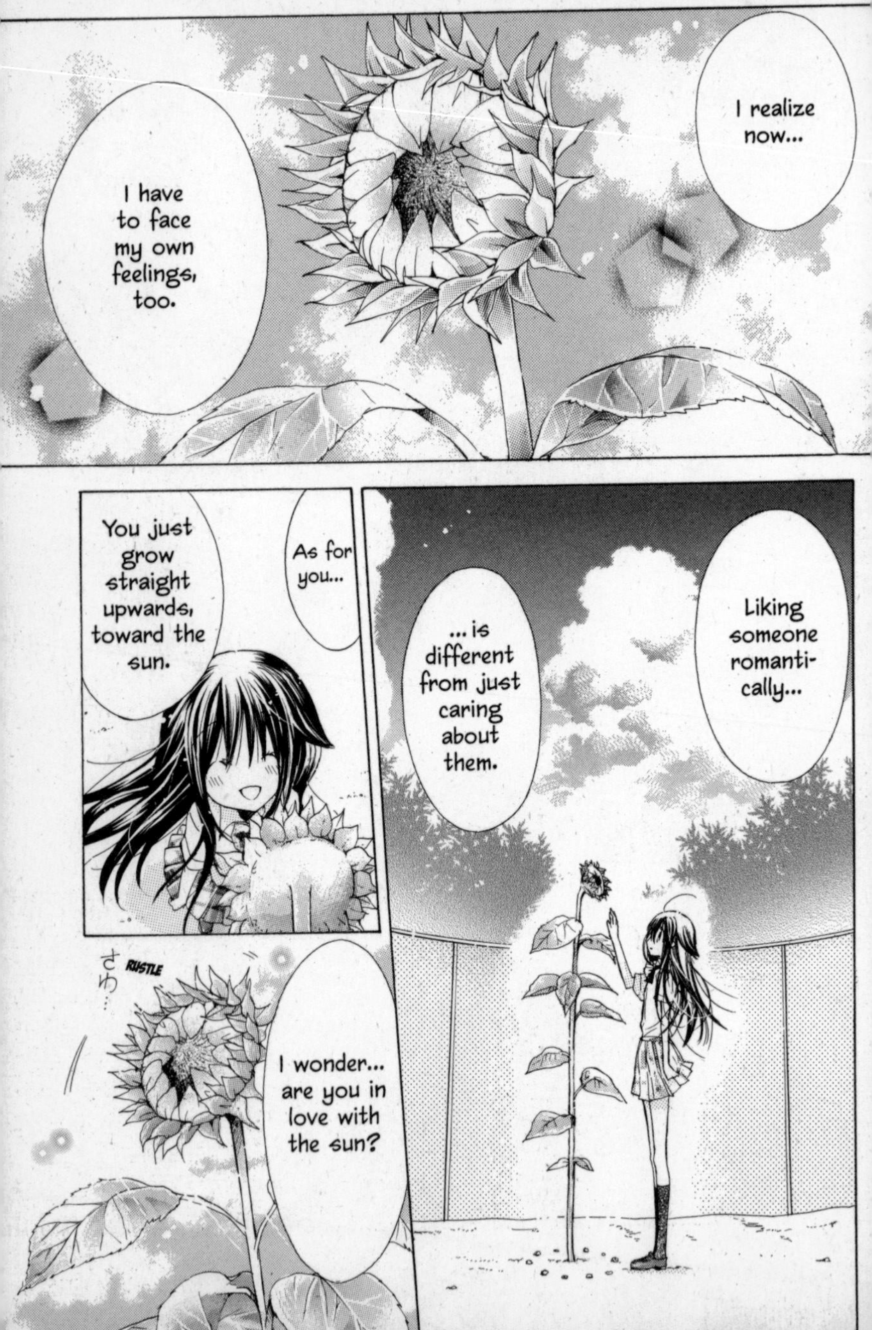
I realize now...
I have to face my own feelings, too.
Liking someone romanti-cally...
... is different from just caring about them.
As for you...
You just grow straight upwards, toward the sun.
さゎ…
RUSTLE
I wonder... are you in love with the sun?

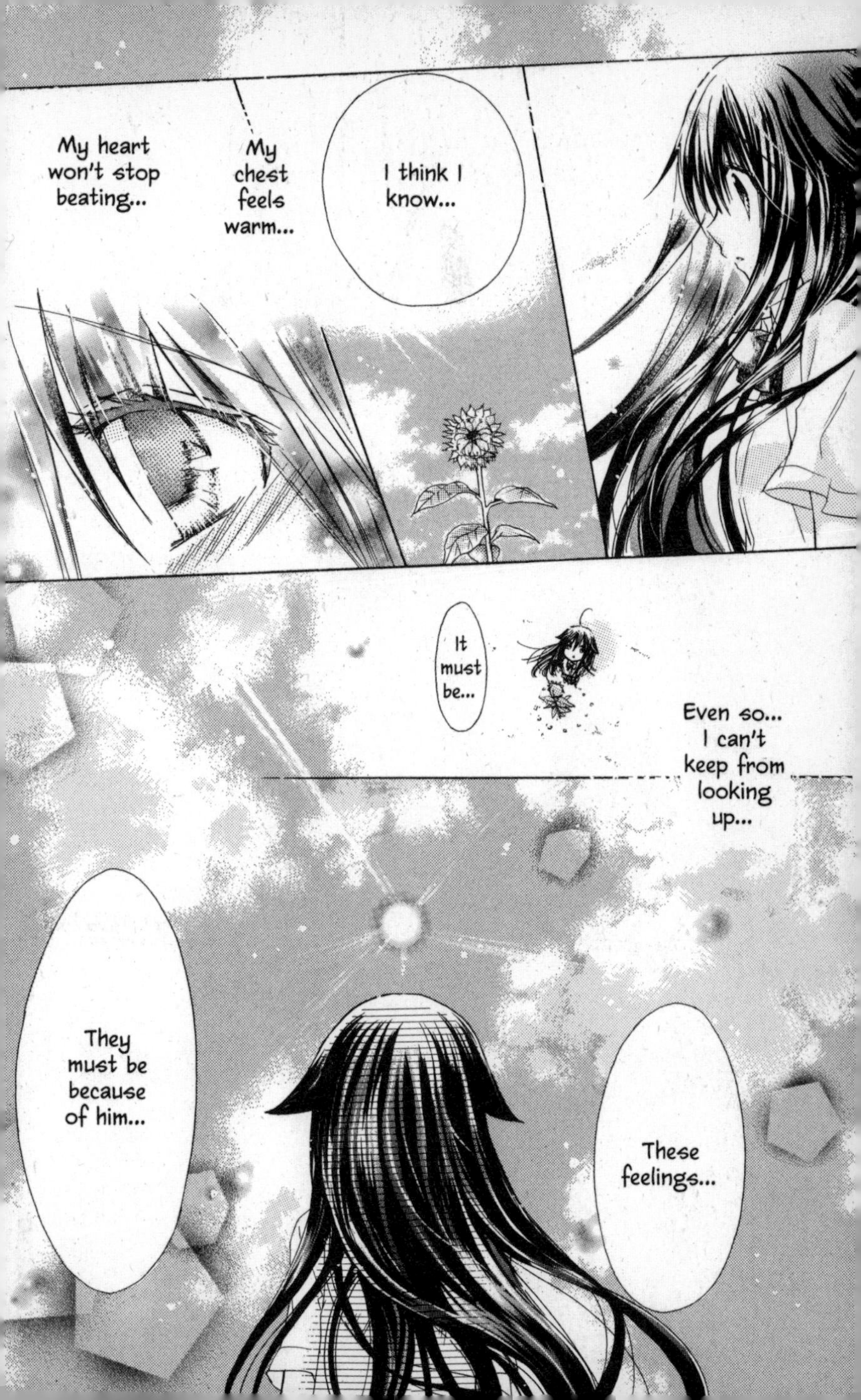

I think I know...
My chest feels warm...
My heart won't stop beating...
Even so... I can't keep from looking up...
It must be...
These feelings...
They must be because of him...

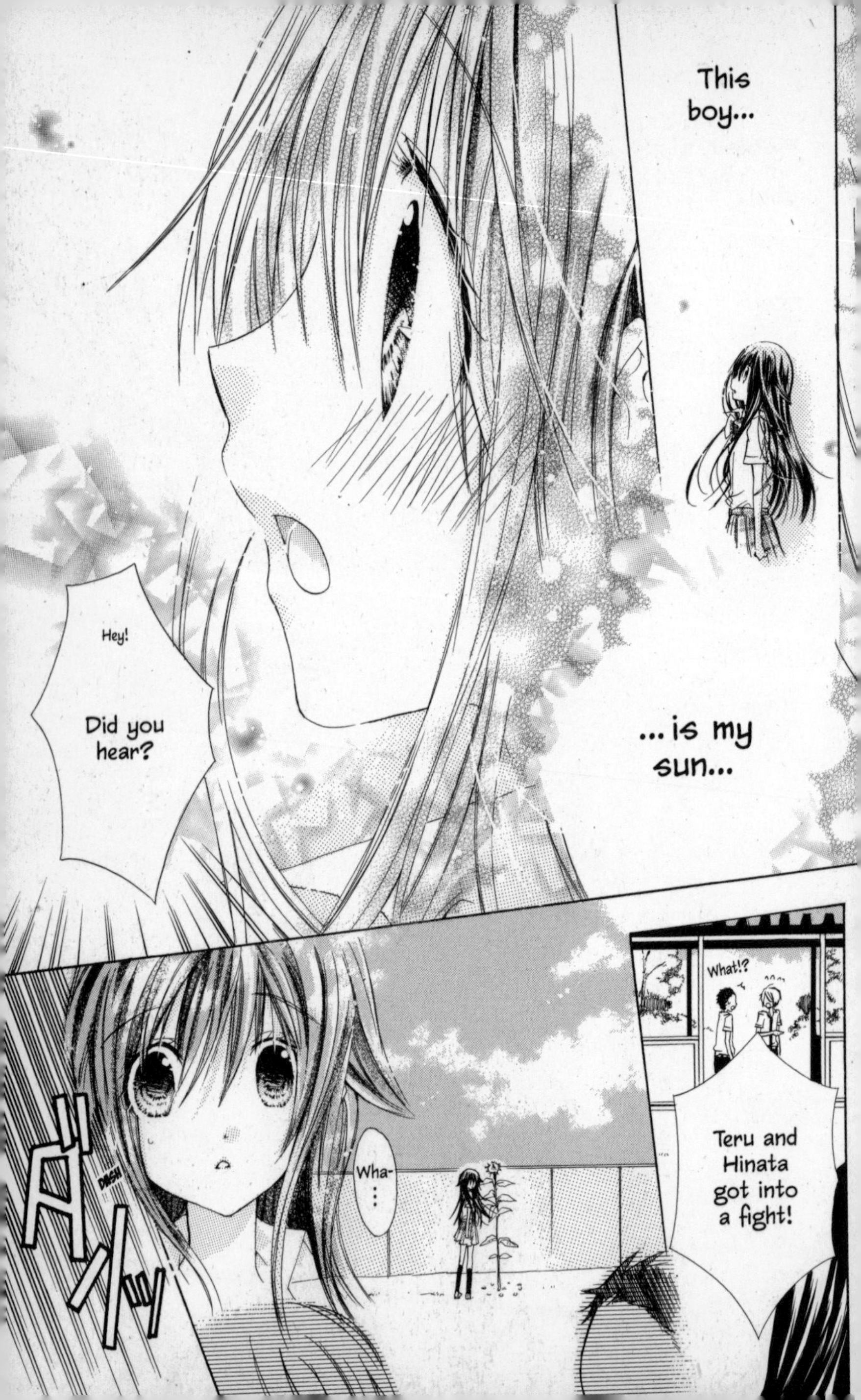
This boy...
... is my sun...
Hey!
Did you hear?
What!?
Teru and Hinata got into a fight!
Wha-...
DASH

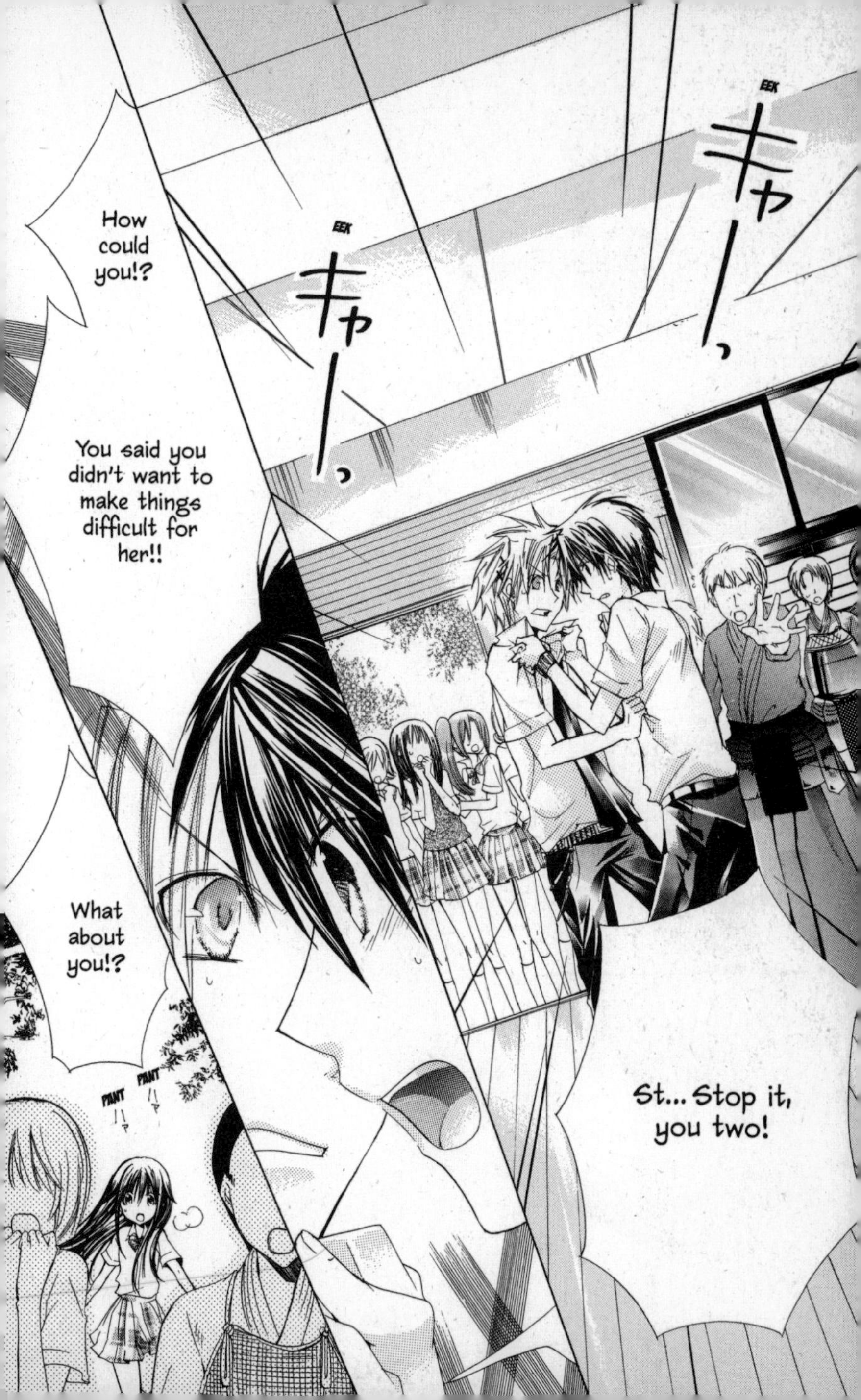
EEK
キャー!
EEK
キャー!
St... Stop it, you two!
How could you!?
You said you didn't want to make things difficult for her!!
What about you!?
PANT
ハァ
PANT
ハァ

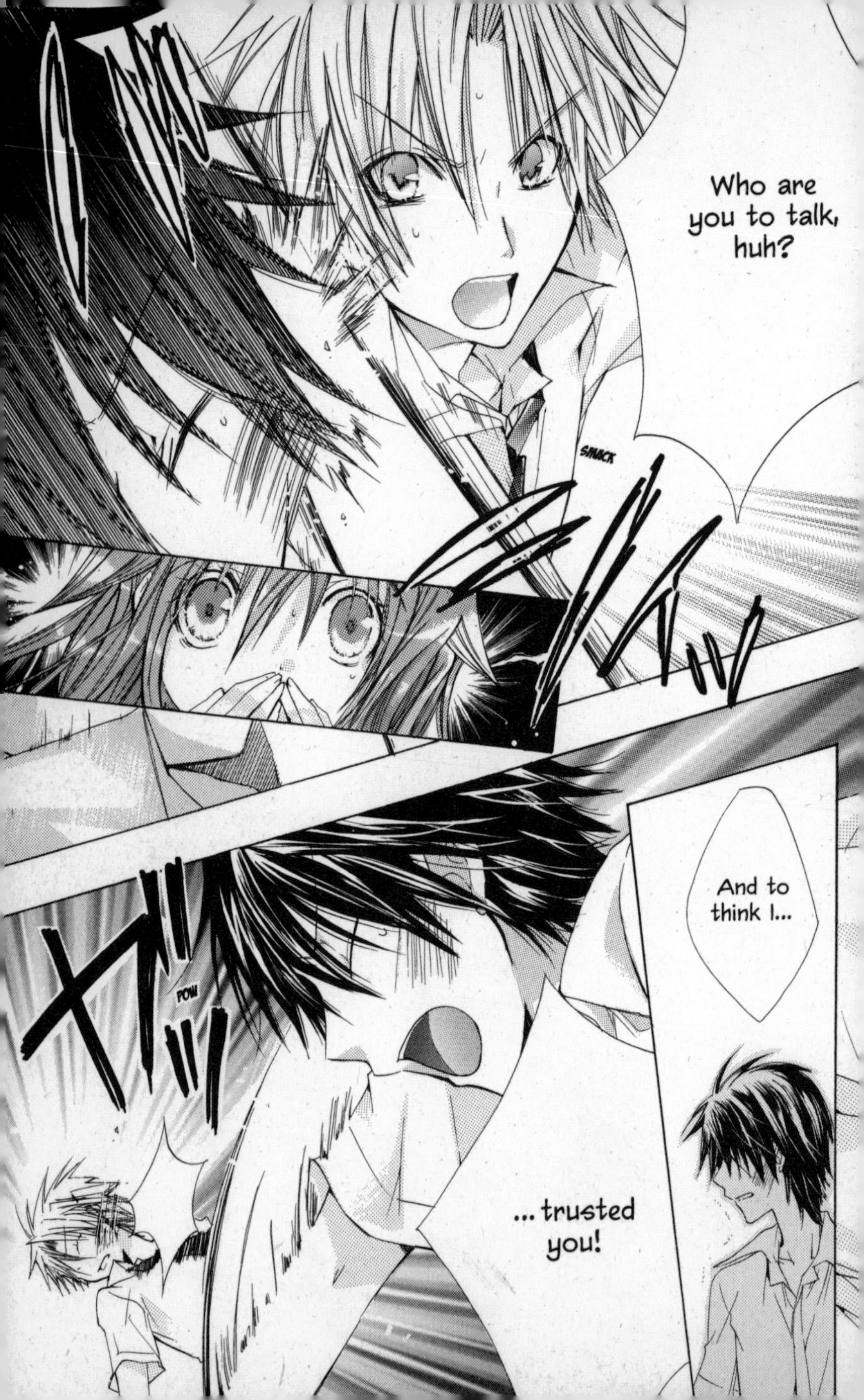
Who are you to talk, huh?
SMACK
And to think I...
POW
... trusted you!

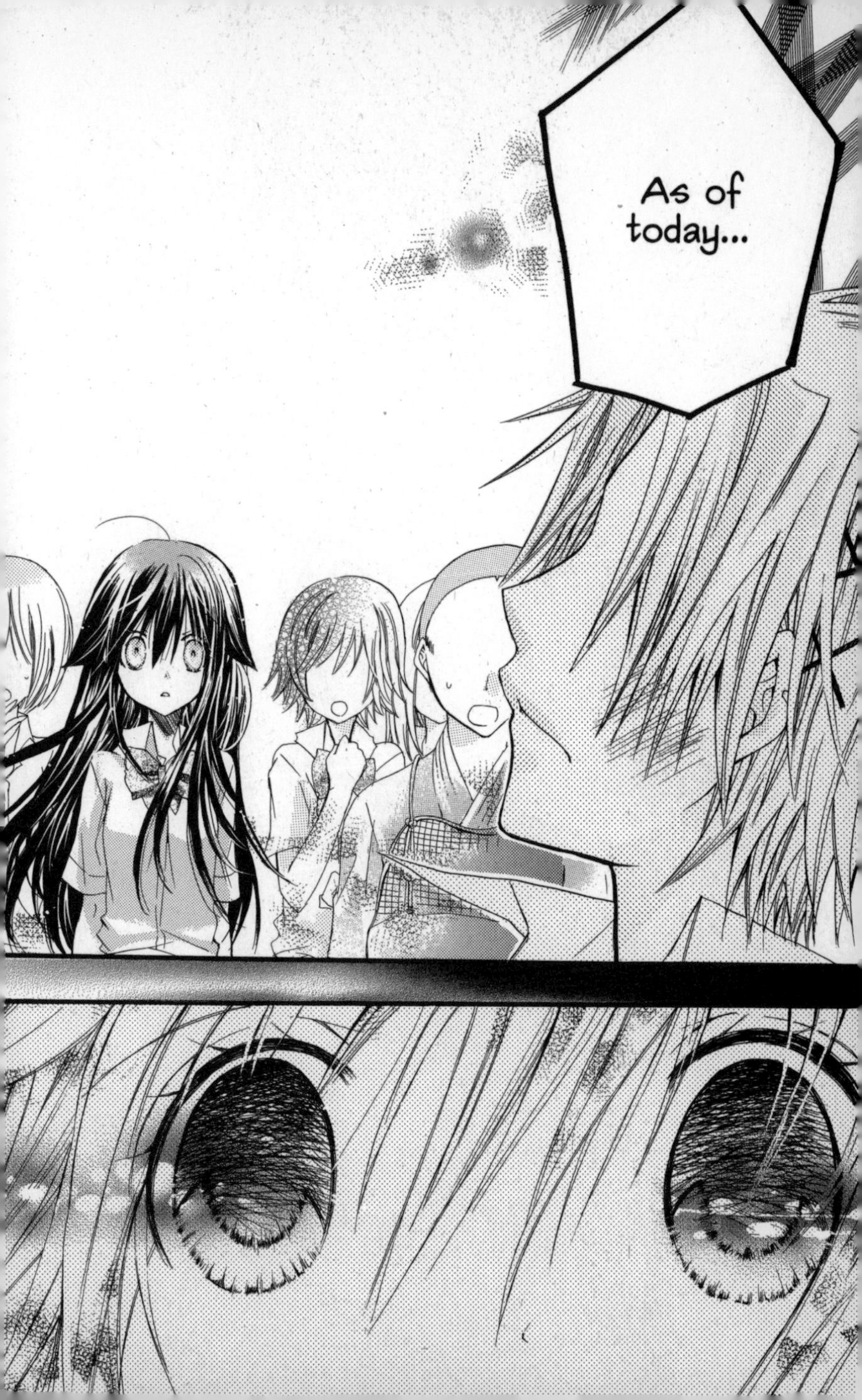
As of today...

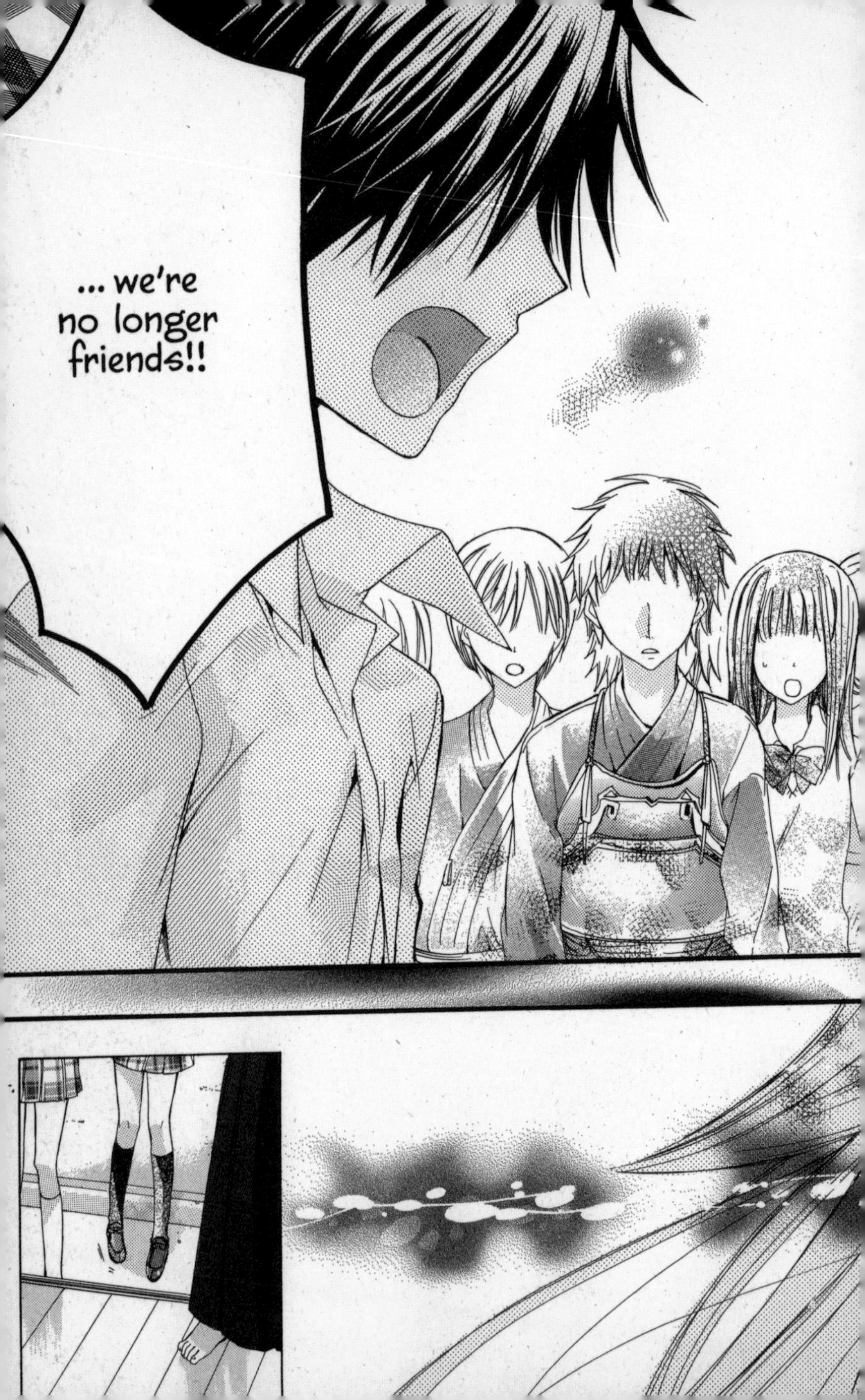
... we're
no longer
friends!!

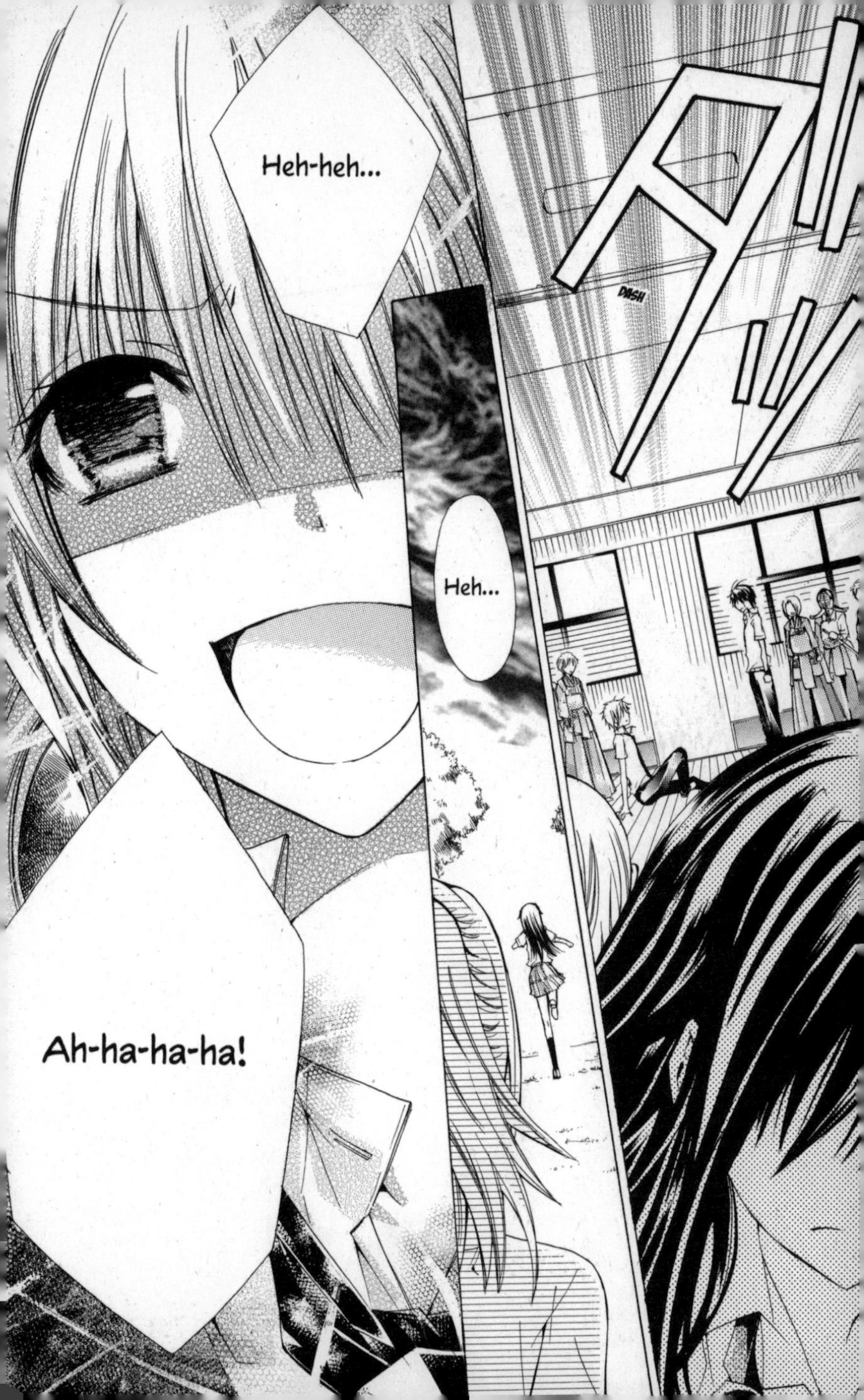
DASH
Heh...
Heh-heh...
Ah-ha-ha-ha!

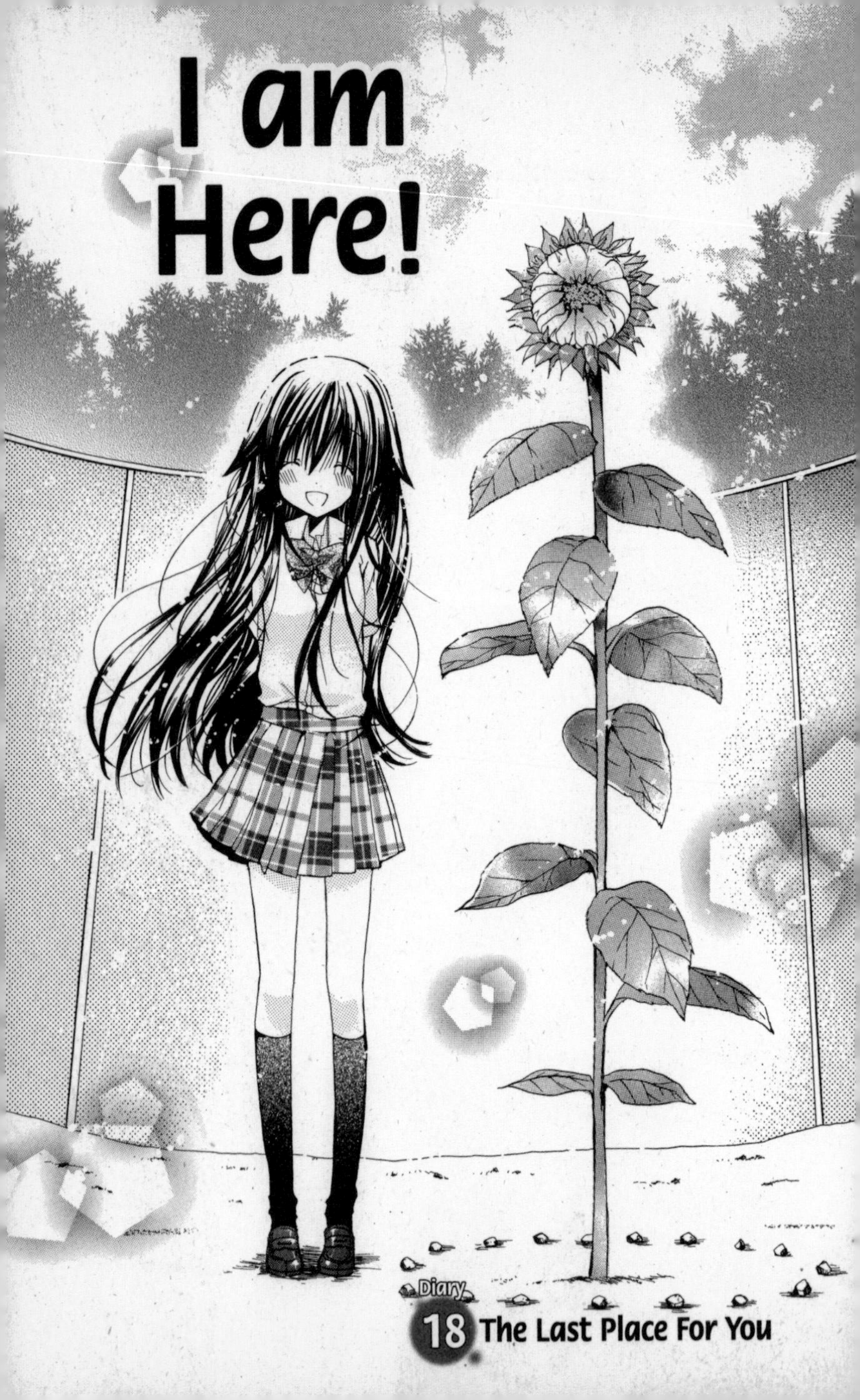
I am Here!
Diary 18 The Last Place For You

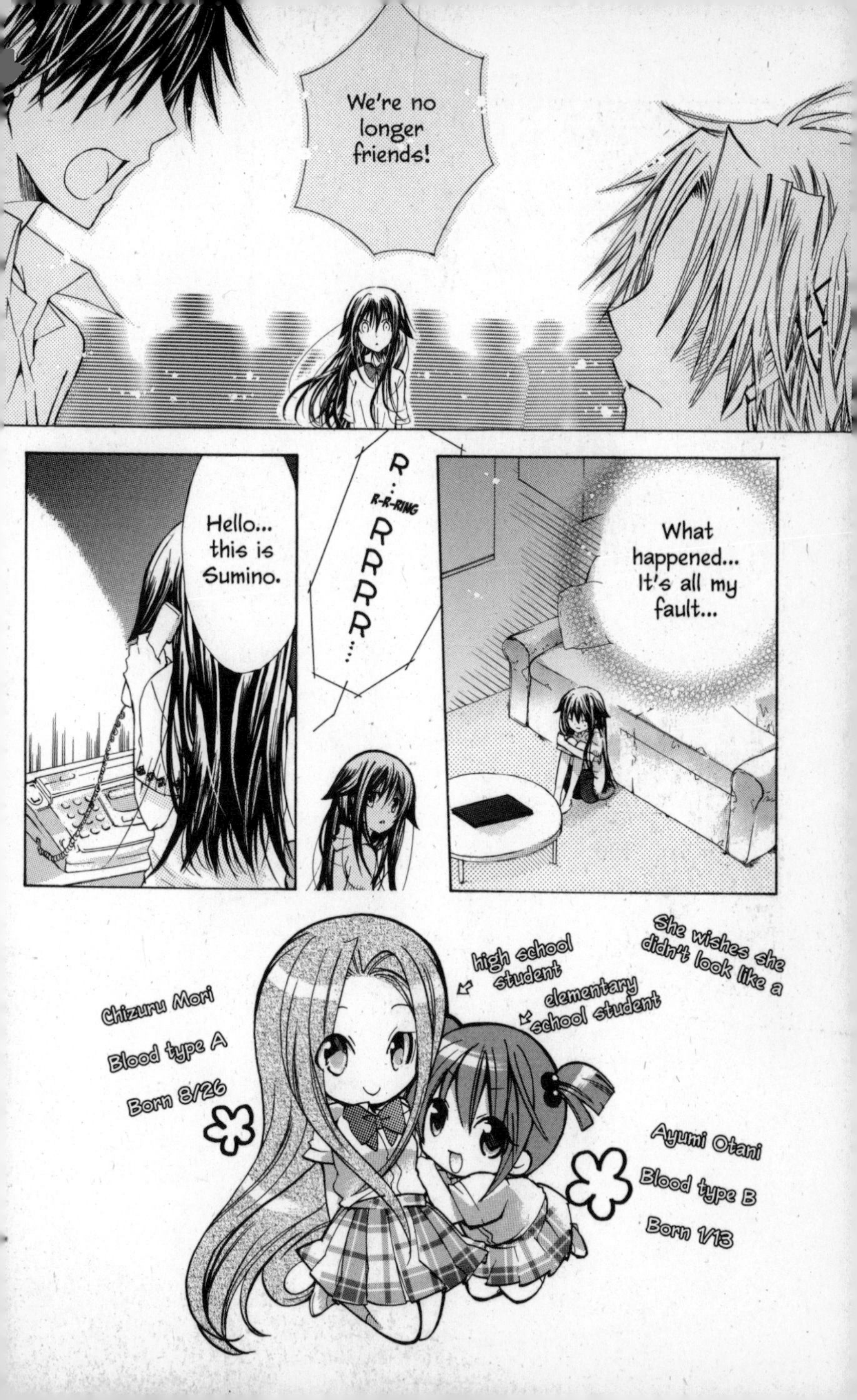
We're no longer friends!
What happened... It's all my fault...
R-R-RING
RRRRR...
Hello... this is Sumino.
She wishes she didn't look like a
elementary school student
high school student
Ayumi Otani
Blood type B
Born 1/13
Chizuru Mori
Blood type A
Born 8/26

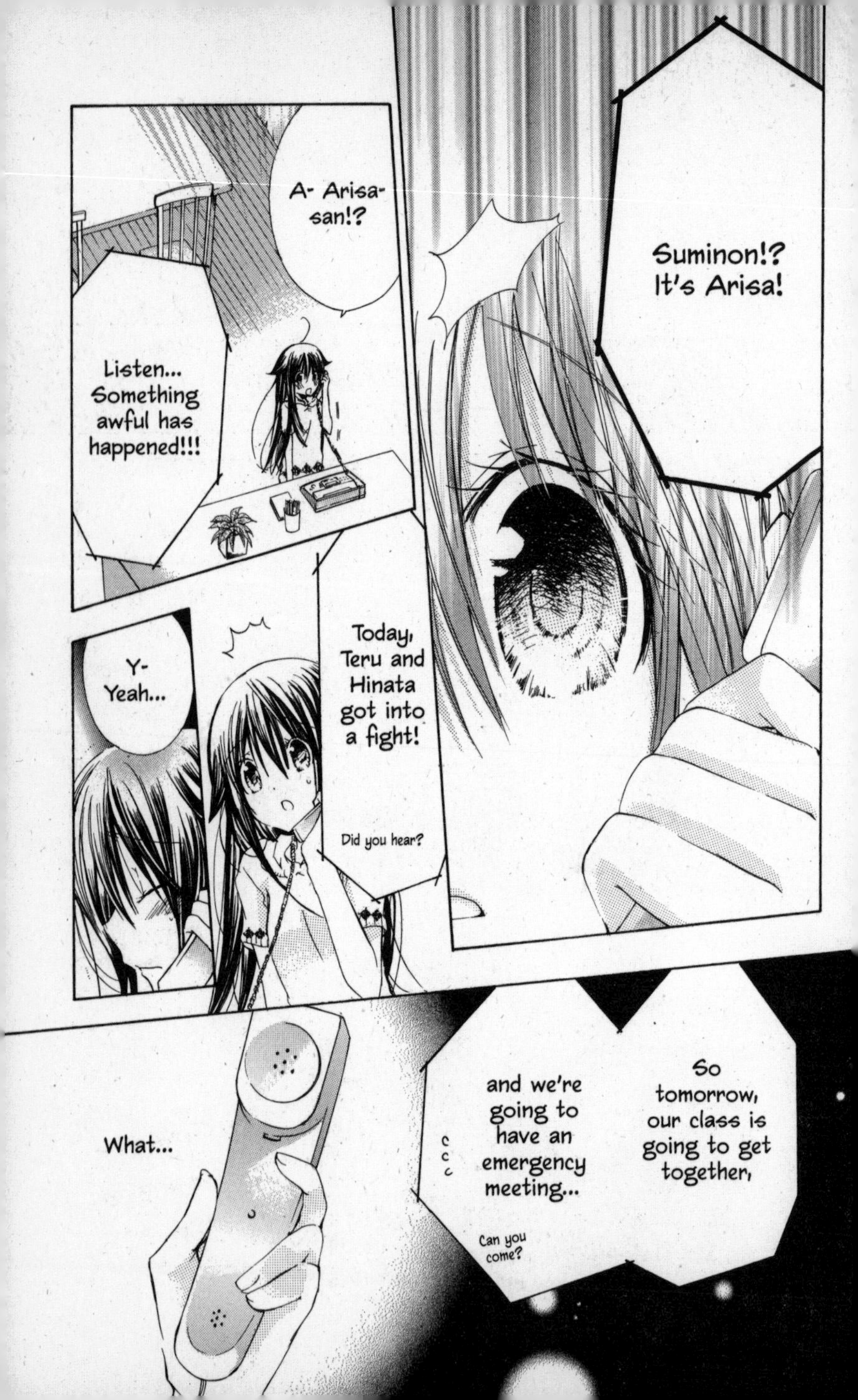
Suminon!? It's Arisa!
A- Arisa-san!?
Listen... Something awful has happened!!!
Today, Teru and Hinata got into a fight!
Did you hear?
Y- Yeah...
So tomorrow, our class is going to get together,
and we're going to have an emergency meeting...
Can you come?
What...

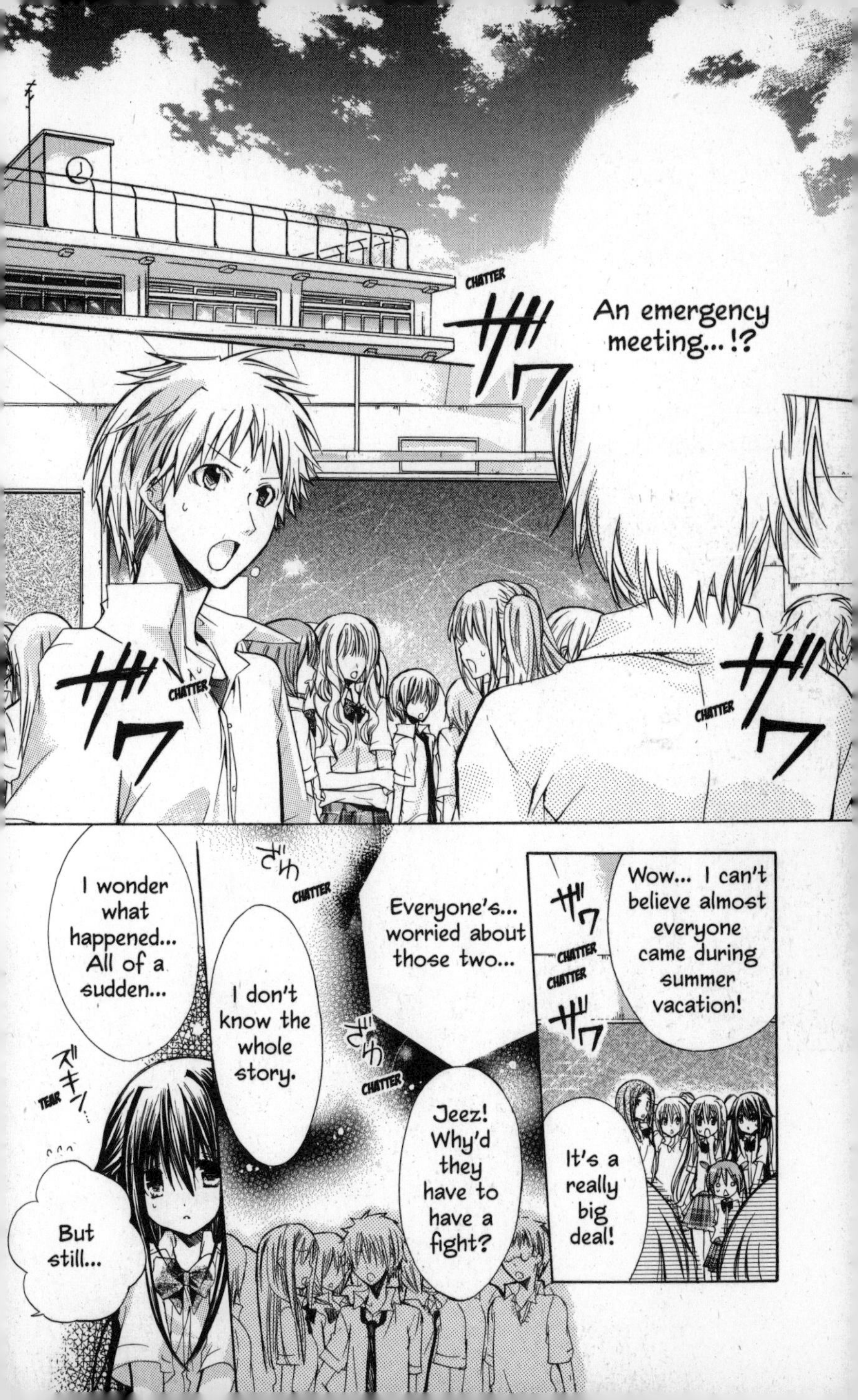
CHATTER
ザワ
An emergency meeting...!?
ザワ
CHATTER
ザワ
CHATTER
Wow... I can't believe almost everyone came during summer vacation!
ザワ
CHATTER
CHATTER
ザワ
It's a really big deal!
ざわ
CHATTER
Everyone's... worried about those two...
I wonder what happened... All of a sudden...
I don't know the whole story.
ざわ
CHATTER
Jeez! Why'd they have to have a fight?
ズキン…
TEAR
But still...

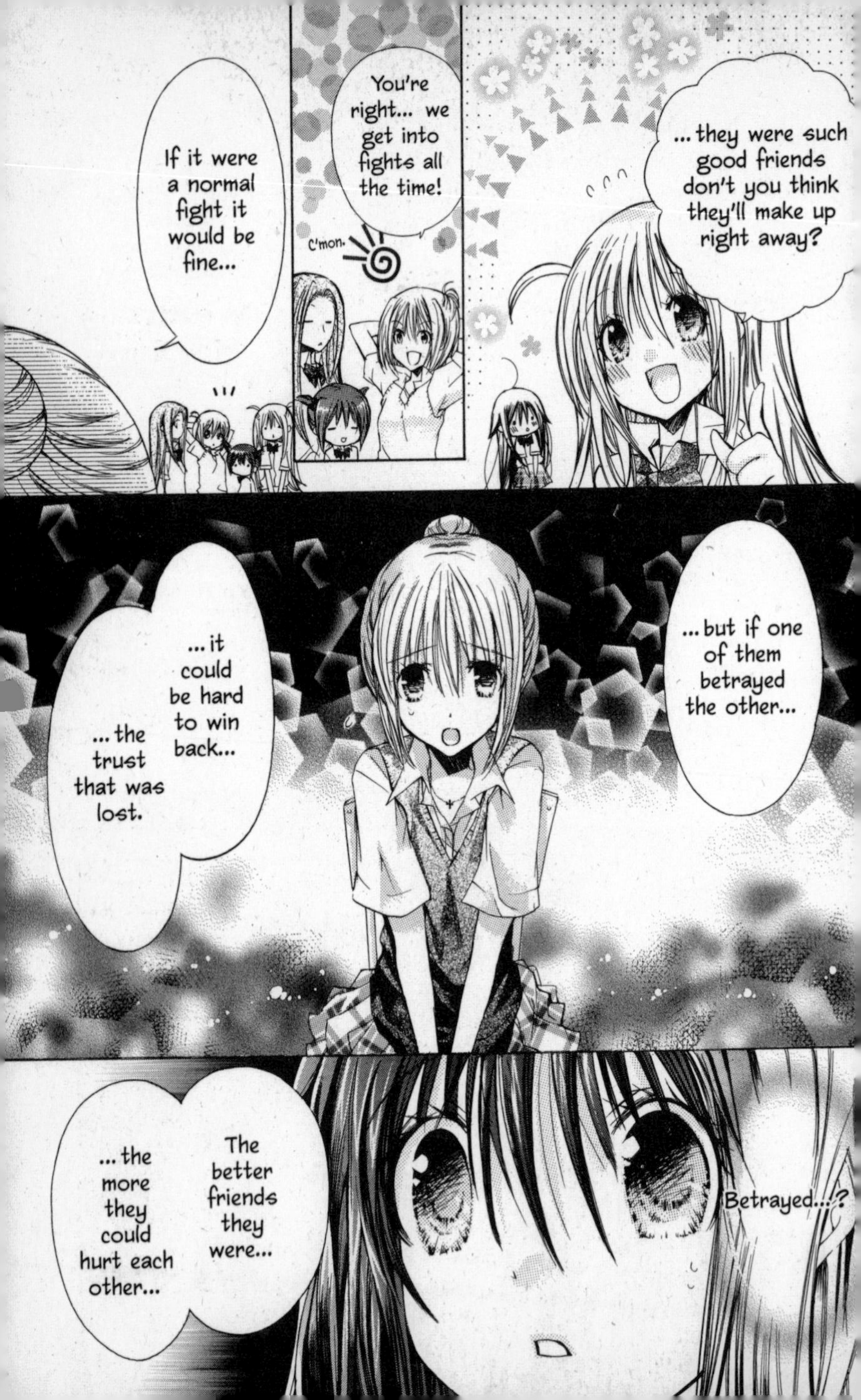
... they were such good friends don't you think they'll make up right away?
You're right... we get into fights all the time!
C'mon.
If it were a normal fight it would be fine...
... but if one of them betrayed the other...
... it could be hard to win back...
... the trust that was lost.
Betrayed...?
The better friends they were...
... the more they could hurt each other...

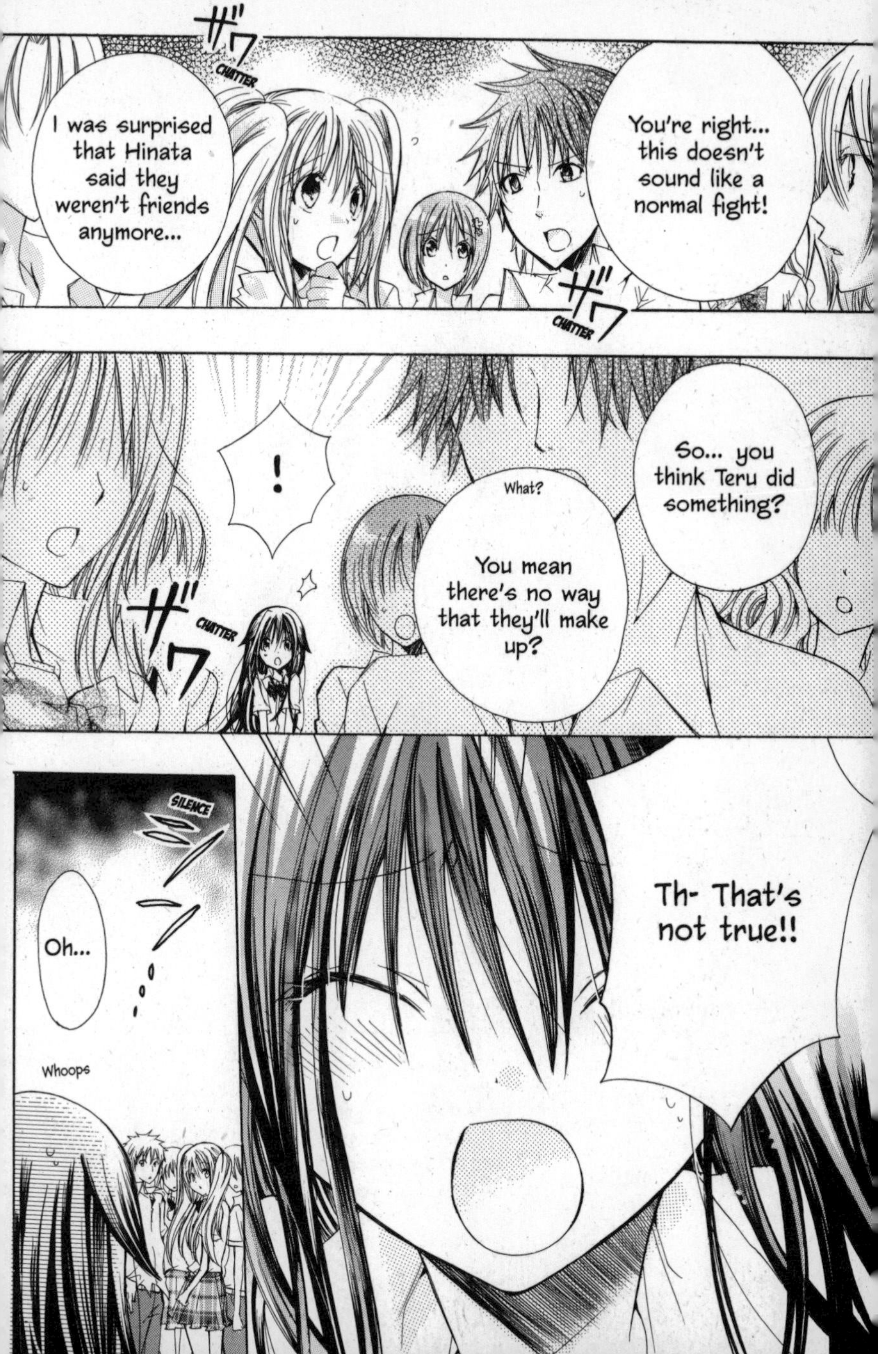

CHATTER
You're right... this doesn't sound like a normal fight!
CHATTER
I was surprised that Hinata said they weren't friends anymore...
So... you think Teru did something?
What?
You mean there's no way that they'll make up?
!
CHATTER
Th- That's not true!!
SILENCE
Oh...
Whoops

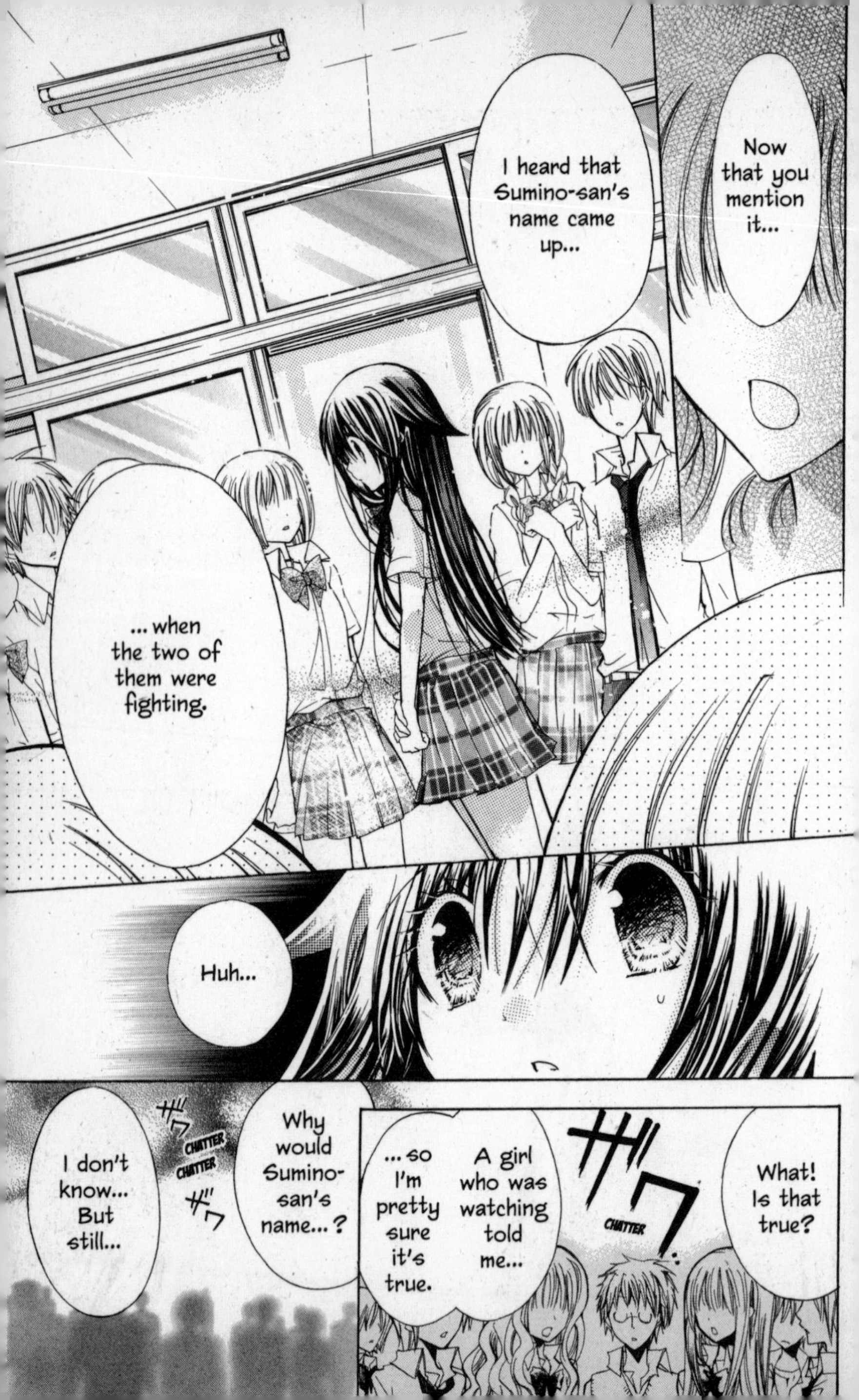
Now that you mention it...
I heard that Sumino-san's name came up...
...when the two of them were fighting.
Huh...
What! Is that true?
CHATTER
A girl who was watching told me...
...so I'm pretty sure it's true.
Why would Sumino-san's name...?
CHATTER
CHATTER
I don't know... But still...

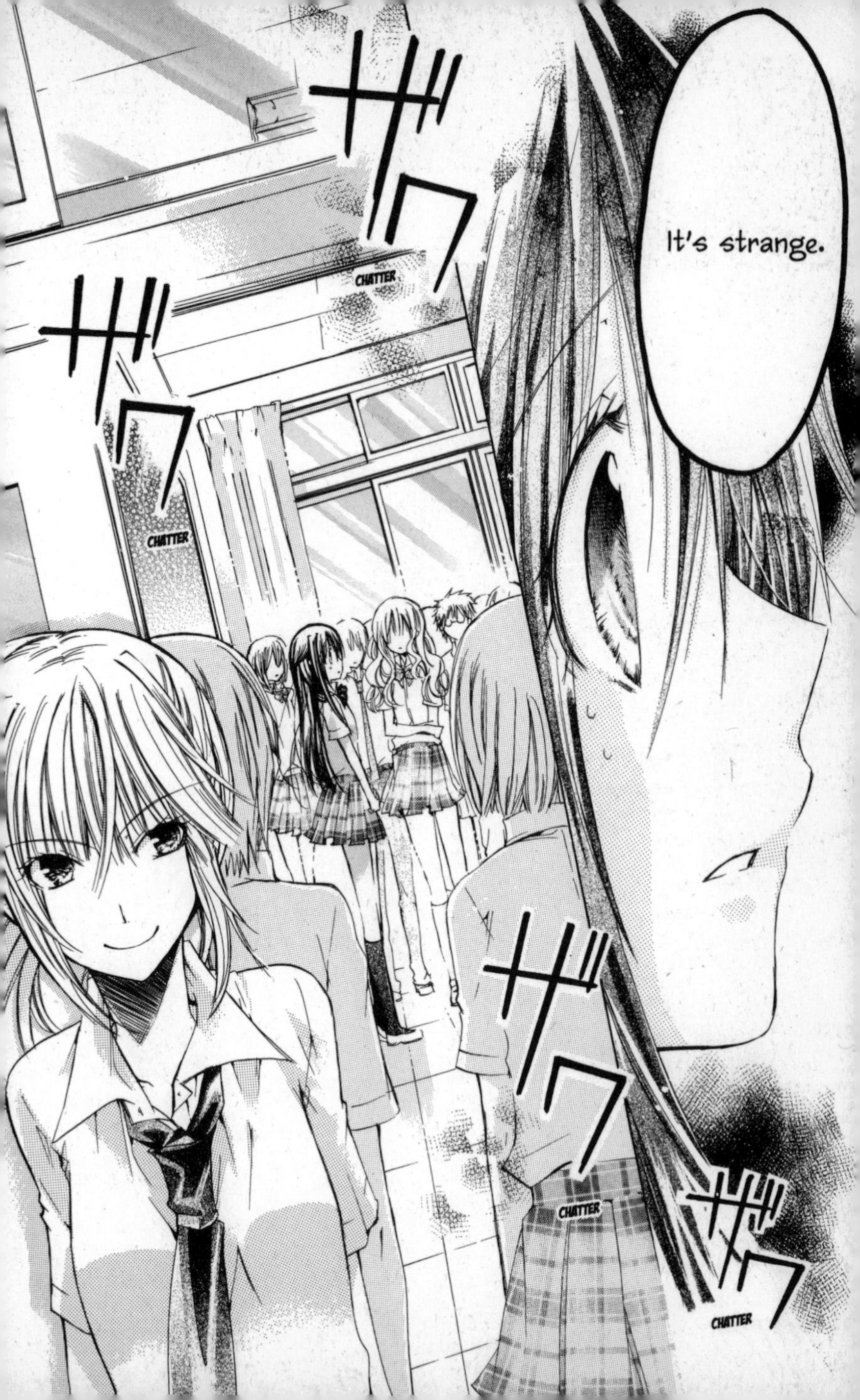

It's strange.
ザワ
CHATTER
ザワ
CHATTER
ザワ
CHATTER
ザワ
CHATTER

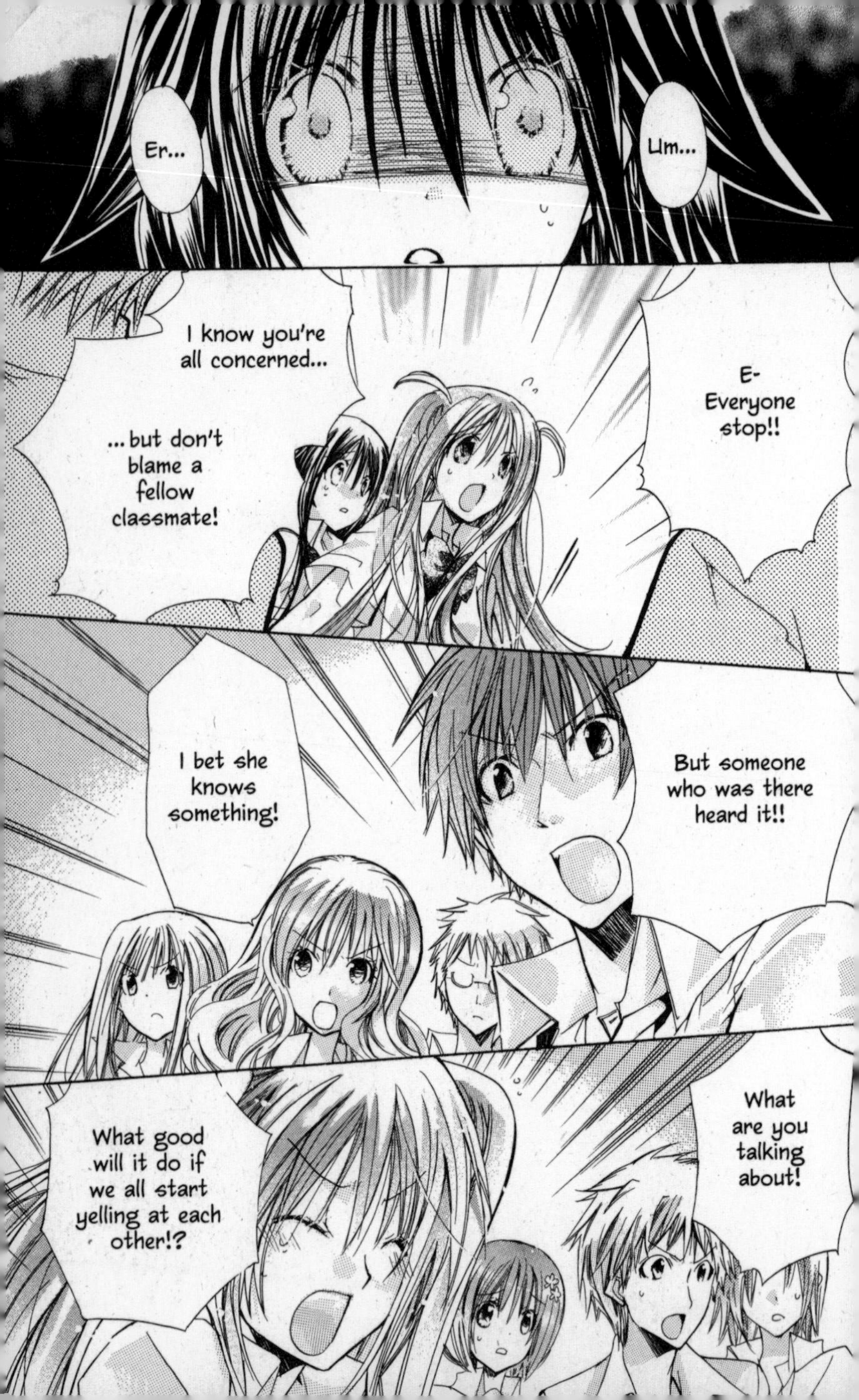
Um...
Er...
E- Everyone stop!!
I know you're all concerned...
...but don't blame a fellow classmate!
But someone who was there heard it!!
I bet she knows something!
What are you talking about!
What good will it do if we all start yelling at each other!?

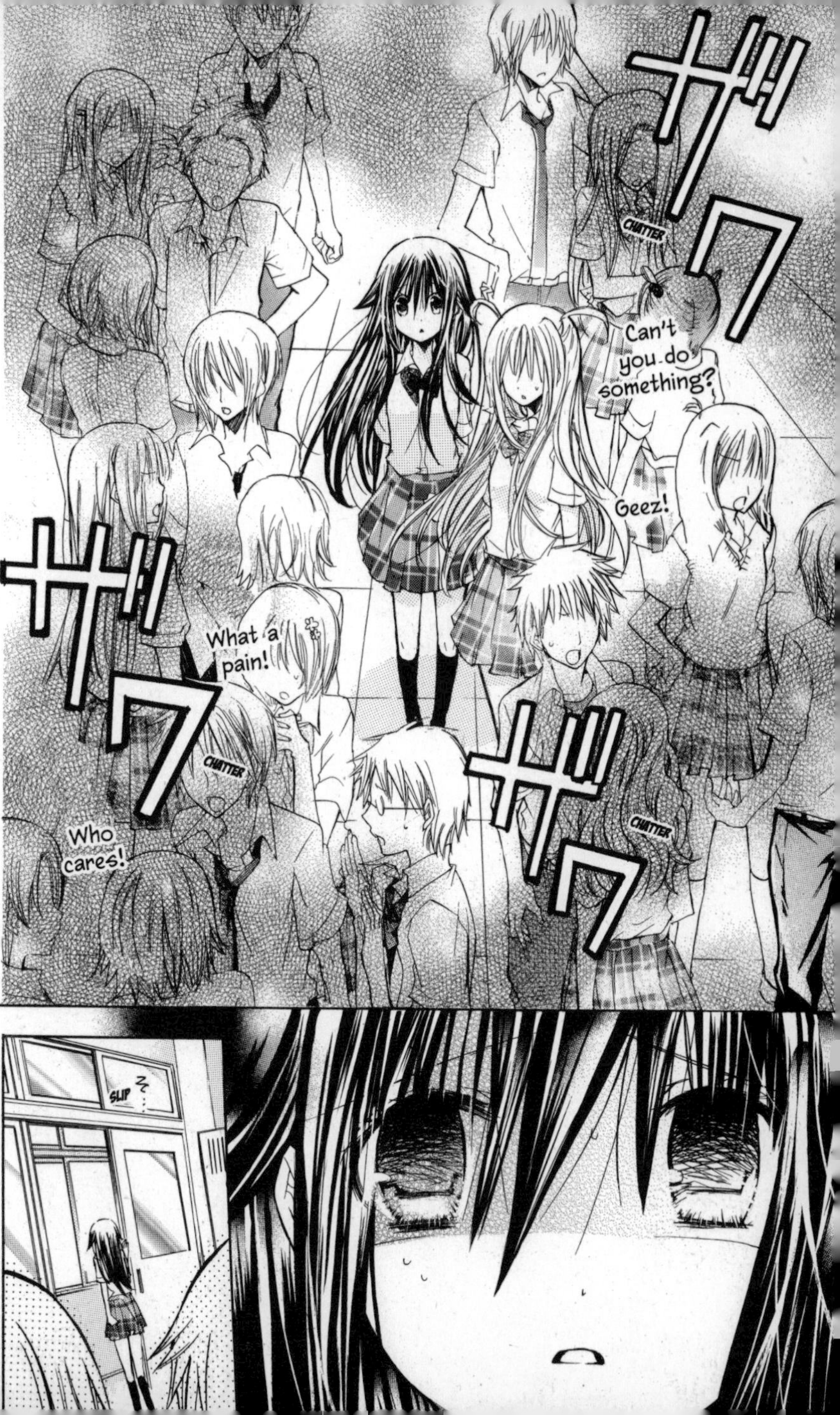
ザワ
CHATTER
Can't you do something?
Geez!
ザワ
CHATTER
What a pain!
ザワ
CHATTER
Who cares!
SLIP

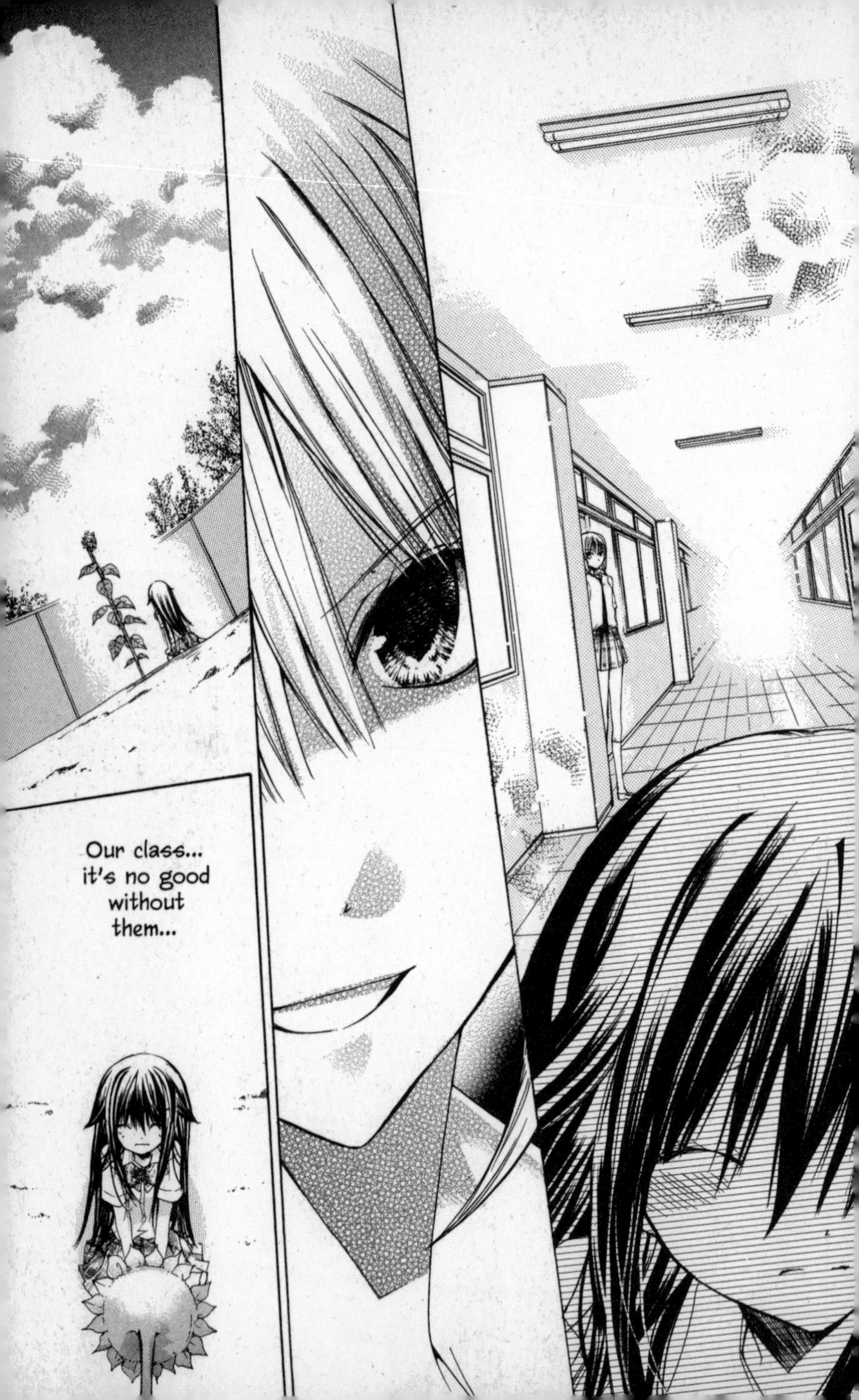
Our class... it's no good without them...

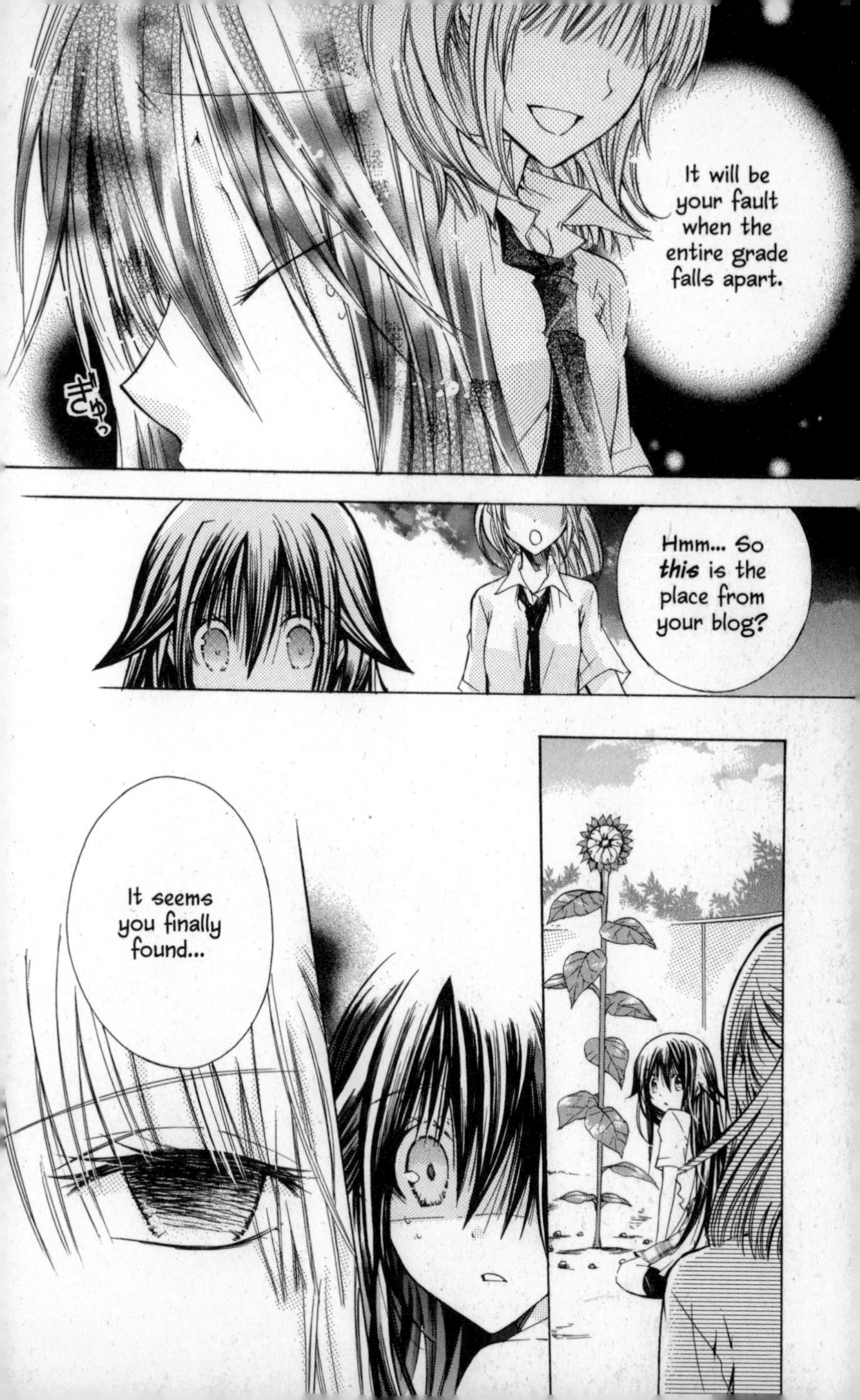
It will be your fault when the entire grade falls apart.
ぎゅっ
Hmm... So *this* is the place from your blog?
It seems you finally found...

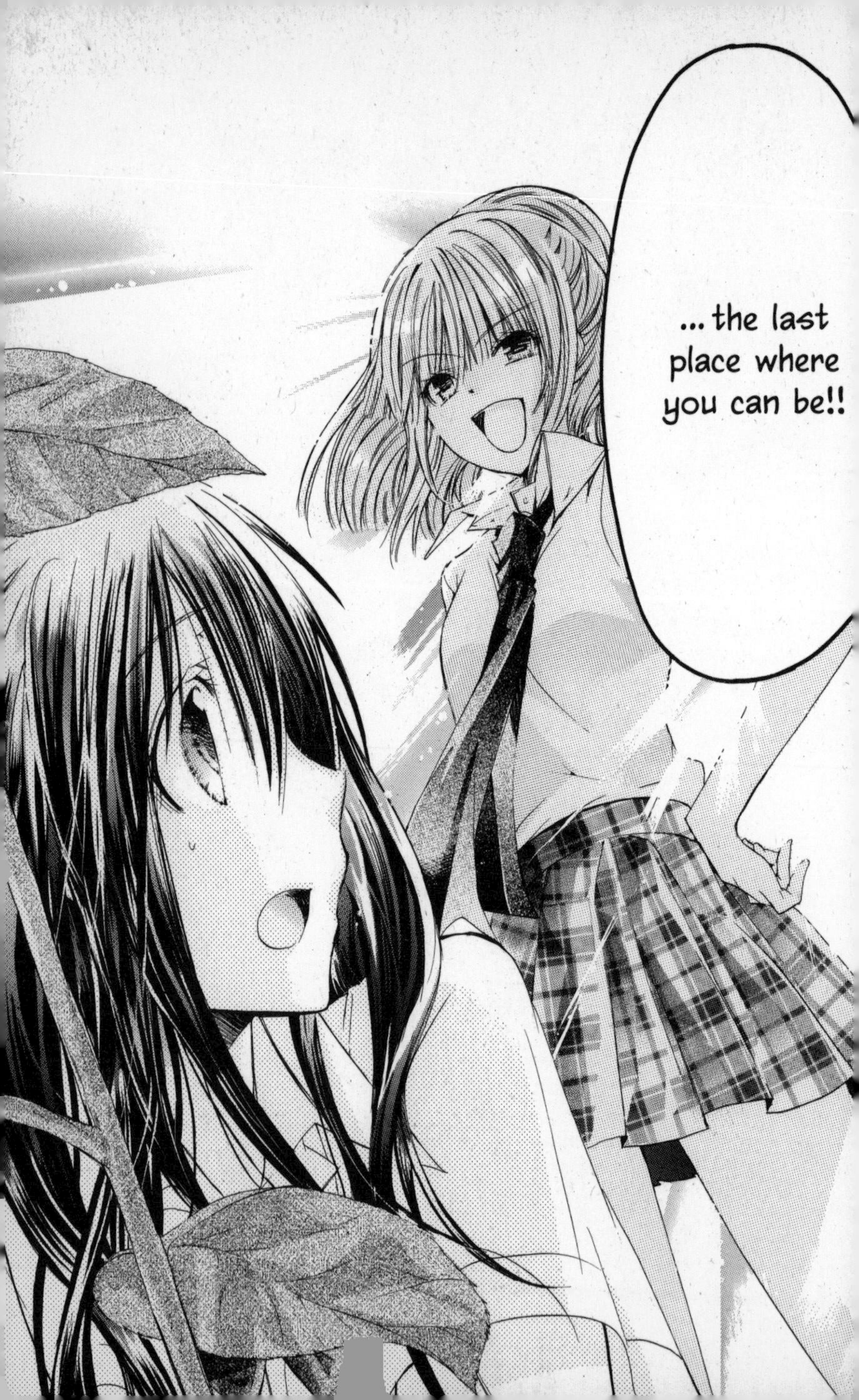
...the last place where you can be!!

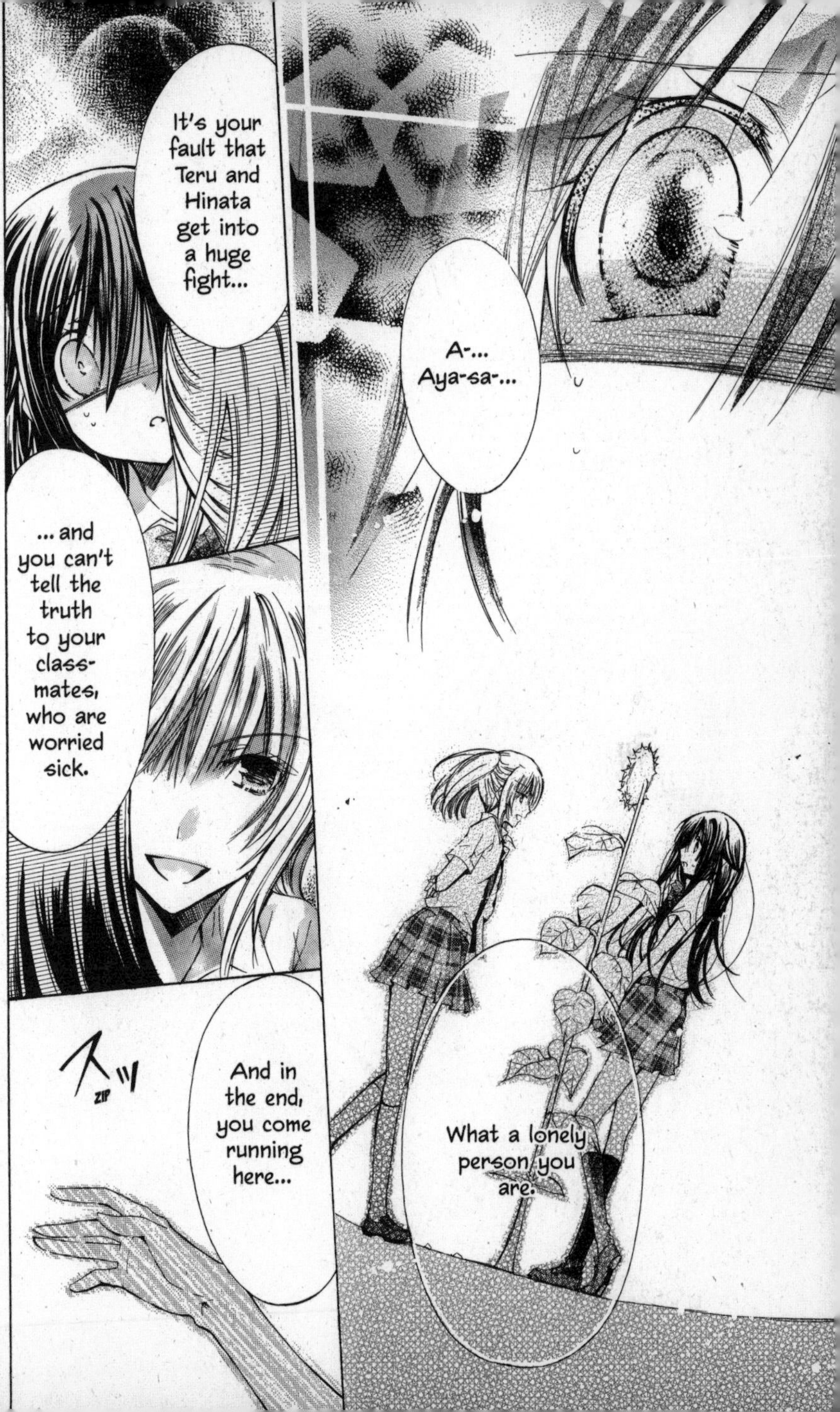
A-... Aya-sa-...
It's your fault that Teru and Hinata get into a huge fight...
... and you can't tell the truth to your class-mates, who are worried sick.
スッ ZIP
And in the end, you come running here...
What a lonely person you are.

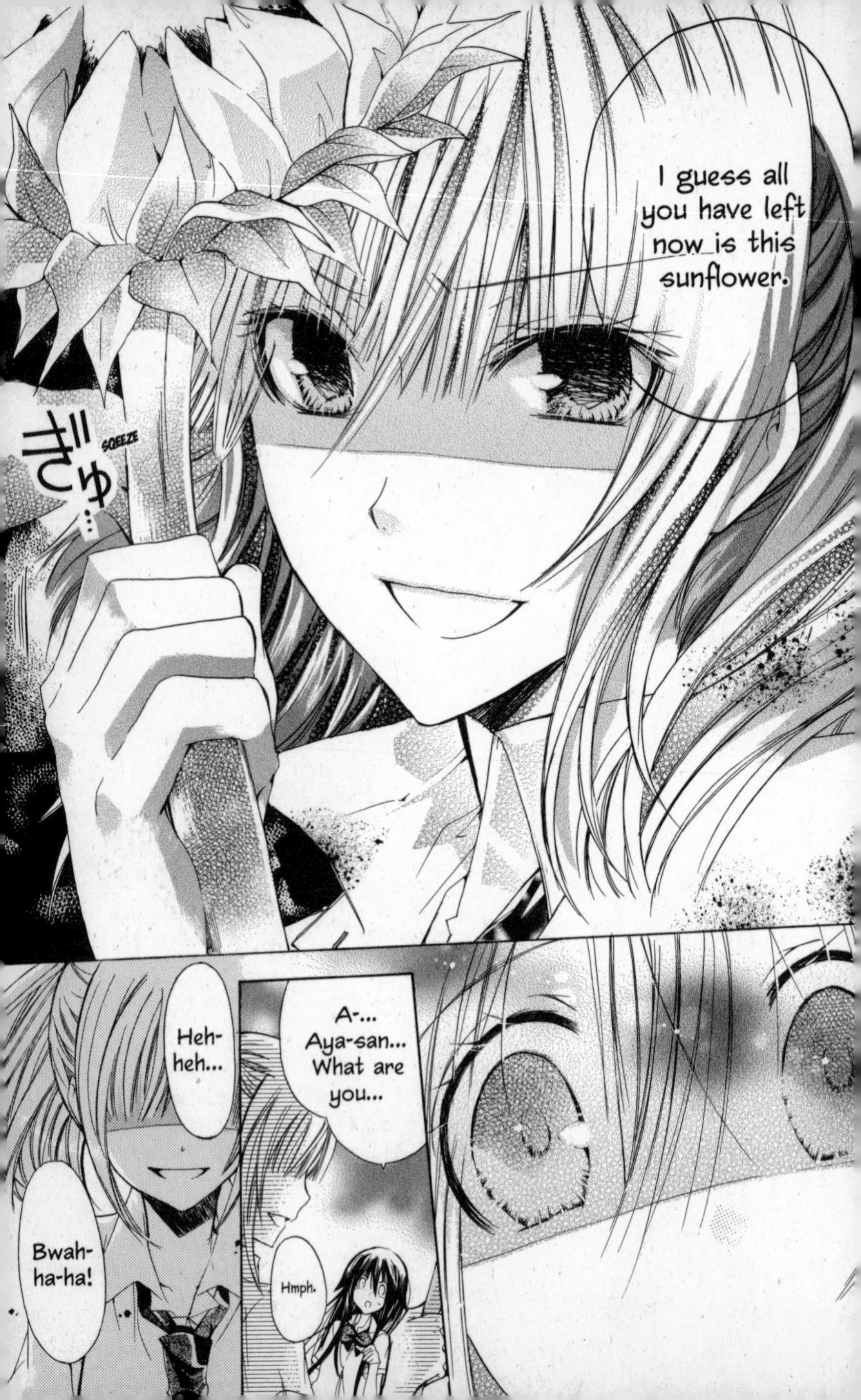
I guess all you have left now is this sunflower.
ぎゅ…
SQEEZE
A-... Aya-san... What are you...
Hmph.
Heh-heh...
Bwah-ha-ha!

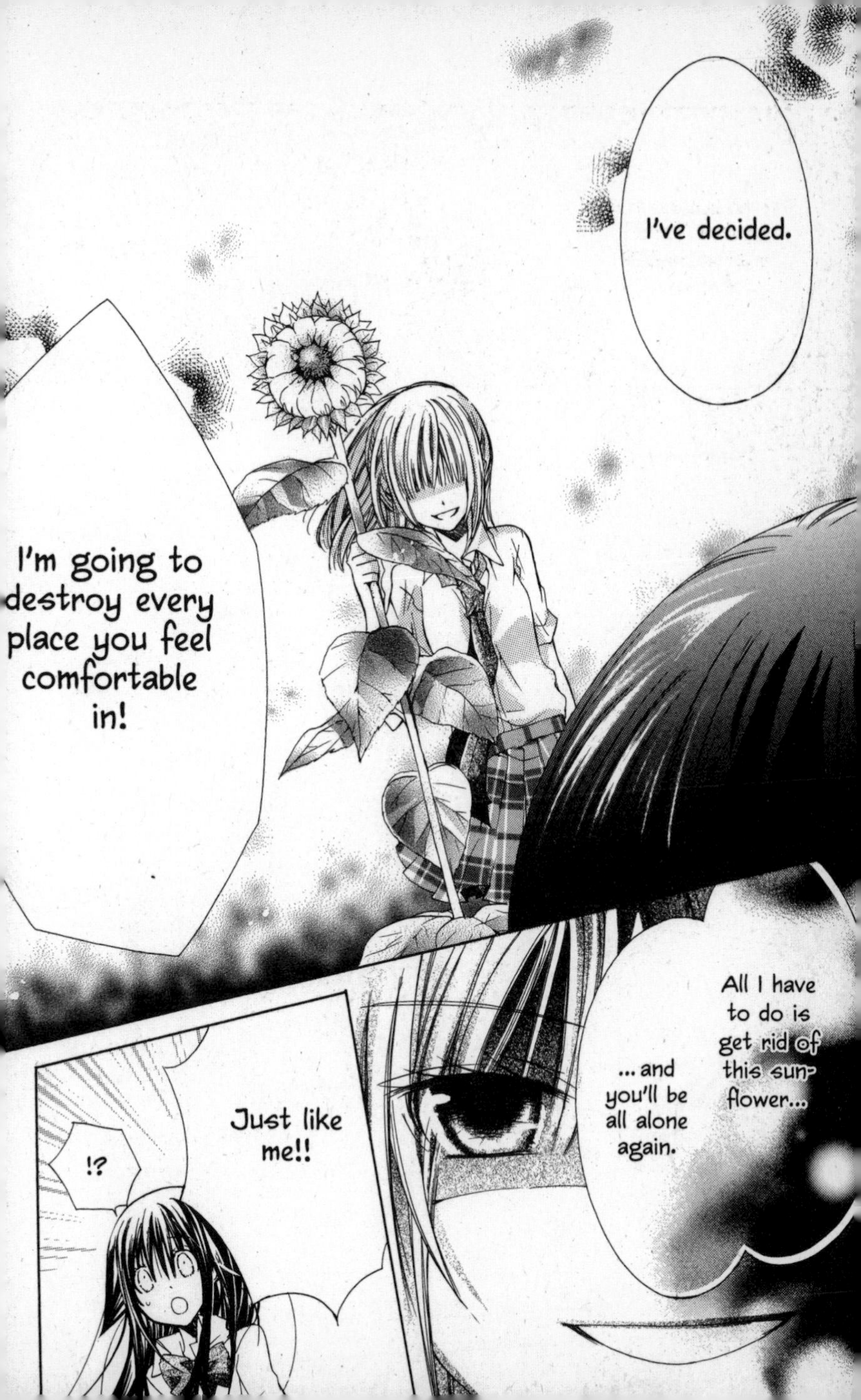
I've decided.
I'm going to destroy every place you feel comfortable in!
All I have to do is get rid of this sun-flower...
...and you'll be all alone again.
Just like me!!
!?

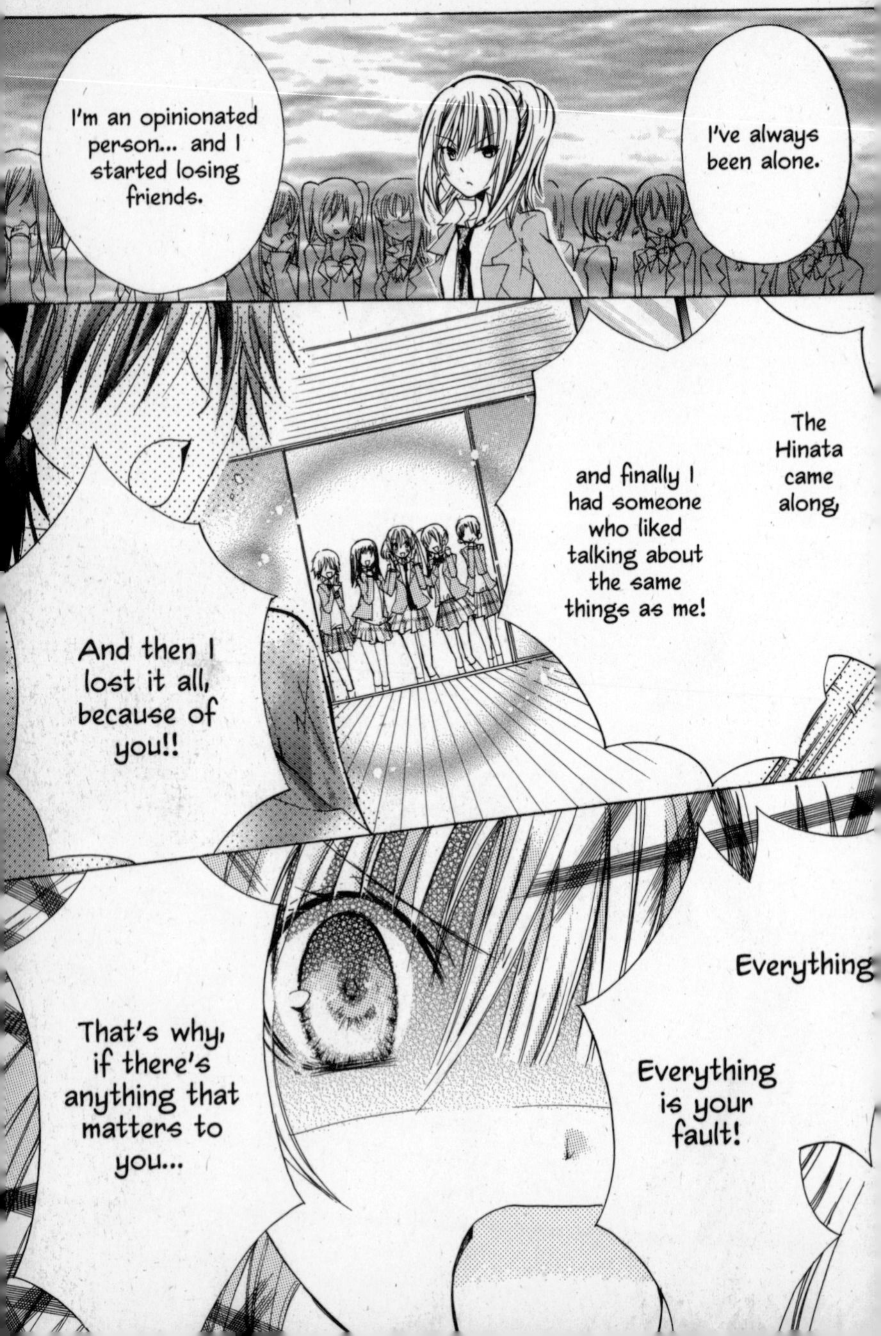
I've always been alone.
I'm an opinionated person... and I started losing friends.
The Hinata came along,
and finally I had someone who liked talking about the same things as me!
And then I lost it all, because of you!!
Everything
Everything is your fault!
That's why, if there's anything that matters to you...

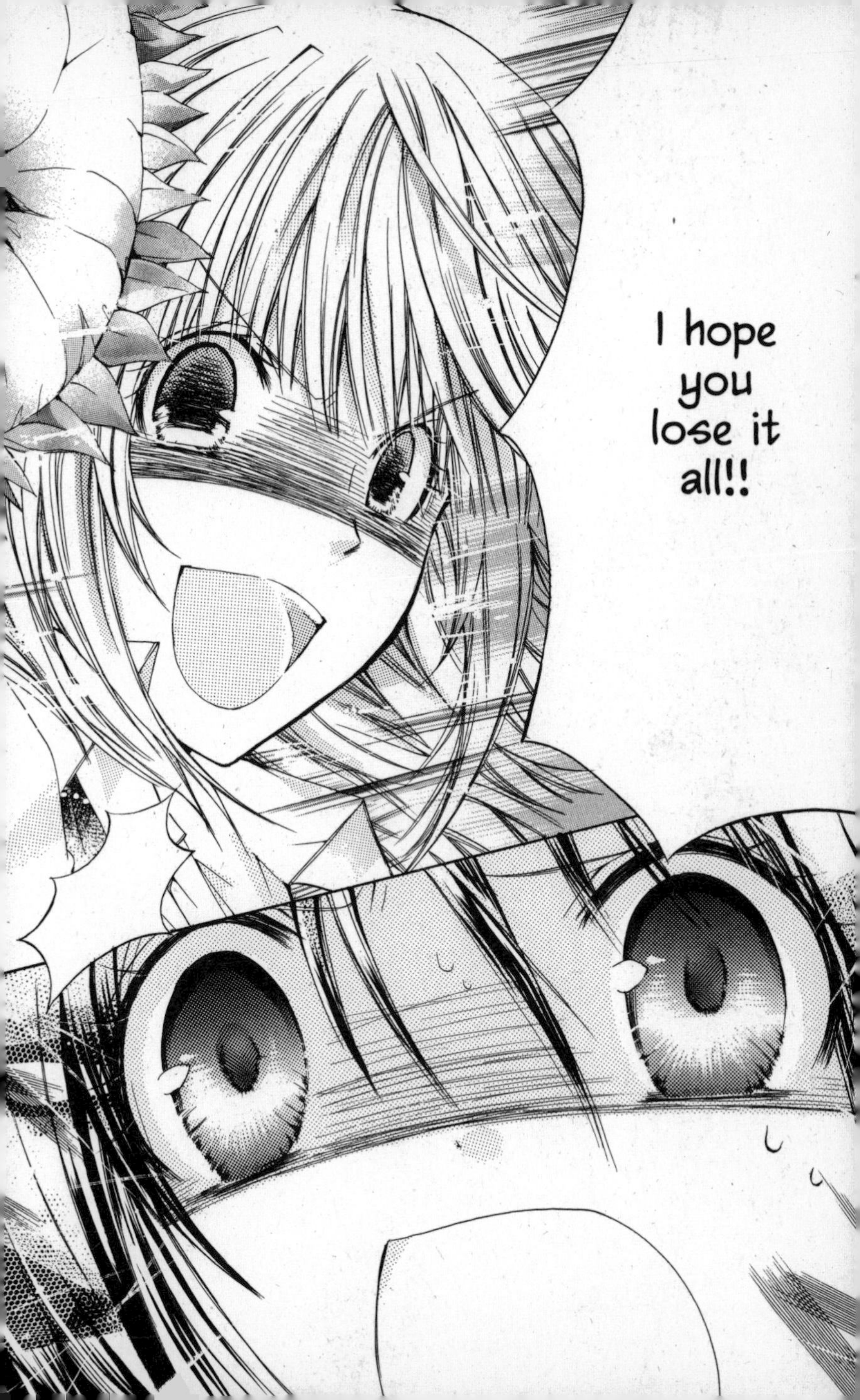
I hope you lose it all!!

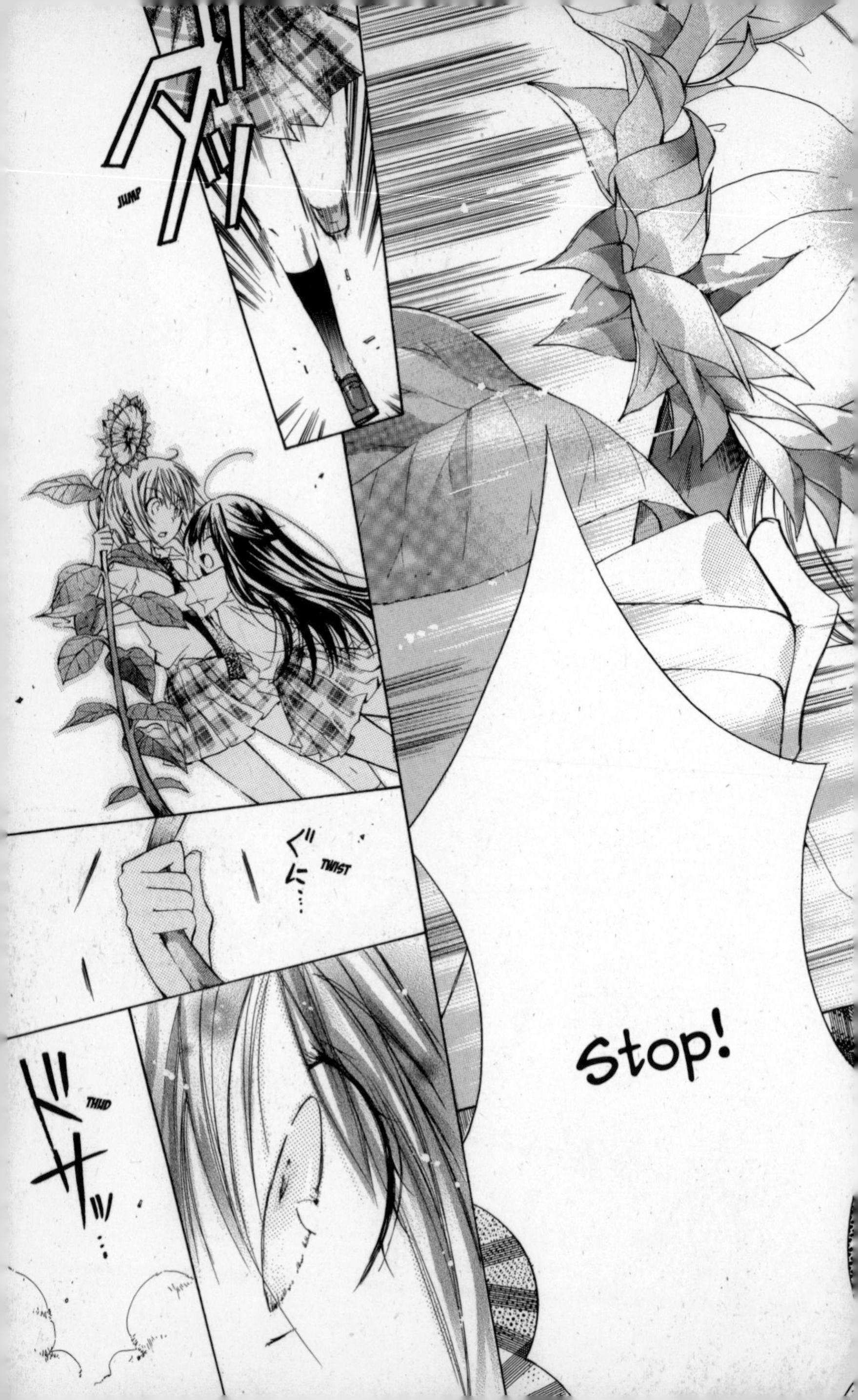
Stop!
JUMP
TWIST
THUD

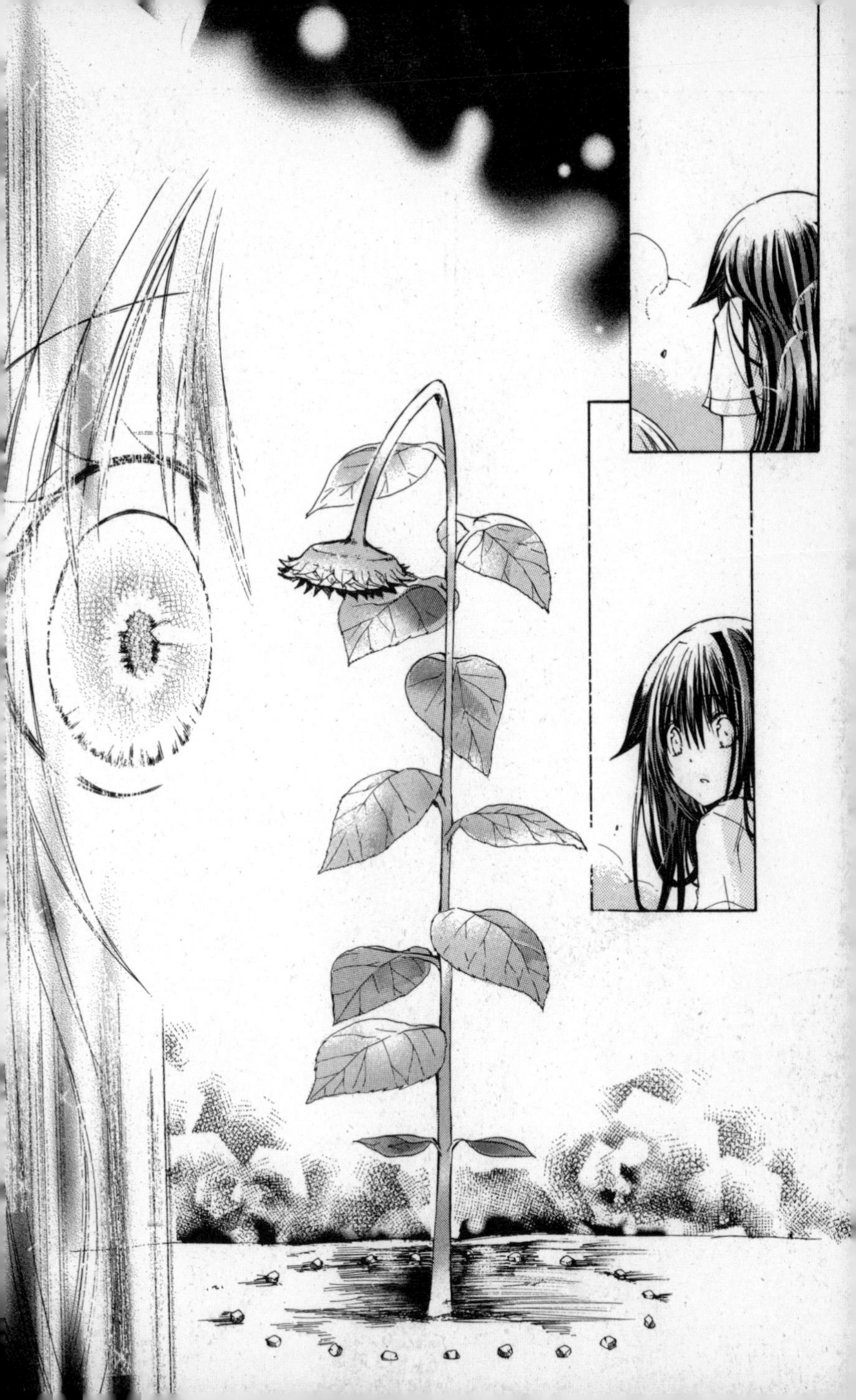

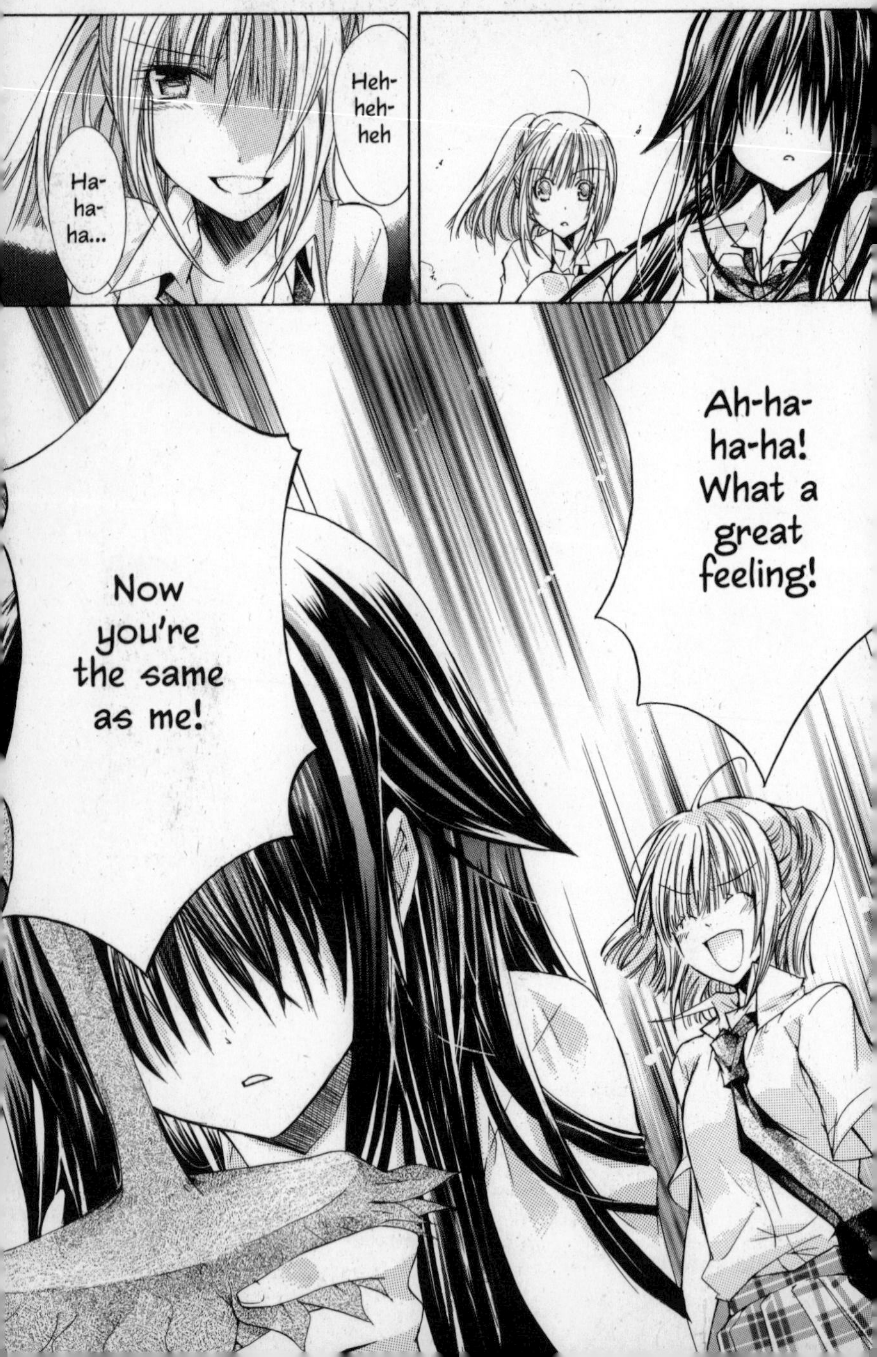
Heh-heh-heh
Ha-ha-ha...
Ah-ha-ha-ha! What a great feeling!
Now you're the same as me!

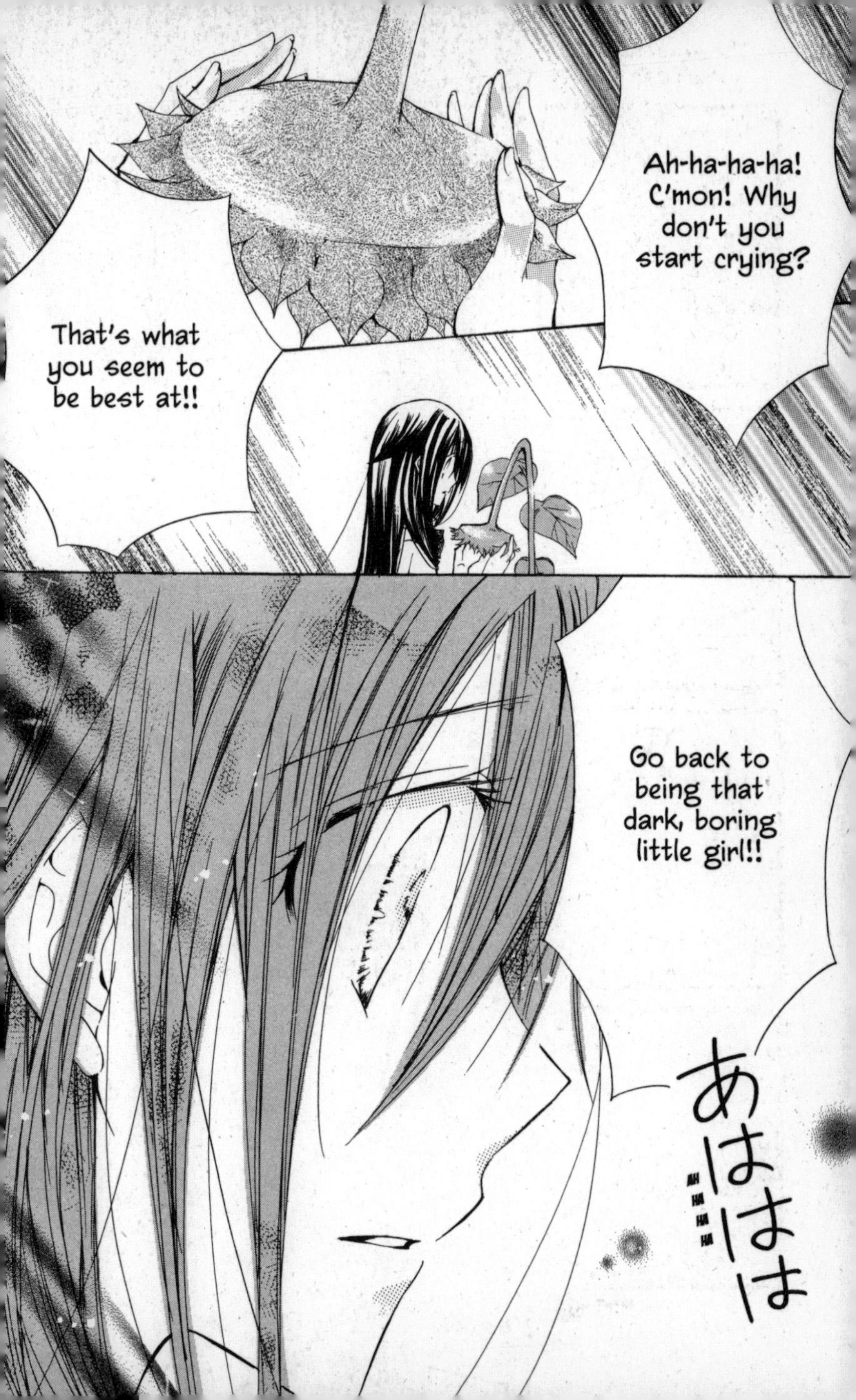
Ah-ha-ha-ha! C'mon! Why don't you start crying?
That's what you seem to be best at!!
Go back to being that dark, boring little girl!!
あはは
AH HA HA HA

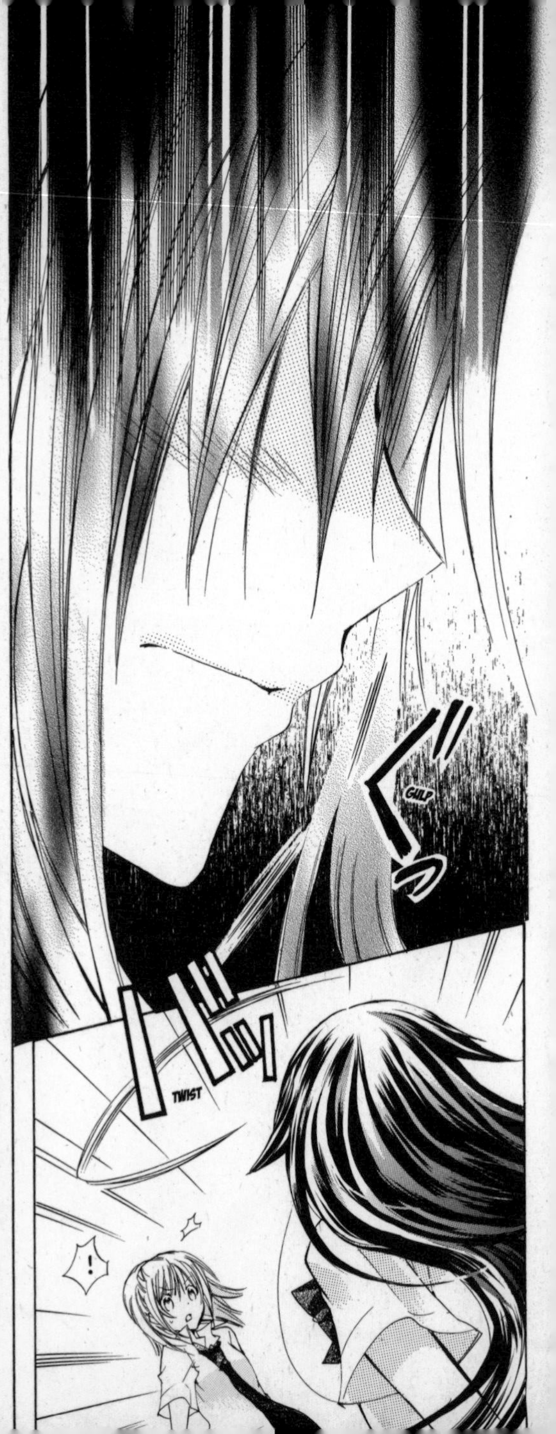
GULP
TWIST

The Adventures of Mahimahi - 7

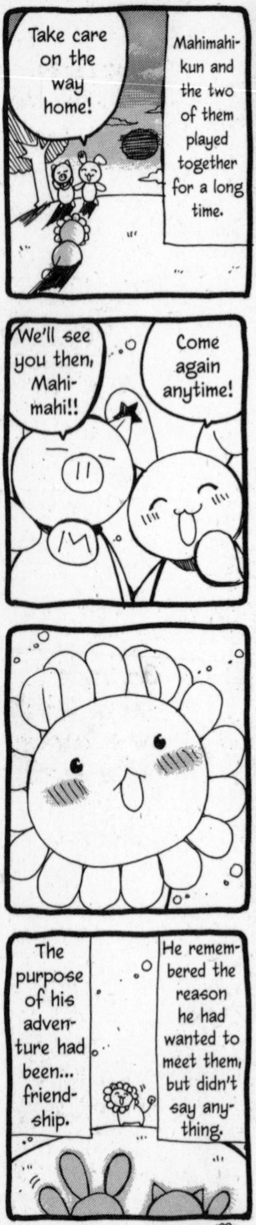
Mahimahi-kun and the two of them played together for a long time.
Take care on the way home!
Come again anytime!
We'll see you then, Mahi-mahi!!
He remembered the reason he had wanted to meet them, but didn't say anything.
The purpose of his adventure had been... friendship.

END

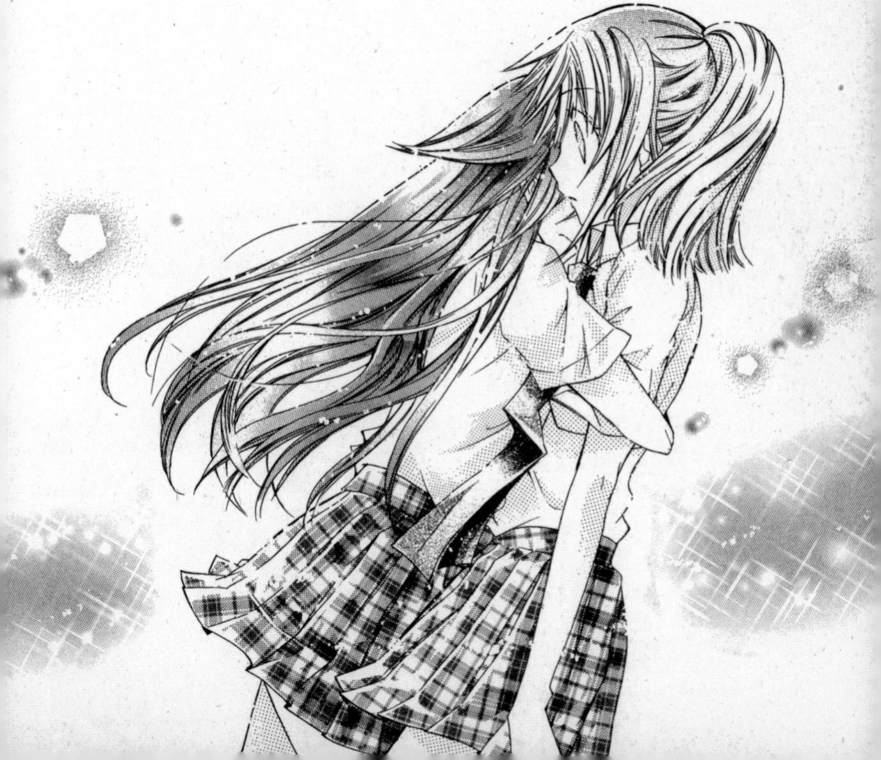

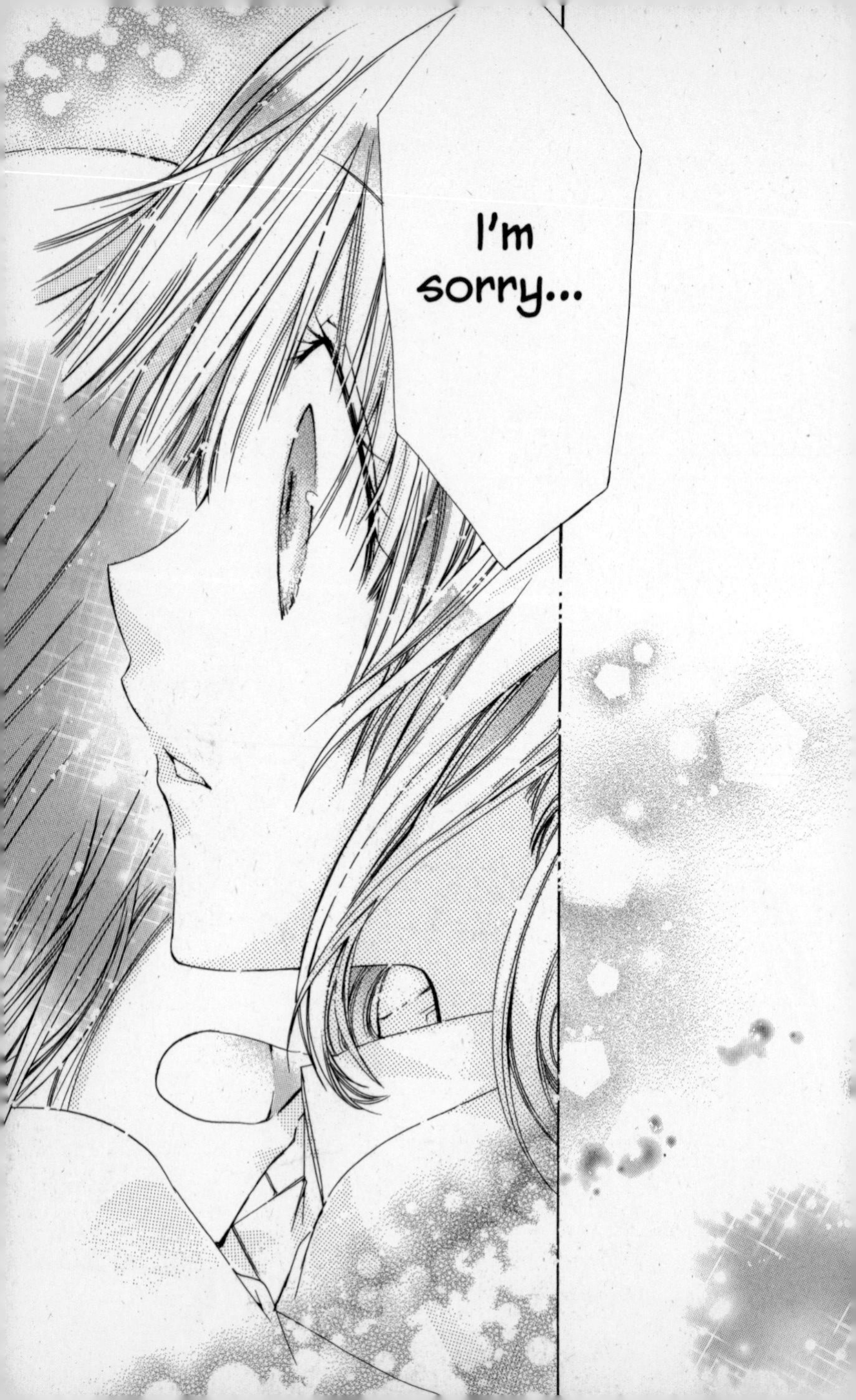
I'm sorry...

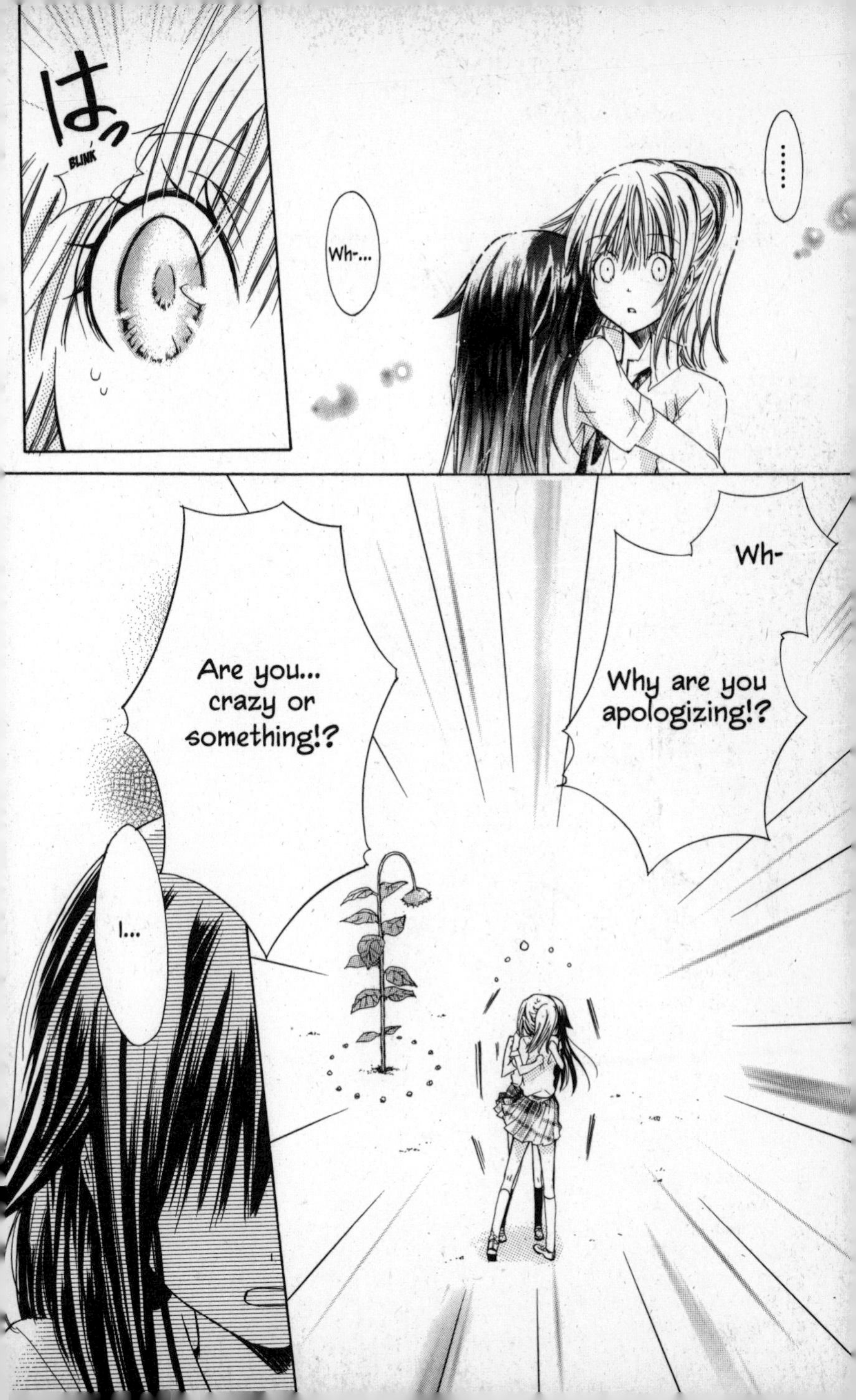
......
Wh-...
はっ
BLINK
Wh-
Why are you apologizing!?
Are you... crazy or something!?
I...

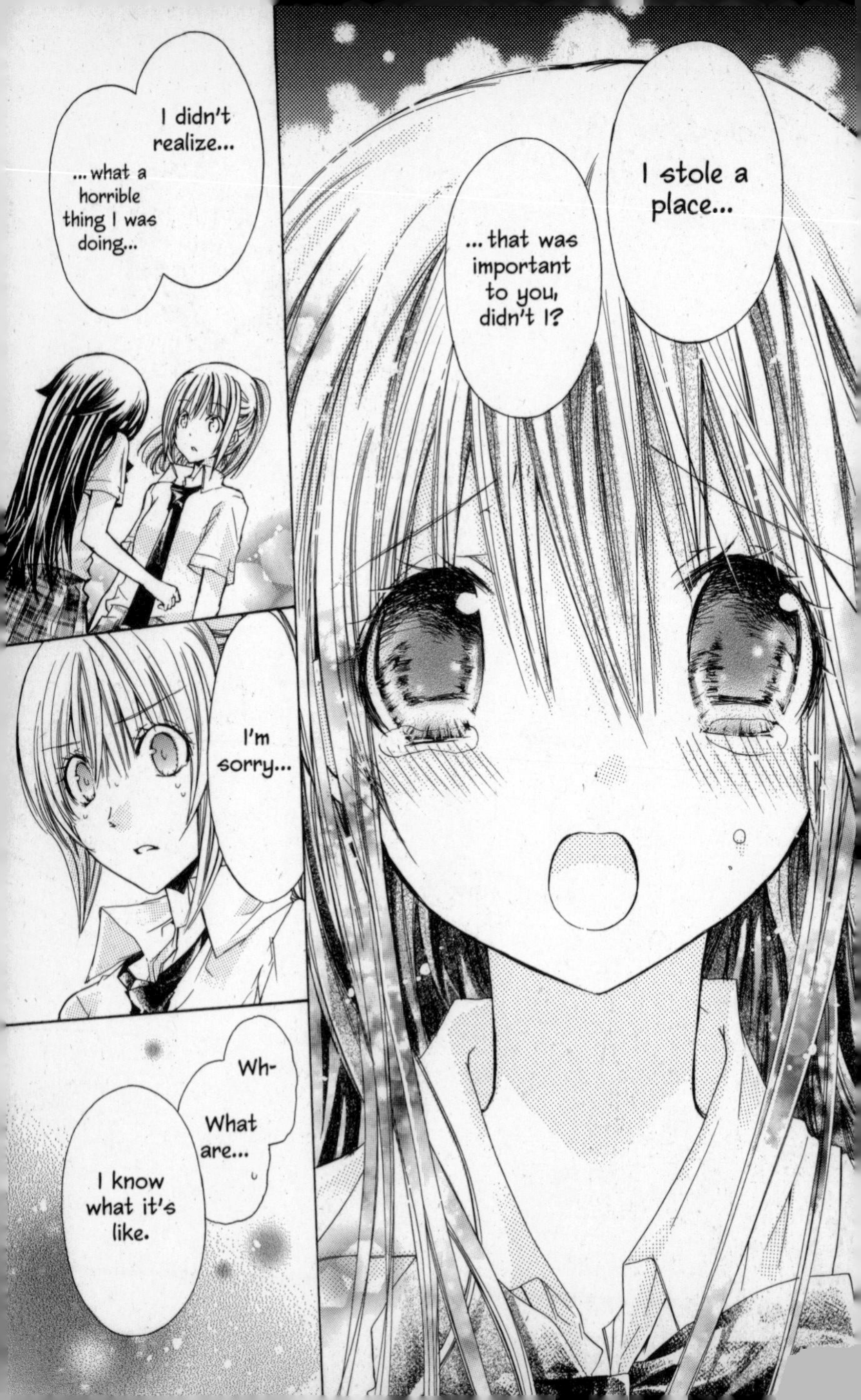
I stole a place...
... that was important to you, didn't I?
I didn't realize...
... what a horrible thing I was doing...
I'm sorry...
Wh-
What are...
I know what it's like.

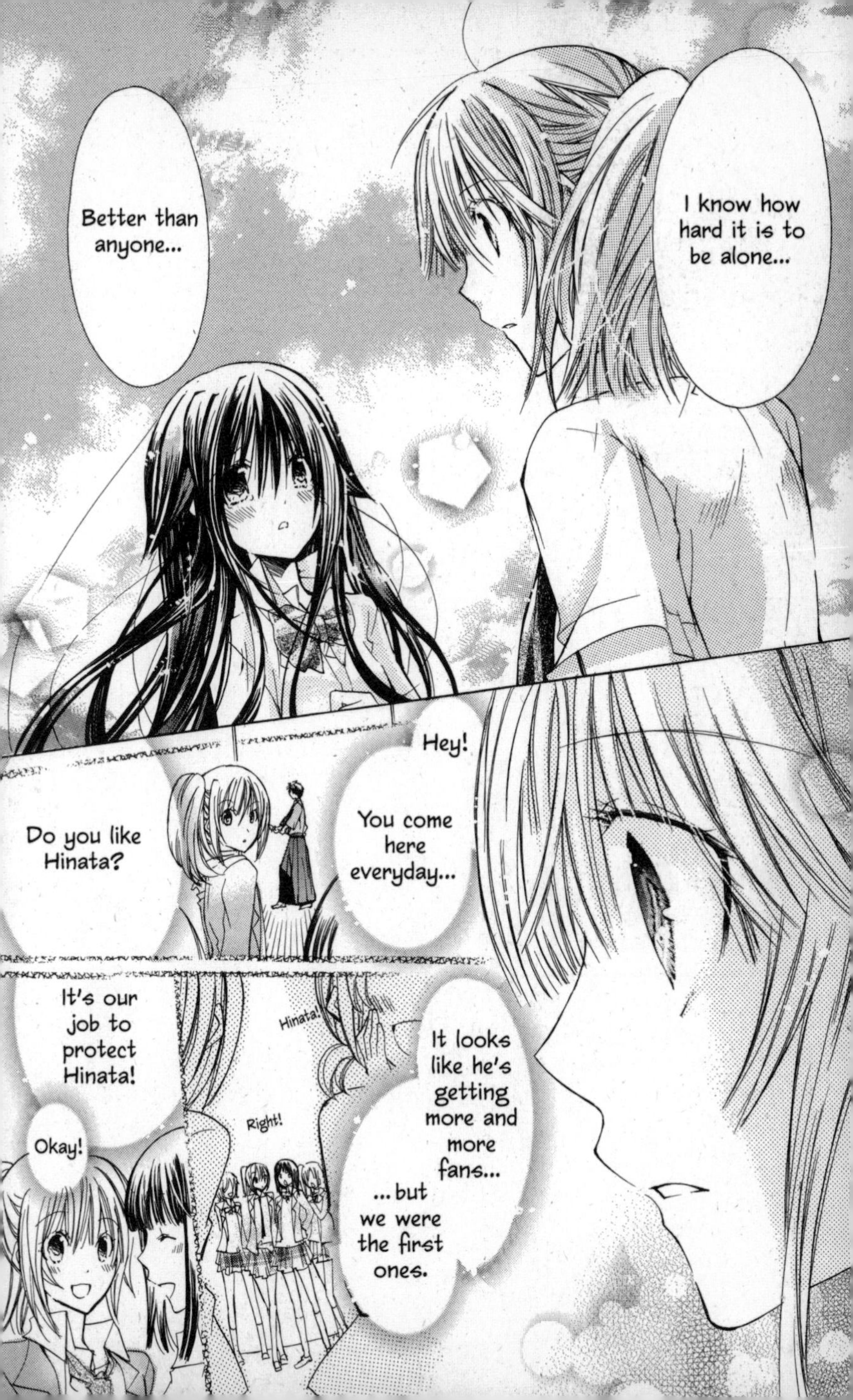
I know how hard it is to be alone...
Better than anyone...
Hey!
You come here everyday...
Do you like Hinata?
It looks like he's getting more and more fans...
...but we were the first ones.
Hinata!
It's our job to protect Hinata!
Right!
Okay!

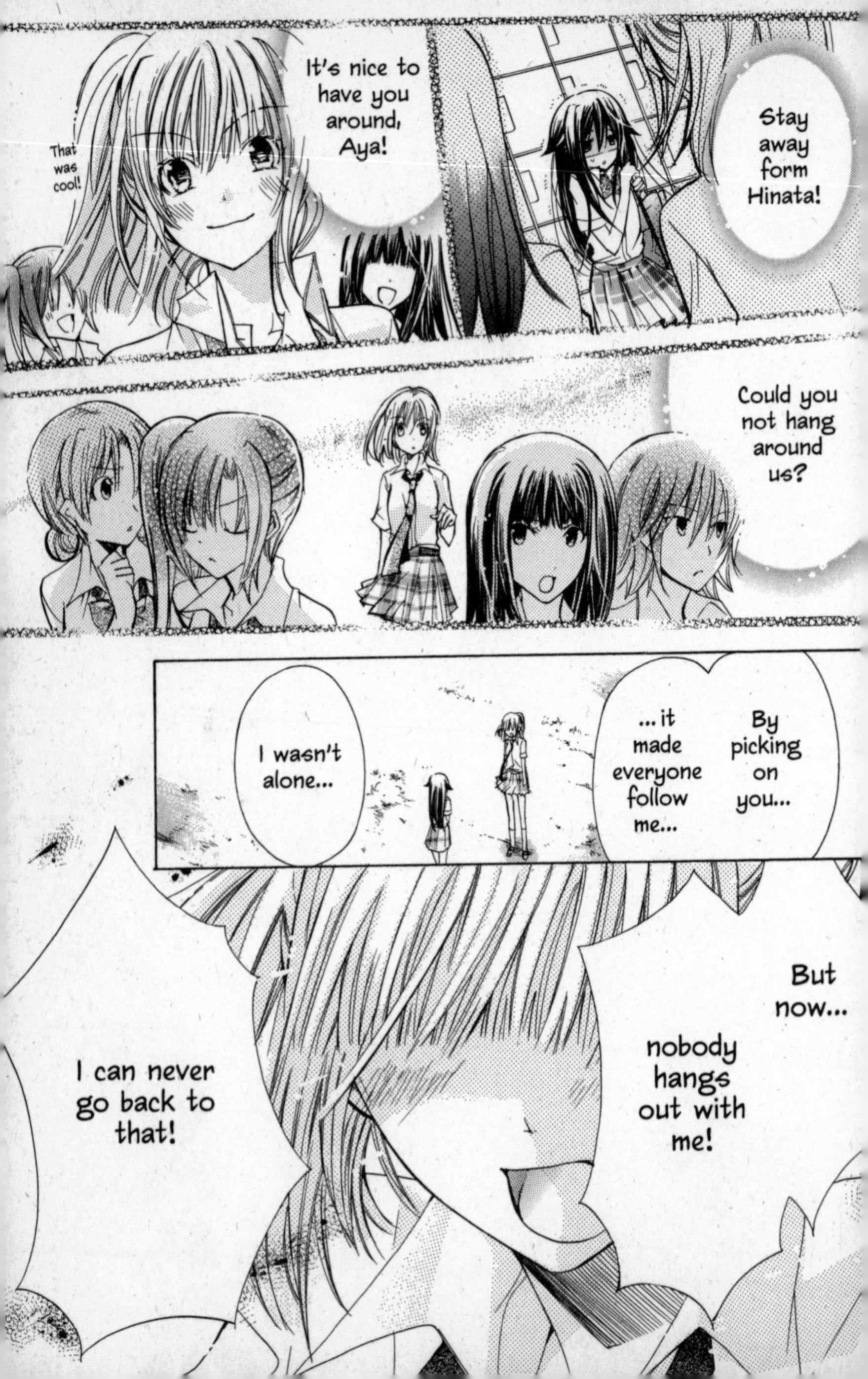

Stay away form Hinata!
It's nice to have you around, Aya!
That was cool!
Could you not hang around us?
By picking on you...
... it made everyone follow me...
I wasn't alone...
But now...
nobody hangs out with me!
I can never go back to that!

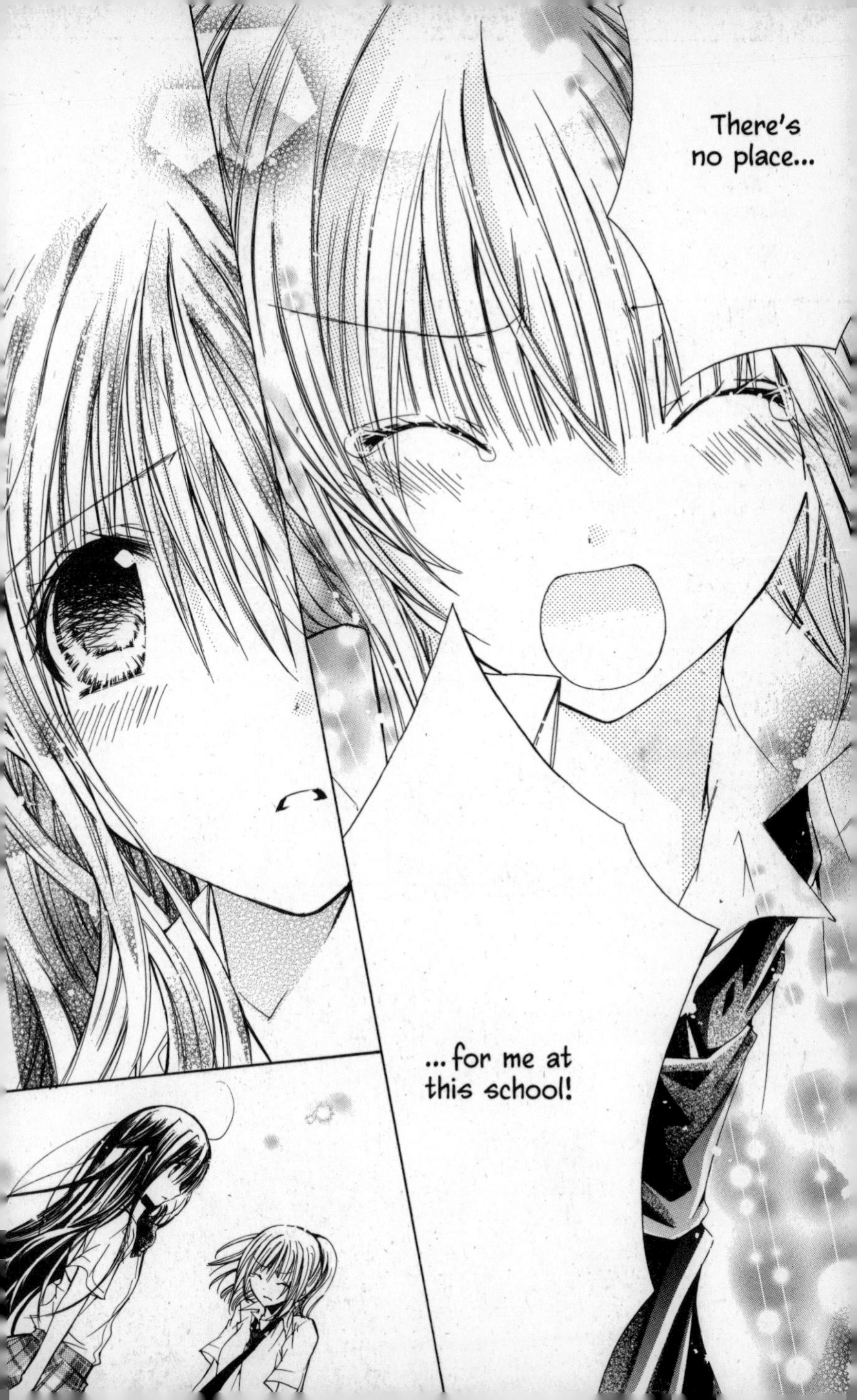
There's no place...
...for me at this school!

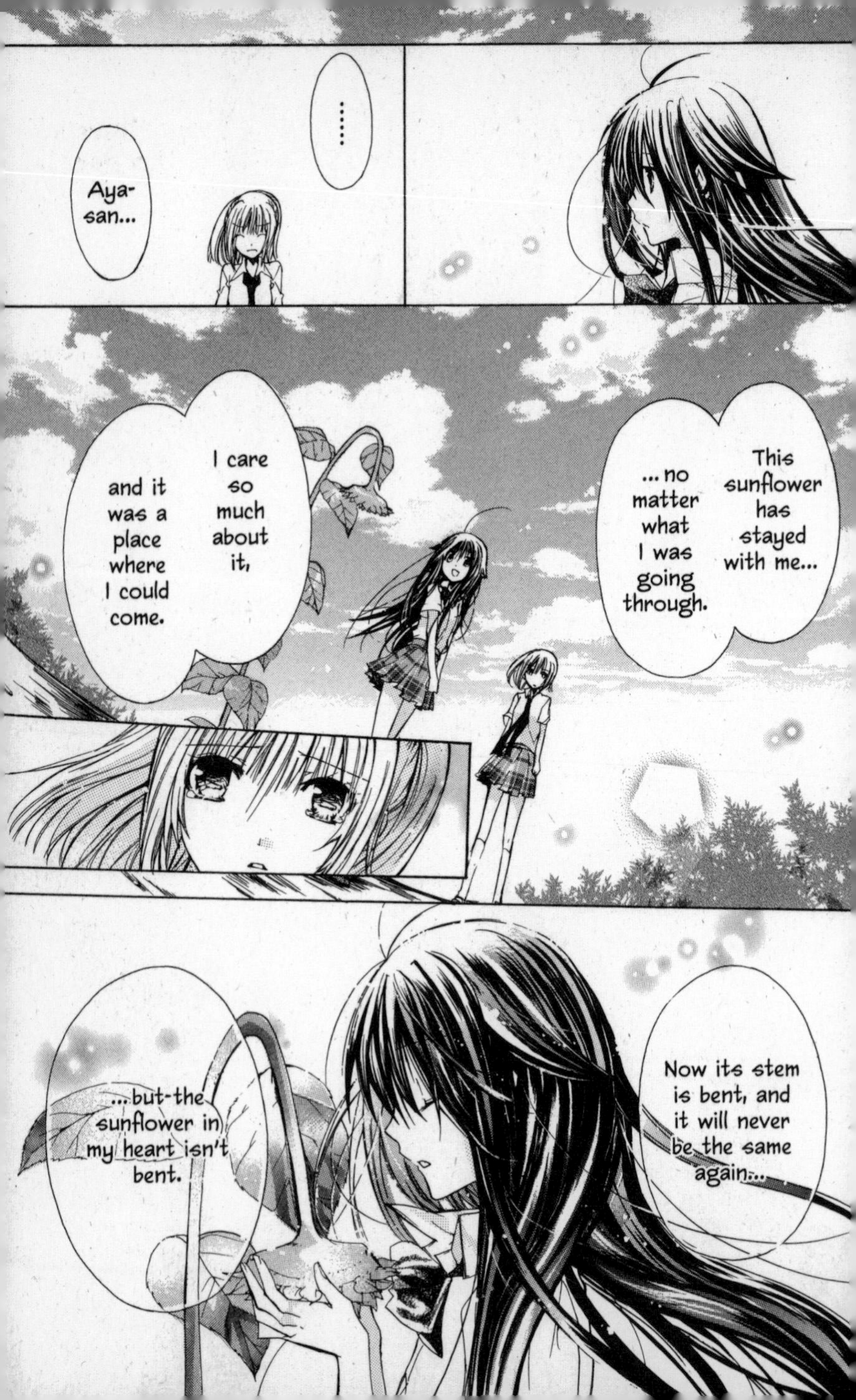
......
Aya-san...
This sunflower has stayed with me... ...no matter what I was going through.
I care so much about it, and it was a place where I could come.
Now its stem is bent, and it will never be the same again...
...but the sunflower in my heart isn't bent.

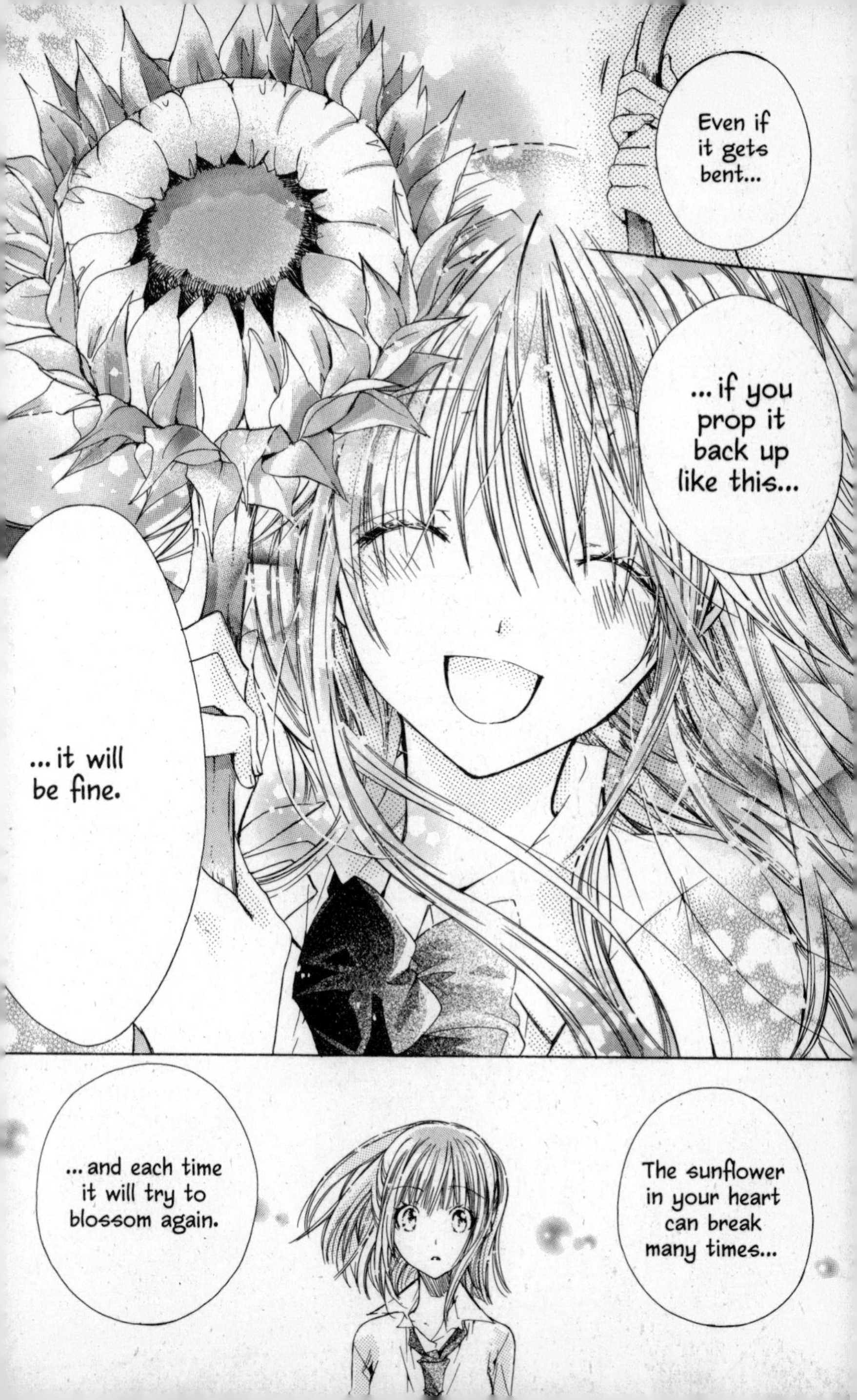
Even if it gets bent...
...if you prop it back up like this...
...it will be fine.
The sunflower in your heart can break many times...
...and each time it will try to blossom again.

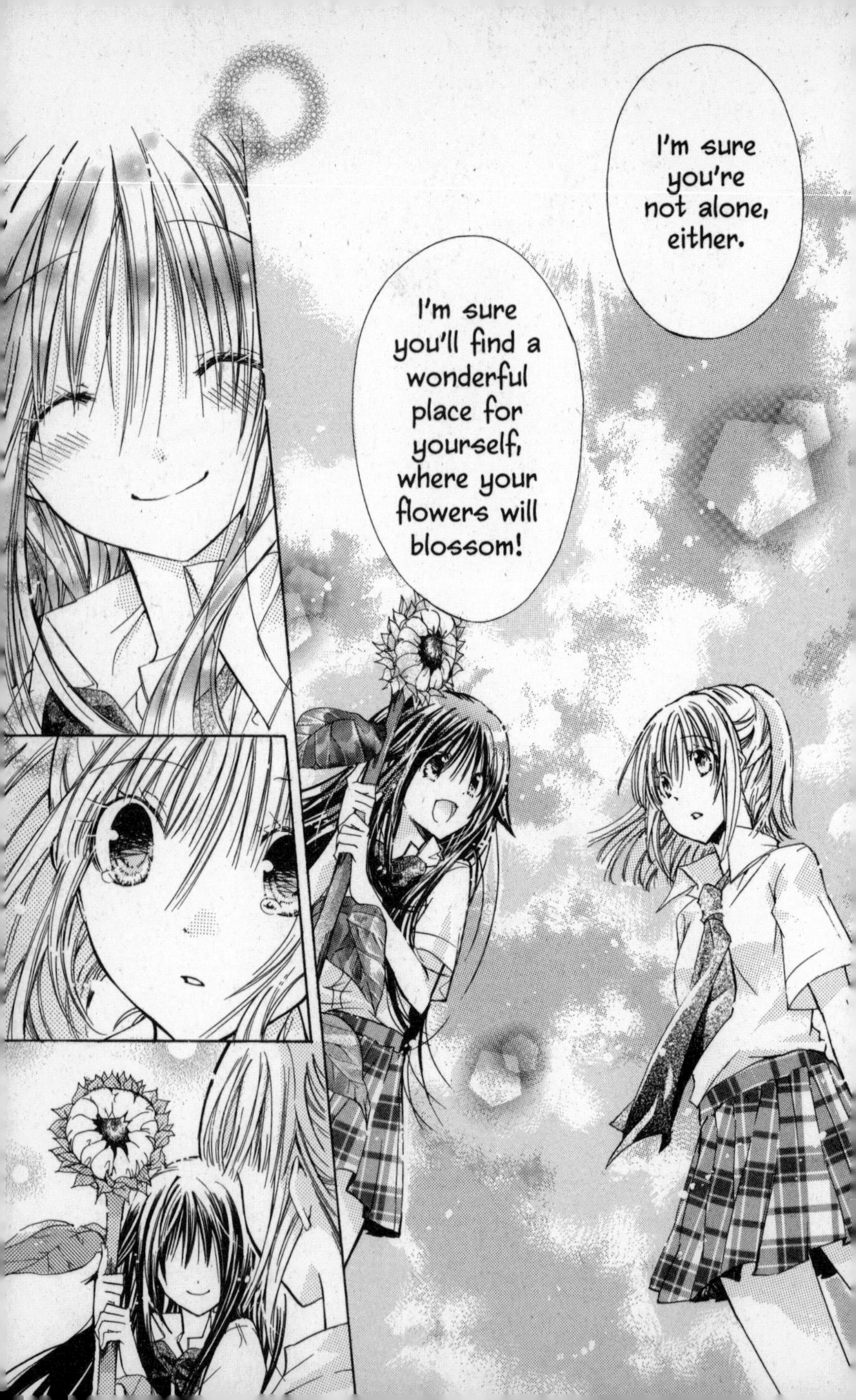
I'm sure you're not alone, either.
I'm sure you'll find a wonderful place for yourself, where your flowers will blossom!

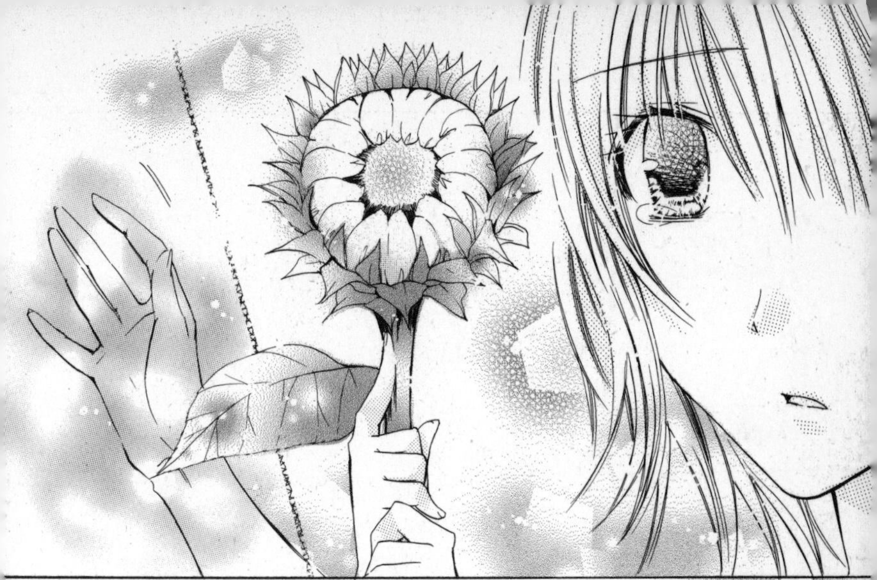
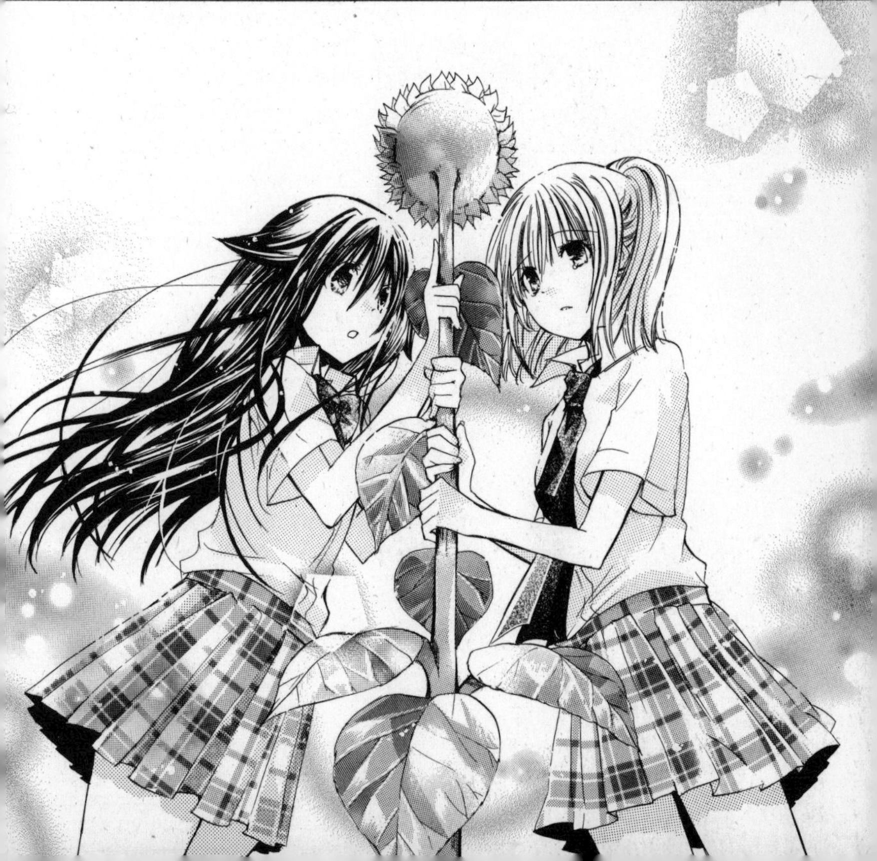

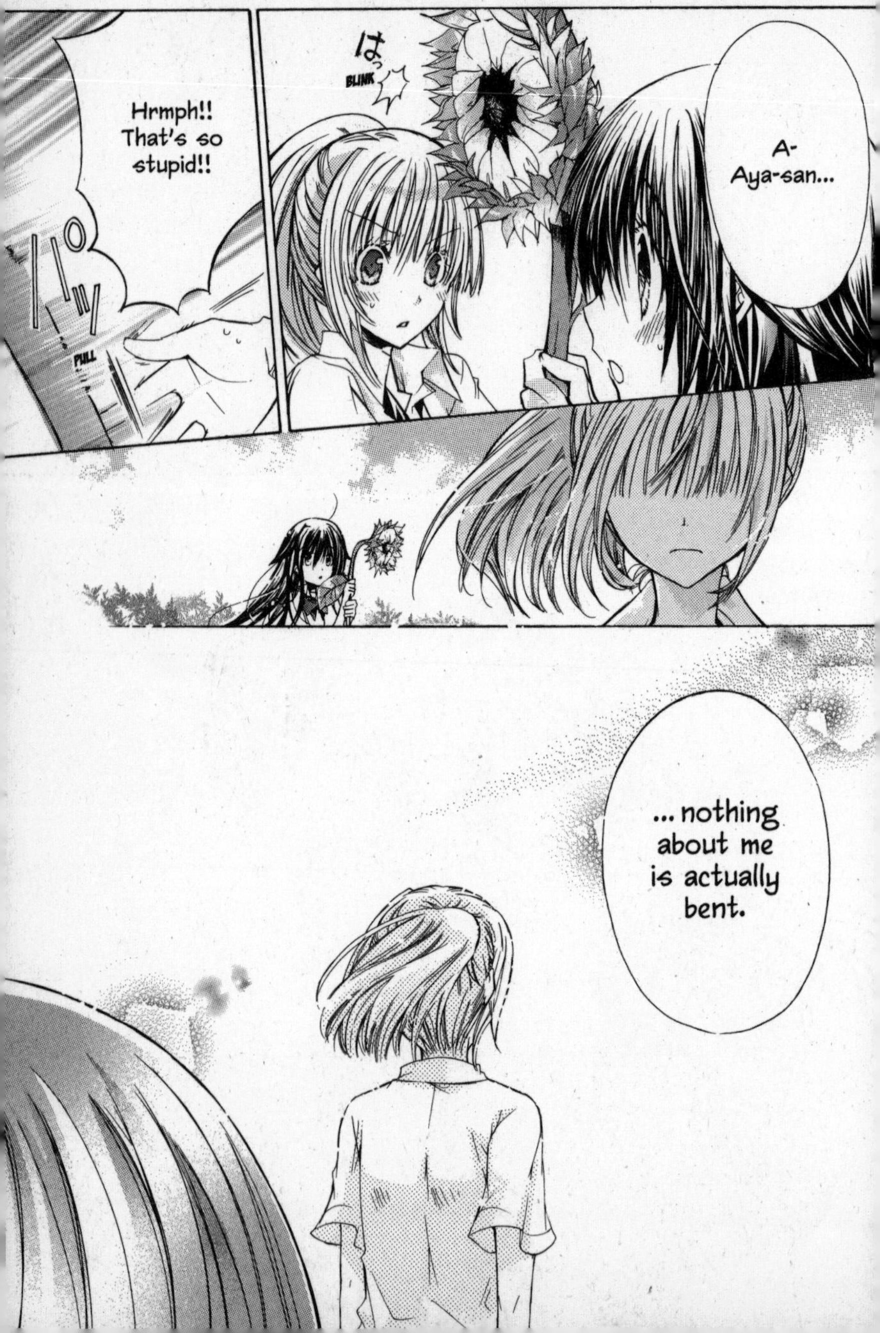
A-
Aya-san...
はっ
BLINK
Hrmph!!
That's so
stupid!!
PULL
...nothing
about me
is actually
bent.

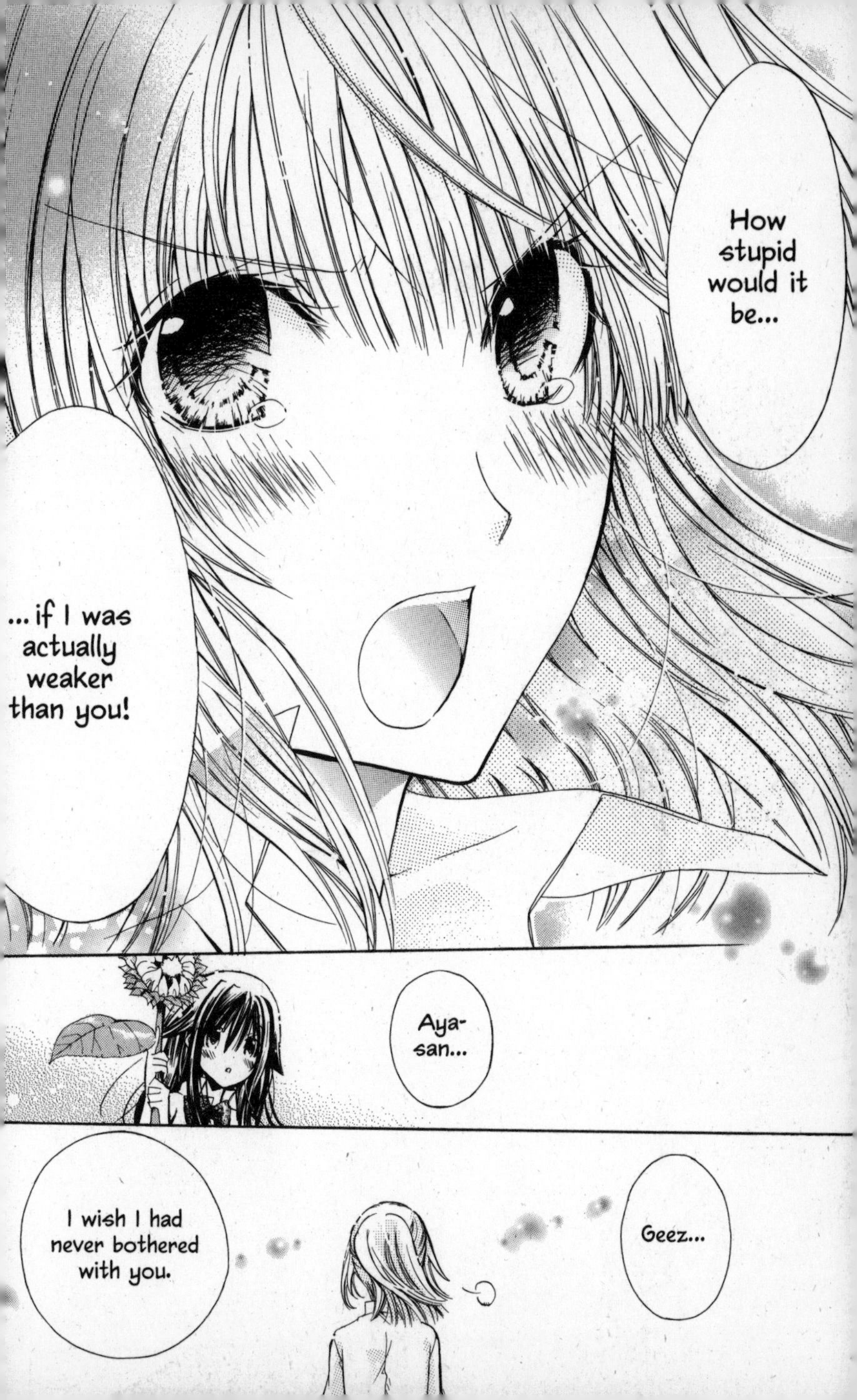
How stupid would it be...
... if I was actually weaker than you!
Aya-san...
Geez...
I wish I had never bothered with you.

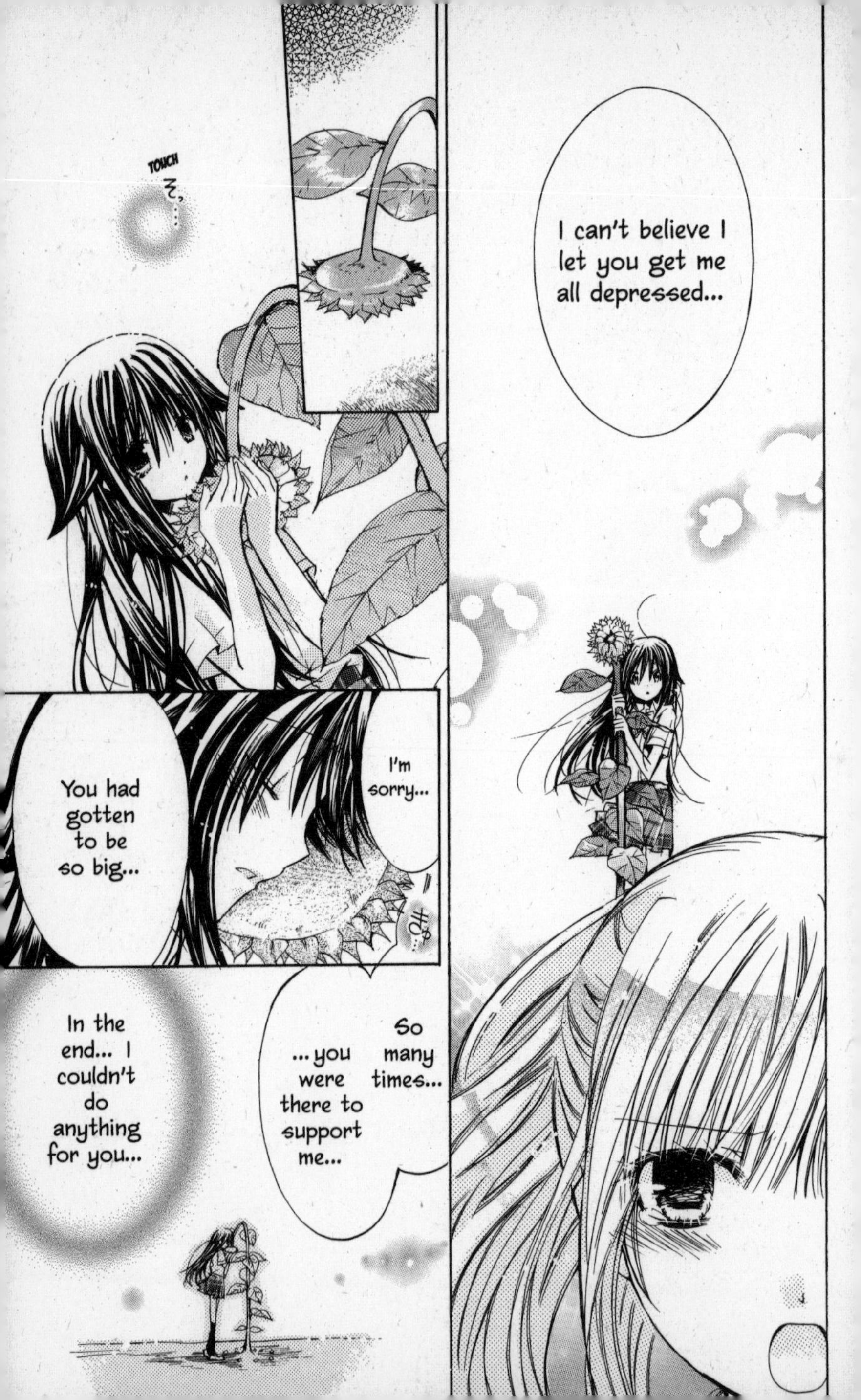
I can't believe I let you get me all depressed...
TOUCH
I'm sorry...
You had gotten to be so big...
So many times...
...you were there to support me...
In the end... I couldn't do anything for you...

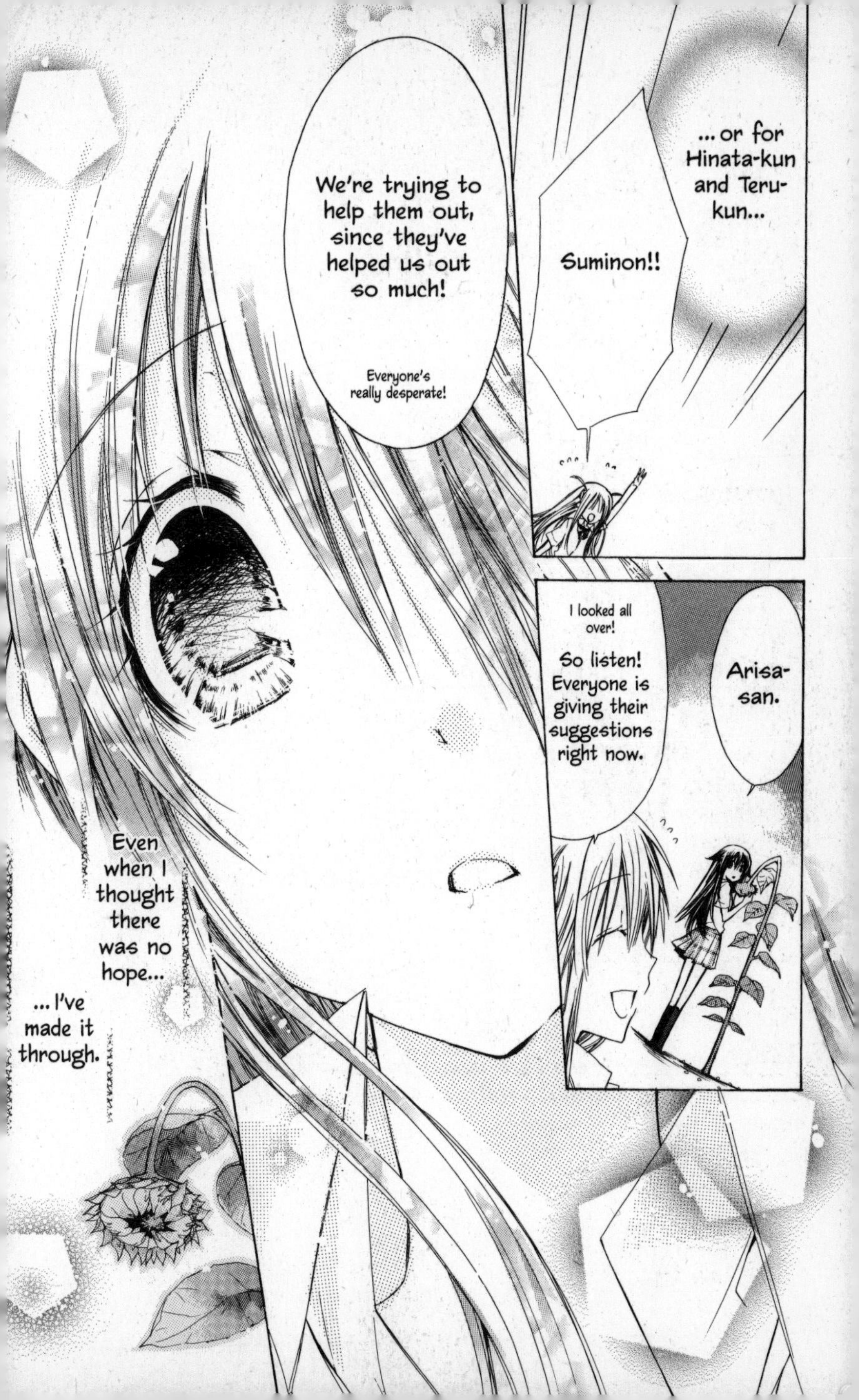
...or for Hinata-kun and Teru-kun...
Suminon!!
Arisa-san.
I looked all over!
So listen! Everyone is giving their suggestions right now.
We're trying to help them out, since they've helped us out so much!
Everyone's really desperate!
Even when I thought there was no hope...
...I've made it through.

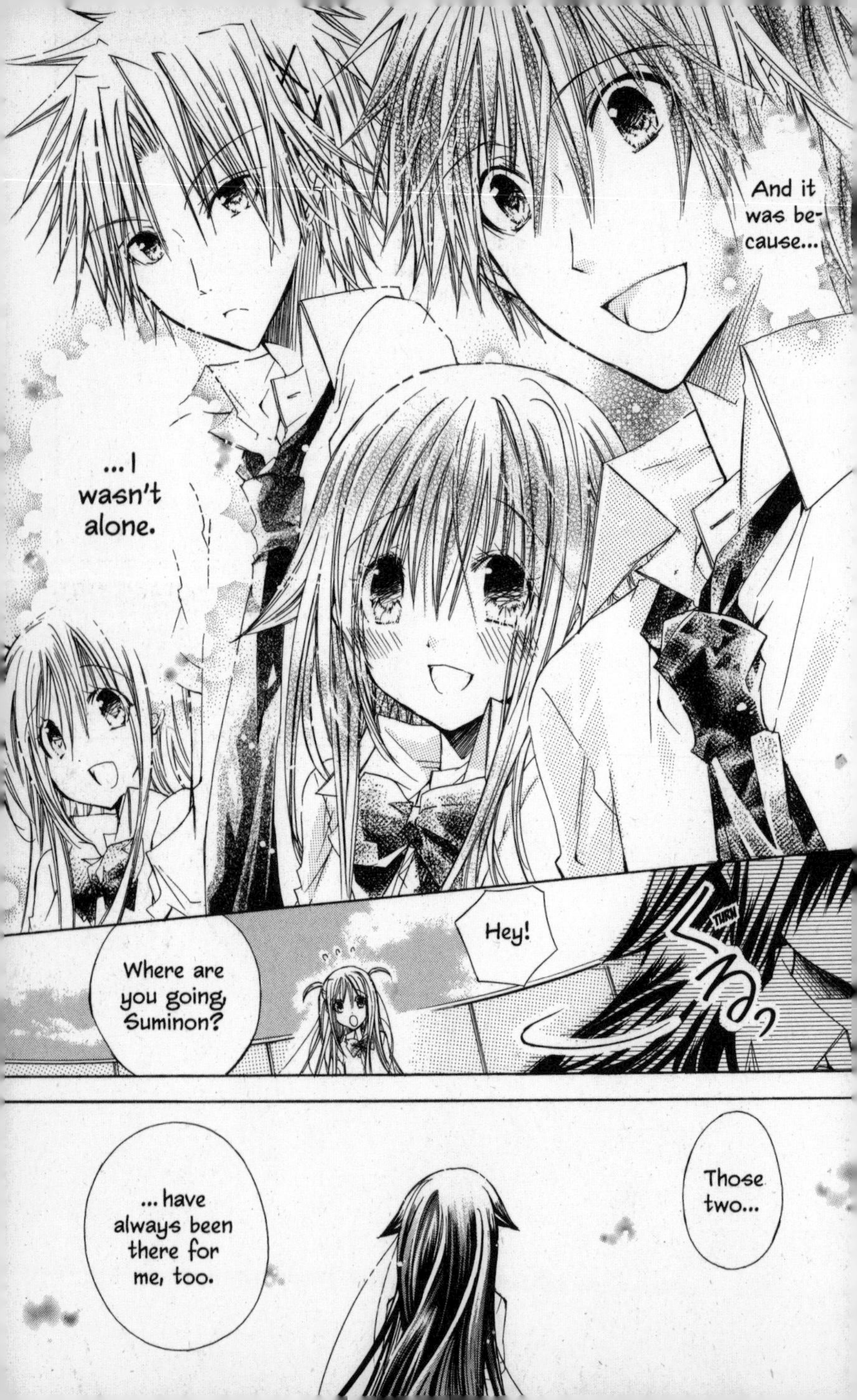
And it was be-cause...
...I wasn't alone.
TURN
Hey!
Where are you going, Suminon?
Those two...
...have always been there for me, too.

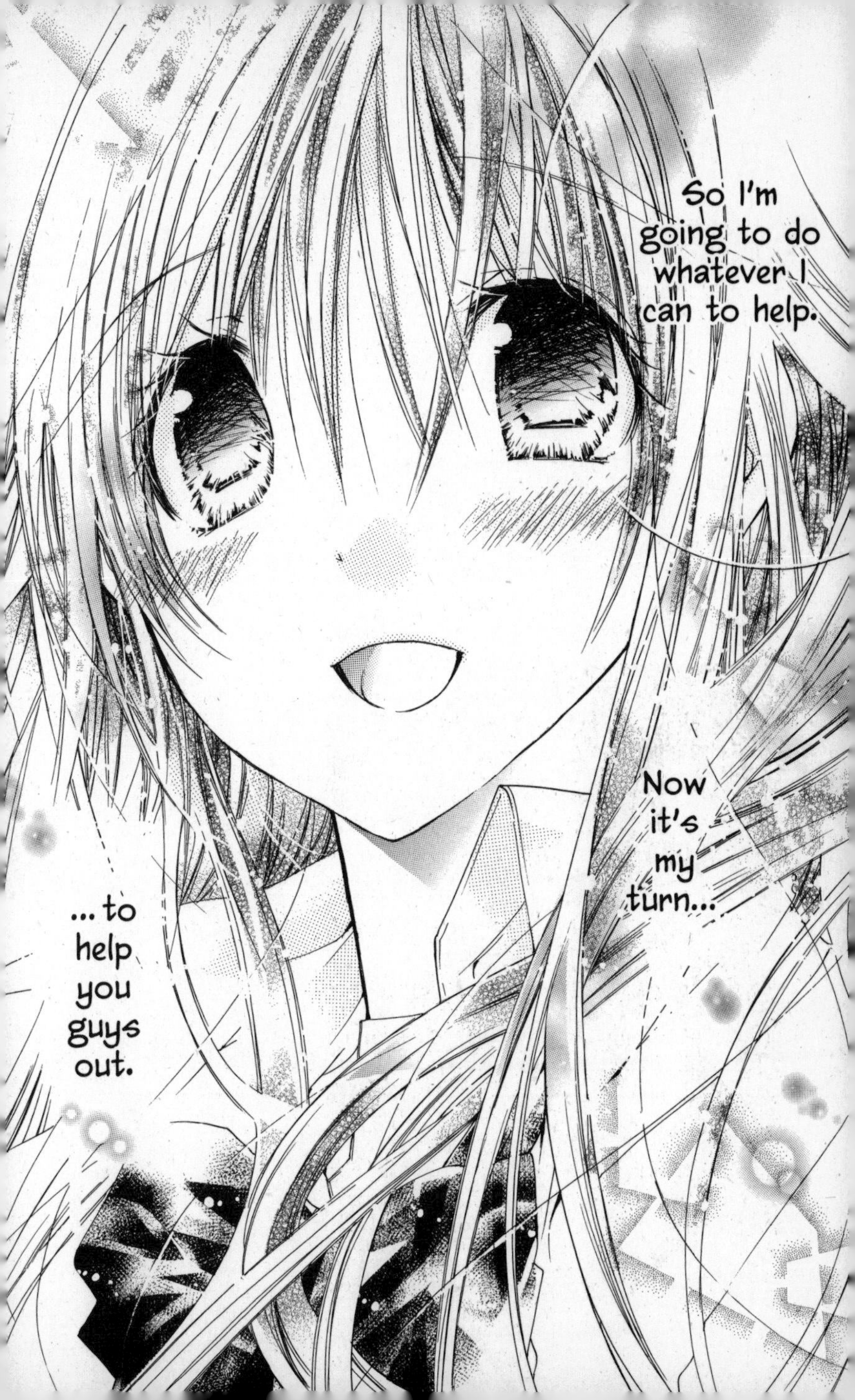
So I'm going to do whatever I can to help.
Now it's my turn...
... to help you guys out.

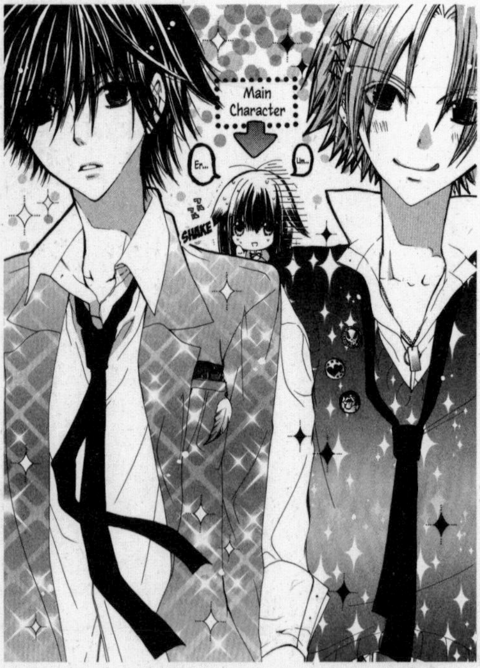
Main Character
Um...
Er...
SHAKE

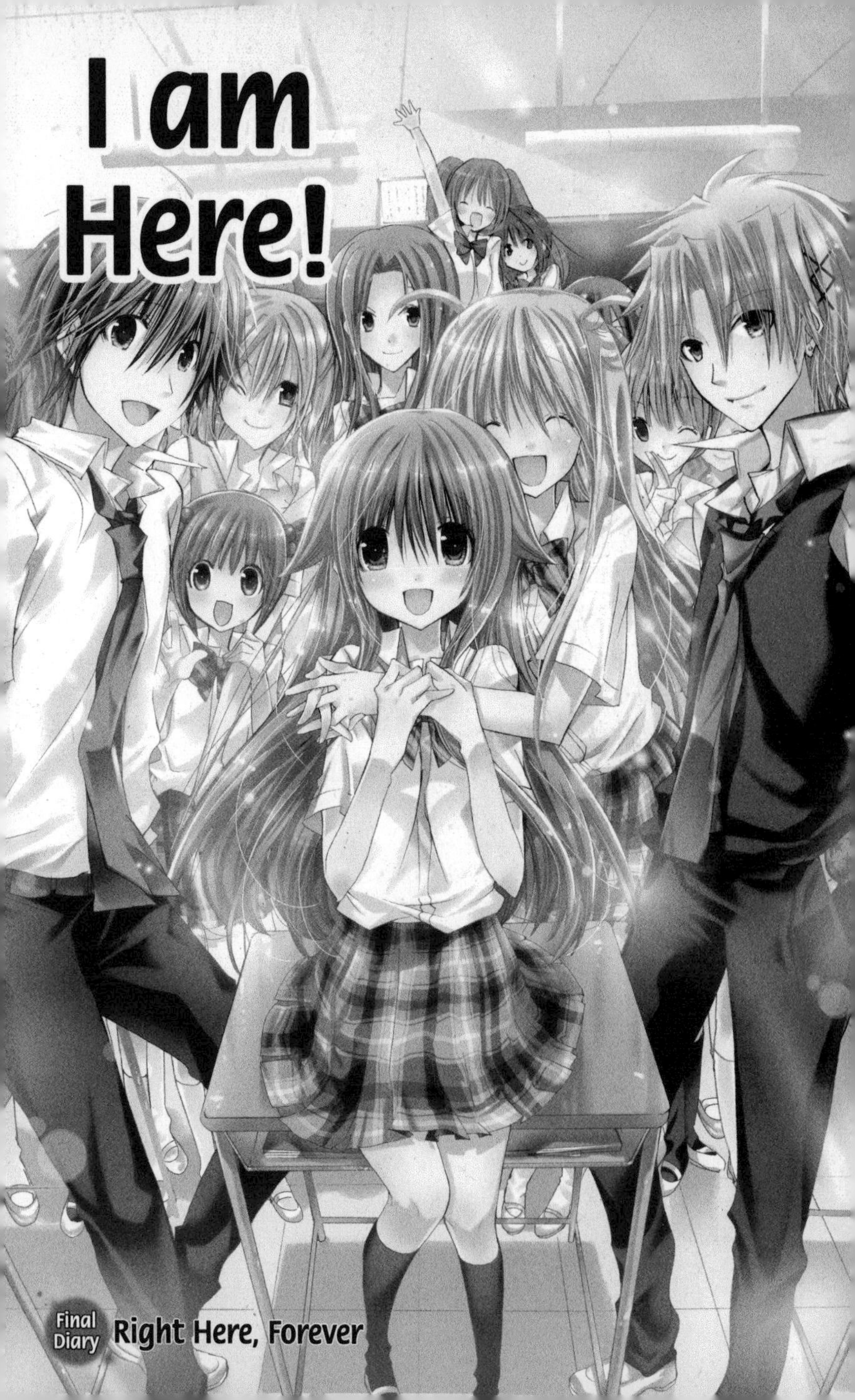
I am Here!
Final Diary
Right Here, Forever

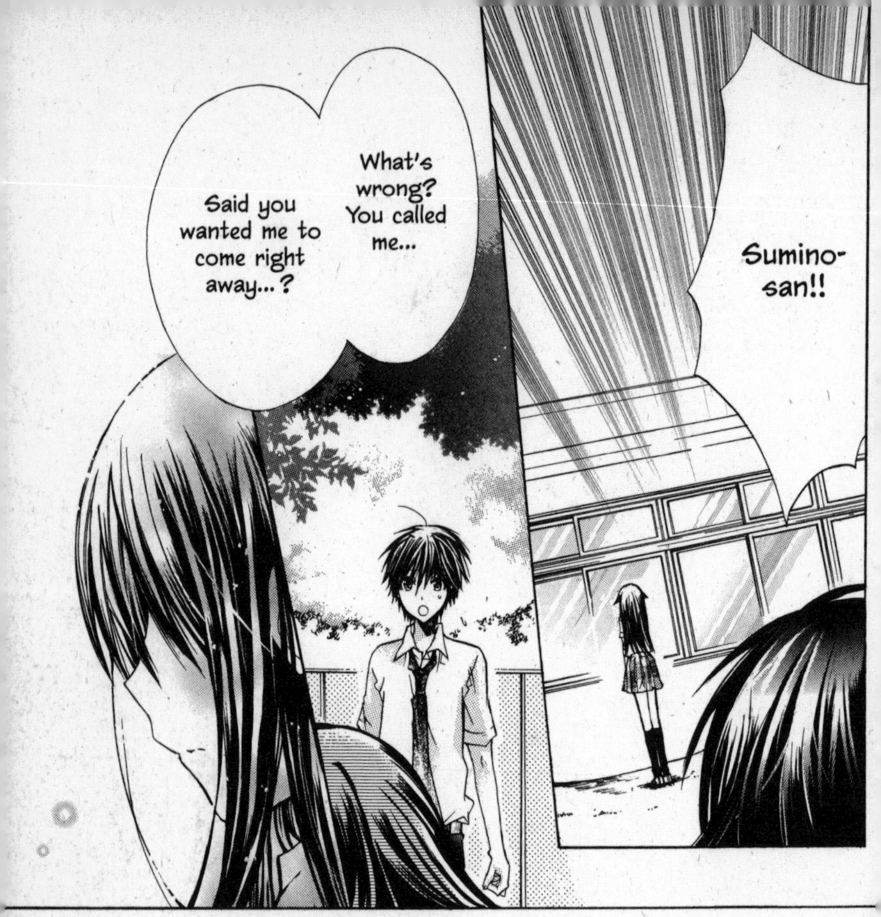
Sumino-san!!
What's wrong? You called me...
Said you wanted me to come right away...?

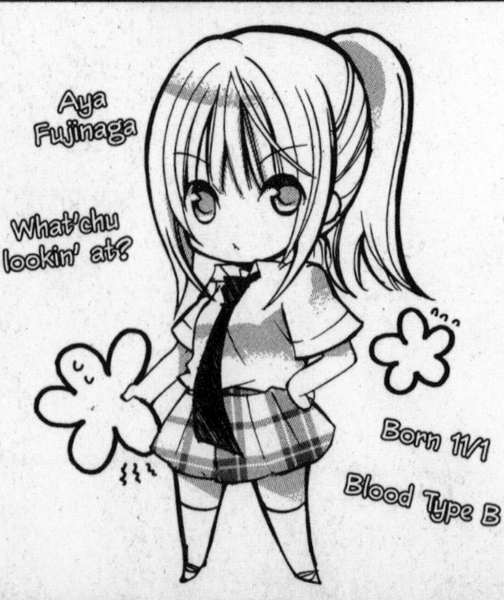
Aya Fujinaga
What'chu lookin' at?
Born 11/1
Blood Type B

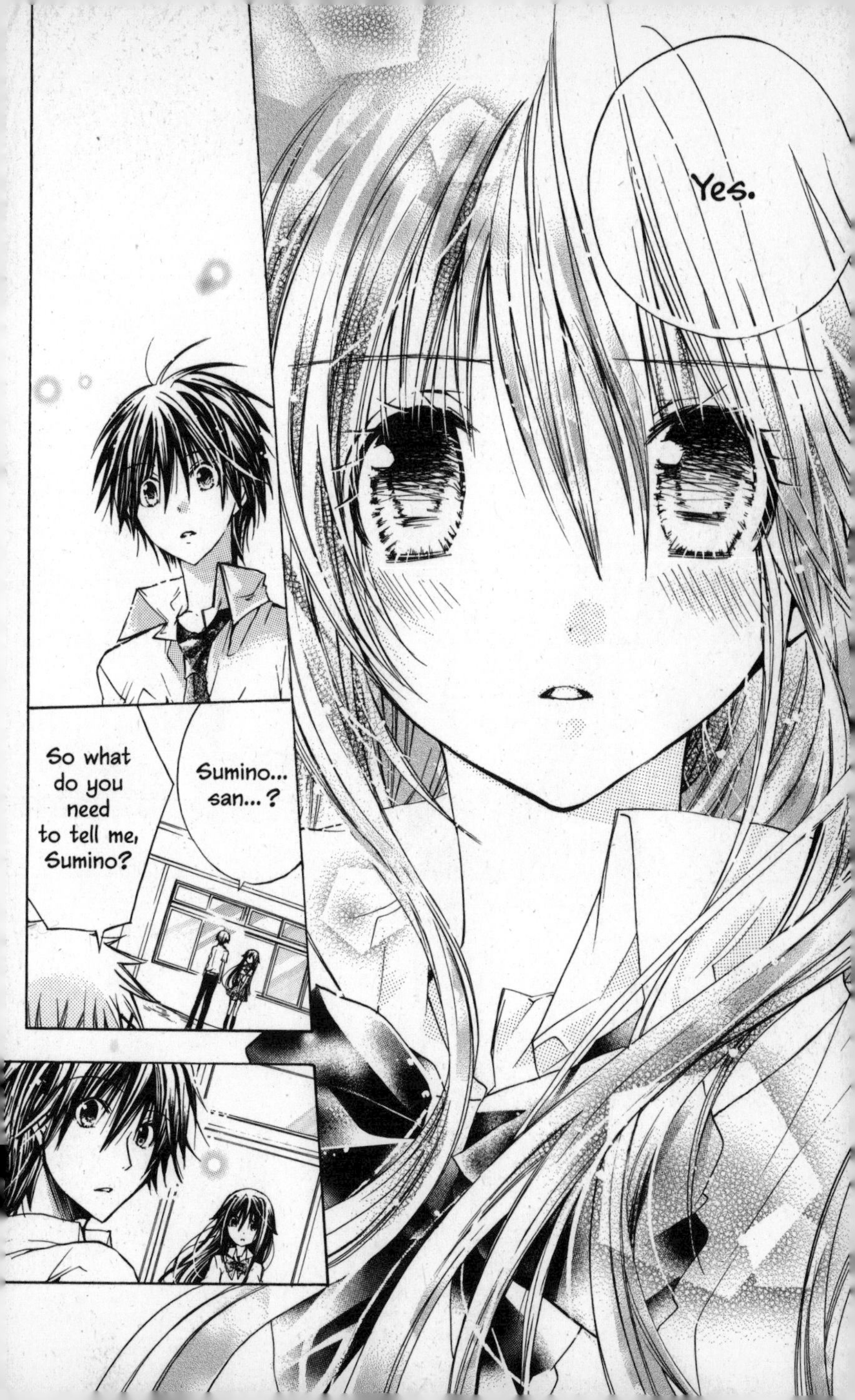
Yes.
Sumino... san...?
So what do you need to tell me, Sumino?

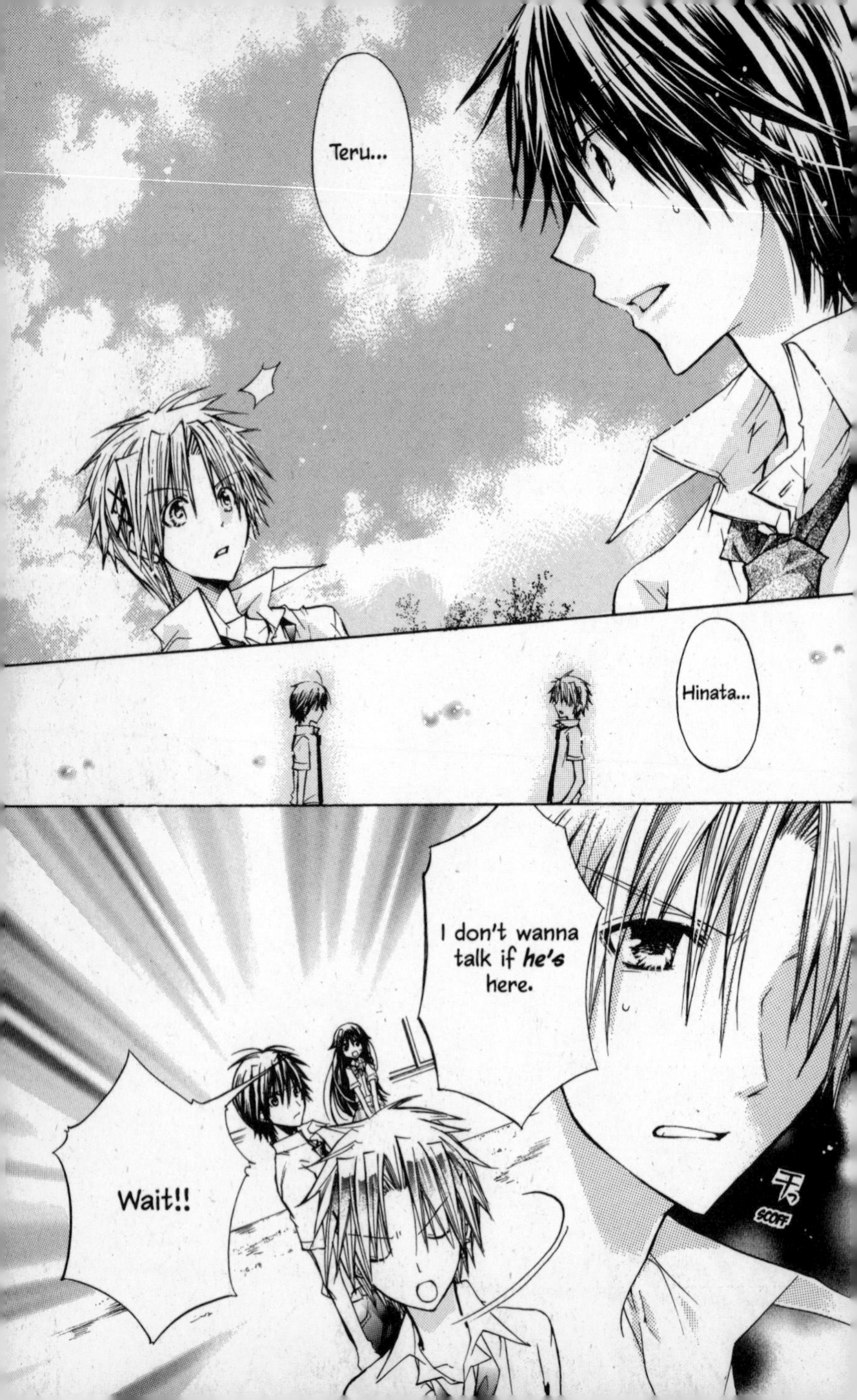
Teru...
Hinata...
I don't wanna talk if *he's* here.
SCOFF
Wait!!

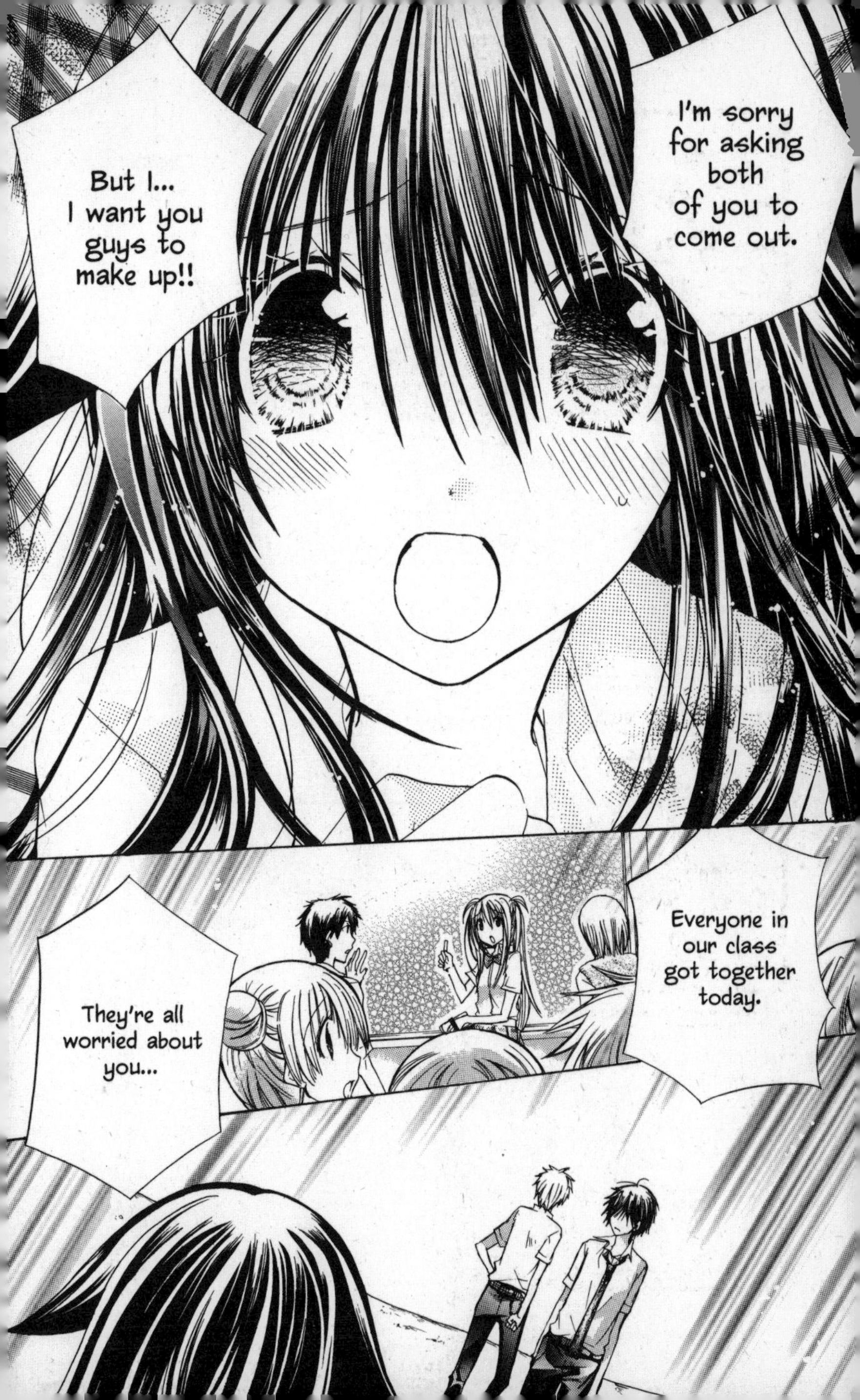
I'm sorry for asking both of you to come out.
But I... I want you guys to make up!!
Everyone in our class got together today.
They're all worried about you...

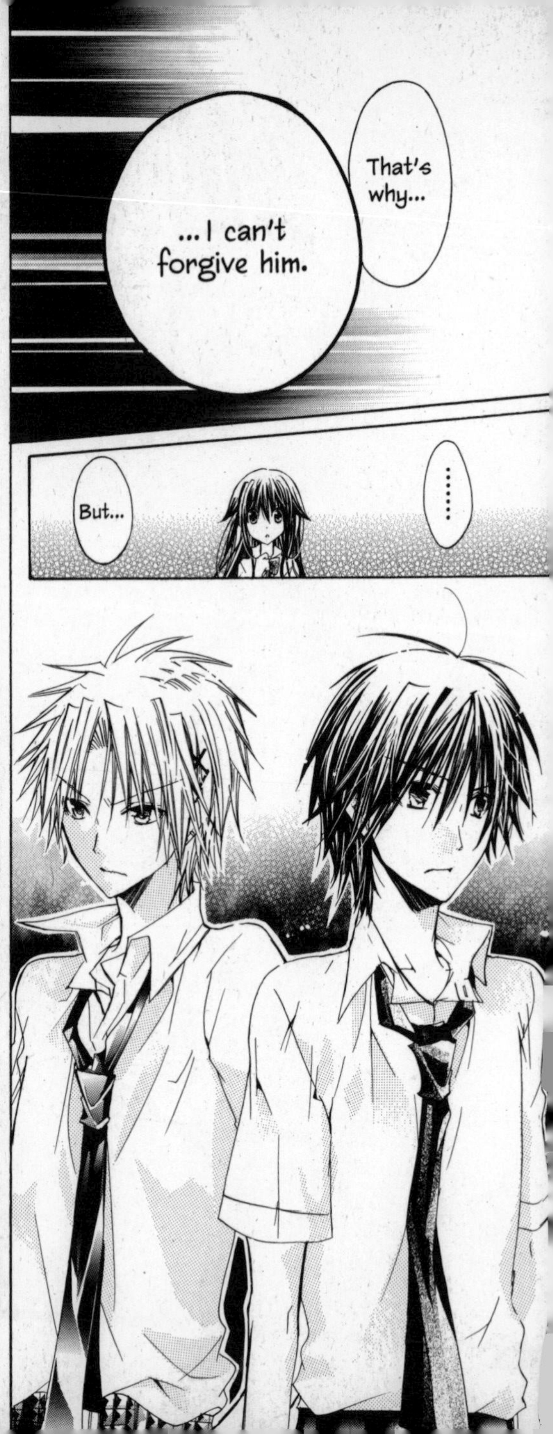
That's why...
...I can't forgive him.
......
But...

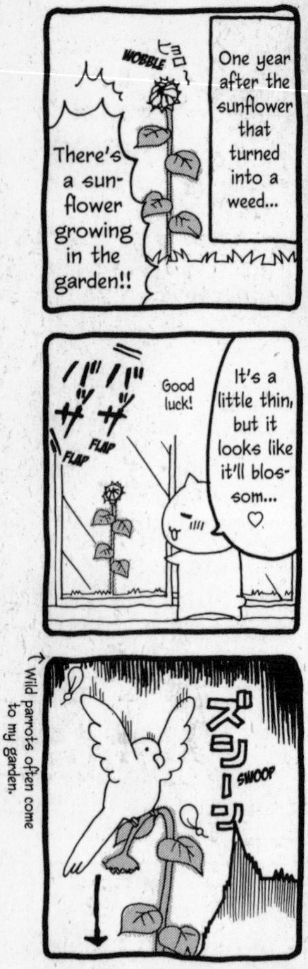
One year after the sunflower that turned into a weed...
WOBBLE
ヒョロ~
There's a sun-flower growing in the garden!!
It's a little thin, but it looks like it'll blos-som... ♡
Good luck!
バサッ バサッ
FLAP
FLAP
ズシーン
SWOOP
Wild parrots often come to my garden.
Arrgh!
FLAP
バッサ
バッサ
FLAP
Appar-ently, sun-flowers will not bloom in my garden...

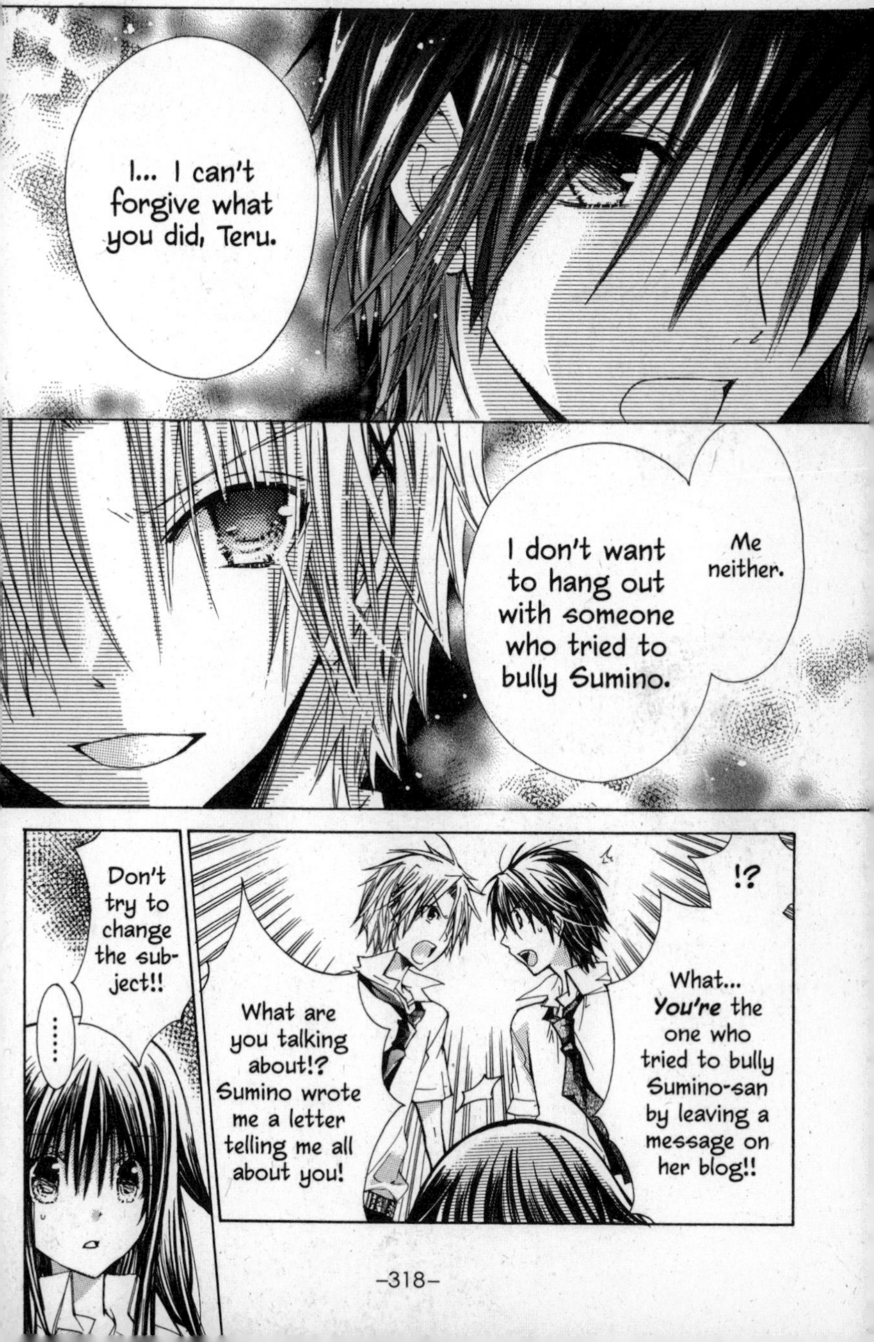
I... I can't forgive what you did, Teru.
Me neither.
I don't want to hang out with someone who tried to bully Sumino.
!?
What... *You're* the one who tried to bully Sumino-san by leaving a message on her blog!!
What are you talking about!? Sumino wrote me a letter telling me all about you!
Don't try to change the subject!!
……

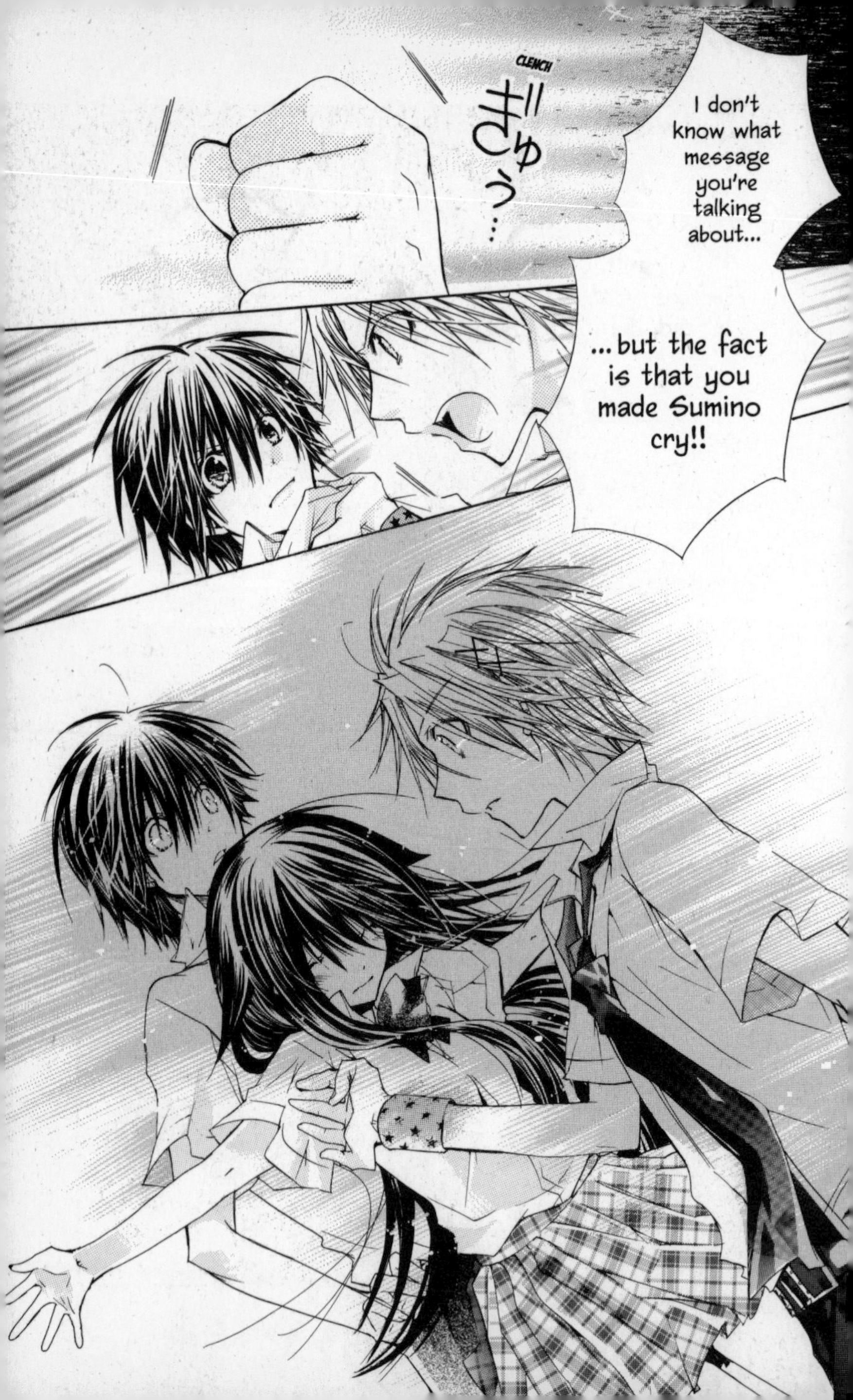
I don't know what message you're talking about...
...but the fact is that you made Sumino cry!!
ぎゅう…
CLENCH

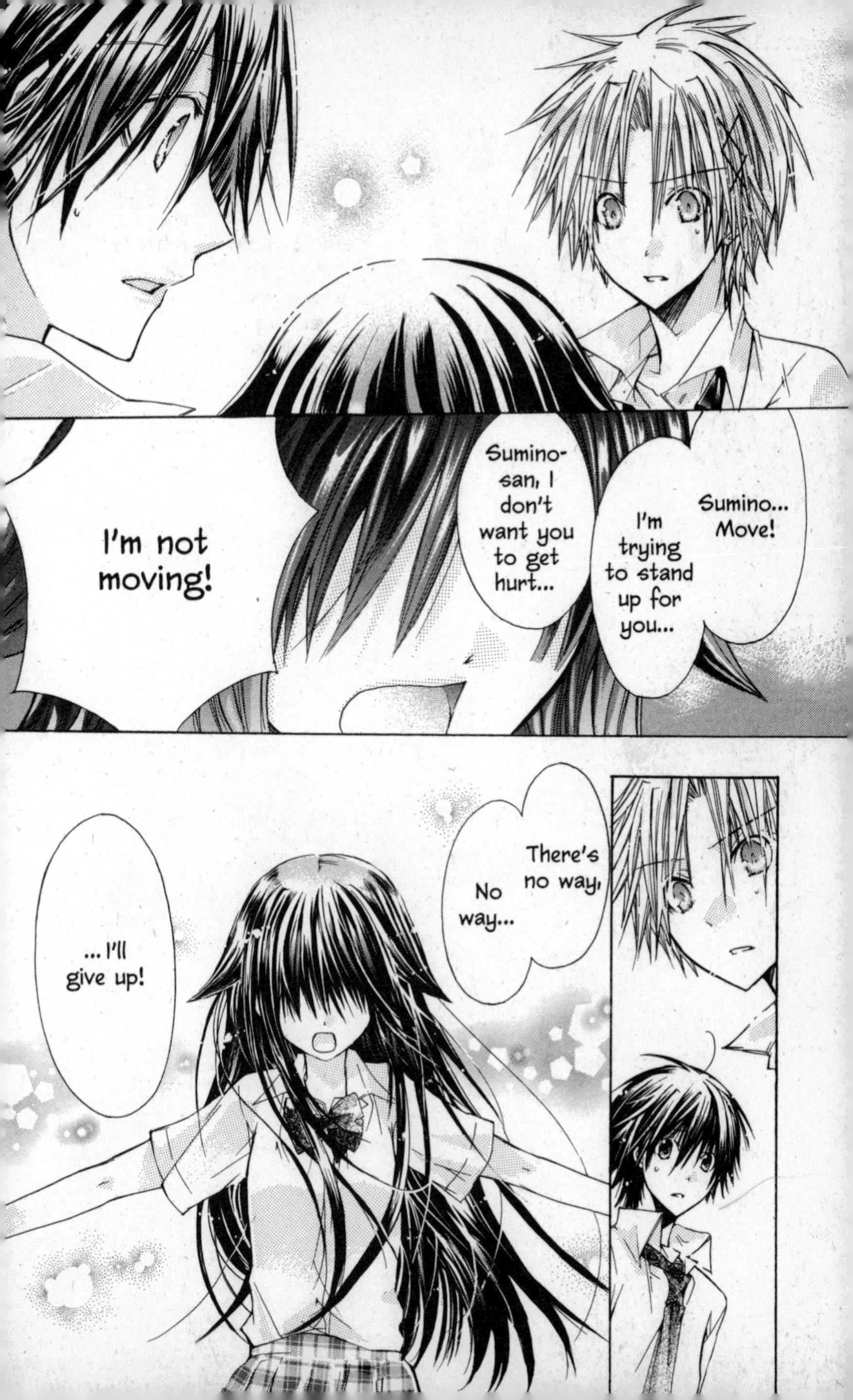

Sumino... Move!
I'm trying to stand up for you...
Sumino-san, I don't want you to get hurt...
I'm not moving!
There's no way,
No way...
... I'll give up!

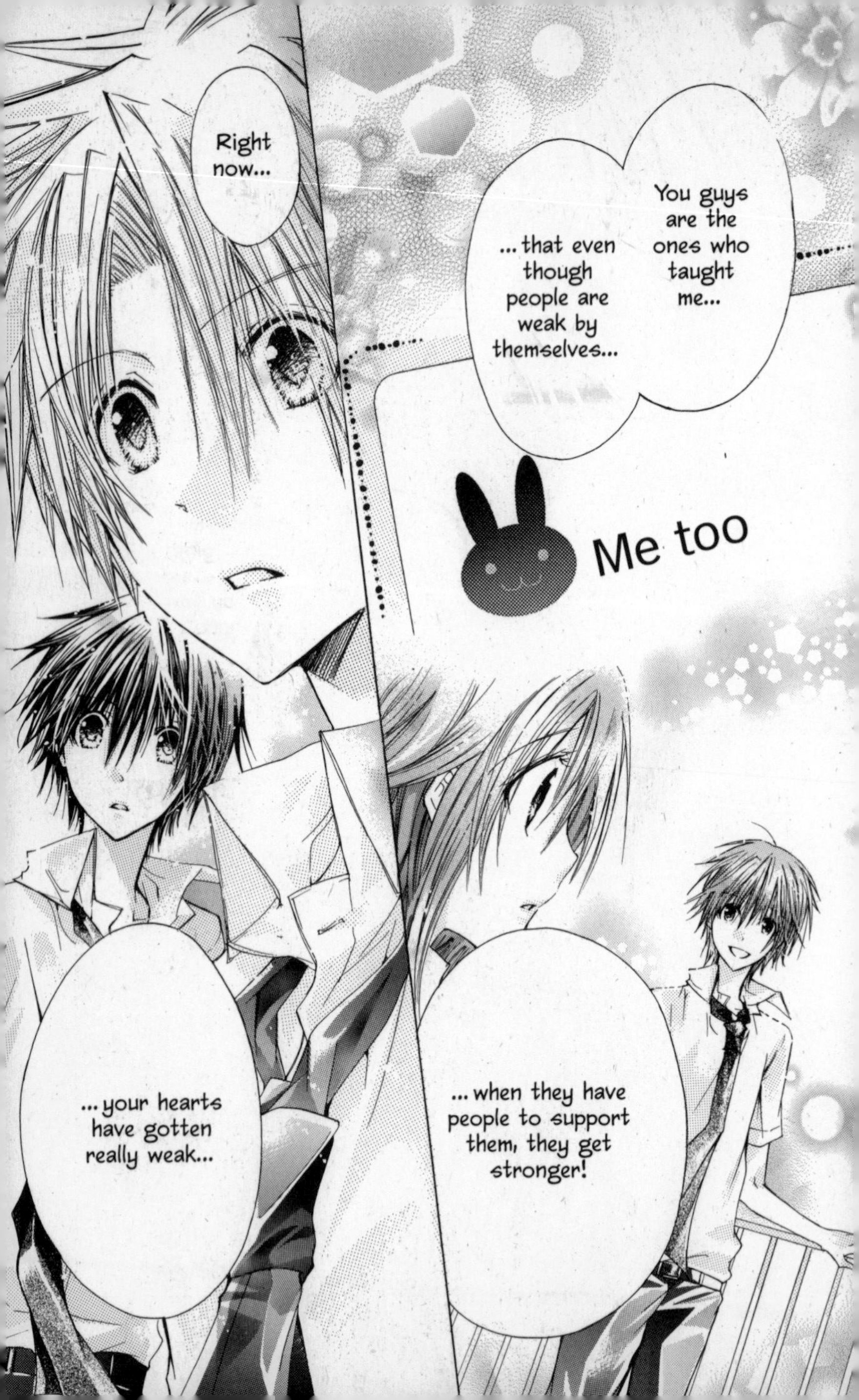
You guys are the ones who taught me...
...that even though people are weak by themselves...
Me too
...when they have people to support them, they get stronger!
Right now...
...your hearts have gotten really weak...

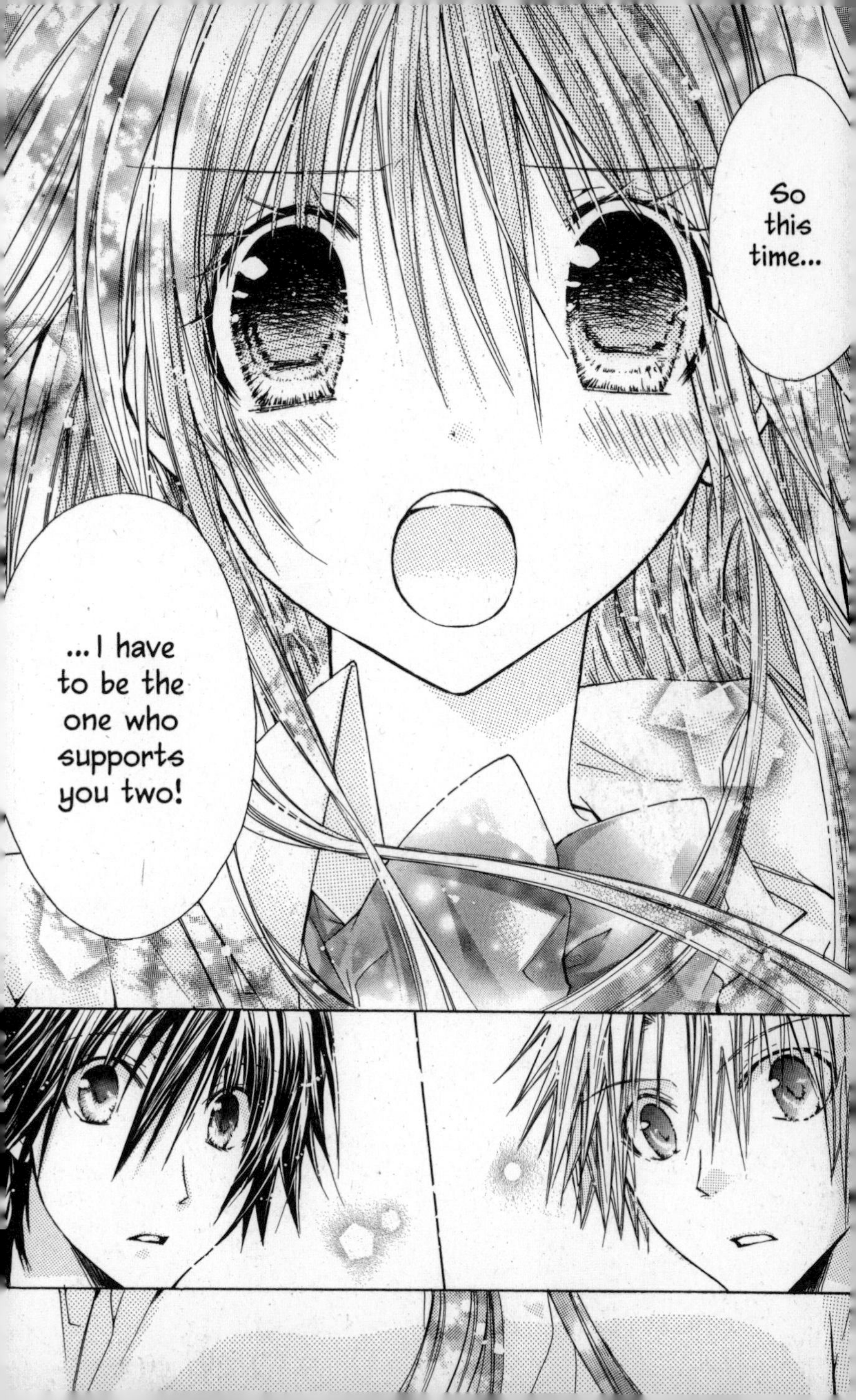
So this time...
...I have to be the one who supports you two!

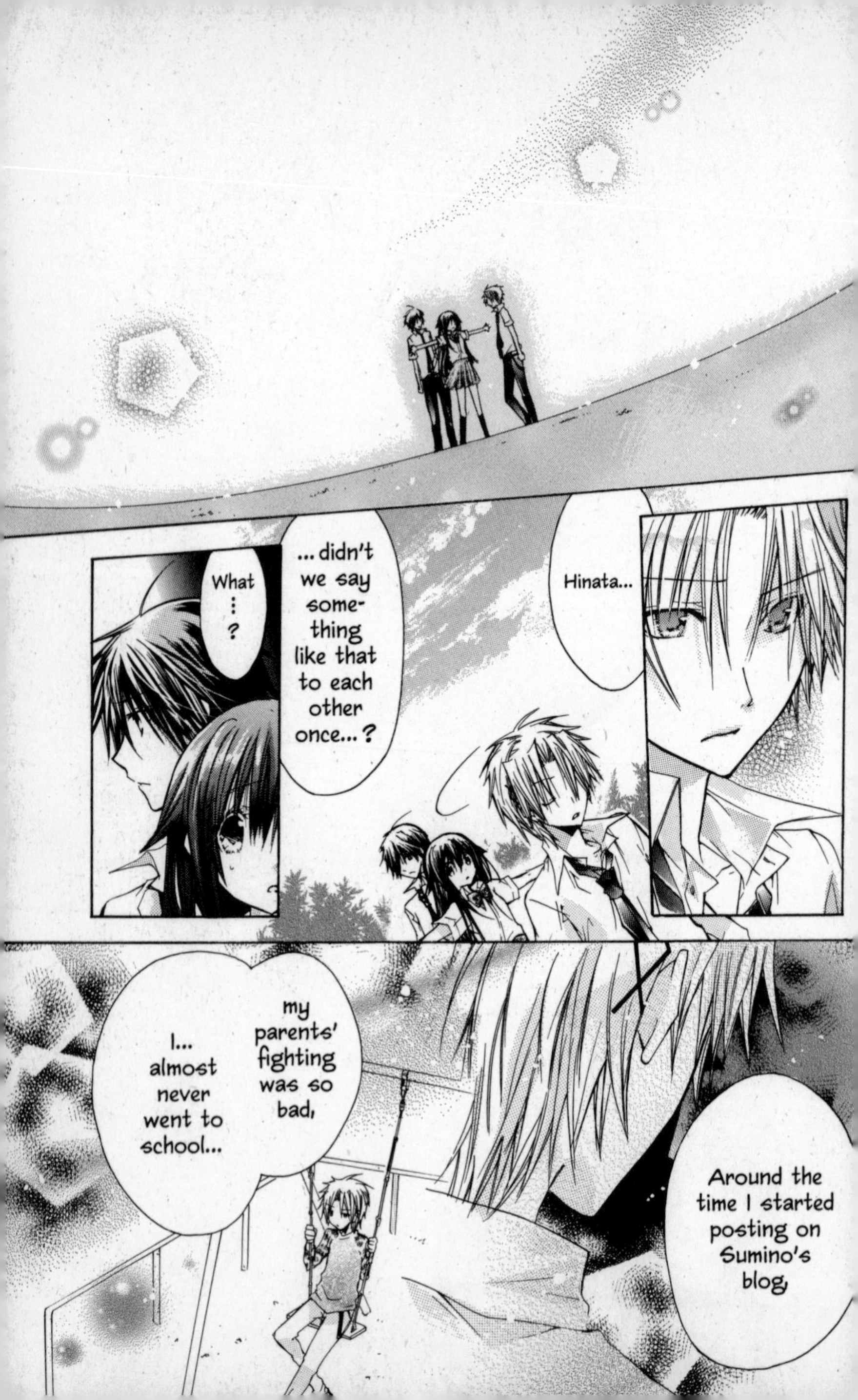
Hinata...
...didn't we say something like that to each other once...?
What...?
Around the time I started posting on Sumino's blog,
my parents' fighting was so bad,
I... almost never went to school...

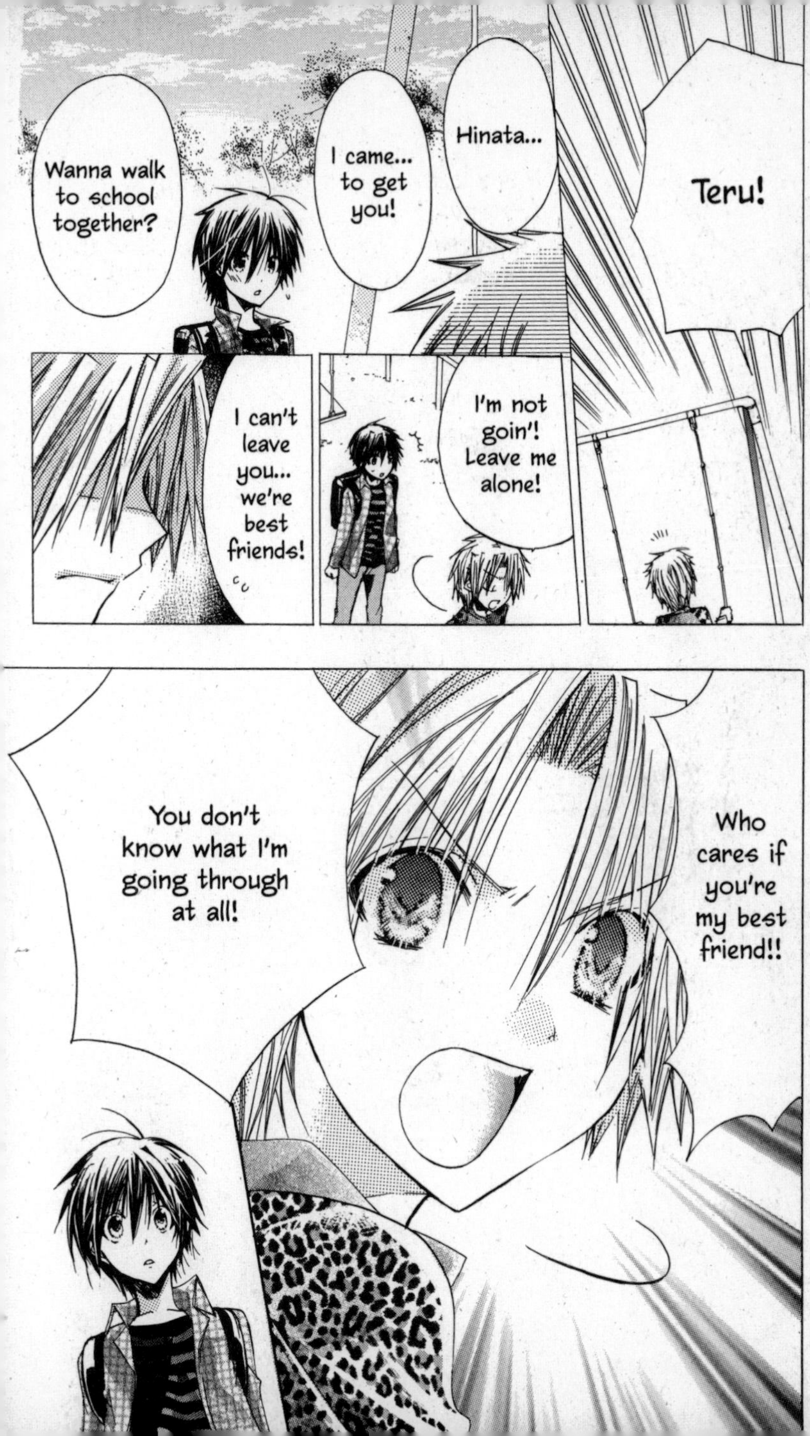
Teru!
Hinata...
I came... to get you!
Wanna walk to school together?
I'm not goin'! Leave me alone!
I can't leave you... we're best friends!
Who cares if you're my best friend!!
You don't know what I'm going through at all!

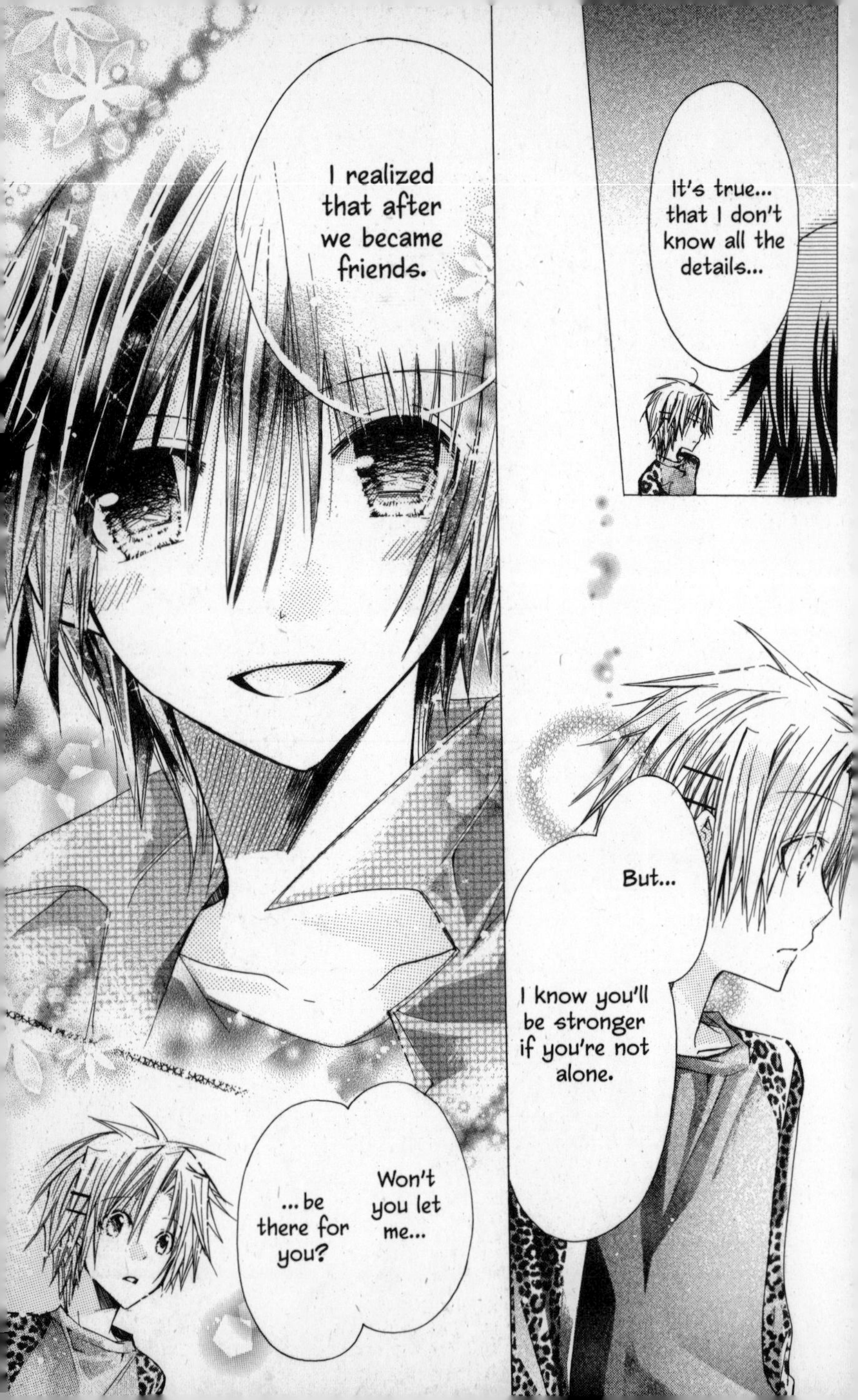
It's true... that I don't know all the details...
But...
I know you'll be stronger if you're not alone.
I realized that after we became friends.
Won't you let me...
...be there for you?

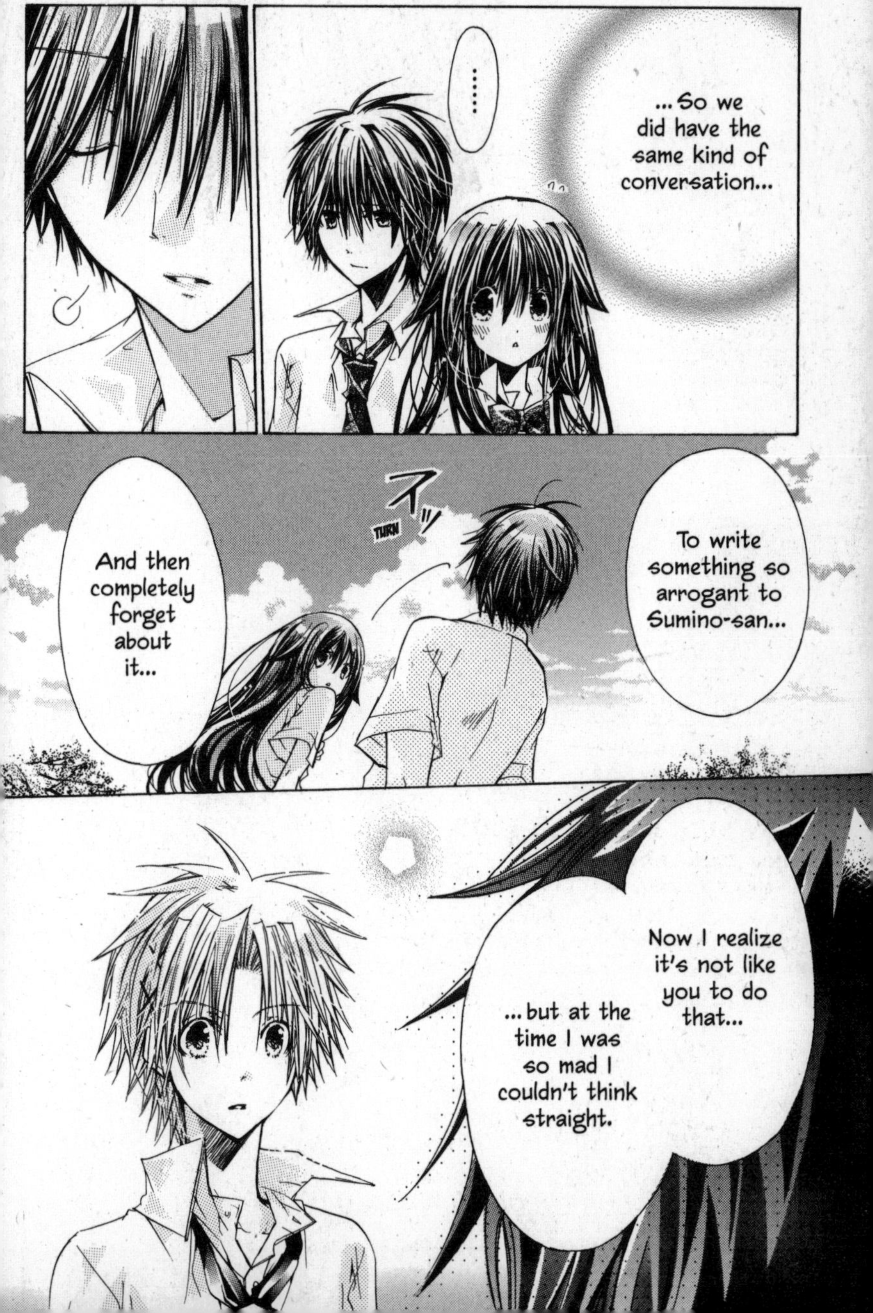
...So we did have the same kind of conversation...
......
To write something so arrogant to Sumino-san...
TURN
And then completely forget about it...
Now I realize it's not like you to do that...
...but at the time I was so mad I couldn't think straight.

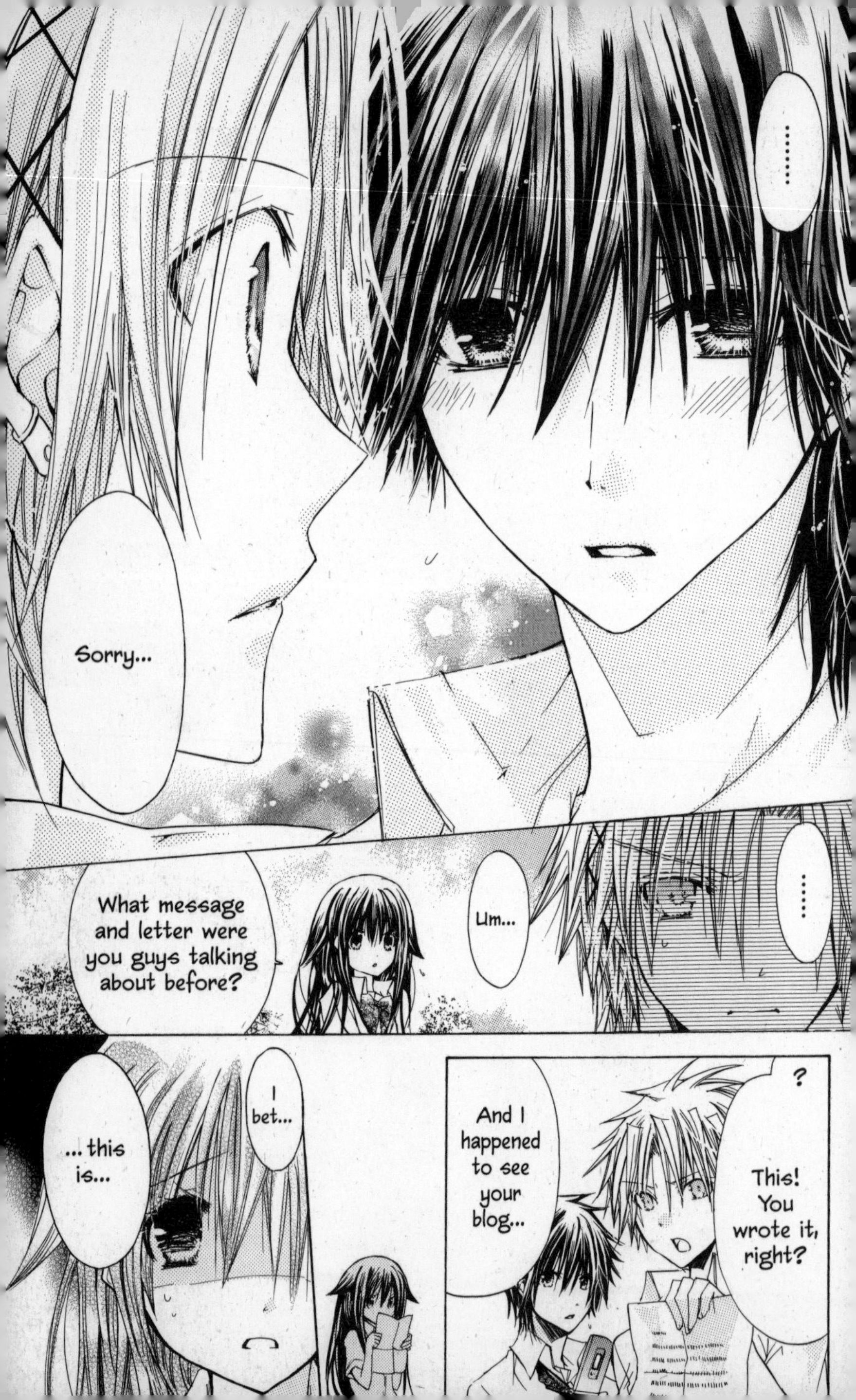
......
Sorry...
......
Um...
What message and letter were you guys talking about before?
?
This! You wrote it, right?
And I happened to see your blog...
I bet...
... this is...

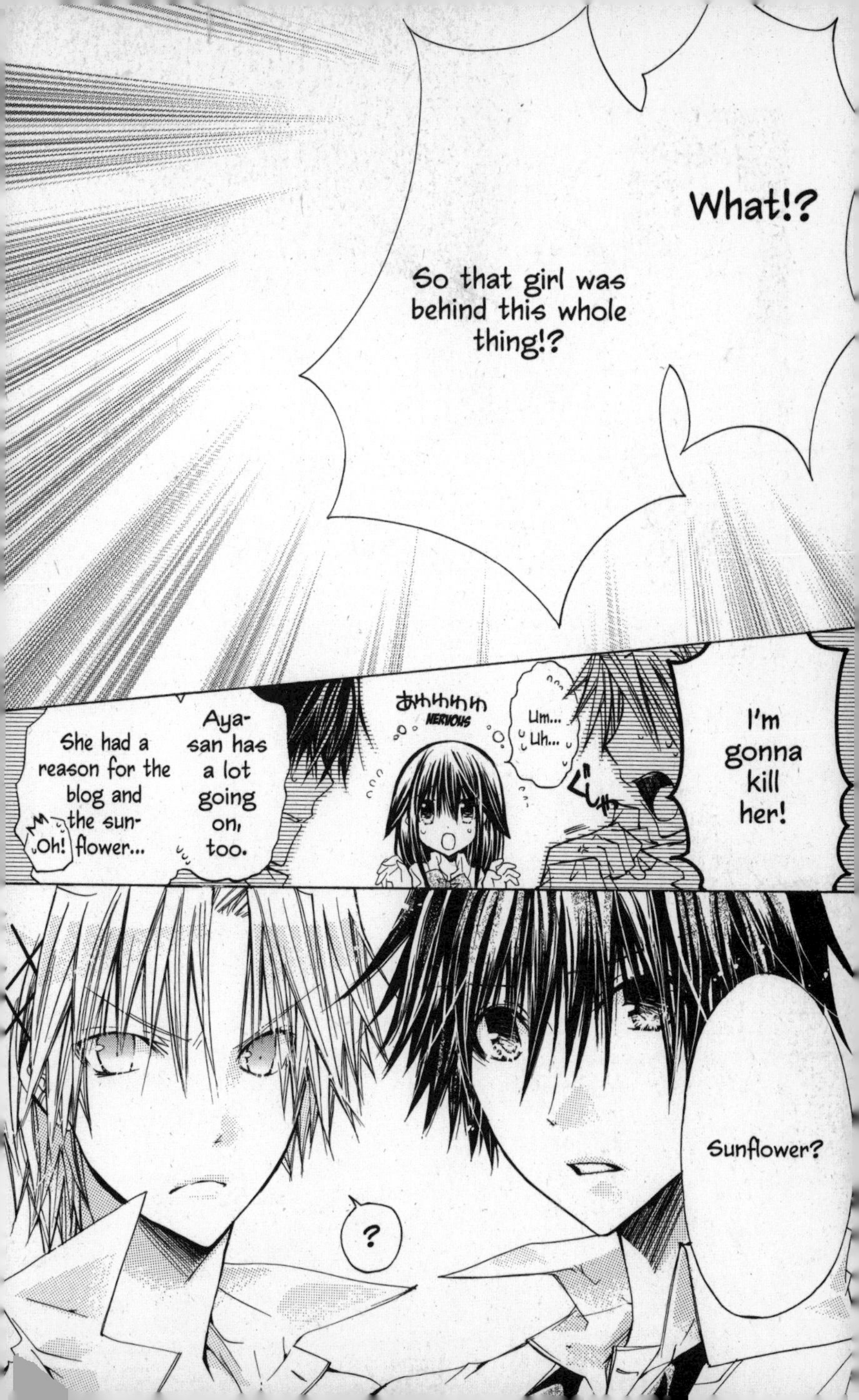
What!?
So that girl was behind this whole thing!?
I'm gonna kill her!
くしゃ
Um... uh...
あわわわわ
NERVOUS
Aya-san has a lot going on, too.
She had a reason for the blog and the sunflower...
Oh!
Sunflower?
?

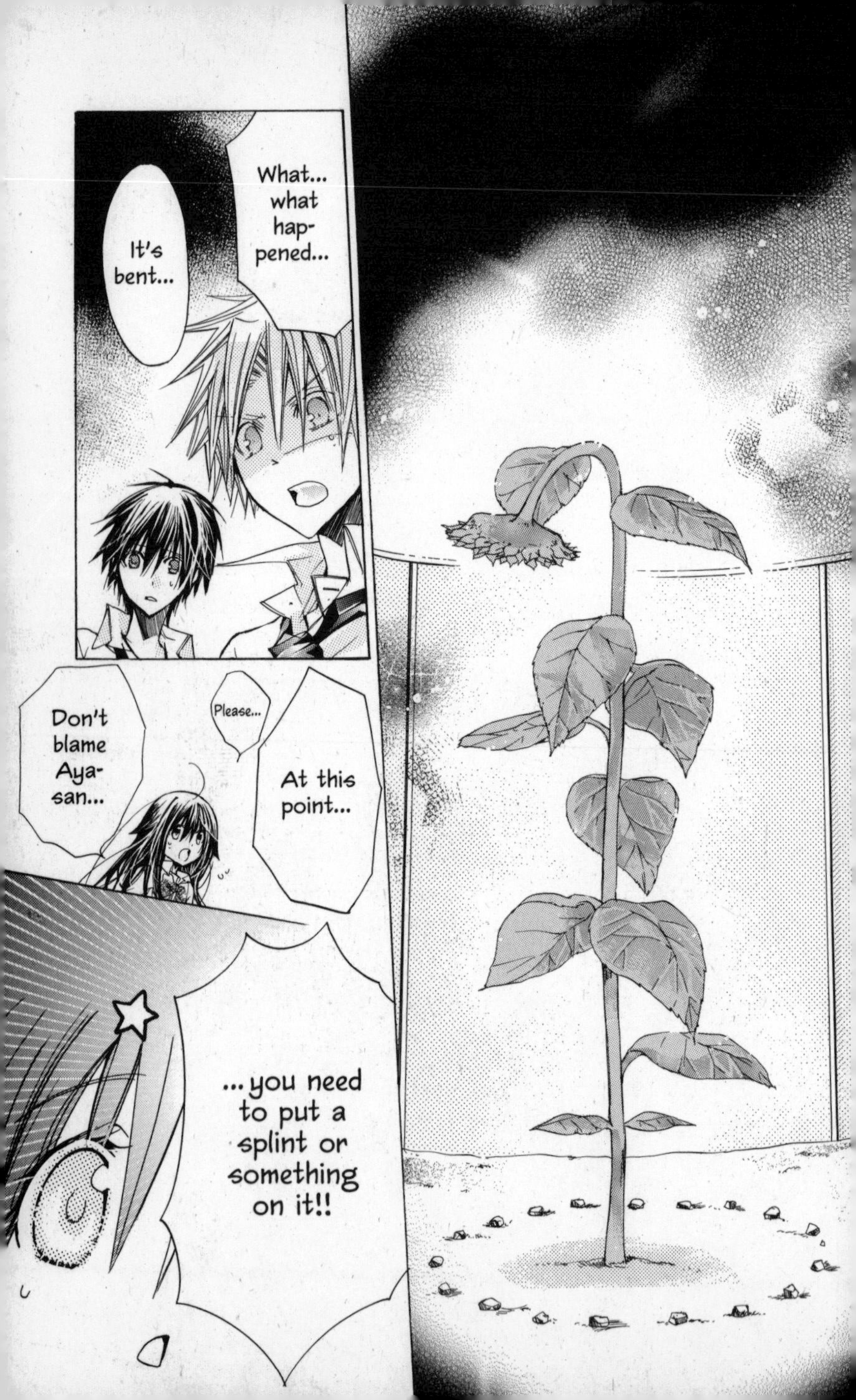
What... what hap-pened...
It's bent...
Don't blame Aya-san...
Please...
At this point...
...you need to put a splint or something on it!!

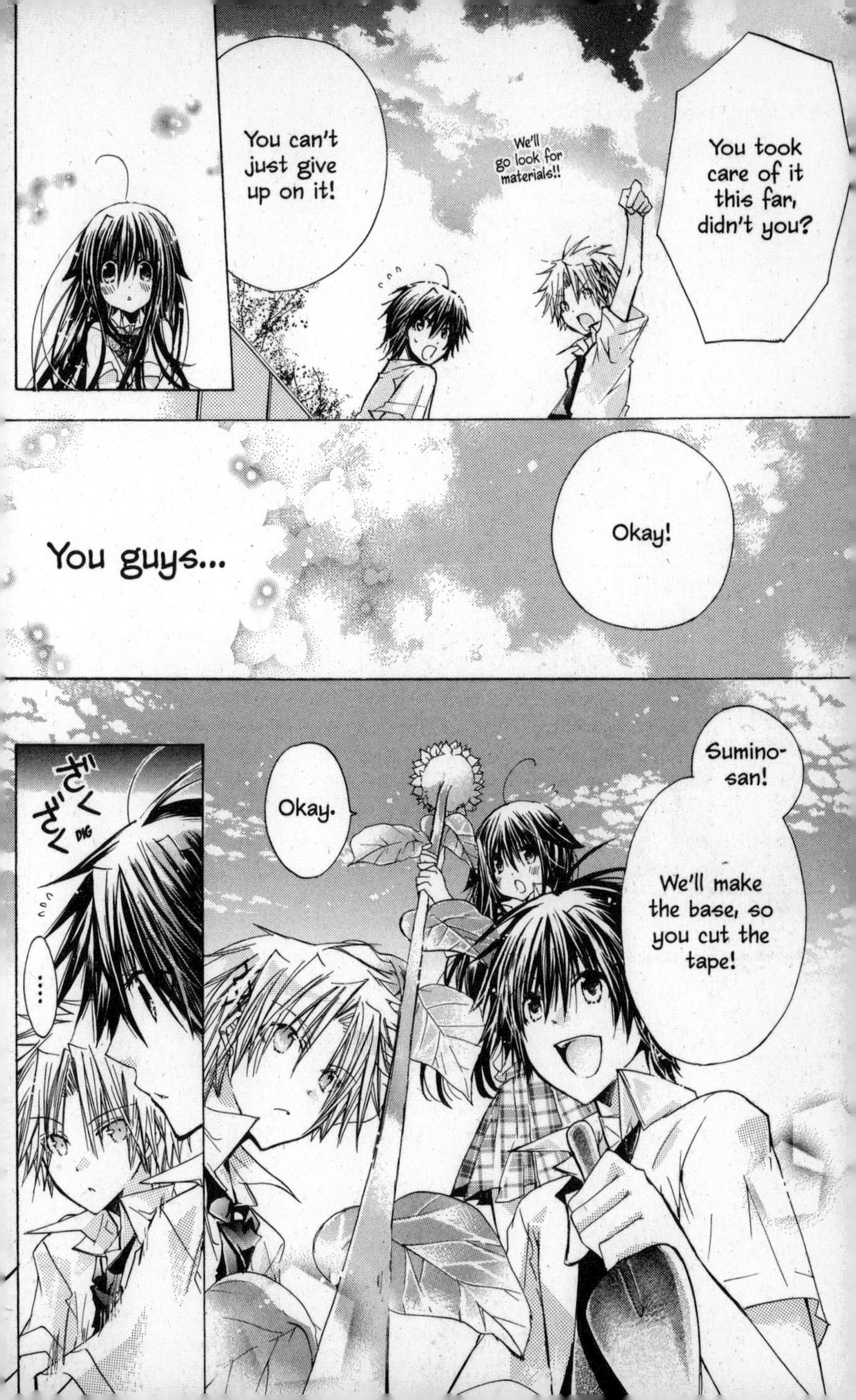
You took care of it this far, didn't you?
We'll go look for materials!!
You can't just give up on it!
Okay!
You guys...
Sumino-san!
We'll make the base, so you cut the tape!
Okay.
ざくざく
DIG
....

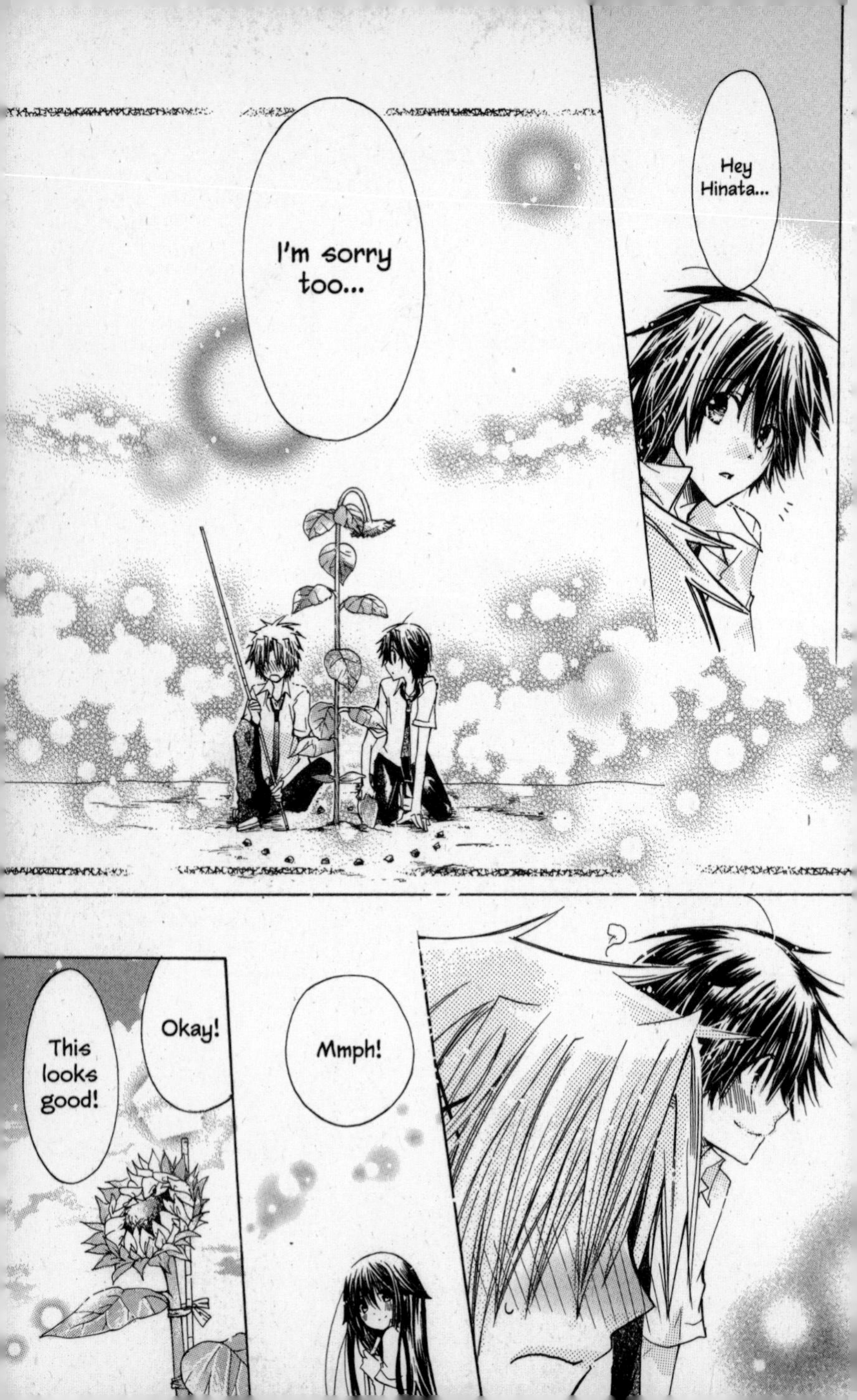
Hey Hinata...
I'm sorry too...
Mmph!
Okay!
This looks good!

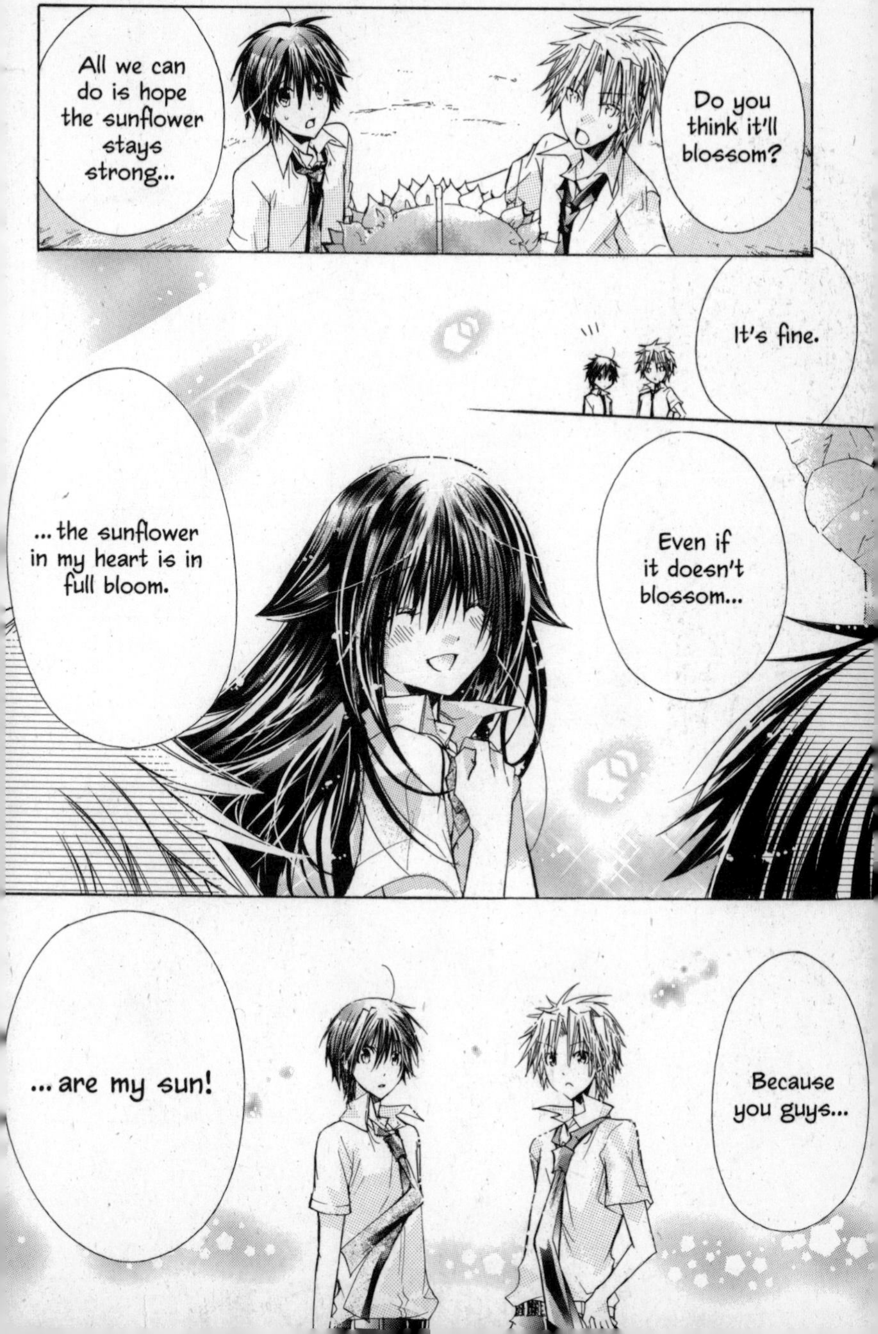
Do you think it'll blossom?
All we can do is hope the sunflower stays strong...
It's fine.
Even if it doesn't blossom...
...the sunflower in my heart is in full bloom.
Because you guys...
...are my sun!

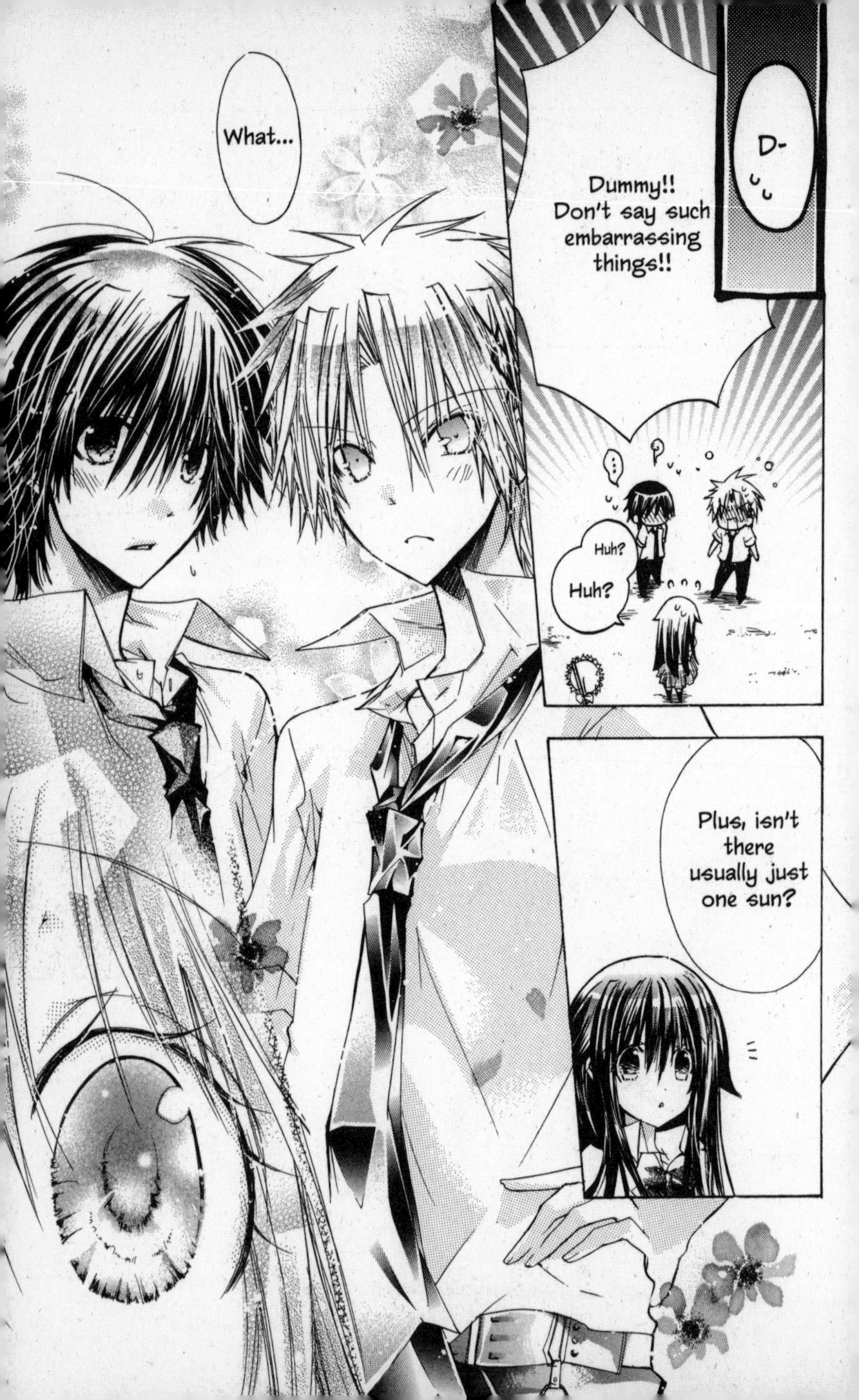
D-
Dummy!! Don't say such embarrassing things!!
Huh?
Huh?
Plus, isn't there usually just one sun?
What...

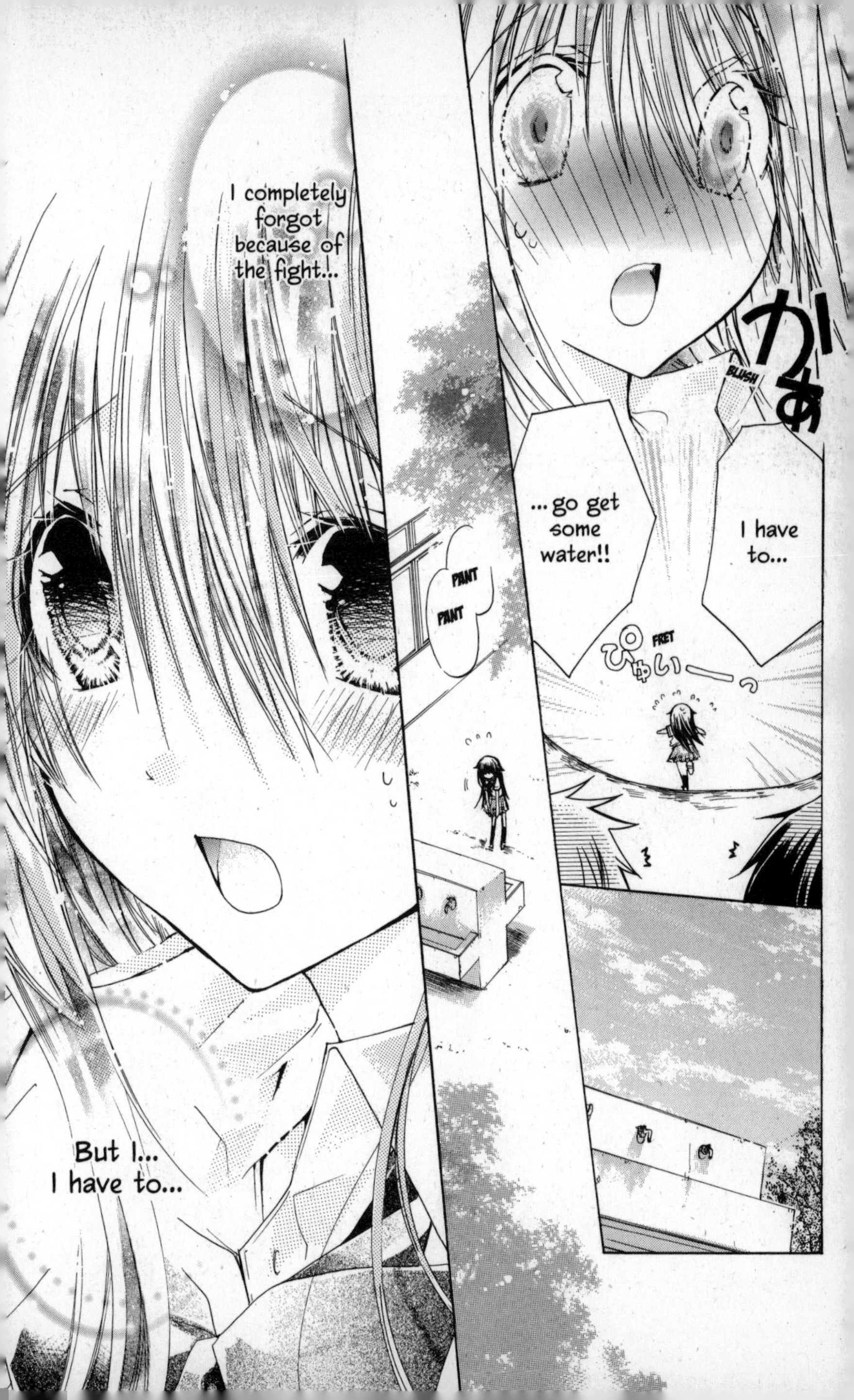
かあ
BLUSH
I have to...
... go get some water!!
ぴゅいーっ
FRET
PANT
PANT
I completely forgot because of the fight...
But I... I have to...

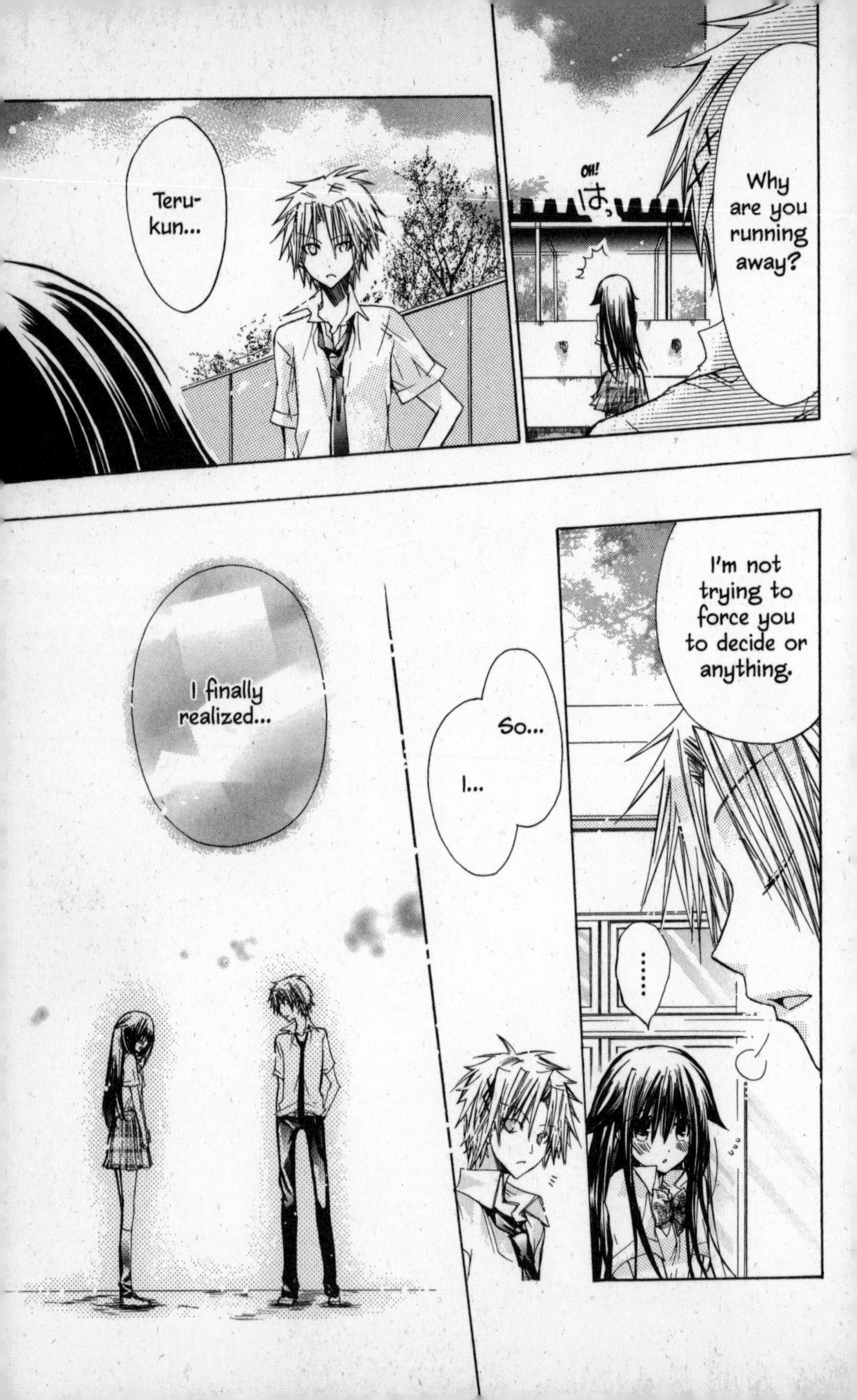
Why are you running away?
OH!
は、
Teru-kun...
I'm not trying to force you to decide or anything.
So...
I...
......
I finally realized...

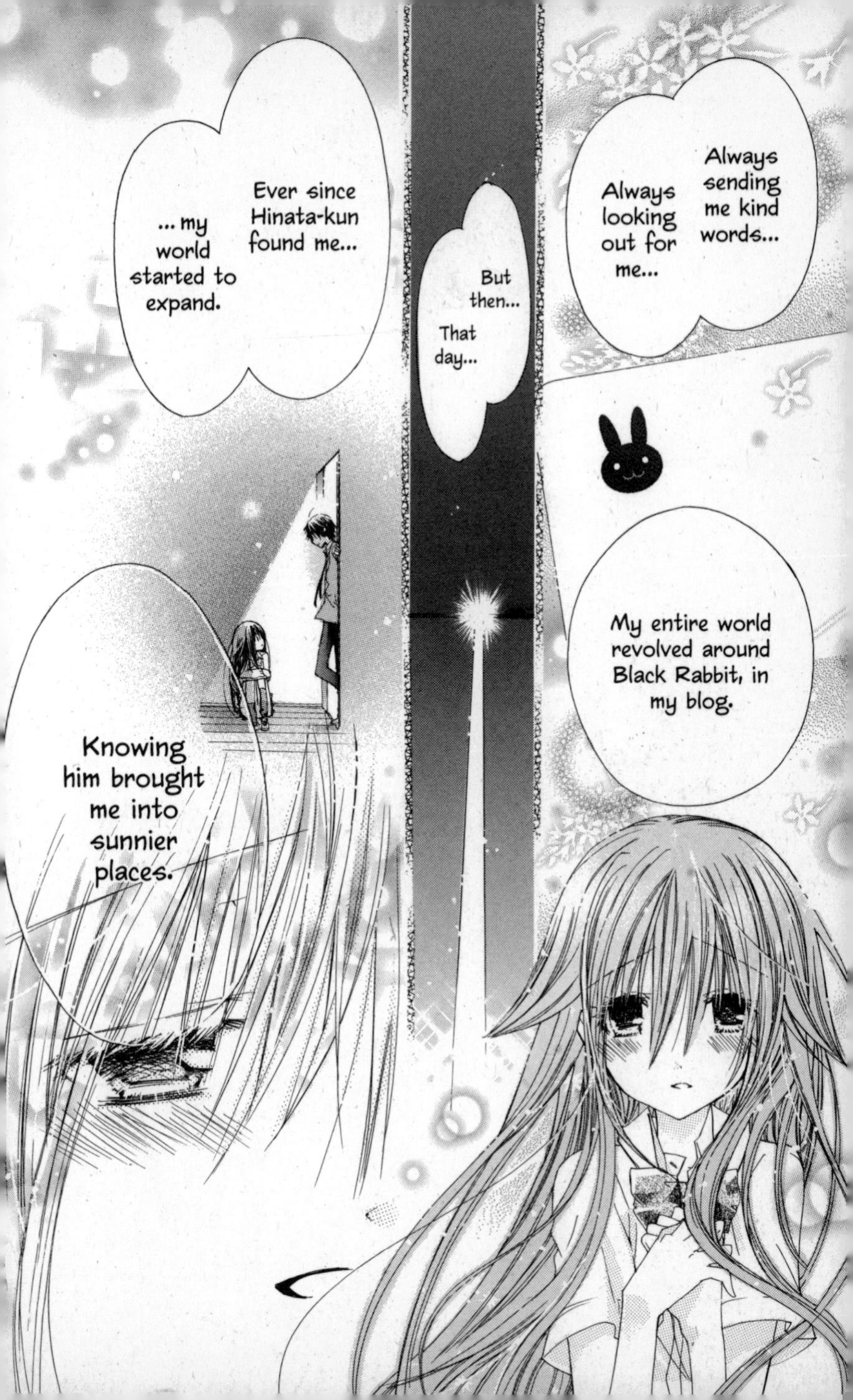
Always sending me kind words...
Always looking out for me...
My entire world revolved around Black Rabbit, in my blog.
But then...
That day...
Ever since Hinata-kun found me...
... my world started to expand.
Knowing him brought me into sunnier places.

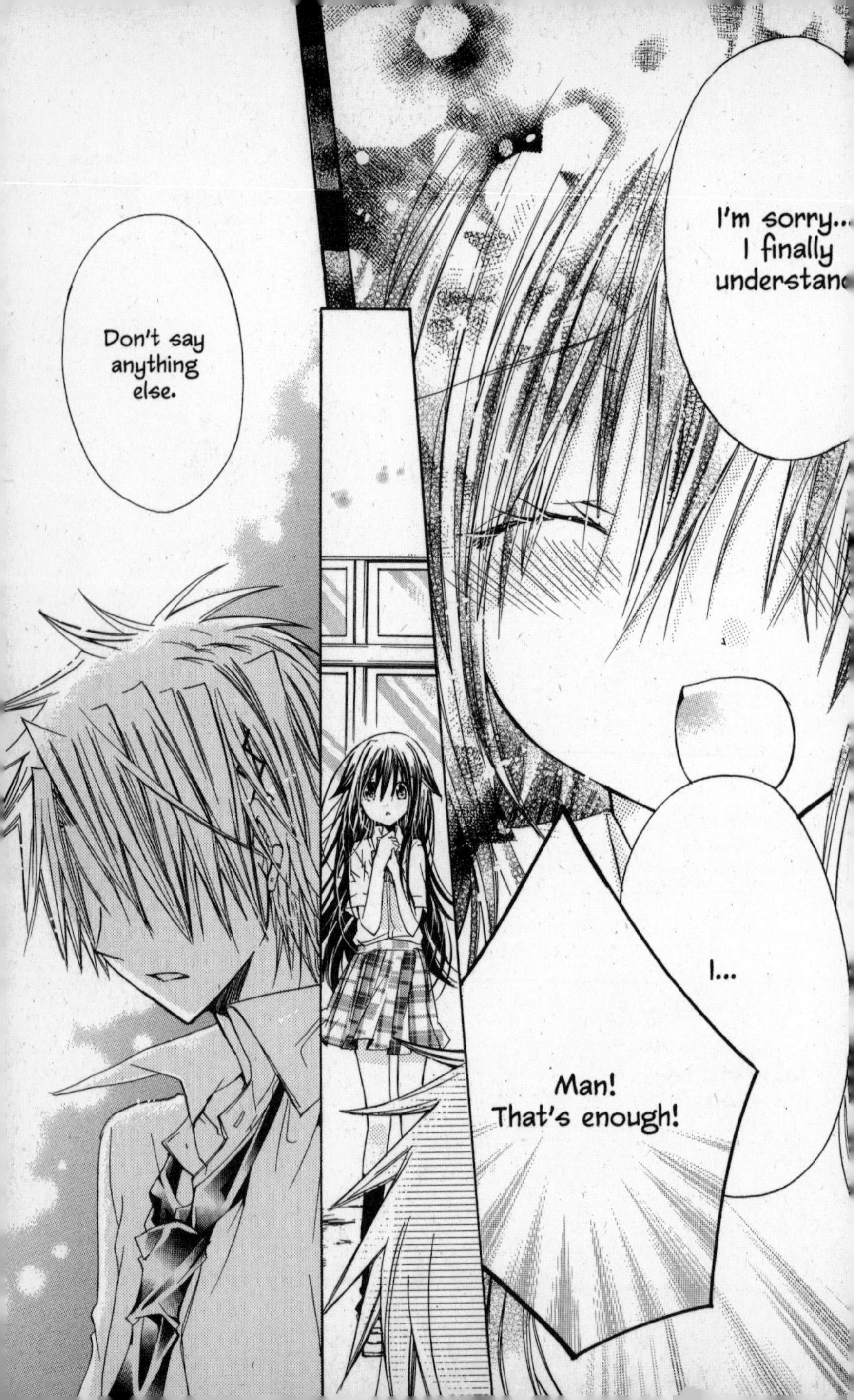
I'm sorry... I finally understan
I...
Man! That's enough!
Don't say anything else.

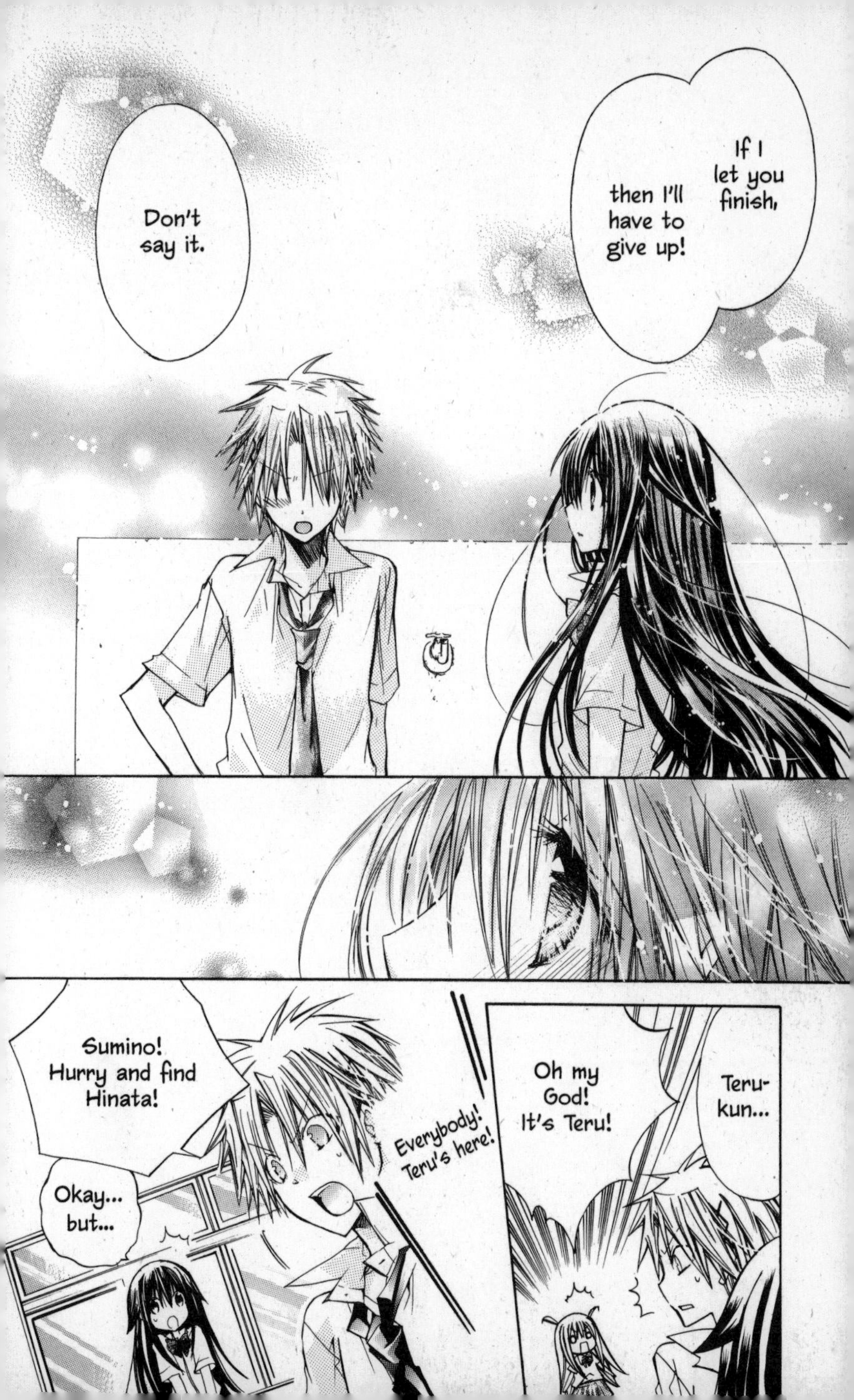
If I let you finish, then I'll have to give up!
Don't say it.
Teru-kun...
Oh my God! It's Teru!
Everybody! Teru's here!
Sumino! Hurry and find Hinata!
Okay... but...

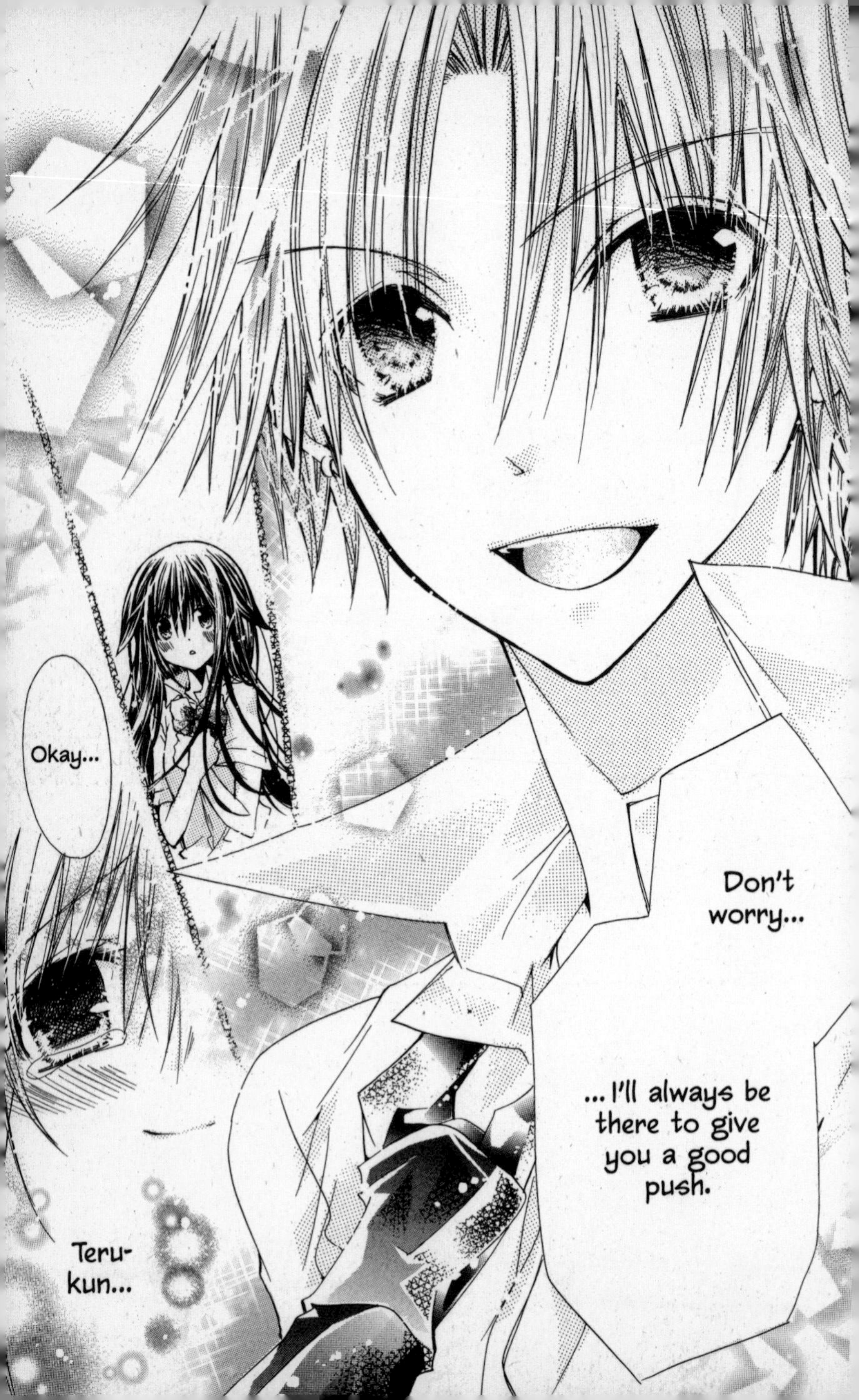
Don't worry...
...I'll always be there to give you a good push.
Okay...
Teru-kun...

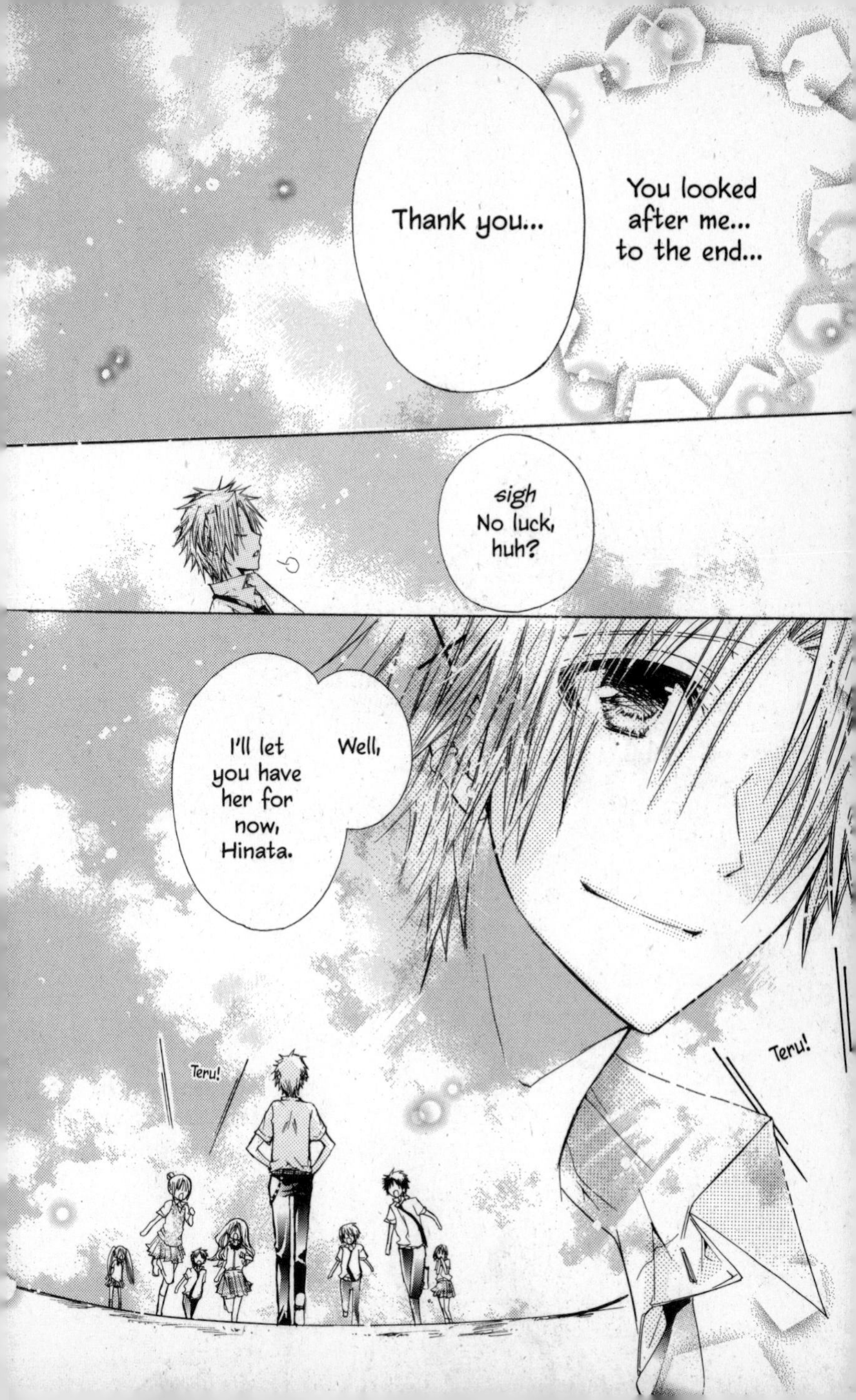
You looked after me... to the end...
Thank you...
sigh No luck, huh?
Well,
I'll let you have her for now, Hinata.
Teru!
Teru!

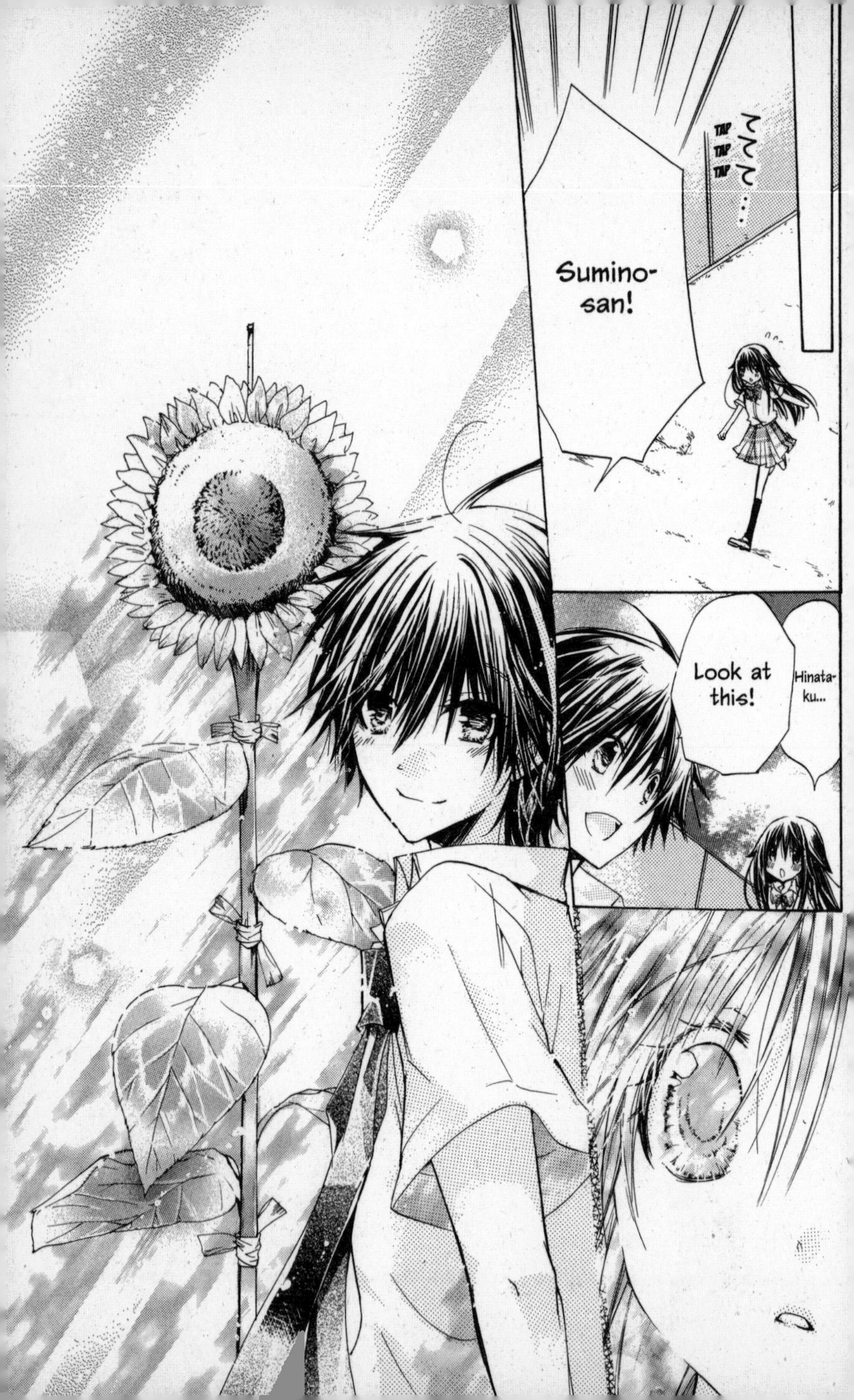

てて…
TAP TAP TAP
Sumino-san!
Hinata-ku...
Look at this!

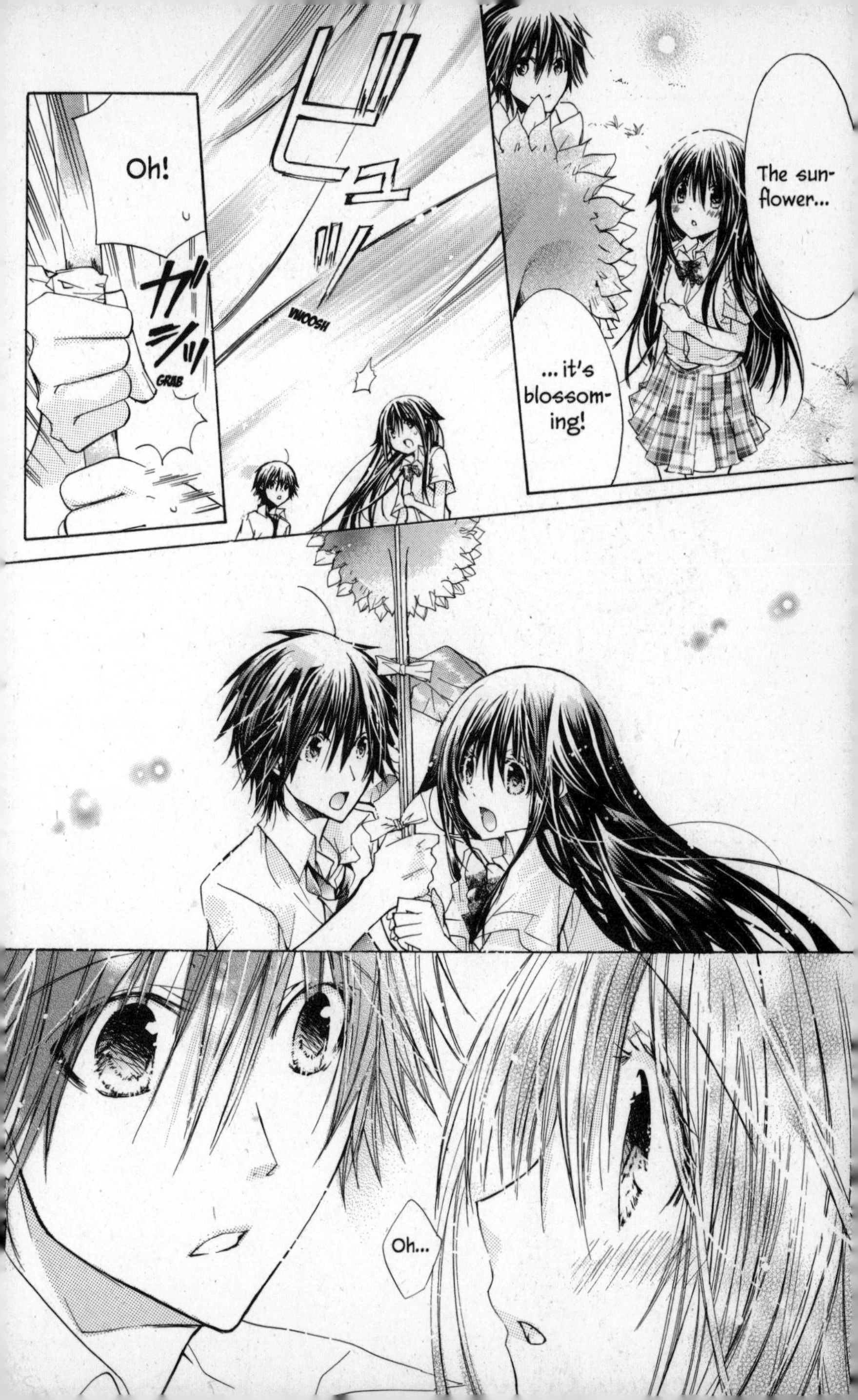
The sun-flower...
... it's blossom-ing!
ヒュッ
VWOOSH
Oh!
ガシッ
GRAB
Oh...

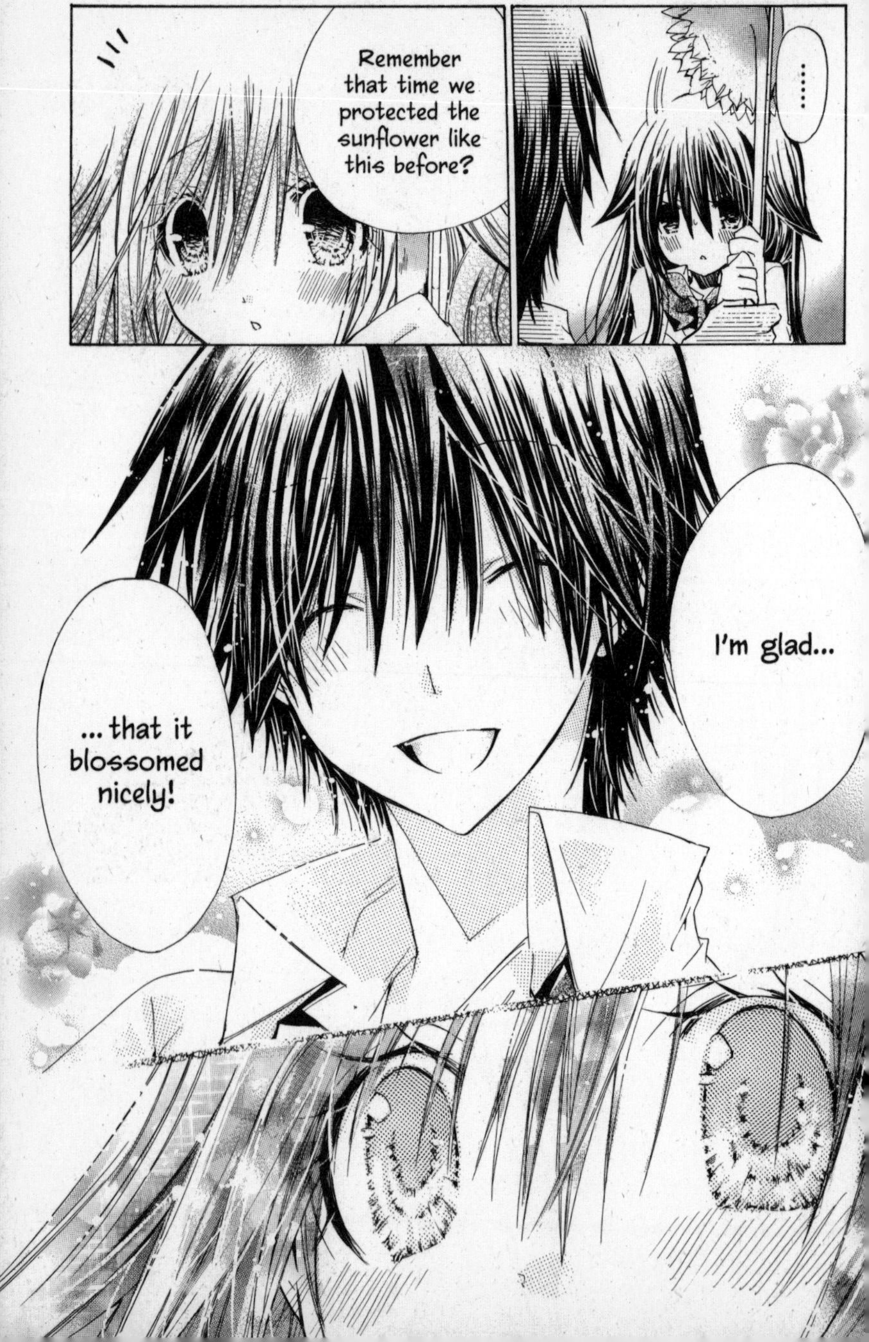
……
Remember that time we protected the sunflower like this before?
I'm glad...
... that it blossomed nicely!

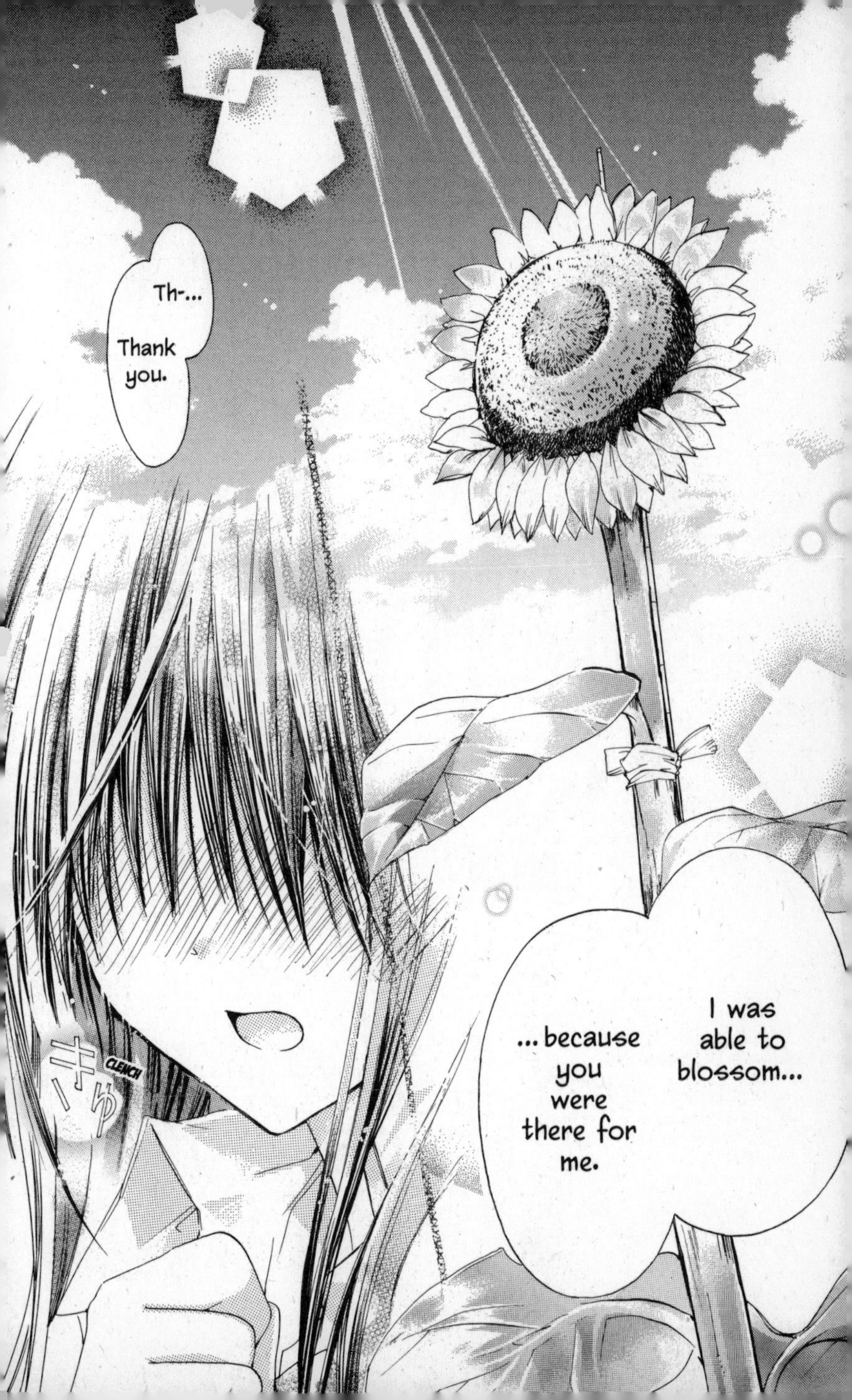
Th-...
Thank you.
I was able to blossom...
...because you were there for me.
CLENCH

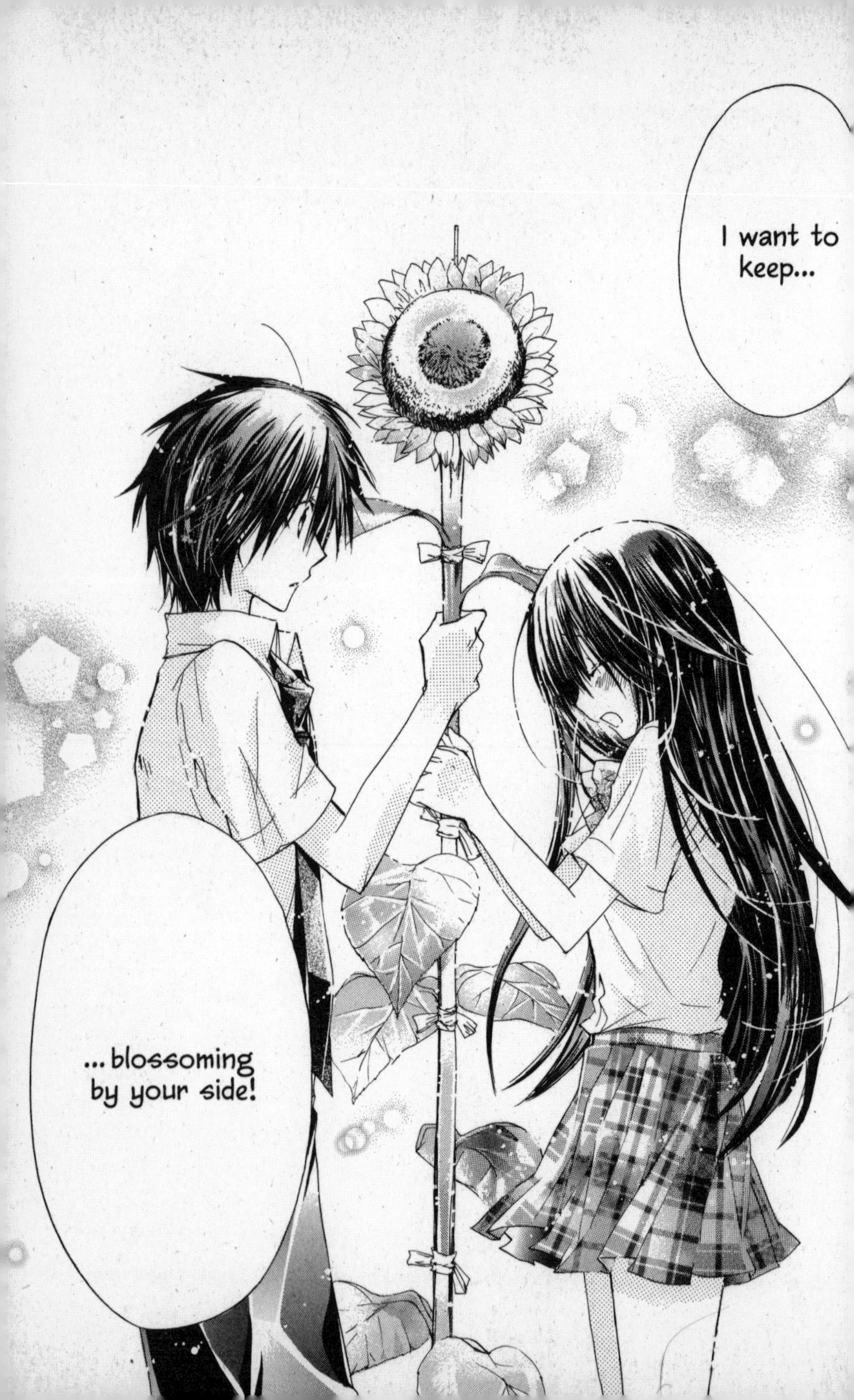
I want to keep...
...blossoming by your side!

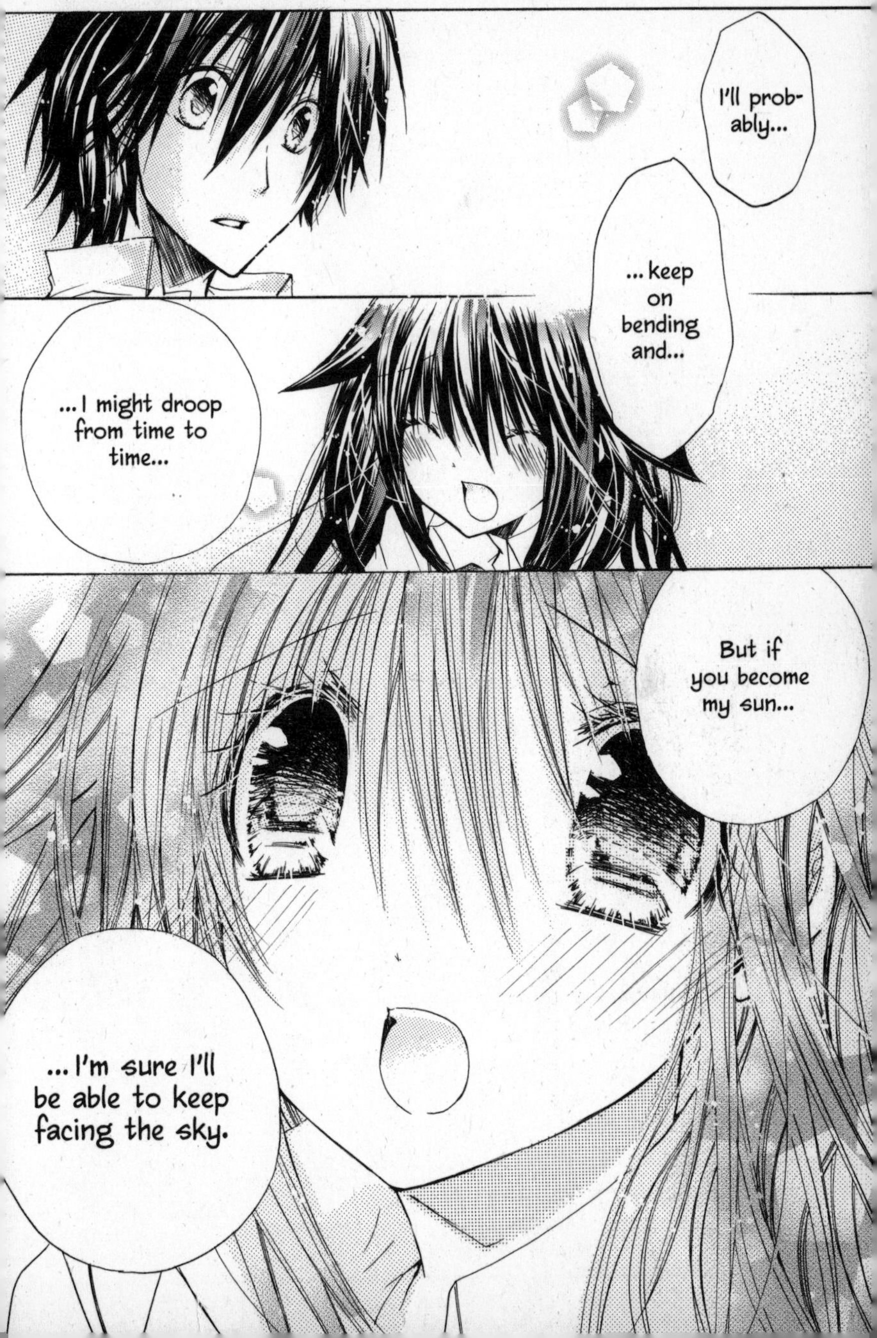
I'll probably...
...keep on bending and...
...I might droop from time to time...
But if you become my sun...
...I'm sure I'll be able to keep facing the sky.

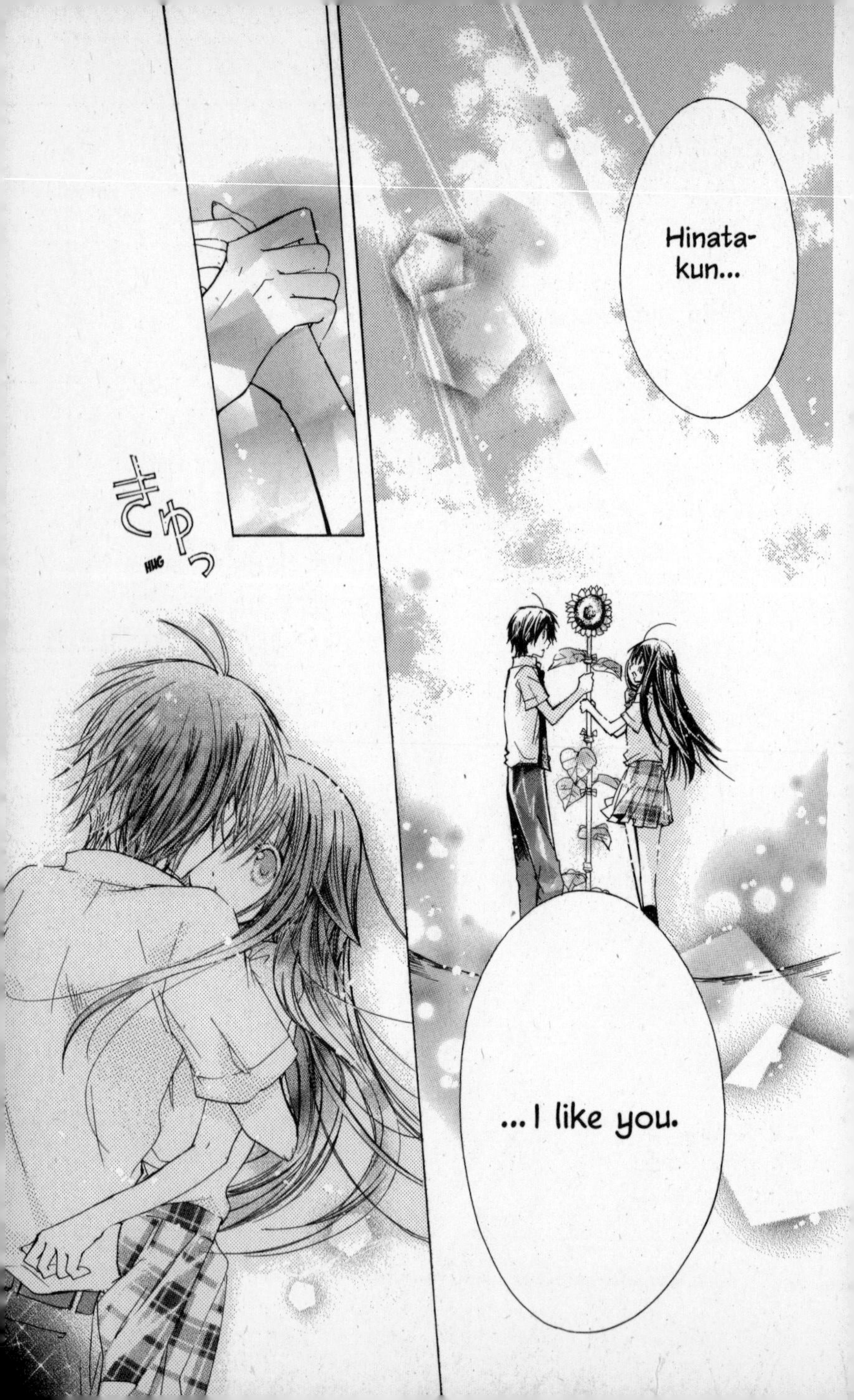
Hinata-kun...
...I like you.
きゅっ
HUG

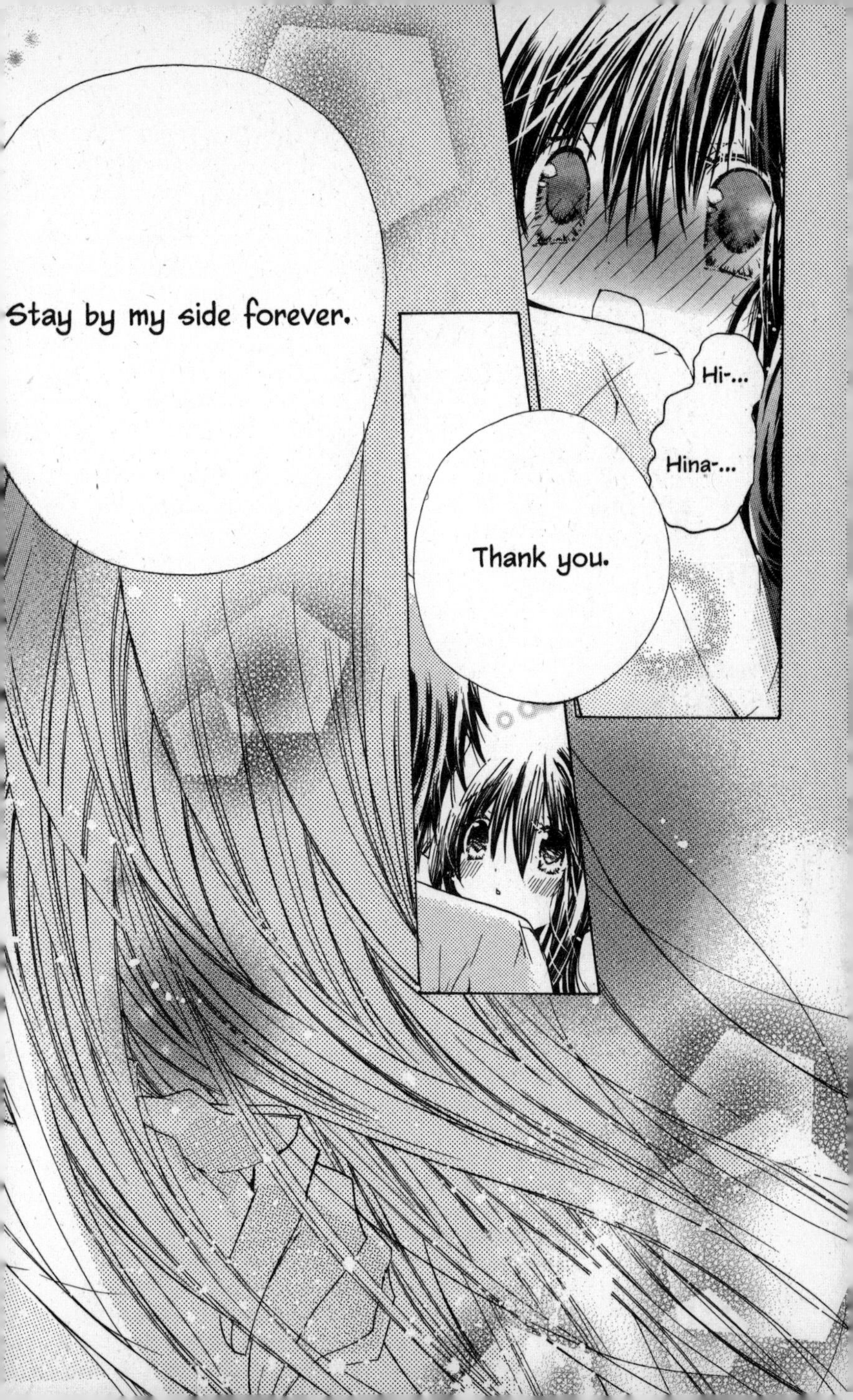
Hi-...
Hina-...
Thank you.
Stay by my side forever.

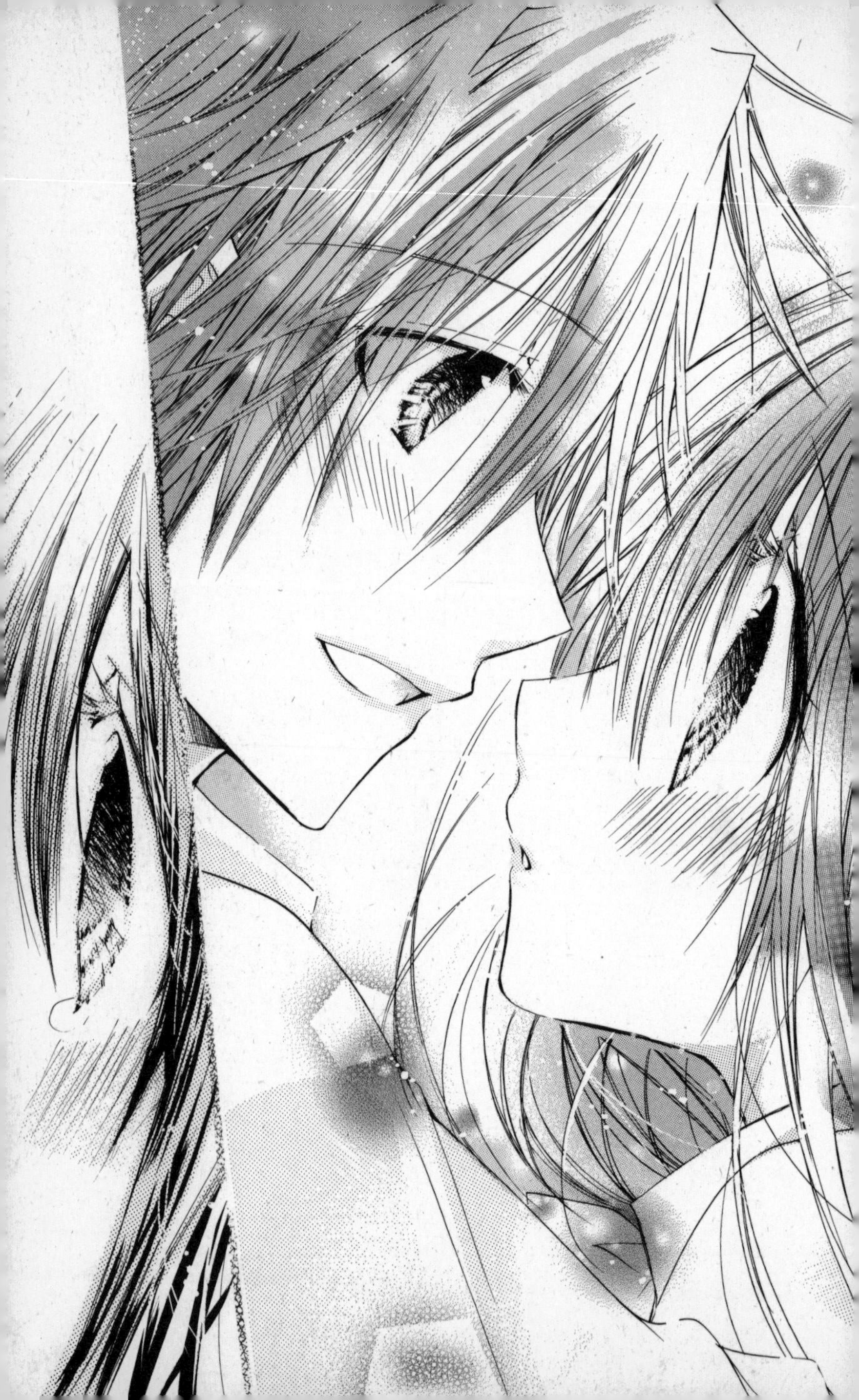

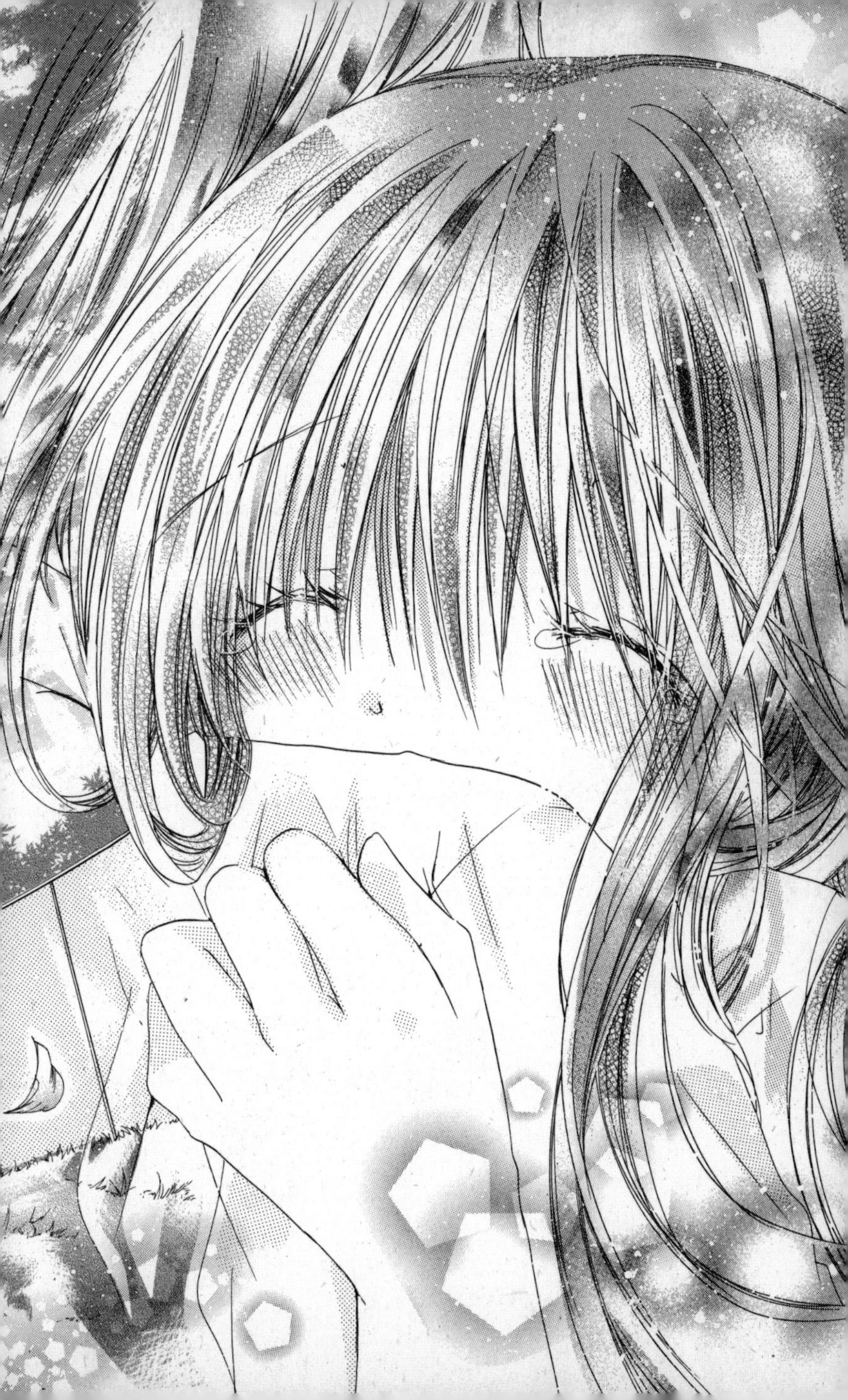

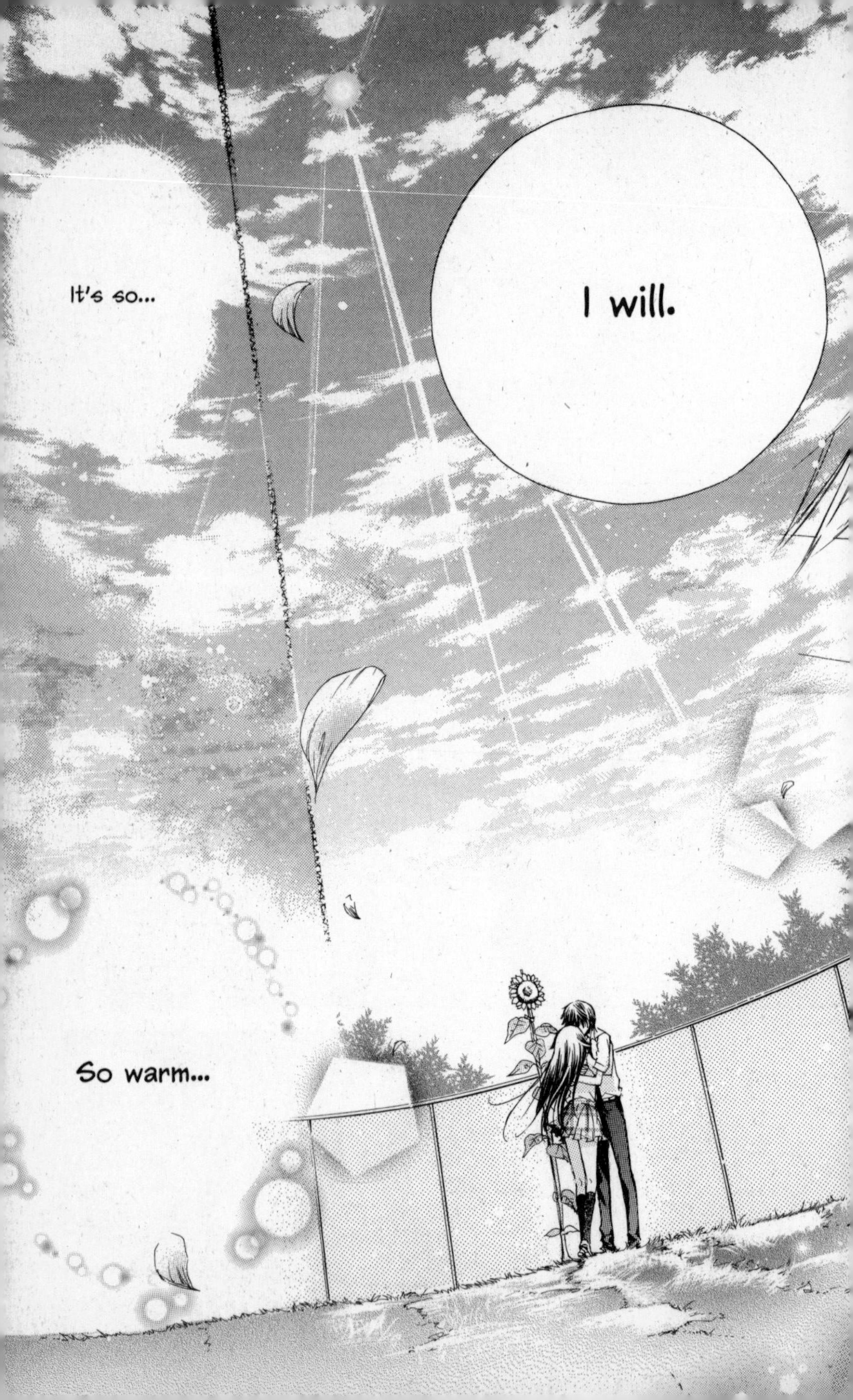
I will.
It's so...
So warm...

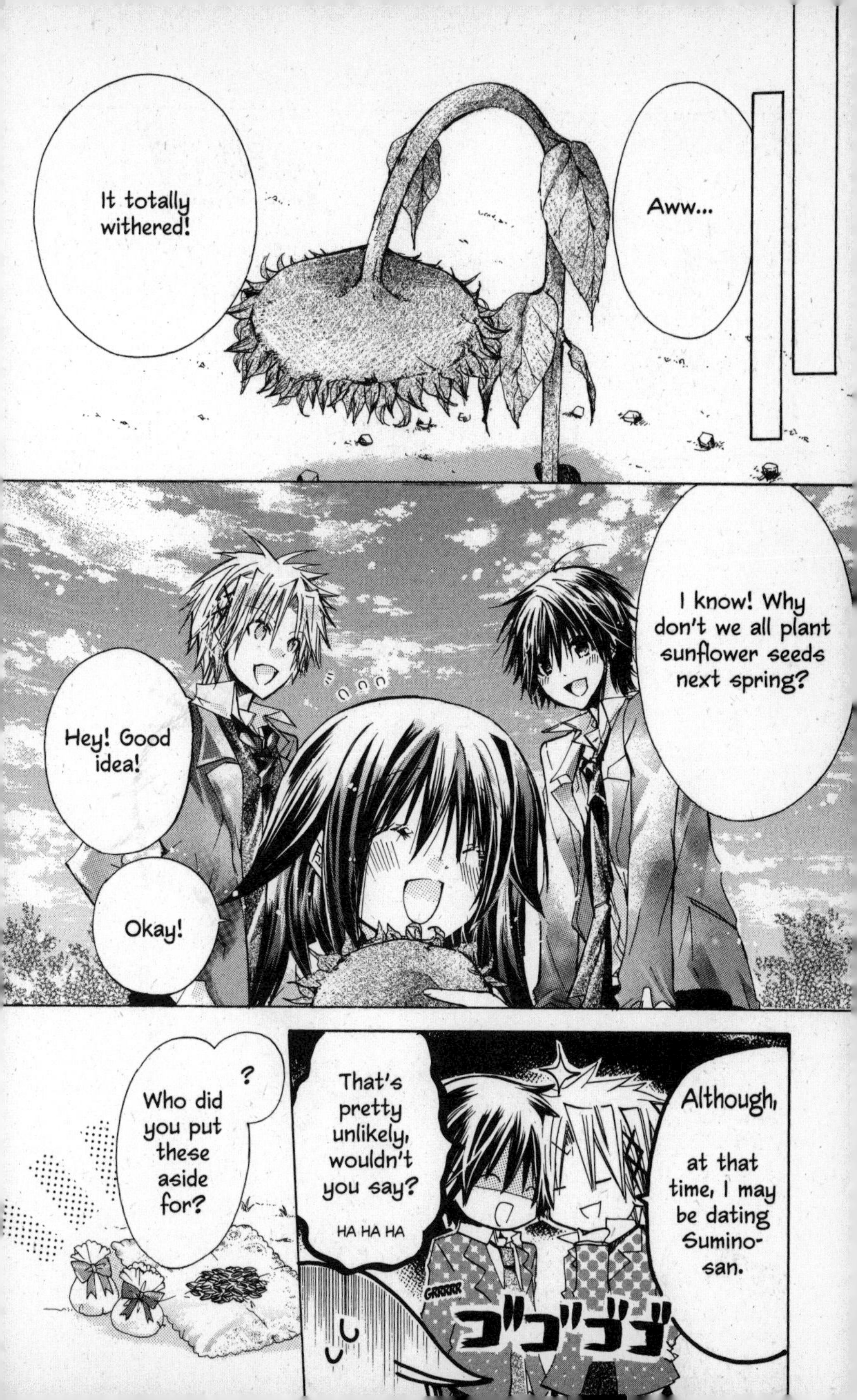
Aww...
It totally withered!
I know! Why don't we all plant sunflower seeds next spring?
Hey! Good idea!
Okay!
Although, at that time, I may be dating Sumino-san.
That's pretty unlikely, wouldn't you say?
HA HA HA
GRRRRR
ゴゴゴゴ
?
Who did you put these aside for?

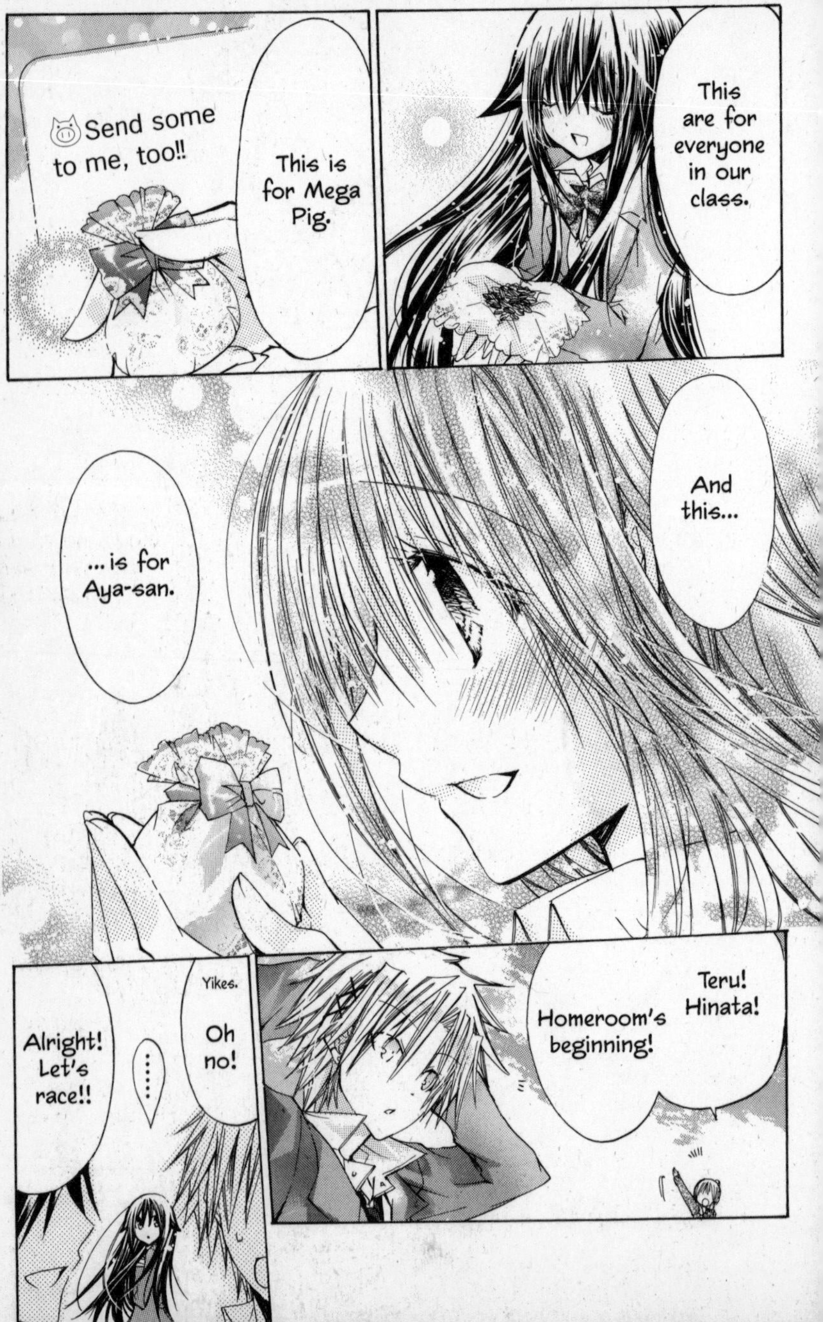
This are for everyone in our class.
This is for Mega Pig.
Send some to me, too!!
And this...
...is for Aya-san.
Teru! Hinata!
Homeroom's beginning!
Yikes.
Oh no!
......
Alright! Let's race!!

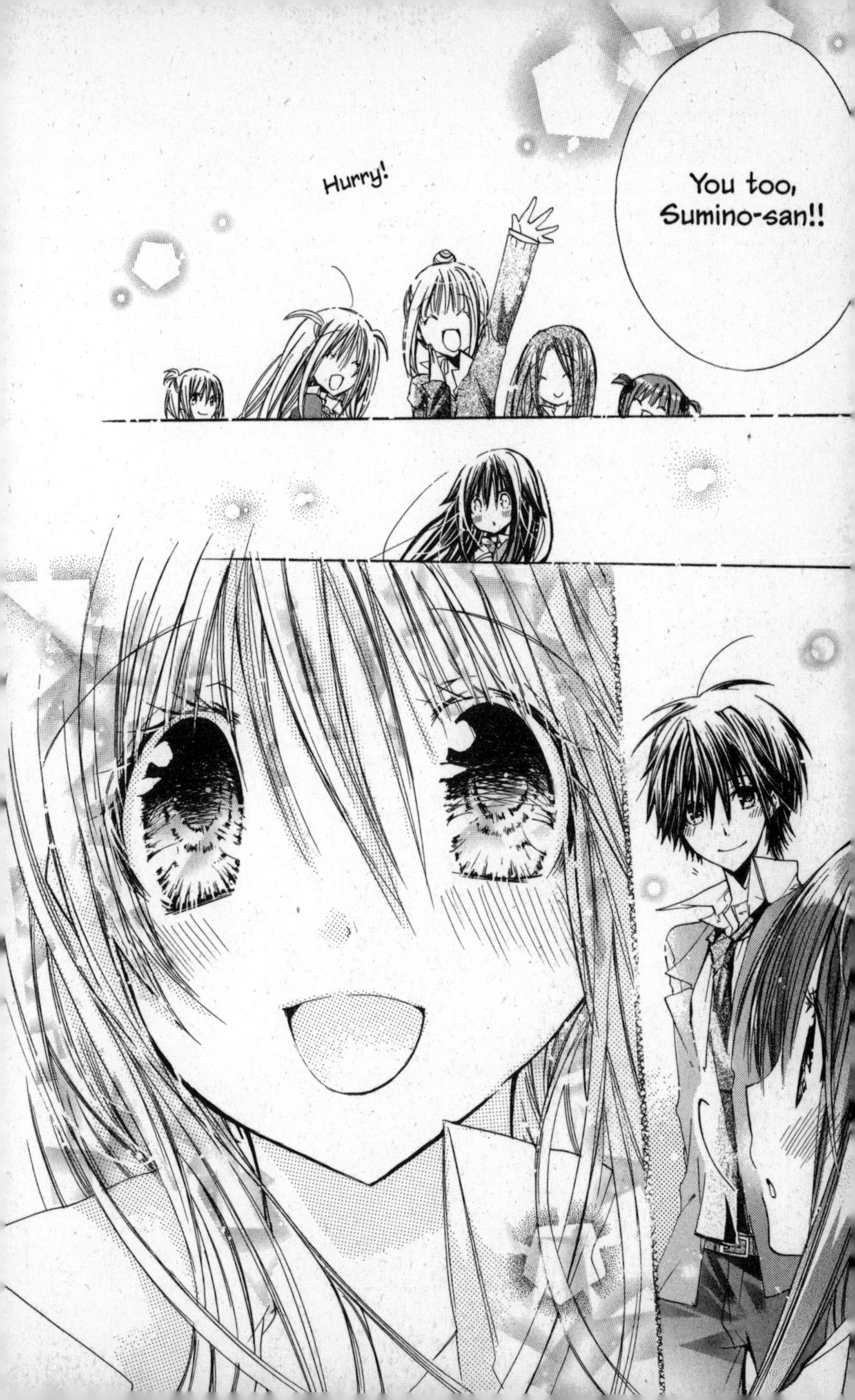
You too, Sumino-san!!
Hurry!

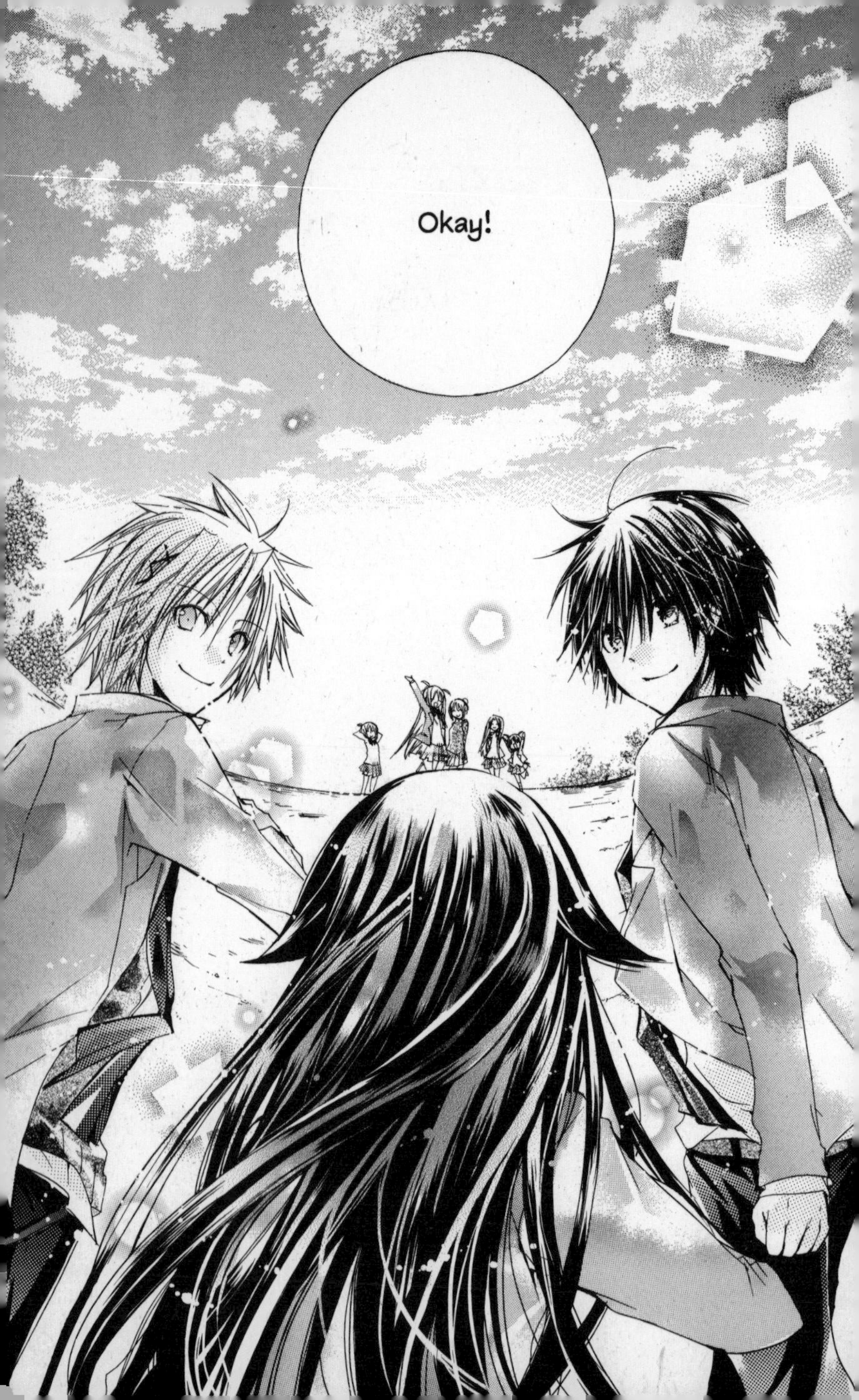
Okay!

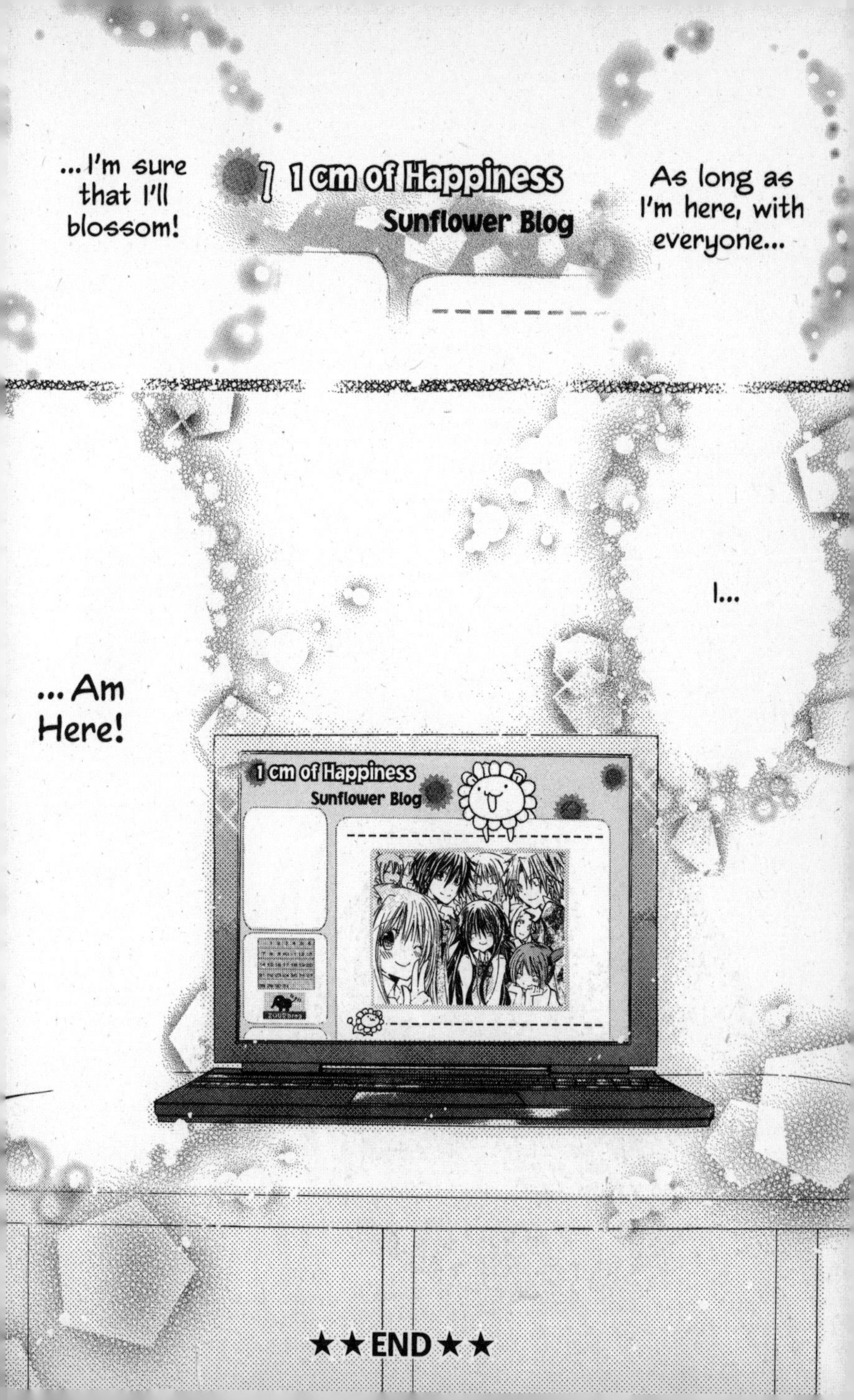
As long as I'm here, with everyone...
1 cm of Happiness
Sunflower Blog
...I'm sure that I'll blossom!
I...
1 cm of Happiness
Sunflower Blog
...Am Here!
★★END★★

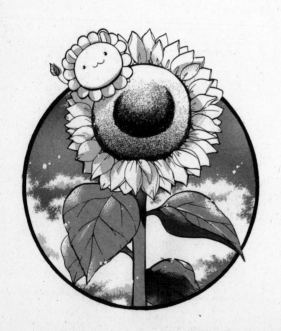

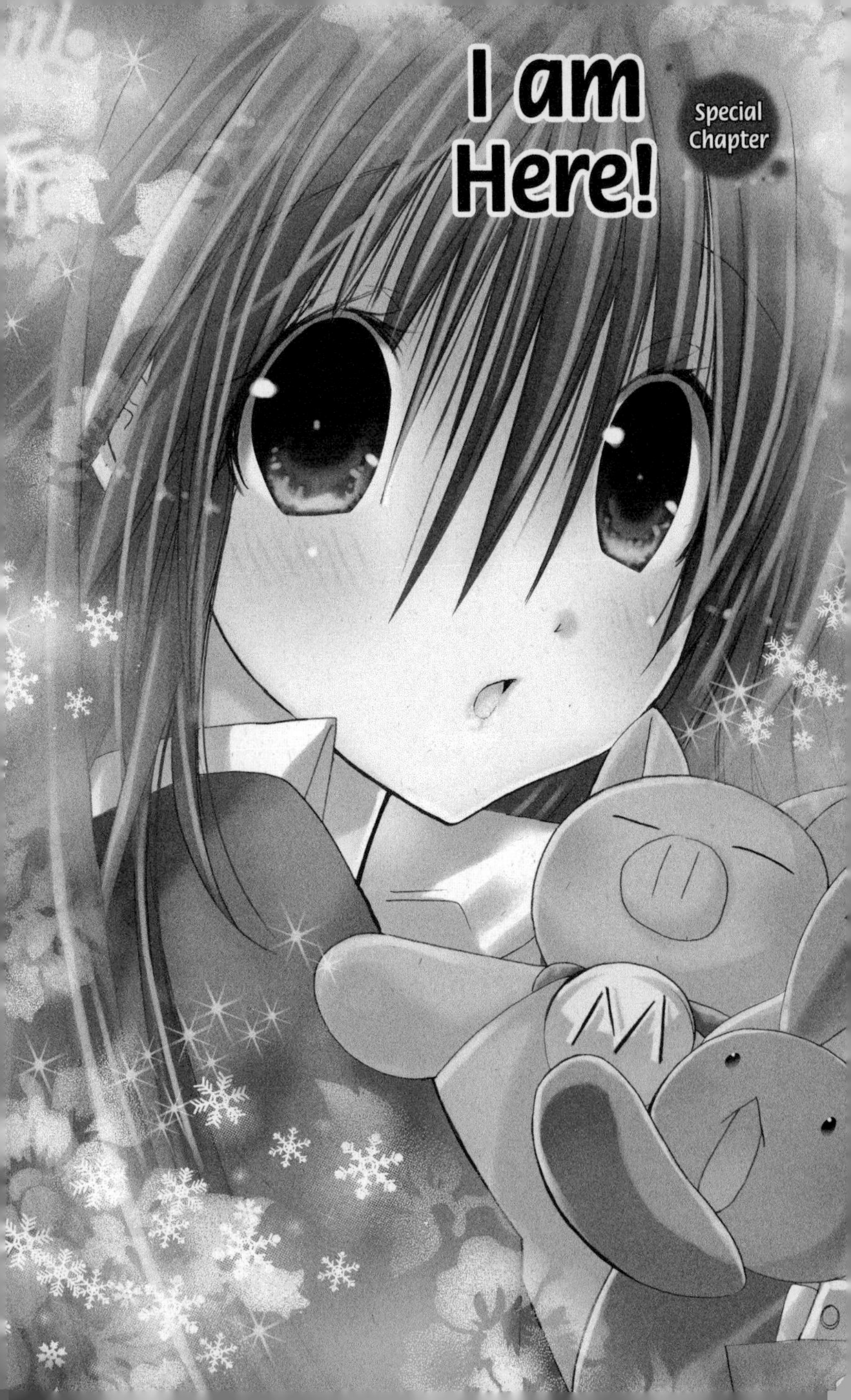
I am Here!
Special Chapter

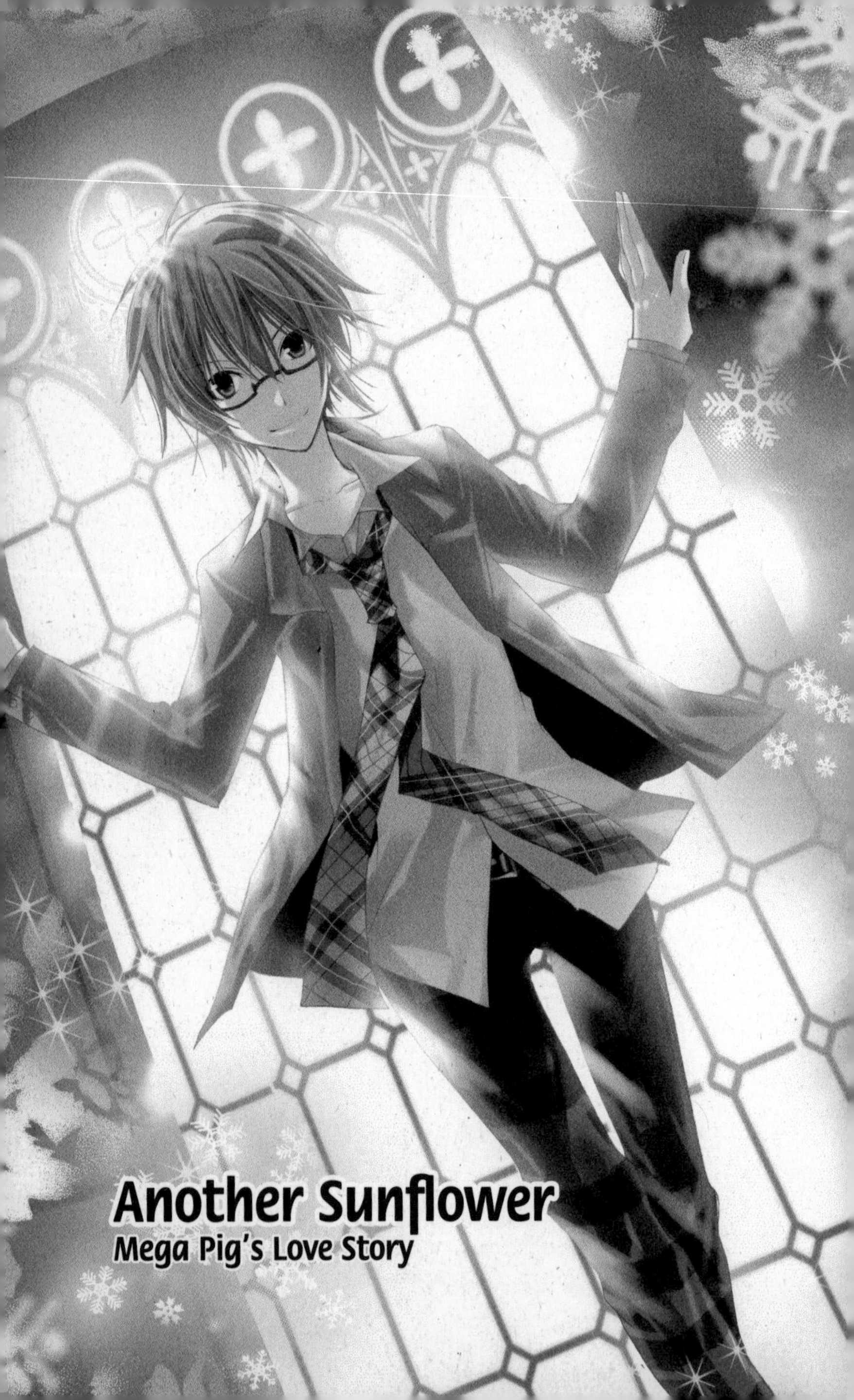
Another Sunflower
Mega Pig's Love Story

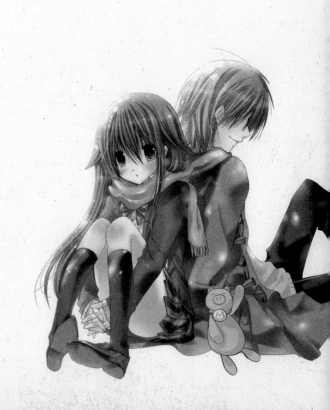

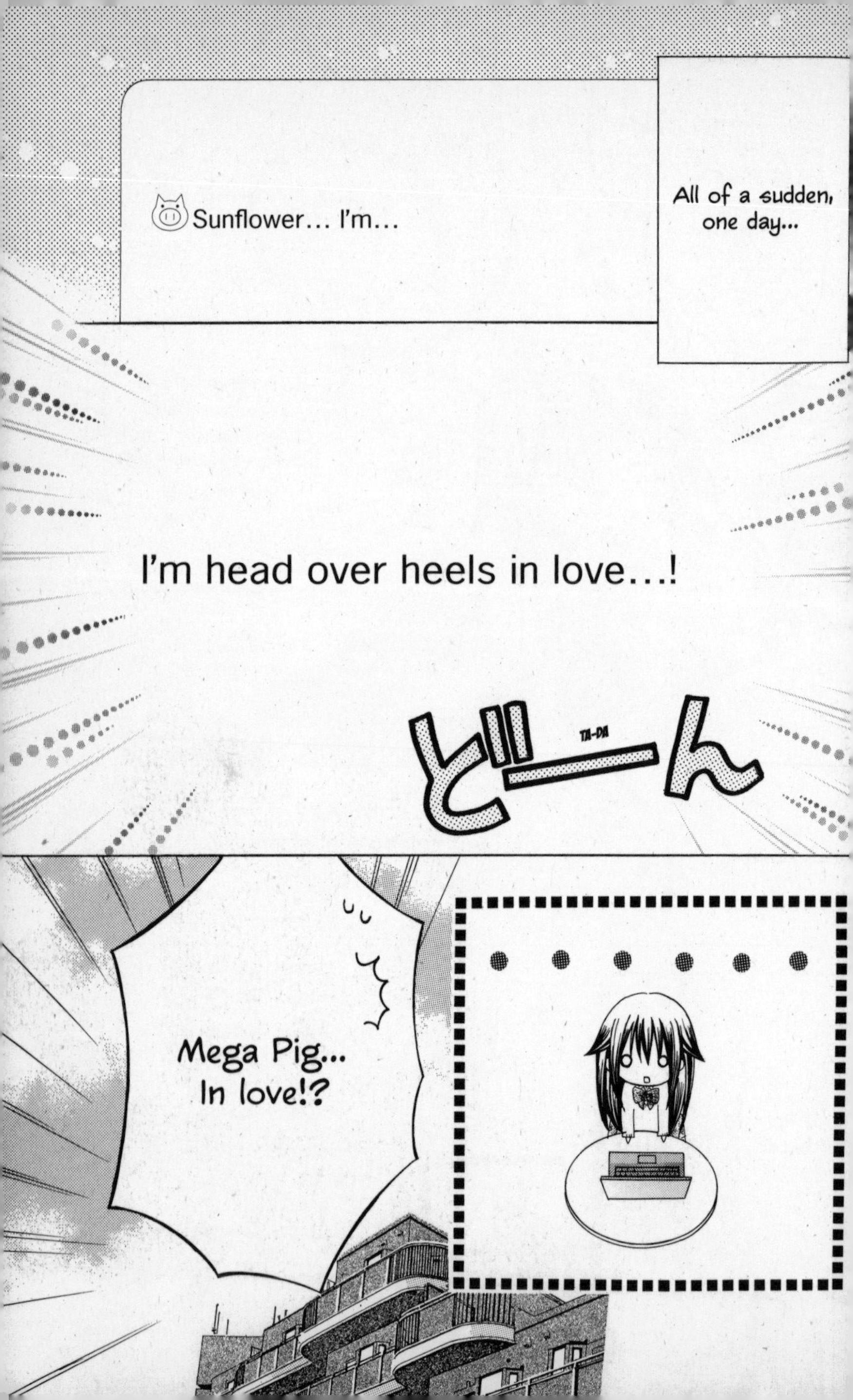
All of a sudden, one day...
Sunflower… I'm…
I'm head over heels in love…!
どーん
TA-DA
Mega Pig... In love!?

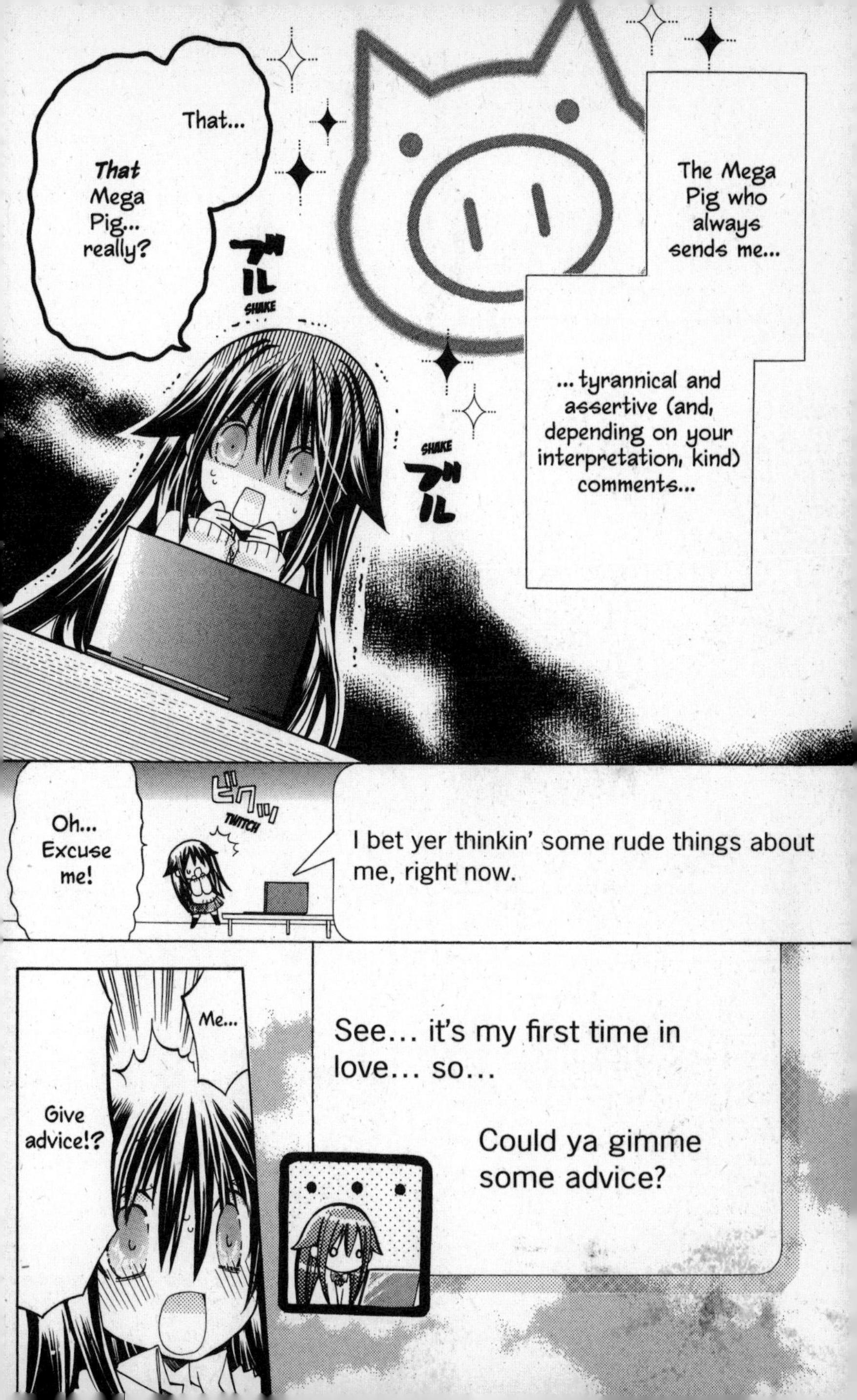
The Mega Pig who always sends me...
...tyrannical and assertive (and, depending on your interpretation, kind) comments...
SHAKE
SHAKE
That...
That Mega Pig... really?
I bet yer thinkin' some rude things about me, right now.
TWITCH
Oh... Excuse me!
See... it's my first time in love... so...
Could ya gimme some advice?
Me...
Give advice!?

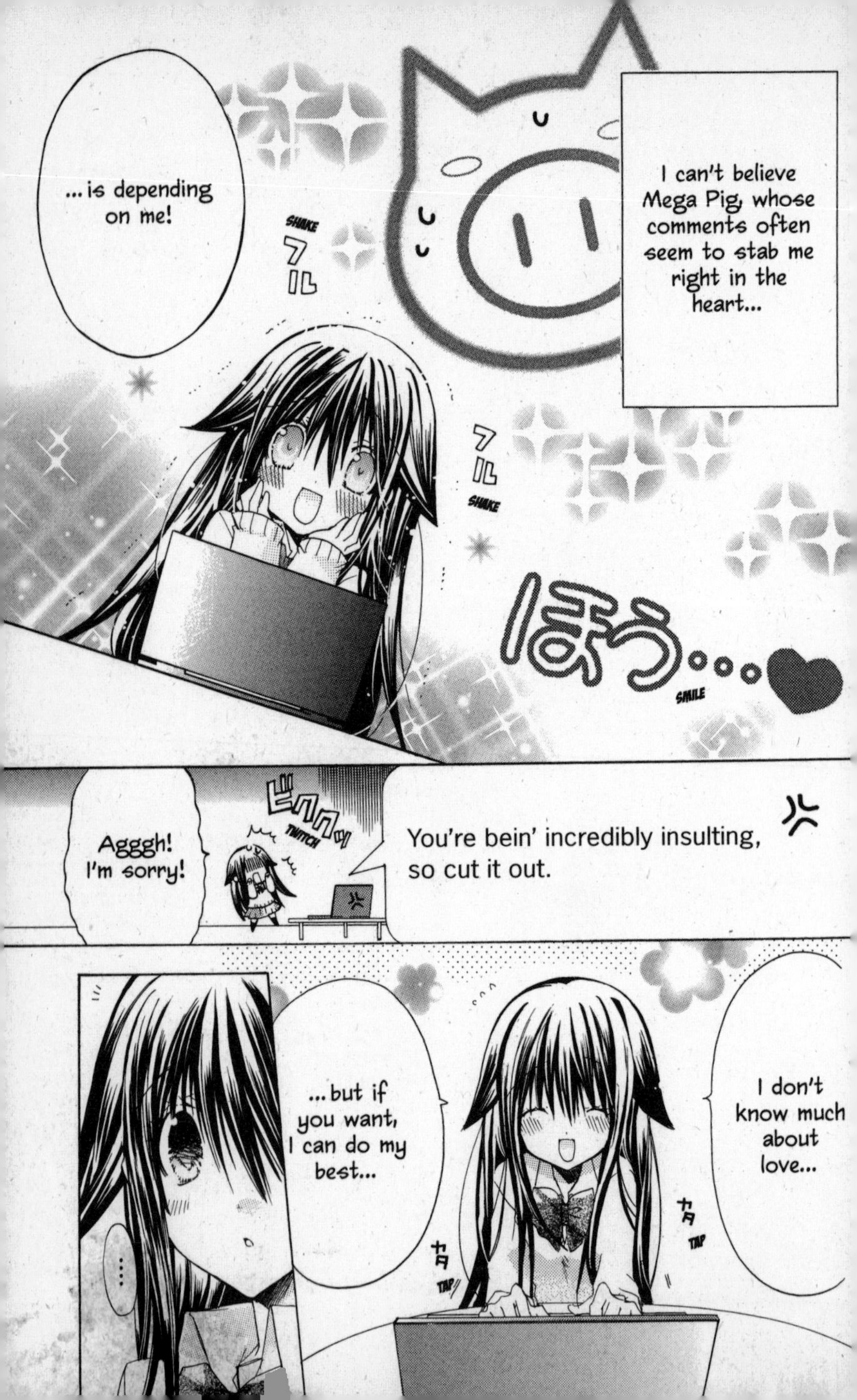
I can't believe Mega Pig, whose comments often seem to stab me right in the heart...
...is depending on me!
SHAKE
フル
フル
SHAKE
ほう…
SMILE
You're bein' incredibly insulting, so cut it out.
TWITCH
Agggh! I'm sorry!
I don't know much about love...
TAP
TAP
...but if you want, I can do my best...
....

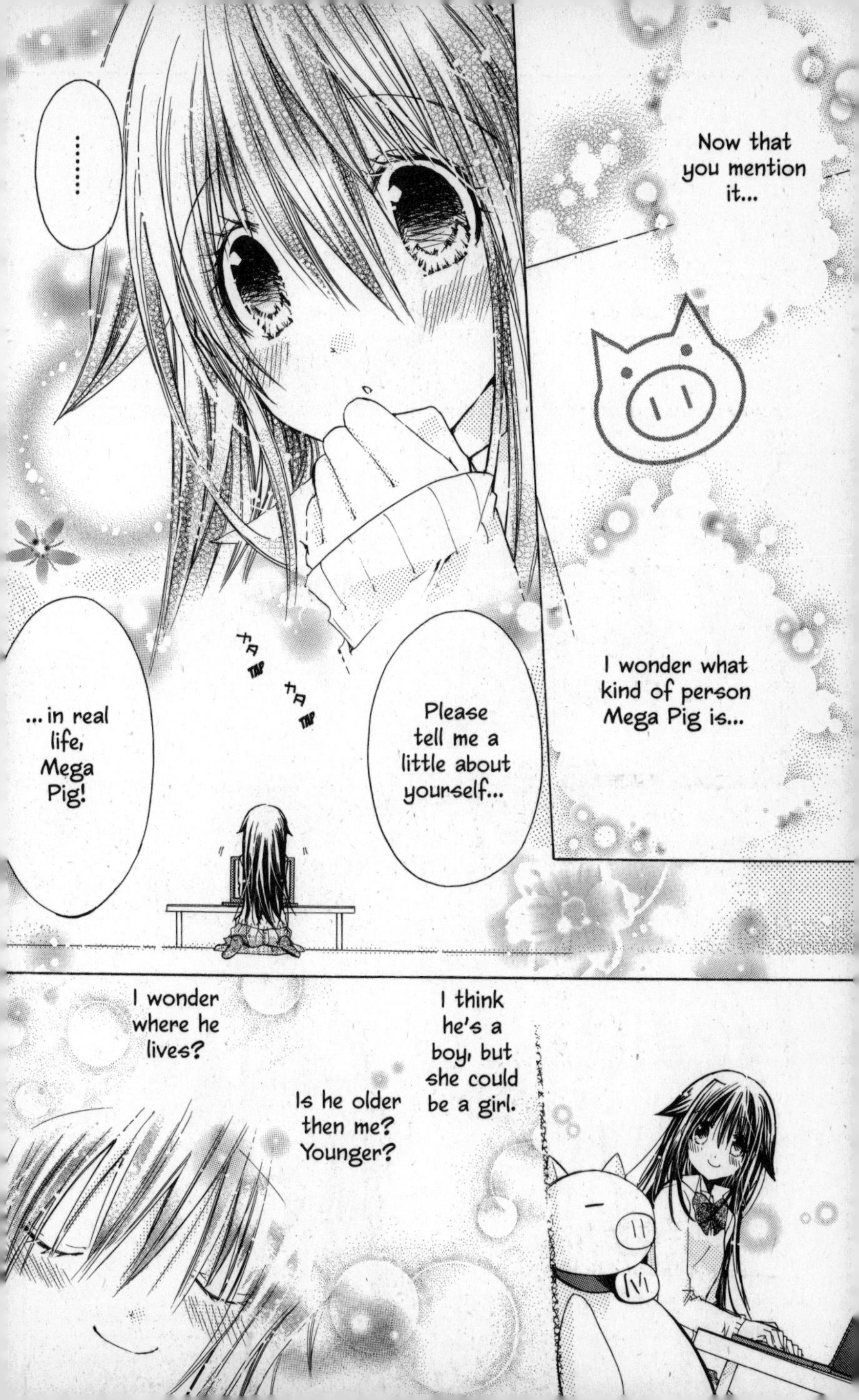
Now that you mention it...
I wonder what kind of person Mega Pig is...
......
Please tell me a little about yourself...
TAP
TAP
...in real life, Mega Pig!
I think he's a boy, but she could be a girl.
I wonder where he lives?
Is he older then me? Younger?

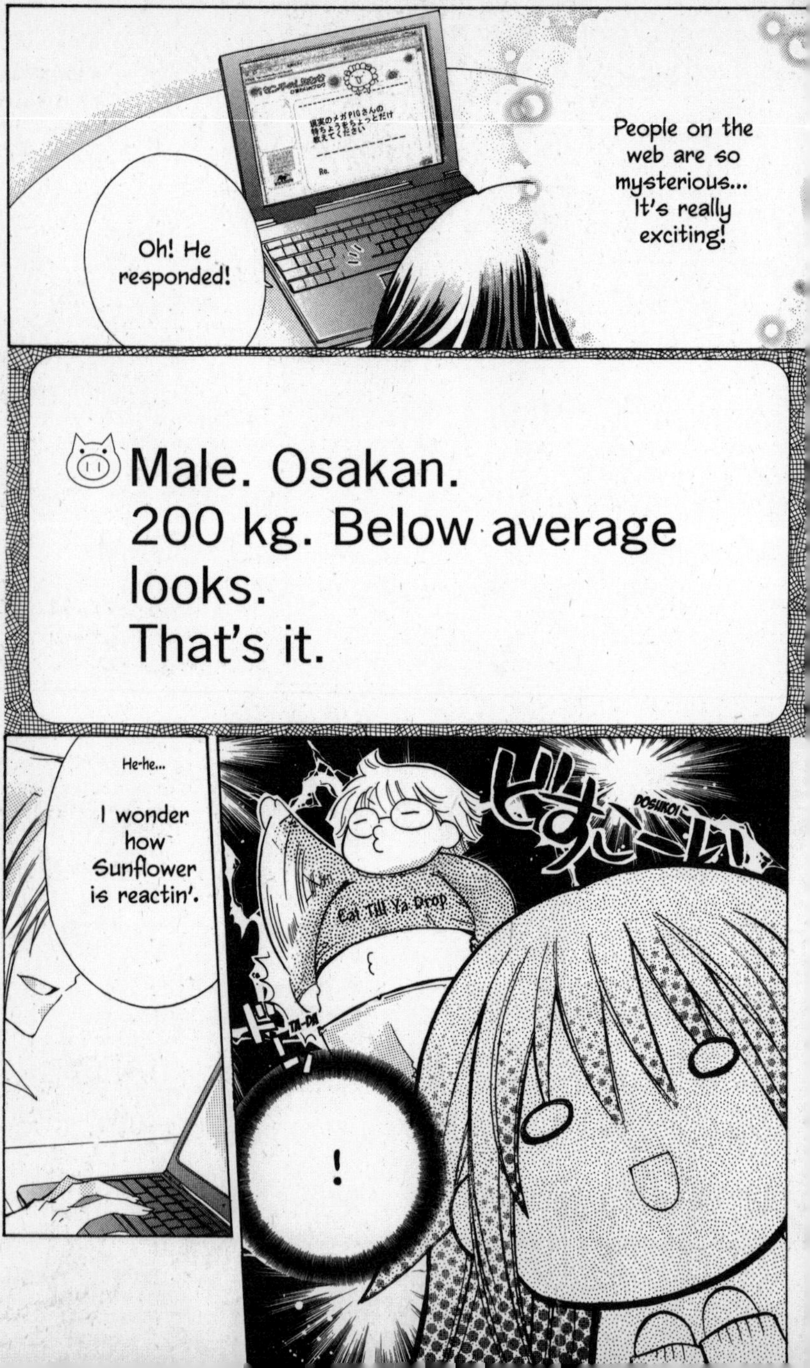
People on the web are so mysterious... It's really exciting!
Oh! He responded!
Male. Osakan. 200 kg. Below average looks. That's it.
DOSUKOI
Eat Till Ya Drop
TA-DA
!
He-he...
I wonder how Sunflower is reactin'.

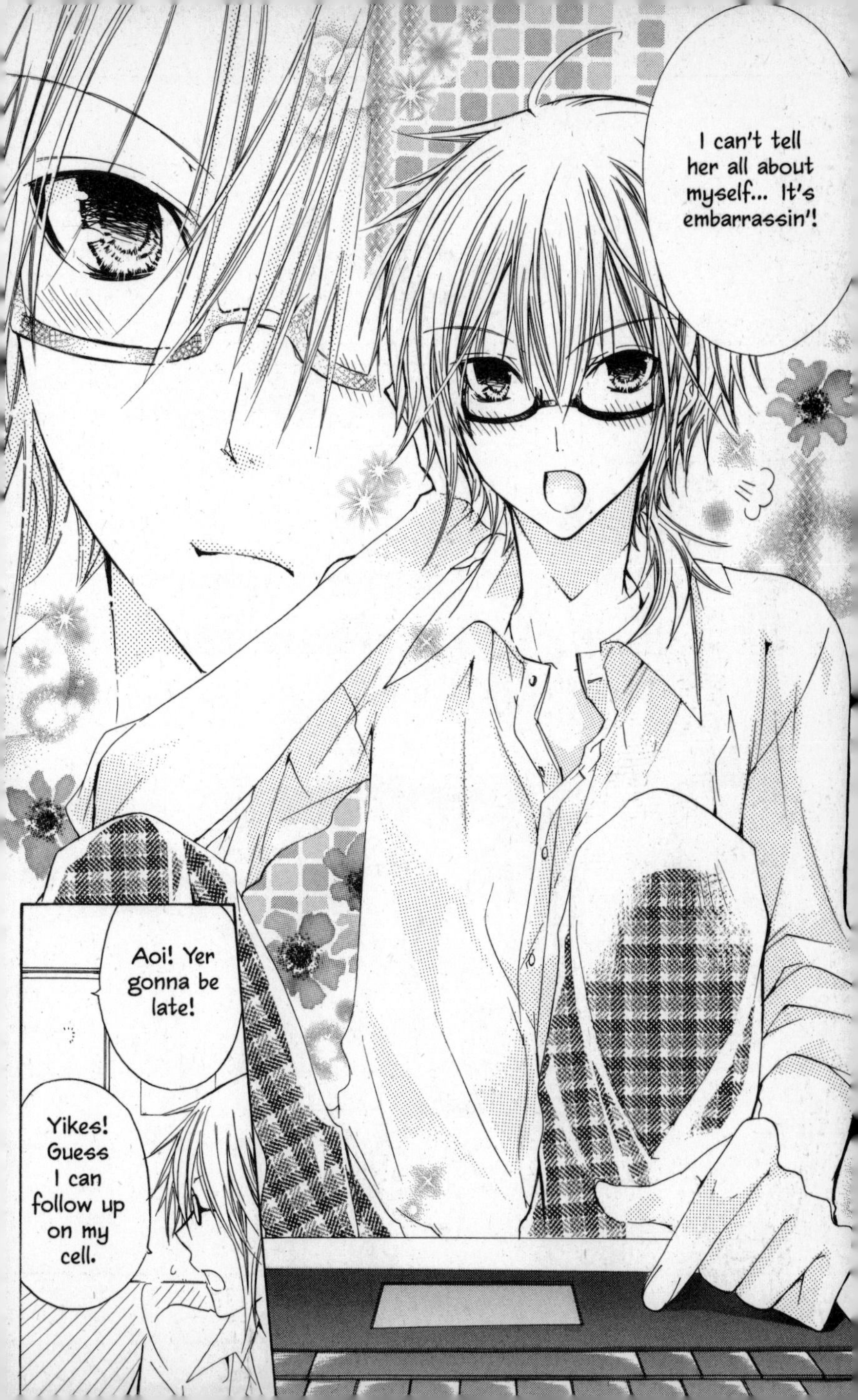
I can't tell her all about myself... It's embarrassin'!
Aoi! Yer gonna be late!
Yikes! Guess I can follow up on my cell.

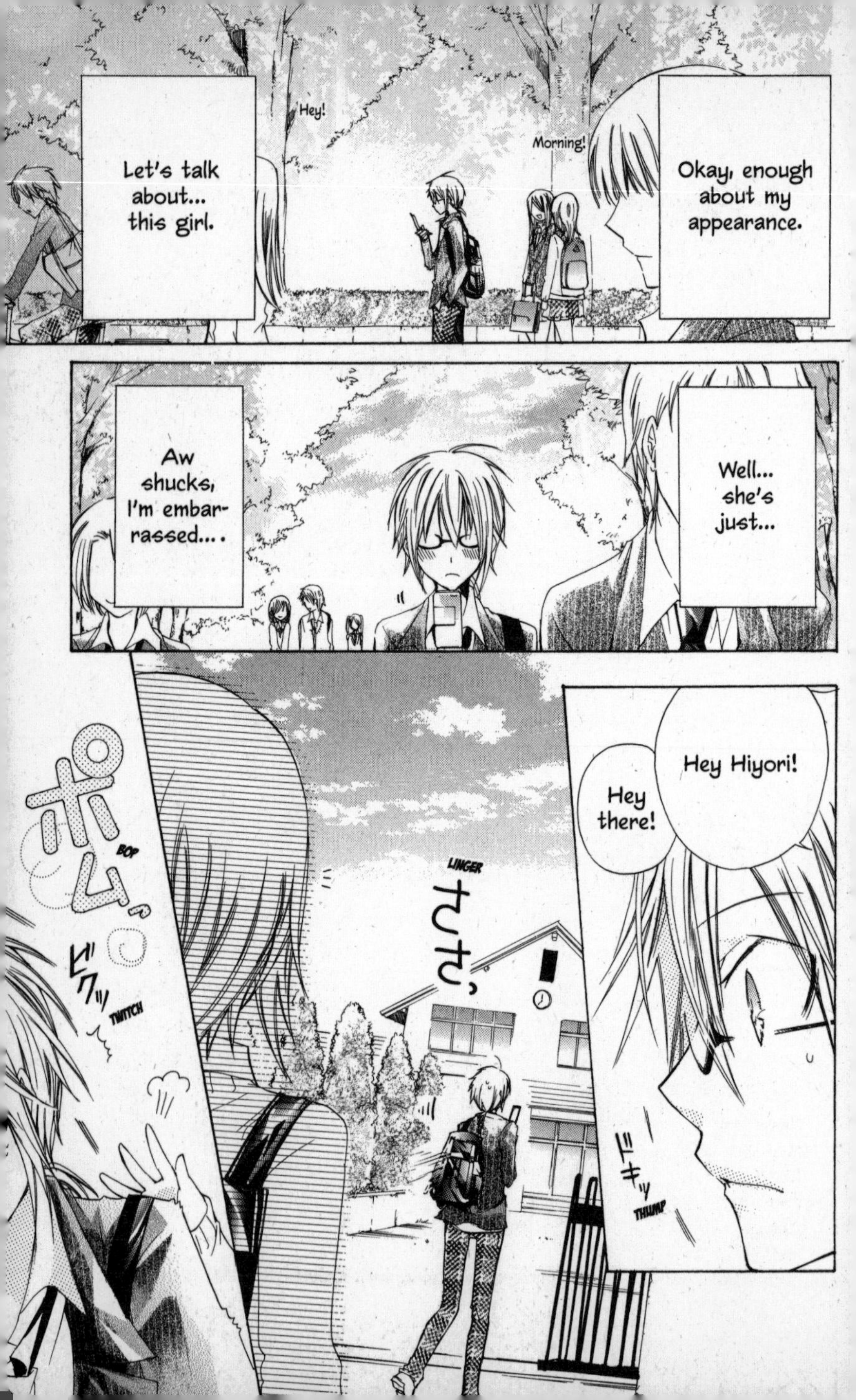
Okay, enough about my appearance.
Morning!
Hey!
Let's talk about... this girl.
Well... she's just...
Aw shucks, I'm embarrassed....
Hey Hiyori!
Hey there!
ドキッ
THUMP
LINGER
ポム
BOP
ビクッ
TWITCH

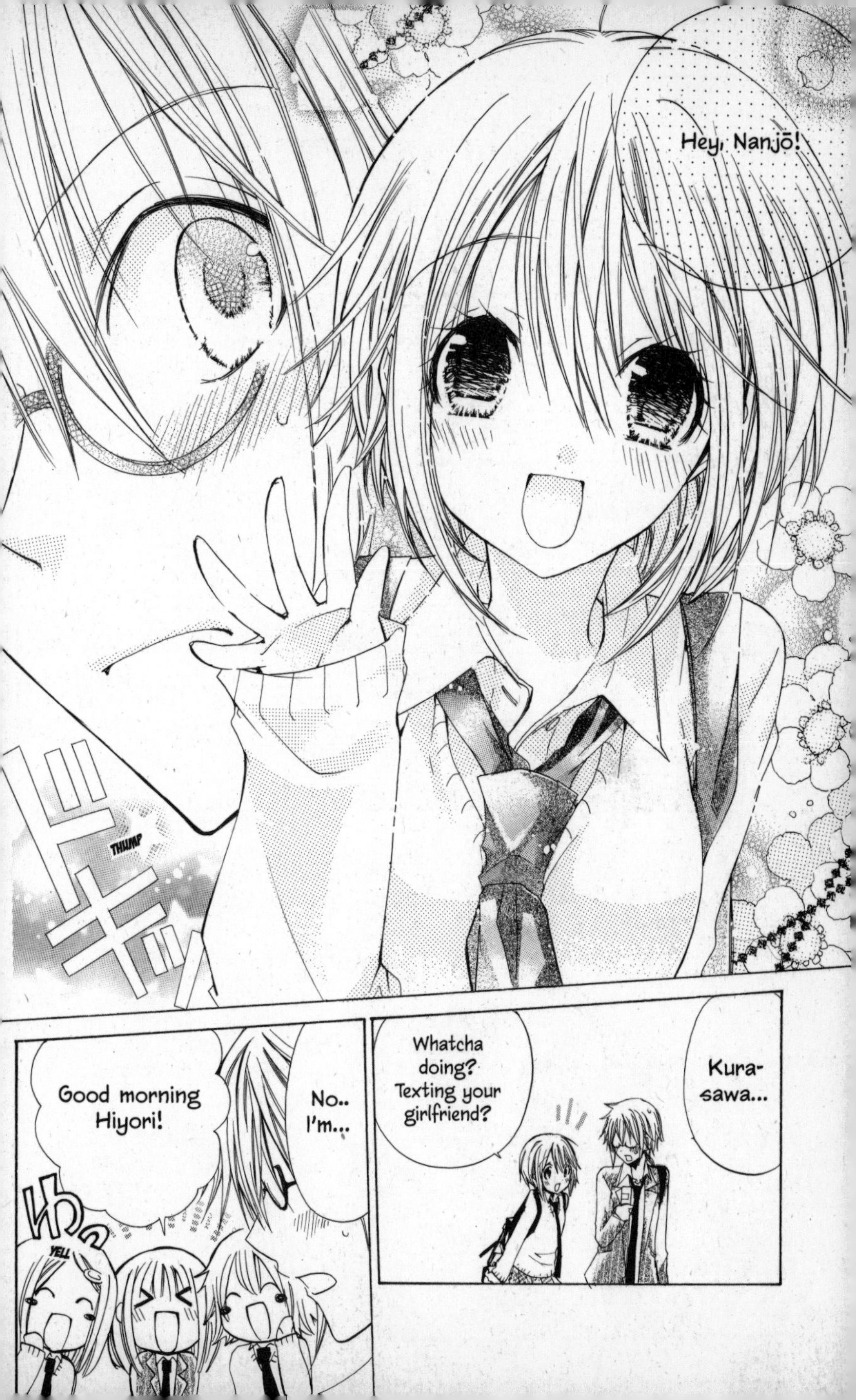
Hey, Nanjō!
THUMP
Kura-sawa...
Whatcha doing? Texting your girlfriend?
No.. I'm...
Good morning Hiyori!
YELL

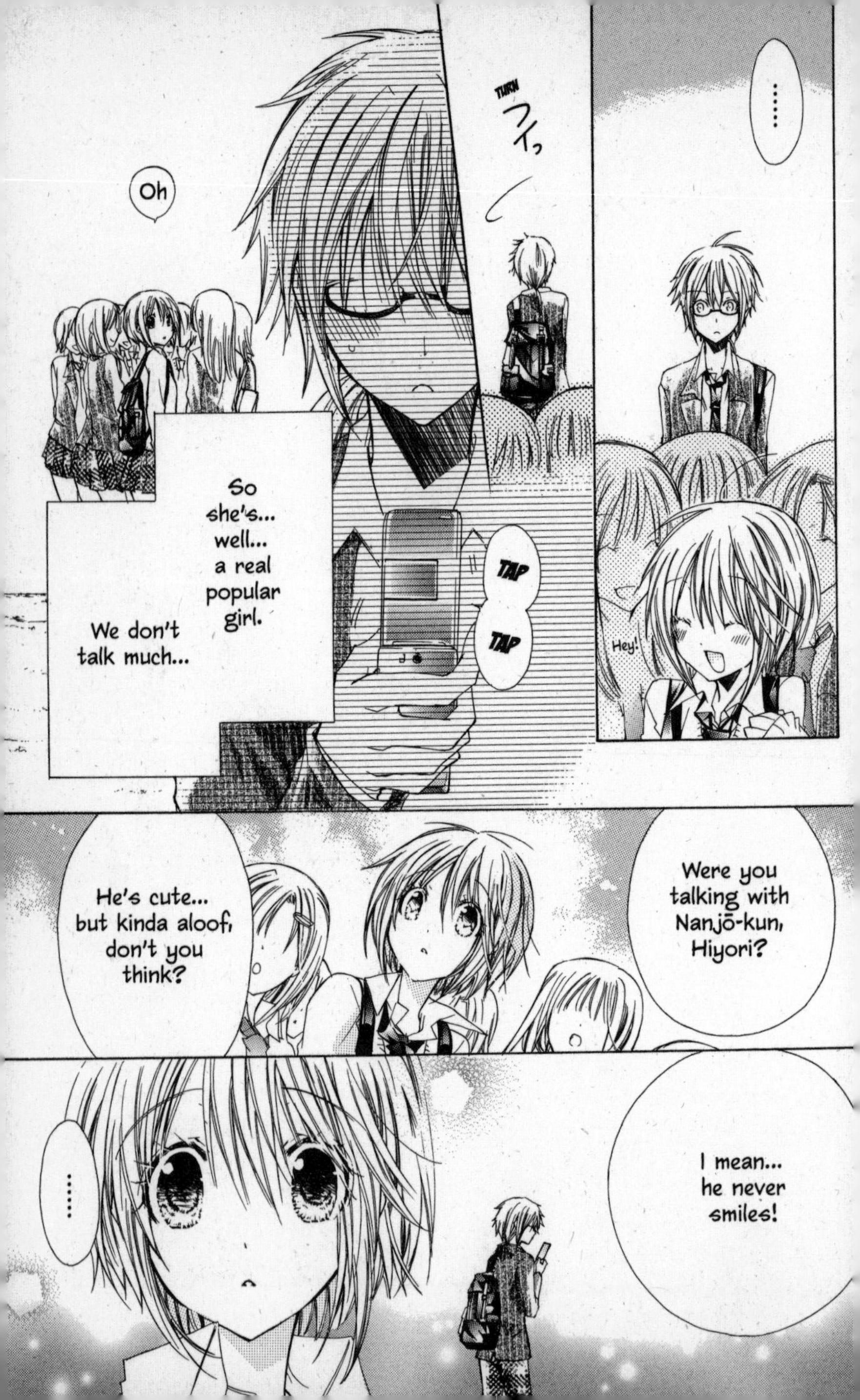

......
Hey!
TURN
フイッ
TAP
TAP
Oh
So she's... well... a real popular girl.
We don't talk much...
Were you talking with Nanjō-kun, Hiyori?
He's cute... but kinda aloof, don't you think?
I mean... he never smiles!
......

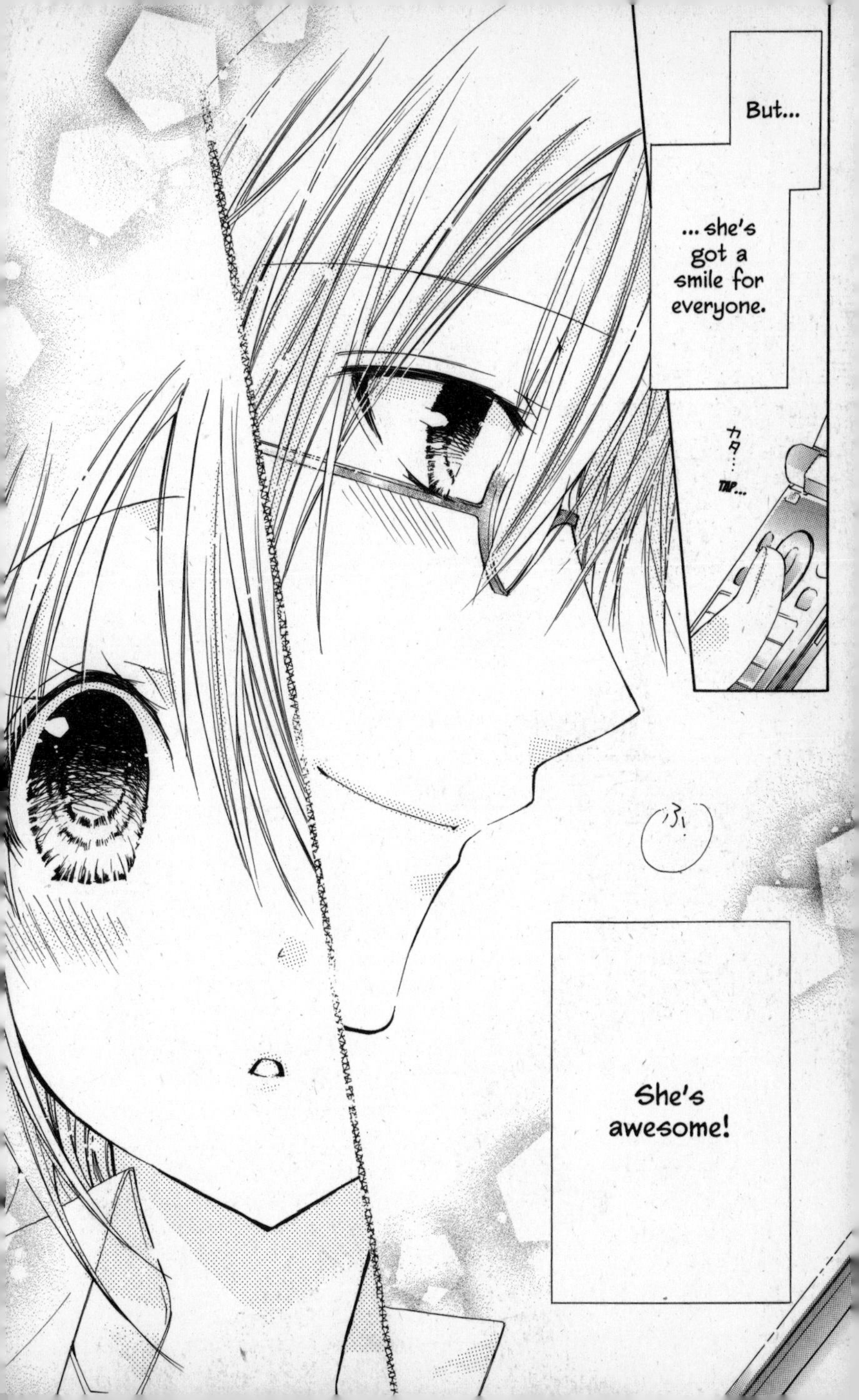
But...
... she's got a smile for everyone.
カタ…
TAP...
ふ
She's awesome!

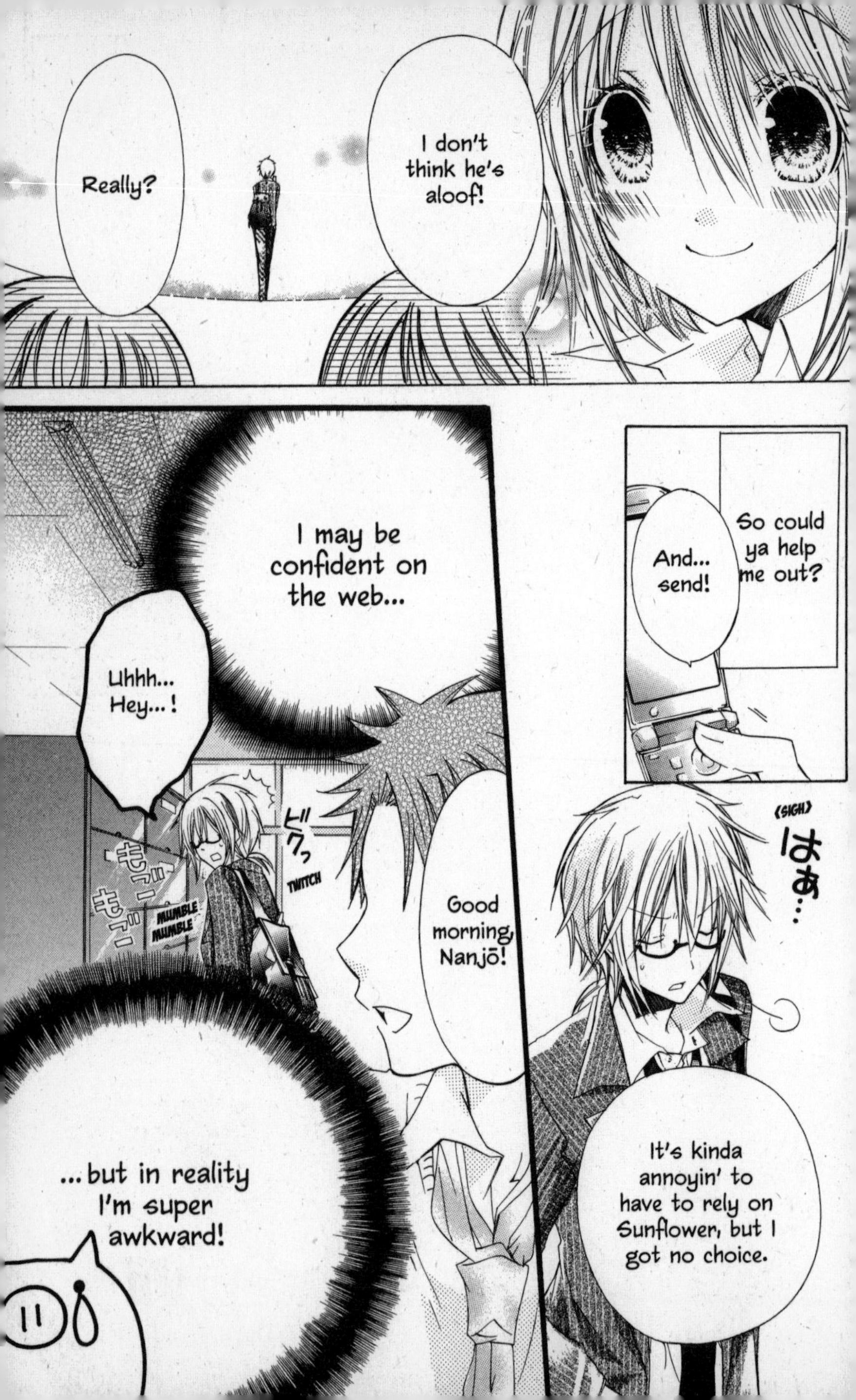
I don't think he's aloof!
Really?
So could ya help me out?
And... send!
(SIGH)
はあ…
It's kinda annoyin' to have to rely on Sunflower, but I got no choice.
I may be confident on the web...
Good morning, Nanjō!
ビクッ
TWITCH
Uhhh... Hey...!
もごーもごー
MUMBLE MUMBLE
...but in reality I'm super awkward!
11

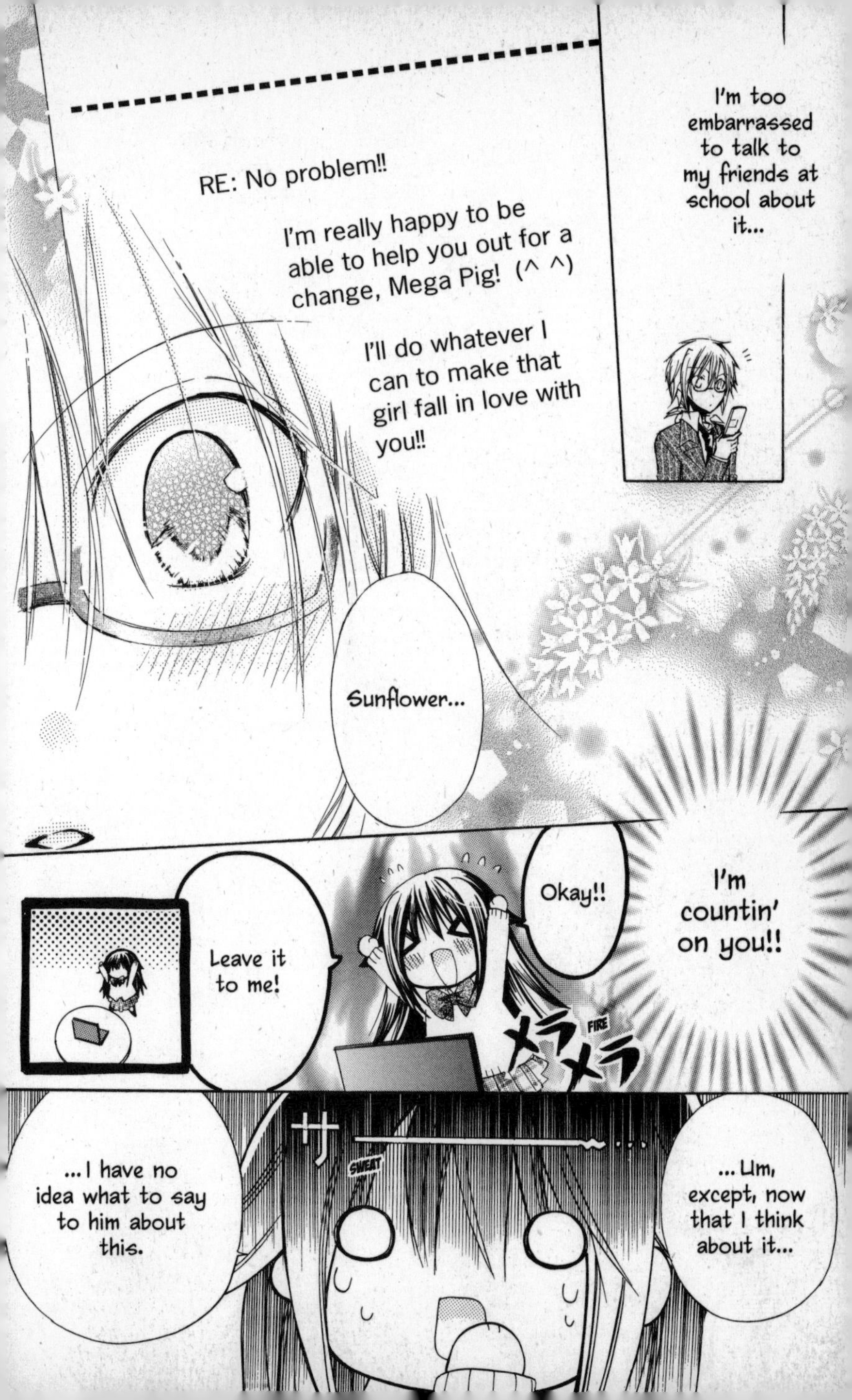
I'm too embarrassed to talk to my friends at school about it...
RE: No problem!!
I'm really happy to be able to help you out for a change, Mega Pig! (^ ^)
I'll do whatever I can to make that girl fall in love with you!!
Sunflower...
I'm countin' on you!!
Okay!!
FIRE
Leave it to me!
...Um, except, now that I think about it...
SWEAT
...I have no idea what to say to him about this.

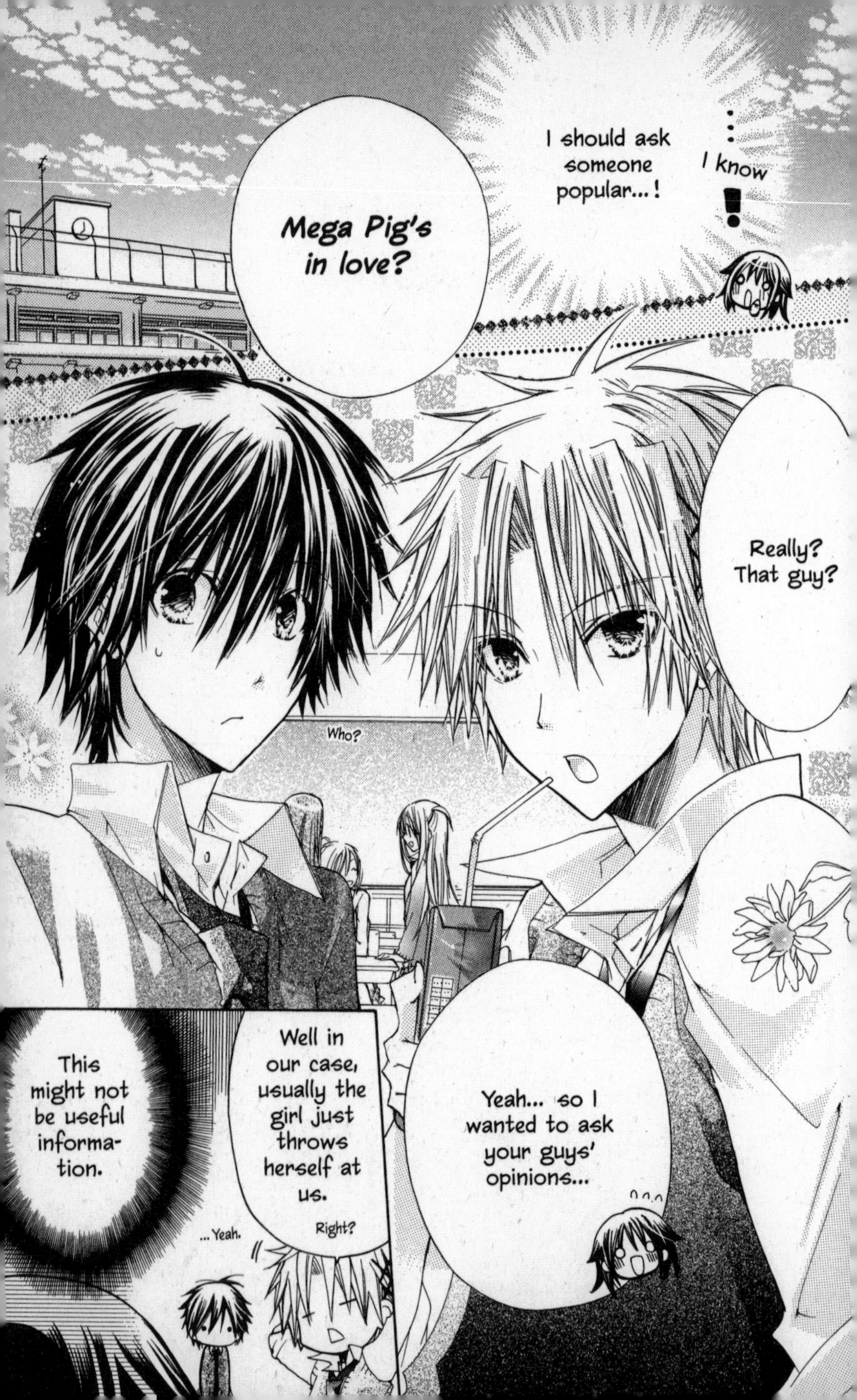

I know!
I should ask someone popular...!
Mega Pig's in love?
Really? That guy?
Who?
Yeah... so I wanted to ask your guys' opinions...
Well in our case, usually the girl just throws herself at us.
Right?
... Yeah.
This might not be useful information.

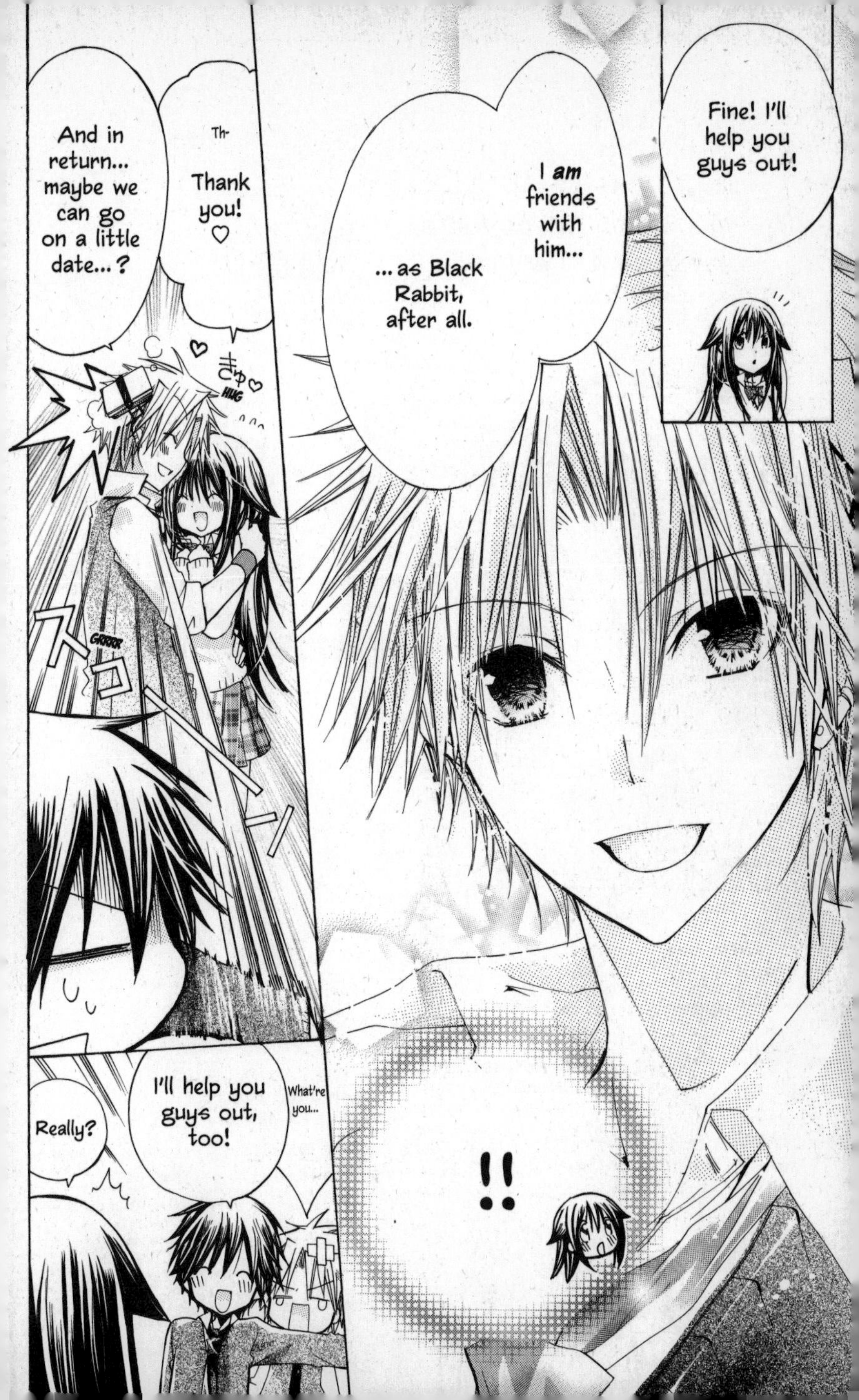
Fine! I'll help you guys out!
I *am* friends with him...
...as Black Rabbit, after all.
!!
Th-
Thank you! ♡
And in return... maybe we can go on a little date...?
きゅ HUG
GRRRR
What're you...
I'll help you guys out, too!
Really?

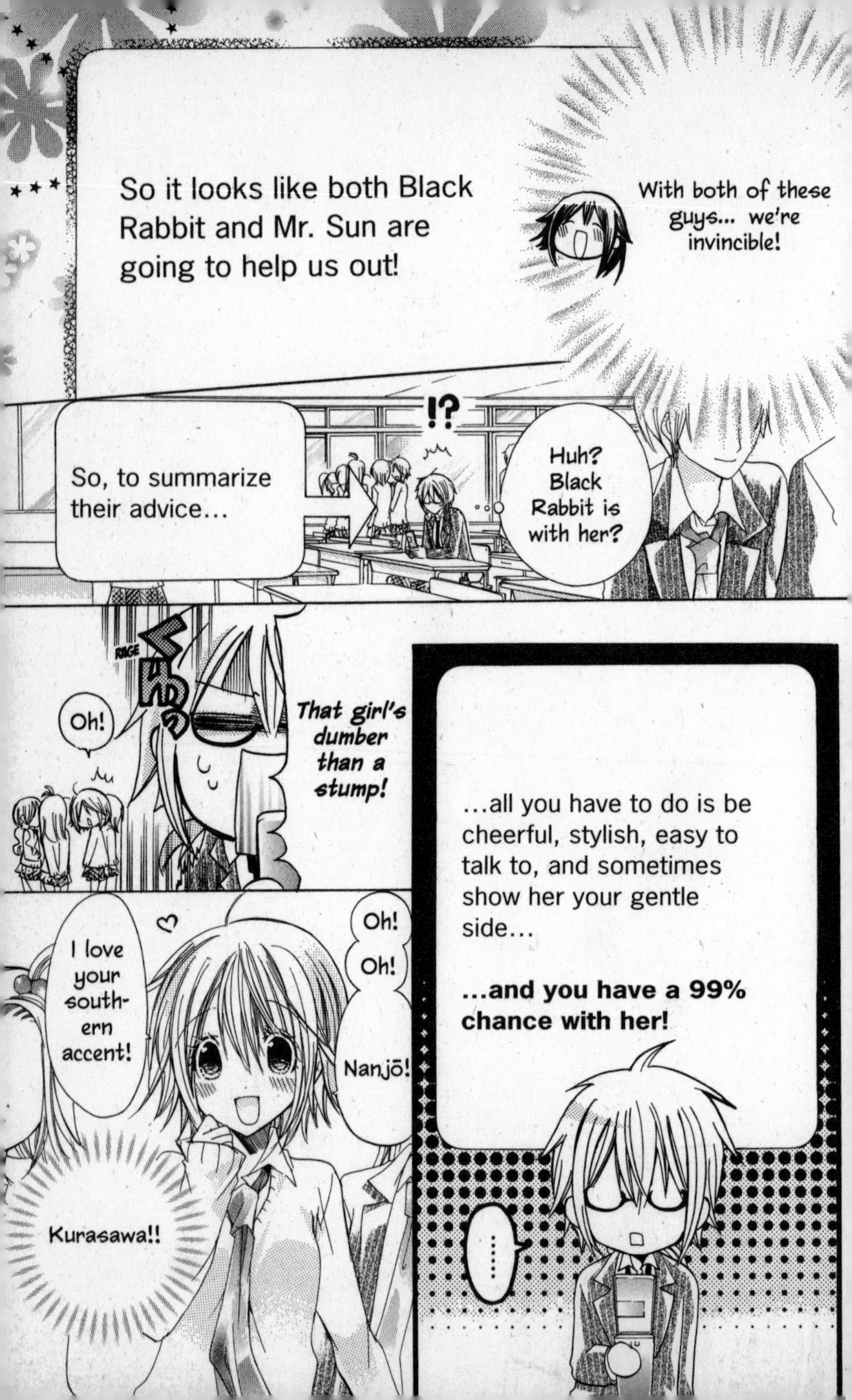
With both of these guys... we're invincible!
So it looks like both Black Rabbit and Mr. Sun are going to help us out!
!?
Huh? Black Rabbit is with her?
So, to summarize their advice...
...all you have to do is be cheerful, stylish, easy to talk to, and sometimes show her your gentle side...
...and you have a 99% chance with her!
......
That girl's dumber than a stump!
RAGE
Oh!
Oh!
Oh!
Nanjō!
I love your southern-ern accent!
Kurasawa!!

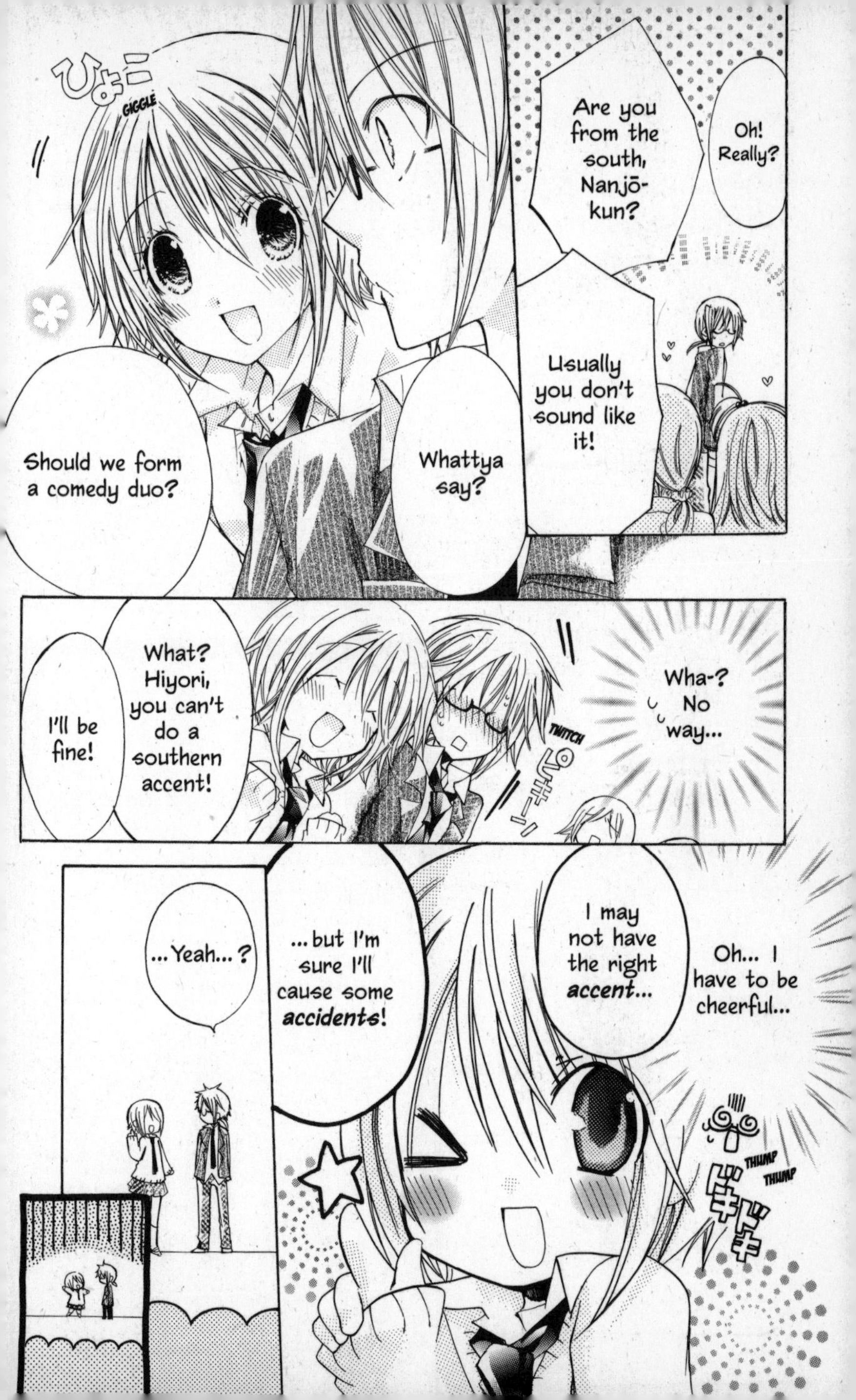
Oh! Really?
Are you from the south, Nanjō-kun?
Usually you don't sound like it!
ひょこ
GIGGLE
Whattya say?
Should we form a comedy duo?
Wha-? No way...
TWITCH
What? Hiyori, you can't do a southern accent!
I'll be fine!
Oh... I have to be cheerful...
I may not have the right **accent**...
THUMP THUMP
...but I'm sure I'll cause some **accidents**!
...Yeah...?

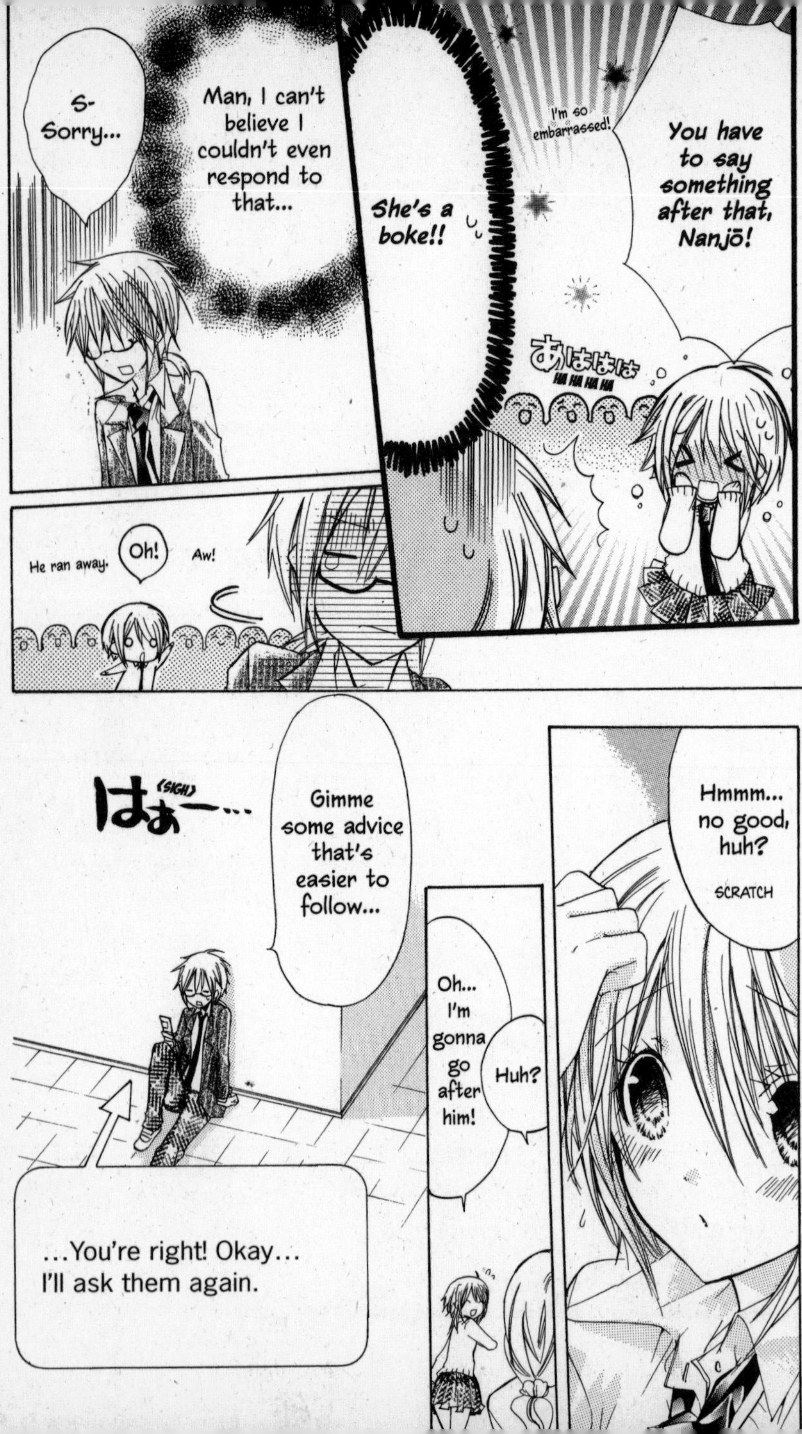
You have to say something after that, Nanjō!
I'm so embarrassed!
She's a boke!!
HA HA HA HA
Man, I can't believe I couldn't even respond to that...
S- Sorry...
Aw!
Oh!
He ran away.
Hmmm... no good, huh?
SCRATCH
Huh?
Oh... I'm gonna go after him!
Gimme some advice that's easier to follow...
(SIGH)
...You're right! Okay... I'll ask them again.

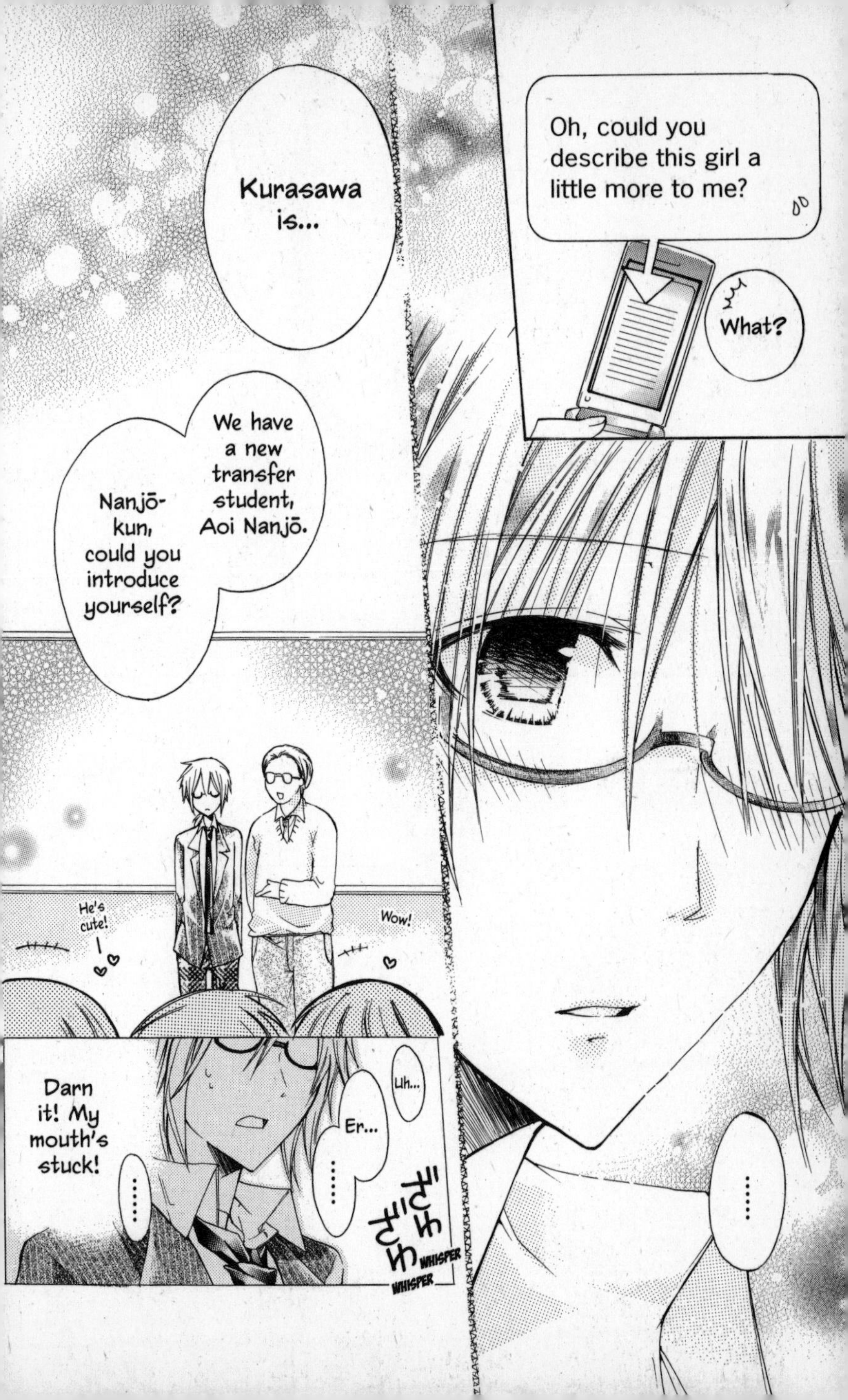
Oh, could you describe this girl a little more to me?
What?
......
Kurasawa is...
We have a new transfer student, Aoi Nanjō.
Nanjō-kun, could you introduce yourself?
Wow!
He's cute!
Uh...
Er...
......
ざわ ざわ WHISPER WHISPER
Darn it! My mouth's stuck!
......

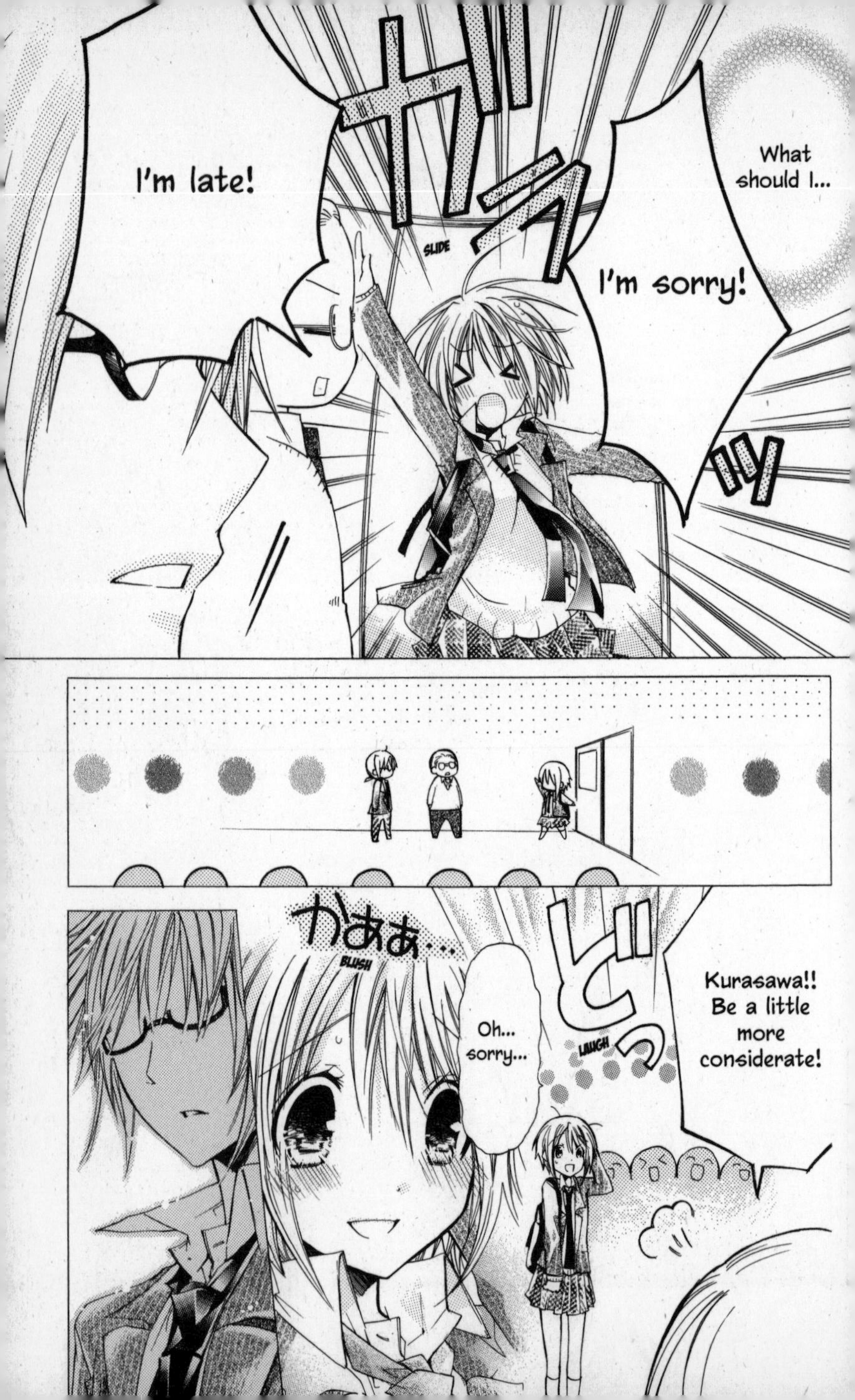
What should I...
I'm sorry!
SLIDE
I'm late!
Kurasawa!! Be a little more considerate!
どっ
LAUGH
Oh... sorry...
かあぁ...
BLUSH

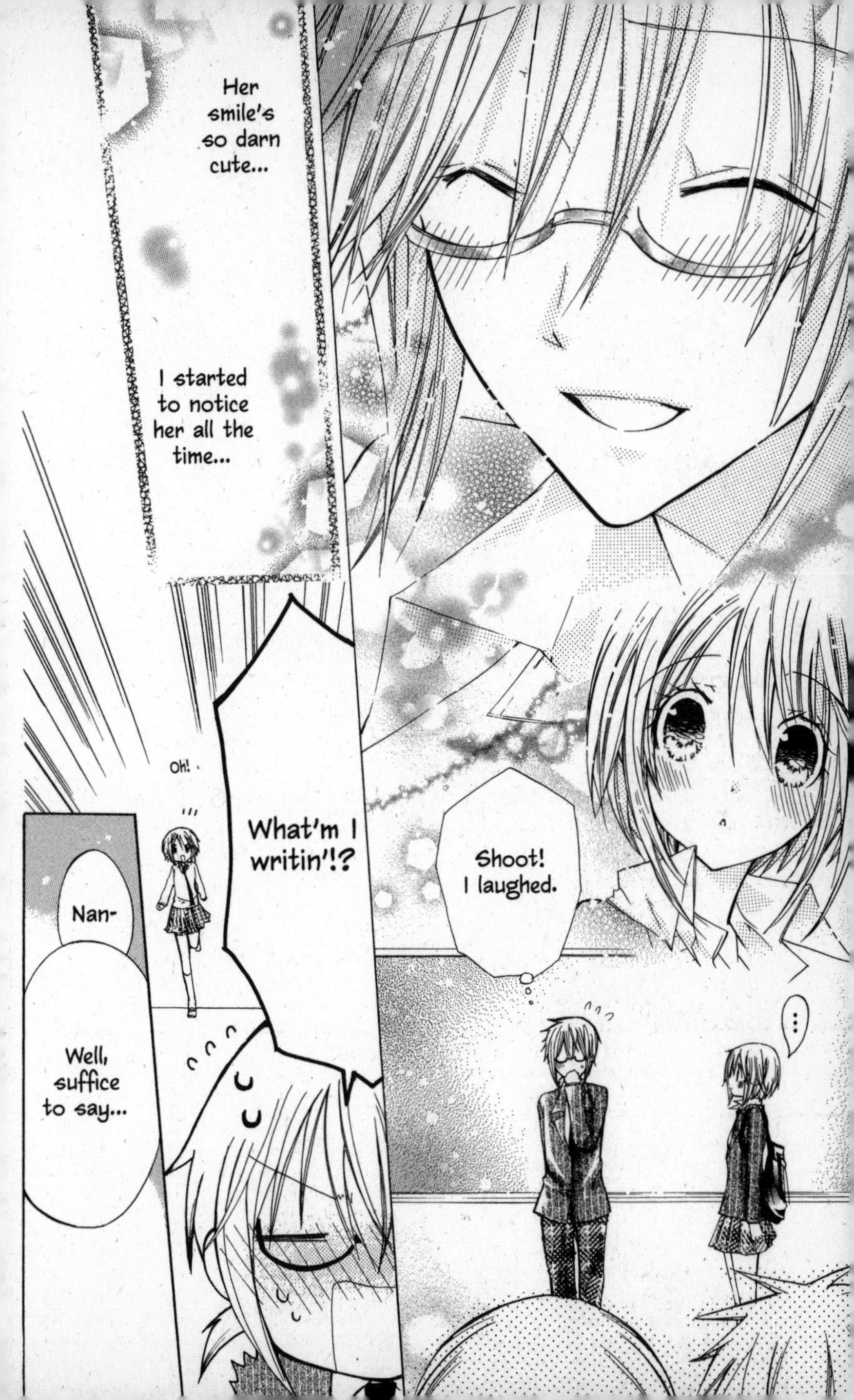
Her smile's so darn cute...
I started to notice her all the time...
Shoot! I laughed.
...
What'm I writin'!?
Oh!
Nan-
Well, suffice to say...

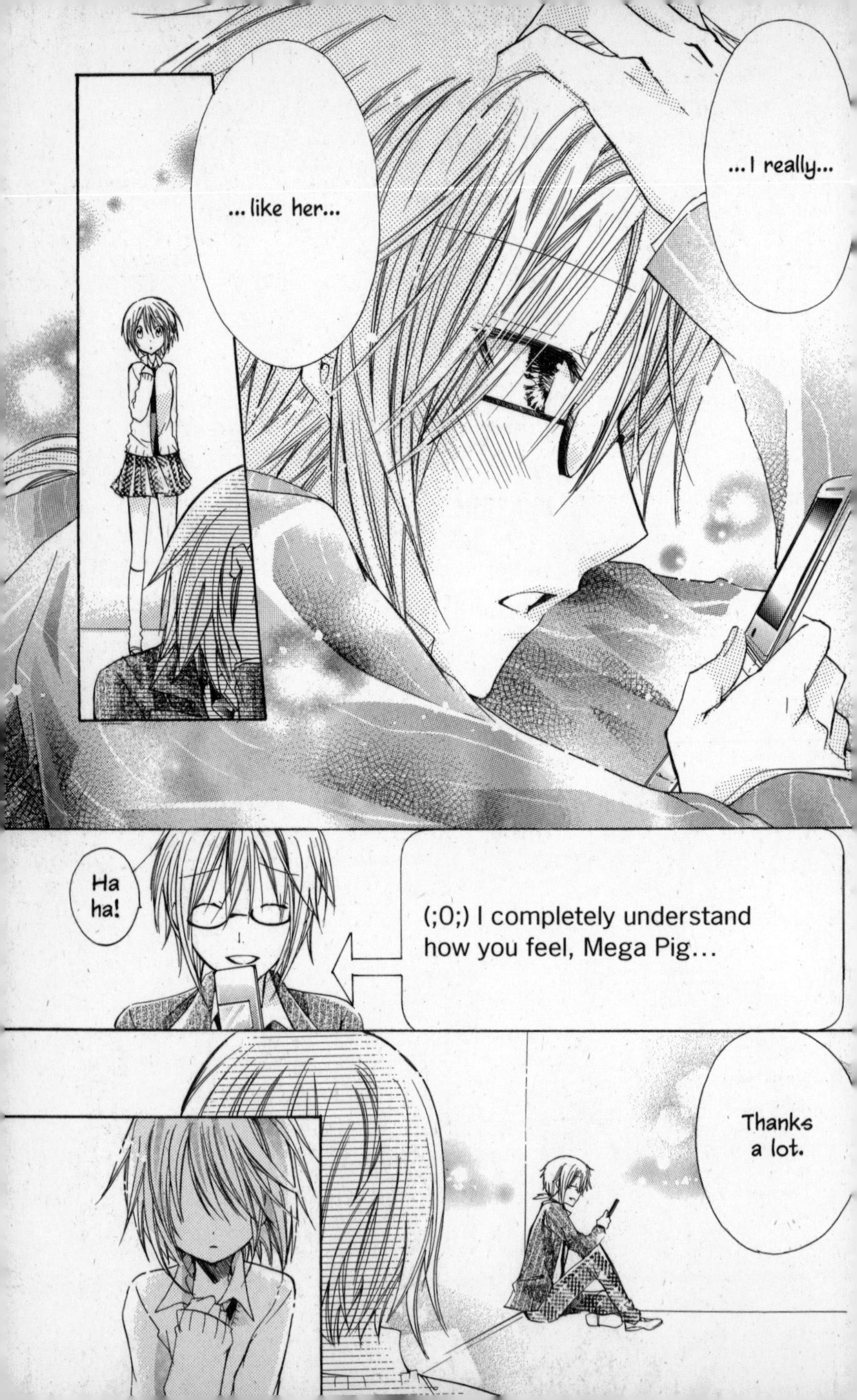
...I really...
...like her...
(;0;) I completely understand how you feel, Mega Pig...
Ha ha!
Thanks a lot.

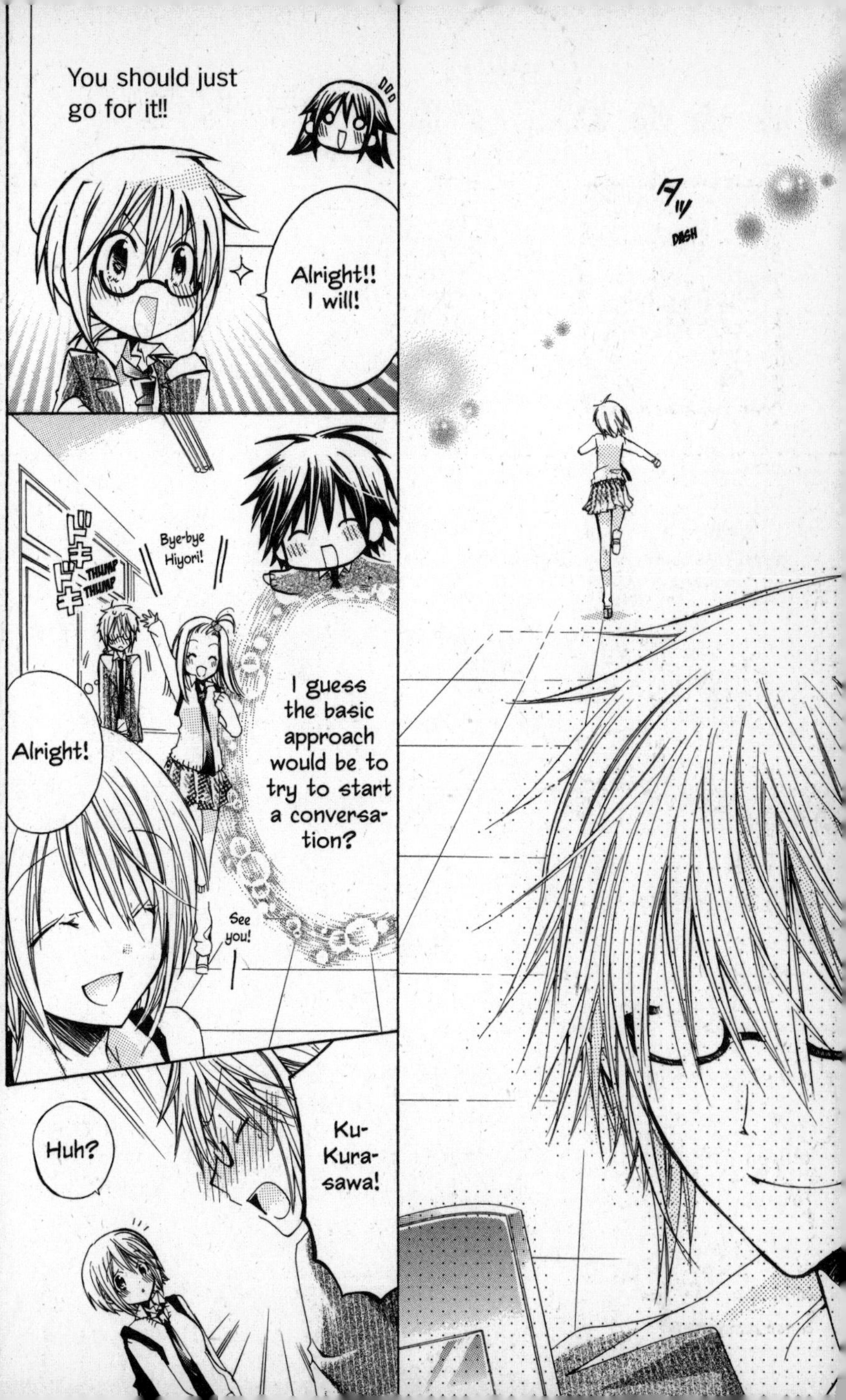
タッ
DASH
You should just go for it!!
Alright!! I will!
Bye-bye Hiyori!
ドキドキ
THUMP THUMP
I guess the basic approach would be to try to start a conversa-tion?
Alright!
See you!
Ku- Kura-sawa!
Huh?

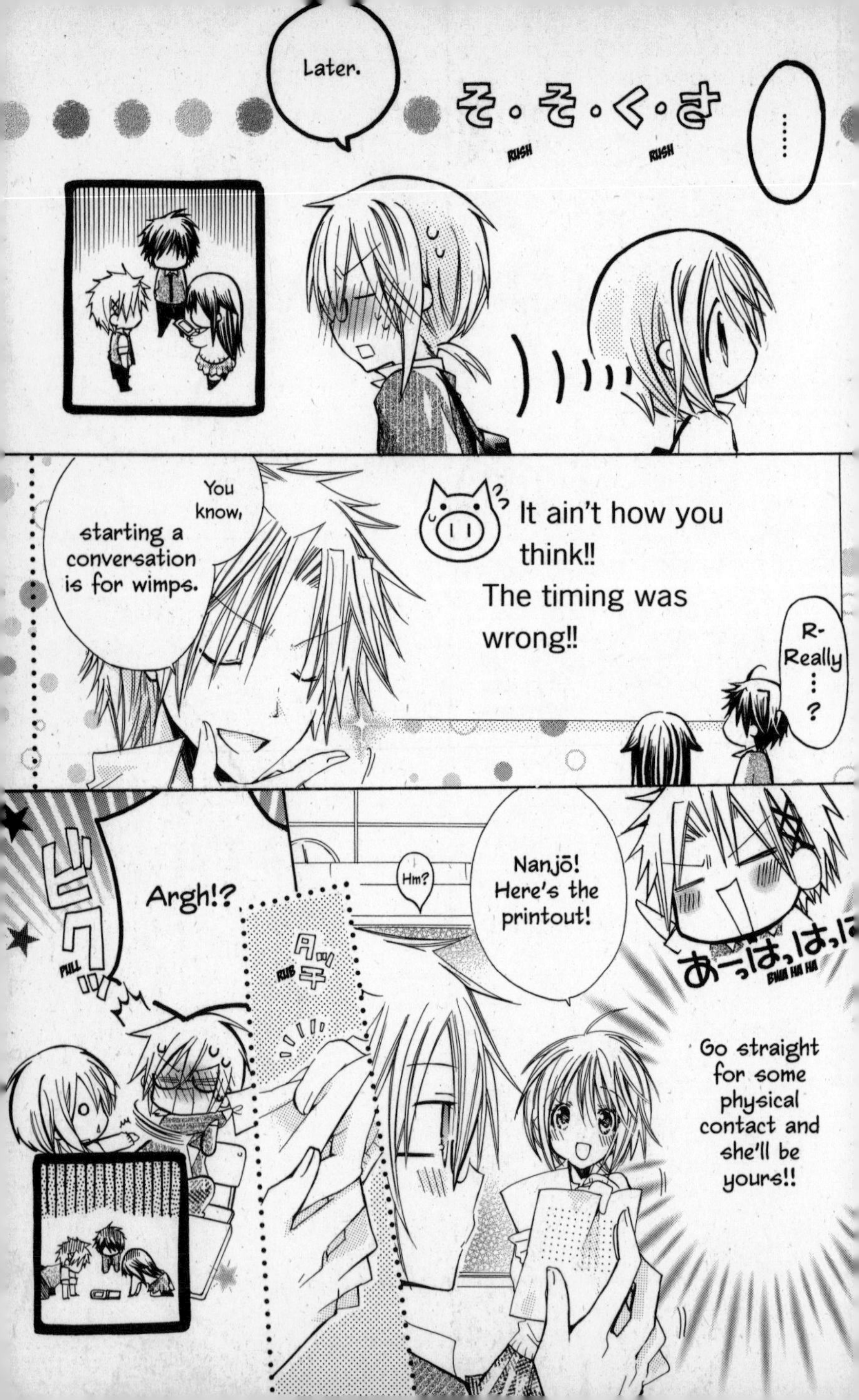
……
そ・そ・く・さ
RUSH
RUSH
Later.
R- Really…?
It ain't how you think!! The timing was wrong!!
You know, starting a conversation is for wimps.
あっはっはっ
BWA HA HA
Go straight for some physical contact and she'll be yours!!
Nanjō! Here's the printout!
Hm?
タッチ
RUB
Argh!?
ビクッ
PULL

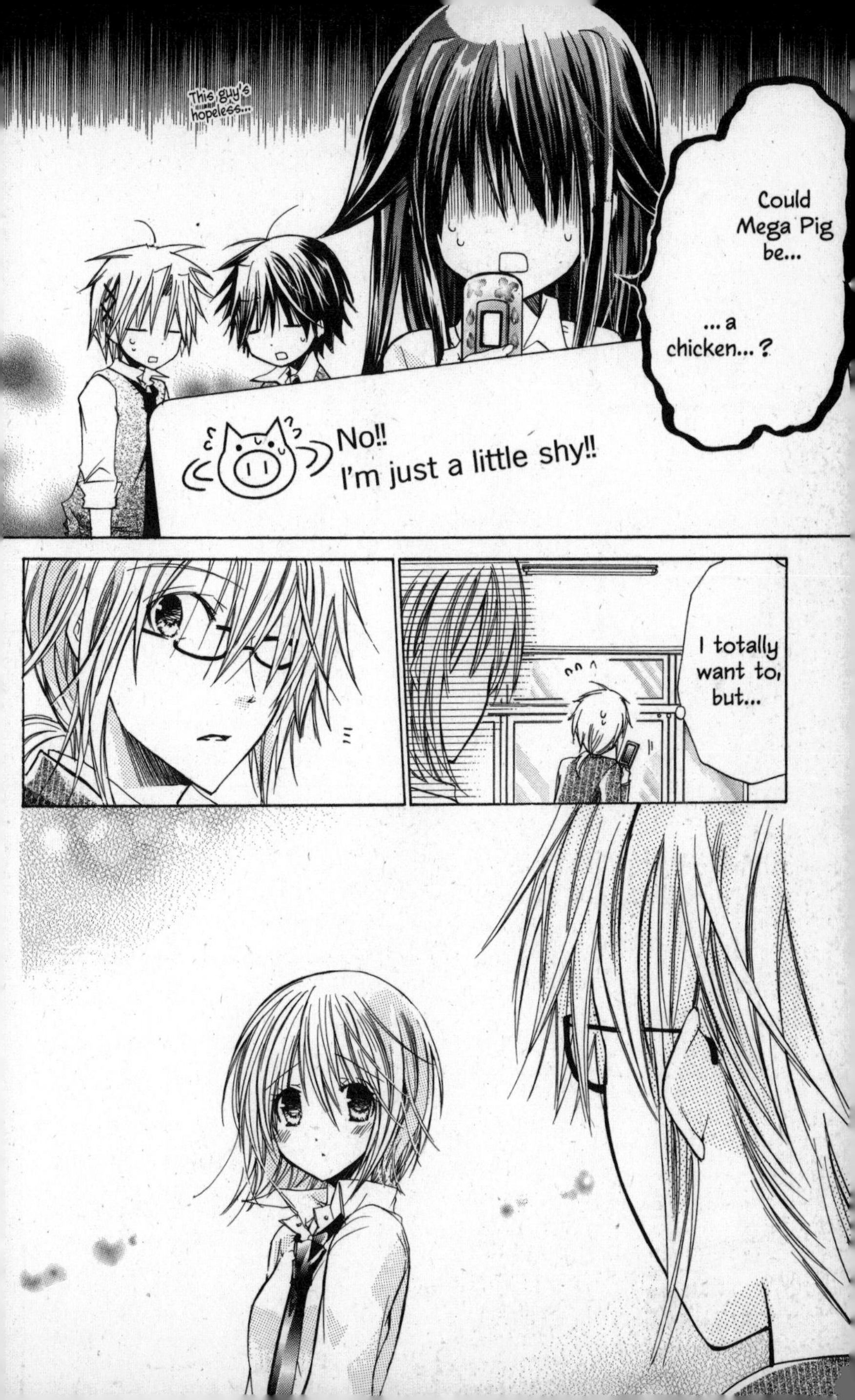
Could Mega Pig be...
... a chicken...?
This guy's hopeless...
No!! I'm just a little shy!!
I totally want to, but...

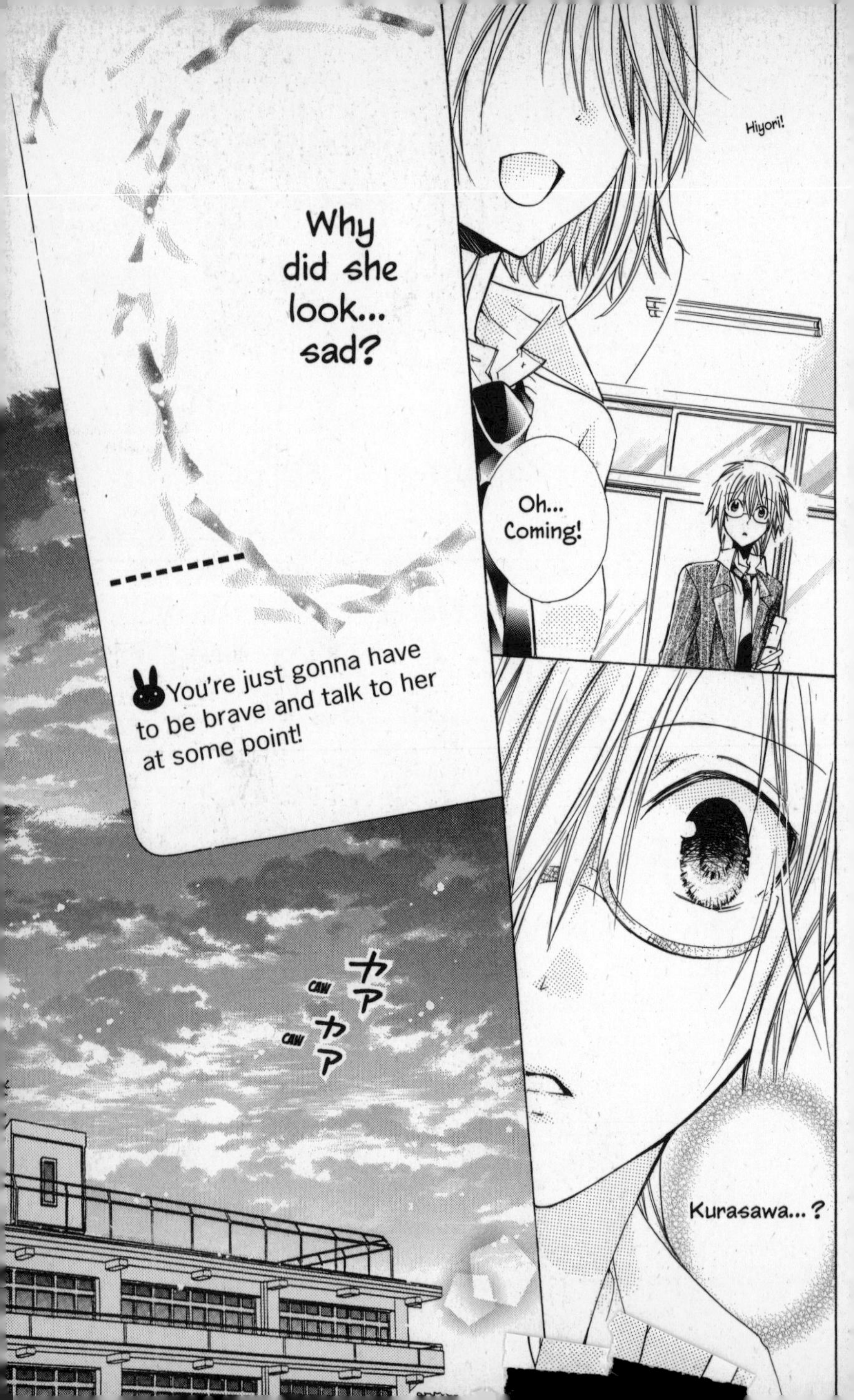
Hiyori!
Oh... Coming!
Kurasawa...?
Why did she look... sad?
You're just gonna have to be brave and talk to her at some point!
カア CAW
カア CAW

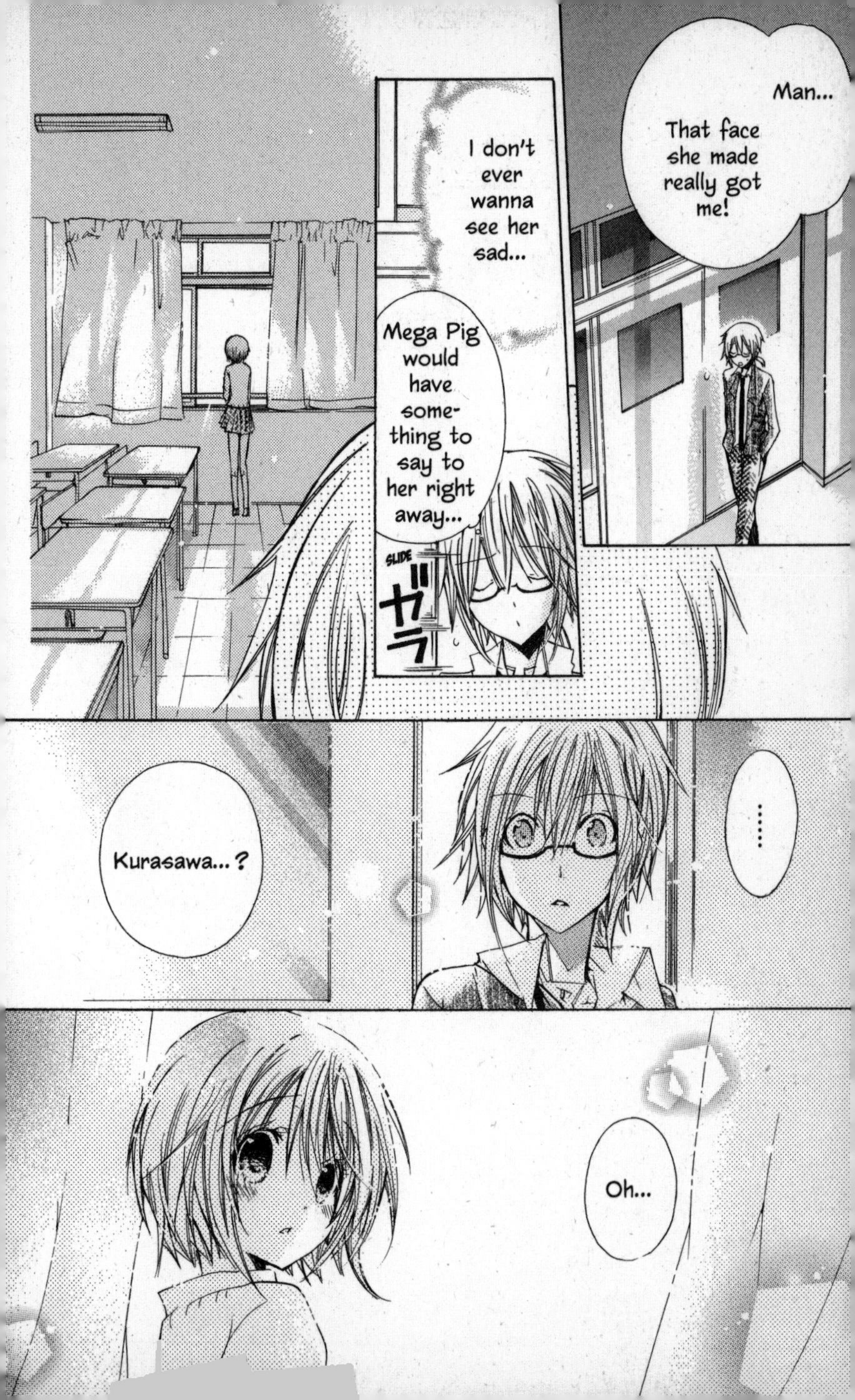
Man...
That face she made really got me!
I don't ever wanna see her sad...
Mega Pig would have some-thing to say to her right away...
SLIDE
ガラ
......
Kurasawa...?
Oh...

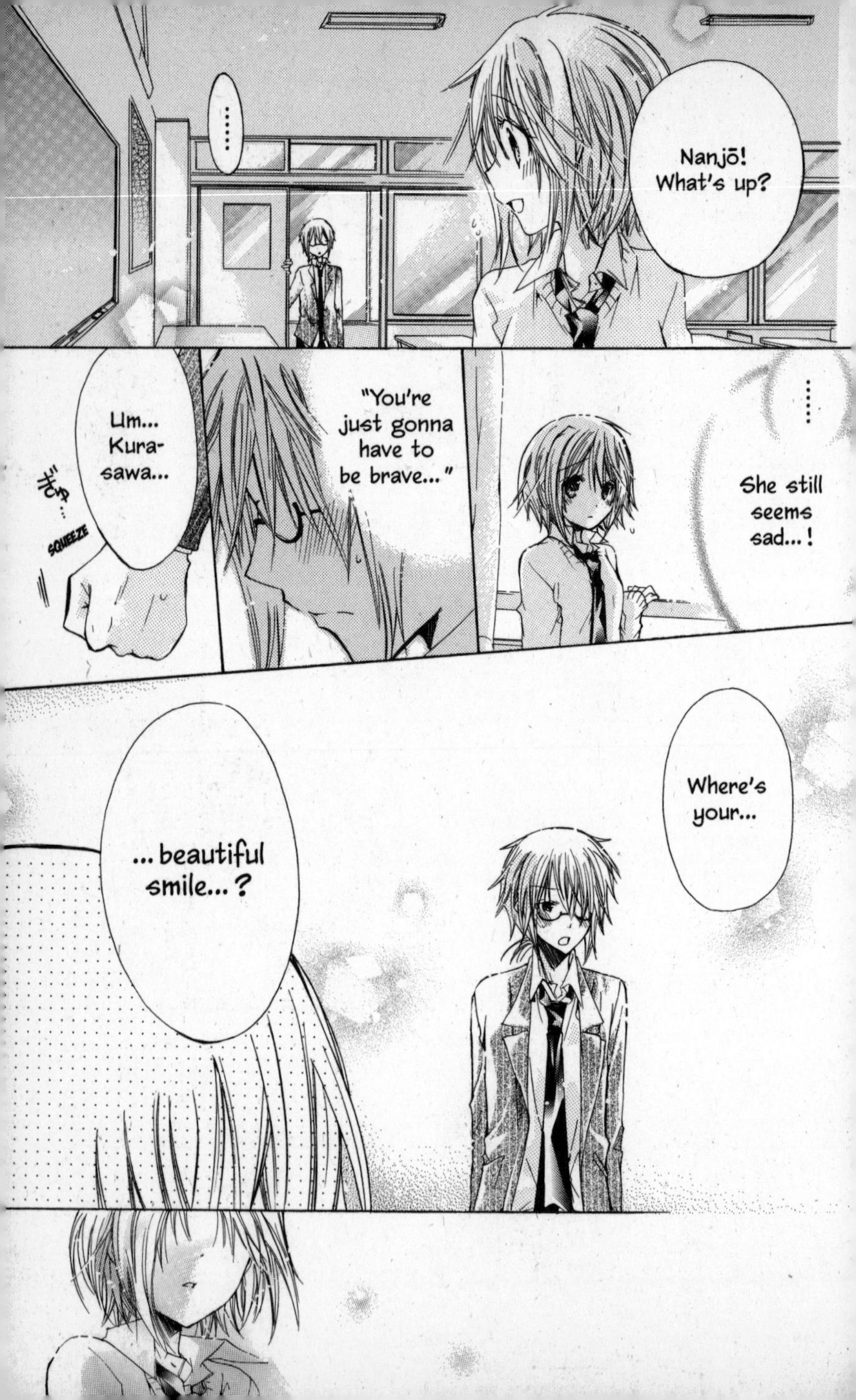
Nanjō! What's up?
......
......
She still seems sad...!
"You're just gonna have to be brave..."
Um... Kura-sawa...
ぎゅ...
SQUEEZE
Where's your...
...beautiful smile...?

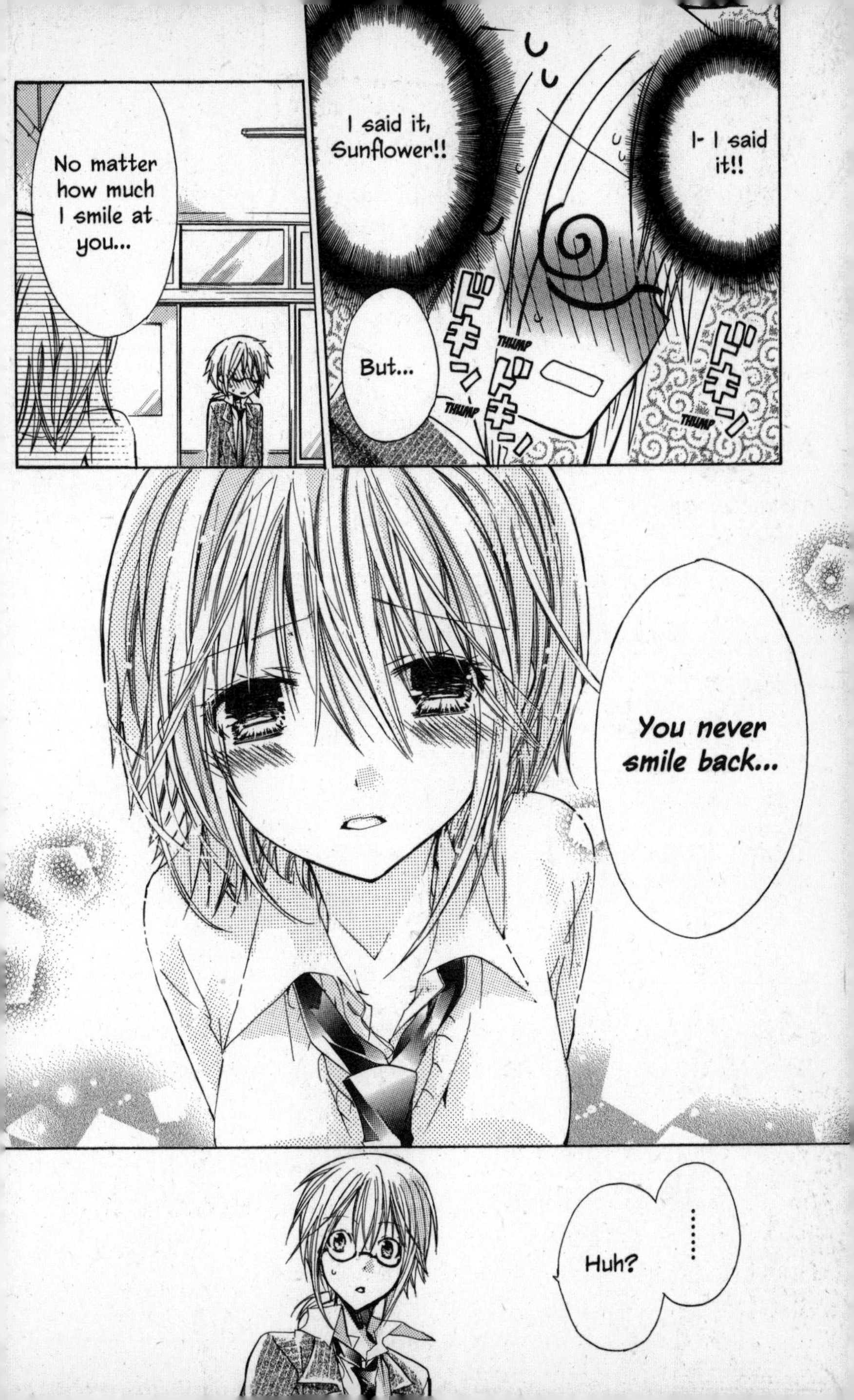
I- I said it!!
I said it, Sunflower!!
ドキーン
THUMP
ドキーン
THUMP
ドキーン
THUMP
But...
No matter how much I smile at you...
You never smile back...
......
Huh?

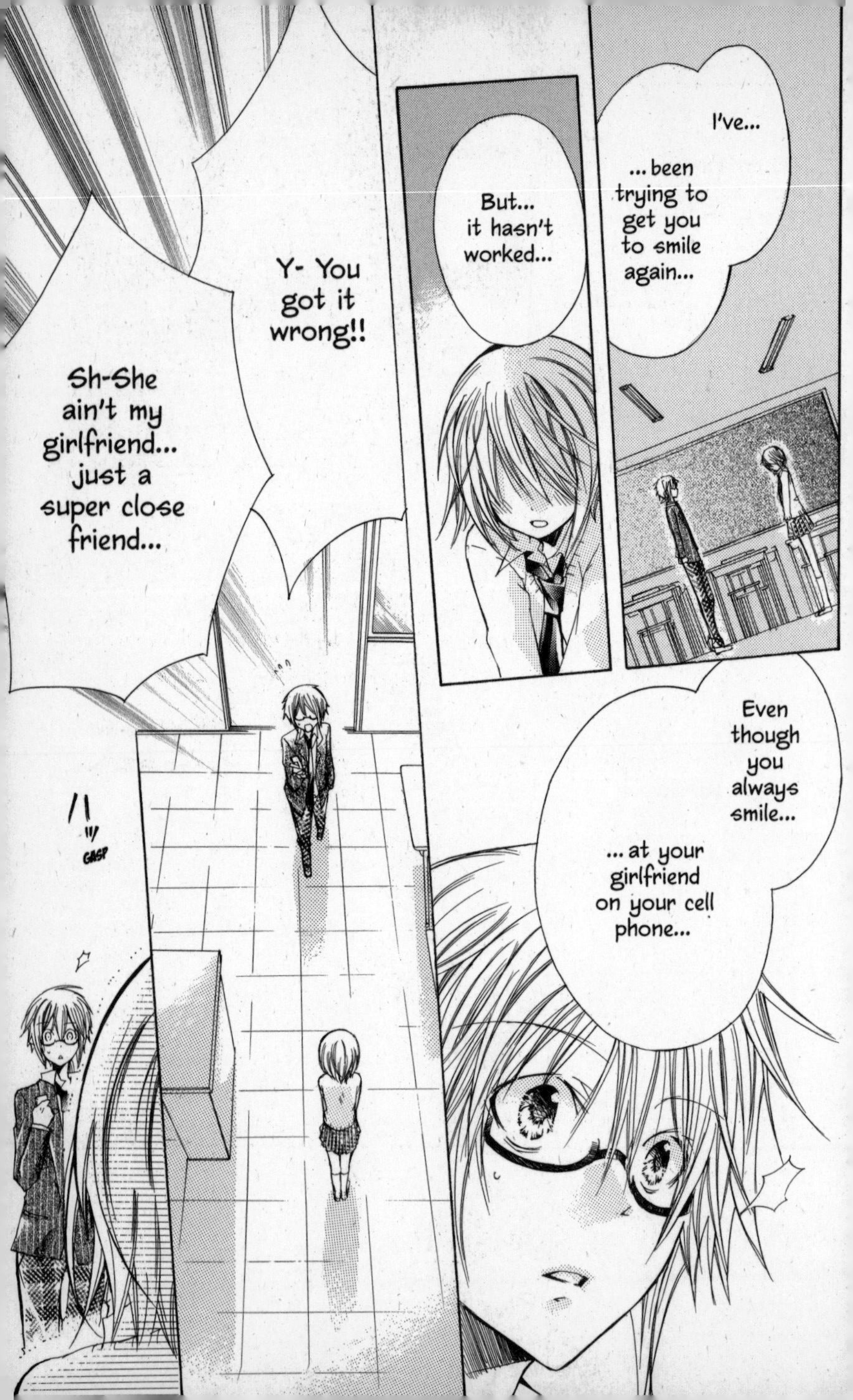
I've...
...been trying to get you to smile again...
But... it hasn't worked...
Even though you always smile...
...at your girlfriend on your cell phone...
Y- You got it wrong!!
Sh-She ain't my girlfriend... just a super close friend...
GASP

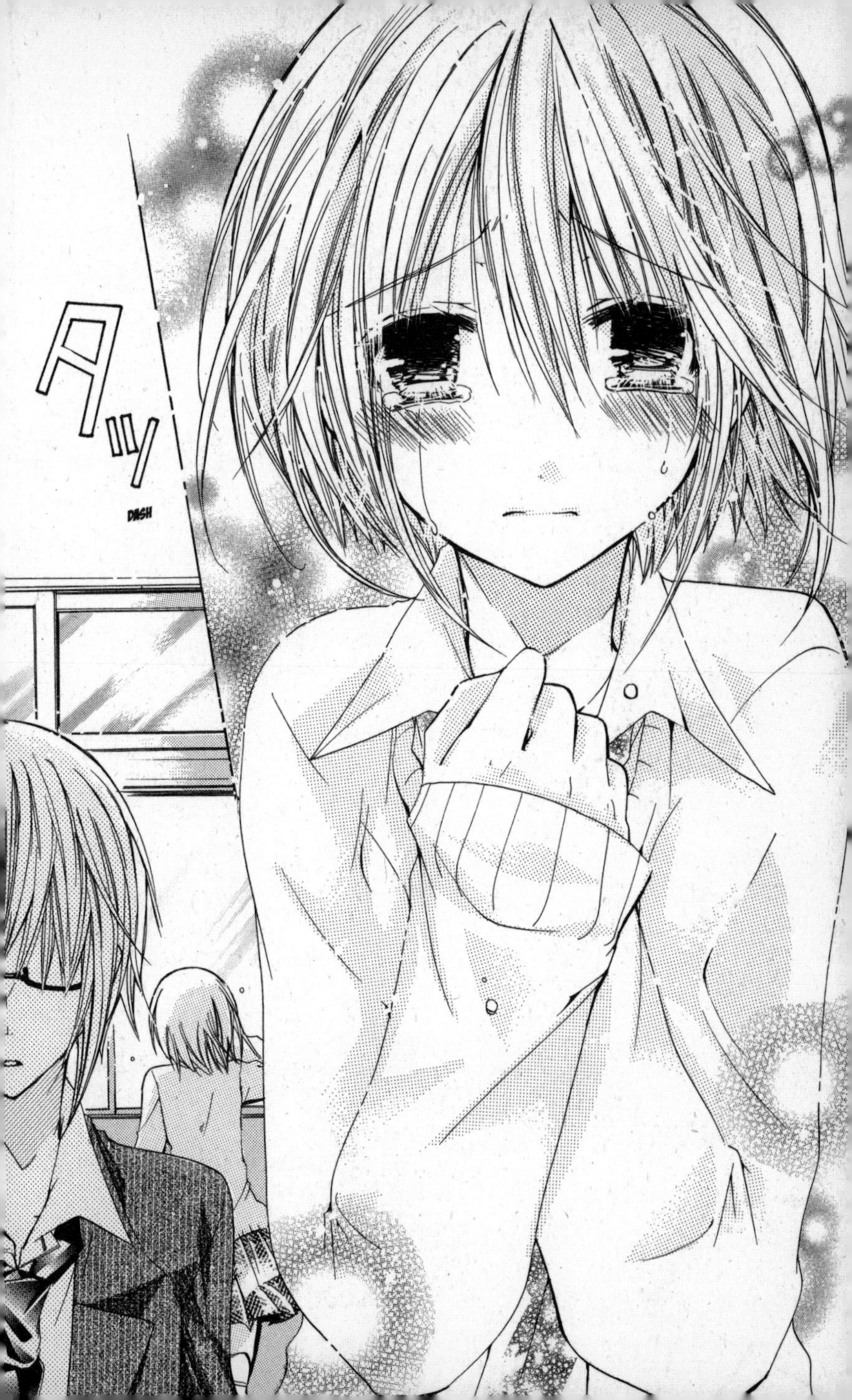
DASH

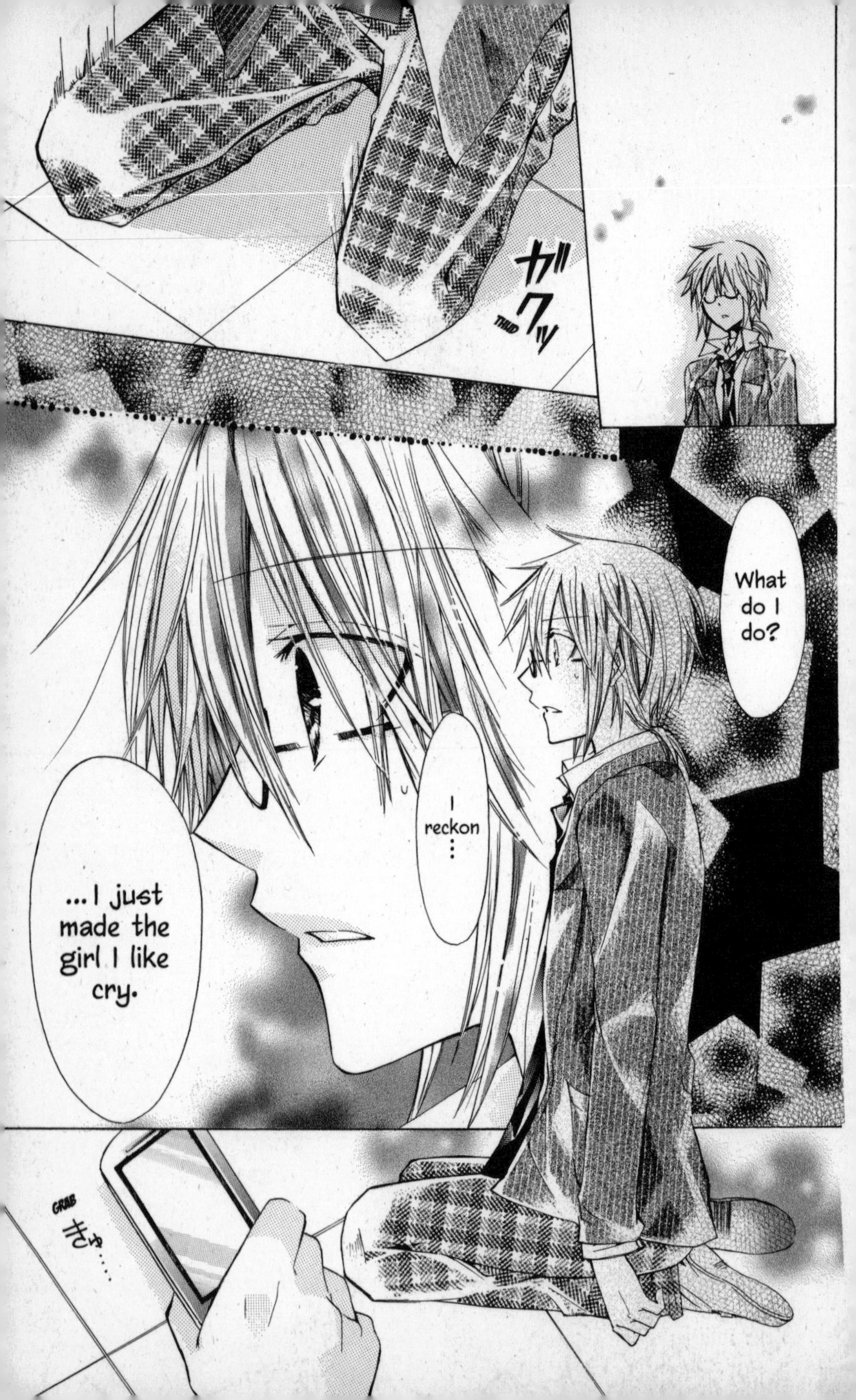
ガクッ
THUD
What do I do?
I reckon...
...I just made the girl I like cry.
GRAB
きゅ……

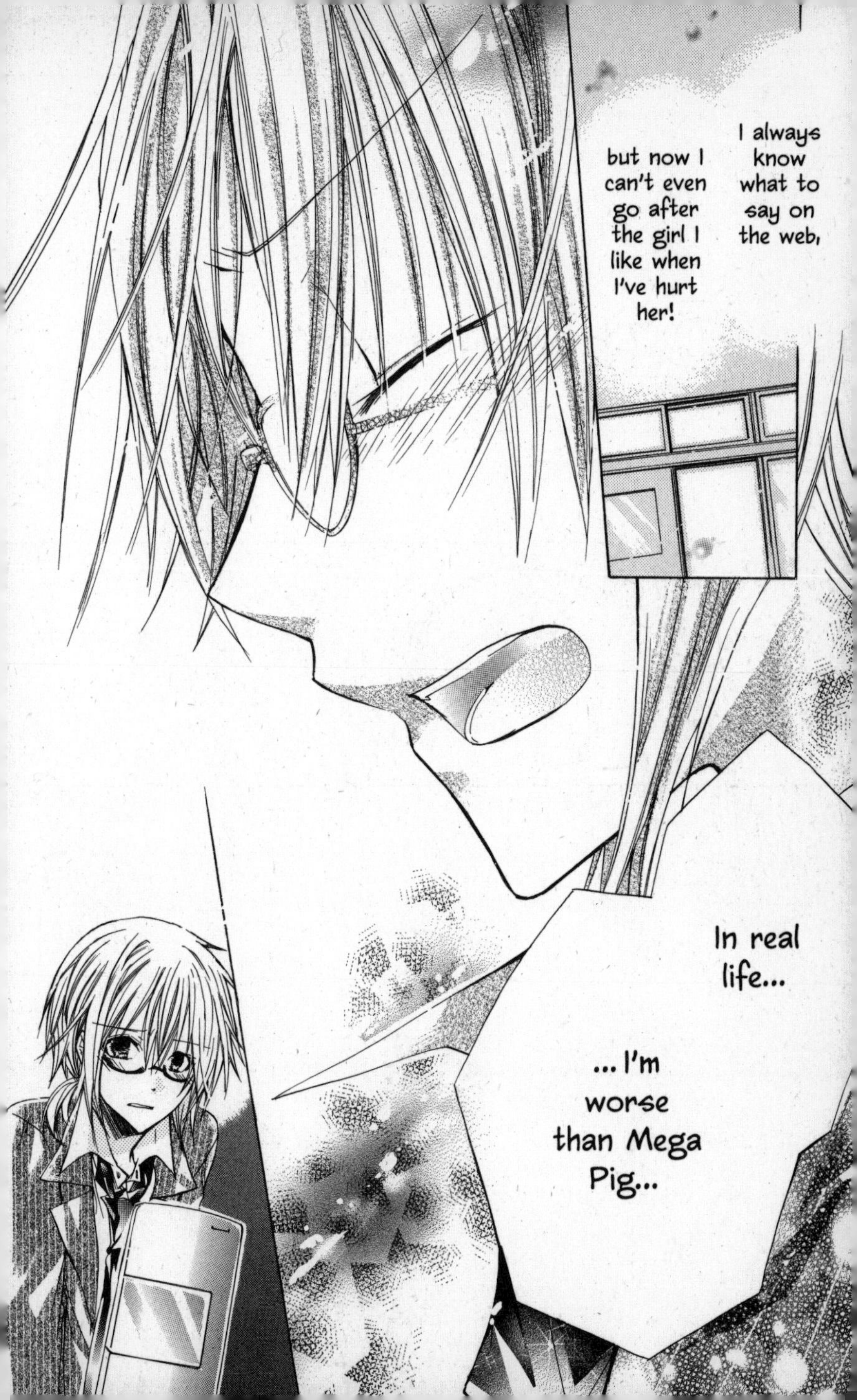
I always know what to say on the web,
but now I can't even go after the girl I like when I've hurt her!
In real life...
...I'm worse than Mega Pig...

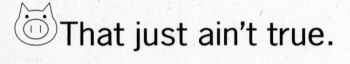That just ain't true.

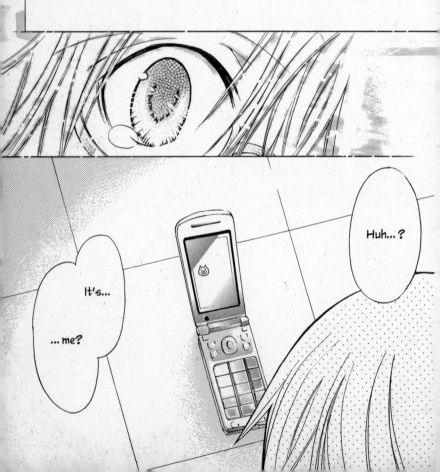

It's...

... me?

Huh...?

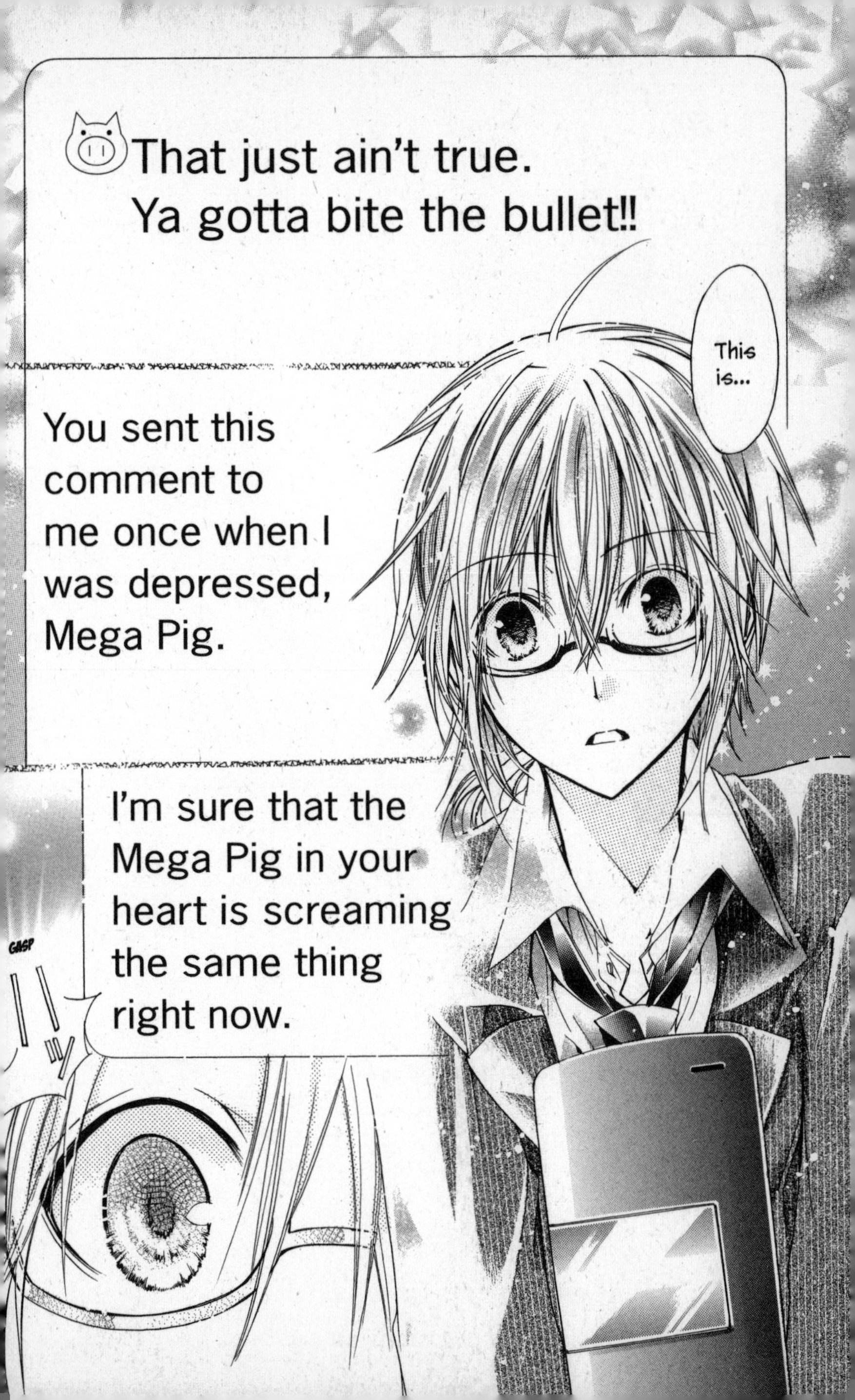
That just ain't true.
Ya gotta bite the bullet!!
This is...
You sent this comment to me once when I was depressed, Mega Pig.
I'm sure that the Mega Pig in your heart is screaming the same thing right now.
GASP

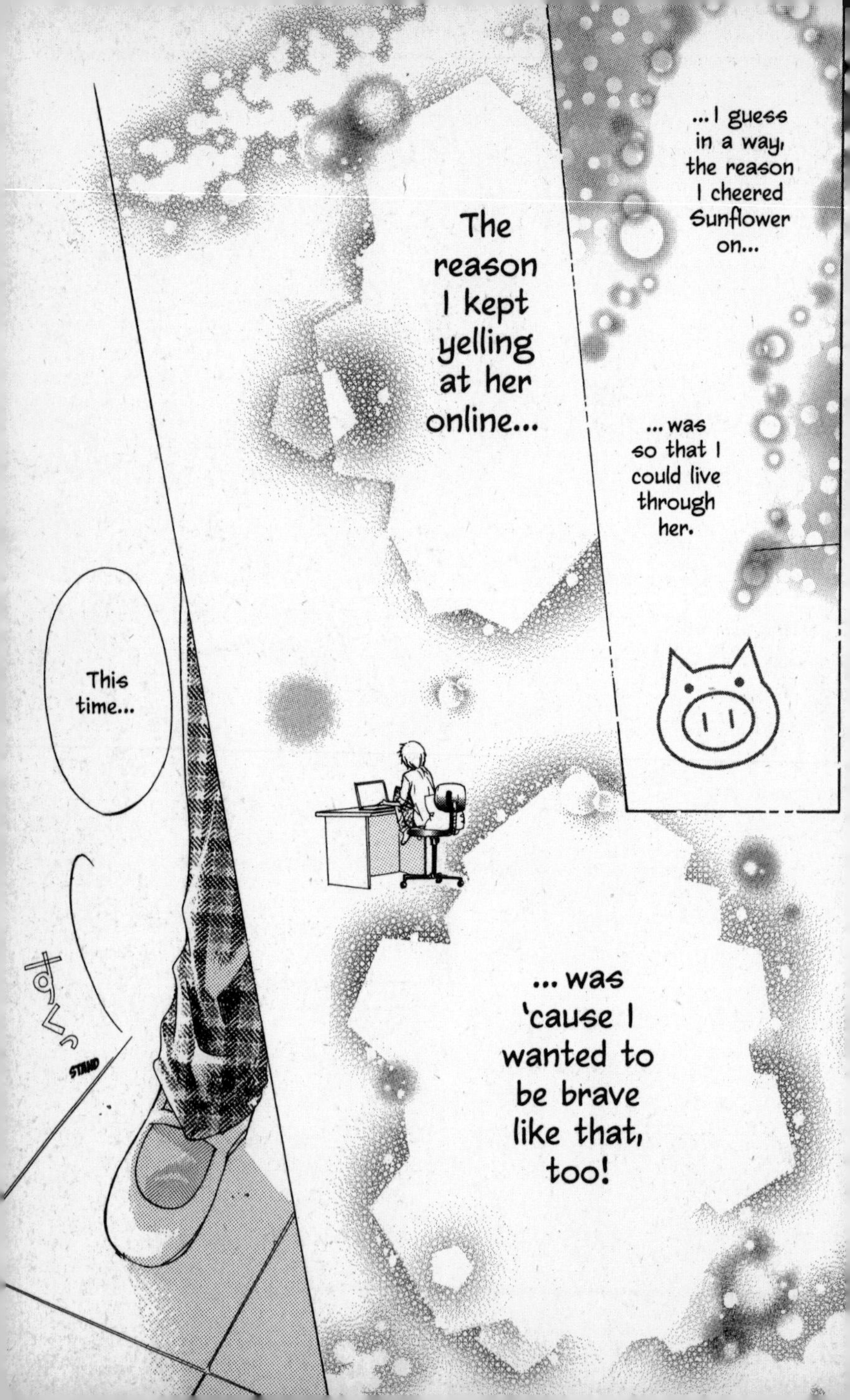
...I guess in a way, the reason I cheered Sunflower on...
...was so that I could live through her.
The reason I kept yelling at her online...
...was 'cause I wanted to be brave like that, too!
This time...
STAND

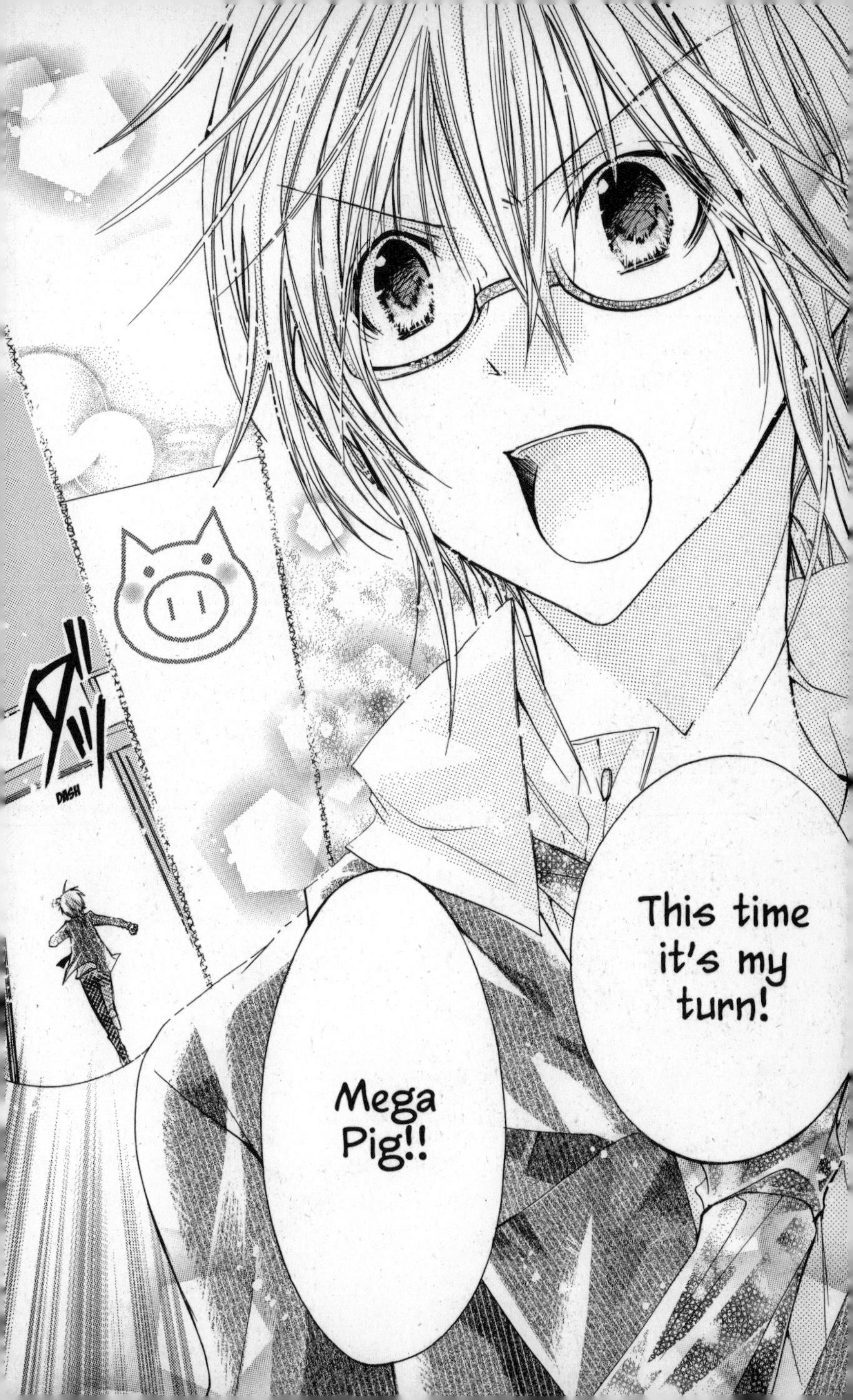
This time it's my turn!
Mega Pig!!
DASH

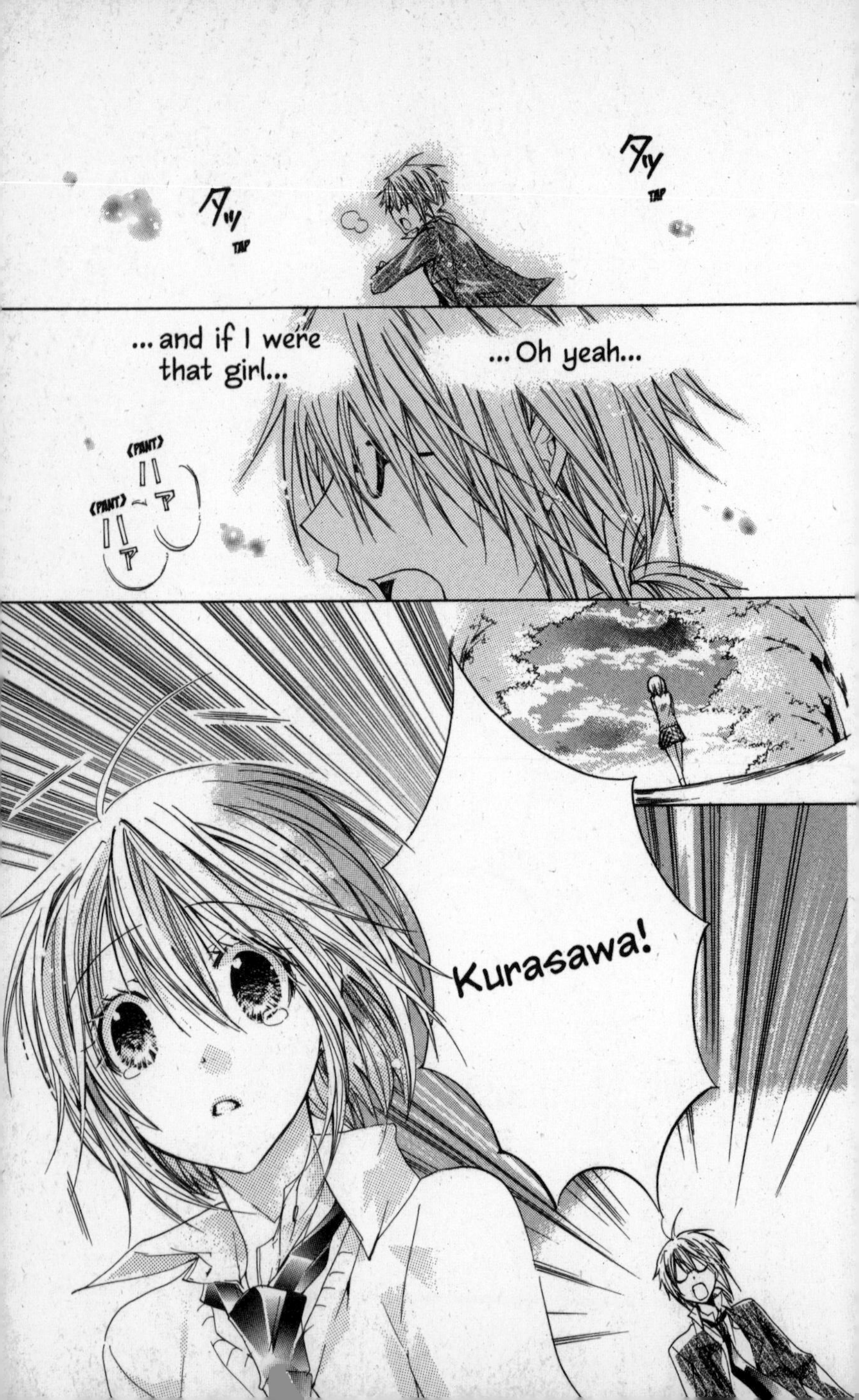

タッ
TAP
タッ
TAP
...Oh yeah...
...and if I were that girl...
(PANT)
(PANT)
Kurasawa!

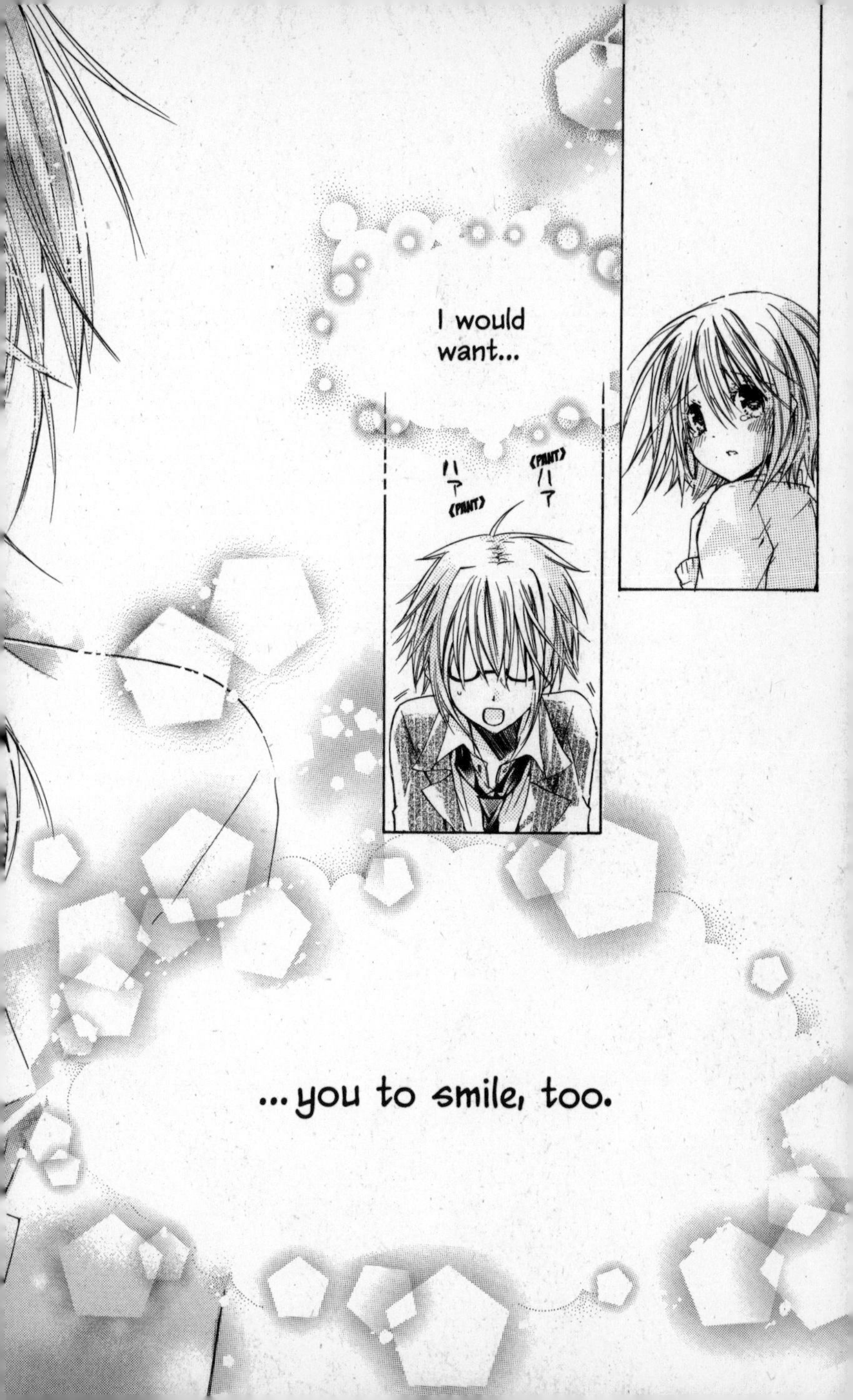
I would want...
ハァ
(PANT)
ハァ
(PANT)
...you to smile, too.

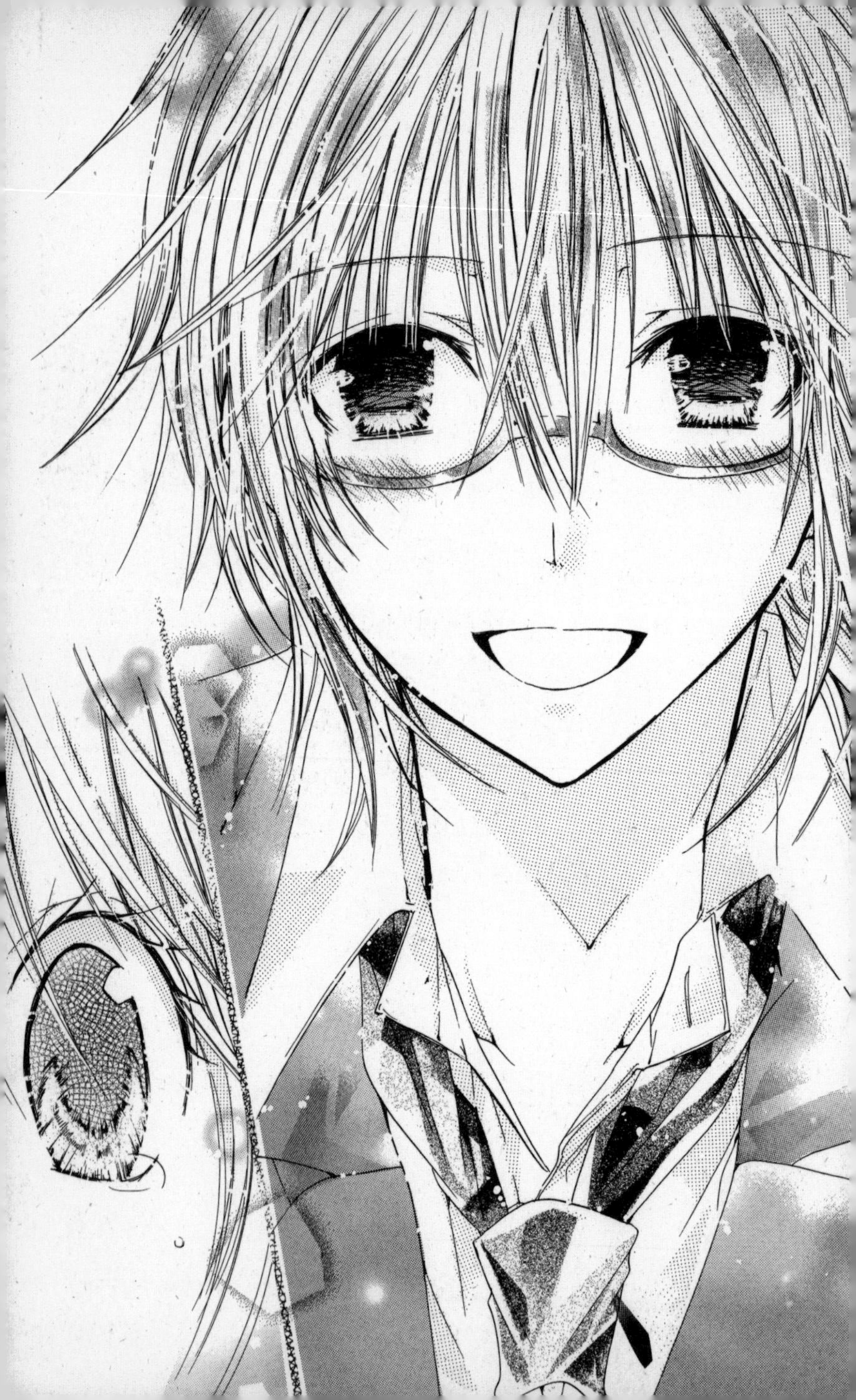

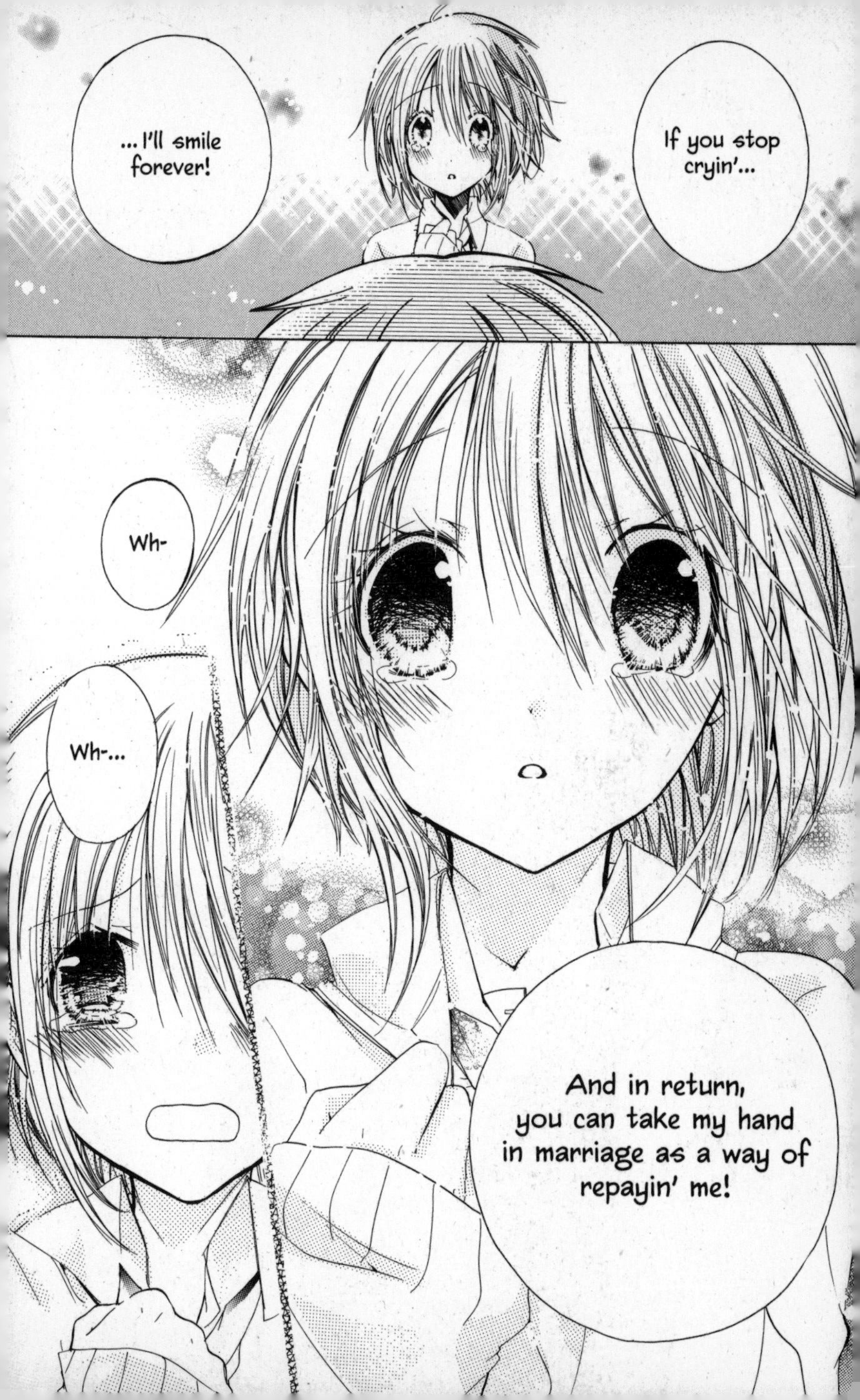
If you stop cryin'...
...I'll smile forever!
And in return, you can take my hand in marriage as a way of repayin' me!
Wh-
Wh-...

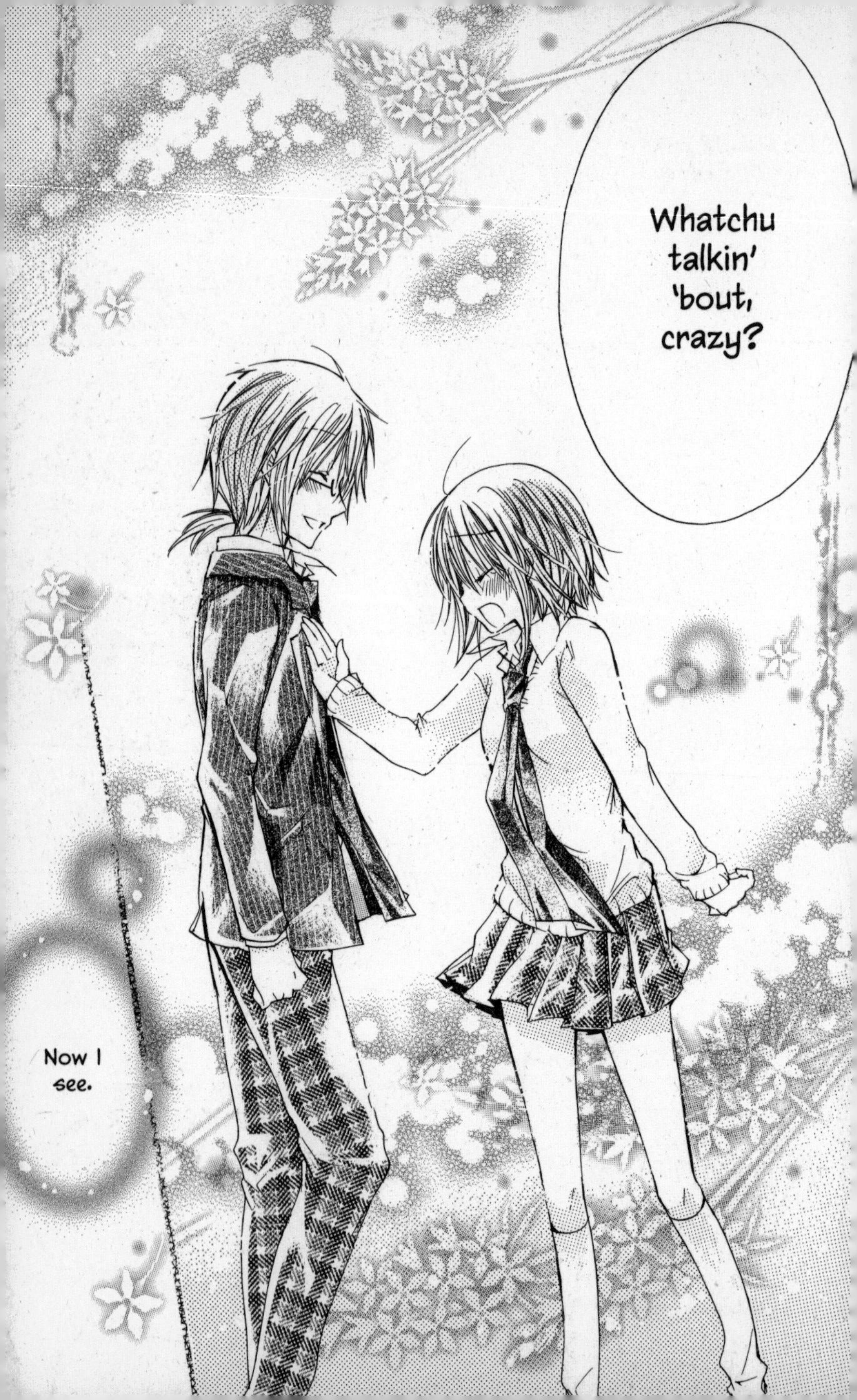
Whatchu talkin' 'bout, crazy?
Now I see.

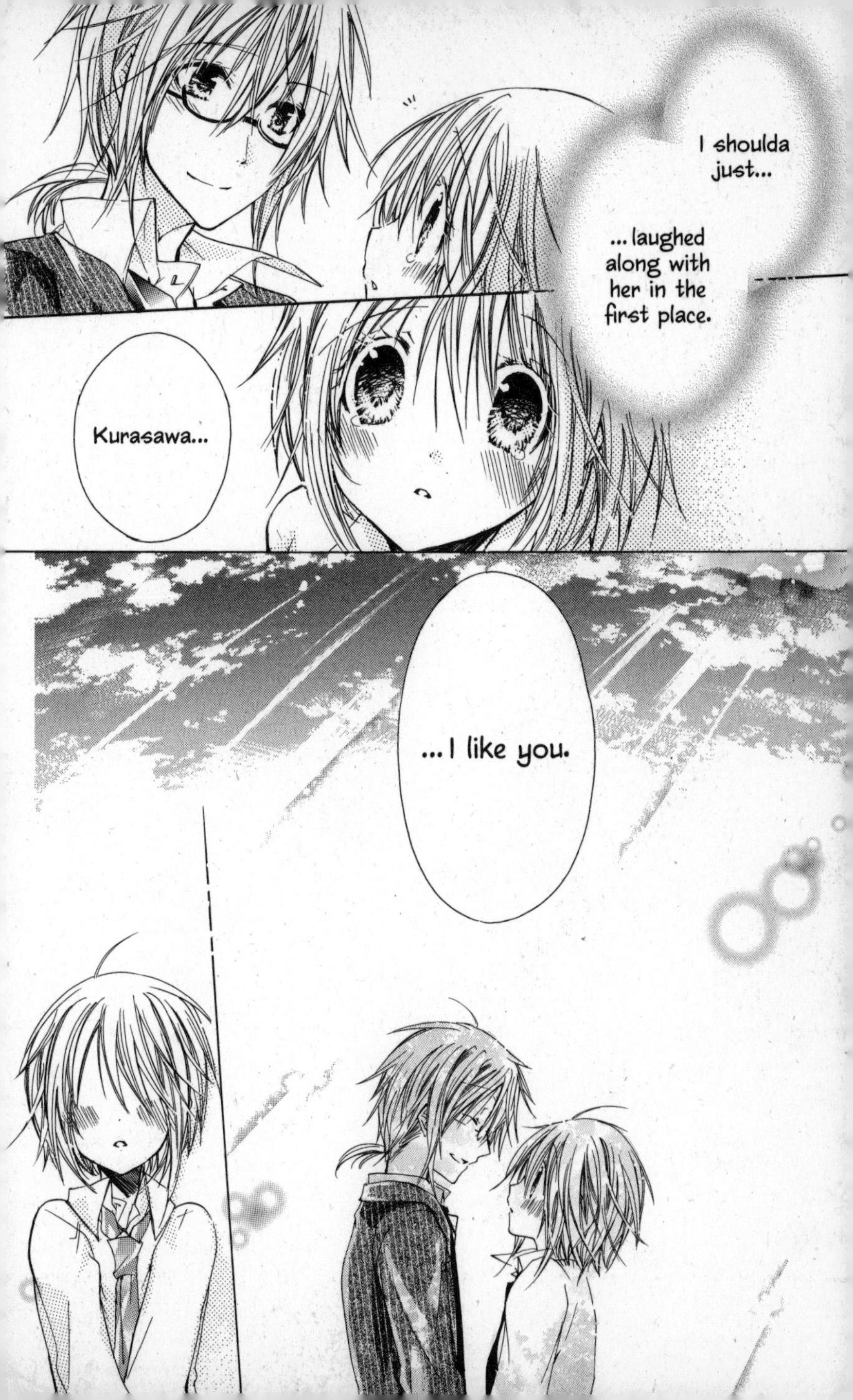
I shoulda just...
...laughed along with her in the first place.
Kurasawa...
...I like you.

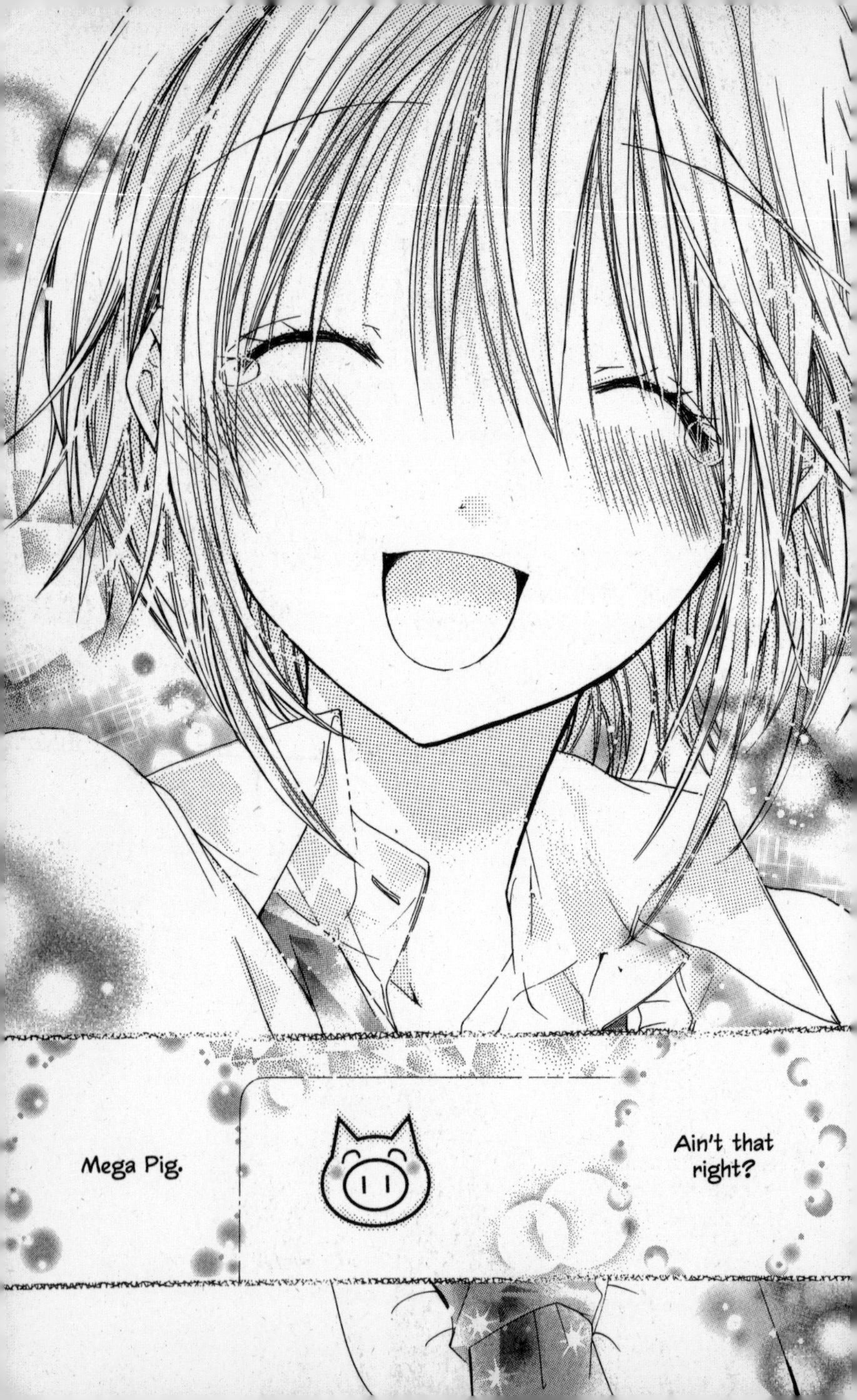
Ain't that right?
Mega Pig.

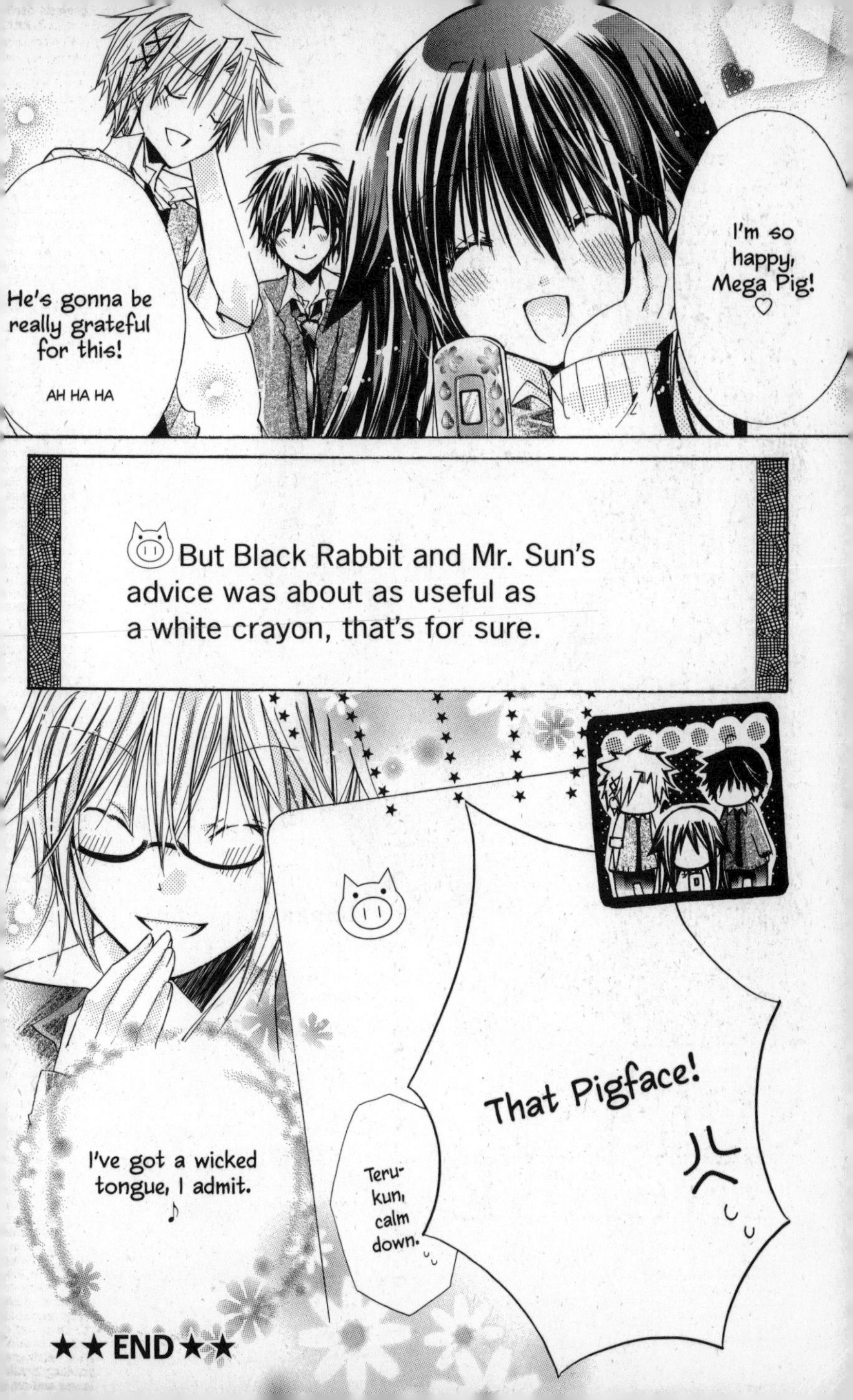
I'm so happy, Mega Pig! ♡
He's gonna be really grateful for this!
AH HA HA
But Black Rabbit and Mr. Sun's advice was about as useful as a white crayon, that's for sure.
That Pigface!
Teru-kun, calm down.
I've got a wicked tongue, I admit. ♪
★★END★★

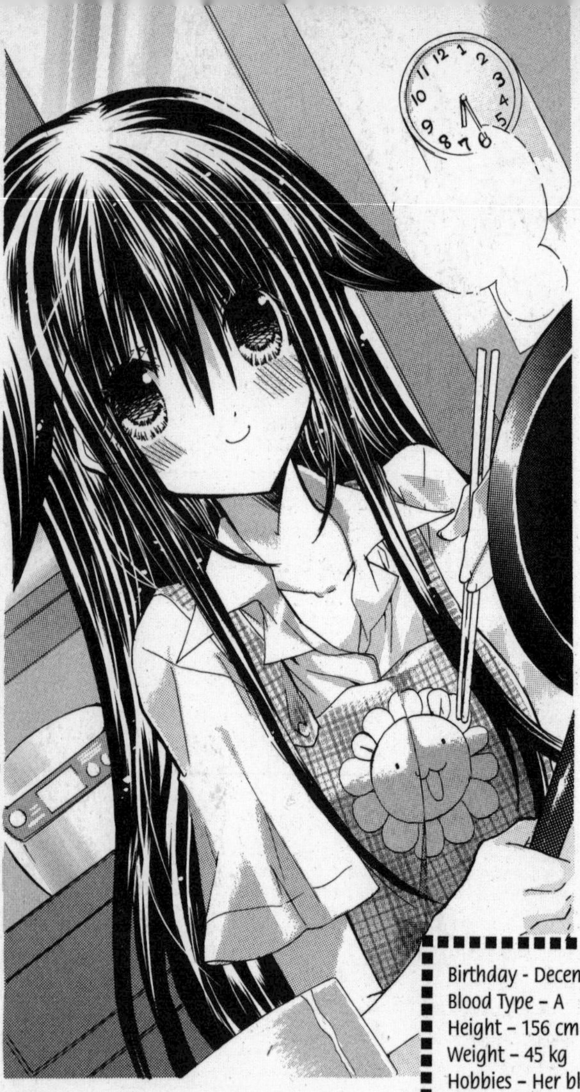

SUMINO HIKAGE

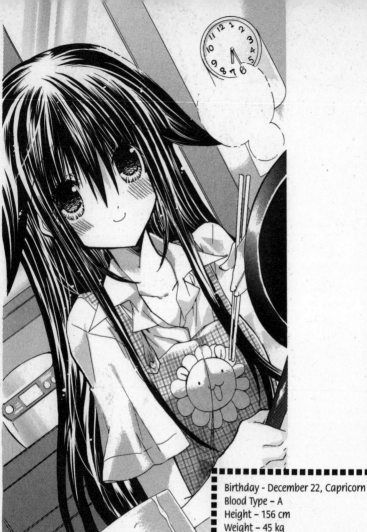

Birthday - December 22, Capricorn
Blood Type – A
Height – 156 cm
Weight – 45 kg
Hobbies – Her blog, surfing the web
Special Ability – Having waiters forget her order
Favorite Foods – Traditional Japanese sweets and Japanese cuisine
Typical Morning – Makes a lunchbox for herself every morning

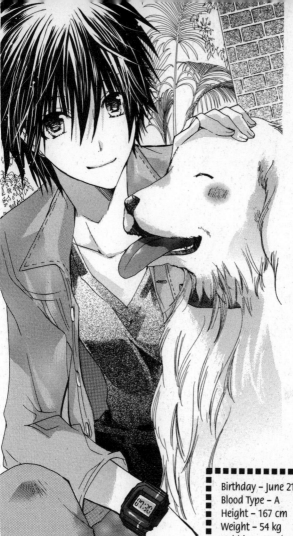

Birthday – June 21, Gemini
Blood Type – A
Height – 167 cm
Weight – 54 kg
Hobbies – Kendo and puzzles
Special Ability – Kendo and English conversation
Favorite Foods – Sushi and seafood
Typical Morning – Jogging and walking the dog at the same time

MUTOU HINATA

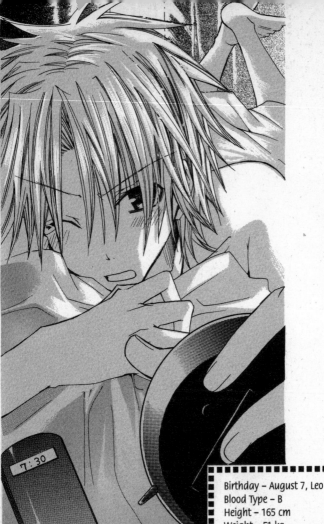

Birthday – August 7, Leo
Blood Type – B
Height – 165 cm
Weight – 51 kg
Hobbies – Hanging out with girls
Special Ability – Snowboarding and
   karaoke
Favorite Foods – Junk food
Typical Morning – Stays in bed right
   until Hinata comes to get him

MIKAMI TERU

Special Short Comic
Hinata and Teru Fourth Grade

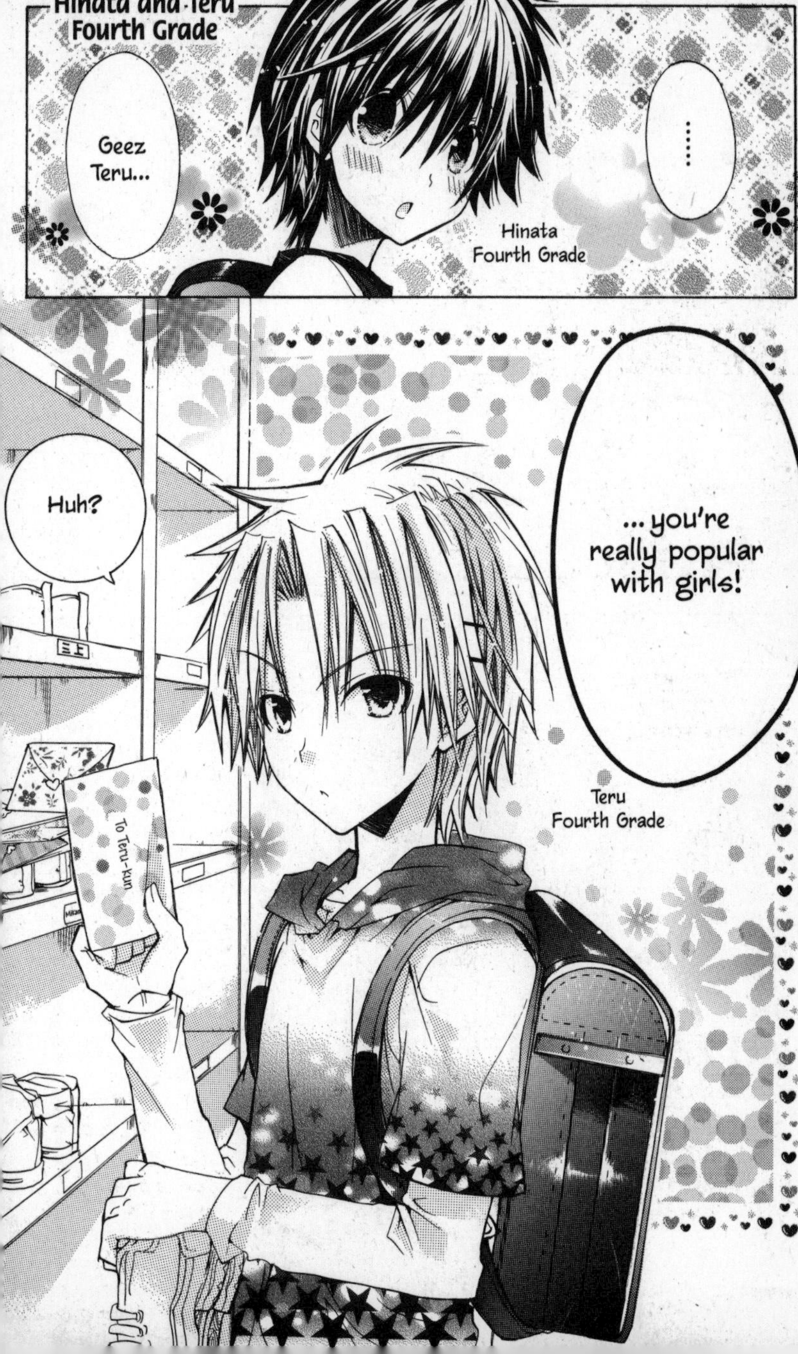
......
Geez Teru...
Hinata Fourth Grade
...you're really popular with girls!
Huh?
Teru Fourth Grade
To Teru-kun

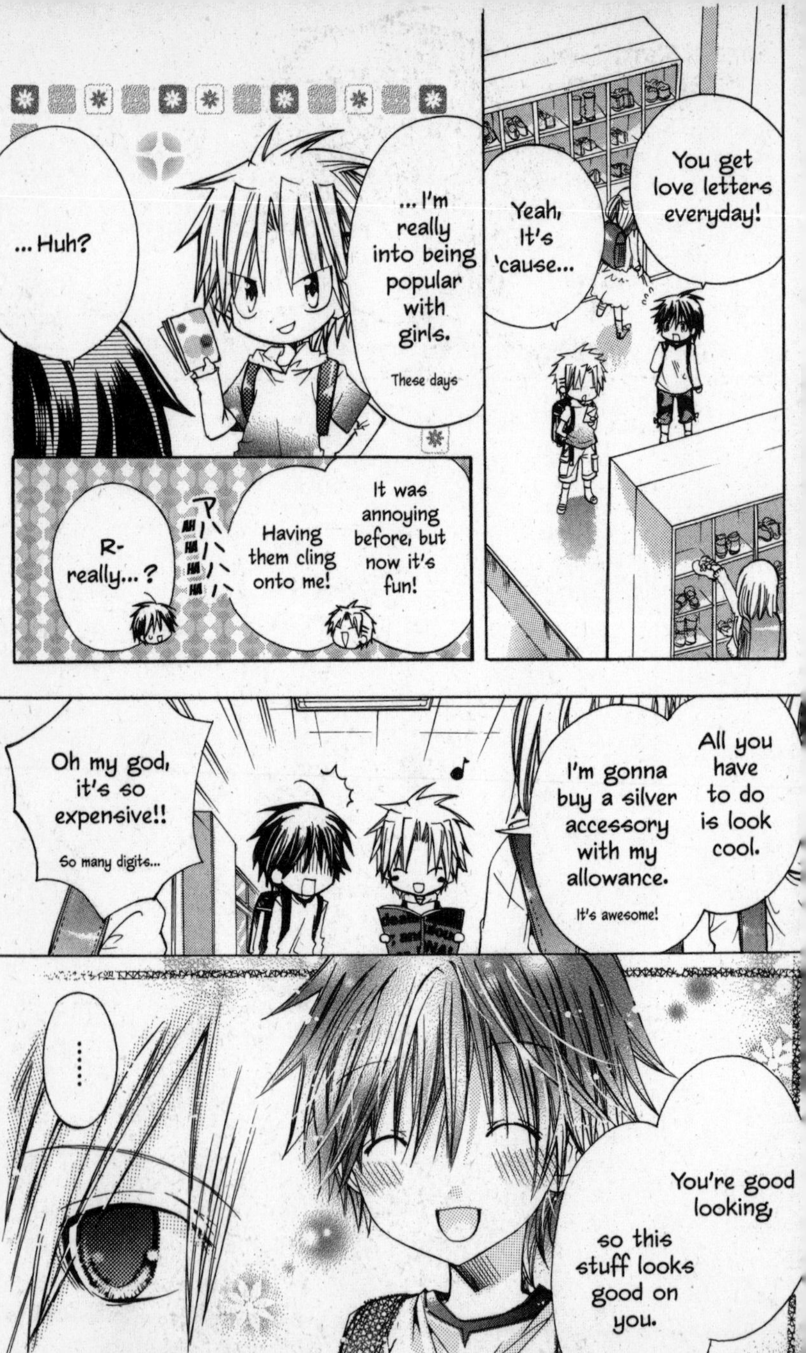
You get love letters everyday!
Yeah, It's 'cause...
... I'm really into being popular with girls.
These days
... Huh?
It was annoying before, but now it's fun!
Having them cling onto me!
AH HA HA HA
R- really... ?
All you have to do is look cool.
I'm gonna buy a silver accessory with my allowance.
It's awesome!
Oh my god, it's so expensive!!
So many digits...
You're good looking,
so this stuff looks good on you.
......

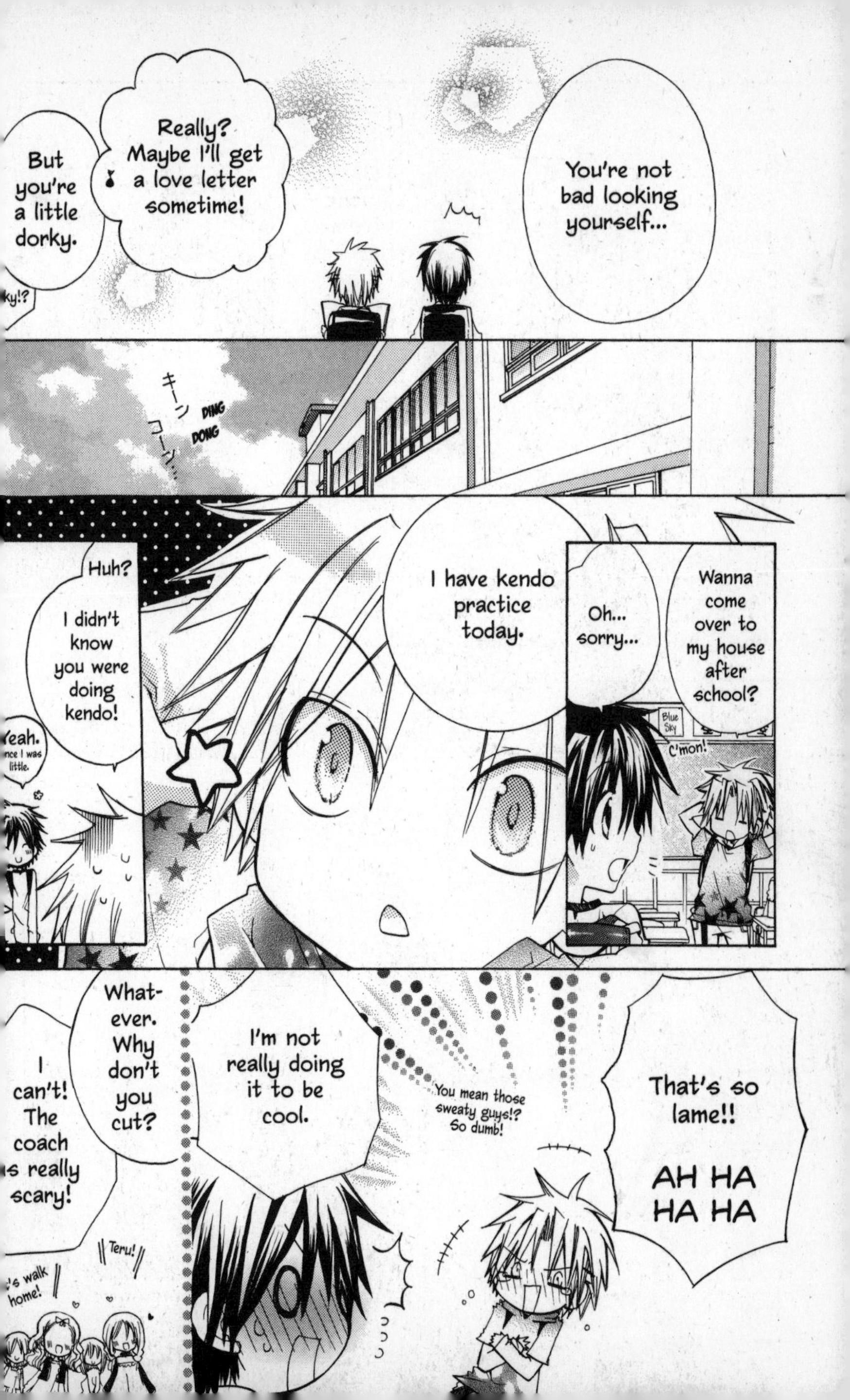
You're not bad looking yourself...
Really? Maybe I'll get a love letter sometime!
But you're a little dorky.
キーンコーン…
DING DONG
Wanna come over to my house after school?
Blue Sky
C'mon!
Oh... sorry...
I have kendo practice today.
Huh? I didn't know you were doing kendo!
Yeah.
That's so lame!! AH HA HA HA
You mean those sweaty guys!? So dumb!
I'm not really doing it to be cool.
What-ever. Why don't you cut?
I can't! The coach is really scary!
Teru!

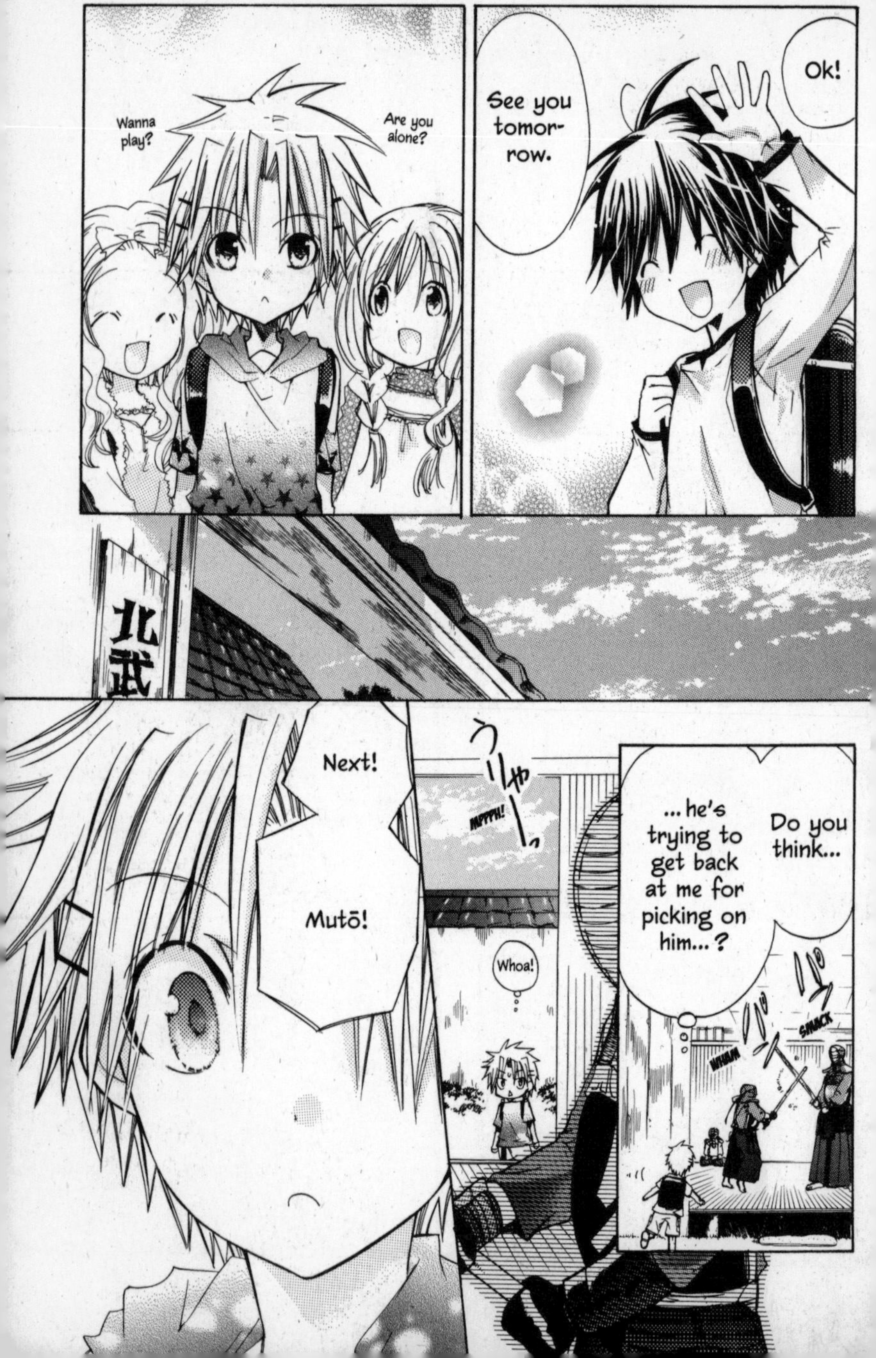
Ok!
See you tomor-row.
Are you alone?
Wanna play?
北武
Do you think...
... he's trying to get back at me for picking on him...?
SMACK
WHAM
うりゃー
MPPPH!
Next!
Mutō!
Whoa!

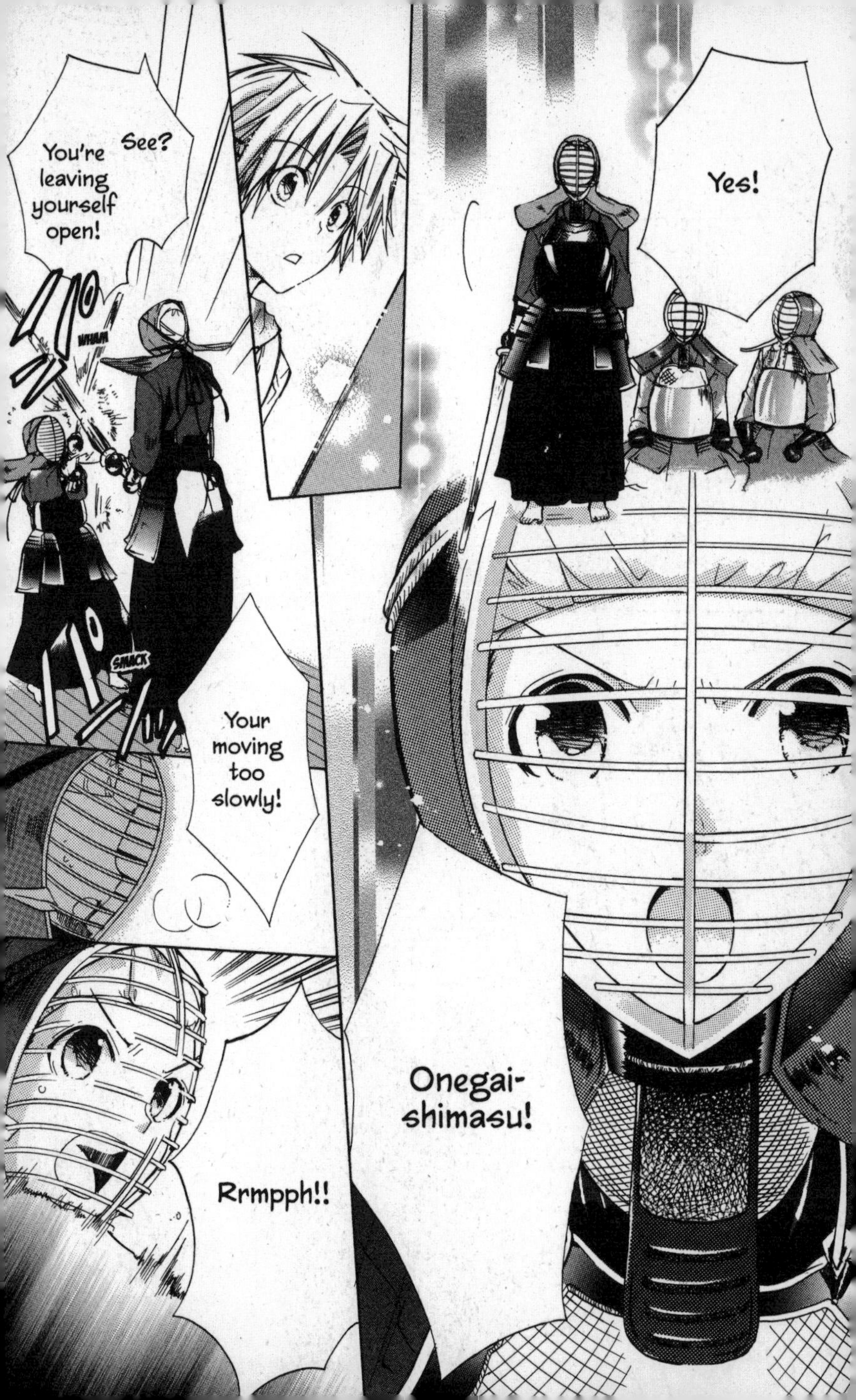
Yes!
See?
You're leaving yourself open!
WHAM
SMACK
Your moving too slowly!
Onegai-shimasu!
Rrmpph!!

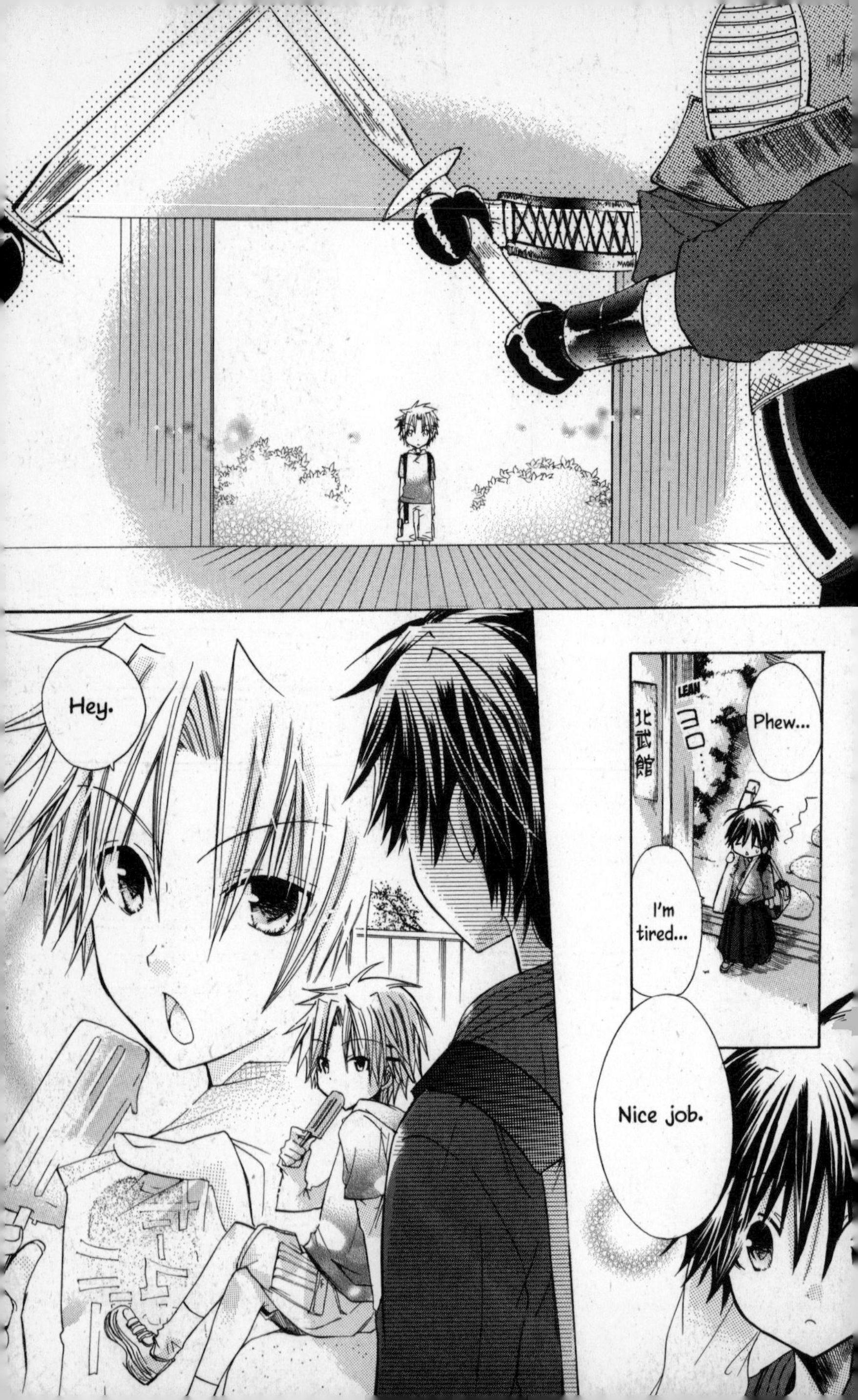
北武館
LEAN
ヨロ…
Phew...
I'm tired...
Nice job.
Hey.

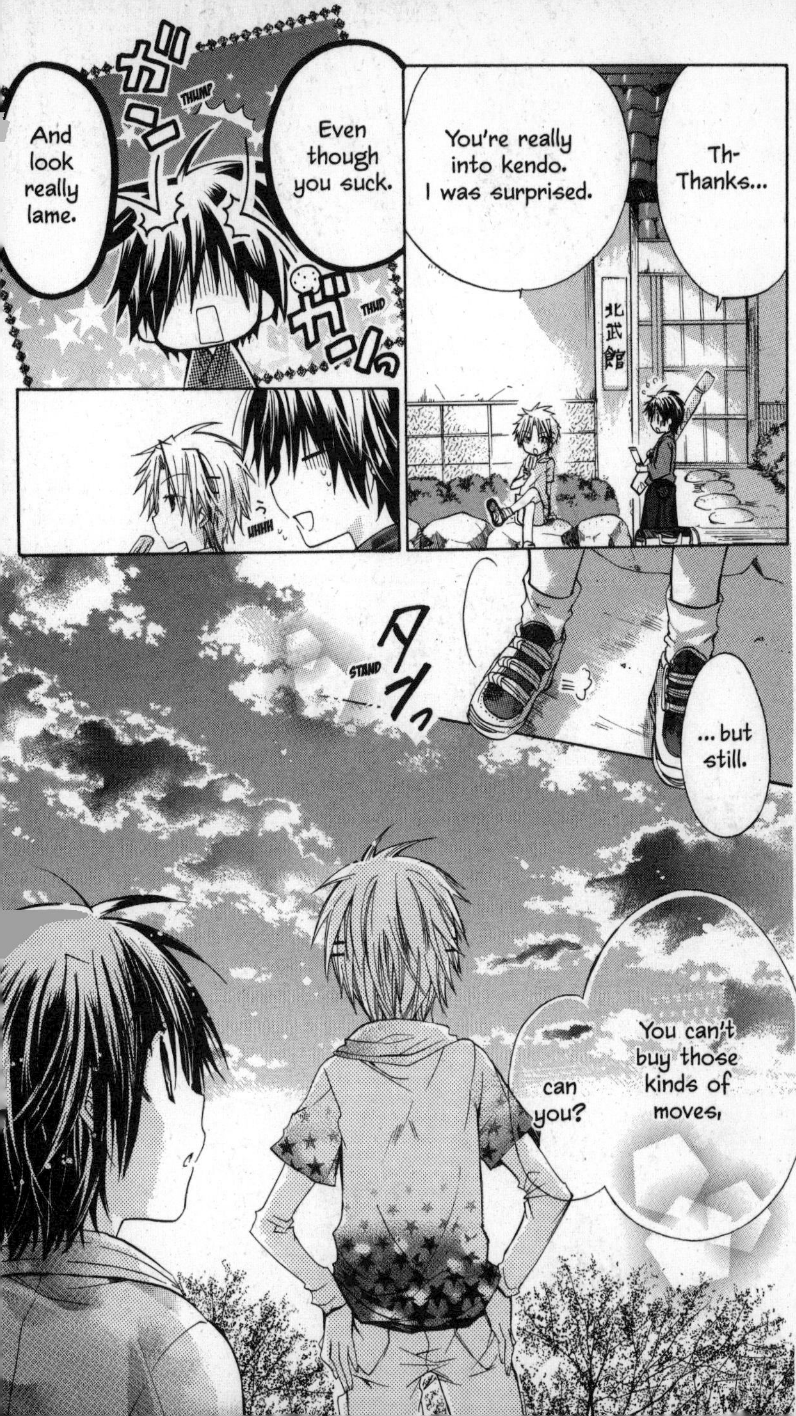
Th- Thanks...
You're really into kendo. I was surprised.
Even though you suck.
THUMP
And look really lame.
THUD
UHHH
... but still.
STAND
You can't buy those kinds of moves,
can you?

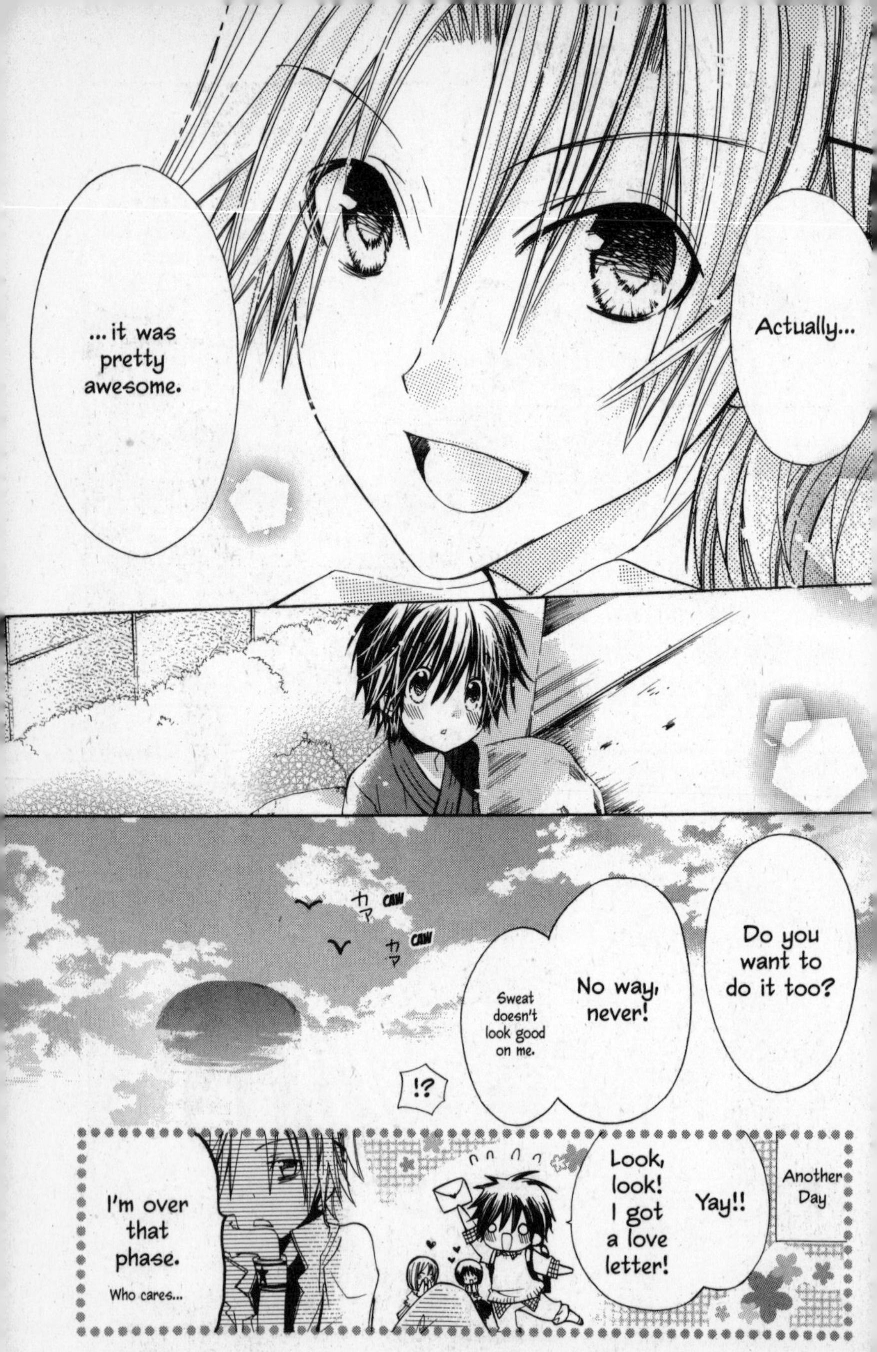
Actually...
...it was pretty awesome.
Do you want to do it too?
No way, never!
Sweat doesn't look good on me.
カア CAW
カア CAW
!?
Another Day
Yay!!
Look, look! I got a love letter!
I'm over that phase.
Who cares...

★★END★★

I Am Here Short

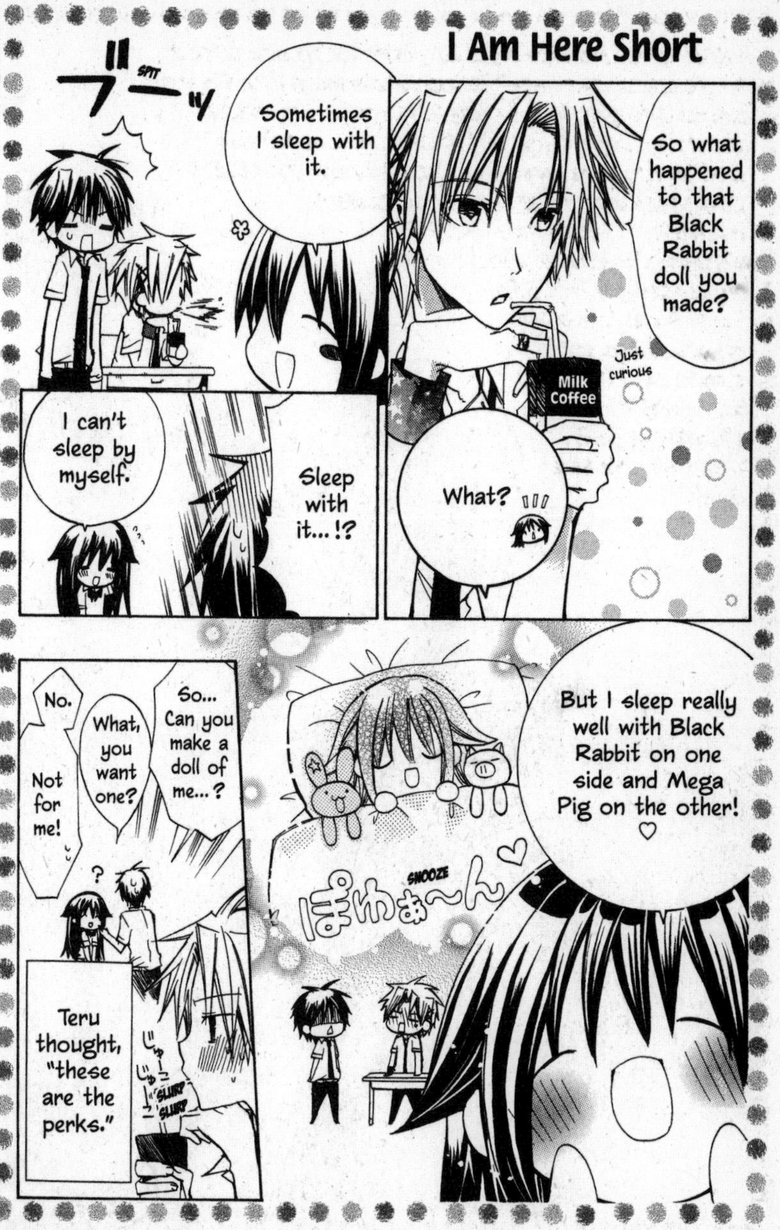
So what happened to that Black Rabbit doll you made?
Just curious
Milk Coffee
What?
Sometimes I sleep with it.
SPIT
Sleep with it...!?
I can't sleep by myself.
But I sleep really well with Black Rabbit on one side and Mega Pig on the other! ♡
SNOOZE
So... Can you make a doll of me...?
What, you want one?
No. Not for me!
SLURP
SLURP
Teru thought, "these are the perks."

END

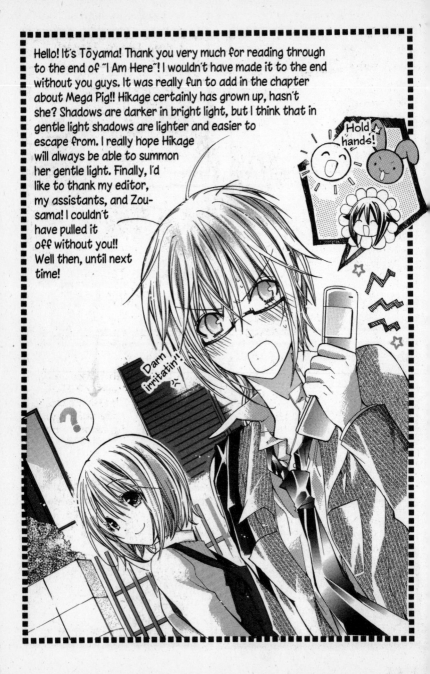

Hello! It's Tōyama! Thank you very much for reading through to the end of "I Am Here~! I wouldn't have made it to the end without you guys. It was really fun to add in the chapter about Mega Pig!! Hikage certainly has grown up, hasn't she? Shadows are darker in bright light, but I think that in gentle light shadows are lighter and easier to escape from. I really hope Hikage will always be able to summon her gentle light. Finally, I'd like to thank my editor, my assistants, and Zou-sama! I couldn't have pulled it off without you!! Well then, until next time!

Hold hands!

Darn irritatin'!

?

I became his girlfriend

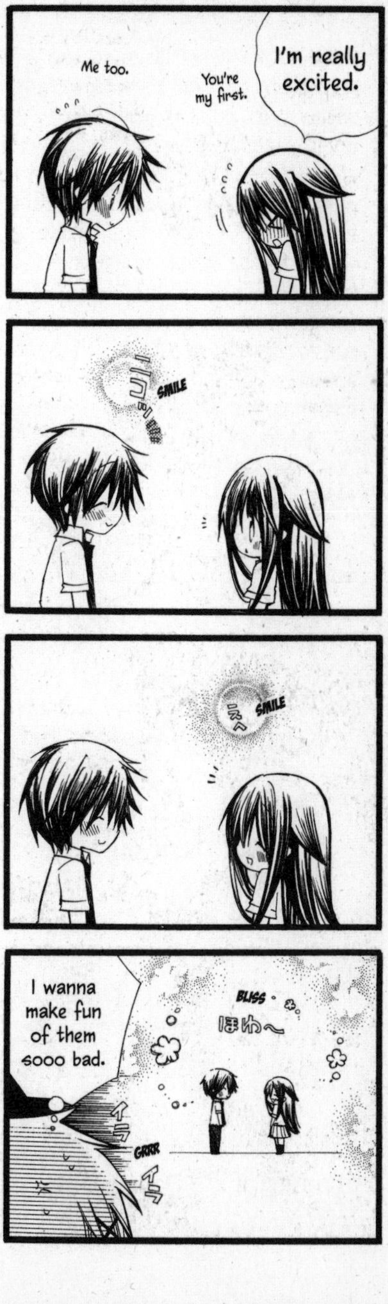
I'm really excited.
You're my first.
Me too.
SMILE
SMILE
BLISS
ほゆ～
I wanna make fun of them sooo bad.
GRRR

I won't lose!

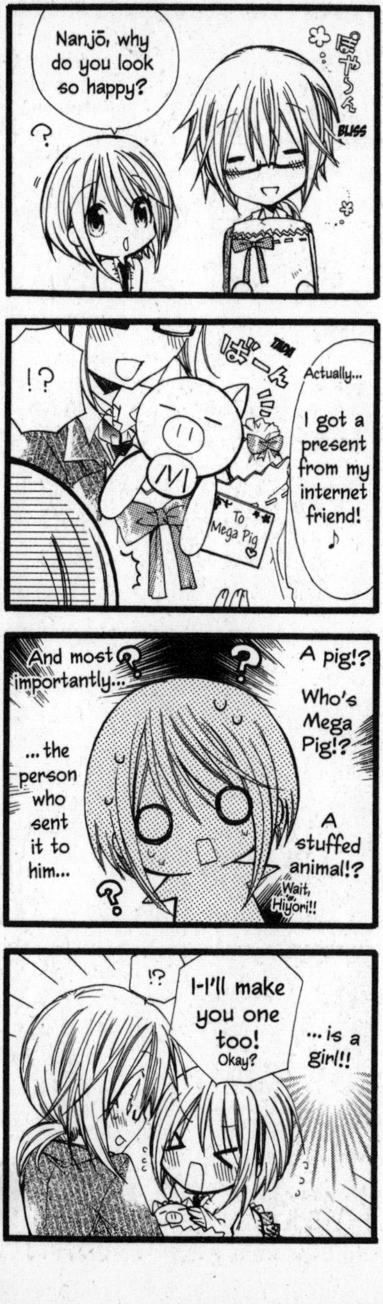
BLISS
Nanjō, why do you look so happy?
?
TADA
Actually...
I got a present from my internet friend! ♪
!?
To Mega Pig
A pig!?
Who's Mega Pig!?
A stuffed animal!?
Wait, Hiyori!!
And most importantly...
... the person who sent it to him...
... is a girl!!
I-I'll make you one too! Okay?
!?

The deciding factor

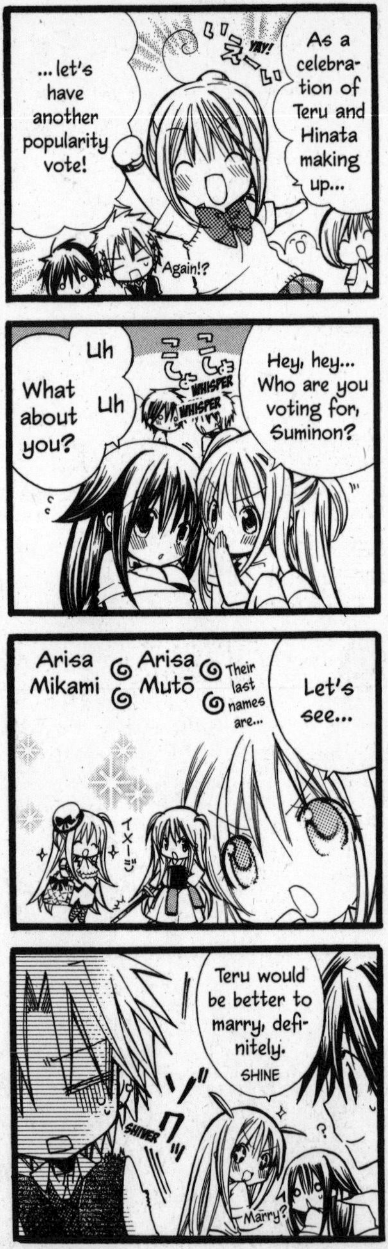
As a celebration of Teru and Hinata making up...
YAY!
... let's have another popularity vote!
Again!?
Hey, hey... Who are you voting for, Suminon?
WHISPER
WHISPER
Uh
Uh
What about you?
Let's see...
Their last names are...
Arisa Mutō
Arisa Mikami
Teru would be better to marry, definitely.
SHINE
SHIVER
Marry?

* Arisa's dream is to marry someone with a wonderful last name.

Have they been convinced...?

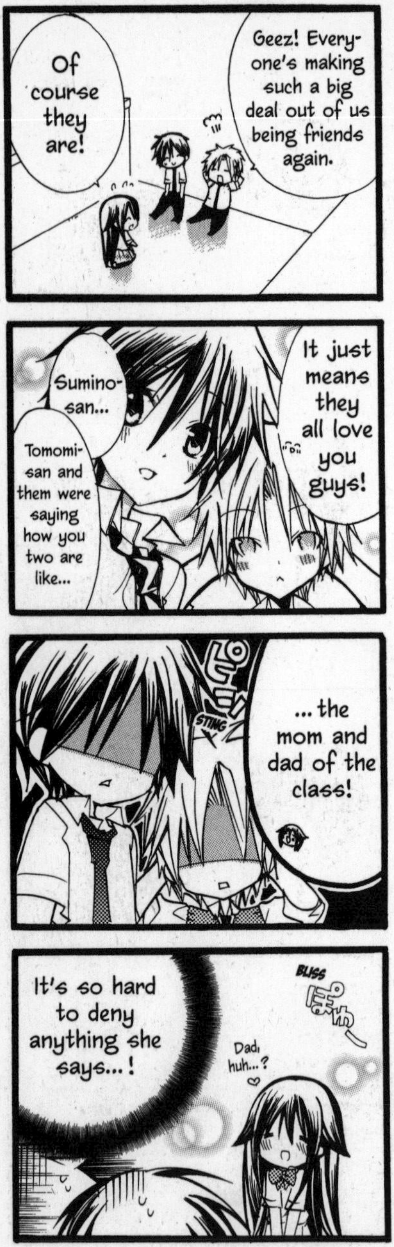
Geez! Everyone's making such a big deal out of us being friends again.
Of course they are!
It just means they all love you guys!
Sumino-san...
Tomomi-san and them were saying how you two are like...
... the mom and dad of the class!
STING
BLISS
Dad, huh...?
It's so hard to deny anything she says...!

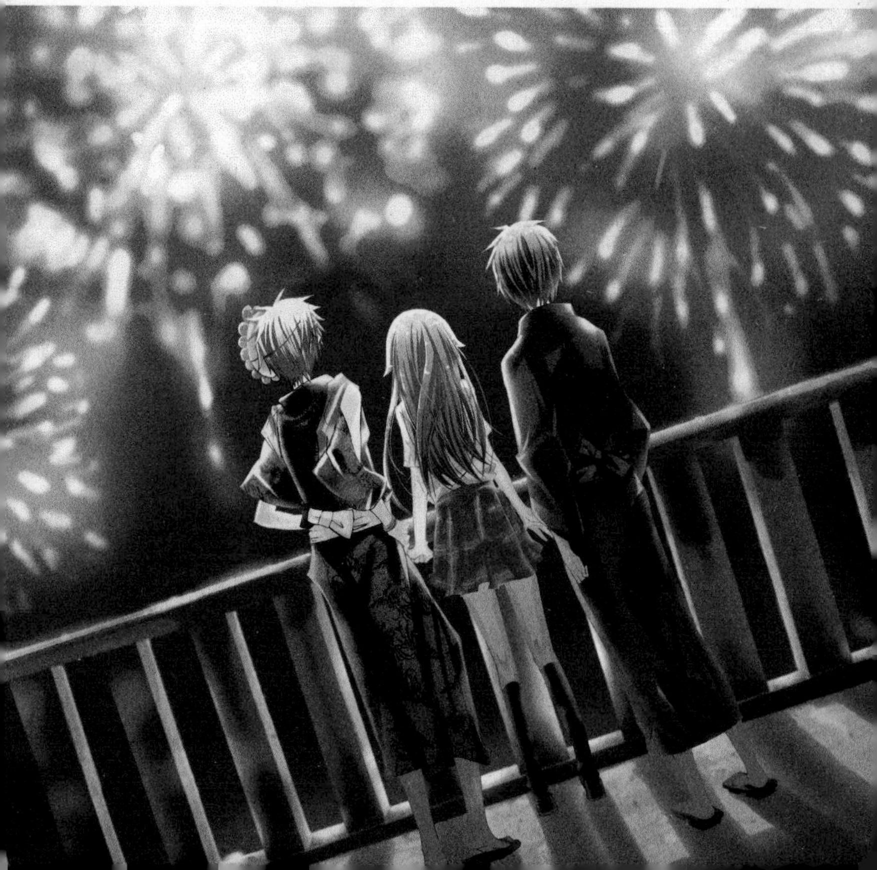

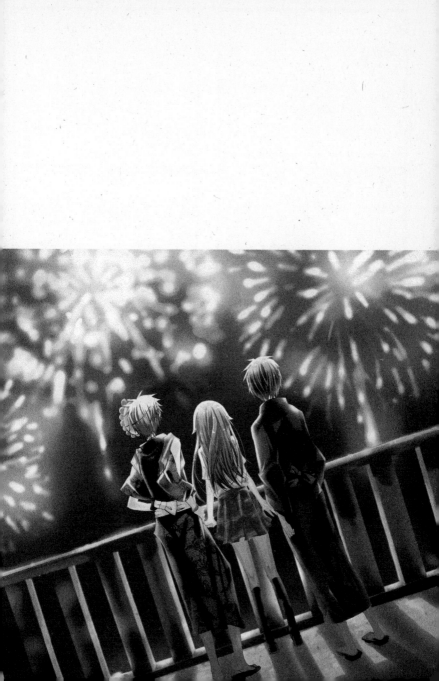

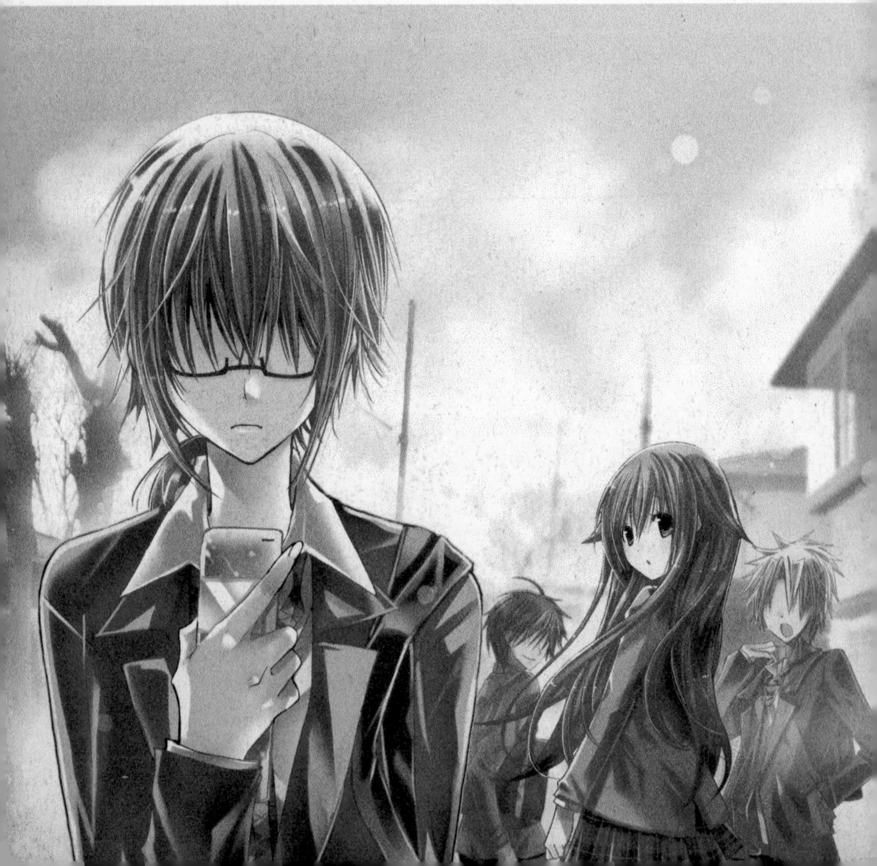

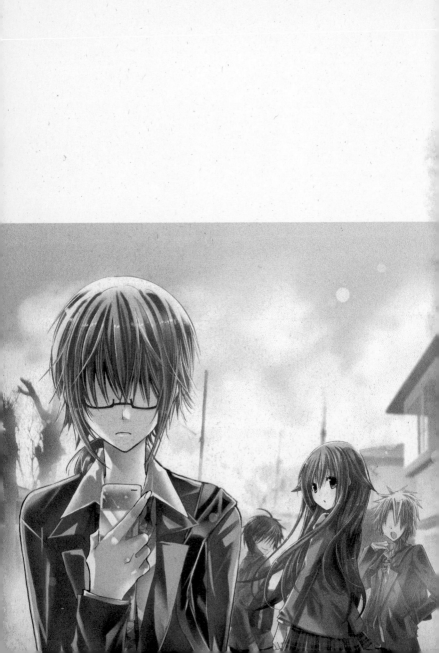

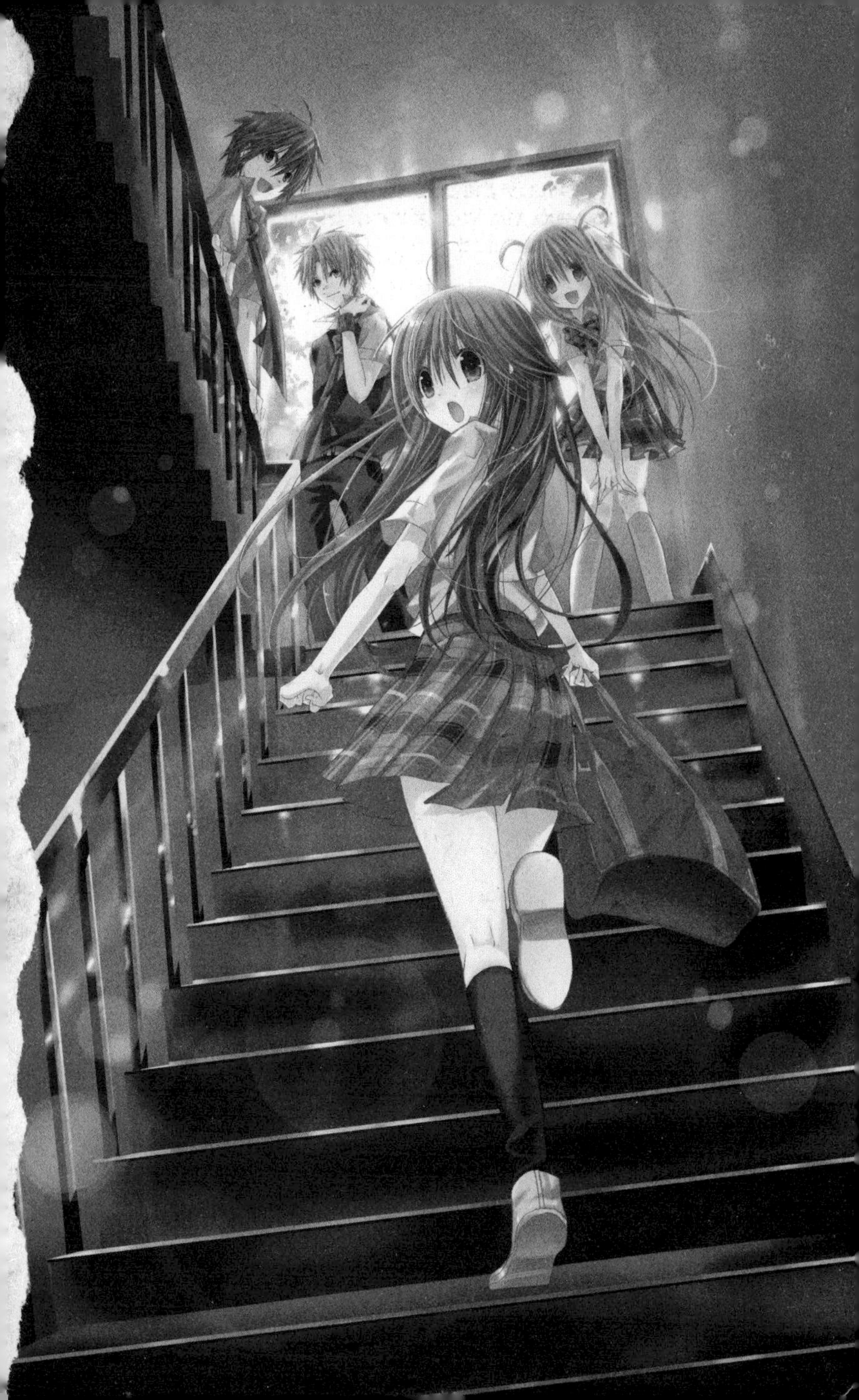

Translation Notes

Japanese is a tricky language for most Westerners, and translation is often more art than science. For your edification and reading pleasure, here are notes on some of the places where we could have gone in a different direction with our translation of the work, or where a Japanese cultural reference is used

Yakitori, page 100
Literally "grilled chicken," yakitori is a Japanese dish made from several bite-sized pieces of chicken meat, or chicken offal, skewered on a bamboo skewer and grilled, usually over charcoal.

Takoyaki, page 100
Takoyaki is a popular Japanese dumpling made of batter, diced or whole baby octopus, tempura scraps, pickled ginger, and green onion, topped with okonomiyaki sauce, ponzu, mayonnaise, green laver, and fish shavings.

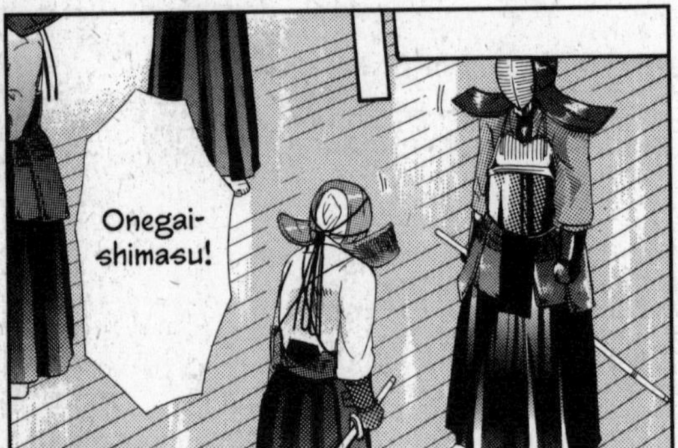
Onegai-shimasu!

Onegai-shimasu, page 131
Onegai-shimasu (literally, "I make a request") is a polite expression used widely in Japan when making a request of another. In kendo, it is said between partners before a spar, as a means of showing respect for each other and for the match.

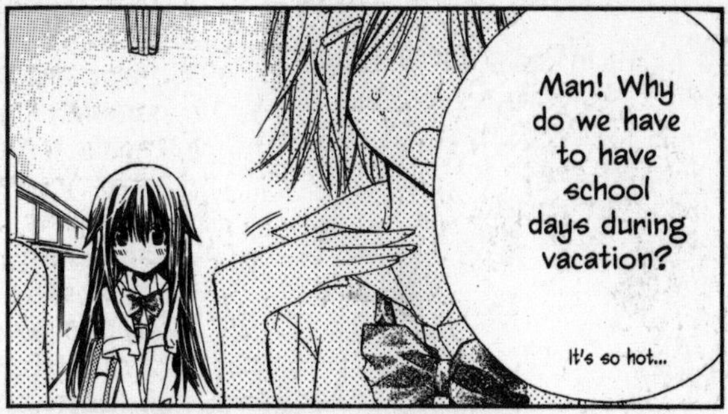
Man! Why do we have to have school days during vacation?
It's so hot...

School days during vacation, page 206
In Japan, there are a few days throughout summer vacation that are designated for students to come into school and take certain classes.

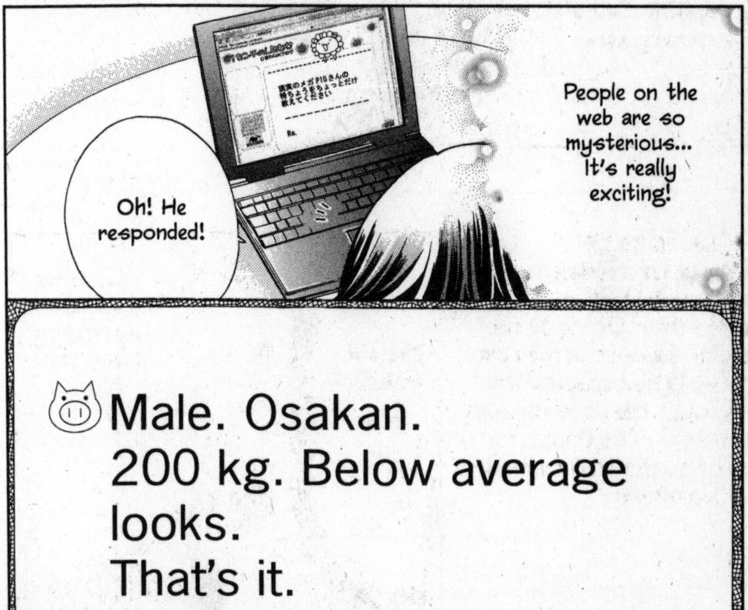
People on the web are so mysterious... It's really exciting!
Oh! He responded!
Male. Osakan.
200 kg. Below average looks.
That's it.

Osakan, page 365
Osakan refers to someone who lives in Osaka. (Like New Yorker, Tokyo-ite...) Osaka is a city in southern Japan with a very distinct accent and vocabulary.

Comedy Duo, page 376

Osaka, and more generally the Kansai Region, is known for producing famous comedians. One common type of comic is the comedy duo, who perform in front of an audience much like standup comedy in the West.

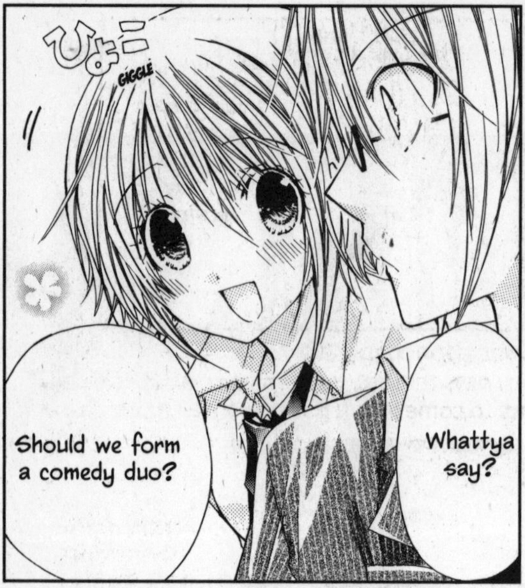
ひょこ
GIGGLE
Whattya say?
Should we form a comedy duo?

Boke, page 377

In comedy duos from Japan, the typical pattern is that one person will be a boke (or "airhead") and the other one will be a tsukkomi (or "poker"). The boke will commonly say silly things, and the tsukkomi will make fun of him or her.

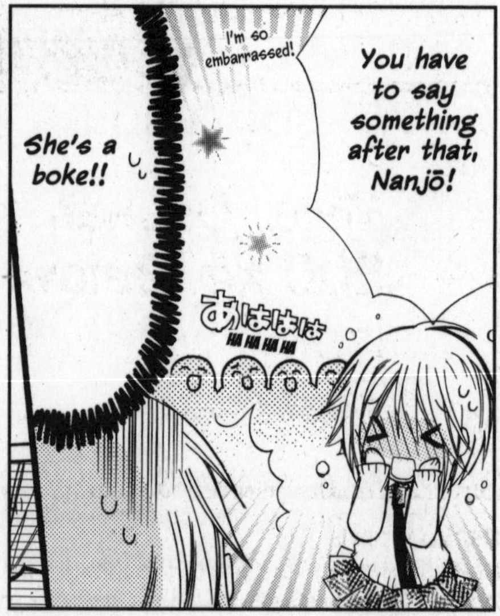
You have to say something after that, Nanjō!
I'm so embarrassed!
She's a boke!!
あははは
HA HA HA HA

TOMARE!

[STOP!]

You are going the wrong way!

Manga is a completely different type of reading experience.

To start at the *beginning*, go to the *end*!

That's right! Authentic manga is read the traditional Japanese way—from right to left, exactly the *opposite* of how American books are read. It's easy to follow: Just go to the other end of the book, and read each page—and each panel—from the right side to the left side, starting at the top right. Now you're experiencing manga as it was meant to be.